EMPLOYMENT LAW

BY THE SAME AUTHOR

Company Law in Ireland (1985, Cork and Dublin)
Cases on Irish Company Law (1986, Cork and Dublin)
Extradition Law in Ireland (1987, Dublin)
Constitutional Law of Ireland (1987, Cork and Dublin)
Commercial Law in Ireland (1990, Dublin)
Bankruptcy Law in Ireland (1990, Cork and Dublin)
Reorganising Failing Businesses: The Legal Framework (1991, Cork and Dublin)
Industrial Relations Law (1991, Dublin)
Commercial and Economic Law—Ireland (1992, Deventer, The Netherlands)

MICHAEL FORDE

Employment Law

WITH A FOREWORD BY

The Honourable Mr Justice Hugh O'Flaherty

of the Supreme Court

THE ROUND HALL PRESS

The book was typeset by
Gilbert Gough Typesetting and
output by Typeset Origination Services Ltd for
The Round Hall Press,
Kill Lane, Blackrock, Co. Dublin.

A catalogue record for this book
is available from the British Library

ISBN 0-947686-86-X

Printed in Ireland by
Colour Books Ltd, Dublin

Foreword

It seems that the print is hardly dry on one work before Dr Forde goes once more into the breach with another valuable legal treatise. His is a truly insatiable talent and dedication. A test of any general work is whether it provides an answer to a problem in a specialised area—one which might have a book to itself. I have found Dr Forde's previous works did meet that test and I have said so. This is a book which will be used on many occasions by practitioners and judges. Dr Forde's style, now well established, is to be economical and to the point.

This is a very thorough book—thorough in its background history, in its research, in its analysis of national law and, perhaps, most of all in putting our labour law in a European context. Once more we are reminded that it is an unjustifiable luxury to regard European law as a separate subject best left to the specialist: rather is it now part of every lawyer's essential baggage. Here in this very basic area of law the European dimension is to be found at every turn.

The book recounts the origin and development of the Employment Appeals Tribunal. The first chairman of its predecessor was my good friend and mentor, former Circuit Court judge, John Gleeson SC. He can be credited with establishing a modern administrative tribunal, combining a lack of formality with adherence to the rules of natural justice. John Gleeson had a remarkable career. He had a rich store of knowledge and experience, having been a senior counsel when I was first called to the bar, then a solicitor, first chairman of the Redundancy Appeals Tribunal and then (having returned to the bar) he was appointed a judge.

It is a sad matter to record that for many people in this country what they desire most is a job because a country can have the fairest employment laws in the world but if there is no employment to go with them they are of little moment to the jobless. This is a problem not solely in the political domain; it must be of concern to us all. The requirement of goodwill on the part of employers and employees is of the essence to give the many who are out of work hope. But it must also mean that the law is not to be stretched so as to frustrate the well-intentioned employer so that he does not feel it is worth his while to lend his strength and resources to the giving of employment.

I have already mentioned practitioners and judges and I add my recommendation to purchase this book to the students, the trade union officers and all who play a part in our estimable dispute-resolving machinery. Indeed, I urge all who are interested in employment—whether as givers or receivers —to support this enterprise. A story about another Michael, Michaelangelo, is worth recalling. As recounted in Vasari's Lives of the *Painters, Sculptors and Architects,* once in Florence, when snow lay on the ground, one of the Medici asked him to construct a snow statue in the palace garden which he did and which proves that a job may be minor and temporary and yet capable of producing a stunning result which, undoubtedly, Michaelangelo's snowman represented. This work is not minor and will not be of short duration but, yes, it too has been executed by a master craftsman.

HUGH O'FLAHERTY

The Supreme Court
Four Courts
Dublin
26 March 1992

For

Jane and Jimmy

Preface

Employment law is a large and somewhat complex subject and no single book could do it full justice. Many of the chapters in this present work really require entire separate books on the topics they cover; that has been done in the areas of sex discrimination (Deirdre Curtin), unfair dismissal (Mary Redmond) and income taxation (Norman Judge); comprehensive treatments of health and safety at work and also of pensions are badly needed. Last year I had published a work on industrial relations law, which deals almost exclusively with the 'collective' side of labour law, i.e., the arrangements between employers and trade unions and other workers' representatives. This present work complements that book and covers the mainly 'individual' side of labour law. Much of the early chapters concern the most obvious matters, such as what is a contract of employment, remuneration, accidents at work, dismissals. The later chapters may be more innovative, especially those on employers' insolvency, occupational pensions, transnational employment, company employees and the public service.

Although I refer extensively to case law decided by the courts not only in this country but also in Britain and occasionally even further afield, no doubt the book will receive some criticism in its treatment of the Employment Appeals Tribunal. In the section on unfair dismissal, I have explained why I refrained from going into that subject in the enormous detail required for a comprehensive treatment of it. If I had done that, the section on unfair dismissal—and also on statutory redundancy—would form a disproportionately large part of the book. I would hope that some diligent scholar will do full justice to the excellent work the Tribunal has been doing since its establishment 25 years ago and am delighted to see the tribute in the foreword paid to the Tribunal's first chairman.

I have sought to state the law up to March 1992.

Many favours were afforded to me in completing this book, for which I am very grateful. Once again, Marie Armah Kwantring did an excellent job with the manuscript and Michael Adams and Bart Daly of Round Hall Press have been most supportive of this endeavour. Simon Jeffreys and Nigel Moore, solicitors of McKenna & Co., London, kindly allowed me to reproduce adapted versions of their employment contract precedents from Longman's Practical Commercial Precedents. My special thanks are due to the Honourable Mr Justice Hugh O'Flaherty of the Supreme Court, not alone for a most complimentary foreword but even more so for the assistance and encouragement he provided me in my early years at the Bar. It needs to be recorded that his Lordship often went out of his way, to an exceptional extent, to help junior barristers get started in the profession; many of my colleagues are equally indebted to his generosity of spirit and wish him every success in his new office. Last, but far from least, are Peter, Patrick and Catherine, whose good humour and support is always an inspiration.

M. F.

Mountain View Road
Dublin 6.
1 April 1992

Contents

FOREWORD   v

PREFACE   ix

TABLES   xxv

1 Introductory   1

2 Personal scope   29

3 Determining the terms   51

4 Incidents of the employment relationship   67

5 Health and safety at work   107

6 Discrimination in employment   126

7 Termination of employment   153

8 Statutory rights on dismissal   180

9 Transfer of employer's business   220

10 Employer's insolvency   232

11 Occupational pensions   243

12 Transnational employment   262

13 Employees and company law   275

14 The public service   288

15 Income tax   328

APPENDIX   357

INDEX   493

1   INTRODUCTORY   1
Historical context   1
Contract, tort and statutory duties   3
   Tort   3
   Statutes   4
   Contract or tort?   4
The Constitution   6
   Non-governmental action   7
   The right to work   9
      Obtaining employment   10
      Dismissal from employment   11
The European Communities   12
   Legislative competence   13
   Legislative techniques   14
International labour standards   16
   European Convention on Human Rights   17
   International Labour Organisation   19
   European Social Charter   19
Adjudication of employment-related disputes   20
   Employment appeals tribunal   22
   Rights Commissioners   24
   Equality Officers   25
   Labour Court   26
   Deciding Officers   27
   Pensions Board   27
   Appeals Commissioners of the Revenue   27
   Social Welfare appeals   27
   Arbitration   27

2   PERSONAL SCOPE   29
Employees and the contract of employment   29
   Purposes of classification   31
   The tests   32
      Control   33
      Integration   34
      Enterprise   35
      Parties' own characterisation   36
   Special features of the relationship   37
      Provide own services   38
      Engagement and dismissal   38
      Remuneration   38

Times of work 39
Workplace 39
Equipment for work 39
Appeals 39
Office-holders 41
Workers 42
Employees excluded from the legislation 42
The Public Service 43
Temporary and part-time workers 44
Beyond retiring age 44
Under-aged workers 45
Employees not insurable for all benefits 45
Employer a close relative 45
Illegal employment 46
Special occupations 46
Trainees and apprentices 47
Out-workers 48
Religious activities 49

3   DETERMINING THE TERMS 51
The employment contract 51
Formality 51
Express terms 52
Implied terms 52
Implied by the facts 53
Implied by law 54
Written statement of particulars 55
Contractual effects 56
Enforcement of obligation 57
Work rules 58
Custom and practice 58
Collective agreements 59
Agency 60
Express incorporation 60
Implied incorporation 61
Problem cases 61
Altering the contract 64
Statutory obligations 65

4   INCIDENTS OF THE EMPLOYMENT RELATIONSHIP   67
The work obligation   68
  Employer providing work   68
  Employee performing work   69
    Competence and care   70
    Obey reasonable orders   71
    Co-operation   71
    Fidelity   72
  Enforcing the work obligation   73
    Resignation/dismissal   73
    Suspension from work   73
    Damages   75
    Reduction of earnings   75
    Injunction   75
The workplace   76
  Changing the workplace   76
  Establishment   76
Times of work   77
  Restrictions on working times   77
    Women   77
    Young persons   78
    Industrial work   78
    Shop work   79
    Bakeries   79
    Drivers   79
  Normal working hours and overtime   79
  Lay offs and short time   81
    Right to lay off   81
    Redundancy payments   82
Remuneration   82
  Defining 'remuneration'   82
  Fixing the remuneration   84
    Minimum wages   84
    Equal pay   85
  Normal remuneration   85
  Sick pay   85
  Paid holidays   87
    Annual leave   87
    Public holidays   87
    Cesser of employment   88
  Modes of payment   88

Workers covered by the Payment of Wages Act ... 89
'Wages' ... 90
Modes of payment ... 90
Deductions from remuneration ... 90
'Deduction' ... 91
Transfer payments ... 92
Court orders ... 92
Rectifying over-payments ... 92
Employee taking industrial action ... 92
Disciplinary measures ... 94
Goods or services necessary to do the work ... 94
Statement of wages and deductions ... 95
Assignment and attachment of remuneration ... 95
Confidential information ... 96
Confidentiality ... 96
Permitted disclosure ... 98
Intellectual property ... 98
Copyright ... 99
Patents ... 100
Post-employment restraints ... 101
Public interest ... 101
Reasonableness inter partes ... 101
Injunction to enforce restraint ... 104
Apprentices and trainees ... 104

5   HEALTH AND SAFETY AT WORK ... 107
The Regulatory System ... 109
The pre-1989 Acts ... 109
The 1989 Act ... 110
The main employers' duties ... 111
Duties to persons who are not employees ... 112
Defective equipment or premises ... 112
Duties of employees ... 113
Elaborating the duties ... 113
Implementation ... 113
The authority ... 113
Inspectors ... 114
Codes of practice ... 114
Prosecution ... 115
Prohibition orders ... 115
Licensing ... 115

Investigations and reports	116
Safety representatives	116
Safety statements	117
Employers' liability	117
Negligence	118
Duty of care	118
Standard of care	118
Causation	119
Defences	119
Tort or contract	120
Breach of statutory duty	120
Occupational diseases	122
Civil liability and the 1989 Act	124
Social welfare benefits	125

6	**DISCRIMINATION IN EMPLOYMENT**	126
	Foreign workers—E.C. nationals	127
	'Worker'	128
	The prohibitions	129
	Exceptions	132
	Sex and marital status	133
	Equal pay	136
	Personal scope	137
	'Pay'	137
	Same employer and workplace	137
	Like work	138
	Grounds other than sex	139
	Transparency	140
	Employment equality	140
	Personal scope	141
	Focus of discrimination	141
	Direct discrimination	143
	Genuine occupational qualification	144
	Indirect discrimination	144
	Essential requirement	146
	Non-retrospective effects	146
	Maternity	147
	Equality legislation	148
	Maternity leave	148
	Fourteen weeks' leave	149

Additional four weeks' leave	149
Time off for ante-natal and post-natal care	150
Return to work	150
Status during absence and leave	150
Resignation	151
Dismissal	151

7	**TERMINATION OF EMPLOYMENT**	**153**
	Modes of termination	153
	Agreement	153
	Dismissal	154
	Repudiation	154
	Frustration	156
	Destruction of the workplace	158
	Employee's illness	158
	Employee's imprisonment	159
	Dissolution of partnerships	159
	Receivership and liquidation	160
	Notice of termination	160
	Notifying resignation	160
	Dismissal notice	161
	Permanent employment	161
	Summary dismissal	163
	Serious misconduct	163
	Grounds stipulated in contract	165
	Dismissal procedures	166
	Public and private sector employment	167
	Fair hearing	168
	Procedures stipulated in contract	170
	Consequences of not affording a hearing	171
	Remedies for wrongful dismissal	172
	Declaration	172
	Injunction	173
	Damages	174
	Remuneration in lieu of notice	175
	Additional damages	175
	Mitigation	176
	Collateral benefits	177
	Taxation	177
	Remedy against employee's wrongful termination	178

8 STATUTORY RIGHTS ON DISMISSAL   180
   Dismissal   180
     Unilateral termination by employer   181
     Contracts for a fixed term or for a specified purpose 181
     Constructive dismissal   182
   Continuity of employment   183
     Date of commencement   184
     Date of dismissal   184
       Dismissal notice   184
       Fixed term or purpose contract   185
     Presumption of continuous employment   185
     Continuity not broken   185
       'Umbrella' contract   185
       Immediate re-employment   186
       Lay-off   186
       Transfer of business   186
     Part-time employment   187
     Absences which are deemed weeks of service   187
     Industrial action   188
   Minimum notice of dismissal   188
     Workers covered   189
     Notice periods   189
     Payment   190
     Peremptory nature   191
   Unfair dismissal   191
     The Unfair Dismissals Act   192
     Employees not covered   193
       Continuity of employment   193
       Public service   194
       Part-time workers   194
       Pensioners   194
       Close family/domestics   195
       Trainees and probationers   195
       Fixed term contracts   195
       Replacement for employees away on maternity leave 196
       Transnationals   196
     Dismissal   196
     Unfair or justifiable?   196
       Determining the reason   198
       Deemed unfair reasons   198
         Trade union membership or activities   199

Race or colour	199
Religion or politics	199
Pregnancy or maternity leave	199
Sex or marital status	199
Proceedings against employer	200
Justifying dismissal	200
Misconduct	200
Incapacity for the job	201
Redundancy	202
Other substantial grounds	202
Redress	203
Reinstatement	204
Re-engagement	204
Compensation	205
Measuring the loss	205
Adding to or subtracting from that sum	205
Ceiling on compensation	205
Redundancy	205
The Redundancy Payments Acts	206
Employees not covered	207
Continuity of employment	207
Public service	208
Part-time workers	208
Pensioners	208
Close family/domestics	208
Transnationals	208
Dismissal and its date	209
Making employees redundant	210
'Redundant'	210
Redundancy notices and certificates	212
Paid time off	212
Lay off and short time	212
Offer of new employment	214
'Suitable' alternative employment	214
'Unreasonable' refusal	215
Offer by associated employer	215
Offer by transferee of business	215
Lump sum payments	216
Continuous employment	216
Normal weekly remuneration	216
Computation	217

Collective redundancies   217
   Consultation with workers' representatives   218
   Notifying and consulting with the Minister   218
   Timing   219

9   TRANSFER OF EMPLOYER'S BUSINESS   220
Special arrangements for employment protection   220
Transfer of undertakings regulations   223
   Interpretation   224
   Relevant 'business transfers'   224
   Workers covered   226
   Continuing rights and duties   228
   Redress for dismissal   229
   Informing and consulting employees' representatives   231

10 EMPLOYER'S INSOLVENCY   232
Impact on employment contract   232
   Bankruptcy   232
   Liquidation   233
   Receivership   234
   Court-supervised examination   235
Transfer of undertakings regulations   235
Preferential debts   237
   Debts to employees   238
      Wages and salary   238
      Holiday pay   239
      Sick pay   239
      Pension contributions   239
      Compensation for dismissal   239
      Compensation for accidents   239
   Sums advanced to pay employees   239
The insolvency fund   240
   Employees covered   240
   Debts payable   240
   Obtaining payments   242

11 OCCUPATIONAL PENSIONS   243
Approved schemes   244
Funding   246
Trustees   247
   Appointment and removal   248

Powers and duties	249
Investment	251
Amendment	252
Employers	253
The surplus	255
Early leavers	257
Assignment and attachment	258
Employer's insolvency	258
Discrimination on grounds of sex and marital status	259
12 TRANSNATIONAL EMPLOYMENT	**262**
Adjudicative jurisdiction	262
E.C.-based defendants	263
Non-E.C.-based defendants	264
Applicable law	265
Contract	265
Tort	267
Statutory rights and duties	267
Territoriality	267
Unfair dismissals	269
Redundancy payments	270
Seafaring	271
Foreign embassy and consular employees	273
13 EMPLOYEES AND COMPANY LAW	**275**
Entitlement to accommodate employees' interests	275
Financial participation by employees	277
Financial assistance to acquire shares	277
Authority and pre-emption when allotting additional shares	278
Share options as remuneration	278
The option price and conditions	279
Selling the shares	280
Termination of employment	280
Directors' services agreements	282
Remuneration	282
'Golden handshakes'	283
'Golden umbrellas'	283
Inspecting service contracts	284
Dismissing directors	284
Right to dismiss	285
Damages	285

14 THE PUBLIC SERVICE   288
Exclusions from employment legislation   288
   Application to the public sector   289
   Categories excluded   289
      'Persons employed by or under the State'   290
      'Officers' of local and regional authorities   291
Public law rights and remedies   291
   Judicial review   292
   Public law or private law dispute?   293
   Political activities   294
   Fair procedures   295
      Matters other than discipline or dismissal   296
      Suspension without pay   296
      Adequate hearing   296
      Absence of bias   300
   Legitimate expectations   300
   Double jeopardy   302
   Grounds for discipline and dismissal   303
The Civil Service   306
   Appointment   308
   Status   309
   Incidents of the office   310
      Altering the incidents   310
      Common law and equitable rights and obligations   311
      Statutory rights and duties   313
   Probation   314
   Discipline and dismissal   314
Local and regional authorities   316
   Appointment   317
   Status   318
   Incidents of the office   318
   Discipline and dismissal   319
Teachers   321
   University teachers   321
   Vocational teachers   322
   National teachers   322
The Garda Síochána   325
The Defence Forces   327

15 INCOME TAXATION 328
Employment or office 328
Taxable benefits 331
Money payments 331
Gifts and other voluntary payments 332
Special contractual payments 334
Payments by third parties 336
Payments to third parties 336
Deductions from remuneration 338
Payments for expenses 338
Benefits in kind 339
Value of benefits 339
Benefits not capable of being converted into money 339
Allowable expenses 341
Necessarily and exclusively incurred 342
Travel expenses 343
Termination payments 345
Taxable emoluments 346
Personal gifts 346
Compensation for loss of rights 346
Golden handshakes 347
P.A.Y.E. 349
Income subject to P.A.Y.E. 350
Impracticable to apply P.A.Y.E. 350
Operating the system 350
Registration by employers 351
Certificates of tax free allowances 351
The P.A.Y.E. tables 351
Taxable pay 351
Benefits in kind, expenses payments etc. 352
Deduction and repayment of tax 352
Year end adjustments 352
Emergency card procedure 353
P.R.S.I. CONTRIBUTIONS AND LEVIES 353
Insured employees' earnings 354
Operating the system 355
Accounting by employers 355
Employees' P.R.S.I. contributions 355
Employers' P.R.S.I. contributions 356
Health contributions 356
Employment and training levy 356

APPENDIX
Standard Terms and Conditions of Employment   359
Executive Employment Agreement   371

Statutes and Regulations
  Redundancy Payments Act, 1967, sections 1-25   387
  Redundancy Payments Act, 1971, sections 10 and 17   402
  Minimum Notice and Terms of Employment Act, 1973,
      sections 1-12 and the schedule   403
  Holidays (Employees) Act, 1973, sections 1-8 and 12
      and the Schedule   409
  Anti-Discrimination (Pay) Act, 1974, sections 1-5 and 11   414
  Protection of Employment Act, 1977, sections 1-2 and 6-16   416
  Unfair Dismissals Act, 1977, sections 1-10 and 13-15   420
  Unfair Dismissals (Claims and Appeals) Regulations, 1977   428
  Unfair Dismissals (Calculation of Weekly Remuneration)
      Regulations, 1977   430
  Employment Equality Act, 1977, sections 1-17   433
  Redundancy Payments Act, 1979, section 7   439
  European Communities (Safeguarding of Employees' Rights
      on Transfer of Undertakings) Regulations, 1980
      (SI No. 306 of 1980), regulations 2-7   440
  Maternity Protection of Employees Act, 1981,
      sections 2-3, 5, 7-23 and 26-27   442
  Protection of Employees (Employer's Insolvency) Act, 1984,
      sections 1 and 3-10   449
  Safety, Health and Welfare at Work Act, 1989, sections 1-2,
      6-15, 27-28, 30-32 and 60   458
  Pensions Act, 1990, sections 2 and 54-74   469
  Worker Protection (Regulation Part-Time Employees) Act,
      1991, sections 1-5   482
  Payment of Wages Act, 1991, sections 1-2 and 4-6   487

Table of Statutes

Truck Act of 1743 (17 Geo. II c.8) 2
Cotton Mills and Factories Act, 1802 (42 Geo. III c.73) 78, 109
Apprentices Act, 1814 (42 Geo. III c.73) 104
Truck Act, 1831 (1 & 2 Will.IV, c.37) 2, 42, 88-89
Superannuation Act, 1834 (4 & 5 Will.IV, c.24) 243
Wages Attachment Abolition Act, 1870 (33 & 34 Vic. c.30) 95
Employers and Workmen Act, 1875 (38 & 39 Vic. c.90) 21, 42
Public Bodies Corrupt Practices Act, 1889 (52 & 53 Vic. c.69) 312, 319
Preferenetial Payments in Bankruptcy (Ireland) Act, 1889 (52 & 53
    Vic. c.60) 238
Trustee Act, 1893 (56 & 57 Vic. c.53) 249
Public Authorites Protection Act, 1893 (56 & 57 Vic. c.61) 313
Merchant Shipping Act, 1894 (57 & 58 Vic. c.60) 51, 52, 109, 271-273
Truck (Amendment) Act, 1896 (59 & 60 Vic.44) .88-89
Workmens' Compensation Act, 1897 (60 & 61 Vic. c.37) 2, 31, 41, 42, 110
Local Government (Ireland) Act, 1898 (61 & 62 Vic c. 37) 319
Merchant Shipping Act, 1906 (6 Edw.7, c. 48) 272
Workmen's Compensation Act, 1906 (6 Ed. 7 c. 58) 268-269
Trade Boards Act, 1909 (9 Edw. c.22) 3
Larceny Act, 1916 (6 & 7 Geo.5, c. 50) 318, 319
Prenvention of Corruption Act, 1916 (6 & 7 Geo. 5 c.64) 312, 319
Sex Disqualification (Removal) Act, 1919 (9 & 10 Geo. 5 c.71) 134
Army Pensions Act, 1923, (No. 26) 243
Garda Síochána Act, 1924 (No. 25) 225
Police Forces (Amalgamation) Act, 1925 (No. 7) 304
Local Authorities (Officers and Employees) Act, 1926 (No. 39) 316
Electricity (Supply) Act, 1927 (No. 27) 206, 222
University College Galway Act, 1929 (No. 35) 132
Vocational Education Act, 1930, (No. 29) 290, 319, 322
Garda Pensions Act, 1933 (No. 32) 243
Workmen's Compensation Act, 1934 (No. 9) 31
Aliens Act, 1935 (No. 14) 127
Conditions of Emplyment Act, 1936 (No. 2) 78-79
Night Work (Bakeries) Act, 1936 (No. 42) 79
Shops (Conditions of Employment) Act, 1938 (No. 4) 45, 109, 122

Shops (Hours of Trading) Act, 1938 (No. 3) 78, 79
Offences Against the State Act, 1939 (No. 13) 308, 317
Trade Union Act, 1941 (No. 22) 6
Local Government Act, 1941 (No. 23) 290, 316-321
Garda Síochána Compensation Act, 1941 (No. 19) 325
Industrial Relations Act, 1966 (No. 26) 26, 84
Conditions of Employment Act, 1944 (No. 12) 79
Vocational Education (Amendment) Act, 1944 (No. 9) 322
Mental Treatment Act, 1945 (No. 19) 243, 258
Merchant Shipping Act, 1947 (No. 46) 273
Solicitors Act, 1954 (No. 36) 52
State Property Act, 1954 (No. 25) 256
Defence Act, 1954 (No. 18) 327
Arbitration Act, 1954 (No. 26) 28
Factories Act, 1955 (No. 10) 70, 109-111, 121
Local Government Act, 1955 (No. 9) 295, 318, 319
Civil Service Regulation Act, 1956 (No. 46) 304, 306-315
Civil Service Commissioners Act, 1956 (No. 45) 307
Statutes of Limitation Act, 1957 (No. 6) 6
Office Premises Act, 1958 (No. 3) 70, 109
Trustee (Authorised Investment) Act, 1958 (No. 8) 251
Garda Síochána Act, 1958 (No. 14) 134, 304
Civil Liability Act, 1961 (No. 41) 117, 120, 239
Copyright Act, 1963, (No. 10) 99
Superannuation Act, 1963 (No. 24) 243
Official Secrets Act, 1963 (No. 1) 313, 319
Companies Act, 1963 (No. 33)
            s.60 277
            s.182 ....285, 287
            s.185 282
            ss.186-189 283
            s.191 ....282, 283
            s.285 .... 34, 238-240, 258
Transport Act, 1964 (No. 30) 222
Patents Act, 1964 (No. 12) 100
Mines and Quarries Act, 1965 (No. 7) 70, 109, 122
Social Welfare (Occupational Injuries) Act, 1966 (No. 16) 2
Industrial Training Act, 1967 (No. 51) 46, 105-106, 289
Income Tax Act, 1967 (No. 6) 27, 328-353
            s.109 329
            s.110 ....31, 329
            s.114 ....283, 345, 348
            s.115 348
            s.117 340-341
            s.118 341

Income Tax Act, 1967 (No. 6) (contd.)

        s.124-127 349

        schedule 2 . . . . 330, 341

Diplomatic Relations and Immunities Act, 1967 (No. 8) 273

Redundancy Payments Act, 1967 (No. 21) 82, 206-217

        s.2 . . . . 44, 184, 185, 187, 208, 209, 289

        s.4 . . . . .44, 187, 207-208, 354

        s.7 . . . . .76, 183, 209, 210-211

        s.9 . . . . .181-182, 209, 214

        s.10 210

        s.11 . . . . 186, 213

        s.12 213

        s.13 213

        s.14 207

        s.15 214

        s.16 . . . . 214, 215

        s.17 . . . . 208, 211

        s.18 211

        s.19 216

        s.20 . . . . 214, 223

        s.21 209

        s.24 216

        s.25 . . . . .208, 270-271

        ss.37-38 . . . . 27, 216

        s.39 . . . . 22, 216

        Schedule 3 . . . . .80, 85, 183, 186, 208, 216-217, 222

Finance Act, 1968, s.37 . . . . 345, 347

Industrial Relations Act, 1969 (No. 14) 24, 290

Health Act, 1970 (No. 1) 222, 293, 316, 320

Redundancy Payments Act, 1971 (No. 20) s.10 . . . . 185, 210

Employment Agency Act, 1971 (No. 27) 000

Dangerous Substances Act, 1972 (No. 10) 122

Finance Act, 1972 (No. 19) 244-246, 337

Minimum Notice and Terms of Employment Act,

    1973 (No. 4) 55-57, 188-191

        s.1 . . . . 30, 189

        s.3 . . . . 55, 189

        s.4 . . . . 188, 190, 191

        s.5 191

        s.6 161

        s.7 191

        s.8 190

        s.9 . . . . 55, 77, 84, 87, 161

        s.10 65

        s.11 57

Minimum Notice and Terms of Employment Act, 1973 (No. 4) (contd.)
        s.12 22
        Schedule 1 .... 185, 186, 187
        Schedule 2 190
Holidays (Employees) Act, 1973 (No. 25) 45, 87-88
        s.1 .... 80, 85, 222
        s.2 .... 48, 290
        s.3 87
        s.4 88
        s.5 88
        s.6 87
        s.12 87
        Schedule 88
Civil Service (Employment of Married Women) Act,
   1973 (No. 17) 127, 139, 304
Anti-Distrimination (Pay) Act, 1974 (No. 15) 85, 136-140
        s.1 .... 30, 82, 137, 181-182
        s.2 .... 65, 136, 138
        s.3 138
        s.4 65
        s.5 65
        s.6 25
Family Law (Maintenance of Spouses and Children) Act,
   1976 (No. 11) 82, 91, 95
Capital Acquisitions Tax Act, 1976 (No. 8) 331
Protection of Employment Act, 1977 (No. 7) 12, 217-219
        s.6 .... 77, 217, 218
        s.7 .... 217, 218
        s.8 218
        s.9 218
        s.10 218
        s.12 .... 212, 218
        s.14 219
        s.15 219
Protection of Young Persons (Employment) Act,
   1977 (No. 9) 11, 45, 46, 47, 48, 78
Unfair Dismissals Act, 1977 (No. 10) 24, 192-205
        s.1 .... 30, 181
        s.2 .... 43, 183, 184, 193-196, 269, 290, 318
        s.3 195
        s.4 195
        s.6 .... 151, 193, 196-203
        s.7 .... 82, 203-205
        s.8 .... 22, 24, 203
        s.9 24

Unfair Dismissals Act, 1977 (No. 10) (contd.)

        s.10 203

        s.14 166

        s.15 203

        s.16(5) 17

Employment Equality Act, 1977 (No. 16) 25, 140-148

        s.1 .... 30, 43, 181-182

        s.2 140

        s.3 .... 140-142, 199

        s.4 65

        s.6 142

        s.8 142

        s.12 .... 141, 289

        s.14 78

        s.16 148

        s.17 144

Agricultural Credit Corporation Act, 1978 (No. 31) 132, 295, 317

Defence (Amendment) Act, 1979 (No. 28) 138, 304, 327

Redundancy Payments Act, 1979 (No. 7) s.7 .... 208, 212

Payments of Wages Act, 1979 (No. 40) 89

Fisheries Act, 1980 (No. 1) 316

Safety in Industry Act, 1980 (No. 9) 70, 109, 122

Arbitration Act, 1980 (No. 7) 264

Finance Act, 1980 (No. 141) s.10 283

Maternity Protection of Employees Act, 1981 (No. 2) 24, 148-151, 199

        s.2 148

        s.8 149

        s.9 149

        s.10 149

        s.11 149

        s.12 149

        s.13 149

        s.14 149

        s.15 150

        s.16 150

        s.17 151

        s.18 151

        s.20 150

        s.21 150

        s.22 150

        s.23 150

Social Welfare (Consolidation Act,

   1981 (No. 1) 27, 31, 46, 50, 81, 125, 353-354

Night Work (Bakeries) (Amendment) Act, 1981 (No. 6) 79

Companies (Amendment) Act, 1982 (No. 10) s.10 238-240

Finance Act, 1982 (No. 14) 339, 341
Companies (Amendment) Act, 1983 (No. 13) 277, 278
Postal Telecommunications Service Act, 1983 (No. 24) 222, 295
Local Authorities (Officers and Employees) Act, 1983 (No. 1) 132, 317
Protection of Employees (Employers' Insolvency) Act,
    1984 (No. 21) 12, 15, 240-242
                s.3 . . . . .240, 354
                s.4 242
                s.6 240-242
                s.7 259
                s.8 242
                s.9 242
                s.10 242
Garda Síochána (Complaints) Act, 1986 (No. 29) 326
Finance Act, 1986 (No. 13) s.9 . . . . .279, 339
Labour Services Act, 1987 (No. 15) 222, 295
Safety, Health and Welfare (Offshore Installations) Act,
    1987 (No. 18) 70, 89, 122
Finance Act, 1988 (No. 12) 91
Bankruptcy Act, 1988 (No. 27) 237
Agriculature (Research, Training and Advice) Act, 1988 (No. 18) 222, 295
Jurisdiction of Courts and Enforcement of Judgments Act,
    1988 (No. 3) 263-265
Safety, Health and Welfare at Work Act, 1989 (No. 7) 70, 109-124
                s.6 111-112
                s.7 112
                s.8 112
                s.9 113
                s.10 112
                s.11 113
                s.12 117
                s.13 116
                s.14-26 . . . . .113, 222
                s.28 124
                s.30 . . . . .113, 114
                s.31 114
                s.60 124
Finance Act, 1989 (No. 10) 339
Defence (Amendment) Act, 1990 327
Industrial Relations Act, 1990 (No. 19) 24, 25, 26, 42, 275, 311
Companies (Amentment) Act, 1990 (No. 27) 172, 235, 237
Pensions Act, 1990 (No. 25) 25, 27, 243-261
                s.8-11 243
                s.27-39 258
                s.40-53 247

Pensions Act, 1990 (No. 25) (contd.)
  s.54 250
  s.55 250
  s.56 250
  s.59 249
  s.60 249
  s.62 253
  s.63 249
  s.64 249
  s.66 260
  s.67 260
  s.68 260
  s.69 260-261
  s.70 260
  s.71 260
  s.72 260
Payment of Wages Act, 1991 (No. 25) 24, 89-95
  s.1 ....83, 89-90
  s.2 90
  s.3 90
  s.4 95
  ss.5 91-95
  s.6 24
Companies Act, 1990 (No. 33)
  s.28 284
  s.50 284
  s.52 276
Social Welfare Act, 1991 (No. 7) ss.39-40 354
Worker Protection (Regular Part-Time Employees) Act,
  1991 (No. 5) 44, 55, 187, 189, 207
Contractual Obligations (Applicable Law) Act, 1991 (No. 8) 266-267

Table of Statutory Instruments

1928 (S.R. & O. No. 37) Prevention of Corruption Acts Adaptation
Order 312, 319
1946 (S.R. & O. No. 395) Aliens Order 127
1959 (No. 227) Factories Act (Building) (Safety, Health and Welfare)
Regulations 122
1960 (No. 28) Income Tax (Employments) Regulations 349-353
1968 (No. 54) Redundancy (Redundancy Appeals Tribunal) Regulations 23
1972 (No. 283) Factories Act (Manual Labour) (Maximum Weights and
Transport) Regulations 122
1975 (No. 128) Aliens (Amendment) Regulations 127
1977 (No. 286) Unfair Dismissals (Claims and Appeals) Regulations ... 23, 203
1977 (No. 287) Unfair Dismissals (Calculation of Weekly
Remuneration) Regulations 80, 85, 205
1979 (No. 107) Health Contributions Regulations 355
1979 (No. 77) Social Welfare (Collection of Employment Contributions
by the Collector General) Regulations 355
1980 (No. 306) E.C. (Safeguarding of Employees' Rights on Transfer
of Undertakings) Regulations 12, 15, 220, 223-231, 235-237
1981 (No. 357) Maternity Protection (Disputes and Appeals)
Regulations 24
1981 (No. 358) Maternity Protection (Time Off for Ante-Natal and
Post-Natal Care) Regulations 150
1982 (No. 84) Youth Employment Levy Regulations 355
1986 (No. 292) E.C. (Major Accident Hazards of Certain Industrial
Activities) Regulations 109, 122
1987 (No. 39) Garda Síochána (Promotion) Regulations 325
1988 (No. 219) E.C. (Protection of Workers) (Exposure to Lead)
Regulations 124
1988 (No. 164) Garda Síochána (Ammissions and Appointments)
Regulations 325
1989 (No. 34) E.C. (Protection of Workers) (Exposure to Asbestos)
Regulations 124
1989 (No. 94) Garda Síochána (Discipline) Regulations 325, 326
1989 (No. 251) E.C. (Protection of Workers) (Exposure to Chemical,
Physical and Biological Agents) Regulations 124

1990 (No. 17) Insolvency Fund (Amendment) Regulations 240
1990 (No. 122) Redundancy (Rebates) Regulations .207
1990 (No. 318) Garda Síochána (Retirement) Regulations 325
1991 (No. 215) Occupational Pension Schemes (Disclosure of
    Information) Regulations 250
1991 (No. 347) Redundancy Certificate Regulations .212
1991 (No. 348) Redundancy (Notice of Dismissal) Regulations 212
1991 (No. 349) Protection of Employees (Employers' Insolvency)
    Forms and Procedure (Amendment) Regulations 242
1991 (No. 351) Payment of Wages (Appeals) Regulations 24

Table of European Community Measures

1957: Treaty Establishing the European Economic Community 12-16
      Art. 48-49 .... 13, 127-128, 132-133
           100-101 13
           118-118A 13
           119 .... 12, 82, 85, 134-140, 259, 261, 289
1968: Regulation No. 1612/68 on the Freedom of Movement for
      Workers Within the Community (O.J. L254/2 of 1968) 127-131
1968: Convention on Jurisdiction and the Enforcement of
      Judgements in Civil and Commercial Matters, as amended
      in 1978 and in 1982 (O.J. C 97/2 of 1983) 263-265
1971: Regulation No. 1408/71 on the Application of Social Security
      Schemes to Employed Persons, to Self-Employed Persons and
      to Members of their Families (O.J. L149/2 of 1971) 128, 270, 354
1975: Directive No. 75/117 on the Approximation of Laws on the
      Application of the Principle of Equal Pay for Men and
      Women (O.J. L 48/29 of 1975) 12, 136-140
1975: Directive No. 75/129 on the Application of Laws Relating to
      Collective Redundancies (O.J. L 48/29 of 1975) 217-219
1976: Directive No. 76/207 on the Implementation of the Principles
      of Equal Treatment for Men and Women as Regards Access
      to Employment, Vocational Training and Promotions, and
      Working Conditions (O.J. L 39/40 of 1976) 12, 140-147
1977: Directive No. 77/187 on the Approximation of Laws Relating
      to the Safeguarding of Employees' Rights in the Event of
      Transfers of Undertakings, Business or Parts of Businesses
      (O.J. L 61/26 of 1977) 223-231, 235-237
1980: Convention on the Law Applicable to Contractual Obligations
      (O.J. L 266/1 of 1980) 266-267
1980: Directive No. 80/987 on the Approximation of Laws Relating
      to the Protection of Employees in the Event of the
      Insolvency of their Employer (O.J. L 283/23 of 1980) .. 232, 240-242
1986: Directive No. 86/378 on the Implementation of the Principle of
      Equal Treatment for Men and Women in Occupational
      Social Security Schemes (O.J. L 225/40 of 1986) 260

Table of Cases

A.C.O.T. v. Doyle [1989] IR 33 140

A.F. Associates Ltd v. Ralston [1973] NI 229 101

Abbott v. Philbin [1961] AC 352; [1960] 3 WLR;
    [1960] 2 All ER 763 . . . . 279, 339

Abels v. Administrative Board of the Bedrijsvereniging Voorde
    Metaal-Industrie (Case 135/83) [1987] 2 CMLR 406 . . . . 226, 236

Addis v. Gramophone Co. [1909] AC 488 . . . . .69, 175-176

Addison v. London Philharmonic Orchestra Ltd [1981] ICR 261 36

Aer Lingus Teo v. Labour Court [1990] ILRM 485 . . . . 135, 146

Aer Rianta cpt v. Labour Court [1989] ILRM 193 135

Ahern v. Minister for Industry & Commerce [1991] IR 291 314

Airfix Footwear Ltd v. Cope [1978] ICR 1210 . . . . 39, 49

Alexander v. Standard Telephone & Cables plc [1990] ICR 291 . . . . 63, 174

Ali v. Southwark LBC [1988] ICR 567 . . . . 170, 171, 174

Allen v. Flood [1898] AC 1 126

Allue and Coonan v. Universita Degli Studi di Venezia (Case 33/88)
    [1991] 1 CMLR 283 . . . . 128, 130

Anderson v. Dalkeith Engineering Ltd [1985] ICR 66 230

Anglia Television Ltd v. Reed [1972] 1 QB 60; [1971] 3 WLR 528;
    [1971] 3 All ER 690 178

Arnott v. Arnott, 58 ILTR 185 (1924) 249

Attorney General v. Cochrane (1810) Wright 10 312

Attorney General v. Dublin Utd. Tramways Ltd [1939] IR 590 325

Attorney General v. Edmunds (1868) LR 6 Eq. 381 312

Attorney General v. Guardian Newspapers Ltd (No.2) [1990] AC 109,
    1988] 2 WLR 805, [1988] 3 All ER 545 312

Attorney General v. Jonathan Cape Ltd [1975] QB 752; [1975] 3 WLR
    606; [1975] 3 All ER 484 312

Attorney General for England & Wales v. Brandon Book Publishers Ltd
    [1987] ILRM 135 312

Auckland Shop Employees' Union v. Woolworths (N.Z.) Ltd [1985] 2
    NZLR 372 181

Australian Iron & Steel Pty Ltd v. Banovic (1990) 64 ALJLR 53 146

B.P. Refinery (Westernport) Pty Ltd v. Shire of Hasings (1978)
    52 ALJR 20 53
Ball v. Johnson (1971) 47 TC 155 333
Bank of Ireland v. Kavanagh [1990] 1 CMLR 87 140
Barber v. Guardian Royal Exchange Insurance Group (Case C–262/88)
    [1990] 2 CMLR 513; [1991] 2 WLR 72;
    [1990] 2 All ER 660 . . . . 137, 259, 261
Barcalys Bank Ltd v. Naylor [1961] 1 Ch 7; [1960] WLR 678; [1960]
    3 All ER 173 337
Barthope v. Exeter Diocesan Board [1979] ICR 900 49
Bartlett v. Kerry CC (UD 178/78) 187
Beets Proper v. F. van Lanschot Bankiers NV (Case 262/84) [1986]
    ECR 773 142
Bell v. Lever Bros. Ltd [1932] AC 161 73
Beloff v. Pressdram Ltd [1973] 1 All ER 241 . . . . 34, 99
Berg v. Ivo Marten Besselsen (Cases 144-145/87) [1989] 3 CMLR 817 229
Berriman v. Delaboe Slate Ltd [1985] ICR 546 230
Berrisford v. Woodword Schools (Midland Division) Ltd [1991]
    ICR 564 203
Bettray v. Staatssecretaris van Justitie (Case 344/87) [1991]
    1 CMLR 459 129
Bilka-Kaufhaus Gmbh. v. von Hartz (Case 170/84) [1987] ICR 110 259
Birch v. University of Liverpool [1985] ICR 470 . . . . 154, 181
Bird v. British Celanese Ltd [1945] 1 KB 336 . . . . 74, 91
Birmingham v. Attorney General [1932] IR 510 206
Blaikston v. Cooper [1909] AC 104 334
Bliss v. South East Thames Regional Health Authority [1987]
    ICR 700 . . . . 155, 176, 183
Blyth v. Scottish Liberal Club (1982) SC 140 163
Bolands Ltd v. Ward [1988] ILRM 382 . . . . 189, 190
Bond v. CAV Ltd [1983] IRLR 360 74
Bork (P.) International A/S v. Foreningen Af Arbejdsledere i Danmark
    (Case 101/87 [1990] 3 CMLR 701 . . . . 225, 227
Botzen Rotterdamsche Droogdok Maatschappij BV (Case 186/83)
    [1986] 2 CMLR 50 225
Boyd Line Ltd v. Pitts [1986] ICR 244 185
Bradley v. C.I.E. [1976] IR 217 118
Briggs v. Oates [1990] ICR 473 160
British Reinforced Concreted Ltd v. Lind (1917) 34 RPC 101 100
British Transport Comm. v. Gourley [1956] AC 185; [1956] 2 WLR 41;
    [1955] 3 All ER 796 177
Brown v. Bullock [1961] 1 WLR 1095; [1961] All ER 129 343
Brown v. Stockton on Tees BC [1989] AC 20; [1988] 2 WLR 935;
    [1988] 2 All ER 129 151
Browne v. Aga Khan (UD 332/87) 203

Browne v. An Bord Pleanála [1990] 1 CMLR 3 16
Browning v. Crumlin Valley Collieries Ltd [1926] 1 KB 522 .... 81, 212
Bruce v. Hatton (1921) 8 TC 180 337
Bull v. Pitney Bowes Ltd [1967] 1 WLR 273; [1966] 3 All ER 384 ... 102, 103
Bullivant (R.) Ltd v. Ellis [1987] ICR 464 98
Bunyan v. United Dominions Trust (Ir) Ltd [1982] ILRM 404 .... 197, 204
Burke v. Minister for Labour [1979] IR 354 6
Burroughs Machinery Ltd v. Timmoney [1976] IRLR 343 63
Burton v. British Railways Board (Case 19/81) [1982] QB 1080;
    [1982] 3 WLR 387; [1982] 3 All ER 537 259
Bushell v. Faith [1970] AC 1099; [1970] 2 WLR 272; [1970]
    1 All ER 53 285
Byrne v. Limerick S.S. Co. [1946] IR 138 .... 157, 272
Byrne v. Ireland [1972] IR 241 .... 288, 291

Caladom Ltd v. Hoare & Kelly (Unrep., 1985) 212
Calder v. H. Kitson Vickers & Sons (Engineers) Ltd [1988] ICR 233 37
Caldwell v. Labour Court [1988] IR 280 135
Callow (F.E.) (Engineering) Ltd v. Johnson [1971] AC 335; [1970] 3
    WLR 932; [1970] 3 All ER 639 110
Calvert v. Wainwright [1947] KB 526 333
Camden Exhibition & Display Ltd v. Lynott [1966] 1 QB 555; [1965]
    3 WLR 763; [1965] 3 All ER 28 63
Cameron v. Prendergast [1940] AC 549 347
Campbell v. Holland Dredging Ltd (Unrep., 3 March 1989) 6
Carvill v. Irish Industrial Bank Ltd [1968] IR 325 .... 73, 161, 164, 286
Cassidy v. Minister for Health [1951] 2 KB 343; [1951] 1 All ER 574 34
Chakki v. United Yeast Co. [1982] ICR 140 159
Chambers v. Mayo Mental Hospital [1930] IR 154 319
Chief Constable v. Evans [1982] 1 WLR 1155; [1982] 3 All ER 141 304
Chomhairle Oilióna Talmhíochta v. Doyle [1989] IR 33 135
City of Boston v. Dolan, 10 NE 2d 275 (1937) 311
Clayton v. Gothorpe [1971] 1 WLR 999; [1971] 2 All ER 1311 335
Clayton & Waller v. Oliver [1930] AC 209 69
Cogan v. Minister for Finance [1941] IR 389 .... 309, 310
Collective Redundancies, Re: E.C. Commission v. Belgium (Case
    215/83) [1985] 3 CMLR 624 217
Collier v. Sunday Referee Publishing Co. [1940] 2 KB 647 .... 68, 69
Collins, Re [1925] Ch 556 232
Collins v. Co. Cork VEC (unrep. 18 Mar. 1983) 299, 322
Collman v. Construction Industry Training Board (1966) 1 ITR 52 234
Compensation to Civil Servants Re [1929] IR 44 206
Connolly v. McConnell [1983] IR 172 169-170
Connor v. Strythclyde Regional Council (1986) SLT 530 296
Conroy v. Commr. Garda Síochána [1989] IR 141 326

Construction Industry Training Board v. Labour Force Ltd [1970]
　　3 All ER 220 38
Cork Corporation v. Cahill [1987] IR 478 135
Corron Works Ltd v. Bell [1967] NI 185 186
Corrigan v. Irish Land Comm. [1977] IR 317 295
Corry v. National Union of Vintners [1950] IR 315 46
Council of Civil Service Unions v. Minister for the Civil Service [1985]
　　AC 374; [1984] 3 WLR 1174; [1984] 3 All ER 935 . . . . 296, 301, 310
Coupland v. Arabian Gulf Petroleum Co. [1983] 3 All ER 226 267
Courage Group's Pension Scheme [1987] 1 WLR 495; [1987]
　　1 All ER 528 252
Courtaulds Northern Spinning Ltd v. Sibson [1988] ICR 451 . . . . . . 76, 154, 182
Cowan v. Scargill [1985] Ch 270; [1984] 3 WLR 501; [1984]
　　2 All ER 750 . . . . 247, 250, 251
Cox v. Electricity Supply Board [1943] IR 94 . . . . 222, 321
Cox v. Electricity Supply Board (No.3) [1944] IR 81 . . . . 74, 320
Cox v. Ireland (unrep., 11 July 1991) 308, 317
Cox v. Phillips Industries Ltd [1976] 1 WLR 638; [1976] 3 All ER 161 176
Crank v. Her Majesty's Stationery Office [1985] ICR 1 185
Cresswell v. Inland Revenue [1984] 2 All ER 713 . . . . 64, 68

DPP v. McLoughlin [1986] IR 355 . . . . 34, 35, 36, 128
Dairy Lee Ltd, Re [1976] IR 314 41
Daly v. Hanson Industries Ltd (U.D. 719/86) 212
Dansk Metalarbejderforbundi Danmark v. Nielsen & Son (Case 284/83)
　　[1986] 1 CMLR 91 218
Davie v. New Merton Board Mills Ltd [1959] AC 604; [1959]
　　59 WLR 1331 [1959] 1 All ER 346 119
Davies v. Braithwaite [1931] 2 KB 628 329
Davies v. Presbyterian Church of Wales [1986] 1 WLR 323; [1986]
　　1 All ER 705 50
David (Laurence) Ltd v. Ashton [1989] ICR 123 104
Davis v. New England College of Arundel [1977] ICR 6 37
Davis v. Richards & Wallington Industries Ltd [1990] 1 WLR 1511;
　　[1991] 2 All ER 563 255
Davis Contractors Ltd v. Fareham UDC [1956] AC 696; [1956]
　　3 WLR 37; [1956] 2 All ER 145 157
Deane v. Wilson [1906] 2 IR 405 91
Dedway Trading Ltd v. Calverly [1973] 3 All ER 776 215
Defrenne v. Sabena (Case 43/75) [1976] ECR 455 . . . . 15, 134, 136
De Lacey Smith v. Attorney General [1934] IR 139 206
Dempsey v. Grant Shopfitting Ltd (UD 554/88) 184
Dekker v. Stichting Vormingscentrum Voor Jonge Volwassen
　　(Case 177/88) [1991] IRL 27 . . . . 142, 147, 148, 151
Derria v. General Council of British Shipping Ltd [1986] 1 WLR 1207 269

Devonald v. Rosser & Sons [1906] 2 KB 728 .... 58, 81, 186, 212
Deyong v. Shenburn [1946] KB 227 53
Dietman v. Brent LBC [1987] ICR 737 .... 171, 172, 174, 298
Dimworth v. Southern Health Board (184/77) 211
Dixon v. B.B.C. [1979] 1 QB 546; [1979] 2 WLR 547; [1979]
    2 All ER 112 195
Dolan v. K. [1944] IR 470 .... 49, 338
Donelan v. Kirby Construction Ltd [1983] IRLR 191 63
Donnelly v. Gleeson (Unrep. 11 July 1978) 233
Donoghue v. Stevenson [1932] AC 562 3
Down County Council v. Irish Insurance Cmrs [1914] 2 IR 110 38
Du Cross v. Ryall (1935) 19 TC 444 347
Duggan v. An Taoiseach [1989] ILRM 710 .... 301-302, 310
Dunk v. George Waller & Sons Ltd [1970] 2 QB 163; [1970]
    2 WLR 1241; [1970] 2 All ER 630 105
Dunne v. Cooney (UD 532/86) 187
Duomatic Ltd, Re [1989] 2 Ch 365; [1969] 2 WLR 114; [1969]
    1 All ER 161 283

Eastham v. Newcastle Utd FC [1964] 1 Ch.413; [1963] 2 WLR 574;
    [1963] 3 All ER 39 104
EC Commission v. Belgium (Case 237/84) [1988] 2 CMLR 865 ...... 133, 227
EC Commission v. France (Case 167/73) [1974] ECR 359 129
EC Commission v. United Kingdom (Case 165/82) [1983] ECR 3431 141
Eaton v. Robert Eaton Ltd [1988] ICR 302 41
Ebbw Vale Steel Co. v. Tew (1935) 79 S.J. 593 178
Educational Co. of Ireland Ltd v. Fitzpatrick (No.2) [1961] IR 345 7
Edwards v. Clinch [1981] 1 Ch 1; [1980] 3 WLR 521; [1980]
    3 All ER 278 .... 41, 330
Edwards v. Skyways Ltd [1964] 1 WLR 349; [1964] 1 All ER 494 60
Egg Stores (Stamford Hill) Ltd v. Leibovici [1977] ICR 260 159
Electrolux Ltd v. Hudson [1977] FSR 312 99
Elwood v. Utitz [1960] NI 93 343
Employees of Consiglio Nazionale delle Ricerche, Re: EC Commission
    v. Italy (Case 225/85) [1987] ECR 2625; [198?] 3 CMLR 635 133
Enderby v. Frenchay Health Authority [1991] ICR 382 140
English v. Donnelly (1958) SC 494 268
English Joint Stock Bank, Re (1867) 3 Eq 341 233
Equal Employment Opportunities Comm. v. Arabian American Oil Co.,
    111 S Ct 1227 (1991) 269
Evans v. London Co-Op. Society Ltd (The Times, 6 July 1976) 251
Evening Standard Ltd v. Henderson [1987] ICR 588 179
Expro Services Ltd v. Smith [1991] ICR 577 225

Faccenda Chicken Ltd v. Fowler [1987] Ch 117; [1986] 3 WLR 288;
    [1986] 1 All ER 617 97
Fall v. Hitchen [1973] 1 WLR 286, [1973] 1 All ER 368 329
Farrer (TN) Re, [1937] Ch 352 233
Ferguson v. John Dawson & Partners (Construction) Ltd [1976]
    1 WLR 1213; [1976] 3 All ER 817 37
Fitzgerald v. Hall, Russell & Co. Ltd [1970] AC 984; [1969] 3 WLR
    868; [1969] 3 All ER 1140 186
Fitzgibbon v. Attorney General [1930] IR 49 206
Fitzpatrick v. Minister for Finance [1946] IR 481 327
Flack v. Kodak [1987] 1 WLR 31; [1986] 2 All ER 1003 186
Flaherty v. Minister for Local Government [1941] IR 587 318
Flanagan v. University College Dublin [1989] ILRM 469 299
Flynn v. An Post [1987] IR 68 . . . . .296, 315
Flynn v. Great Northern Rly (Irl) Ltd,
    89 ILTR 46 (1955) 86, 159, 162, 168, 170
Flynn v. Power [1985] IR 648 . . . . .17, 67, 71, 151, 199, 203, 304
Folami v. Nigerline (U.K.) Ltd [1978] ICR 272 41
Foreningen Af Arbejdsledeve i Danmark v. Daddy's Dance
    Hall A/S (Case 324/86) [1989] 2 CMLR 517 . . . . .223, 225, 229
Ford Motor Co. v. Amalg. Union Engineering Workers [1969]
    2 QB 303; [1969] 1 WLR 339; [1969] 2 All ER 481 59
Ford v. Warwickshire CC [1983] 2 AC 71; [1983] 2 WLR 399,
    [1983] 1 All ER 783 186
Foster & Clarke Ltd's Indenture Trusts [1966] 1 WLR 125; [1966]
    1 All ER 43 234
Foster v. British Gas Corp. (Case C-188/89) [1990]
    2 CMLR 833 . . . . .16, 44, 132, 140
Fowler v. Commercial Timber Co. [1930] 2 KB 1 233
French Nurseries, Re: EC Commission v. France (Case 307/89) [1987]
    3 CMLR 555 133

Gallagher v. Revenue Comrs. [1991] ILRM 632 299
Galvin v. Minister for Industry & Commerce [1932] IR 216 41
Garvey v. Ireland [1981] IR 75 . . . . .41, 167, 171, 297-298, 204, 315, 325
Gascol Conversions Ltd v. Mercer [1974] ICR 420 . . . . .63, 80
Gearons v. Dunnes Stores Ltd (UD 367/1988) 198
General Electric Co. v. Gilbert, 429 US 125 (1976) 142, 147
General Rolling Stock Co., Re (1866) 1 LR Eq 346 .233
Gibney v. Riverside Mfg. Co. (Ir) Ltd (UD 732/87) 204
Gibson v. Motortune Ltd [1990] ICR 740 223
Girls Public Day School Trust v. Khanna [1987] ICR 339 187
Given, Re [1936] IR 20 000
Glantree Engineering Ltd v. Goodhand [1983] 1 All ER 542 334
Glasenapp v. Germany, 9 EHRR 25 304

Glover v. B.L.N. Ltd [1973] IR 388 .... 164, 165-166, 167, 169, 173, 286, 287
Glover v. B.L.N. Ltd (No. 2) [1973] IR 432 .... 177, 346
Glynn v. CIR [1990] 2 AC 298, [1990] 2 WLR 633 336
Gormley v. McCartin Bros. (Engineering) Ltd [1982] ILRM 215 208
Gothard v. Mirror Group Newspapers Ltd [1988] ICR 729 236
Goulding Chemicals Ltd v. Bolger [1977] IR 211 .... 60, 206
Government of Canada v. Employment Appeals Tribunal
    (unrep., 12 Mar. 1992) 274
Graham v. Minister for Industry & Commerce [1933] IR 156 .... 32, 38, 40
Greater London Council v. Minister for Social Security [1971]
    1 WLR 641; [1971] 2 All ER 285 34
Grehan v. North Eastern Health Board [1989] IR 422 .... 52, 162, 303
Griffiths v. Secretary of State [1974] 1 QB 468; [1973] 3 WLR 831;
    [1973] 3 All ER 1184 .... 234, 286
Groener v. Minister for Education (Case 379/87)
    [1990] 1 CMLR 401 .... 132, 317
Gunn v. Bord Cholaiste Naisiónta Eolaine is Dearta [1990]
    2 IR 168 .... 167, 322
Gunton v. Richmond upon Thames LBC [1981] Ch 448; [1980]
    3 WLR 714; [1980] 3 All ER 577 .... 154, 171

Hadley v. Baxendale (1854) 9 Ex 341 176
Hafner, Re [1943] IR 426 280
Halal Meat Packers (Ballyhaunis) Ltd v. Employment Appeals Tribunal
    [1990] ILRM 293 .... 23, 193, 203
Hales v. Minister for Industry and Commerce [1967] IR 50 46
Hallinan v. Gilligan (UD 564/81) 211
Hamblett v. Godfrey [1987] 1 WLR 357; [1987] 1 All ER 916 335
Handels-Og Kontorfunktionaerernes Forbund Danmark v. Dansk
    Arbejdsgiverforforening (Case 109/88) [1991] 1 CMLR 8 ... 139, 140, 151
Hanley v. Pease & Partners [1915] 1 KB 698 .... 74, 81
Hare v. Murphy Bros. Ltd [1974] 3 All ER 940 159
Harman v. Flexible Lamps Ltd [1980] IRLR 418 158
Harmer v. Cornelius (1858) 5 C.B. (NS) 236 .... 70, 165
Harrington v. Minister for Finance [1946] IR 320 326
Harrison v. Nortland Polytechnic Council [1991] 2 NZLR 593 303
Hart v. A.R. Marshall & Sons (Bulwell) Ltd [1977] 1 WLR 1067;
    [1978] 2 All ER 413 159
Harte v. Telecard Holdings Co. (unrep., 18 May 1979) 188
Harvey v. R.G. O'Dell Ltd [1958] 2 QB 78, [1958] 2 WLR 473;
    [1958] 1 All ER 657 70
Haughton v. Olau Line (U.K.) Ltd [1986] 1 WLR 502; [1986]
    2 All ER 47 .... 269, 272
Hayward v. Cammell Laird Shipbuilders Ltd [1988] AC 894; [1988]
    2 WLR 1134; [1988] 2 All ER 257 138

Heaton v. Bell [1969] 2 WLR 754; [1969] 2 All ER 70 . . . . 338, 339, 340
Hellyer Bros. Ltd v. McLeod [1987] 1 WLR 726 186
Heneghan v. Western Regional Fisheries Board [1986] ILRM 225 300
Henley v. Murray [1950] 1 All ER 908 346
Hennessy v. Read & Write Shop Ltd (UD 192/78) 201
Henry v. Foster (1931) 16 TC 605 347
Herman v. Owners of S.S. Vica [1942] IR 305 . . . . 157, 172, 272
Heyman v. Darwins Ltd [1942] AC 356 171
Hewlett v. Allen & Son [1892] 2 QB 662, aff'd; [1894] AC 383 . . . . 89, 92
Hickey v. Eastern Health Board [1991] IR 208 . . . . 298, 324
Hilder v. Dexter [1902] AC 474 279
Hill v. C.A. Parsons Ltd [1972] 1 Ch 305; [1971] 3 WLR 995; [1971]
    3 All ER 1345 174
Hines v. Birkbeck College [1986] Ch. 526; [1986] 2 WLR 527; [1985]
    3 All ER 156 322
Hitchcock v. Post Office [1980] ICR 100 34
Hivac Ltd v. Park Royal Scientific Instruments Ltd [1946] 1 Ch 169;
    [1946] 1 All ER 350 . . . . 72, 101
Hochstrasser v. Mayes [1960] AC 376; [1960] 2 WLR 63; [1959]
    3 All ER 817 . . . . 331-332, 334, 348
Hofman v. Barmer Ersatzkasse (Case 184/83) [1984] ECR 3047 148
Hogg v. Dover College [1990] ICR 39 154
Holdsworth (Harold) & Co. (Wakefield) Ltd v. Caddies [1955]
    1 WLR 352; [1955] 1 All ER 725 286
Holland v. Geoghegan [1972] 1 WLR 1473; [1972] 3 All ER 333 335
Home Counties Dairies Ltd v. Skilton [1970] 1 WLR 526; [1970]
    1 All ER 1227 . . . . 102, 103
Horlock v. Beale [1916] 1 AC 486 158
House of Spring Gardens Ltd v. Point Blank Ltd [1984] IR 611 96
Hubbard v. Vosper [1972] 2 QB 84; [1972] 2 WLR 389; [1972]
    1 All ER 1023 98
Hughes v. Dept. Social Security [1985] 1 AC 776; [1985] 2 WLR 866 195
Hughes v. Quinn [1917] 2 IR 442 39
Hughes (C. & W.) Ltd, Re [1966] 1 WLR 1369; [1966] 2 All ER 702 38
Hugh-Jones v. St. John's College Cambridge [1979] ICR 848 48
Humphries v. Iarnod Eireann (UD 1099/88) 194
Hunter v. Dewhurst (1932) 16 TC 605 . . . . 347, 348
Hutton v. West Cork Rly (1883) 23 Ch D 654 276
Hyland v. J.H. Barker (North West) Ltd [1985] ICR 861 46
Hynes v. Garvey [1978] IR 174 305

Imperial Group Pension Trust Ltd v. Imperial Tobacco Ltd [1990]
    1 WLR 589, [1991] 2 All ER 597 . . . . 248, 253-254
Imperial Hydropathic Hotel Co. v. Hampson (1882) 23 Ch D 1 285

Industrial Development Consultants Ltd v. Cooley [1972] 1 WLR 443;
    [1972] 2 All ER 162 72
Industrial Yarn's Ltd v. Greene [1984] ILRM 15 .... 189, 191, 213
Ingram v. Foxan [1984] ICR 685 188
Initial Services Ltd v. Putterill [1968] 1 QB 396; [1967] 3 WLR 1032;
    [1967] 3 All ER 145 98
Inland Revenue v. Brander & Cruikshank [1971] 1 WLR 212; [1971]
    1 All ER 36 331
Irani v. Southampton & South West Hampshire Health Autority [1985]
    ICR 590 171
Irish Insurance Cmrs. v. Craig [1916] 2 IR 59 318
Irish Leathers Ltd v. Minister for Labour
    [1986] IR 177 .... 178, 186, 189, 191, 213, 241
Irish Shipping Ltd v. Byrne [1987] IR 468 191
Ivory v. Ski Line Ltd [1988] IR 399 .... 150, 152

Jackson v. John Mc Carthy & Co. (UD 297/78) 202
Janata Bank v. Ahmed [1981] ICR 791 270
Jardine v. Gillespie (1906) 6 TC 263 344
Jarrold v. Boustead [1964] 1 WLR 1357; [1964] 3 All ER 76 .... 334, 348
Jenkins v. Kingsgate (Clothing Productions) Ltd (Case 96/80)
    [1981] ECR 911 138
Johnston v. Chief Constable of the RUC (Case 222/84) [1986] ECR
    165; [1987] QB 129 .... 141, 313
Johnston v. Cliftonville F.C. Ltd [1984] NI 9 104
Johnstone v. Bloomesbury Health Authority [1991] 2 WLR 1362;
    [1991] 2 All ER 293 .... 52, 70, 71
Jones v. Associated Tunnelling Ltd [1981] IRLR 477 .... 57, 76, 154

Keegan v. Dawson [1934] IR 232 268-269
Keenan v. Miller Insulation Engineering Ltd
    (unrep., 8 December 1987) 124
Kelleher v. St. James Hospital Board (59/77) 211
Kelly v. Donegal CC [1946] IR 228 31
Kelly v. Owners of the Ship 'Miss Evans' [1913] 2 IR 385 38
Kelly v. Quinn [1964] IR 488 342
Kemp v. New Zealand R.F. League Inc. [1989] 3 NZLR 463 104
Kempf v. Staatssecretaris van Justitie (Case 139/85) [1974] ECR 359 128
Kennedy v. Hughes Dairy Ltd [1989] ILRM 122 118
Kenny v. An Post [1988] IR 285 64
Kenyon v. Darwen Cotton Mfg. Co. [1936] 2 KB 193 89
Kingston v. Irish Dunlop Co. Ltd [1969] IR 233 173
Kirby v. Burke [1944] IR 207 3
Knox v. Down District Council [1981] IRLR 452 .... 52, 61
Kowalska v. City of Hamburg (Case C-33/89) [1992] ICR 29 139

Laider v. Perry [1966] AC 16, [1964] 3 WLR 709, [1964] 3 All ER 329 333
Landers v. Attorney General, 109 ILTR 1 (1975) 11
Landsorganisationen i Danmark v. Ny Molle Kro (Case 287/86) [1989]
    2 CMLR 468 225
Lansing Linde Ltd v. Kerr [1991] 1 WLR 251 104
Lavery v. Plessey Telecommunications Ltd [1983] ICR 534 150
Lawrie-Blum v. Land Baden-Wurttenberg (Case 66/85) [1986] ECR
    2121; [1987] 3 CMLR 389 .... 128, 133
Laws v. London Chronicle Ltd [1959] 1 WLR 698; [1959] 2 All ER 285 ... 164
Lee Ting Sang v. Chung Chi Keung [1990] 2 AC 374; [1990]
    2 WLR 1173 .... 32, 41
Leverton v. Clwyd County Council [1990] AC 706; [1989] 2 WLR 47;
    [1989] 1 All ER 78 138
Levin v. Secretary of State (Case 53/81) [1982] ECR 1035 128
Lewis v. Motorworld Garages Ltd [1986] ICR 158 .... 154, 182
Lewis v. Squash (Ireland) Ltd [1983] ILRM 363 46
Leyden v. Attorney General [1926] IR 334 323
Limerick County Council v. Irish Insurance Cmrs [1934] IR 364 38
Limerick Health Authority v. Ryan [1969] IR 194 .... 187, 210
Lion Laboratories Ltd v. Evans [1985] 1 QB 526; [1984] 3 WLR 539;
    [1984] 2 All ER 417 98
Liscoe v. Henry [1926] IR 137 38
Lister v. Romford Ice & Cold Storage Co. [1957] AC 555; [1957]
    2 WLR 158; [1957] 1 All ER 125 54
Listster v. Forth Dry Dock & Engineering Co. [1990] 1 AC 547;
    [1989] 2 WLR 634; [1989] 1 All ER 1134 .... 224, 228, 237
Littlewoods Organisation Ltd v. Harris [1977] 1 WLR 1472; [1978]
    1 All ER 1028 103
Lloyds Bank v. Secretary of State [1979] 1 WLR 498; [1979]
    2 All ER 573 188
Loat v. Andrews [1986] ICR 679 290
Loftus and Healy v. An Bord Telecom (unrep. 13 Feb. 1987) 198
Logue v. Pentland [1930] IR 6 38
London Transport Executive v. Clarke [1981] ICR 355 156
Lonsdale v. Attorney General [1928] IR 35 206
Looney v. Looney (UD 843/1984) 197
Lord Advocate v. Scotsman Publications Ltd [1990] AC 812; [1989]
    2 WLR 358; [1989] 2 All ER 852 312
Lucas (T.) & Co. v. Mitchell [1972] 1 WLR 938; [1972] 2 All ER 1035 103
Lupton v. Potts [1969] 1 WLR 1749, [1969] 3 All ER 1083 343
Lynch v. Limerick County Council [1926] IR 176 41
Lynch v. Sunbeam Ltd (U.D. 20/77) 204

M, Re [1955] NI 182 238
McCabe v. Lisney & Co. [1981] ILRM 289 .... 23, 40, 203

McCarroll v. Hickling Pentecost & Co. [1971] NI 250 64
McCarthy v. CIE (unrep., 10 May 1985) 198
McCormac Products Ltd v. Monaghan Co-Op. Ltd [1988] IR 304 264
McClaren v. Home Office [1990] ICR 824 293
McClelland v. Northern Ireland General Health Services Board
    [1957] 1 WLR 594; [1957] 2 All ER 129 . . . . .162-163, 303
McCreery v. Bennett [1904] 2 IR 69 95
McDermid v. Nash Dredging & Reclaimation Ltd [1987] AC 906;
    [1987] 3 WLR 212; [1987] 2 All ER 878 120
McDermott v. Loy (Unrep., 29 July 1982) 36, 39, 40, 329
McDonald v. Des Gibney Ltd (UD 329/85) 204
McDonnell v. Minister for Education [1940] IR 316 161
McDonough v. Minister for Defence [1991] ILRM 115 . . . . 299, 327
McEllistrim v. Ballymacelligot Co-op Agricultural & Dairy Soc. Ltd
    [1919] AC 548 101
McEneaney v. Minister for Education [1941] IR 430 . . . . 323, 324
McEvanhenry Ltd, Re (Unrep., 15 May 1986) 233
McGarry v. R. [1954] IR 64 346
McGowan v. Wren [1988] ILRM 744 298
McGrath v. Comr. Garda Síochána [1991] 1 IR 69 302
McGrath v. Maynooth College [1979] ILRM 166 . . . . 8, 321
McGregor v. Randall [1984] 1 All ER 1092 335
McHugh v. Comr. Garda Síochána [1986] IR 228 326
McLoughlin v. Great Southern Railways Co. [1944] IR 479 . . . . 162, 170
McLoughlin v. Minister for Social Welfare [1958] IR 1 306-307
McLoughlin v. Minister for Public Service [1985] IR 631 326
McMillan v. Guest [1942] AC 561 331
McSweeney v. O.K. Garages Ltd (U.D. 107/78) 202
Mack Trucks (Britain) Ltd Re, [1967] 1 WLR 780;
    [1967] 1 All ER 977 235
Maguire v. P.J. Langan (Contractors) Ltd [1976] NI 49 31
Maher v. Attorney General [1973] IR 140 314
Mahon v. McLoughlin (1926) 11 TC 83 338
Malloch v. Aberdeen Corp. [1971] 1 WLR 1578; [1971]
    2 All ER 1278 . . . . 298, 315
Manning v. Mullins [1898] 2 IR 34 258
Marbe v. George Edwards (Day's Theatre) Ltd [1928] 1 KB 269 69
Market Investigations Ltd v. Minister for Social Security [1969]
    2 QB 173 [1969] 2 WLR 1; [1968] 3 All ER 732 . . . . 33, 39
Marks v. Wellman [1970] NI 236 215
Marlborough Harbour Board v. Goulden [1985] 2 NZLR 378 . . . . 170, 171
Marley v. Forward Trust Ltd [1986] ICR 891 62
Marrison v. Bell [1939] 2 KB 187 86
Marsden v. IRC. [1965] 1 WLR 734, [1965] 2 All ER 364 344

Marshall v. Harland & Wolff Ltd [1972] 1 WLR 899; [1972]
  2 All ER 715 159
Marshall v. Southampton & South West Herts. Health Authority (Case
  152/84) [1986] ECR 723 16
Marshall (Thomas) (Exports) Ltd v. Guinle [1979] Ch 227; [1978]
  3 WLR 116; [1978] 3 All ER 193 . . . . 4, 54, 96
Mason v. Provident Clothing & Supply Co. [1913] AC 724 . . . . 101, 103
Massey v. Crown Life Insurance Co. [1978] 1 WLR 676; [1978]
  2 All ER 576 37
Matthews v. Kuwati Bechtel Corp. [1957] 2 QB 57; [1959]
  2 WLR 702; [1959] 2 All ER 345 . . . . 4, 70, 120
Mauldon v. British Telecommunications plc. [1987] ICR 450 194
Maulik v. Air India [1974] ICR 528 270
Maunsell v. Minister for Education [1940] IR 213 . . . . 296, 298, 303, 324
Mears v. Safecar Security Ltd [1983] 1 QB 54; [1982]
  3 WLR 366; [1982] 2 All ER 865 . . . . 54, 56, 86
Meek v. Port of London Authority [1918] 1 Ch 415 59
Melon v. Hector Powe Ltd [1981] 1 All ER 313 215
Merrigan v. Home Counties Cleaning Ireland Ltd (UD 904/84) 202
Meskell v. CIE [1979] IR 121 8
Mettoy Pension Trustees Ltd v. Evans [1990] 1 WLR 1587; [1991]
  2 All ER 513 . . . . 249, 253, 256
Micklefield v. S.AC Technology Ltd [1991] 1 All ER 275 281
Midland Counties Bank v. Attwood [1905] 1 Ch 357 234
Midland Sinfonia Concert Soc. v. Secretary of State [1981] ICR 454 36
Mikkelsen v. Danmols Inventar A/S (Case 105/84) [1986] 223, 227
Miles v. Wakefield Council [1987] AC 539, [1987] 2 WLR 795;
  [1987] 1 All ER 1089 . . . . 75, 93
Minister for Industry & Commerce v. Hales [1967] IR 50 39
Minister for Industry & Commerce v. Healy [1941] IR 545 . . . . 39, 49
Minister for Industry & Commerce v. Jones [1927] IR 216 38
Minister for Industry & Commerce v. Ussher [1948] IR 133 83
Minister for Labour v. Costello [1988] IR 235 85
Mirror Group Newspapers Ltd v. Gunning [1985] 1 WLR 394 . . . . . 30, 137, 141
Mitchell & Eldon v. Ross [1960] Ch 145; [1961] 3 WLR 411;
  [1961] 3 All ER 49 . . . . 41, 331
Morgan v. Manser [1948] 1 KB 184; [1947] 2 All ER 666 159
Morren v. Swinton & Pendlebury BC [1965] 1 WLR 576; [1965]
  2 All ER 349 34
Morris v. C.H. Bailey Ltd [1969] 2 LlLR 215 63
Motokov Foreign Trade Corp. v. Fermoyle Investments Ltd
  (Unrep., 25 Jan. 1985) 272
Mulcahy v. O'Sullivan [1944] IR 336 . . . . 53, 84
Mulvey v. Coffey [1942] IR 277 . . . . 333, 346, 348
Murco Petroleum Ltd v. Forge [1987] ICR 282 154

Murphy v. Minister for Social Welfare [1987] IR 295 .... 307, 309
Murphy v. Stewart [1973] IR 97 11
Murphy v. Telecom Éireann [1986] ILRM 483, reversed;
    [1988] ILRM 53 139
Murtagh Properties Ltd v. Cleary [1972] IR 330 .... 7, 10-11
Mythen v. Employment Appeals Tribunal [1989] ILRM 844 ..... 226, 230, 237
Narich Pty Ltd v. Commr. Pay Roll Tax [1984] ICR 286 .... 34, 37, 329
National Coal Board v. Galley [1958] 1 WLR 16; [1958] 1 All ER 91 ... 61, 75
National Coal Board v. National Union of Mineworkers [1986] ICR 736 63
National Insurance Act, 1911—Officers of South Dublin Union, Re
    [1913] 1 IR 244 318
National Maternity Hospital v. Minister for Social Welfare
    [1960] IR 74 .... 47, 105
National Union of Railwaymen v. Sullivan [1947] IR 354 6
Nelson v. Saudi Arabia, 923 F 2d 1528 (1991) 274
Nethermere (St. Neots) Ltd v. Gardiner [1984] ICR 612 .... 39, 49
New Zealand Educational Institute v. Director General of Education
    [1981] 1 NZLR 538 48
Newell v. Starkie [1917] 2 IR 73 312
Newman (R.S.) Ltd, Re [1916] 2 Ch 309 233
Ni Bheolain v. Dublin VEC (Unrep., 28 Jan. 1983) 322
Nokes v. Doncaster Amalg. Collieries Ltd [1940] AC 1014 .... 221, 228
Norris v. Attorney General [1984] IR 36 142
North East Coast Shiprepairers Ltd v. Secretary of State
    [1978] ICR 755 105
North Island Wholesale Groceries Ltd v. Hewin [1982]
    1 NZLR 176 .... 164, 177
North Western Health Board v. Martyn [1987] IR 565 .... 25, 135, 145, 146
Norwest Holst Group Administration Ltd v. Harrison [1985] ICR 668 154
Notcutt v. Universal Equipment Co. (London) Ltd [1986] 1 WLR 641;
    [1986] 3 All ER 582 158
Nova Colour Graphic Supplies Ltd v. Employment Appeals Tribunal
    [1987] IR 426 .... 186, 215, 223
Nurse v. Morgan Crucible Ltd [1989] AC 692; [1989] 2 WLR 82;
    [1989] 1 All ER 113 124

O'Brien v. Associated Fire Alarms Ltd [1968] 1 WLR 1916; [1969]
    1 All ER 93 .... 54, 76, 154
O'Brien v. Minister for Finance [1944] IR 392 326
O'Brien v. Minister for Finance (No.2) [1946] IR 314 326
O'Brien v. Tipperary (South Riding) Board of Health [1938] IR 761 41
O'Broin v. McGiolla Merdhre [1959] IR 98 342
O'Callaghan v. Irish Insurance Cmrs. [1915] 2 IR 262 318
O'Callaghan v. Meath VEC (Unrep., 20 Nov. 1990) 322
O'Callaghan v. Minister for Education (Unrep., 30 Nov. 1955) 324

O'Coindealbhain v. O'Carroll [1989] IR 229 338
O'Coindealbhain v. Mooney [1990] 1 IR 422 36
O'Donoghue v. Vetinary Council [1975] IR 398 300
O'Driscoll v. Cork CC [1931] IR 92 206
O'Flynn v. Mid Western Health Board [1989] IR 429 299
O'Friel v. St. Michael's Hospital [1982] ILRM 260 . . . . 34, 39
O'Grady v. Saper Ltd [1940] 2 KB 469 86
O'Kelly v. Trusthouse Forte Ltd [1984] 1 QB 90; [1983] 3 WLR 605;
      [1983] 3 All ER 456 21
O'Looney v. Minister for Public Service [1986] IR 543 326
O'Mahony v. Henry Ford & Son Ltd [1962] IR 146 . . . . 119, 123
O'Neill v. Beaumont Hospital Board [1990] ILRM 419 . . . . 294, 300
O'Neill v. Iarnrod Eireann [1991] ILRM 129 294
O'Neill v. Tipperary CC (South Riding) [1926] IR 397 206
O'Rourke v. Talbot Motors Ltd [1984] ILRM 587 60
O'Sullivan v. Limerick CC [1928] IR 493 206
Octavius Atkinson & Sons Ltd v. Morris [1989] ICR 431 184
Orman v. Saville Sportswear Ltd [1960] 1 WLR 1055, [1960]
      3 All ER 105 . . . . 53, 86
Ottoman Bank v. Chakarin [1930] AC 277 71
Owen v. Burden [1972] 1 All ER 356 342
Owen v. Pook [1970] AC 244; [1969] 2 WLR 775; [1969]
      2 All ER 1 . . . . 338, 344, 345

Pambankien v. Brentford Nylons Ltd [1978] ICR 665 . . . . 215, 220
Parcelli v. Strathclyde Regional Council [1986] ICR 564 142
Paris v. Stepney Borough Council [1951] AC 367 . . . . 70, 118
Parke v. Daily News Ltd [1962] Ch 927; [1962] 3 WLR 966; [1962]
      2 All ER 927 275
Parsons v. Albert J. Parsons & Sons [1979] ICR 271 41
Parsons v. B.N.M. Laboratories Ltd [1964] 1 QB 95; [1963] 2 WLR
      1273; [1963] 2 All ER 658 . . . . 177, 241
Patchett v. Sterling (1955) 72 RPC 50 100
Paterson (Andrew M.) Ltd, Re [1981] 2 NZLR 289 62
Pearce v. University of Aston, [1991] 2 All ER 461, 469 322
Penman v. Fife Coal Co. [1936] AC 45 92
People v. Warren [1945] IR 24 . . . . 41, 318, 319
Pepper v. Webb [1969] 1 WLR 514; [1969] 2 All ER 216 . . . . 73, 163
Pereira v. Hotel Jayapuri Bhd. [1986] 1 WLR 449 83
Perrons v. Spackman [1981] 1 WLR 1411 245
Petrie v. Mac Fisheries Ltd [1940] 1 KB 258 . . . . 58, 87
Phelan v. Minister for Local Government [1930] IR 542 318
Phillipps v. Keane [1925] IR 48 344
Pickstone v. Freemans plc [1989] AC 66; [1988] 3 WLR 265; [1988]
      2 All ER 803 . . . . 138, 139

Picton v. Cullen [1900] 2 IR 612 95
Polkey v. A.E. Dayton Services Ltd [1988] 1 AC 344; [1987]
    3 WLR 1153; [1987] 3 All ER 947 198
Poussard v. Spiers (1876) 1 QBD 410 158
Powell v. Brent LBC [1988] ICR 176 174
President of Methodist Conference v. Parfitt [1984] 1 QB 368; [1984]
    2 WLR 84; [1983] 3 All ER 747 50
Price v. Movat (1862) CB (NS) 508 165
Provident Financial Group plc v. Hayward [1989] ICR 160 179
Public Employees, Re: E.C. Commission v. Belgium (Case 149/79)
    [1980] ECR 3881 000
Pupil Teachers and Monitors, Case of [1913] 1 IR 219 47

Qualcast (Wolverhampton) Ltd v. Haynes [1959] AC 743; [1959]
    2 WLR 510; [1959] 2 All ER 38 119

R. v. Bembridge (1783) 3 Doug KB 327 311
R. v. Chief Constable of Thames Valley Police, ex p. Cotton [1990]
    IRLR 344 293
R. v. Civil Service Appeal Board, ex p. Bruce [1988] ICR 649 309
R. v. Derbyshire C.C., ex p. Noble [1990] ICR 808 293
R. v. Hillingdon Health Authority, ex p. Goodwin [1984] ICR 800 296
R. v. Llellwyn-Jones [1968] 1 QB 429; [1967] 3 WLR 1298; [1967]
    3 All ER 225 312
R. v. London Transport C'tee, ex p. Freight Transport Assn. Ltd [1990]
    3 CMLR 495 16
R. v. Minister for Agriculture, ex p. Agegate Ltd (Case C-3/87) [1990]
    1 CMLR 366 .... 128, 130
R. v. National Coal Board, ex p. National Union of Mineworkers [1986]
    ICR 791 296
R. v. Newbould Ltd [1962] 2 QB 102; [1962] 2 WLR 648; [1962]
    1 All ER 693 293
R. v. Secretary of State, ex p. Thornton [1987] QB 36; [1987]
    3 WLR 158; [1986] 2 All ER 641 303
R. v. Trinity House London Pilotage C'tee [1985] 2 CMLR 413 129
R. v. Welch (1853) 2 E & B 357 68
R. (Dillon) v. Minister for Local Government [1927] IR 474 318
R. (in right of the Province of Ontario) v. Jennings (1966)
    57 DLR 2d 644 177
R. (McMorrow) v. Fitzpatrick [1918] 2 IR 103 304
Rainey v. Greater Glasgow Health Board [1987] AC 224; [1986]
    2 WLR 1087; [1987] 1 All ER 65 140
Rank Xerox Ltd v. Churchill [1988] IRLR 280 76
Reading v. Attorney General [1951] AC 507; [1951] 1 All ER 617 .... 312, 327

Ready Mixed Concrete (South East) Ltd v. Minister of Pensions and
    Social Security [1968] 2 QB 497; [1968] 2 WLR 775; [1968]
    1 All ER 433 . . . . 33, 37, 38, 39
Reed v. Seymour [1927] AC 554 332
Reid v. Explosives Co. (1887) 19 QBD 264 235
Reid v. Rush & Tomkins Group plc [1990] 1 WLR 212; [1989]
    3 All ER 228 . . . . 53, 118
Reigate v. Union Mfg. Co. [1918] 1 KB 592 234
Rendell v. Went [1964] 1 WLR 650; [1963] 3 All ER 325 337
Revenue Comrs. v. Kelly (EE 9/1987) 146
Richards v. Hayward (1841) 2 M & G 574 178
Ricketts v. Colquhoun [1926] AC 1 . . . . 342, 343
Rigby v. Ferodo Ltd [1988] ICR 29 . . . . 154, 155, 182
Riley v. Coglan (1967) 44 TC 481 334
Rinner-Kuhn v. FWW Spezial-Gebaudereinigung Gmbh
    (Case 171/89) [1989] IRLR 493 139
Robb v. Green [1895] 2 QB 315 96
Robb v. Hammersmith & Fulham LBC [1991] ICR 514 171
Robertson v. British Gas Corp. [1983] ICR 351 62
Roche v. Kelly [1969] IR 100 33
Rubel Bronze & Metal Co., Re [1918] 1 KB 315 . . . . 68, 73
Rummler v. Dato-Druck Gmbh (Case 237/85) [1987] 3 CMLR 127 139

Sagar v. Ridehalgh Ltd [1931] 1 Ch 310 . . . . 58, 91
Santokh Singh v. Guru Nanak Gurdwara [1990] ICR 309 50
Santry v. Coast Lines Ltd [1964] IR 439 268
Sayers v. International Drilling Co. NV [1971] 1 WLR 1176; [1971]
    3 All ER 163 . . . . 266, 267
Scally v. Southern Health & Social Services Board [1991] 3 WLR 778;
    [1991] 4 All ER 563 . . . . 4, 5, 57
Scanlon v. Hartlepool SS Co. [1929] IR 96 268
Secretary of State v. A.S.L.E.F. (No.2) [1972] 2 QB 455; [1972]
    2 WLR 13700; [1972] 2 All ER 949 . . . . 52, 72
Secretary of State v. Cheltenham Computer Bureau [1985] ICR 381 207
Secretary of State v. Cooper [1987] ICR 766 242
Seltz's Application, Re (1954) 71 RPC 50 100
Sengupta v. Republic of India [1983] ICR 221 274
Sex Discrimination in the Civil Service, Re (Case 318/86) [1989]
    3 CMLR 663 141
Sheering Chemicals Ltd v. Falkman Ltd [1982] 1 QB 1; [1981] 2 WLR
    848; [1981] 2 All ER 321 98
Shepherd (F.C.) Ltd v. Jerrom [1987] 1 QB 301; [1986] 2 WLR 101;
    [1986] 3 All ER 589 . . . . 156, 159
Shilton v. Wilmhurst [1991] 1 AC 684; [1991] 2 WLR 530; [1991]
    3 All ER 148 336

Shipsey v. British & South American Steam Navigation Co.
[1936] IR 65 265
Shirlaw v. Southern Foundries (1926) Ltd [1939] 2 KB 206 53
Shove v. Downs Surgical plc. [1984] ICR 532 .... 176, 177
Sim v. Rotherham Metropolitan BC [1987] 1 Ch 216; [1986]
2 WLR 851; [1986] 3 All ER 387 .... 75, 90, 93
Simpson v. Tate [1925] 2 KB 214 342
Sinclair v. Dublin City VEC (UD 349/86) 187
Siney v. Dublin Corp. [1980] IR 400 54
Singh v. British Steel Corp. [1974] IRLR 131 63
Sister Dolores v. Minister for Social Welfare [1960] 2 IR 77 .... 47-48, 105
Society for the Protection of Unborn Children (Ireland) Ltd v. Open
Counselling Ltd [1988] IR 593 8-9
Soc. Sanicentral v. Collins (Case 25/79) [1979] ECR 3423 263
Solus Teo., Re [1990] ILRM 180 242
Somali Bank v. Rahman [1989] ICR 314 270
Spijkers v. Gebroeders Benedik Abattoir BV (Case 24/85) [1986]
2 CMLR 296 225
Stakelum v. Canning [1976] IR 314 238
State (Curtin) v. Minister for Health [1953] IR 93 .... 320, 321
State (Cussen) v. Brennan [1981] IR 181 317
State (Daly) v. Minister for Agriculture [1987] IR 165 .... 305, 314, 315
Stae (Donegal VEC) v. Minister for Education [1985] IR 56 322
State (Gleeson) v. Minister for Defence
[1976] IR 280 ....11-12, 167, 297, 327
State (IBM Ireland Ltd) v. Employment Appeals Tribunal [1984]
ILRM 31 203
State (Irish Pharmaceutical Union) v. Employment Appeals Tribunal
[1987] ILRM 36 .... 23, 168, 204
State (Kerry County Council) v. Minister for Local Government [1933]
IR 517 292
State (McGarrity) v. Deputy Comr. Garda Síochána, 112 ILTT 25
(1978) 305
State (Minister for Local Government) v. Cork Mental Hospital [1932]
IR 207 317
State (Minister for Local Government) v. Ennis Mental Hospital [1939]
IR 258 317
State (O'Callaghan) v. O'Huadaigh [1977] IR 42 302
State (Raftis) v. Leonard [1960] IR 381 318
Stenhouse Australia Ltd v. Phillips [1974] AC 391; [1974] 2 WLR 134;
[1974] 1 All ER 117 .... 102, 103
Stenson v. CIE [1967] IR 409 206
Stevenson, Jordan & Harrison Ltd v. Mucdonald & Evans
[1952] TLR 101 000
Stevens v. Brodribb Sawmilling Co. Pty Ltd (1986) 160 CLR 16 120

Stroker v. Doherty [1991] 1 IR 23 . . . . 304, 305, 326
Suffolk C.C. v. Secretary of State [1984] ICR 882 187
Sunday Tribune Ltd, Re [1984] IR 505 . . . . 34, 35, 37, 99, 238
Sweeney v. Duggan (Unrep., 31 July 1991) 118
Sybron Corp. v. Rochem Ltd [1984] 1 Ch 112; [1983] 3 WLR 113;
    [1983] 2 All ER 707 72
System Floors (UK) Ltd v. Daniel [1982] ICR 54 56

Tadd v. Eastwood [1983] IRLR 320 63
Tai Hing v. Cotton Mill Ltd v. Liv Chong Hing Bank Ltd [1986]
    AC 80, [1978] 2 WLR 62, [1978] 1 All ER 515 5
Taylor v. Caldwell (1863) 3 B. & S. 826 158
Taylor v. Provan [1975] AC 194, [1974] 2 WLR 394, [1974]
    1 All ER 1201 345
Tennant v. Smith [1892] AC 150 339
Thistle v. Monaghan County Council [1931] IR 381 319
Thomas v. University of Bradford [1987] AC 795, [1987] 2 WLR 677;
    (1987) 1 All ER 834, R. 517, IR 207 . . . . 321, 322
Thompson v. ASDA–MFI Group plc [1988] 1 Ch 241; [1988]
    2 WLR 1093; [1988] 2 All ER 722 279
Thompson v. Smith Shiprepairers (North Shields) Ltd [1984] QB 405,
    [1984] 2 WLR 522, [1984] 1 All ER 881 . . . . 118, 123
Tilley v. Wales [1943] AC 386 347
Todd v. British Midland Airways Ltd [1978] ICR 959 270
Tomalin v. Pearson & Son Ltd [1909] 2 KB 61 268
Turner v. Goldsmith [1891] 1 QB 544 69
Turner v. Sawdon & Co. [1901] 2 KB 653 . . . . 68, 69
Tyne & Clyde Warehouses Ltd v. Hamerton [1978] ICR 661 37

Union Nationale de Entraineurs v. Heylers (Case 222/86) [1989]
    1 CMLR 901 130
United States v. Silk, 331 US 704 (1946) 36
United States Civil Service Comm. v. National Assn. of Letter Carriers,
    413 US 548 (1973) 304

Van der Mussele v. Belgium 6 EHRR 163 (1983) 17
Van Duyn v. Home Office (Case 41/74) [1974] ECR 1337 128
Vaughan-Neill v. Inland Revenue [1979] 1 WLR 1283; [1979]
    3 All ER 481 334
Vorvis v. Insurance Corp. of British Columbia [1989] SCR 1085 176

Waikato Savings Bank v. Andrews Furniture Ltd [1982] 2 NZLR 520 240
Waite v. Government Communications Headquarters [1983] 2 AC 714;
    [1983] 3 WLR 389; [1983] 2 All ER 1013 194

Walgrave & Koch v. Assn. Union Cycliste (Case 36/74) [1974]
ECR 1405 15
Wallace v. South Eastern Education and Library Board [1980] NI 38 142
Walsh v. Cassidy & Co. [1951] I Jur Rep 47 280-281
Walsh v. Dublin Health Authority, 98 ILTR 82 (1964) 161
Warren v. Mendy [1989] 1 WLR 853, [1989] 3 All ER 103 ...... 104, 173, 178
Webb v. (Ireland) [1988] IR 353 301
Wendelboe v. L.J. Music Aps (Case 19/83) [1986] 1 CMLR 476 227
West v. Kneels Ltd [1987] ICR 146 185
Westall Richardson Ltd v. Raulson [1954] 2 All ER 448 39
Western Health Board v. Quigley [1982] ILRM 390 318
Westwood v. Secretary of State [1985] AC 20; [1984] 2WLR 418;
[1984] 1 All ER 719 .... 191, 241
WHPT Housing Assn. v. Secretary of State [1981] ICR 737 34
Wheelan v. Minister for Justice (unrep., 29 June 1990) 314
Wheeler v. Patel [1987] ICR 631 230
White (Marian) Ltd v. Francis [1972] 1 WLR 423; [1972] 3 All ER 587 ... 102
Whitwood Chemical Co. v. Hardman [1891] 2 Ch 416 104
Wickers v. Champion Employment [1984] ICR 365 38
Wigg v. Attorney General [1927] IR 285 206
Wilkins v. Rogerson [1961] 1 Ch 133; [1961] 2 WLR 102; [1961]
1 All ER 358 339
Williams v. North's Navigation Collieries (1889) Ltd [1906] AC 136 92
Wilson v. Maynard Shipbuilding Consultants Ltd [1978] 1 QB 665;
[1978] 2 WLR 466; [1978] 2 All ER 78 269-270
Wilsons & Clyde Coal Co. v. English [1938] AC 57 .... 4, 118
Wilts Police Authority v. Wynn [1981] 1 QB 95 [1980] 3 WLR 445 48
Wiluszynske v. Tower Hamlets BC [1989] ICR 493 75
Winfield v. London Philharmonic Orchestra Ltd [1979] ICR 726 36
Wing v. O'Connell [1927] IR 84 333
Wislang's Application, Re [1984] NI 63 322
Withers v. Teachers Retirement System of New York, 447 F Supp 1248
(1978) 251
Wood v. Cunard Line Ltd [1991] ICR 13 272
Woods v. Dublin Corp. [1931] IR 396 319
Woods v. W.M. Car Services (Peterborough) [1982] ICR 693 154
Worthington v. Moore (1903) 20 RPC 41 100
Wright v. Boyce (1958) 38 TC 138 334
Wrights v. Day [1895] 2 IR 337 50
Wyatt v. Kreglinger & Fernau [1933] 1 KB 793 103

X. v. Ireland (1971) 14 Y B'k ECHR 118, 198 17-18

Young v. Canadian Northern Rly. Co. [1931] AC 83 62

1

Introductory

Employment law is concerned with the relations existing between employers and their employees. The employment relationship is governed principally by the contract of employment between the employer and his employee; the rights and responsibilities of employees derive from this contract and also from various Acts which lay down employment standards. Just as the relationships between members of families have generated their own body of law, based on an amalgam of contractual obligations, equitable principles and statutory provisions, the relations between employers and workers have given rise to their own distinctive set of legal rules. Indeed in some Continental European countries there is an entirely separate tier of courts for dealing with practically all labour law questions. The Employment Appeals Tribunal, which deals with many issues under the more important pieces of employment protection legislation,[1] is a much diluted version of the Continental labour courts.

HISTORICAL CONTEXT

On the eve of the industrial revolution and indeed for many decades later, employment law was regarded in much the same light as family law. In his masterly account of the 'Laws of England',[2] which perhaps is the most important law book ever to be published in the English-speaking world, the great jurist Blackstone, writing in the eighteenth century, placed his account of the law of 'Master and Servant' in his first book, dealing with the 'Law of Persons', in between sections on 'Army and Navy' and on 'Husband and Wife'. According to Blackstone, the great relationships in private life are the family relationship and the employment relationship. Regarding the latter, he observed that it is 'founded in convenience, whereby a man is directed to call in the assistance of others, where his own skill and labour will not be sufficient to answer the cares incumbent on him.'[3] He listed four

1. See infra p.22.
2. W. Blackstone, *Commentaries on the Laws of England* (4 vols., 1765-69).
3. Vol. I at p.422 (ibid. 1825).

principal categories of employees of his time; domestic or menial servants, apprentices, labourers hired by the day or by the week and 'superior servants', like stewards, bailiffs etc. The vast majority of employees or servants at the time were either domestics or farm labourers. Most persons carrying on a trade or a profession were self-employed. Outside of domestic service, women workers hardly featured in the labour market. Although he did not refer to them, even by Blackstone's time a significant number of persons worked in industry and commerce. The main feature of the labour market since that time has been the steady contraction in the number of domestic and agricultural workers, matched with an expansion of employment in trade, particularly in the service of limited companies, and also the emergence of the State, either at central or local government level, as a major employer.

By the middle of the last century it was generally recognised that the legal lynchpin of the employment relationship was the contract which the employer and employee entered into, to provide services in return for remuneration. Occasionally, there might be an actual written agreement spelling out in detail the rights and obligations of the parties. More often, the contract would be oral, with the parties agreeing that the terms of employment shall be the same as apply to others then employed at the same kind of work. Most of the labour legislation in the nineteenth century was concerned with industrial relations and trade unionism. As is explained elsewhere,[4] workers would band together in trade unions in order to seek for themselves improved terms and conditions of employment. Because the great majority of workers then did not have the franchise, they did not possess the political influence to secure the enactment of legislation that would significantly improve their rights over those of their employers. However, some protective measures were enacted in the Victorian era.

An important measure, which remained on the statute book up to July 1991, is of a slightly earlier vintage, the Truck Act, 1831.[5] Among the main measures adopted in the last century affecting employees (other than trade union legislation) were the several Factories Acts, which laid down minimum standards of safety in factories, and the Workmen's Compensation Act of 1897, which established a no-fault compensation system for workers who were injured during the course of their employment.[6] In 1909 the trade

---

4. *Industrial Relations Law* (1991)—hereinafter referred to as *Industrial Relations Law*.
5. There was an earlier Truck Act, of 1743 (17 Geo. II c.8).
6. See generally, B. Shillman, *Employers' Liability and Workmen's Compensation in Ireland* (2nd ed. 1942). In 1966 the workmen's compensation system was replaced entirely by social welfare occupational injury benefits: Social Welfare (Occupational Injuries) Act, 1966.

boards system was established which sought to set minimum wages for badly paid workers who were not unionised.[7] In the 1930s measures were enacted dealing with matters like employment conditions in industrial establishments, in shops and in bakeries, and with minimum wages for agricultural workers. Most of the employment legislation now in force was enacted in the 1970s, notably, the Unfair Dismissals Act, 1977, measures dealing with sex discrimination in work, redundancy payments and minimum notice of dismissal from employment. Many of the measures adopted in the 1980s were prompted by E.C. Directives.

CONTRACT, TORT AND STATUTORY DUTIES

As has been stated, the legal kernel of the employment relationship is the contract of employment. This may be written or unwritten; its main terms may have been the subject of express agreement between the parties or they may be implied from the surrounding circumstances, such as collective agreements with trade unions, works or office rules, custom and practice at the workplace. Where either party contravenes any of the terms of their contract, the other party can seek redress by suing for breach of contract and will recover damages for any consequent losses suffered. Exceptionally, breach of the contract may be enjoined or be sanctioned by an employer refusing to pay wages for work that is not done. The general principles of the law of contract, therefore, have a very strong bearing on employment law.[8]

Tort The employment relationship is also affected by the law of tort. Tort law is concerned with a variety of duties which the common law imposes on persons over and above whatever obligations they may have assumed under contracts.[9] By far the most important of these duties in the employment relationship is the duty of care that employers owe for their employees' safety while at work. Long before the famous 'snail in the ginger ale bottle' case[10] and its Irish counterpart, the 'maggot in the jam jar' case,[11] were decided, the courts laid down a variety of obligations in tort in respect of

---

7. Trade Boards Act, 1909. These were replaced by joint labour committees: see *Industrial Relations Law*, pp. 218-220.
8. A comprehensive account is contained in M. Freedland, *The Contract of Employment* (1976).
9. See generally, B. McMahon & W. Binchy, *Irish Law of Torts* (2nd ed. 1990).
10. *Donoghue v. Stevenson* [1932] AC 562.
11. *Kibry v. Burke* [1944] IR 207.

employees' safety at work and these duties were supplemented and expanded by statutory provisions.[12]

Statutes Legislative provisions concerning employment-related matters, be they contained in Acts of the Oireachtas or of previous Parliaments or in regulations made under Acts, affect employers and workers in several different ways. The standard of conduct prescribed in the Act may be deemed to be a term of the employment contract and thereby become enforceable like any other contractual term.[13] Alternatively, the Act may establish or incorporate some special mode or process by which its requirements may be enforced. Or the Act may simply render certain conduct a criminal offence. The Act may even lay down some standard of conduct but not indicate when or in what manner its requirements may be enforced. Thus, the vexed question of when do statutory obligations give persons a civil right of action in the ordinary courts whenever the legislative requirements have been contravened. In other words, although perhaps oversimplifying the question, when are criminal or regulatory offences, or other statutory obligations, also actionable torts? [14] In the employment law field, this question arises most frequently in connection with prescribed safety standards where the plaintiff suffered injury because those standards were not complied with.[15]

Contract or Tort? Occasionally conduct which is actionable as a tort may also be actionable as a breach of an express or an implied term of a contract. Accordingly, the party affected by the breach of duty in question can sue either in contract or in tort. This is very much the case with the employer's duty of care, which requires that workers be provided with safe tools, a safe workplace, a safe system of working and safe fellow-employees. Normally this duty is regarded as arising in tort.[16] But the duty of care is equally an implied term of the employment contract.[17] Another such duty is that which forbids the disclosure of or exploitation of confidential information obtained in the course of employment. Where that obligation is not expressly stipulated in the employment contract, the duty is an implied term of that contract and also is imposed extra-contractually.[18]

12. See post p.118.   13. E.g. Anti-Discrimination (Pay) Act, 1974.
14. See generally, Buckley, 'Liability in Tort for Breach of Statutory Duty', 100 *LQR* 204 (1984). Cf. *Scally v. Southern Health and Social Services Board* [1991] 4 All ER 563, at pp.573-576.
15. See post p. 120
16. *Wilsons & Clyde Coal Co. Ltd v. English* [1938] AC 57.
17. *Matthews v. Kuwait Bechtel Corp.* [1957] 2 QB 57.
18. *Thomas Marshall (Exports) Ltd v. Guinle* [1979] Ch. 227.

In *Scally v. Southern Health and Social Services Board*,[19] the plaintiffs had lost certain pension entitlements under a pension scheme, the terms of which had been made part of their contracts. Had they been informed by the employer of changes which had been made in the contribution rules for that scheme, they would have made additional contributions and thereby would have obtained the benefits which were lost. They sued their employer for damages in respect of those lost benefits, basing their claim in contract, in tort and for breach of statutory duty. It was held that, generally, in disputes between employees and their employer, it is preferable to analyse the issues by reference to the law of contract rather than the tort of negligence. The following statement of principle was approved:

> there is [no]thing to the advantage of the law's development in searching for a liability in tort where the parties are in a contractual relationship. This is particularly so in a commercial relationship. Though it is possible as a matter of legal semantics to conduct an analysis of the rights and duties inherent in some contractual relationships . . . either as a matter of contract law when the question will be what, if any, terms are to be implied or as a matter of tort law when the task will be to identify the duty arising from the proximity and character of the relationship between the parties, . . . it [is] correct in principle and necessary for the avoidance of confusion in the law to adhere to the contractual analysis: on principle because it is a relationship in which the parties have, subject to a few exceptions, the right to determine their obligations to each other, and for the avoidance of confusion because different consequences do follow according to whether liability arises from contract or tort, e.g. in the limitation of actions. . . . Since, in modern times, the relationship between master and servant, between employer and employee, is inherently one of contract, it [is] entirely correct to attribute the duties which arise from that relationship to implied contract.[20]

Ordinarily, it will not matter if a claim for breach of the duty in question is brought in contract or in tort; at one time the distinction was vital but the old system of formal pleading was abolished in the 1850s. Occasionally, however, it can be decisive how the action is framed; most notably, where the defendant is in some non-E.C. Member State and notice of the proceedings must be served on him. In one such case, Keane J held that a claim for damages for 'breach of duty', where the plaintiff was fatally injured in

19. [1991] 4 All ER 563.
20. Id. at p.568, from *Tai Hing Cotton Mill Ltd v. Liu Chong Hing Bank Ltd* [1986] AC 80, at p.107.

the course of his work, was a claim in tort and not one for breach of contract.[21] Accordingly, the rules for service outside the jurisdiction in tort cases applied. The contract/tort distinction can also be relevant for the purposes of statutes of limitation.[22] But where the claim is in respect of personal injuries there is the one limitation period regardless of how the claim is framed,[23] that is whether the action is one for breach of contract, tort or breach of statutory duty.

THE CONSTITUTION

The Constitution affects employment law in several ways. Laws and regulations will be declared invalid where they contravene some provision of the Constitution; for instance, in 1946 Part III of the Trade Union Act, 1941, was condemned because it infringed the guarantee of freedom of association[24] and in 1978 a minimum wage order for the hotels industry was condemned because employers who would be adversely affected by that order had not been given adequate opportunity to air their objections to it.[25] The basis for constitutional challenge to measures can be that they contravene the separation of powers between the legislature and the executive and the courts, that they impose unfair procedures, that they discriminate unfairly or that they infringe one of the other specified or unspecified rights, like the right to work. Very few measures dealing with employment questions have been struck down in this manner. As is explained elsewhere,[26] industrial action by trade unions can be unlawful because it contravenes the constitutional right of persons affected by that action, such as women workers being prevented from getting jobs and primary school children being prevented from receiving education.

The extent to which the Constitution affects relations between employers and workers, outside the industrial action and trade union sphere, is largely unexplored territory. One reason perhaps for the dearth of authority on the question is that many of the matters which might give rise to a constitutional right have been made the subject of legislative provision. Thus, the extent to which the Constitution guarantees non-discrimination between the sexes in the workplace is no longer of great practical importance because the matter of discrimination is regulated by two enactments, as well as by

21. *Campbell v. Holland Dredging Ltd* (3 March 1989).
22. Statute of Limitations, 1957, s.11.   23. Id. s.11(2)(b).
24. *National Union of Railwaymen v. Sullivan* [1947] IR 354.
25. *Burke v. Minister for Labour* [1979] IR 354.
26. *Industrial Relations Law*, pp.19-22.

Article 119 of the E.E.C. Treaty and several E.C. Directives.[27] Two general points arising under the Constitution call for brief consideration at this stage, viz. the non-governmental action question and the right to work.

Non-governmental action The State, in the guise of the legislature, the executive and other public authorities, is bound by the various obligations imposed by the Constitution. The principal purpose of having a Constitution which gives persons entrenched rights is to ensure that the State is properly run and to protect individuals from abuses of power by the State and its agencies. A matter which still requires some clarification, however, is to what extent private individuals and organisations, notably employers and employees, are bound by the Constitution in their dealings with each other.[28] Assuming that a certain practice would constitute unfair discrimination or unfair procedures or other unconstitutional action on the part of a public sector employer, does a private employer who engages in that practice violate the Constitution? A categorical answer has not yet been given to this question, although on several occasions it has been held that industrial action being taken by trade unions contravened others' constitutional rights.[29]

In the light of what was said in some of the trade union cases, it would seem that private sector employers are bound by the Constitution. According to Budd J in a case concerning picketing to enforce a closed shop,

> If an established right in law exists a citizen had the right to assert it and it is the duty of the Courts to aid and assist him in the assertion of his right. The Court will therefore assist and uphold a citizen's constitutional rights, obedience to the law is required of every citizen, and it follows that if one citizen has a right under the Constitution there exists a correlative duty on the part of other citizens to respect that right and not to interfere with it. To say otherwise would be tantamount of saying that a citizen can set the Constitution at nought and that a right solemnly given by our fundamental law is valueless. It follows that the Courts will not so act as to permit any body of citizens to deprive another of his constitutional rights and will in any proceedings before them see that these rights are protected, whether they be assailed under the guise of a statutory right or otherwise.[30]

And according to Walsh J in another closed shop case,

> If the Oireachtas cannot validly seek to compel a person to forego a

27. See post p.134 et seq.
28. See generally, M. Forde, *Constitutional Law of Ireland* (1987) ch.26.
29. E.g. *Murtagh Properties Ltd v. Cleary* [1972] IR 330.
30. *Educational Co. Ireland Ltd v. Fitzpatrick (No.2)* [1961] IR 345, at p.368.

constitutional right, can such a power be effectively exercised by some lesser body or by an individual employer? To exercise what may be loosely called a common law right of dismissal as a method of compelling a person to abandon a constitutional right, or as a penalty for him not doing so, must necessarily be regarded as an abuse of the common law right because it is an infringement, and an abuse, of the Constitution which is superior to the common law and which must prevail if there is a conflict between the two.[31]

However, what was decided in these cases is not authority for the proposition being canvassed here; one of them involved picketing which was expressly authorised by the terms of the Trade Disputes Act, 1906, and the employer in the second case was the State-owned public transport monopoly, Córas Iompair Éireann.

In the only reported case where the Supreme Court had to consider whether a private employer is bound by the Constitution, the Court found in favour of the employer. That was *McGrath v. Maynooth College*,[32] where the two plaintiffs were dismissed from their posts as professors in Maynooth College. This College was founded in 1795 as a seminary for training Catholic priests and until 1966 it admitted only clerical students and all its teaching staff were clerics. It then became empowered to grant degrees from the National University of Ireland and it hired some non-clerical teachers. The plaintiffs had been priests and full-time teaching officers of the College until they were dismissed from their posts in 1976 for breaking several College regulations. It was contended, unsuccessfully, that their dismissal was unlawful because it contravened their freedom of religion, on the grounds that the regulations they had broken forbade them from publishing matter without the consent of the College authorities and forbade wearing non-clerical dress in the College. Their dismissal was upheld principally because the guarantee of freedom of religion entitled the College to take measures which would safeguard the institution's special religious ethos. Kenny J took the view that, in any event, the guarantee of freedom of religion 'is confined to the State' and does not even apply to bodies which obtain financial subventions from the State.[33] None of the other judges addressed this point.

The most detailed pronouncement on the *drittwirkung* question was in *Society for the Protection of Unborn Children (Ireland) Ltd v. Open Counselling Ltd*,[34] where the defendants, two private companies, were sued for giving advice to pregnant women about abortion facilities in England.

31. *Meskell v. C.I.E.* [1973] IR 121, at p.135.   32. [1979] ILRM 166.
33. Id. at p.214.   34. [1988] IR 593.

It was held that such action contravened the 'right to life' guarantee. Answering the contention that, by its very terms, this guarantee only bound the State and it did not impose duties on private individuals and organisations, Hamilton P held that the courts are also an organ of the State and, accordingly, are obliged to protect the guaranteed rights. According to the learned President of the High Court,

> the courts will provide a procedure for the enforcement and protection of personal rights and the powers of the courts in this regard do not depend on legislation . . . .
>
> Under the Constitution . . . the State's powers of government are exercised in their respective spheres by the legislative, executive and judicial organs established under the Constitution and the courts will act to protect and enforce the rights of individuals and the provisions of the Constitution. . . .
>
> [T]he judicial organ of Government is obliged to lend its support to the enforcement of the right to life of the unborn, to defend and vindicate that right and, if there is a threat to that right from whatever source, to protect that right from such threat, if its support is sought.[35]

It, therefore, would seem that the courts will hold private sector employers to terms of the Constitution. However, the full rigours of constitutional obligation may not obtain in private sector employment because employers will invoke their own countervailing guaranteed rights of private property; the right to conduct their business affairs as they choose, subject to whatever duties are imposed on them by legislation and the common law and any obligations they may assume under contract. The position may very well be that it is an implied term of the employment contract that employees' constitutional rights will be respected, except where the contrary is expressly stipulated by the parties. This then leads on to the question of to what extent constitutional rights can be waived by contract, another matter about which there is a dearth of authority.

The right to work The expression the right to work means different things to different people. For the Paris revolutionaries of 1848 the *droit au travail* meant an obligation on the State to provide employment for everybody who needed a job. In the old Soviet Constitution that right was defined as the right to 'guaranteed employment and pay in accordance with the quantity and quality of their work, and not below the state-established minimum'. The term also signifies a right to an income from the State when one is

35. Id. at p.599.

unemployed, i.e. social security during unemployment. It also means a right not to be unfairly excluded from a job, or at the least not to be unfairly deprived of a job one already holds.

The right to work as envisaged by Article 1 of the European Social Charter[36] is formulated as follow:

> With a view to ensuring the effective exercise of the right to work, the Contracting Parties undertake:
> (1) to accept as one of their primary aims and responsibilities the achievement and maintenance of as high and stable a level of employment as possible, with a view to the attainment of full employment;
> (2) to protect effectively the right of the worker to earn his living in an occupation freely entered upon;
> (3) to establish or maintain free employment services for all workers;
> (4) to provide or promote appropriate vocational guidance, training and rehabilitation.

There is no express reference in the European Convention on Human Rights to employment as such (apart from trade union questions) and the only reference to employment in the Constitution is contained in the 'directive principles' in Article 45, which cannot be invoked by the courts in order to strike down post-1937 legislation. These principles state, *inter alia*,

> The State shall ... direct its policy towards securing: That the citizens (all of whom, men and women equally, have the right to an adequate means of livelihood) may through their occupations find the means of making reasonable provisions for their domestic needs.

But it has been held that the right to work is one of the unspecified rights under Article 40.3 of the Constitution.

Obtaining employment: In the first case in which the constitutional right to work obtained judicial recognition, that right was not founded on Article 40.3 but on the Article 45.2 'directive principle' quoted above; indeed the outcome of the case could also have been justified under Article 40.1, the equality clause. That was *Murtagh Properties Ltd v. Cleary*,[37] where trade union members picketed the plaintiff's property, a public house, in order to prevent non-union bar staff from being employed there. Since the union's membership was all male and it would not accept women into its membership, the picketers effectively sought to prevent women from being employed by the plaintiff. Kenny J held that Article 45.2 clearly means that 'in

36. Adopted, 18 Oct. 1961, [1965] IrTS no.3; see post p.19.
37. [1972] IR 330.

stipulates that laws and regulations 'necessitated by the obligations of [E.C.] membership' cannot be declared unconstitutional. What kinds of measures are so necessitated and who has final say in determining that question are matters of Community law and constitutional law beyond the scope of this book.[53]

Legislative competence Community institutions do not have authority to legislate for each and every aspect of employment law; their competence in this regard is defined by the Treaty of Rome, as amended. One of the principal objectives of the Community is fostering the free movement of workers between E.C. Member States and, in particular, preventing discrimination on the grounds of nationality against citizens of E.C. States in relation to employment. Several Regulations and Directives have been adopted giving effect to the principle of free movement, as set out in Articles 48 and 49 of the Treaty.[54] As has been observed, Article 119 also has been the subject of secondary Community legislation. Another source of community authority is Articles 100-101 of the Treaty dealing with the approximation or harmonisation of laws, whereby Member States can be required to adopt similar rules for various matters in order to facilitate 'the establishment or the functioning of the common market'.

Finally, under Article 118 of the Treaty, the Commission is given the task of promoting close co-operation between Member States in the social field, particularly in matters relating to

- — employment;
- — labour law and working conditions;
- — basic and advanced vocational training;
- — social security;
- — prevention of occupational accidents and diseases;
- — occupational hygiene;
- — the right of association and collective bargaining between employers and workers.

Article 118A, which was inserted by the Single European Act, calls on Member States to

pay particular attention to encouraging improvements, especially in the working environment, as regards the health and safety of workers,

52. See post p.223.
53. See generally, M. Forde, *Constitutional Law of Ireland* (1987) pp.224-226.
54. See post p.128.

and shall set as their objective the harmonisation of conditions in this area, while maintaining the improvements made.

Measures being proposed to improve the working environment, as defined here, do not need the unanimous support of members of the E.C. Council of Ministers; a qualified majority suffices. Following the 'first stage', where differences in laws are 'distorting the conditions of competition in the common market' and those conditions should be eliminated, the Council by a qualified majority can take appropriate measures to put an end to that distortion.

Exactly what role the Charter of Fundamental Social Rights[55] will play in the expanding E.C. social law remains to be seen. This document, which was adopted by all the E.C. Member States in 1989, proclaims in somewhat general terms a number of social rights. These are freedom of movement, employment and remuneration, an improvement of living and working conditions, social protection, freedom of association and collective bargaining, vocational training, equal treatment between men and women, health protection and safety at the workplace, protection of children and adolescents and rights for the elderly and the disabled. The objective of the Charter is to develop these rights, in conjunction with realising the single market. To that end, the Member States committed themselves to 'take such steps as are appropriate and to mobilise all the resources that may be necessary in order to guarantee [these] rights . . . and full implementation of the social measures indispensable to the efficient operation of the single market.'[56] An action programme, to give practical effect to the Charter's provisions, has been drawn up by the E.C. Commission.[57]

But the Charter does not authorise the E.C. institutions to implement its provisions by way of Regulations and Directives. Rendering the Charter's provisions legally enforceable in the courts by employees and others is the responsibility of the Member States, who undertook to act appropriately either by way of legislation or industry-wide collective agreements. However, some implementing role is envisaged for the E.C. institutions, because the Charter's preamble speaks of '[r]esponsibility for the initiatives to be taken . . . lies, according to the circumstances, with the Member States . . . or with the Community.'

Legislative techniques Although the Irish Constitution adopts a 'dualist' stance regarding when international treaties become part of domestic law,[58] special provision is made for incorporating into Irish law the E.C. Treaties

55. Ante n.47.   56. Art. 32.
57. See Hepple, supra n.47.   58. See Forde, supra n.53, pp.206-209.

and measures adopted under them. Certain provisions of the Treaty of Rome have been held to have 'direct effect' in the laws of E.C. Member States; i.e. these provisions can be immediately enforced in the courts without the Community institutions or the States adopting legislative measures rendering them enforceable. Perhaps over-simplifying the position, Treaty clauses which are clear and unambiguous, unconditional and not dependent on any further action to give them reasonably precise content, are directly enforceable in the Irish courts.[59] In the employment law area, such clauses include Article 48 on the free movement of workers and Article 119 on equal pay for equal work.[60] The principal Community form of legislation is the Regulation, and the requirements set out in E.C. Regulations can be enforced in the Irish courts in the same way as domestic legislation.[61] Apart from measures dealing with the free movement of workers and the social security entitlements of migrant workers and their families, there have been no major Regulations so far in the employment field.

The form of secondary legislation most frequently adopted by the Community in this area is the Directive. These are directions to Member States' governments to adopt appropriate legislative measures so as to give effect to their substantive requirements.[62] Generally, Directives do not confer rights on nor impose obligations on individuals or organisations until an Act is passed or a statutory instrument is adopted which gives effect to them—for instance the 1980 Employers' Insolvency Act and the 1984 Transfer of Undertakings Regulations.[63] Implementation of Directives by statutory instrument rather than by way of legislation is authorised by the European Communities Act, 1972, as amended in 1973.

However, where a Directive purports to impose specific obligations on *inter alia* the State or other public authority, and these institutions then do not do what the Directive requires, they will not be permitted to hide behind the failure to implement the E.C. measure into Irish law. This is the 'horizontal effect' principle, by which unambiguous requirements set out in Directives are directly applicable in the courts and enforceable against public authorities.[64] The principle holds that a Member State 'which has not

59. See generally B. McMahon & F. Murphy, supra n.46, pp.245-251. Cf. Wyatt, 'Enforcing E.C. Social Rights in the United Kingdom' 18 *Ind. L. J. 197* (1989).

60. *Walgrave & Koch v. Assn. Union Cycliste* (Case 36/74) [1974] ECR 1405 and *Defrenne v. Sabena* (Case 43/75) [1976] ECR 455.

61. Treaty of Rome (E.E.C) Art. 189.

62. Id. Art. 189.

63. Discussed post chapters 10 and 9.

64. See generally, B. McMahon & F. Murphy, supra n.46 pp.253-255 and Curtin, 'The Province of Government: Delimiting the Direct Effect of Directives in the Common Law Context', [1990] *Eur. L. Rev.* 195.

adopted the implementing measures required by the Directive within the prescribed period may not plead, as against individuals, its own failure to perform the obligations which the Directive entails.'[65] Because the State and public agencies are very large employers, this principle has particular relevance in the employment field. Accordingly, although the State may decide to delay giving effect to E.C. Directives for some years, nevertheless clear and unconditional requirements laid down in them can be enforced against it *qua* employer.

Whether State-owned industrial and commercial employers like Radio Telefís Éireann, Córas Iompair Éireann and Aer Lingus, fall within the horizontal effect principle remains to be seen. It was held by the European Court of Justice in *Foster v. British Gas plc*,[66] that any body which performs a public service and is controlled by the State is an emanation of the State for this purpose. This case concerned whether British Gas Corp., which at the time was a State-owned public utility with a monopoly in the supply of gas, could be held bound by one of the Directives against sex discrimination. According to the Luxembourg Court,

> a body, whatever its legal form, which has been made responsible, pursuant to a measure adopted by the State, for providing a public service under the control of the State and has for that purpose special powers beyond those which result from the normal rules applicable in relations between individuals is included in any event among the bodies against which the provisions of a Directive capable of having direct effect may be relied upon.[67]

It was then left for the English courts to determine whether British Gas met this description.[68]

INTERNATIONAL LABOUR STANDARDS

Apart entirely from the European Communities, Ireland is a party to several international treaties that impose obligations on the State in connection with employment matters.[69] These obligations exist at the public international

65. *Marshall v. Southampton & South West Herts. Health Authority* (Case 152/84) [1986] ECR 723, at p.7 (para 47).
66. (Case C-188/89) [1990] 2 CMLR 833.
67. Id. at p.857 (para.20).
68. [1991] 2 WLR 1075. Compare *Browne v. An Bord Pleanala* [1990] 1 CMLR 3 with *R. v. London Borough Transport C'tee, ex p. Freight Transport Ass'n Ltd* [1990] 3 CMLR 495.
69. See generally, N. Valticos, *International Labour Law* (1979)

law level and cannot be enforced directly in the Irish courts. It is possible, however, that comparable provisions of the Constitution or of legislation would be interpreted to bring about outcomes which would be consistent with those required by the international measures. Some of these treaties contain a mechanism, either judicial or administrative, for ensuring that State parties comply with the substantive rights proclaimed by them.

A feature of many of the employment protection Acts passed in recent years is that they authorise their own amendment by regulation in order that their requirements be in line with any international obligations assumed by the State. For instance, s.16(5) of the Unfair Dismissals Act, 1977, authorises the Minister by order to amend any provision of that Act 'so as to comply with any international obligations in relation to dismissals that the State has decided to assume.' It has never been determined whether, under the Constitution, Acts of the Oireachtas may be amended in this manner and, if they can be so amended, the extent to which they can be so changed.

European Convention on Human Rights By far the most important of the international treaties is the European Convention on Human Rights,[70] to which Ireland was one of the original parties in 1950, but it is of little direct relevance to employment questions apart from trade union rights. It also forbids forced and compulsory labour,[71] which is not really a problem in Ireland, and it guarantees freedom of opinion, of expression and of religion as well as the right to privacy, which occasionally can have employment law ramifications.[72] The obligations imposed by the Convention apply principally to the State or other governmental action, in the sense that ordinarily only action done by or on behalf of the State can be the subject of a complaint, investigation and adjudication under the Convention.[73] For practical purposes, therefore, it is virtually inapplicable to the private sector workplace.

Even in the case of State-owned industrial and commercial undertakings, it would seem that the Convention's requirements do not ordinarily apply to them unless the Government can be directly implicated in the very action being complained of. A decision of the European Commission of Human Rights, concerning the admissibility of complaints made of breaches of the Convention, provides an excellent illustration of the position. In *X v. Ireland*,[74] the Commission indicated where State parties may incur respon-

70. Adopted 4 Nov. 1950, [1953] IrTS No.12.
71. Art. 4. Cf. *Van der Mussele v. Belgium*, 6 EHRR 163 (1983).
72. E.g. *Flynn v. Power* [1985] IR 648.
73. See generally, Forde, 'Non-Governmental Interferences with Human Rights', 56 *B.Y.B.I.L.* 253 (1986).
74. Decisions of 24 July 1970 and 1 Feb. 1971, 14 *Y. B'r E.C.H.R.* 118 and 198 (1971).

sibility under the Convention for *prima facie* violations of its requirements committed by State-owned employers. The applicant there complained *inter alia* that the Electricity Supply Board (E.S.B.), a statutory public corporation with a practical monopoly in the supply of electricity, discriminated against him on account of his trade union activities, in violation of Article 11. The Irish Government contended that it could not be held responsible for the activities of the E.S.B.; that

> the Board is . . . a body established by a statute which sets out its essential features and functions and is financed, at least in the first instance by public funds . . . and it is clear from the provisions of the statute that the Board is solely responsible for matters relating to exercise of its functions, including the relationship between the Board and its employees. . . . Accordingly, the applicant's complaint is in respect of alleged actions by or on behalf of a body independent of the Government and such actions cannot involve the direct responsibility of the Government under the Convention.[75]

Against this, the applicant emphasised that a Government Minister appoints the board of the E.S.B., including its Chairman, and reference was made to a letter of that Minister which stated that he exercised general supervision over the Board's policies.

The Commission decided that, even assuming the Government was responsible, in the circumstances the action complained of was not a violation of the substantive rights guaranteed by Article 11. Consequently, there was no need to consider the question of Government liability for the E.S.B.'s actions, except to observe that 'the Government exercises at least general supervision over the policy of the Board, the day to day administration is solely in the hands of the Board; [but] the acts alleged by the applicant clearly fall within the domain of such day to day administration for which the Government is not directly responsible.'[76] However, the Commission suggested that a State might still be 'indirectly' responsible for infringements committed by non-governmental actors if its own laws did not adequately protect against interferences with the guaranteed right; that

> insofar as the acts alleged have not been committed in circumstances involving the direct responsibility of the Government, a breach by the Government in connection with these acts may not be established otherwise than by showing either that the domestic law does not protect a right or freedom guaranteed by the Convention which has

---

75. Id. at p.218.   76. Ibid.

been infringed or that there is no adequate remedy for enforcing the law's protection in this respect....[77]

International Labour Organisation Another expressly proclaimed source of inspiration for the E.C.'s Charter of Fundamental Rights are the many conventions and recommendations which were adopted by the Geneva-based International Labour Organisation. This body was established in 1919 as an autonomous body associated with the League of Nations to promote progress in the areas of employment, trade unions and social security. Ireland has had a long association with the I.L.O. in that the organisation's very first official was Edward Phelan, who was born in Waterford in 1888. Before working for the I.L.O., Phelan had studied at Liverpool University and he joined the British Intelligence Service in 1916. Ireland has become a party to numerous conventions sponsored by that organisation.[78] None of these conventions are directly enforceable in the courts but legislation has been enacted to give effect to many of their requirements, most notably conventions dealing with protection for merchant seamen.

European Social Charter The European Social Charter[79] should not be confused with the E.C.'s Charter of Fundamental Rights, although there is a marked resemblance between the substantive provisions of these measures. Indeed the E.C. Charter, in its preamble, states that its framers drew inspiration from the Council of Europe's Social Charter, which was adopted almost thirty years earlier and to which Ireland became a party in 1965. The Social Charter's general tenor resembles the directive principles of social policy in Article 45 of the Irish Constitution and its contents are similar to the 'economic and social principles' contained in the preamble to the French Constitution. Ireland is not bound by each and every right proclaimed in the Social Charter; State Parties are given some freedom to choose which rights they undertake to respect. Ireland has agreed to respect the right to work (art. 1), to organise and to bargain collectively (arts. 5 and 6), to social and medical assistance (art. 13), to protection for the family (art. 16), to protection for married workers and their families (art. 19), to just conditions of work (art. 2), to healthy working conditions (art. 3), to a fair remuneration (art. 4), to protection for children and young persons (art. 7), to protection for employed women (art. 8), to vocational guidance and training (arts. 9 and 19), to protection against diseases (art. 11(3)), to social

---

77. Id. at p.220.
78. Valticos, supra n.69, provides a detailed exposition of the Organisation's work.
79. Adopted 18 Oct. 1961, [1965] IrTS No.3.

security (art. 12), to benefit from the social welfare services (art. 14), to rehabilitation for disabled persons (art. 15), to protection for mothers and children (art. 17) and to permit nationals of other State Parties to work in this country (art. 18).

The mechanisms used for ensuring that these rights are rendered effective resemble those used for monitoring compliance with the I.L.O.'s trade union conventions. In brief, the State Parties must make reports to the Council of Europe every two years concerning their laws and practices that touch on the guaranteed rights. These reports are then examined by a committee of independent experts which issues conclusions on the national reports. Those conclusions and reports in turn are forwarded to a sub-committee of the Council of Europe's Social Committee and to its Consultative Committee. The final tier in this elaborate process is the Council of Europe's Committee of Ministers. If the Ministers by a two-thirds majority form the view that certain rights are not being respected, they are authorised to make necessary recommendations to the state in question. There is no provision for employers' organisations and trade unions to complain to the Council of Europe about breaches of the Social Charter. But copies of the biennial national reports must be given to each State Party's representative employers' organisations and trade unions, and any comments made by these bodies on the reports must be forwarded to the Council of Europe along with the reports.

ADJUDICATION OF EMPLOYMENT-RELATED DISPUTES

Where employers and workers cannot resolve between themselves whatever differences they may have and they prefer to avoid resort to industrial action, the matter most likely will end up in the courts or in some other tribunal. Actions for breach of contract and for tort will be brought in the ordinary courts—in the District Court, the Circuit Court or the High Court, as the case may be. Prosecutions for breach of the employment legislation will always be brought in one of those courts. However, Article 37 of the Constitution authorises the establishment of subordinate tribunals, outside the court system, to exercise 'limited functions and powers of a judicial nature' in non-criminal matters. Several tribunals have been established to deal with employment-related matters.

The establishment of specialised judicial bodies to determine disputes of that nature is a feature of most advanced industrial societies. In Britain, these matters are dealt with by the industrial tribunals; in France by the *Conseils des Prud'hommes*, in Germany by the *Arbeitsgerichts*. Exactly what matters come within the exclusive or optional jurisdiction of these bodies varies considerably. For instance, in Britain the tribunals have exclusive jurisdiction over claims under most of the legislation which provides protection for individual employees, but actions for breach of the employment contract must be brought in the ordinary courts. In France, the *Conseils* also have jurisdiction over breach of contract claims but several of the statutory protection regimes are enforced only in the administrative courts, which are separate from the *Conseils* and the ordinary civil courts. Each society tends to develop its own unique structure for adjudications in this field, which evolves piece-meal over time. Even in the last century, under the Master and Servant Act, 1867, and the Employers and Workmen Act, 1875, special procedures were laid down for hearing employment-related disputes in the county courts and the magistrates courts. Section 23 of the former Act sought to exclude all judicial review in the High Court of decisions reached by those courts in employment cases.

None of the present day specialised tribunals are entirely isolated from the ordinary courts. Decisions of almost all of them are subject to an express right of appeal, usually to the High Court, although that right is often confined to a question of law as opposed to the facts. Yet differences concerning factual issues can also constitute disputes about matters of law in appropriate cases.[80] Furthermore, all of these tribunals are subject to judicial review by the High Court. Any attempt to entirely exclude judicial review, as was done in the past, most likely would be unconstitutional. The scope of judicial review does not extend, however, to all types of errors in decisions which could be corrected in a full appeal. Review is concerned primarily with circumstances where a tribunal either exceeded its very jurisdiction or it followed unfair or improper procedures.

A feature of employment tribunals in most countries is their tripartite composition, representing employers' and employees' interests, often with an independent individual chairing the bench. How the representatives of employer and employee interests are chosen varies considerably. In France, for instance, the method is direct election by the workforce and also by the employers. In this country the usual practice is that each 'side', although appointed by the Government or a Minister or some public agency, is nominated by the main employees' and employers' organisations—the Irish Congress of Trade Unions and the Irish Union of Employers. It is assumed that, with each side of industry being represented on the tribunal, the bench will have a greater practical understanding of the background to the dispute and the issues involved than would adjudicators whose entire professional

80. Cf. *O'Kelly v. Trusthouse Forte p.l.c.* [1984] 1 QB 90. See generally, G. Hogan & D. Morgan, *Administrative Law in Ireland* (2 ed. 1991) pp.392-396.

life was involved in the law. The expectation is that the tripartite body will administer a more sensitive and fairer form of industrial justice.

Employment Appeals Tribunal The Employment Appeals Tribunal ('E.A.T.') was established by s.39 of the Redundancy Payments Act, 1967, initially in order to administer the system of redundancy compensation introduced by that Act. Its jurisdiction was extended by the Minimum Notice and Terms of Employment Act, 1973, to several of the matters arising under that Act.[81] That jurisdiction was further and very significantly expanded by the Unfair Dismissals Act, 1977, and a large proportion of the E.A.T.'s present workload is dealing with unfair dismissal claims. Section 18 of that Act changed its name from the Redundancy Appeals Tribunal to its present name. Among the other claims which can be brought before the E.A.T. are under the Maternity Protection of Employees Act, 1981, the Protection of Employees (Employer's Insolvency) Act, 1984, and the Payment of Wages Act, 1991. One of these Acts requires that the claim must first be submitted to a rights commissioner, with a right of appeal to E.A.T. (payment of wages). Others give persons the option of presenting their claim first to a rights commissioner, with an appeal to the E.A.T., or commencing before the E.A.T. (unfair dismissals and maternity protection).

The composition and method of appointing members of the E.A.T. remains governed by s.39 of the Redundancy Payments Act, 1967. Its members are appointed by the Minister for Labour. There are two principal categories of member. One is the chairman and vice chairmen. The former must be someone who practised as a barrister or a solicitor for at least seven years. In practice, the vice-chairmen are also persons with some degree of legal experience, but there is no express requirement that they be lawyers, let alone lawyers with some actual experience in court work or in employment law. The other category are the ordinary members, half of whom are appointed on the nomination of the trade unions and the other half on the employers' nomination. There is no statutory ceiling to the terms of office of any of the members, which can be fixed by the Minister.

Section 39(17) of the Redundancy Payments Act, 1967, sets out the principal judicial powers which are conferred on the E.A.T., being to administer oaths and take evidence on oath, compel the attendance of witnesses and the production of relevant documentation.[82] Witnesses enjoy the same privileges and immunities as if they were giving evidence in the High Court.[83] Rules of procedure for the E.A.T. have been adopted, in the

81. All matters other than the written statement of particulars required by s.9 of that Act; for s.9, see post p55.
82. Unfair Dismissals Act, 1977, s.8(9).   83. Ibid.

Redundancy (Redundancy Appeals Tribunal) Regulations, 1968,[84] the Unfair Dismissals (Claims and Appeals) Regulations, 1977,[85] and the Maternity Protection (Disputes and Appeals) Regulations, 1981.[86] These are not alone supplemented by but are subject to the fundamental principles of fair procedures, often called constitutional or natural justice. That these principles are paramount was emphasised on at least two occasions by the Supreme Court, in *State (Irish Pharmaceutical Union) v. Employment Appeals Tribunal*[87] and again in *Halal Meat Packers (Ballyhaunis) Ltd v. Employment Appeals Tribunal.*[88] One of the principal objectives for having tribunals like the E.A.T. is to ensure that justice will be administered with far less formality than in the courts, so that the ordinary employer or worker will feel more at ease during the course of the proceedings and matters could be dealt with more flexibility. Yet at times informality presents a considerable threat to ensuring fair procedures for all parties, so that tribunals must maintain a difficult balance between a relaxed atmosphere and proceedings and, on the other hand, due process of law.

In the *Halal Meat Packers* case, the E.A.T. went to the very opposite extreme. There an employer, against whom a claim had been brought, did not enter a formal appearance to the claim but was present at the tribunal when the hearing commenced and sought to participate. Because it did not enter the proper appearance, it was not allowed by the Tribunal to defend the claim. Of those events, Walsh J observed that the 'present case indicates a degree of formality, and even rigidity, which is somewhat surprising. It is a rather ironic turn in history that this tribunal which was intended to save people from the ordinary courts would themselves fall into a rigidity comparable to that of the common law before it was modified by equity.'[89] The tribunal's decision was set aside because it disregarded the most fundamental maxim of fair procedures, *audi alteram partem*—the two parties should be heard.

Determinations of the E.A.T. under the unfair dismissals and the maternity protection legislation can be appealed to the Circuit Court.[90] That appeal is by way of a full re-hearing. Furthermore, the Circuit Court's decision, on appeal, can itself be appealed to the High Court in the same way as almost all other Circuit Court judgments are appealable. In *McCabe v. Lisney*,[91] it was held that there was nothing in the 1977 Act which excluded from it the general provision for circuit appeals to the High Court.

---

84. SI No. 24 of 1968
85. SI No. 286 of 1977. See generally, M. Redmond, *Dismissal Law* (1982) pp.121-127.
86. SI No. 357 of 1981.   87. [1987] ILRM 36.
88. [1990] ILRM 293.   89. Id. at pp.305-306.
90. 1977 Act s.10(4) and 1981 Act s.27(3).   91. [1981] ILRM 289.

A frequent criticism of the Unfair Dismissals Act is that it can take three full hearings of a case—before the E.A.T., then the Circuit Court and after it the High Court—before a final determination on the evidence can be made.

This is not the case with claims under the Redundancy Payments Acts, 1967-1979, the Minimum Notice etc. Act, 1973, and the Payments of Wages Act, 1991. There is no right of appeal to the Circuit Court and the only right of appeal is to the High Court on a point of law.[92]

Rights Commissioners The office of rights commissioner was first provided for by s.13 of the Industrial Relations Act, 1969. At that time rights commissioners were attached to the Labour Court and their task was to intervene in and investigate industrial disputes, with a view to promoting a settlement. They played a particularly valuable role in resolving disputes which were caused by incidents with one or a small group of employees, for instance, dismissals. Since 1990, the commissioners have operated as a service of the Labour Relations Commission.[93] They are appointed by the Minister for Labour from a panel submitted to him by the Commission.[94] They are authorised to regulate how proceedings before themselves are to be conducted, including the circumstances when legal representation will be allowed.

In 1977 the rights commissioners' functions were radically transformed when they were given jurisdiction to hear claims under the Unfair Dismissals Act of that year.[95] Employees who wish to seek reinstatement, reengagement or compensation under that Act were given a choice of forum; they could bring their claim before a commissioner, whose decision could be appealed to the E.A.T.[96] One of the possible advantages of proceedings before a commissioner is that they are not heard in public.[97] Rights commissioners are also authorised to hear claims under the Maternity Protection of Employees Act, 1981,[98] and the Payment of Wages Act, 1991;[99] again, there is a right of appeal from their decisions to the E.A.T. Claimants under any of these Acts, of course, can by-pass the commissioners entirely and go straight to the E.A.T. Decisions made by commissioners, described as recommendations, do not have any legally binding effect but in practice they are observed by employers. Usually where an employer might be mindful to disregard their recommendation, he would have notified them of his

92. 1967 Act s.39(14), 1973 Act s.11(2) and 1991 Act s 7(4)(b).
93. Industrial Relations Act, 1990, s.35.   94. Id. s.34.
95. 1977 Act s.8. See S.I. No. 286 of 1977.
96. Id. s.9.   97. Id. s.8(6).
98. S.27. See S.I. No. 357 of 1981.   99. S.6. See S.I. No. 351 of 1991.

objection to their hearing the claim; in that event, the claim must be brought before the E.A.T.[1]

Equality Officers Claims in respect of unlawful sex discrimination can be referred to equality officers. These were established by s.6 of the Anti-Discrimination (Pay) Act, 1974, under the name of equal pay officers attached to the Labour Court. Since 1990, they are officers of the Labour Relations Commission but, by statute, they are 'independent in the performance of [their] functions'.[2] Where the claim is for breach of the equal pay provisions, it may be referred directly to an equal pay officer for investigation and recommendation.[3] The same applies to some claims under the equal treatment provisions of the Pensions Act, 1990;[4] other claims under these provisions are determined by the Pensions Board.[5] In the case of claims under the Employment Equality Act, 1977, the dispute may be referred to the Labour Court, which then may decide to refer it to an equality officer to be investigated and for a recommendation.[6] Where the officer makes a recommendation on the matter, it can be appealed to the Labour Court. Where an officer's recommendation has not been implemented, that question too can be referred to the Labour Court. There is a right of appeal to the High Court on a point of law from a determination of the Labour Court on any of these issues.[7] It is expected that legislation will be enacted in the near future reforming this somewhat Byzantine disputes-resolution mechanism.[8]

In *North Western Health Board v. Martyn*,[9] the Supreme Court indicated the best way for equality officers to set out the conclusions of their investigation into a claim for redress under these Acts. According to Finlay CJ,

> it is the essence of the procedures laid down by the Act of 1977 that they commence at least in a relatively informal form and that in particular the function of the equality officer to whom the Labour Court may refer a complaint is partly conciliatory and only partly that of an arbitrator. Notwithstanding these considerations, however, it seems to me desirable that an equality officer should in his or her report set out the facts as found and, in short terms, the evidence upon which

1. 1977 Act s.8(3)(b) and (5)(b).
2. Industrial Relations Act, 1990, s.37.
3. Anti-Discrimination (Pay) Act, 1974, s.7.   4. S.76.
5. S.75; see infra p.27.   6. S.19.
7. 1974 Act s.8(3), 1977 Act s.21(4) and 1991 Act, s.77(5).
8. For a detailed account of the present judicial and administrative proceedings, see D. Curtin, *Irish Employment Equality Law* (1989) ch.9.
9. [1987] IR 565.

they have found. If a party appealing the ruling or recommendations of an equality officer to the Labour Court seeks to put in issue any of the facts so found, they should unequivocally do so in their notice of appeal and, in turn, the Labour Court, upon the conclusion of its hearing, should in an unambiguous fashion state the facts which it has found and the evidence upon which it has found them.[10]

Labour Court The Labour Court was established by Part II of the Industrial Relations Act, 1946, and its role in the labour relations system was expanded significantly by the Industrial Relations Act, 1967. It is not a court in the strict sense of a court having authority under Article 34 of the Constitution to exercise what may be termed plenary judicial powers. It is not staffed by judges appointed in accordance with Article 34 and solicitors and barristers rarely appear professionally before it. Its main function, according to the preamble to the 1946 Act, is to 'promote harmonious relations between workers and employers'. It has been assigned a multiplicity of tasks by the various Industrial Relations Acts.[11] In 1990 several of its functions were assigned to a new body, the Labour Relations Commission.[12] As has been observed above, rights commissioners and equality officers are now attached to that Commission.

As regards adjudicating claims under the legislation which gives rights to individual employees, the Labour Court's role is confined entirely to the sex discrimination field. Claims for breach of the Employment Equality Act, 1977, may be referred to the Court, which may then refer the matter to an equality officer for investigation and recommendation.[13] Recommendations by these officers under that Act, and also under the legislation on equal pay and on equality in pension schemes, may be appealed to the Court.[14] It also hears claims that any of these officers' recommendations has not been implemented.

The Court's hearings are in private unless any of the parties request for the matter to be heard in public.[15] Witnesses may be summoned by the Court and be examined on oath, and they may be required to produce all relevant documents in their possession or control.[16] They enjoy the same privileges and immunity as witnesses in the High Court.[17] There is a right of appeal from the Labour Court to the High Court on a point of law.

10. Id. at p.579.   11. See generally, *Industrial Relations Law*, pp.34-40.
12. Ibid.   13. S.19.   14. Supra n.27.
15. 1974 Act s.8(1)(c), 1977 Act s.21(3)(a)(b) and 1990 Act s.77(3)(a)(b).
16. Industrial Relations Act, 1946, s.21(1).
17. Id. s.21(2).

Deciding Officers Section 37 of the Redundancy Payments Act, 1967, provides for the appointment of deciding officers to determine a variety of claims and disputes arising under that Act, as amended. These officers' jurisdiction is defined in s.38 of that Act as to determine who is an employee's employer and such other matters as the Minister may prescribe. In an appropriate case, instead of deciding any matter themselves, an officer may refer it to the E.A.T. for decision.[18]

Pensions Board The Pensions Board was established by the Pensions Act, 1990, and was given a very extensive role in the supervision of occupational pension schemes. Part VI of this Act deals with equality between the sexes in pension schemes. Section 75 of the Act gives the Board jurisdiction over three categories of dispute, viz. whether the scheme is a 'defined contribution' scheme, whether a scheme's rules comply with the equal treatment principle and whether or to what extent a scheme's rules are null and void for contravening that principle. Decisions of the Board can be appealed to the High Court on a point of law.

Special Commissioners of the Revenue Appeals against assessments to income tax and in connection with most other determinations by the Revenue regarding taxation are heard by the Special Commissioners. The relevant procedures are laid down in Part XXVI (ss.415-432) of the Income Tax Act, 1967. An aggrieved taxpayer can appeal the Commissioner's decision to the Circuit Court, where the matter will be reheard *de novo*. Either the taxpayer or the Revenue can appeal the Commissioner's decision to the High Court on a point of law by way of case stated.

Social Welfare appeals The decision-making structure in relation to social welfare claims is contained in Part VIII (ss.295-309) of the Social Welfare (Consolidation) Act, 1981. Claims are first determined by a deciding officer, whose decision can be appealed to an appeals officer, from whom there is an appeal to the High Court on a point of law.[19]

Arbitration Where the employer and employee have so agreed in writing, their differences can be submitted for resolution by way of binding arbitration. The arbitrator is whoever they choose for that purpose; he may be a named individual or the person designated by the individual or body authorised by the parties to make the appointment. What procedure should be followed depends principally on what the parties have agreed on, subject

18. S.39(16).
19. See generally Hogan & Morgan, supra n.80, pp.241-248.

to the observation of natural justice. It is unusual for employment contracts in this country to contain arbitration clauses, partly because the Arbitration Act, 1954, does not apply to labour arbitration. According to s.5 of that Act, it does not apply to 'arbitration of any question relating to the terms or conditions of employment or the remuneration of any employees . . . .' The precise status of an arbitration which is not within this Act appears never to have been considered by the courts here.

2

Personal scope

The question of the personal scope of a body of law concerns who are directly affected by those laws; what persons are the subjects of the rights and duties thereby imposed. Company law is concerned mainly with registered companies, their shareholders, directors and creditors; family law regulates the rights and responsibilities of members of families. Employment law applies principally to employers and employed persons.

EMPLOYEES AND THE CONTRACT OF EMPLOYMENT

Those who work for others fall into two main legal categories. They may be employees, that is persons who work under what is known as a contract of employment or of service. Alternatively, they may be self-employed, working for numerous persons. A typical employee works only for one employer, arrives at and departs from the job at pre-ordained times, is paid a fixed rate, which is usually based on the hours spent working, and takes instructions from the employer on how the work is to be done. Examples include regular factory workers, clerks and the like. However, there are significant numbers of what may be described as atypical workers, who are neither obviously employees nor self-employed. It is probable that developments in the labour market in recent years, like the greater use of employment agency personnel, the trend towards flexible service arrangements and the increased integration of professional persons into large bureaucratic institutions, has considerably expanded the numbers of atypical workers. Much of the case law is concerned with which of the two categories these workers should be classified into.

So far as most contractual rights and obligations are concerned, it matters little whether the person who is engaged to perform work for another is classified as an employee or as self-employed. Because of its very nature, however, certain terms will be implied into a contract of employment, notably, the employer's extensive obligations regarding safety at work[1] and

1. See post p.118.

the employee's obligation of fidelity.[2] The employee/self-employed distinction is important in the law of tort because an employer is vicariously liable for the wrongs committed by his employees in the course of their work but not generally for the wrongs of those he engaged under a contract for services.[3]

It is in respect of the many statutory rights and duties that the distinction between the two categories is particularly significant, because most of the modern employment protection legislation applies only to employer-employee relationships and not to independent contractors. Thus, the Unfair Dismissals Act, 1977, applies only to employees, who are defined as any 'individual who has entered into or works under . . . a contract of employment.'[4] When dealing with disputes concerning relations between persons who hire others to work and those who are hired, a vital preliminary question therefore is whether the hiring is under a contract of employment or under a contract for services; whether the person hired is an employee or is self-employed. If he is an employee then, subject to exceptions, the full panoply of employment law should govern his circumstances. If he is self-employed, most employment laws do not directly affect him.

A few employment protection laws apply to some self-employed workers as well as to employees because of the way in which those Acts define the term 'employed' and 'employee'. The Anti-Discrimination (Pay) Act, 1974, which applies to 'employed persons', defines employed as 'mean[ing] employed under a contract of service or apprenticeship or a contract personally to execute any work or labour.'[5] This definition embraces the self-employed provided that, under their terms of engagement, they must perform the work themselves rather than have the option of hiring others to do whatever the job undertaken requires.[6] The Minimum Notice and Terms of Employment Act, 1973, and the Redundancy Payments Acts, 1967-1979, define the term employee for their purposes as any person working under a 'contract with an employer . . ., whether it is a contract of service or of apprenticeship or otherwise. . . .'[7] The 'or otherwise' here suggests that these Acts may apply to self-employed persons who are hired by an employer, especially when this definition is contrasted with a similar one in the Employment Equality Act, 1977, except the later Act goes on to add that the term 'employer' in relation to an employee means 'the person by whom the employee is . . . employed under a contract of employment. . . .'[8] While

2. See post p.96.
3. See generally, B. McMahon & W. Binchy, *Irish Law of Torts* (2nd ed. 1990) ch.43.
4. S.1.   5. S.1(1).
6. Cf. *Mirror Group Newspapers Ltd v. Gunning* [1986] ICR 145.
7. S.1.   8. S.1(1).

the literal meaning of the definition in the Minimum Notice and in the Redundancy Acts includes some self-employed workers, it is probable that the courts would conclude that these Acts apply only to employees, on the grounds that if the Oireachtas really intended to extend them to the self-employed it would have said so in a more direct manner. Employees within the Payment of Wages Act, 1991, include those who have agreed 'to do or perform personally any work or service for a third person';[9] this does not include a professional person-client relationship or a business under-taking–customer relationship.

Purposes of classification Disputes about whether someone is or was an employee or self-employed arise in a variety of contexts and these disputes are not always between the employer and his alleged employee or self-employed helper. At times, the plaintiff is someone who never had any dealings with the alleged employer, such as someone injured in an accident and who claims that the defendant is the wrongdoer's employer and, accordingly, is vicariously liable for the loss suffered.[10] Many of the older cases concern claims under the since-repealed Workmen's Compensation Acts; if the plaintiff was indeed the defendant's employee, under those Acts he was entitled to be compensated for the injuries suffered in the course of his employment regardless of who was at fault.[11] Many of the more recent cases arise under the social security laws and the tax laws. The Social Welfare (Consolidation) Act, 1981, requires that social insurance con-tributions be paid in respect of persons employed 'under any contract of service or apprenticeship'.[12] Some of the employment protection legislation applies only to workers who are insured under the Social Welfare Acts, notably the Redundancy Payments Acts, 1967-1979,[13] the protection of Employees (Employers' Insolvency) Act, 1984,[14] and the Maternity Protection of Employees Act, 1981.[15]

The Finance Act, 1967, imposes income tax under Schedule E on *inter alia* 'emoluments' paid to employees, which are defined as 'all salaries, fees wages, prerequisites or profits or gains whatsoever arising from an office or employment'.[16] The earnings of self-employed persons are taxed under Schedule D, which, from the taxpayer's perspective, is a more favourable

9. S.1.
10. See supra n.3; cf. *Maguire v. P.J. Langan (Contractors) Ltd* [1976] NI 49.
11. Workmen's Compensation Acts, 1934-1953, esp. 1934 Act s.15. Cf. *Kelly v. Donegal C.C.* [1946] IR 228, where the plaintiff's contract was a composite one, being partly of service and partly for services.
12. S.5(1) and sched. I.
13. S.4 (insured for all benefits).
14. S.3 (insured for all benefits).
15. S.2(1) (see post p.148).
16. Ss.110 and 111(4).

arrangement. Thus, in many of the cases, a person working is claiming that he is not an employee, in order that he will not be taxed under Schedule E and be subject to P.A.Y.E., or his employer is claiming that he is not an employee so that P.R.S.I. contributions do not have to be paid in respect of him. Although it has never been so held,[17] it would seem that the purpose for which the classification is being determined—for vicarious liability, employment protection, social security or taxation—in practice may have some bearing on how the person is categorised by a court.

The tests Various tests are applied in order to determine whether in the circumstances an individual is an employee or is self-employed. There is no simple master test; at times greater emphasis is placed on one test over the others. The proper approach to questions of classification was put by Kennedy CJ in *Graham v. Minister for Industry and Commerce* as follows:

> No exhaustive definition of either category has yet been settled and established either by statute or by judicial decision and there is a zone of uncertainty. A commonly accepted test is that of control. Is the alleged 'employed person' ... subject to be controlled by the employer in executing the work, e.g. as to the order and manner in which he carries out the work in detail? As to the disposal of his time while engaged in it? This, the most usual test, is . . . far from sufficient as a single test. . . . [T]here are other and equally important tests, e.g. is the 'engaged person' engaged to execute the whole of a given piece of work? Can the engagement be terminated before completion of the piece of work without cause assigned, or only for misconduct or for malperformance of the work? Is the agreed remuneration on a wage basis or on a percentage or other commercial profit basis? Are the necessary materials to be procured by the engaged person on his own account and, if necessary, his own credit? Are such other workmen (if any) as have been taken into employment upon the work by the engaged person so employed by him as agent for the principal, or are they his own employees paid by and subject to him? Is the engaged person required to give all the time of his working day to the work until completed, or is he free to arrange his own time as he pleases? Is he a member of a trade union and are trade union rules and conditions applicable to the work.[18]

17. Indeed, the contrary has been stated: *Lee Ting Sang v. Chung Chi Keung* [1990] 2 AC 374.
18. [1933] IR 156, at pp.159-160.

A similar approach has been adopted in Britain: in the *Market Investigations* case:

> The fundamental test to be applied is this: 'Is the person who has engaged himself to perform these services performing them as a person in business on his own account?' If the answer to that question is 'yes', then the contract is a contract of services. If the answer is 'no', then the contract is a contract for service. No exhaustive list has been compiled and perhaps no exhaustive list can be compiled of the considerations which are relevant in determining that question, nor can strict rules be laid down as to the relative weight which the various considerations should carry in particular cases. The most that can be said is that control will no doubt always have to be considered, although it can no longer be regarded as the sole determining factor; and factors which may be of importance are such matters as whether the man performing the services provides his own equipment, whether he hires his own helpers, what degree of financial risk he takes, what degree of responsibility for investment and management he has, and whether and how far he has an opportunity of profiting from sound management in the performance of his task.[19]

Control: The most commonly used test is that of control: whether under the terms of the contract, express or implied, the employer has 'the power of deciding the thing to be done, the way in which it shall be done, the means to be employed in doing it, the time when and the place where it shall be done.'[20] In *Roche v. Kelly,*[21] a vicarious liability case, Walsh J observed that '[w]hile many ingredients may be present in the relationship of master and servant, it is undoubtedly true that the one principal one, and almost invariably the determining one, is the fact of the master's right to direct the servant not merely as to what is to be done but as to how it is to be done. The fact that the master does not exercise the right, as distinct from possessing it, is of no weight if he has the right.'[22] If the contract gives the employer extensive control over the work to be done or spells out in detail how it is to be done, the presumption is that it is a contract of employment, absent strong indications to the contrary from other features of the relationship. That the parties may have formally designated their relationship as one of independent contract is not conclusive.[23]

19. *Market Investigations Ltd v. Minister for Social Security* [1969] 2 QB 173, at pp.184-185; also *Lee Ting Sang* case, supra n.17.
20. *Ready Mixed Concrete (South East) Ltd v. Minister of Pensions and Social Security* [1968] 2 QB 497, at p.515.
21. [1969] IR 100.   22. Id. at p.108.   23. Infra p.37.

However, an employer-employee relationship can exist without there being any right of extensive control. In the case of highly skilled personnel, especially those doing work of a professional nature, the employer may exercise very little control. Carroll J in *In re Sunday Tribune Ltd*, remarked that '[i]n the present day when senior staff with professional qualifications are employed, the nature of their employment cannot be determined in such a simplistic way' as the control test.[24] The issue there was whether several journalists who worked for a Sunday newspaper were employees; if they were, their unpaid wages would be preferred debts in the winding up of their employer.[25] Although the company exercised relatively little control over them, Carroll J, using a different test, concluded that two of them were indeed employees. There are numerous reported decisions in the same vein concerning doctors in hospitals,[26] dentists engaged by local authorities,[27] engineers,[28] architects,[29] lecturers,[30] authors.[31] There may be certain other features of the job which explain why the employer has very little detailed control and yet the relationship will be classified as one of employment.[32]

On the other hand, there can be extensive control but the engaged person is nevertheless an independent contractor. For instance in *D.P.P. v. McLoughlin*,[33] it was held that share fishermen who worked for the defendant were not his employees. The defendant, as skipper of the fishing boat, exercised extensive control over the men while at sea but that right 'arose as much from the nature of the operations being carried on as from the contractual relationship which existed' between the parties.[34] A similar analysis was applied in an English case, *Hitchcock v. Post Office*,[35] which concerned the status of a postmaster engaged by the Post Office. Although the terms of his engagement set out in great detail how the plaintiff should do the work, it was held that several other features of the relationship showed that it was not a contract of employment.

Integration: Another commonly used test is that of integration: whether the engaged person is 'employed as part of the business, and his work done as

24. [1984] IR 505, at p.508.
25. Companies Act, 1963, s.285(2)(b).
26. *O'Friel v. St. Michael's Hospital* [1982] ILRM 260 and *Cassidy v. Minister for Health* [1951] 2 KB 343.
27. *Greater London Council v. Minister for Social Security* [1971] 1 WLR 641.
28. *Morren v. Swinton and Pendlebury B.C.* [1965] 1 WLR 576.
29. *WHPT Housing Ass'n Ltd v. Secretary of State* [1981] ICR 737.
30. *Narich Pty. Ltd v. Commissioner of Pay Roll Tax* [1984] ICR 286.
31. *Beloff v. Pressdram Ltd* [1973] 1 All ER 241.
32. E.g. *Market Investigation* case, supra n.2.
33. [1986] IR 355.   34. Id. at p.360.   35. [1980] ICR 100.

an integral part of the business', as apposed to being 'not integrated into but only accessory to' the business.[36] The usefulness of this test is debatable; one judge has remarked that it 'raises more questions than I know how to answer'.[37] But it was applied in *In re Sunday Tribune Ltd*[38] in order to determine which category several journalists fell into. One of the journalists wrote a column for the Sunday newspaper for 50 out of the 52 weeks in the year and took part in editorial conferences and received holiday pay. She was held to be 'an integral part of the business of the newspaper' and, accordingly, one of its employees.[39] Another of them wrote for the paper on a regular basis but her contributions were not published virtually every week; she visited the paper's offices, usually once a week, to suggest a topic for contribution or to be requested to make a contribution, although she would not work on a contribution until it was commissioned by the editor. She was paid not at a rate per word but on the basis of a collective agreement with the National Union of Journalists. Carroll J concluded that she was 'not an integral part of the business' of the newspaper and, therefore, was an independent contractor in respect of her dealings with the company.

Significant integration in the employer's business operations may make up for a lack of detailed control by the employer. However, self-employed persons can be highly integrated in another's commercial operations, for instance, the second journalist in the *Sunday Tribune Ltd* case and the share fishermen in the *McLoughlin* case. The very nature of the business activity may require a high degree of integration. The difficulty with this test for identifying employees is that the courts have not spelt out in general terms what is meant by integration. As is explained below, if the engaged person assumes some commercial risk in doing the job, he most likely will be classified as self-employed regardless of how integrated he is in the employer's business.

Enterprise: Another test that is used, and perhaps the most important test, is the entrepreneurial criterion: 'is the person who has engaged himself to perform these services performing them as a person in business on his own account.'[40] If the engaged person's performance of the task requires significant capital investment on his part and especially if he is on risk, in the sense of standing to make a sizeable profit or incur a substantial loss,

36. *Stevenson, Jordan and Harrison Ltd v. Macdonald and Evans* [1952] 1 TLR 101, at p.121.
37. *Ready Mixed Concrete* case [1968] 2 QB at p.524.
38. [1984] IR 505.
39. Similarly, *Beloff v. Pressdram Ltd* [1973] 1 All ER 241.
40. *Market Investigations Ltd v. Minister of Social Security* [1969] 2 QB 173, at p.184; see too *Lee Ting Sang v. Chung Chi-Keung* [1990] 2 AC 374.

depending on how efficiently he does the job, he will be regarded as an independent contractor. As the United States Supreme Court once put it, are the engaged persons 'small business men'?[41] Where this enterpreneurial element is present, as a rule it points to a contract for services regardless of how much control is exercised over one party or how much integration there may be. In *McDermott v. Loy*,[42] which concerned classification for the purposes of income tax, the respondent's occupation was collecting premiums for a life insurance company. He had to buy the 'collection book', he had no fixed hours, he could canvass business wherever and whenever he wished, he could employ somebody else to collect the premiums for him and he could sell the collection book; he was also a trade union member and a member of the company's pension fund. Barron J upheld the Appeal Commissioners' decision that he was self-employed. Similarly, in *O'Coindealbhain v. Mooney*,[43] the respondent's job was as branch manager of the social welfare office in a country town; his remuneration comprised certain allowances and a fixed fee related to the volume of work performed; he was required to provide and furnish his own premises and to employ competent assistants. He was held to be self-employed, principally because 'his profit is the amount by which his remuneration exceeds his expenses; the lower he can keep his expenses the greater the profit.'[44]

Even when the engaged person has not undertaken investment in his function, he may be self-employed under this test, such as the share fishermen in *D.P.P. v. McLaughlin*.[45] When the defendant took his fishing boat to sea, he usually had a crew of five persons. They were engaged on a voyage basis, although the same persons went on most voyages. Their remuneration was based on a sharing arrangement dependent on the size of each catch; after deducting the expenses of the trip, about half of the gross proceeds of a catch would be divided among them and the skipper, the precise proportion to be determined by consultation with him. If there was a poor catch they would not be remunerated but they were not required to contribute towards any loss incurred in a voyage. Costello J held that the relationship between them and the defendant was not one of employer and employee; they were partners in an enterprise and, accordingly, were self-employed.[46]

Parties' own characterisation: In an evenly balanced situation, where

41. *United States v. Silk*, 331 US 704 (1946).   42. Barron J, 29 July 1982.
43. [1990] 1 IR 422.   44. Id. at p.432.   45. [1986] IR 355.
46. Cf. several cases concerning players in orchestras, *Winfield v. London Philharmonic Orchestra Ltd* [1979] ICR 726, *Addison v. London Philharmonic* [1981] ICR 261 and *Midland Sinfonia Concert Soc. Ltd v. Secretary of State* [1981] ICR 454.

several features point to employee status but others just as convincingly point to self-employed status, account will be taken of how the parties themselves decided to characterise their relationship. Thus, in *Massey v. Crown Life Insurance Co. Ltd*[47] the plaintiff had managed an insurance company's branch office for two years and, although he was then classified as an employee, he was paid partly on commission and he was permitted to do work for an outside insurance broker. On being advised by his accountant that there were tax advantages for him in changing his status, he and the company agreed that thenceforth he would be treated as self-employed. There was no other material change in the terms of his engagement. On the question of whether he still was an employee for the purposes of the Unfair Dismissals Act, it was held that, in the circumstances, the parties' own classification of their relationship was determinative. According to Lord Denning MR, provided that 'their relationship is ambiguous and is capable of being one or the other, then the parties can remove that ambiguity, by the very agreement itself which they make with one another. The agreement then becomes the best material from which to gather the true legal relationship between them.'[48]

But the self-classification is only decisive in relatively evenly balanced situations. The law is that 'if the true relationship of the parties is that of master and servant under a contract of service, the parties cannot alter the truth of that relationship by putting a different label upon it. ...'[49] As Carroll J put it in *In re Sunday Tribune Ltd* '[t]he Court must look at the realities of the situation in order to determine whether the relationship of employer and employee in fact exists, regardless of how the parties describe themselves.'[50] It was held there that the fact that the journalists opted for self-employed status for the purposes of income tax was not determinative; that was merely a convenient arrangement agreed by the Revenue for journalists who would be contributing material to several newspapers at any one time.

Special features of the relationship In applying the above tests, the court or tribunal will consider several key aspects of the contractual terms, which, if not express, will be implied.

47. [1978] 1 WLR 676.
48. Id. at p.679. See too, *Ready Mixed Concrete* case [1968] 2 QB 497 and *Calder v. H. Kitson Vickers & Sons (Engineers) Ltd* [1988] ICR 233.
49. *Massey* case [1978] 1 WLR at p.679.
50. [1984] IR at p.508. See too, *Narich Pty. Ltd v. Commr. Pay Roll Tax* [1984] ICR 286, *Ferguson v. John Dawson & Patners (Construction) Ltd* [1976] 1 WLR 1213, *Davis v. New England College of Arundel* [1977] ICR 6, *Tyne & Clyde Warehouses Ltd v. Hamerton* [1978] ICR 661.

Provide own services: If the engaged person is permitted to get somebody else to do all or any of the work contracted for, the relationship is that of employer and independent contractor. Perhaps the key feature of the contract of employment is that the employee agrees to 'provide his own work and skill in the performance of some service' for the employer.[51]

Engagement and dismissal: Where the worker is engaged by somebody other than the alleged employer or his agent, that often indicates, if anything, that he is employed by the person who did the hiring.[52] Thus, workers in the building industry engaged by 'labour only sub-contractors' have been held not to be employees of the construction firm which contracted the work out to the 'subbie'.[53] Yet circumstances can arise where the construction firm exercises such close control over the work being done and actually pays the engaged persons their remuneration and becomes entitled to dismiss them that they become its employees.[54] In appropriate circumstances, the 'subbie' who hired those workers and who works along with them may even be an employee of the construction firm which awarded him the contract.[55] Where staff are supplied to an enterprise by an employment agency, who their employer is depends on the nature of the arrangements regarding performing the work, remuneration, discipline, dismissal and the like made between the agency and the enterprise.[56]

Remuneration: If the work is performed gratuitously, the relationship cannot be that of employer and employee;[57] one party must have agreed to work 'in consideration of a wage or other remuneration.'[58] Often significance will be attached to the method agreed for calculating the remuneration. If payment is based on the amount of time spent doing the job, such as a rate per day, per week etc., the tendency is to regard the relationship as one of employment.[59] Of course, many employees are paid on the basis of piece rates or their remuneration is determined by reference to the profits made in the employing enterprise. Where the remuneration is paid in aggregate to

---

51. *Ready Mixed Concrete* case [1968] 2 QB at p.515.
52. Cf. *Kelly v. Owners of the Ship 'Miss Evans'* [1913] 2 IR 385
53. *Re C.W. & L. Hughes Ltd* [1966] 1 WLR 1369.
54. Compare *Limerick County Council v. Irish Insurance Comrs.* [1934] IR 364 with *Down County Council v. Irish Insurance Comrs.* [1914] 2 IR 110; cf. *Graham v. Minister for Industry & Commerce* [1933] IR 156.
55. *Limerick County Council v. Irish Insurance Comrs.* [1934] IR 364.
56. Cf. *Construction Industry Training Board v. Labour Force Ltd* []1970] 3 All ER 220 and *Wickers v. Champion Employment* [1984] ICR 365.
57. Cf. discussion of trainees and apprentices, infra p.47.
58. *Ready Mixed Concrete* Case [1968] 2 QB at p.515; compare *Liscoe v. Henry* [1926] IR 137 with *Minister for Industry and Commerce v. Jones* [1927] IR 216.
59. E.g. *Logue v. Pentland* [1930] IR 6.

those engaged as a group and they decide how it should be divided up between them, that is a strong indication that they are not employees.[60]

Times of work: The greater the choice an engaged person has over when the work shall be done, the more likely it is that he will be an independent contractor.[61] Similarly, if the agreed duration of the work is short, the likelihood is that he is self-employed. But there are instances where the engaged person had considerable freedom when to work being held to be an employee.[62] Recently, so-called flexi-time has become a feature of many employments.

Workplace: The typical employee attends the employer's factory, office, shop or whatever and performs the work there. But the very nature of certain jobs may require that the work is done away from the employer's establishment, like interviewing for a market research agency[63] or collecting contributions to be paid into a fund.[64] Where it is convenient for the employer to have the work done outside his establishment, like in the worker's own home, the general tendency is to regard the arrangement as one for services, especially because, in those situations, the engaged person usually will have considerable freedom when to do the work, will be paid on the basis of the work actually done and may even get assistance from others in doing the work.[65] But in appropriate circumstances 'outworkers' can be employees, notably where they have undertaken to do a specified quantity of work in a period and that arrangement subsists over a long duration.[66]

Equipment for the work: Where the equipment necessary to do the work in question requires considerable capital investment, significance will be attached to who is to pay for the equipment. If it is the engaged person who must pay, that tends to indicate that he falls on the self-employed side of the line.[67]

Appeals It is a matter of some debate whether the question about a worker's

60. E.g. *O'Friel v. St. Michael's Hospital* [1982] ILRM 260.
61. *Minister for Industry and Commerce v. Hales* [1967] IR 50, at p.69; e.g. *O'Friel* case, supra n.60.
62. E.g. *Market Investigations Ltd v. Minister of Social Security* [1969] 2 QB 173.
63. Ibid.
64. E.g. *Hales* case, supra n.61 and *McDermott v. Loy* (Barron J 29 July 1982).
65. E.g. *Minister for Industry and Commerce v. Healy* [1941] IR 545 and *Westall Richardson Ltd v. Roulson* [1954] 2 All ER 448.
66. E.g. *Airfix Footwear Ltd v. Cope* [1978] ICR 1210 and *Nethermere (St. Neots) Ltd v. Gardiner* [1984] ICR 612.
67. E.g. *Readymix Concrete* case [1968] QB 497 and *Hughes v. Quinn* [1917] 2 IR 442.

classification, whether he is an employee or is self-employed, is a question of fact or one of law or is it what may be termed a mixed question of fact and law. If it is a question of law, the principal practical consequence is that it is far easier for appellate tribunals to overrule decisions made by subordinate tribunals regarding this matter; for most subordinate tribunals' decisions are subject to an appeal on a point of law. But if the classification is a question of fact, then such determinations by subordinate tribunals can only be overturned on appeal in very limited circumstances. The vast majority of claims made under the employment legislation are determined initially by the Employment Appeals Tribunal, so that the legal or factual nature of the decision concerning the worker's classification affects the extent to which the E.A.T.'s decisions in particular instances can be set aside on appeal.[68] It was held by the Supreme Court in *Graham v. Minister for Industry and Commerce,*[69] which concerned appealing a determination made under social insurance legislation, that the classification question is one of fact. As Kennedy CJ put it, '[t]he question whether a particular individual is an "employed person" . . . or is an independent contractor, is a question of fact often difficult of solution depending in each case on the particular facts of that case.'[70] This view was reiterated by Barron J in *McDermott v. Loy,*[71] which concerned a determination about a taxpayer's status, whether he was subject to schedule D or schedule E. There is no authority that deals with this matter exhaustively in the context of appeals from decisions of the E.A.T. A strong case could be made that the question is one of law and not of fact, on the grounds that determining what class other types of contracts fall into is regarded generally as a question of law; for instance whether a contract is one for the sale of goods or is one for work and materials or is a contract for the sale of land.

Classification of a worker's legal status being regarded as a matter of fact does not render the E.A.T.'s or other decision-maker's (such as the Social Welfare Appeals Tribunal or the Income Tax Special Commissioners) determination on this matter entirely unappealable. In the first place, appeals from the E.A.T.'s determinations under the Unfair Dismissals Act, 1977, to the Circuit Court are by way of a full re-hearing, and appeals from the Circuit Court to the High Court under that Act are also by way of a re-hearing of the entire evidence.[72] Where, as is generally the case, the right of appeal is confined to points of law, a determination about a worker's classification

68. Appeals under the Unfair Dismissals Act, 1977, are by way of a complete re-hearing of the case.
69. [1933] IR 156.   70. Id. at p.159; see also FitzGibbon J at p.162.
71. Barron J, 29 July 1982.
72. *McCabe v. Lisney & Co.* [1981] ILRM 289.

will be set aside if the subordinate tribunal applied the wrong legal test or if, on the evidence before that body, the appellate tribunal concludes that no reasonable decision-maker would have made the determination in question.[73]

Office-holders At times a distinction is drawn between employees and office-holders; on other occasions office holders are regarded as a particular species of employee. An office has been described as 'a position or place to which certain duties are attached, especially of a more or less public character; a position of trust, authority or service under constituted authority; a place in the administration of government, the public service, the direction of a corporation, company, society etc.'[74] Most senior public sector appointees are office-holders; numerous what may be termed intermediate public sector posts are classified by legislation as offices.[75] Whether these office-holders are employees for the purposes of the general employment protection legislation rarely arises because many of those Acts do not apply to non-industrial public service workers.[76] On occasions, office holders have been held not to be employees; for instance, the Commissioner of the Garda Síochána was held not to be a mere servant or employee of the State,[77] a rate collector was held not to be a 'clerk or servant' of the corporation which appointed him[78] and a district health nurse was held not to be a 'workman' for the purposes of the Workmen's Compensation Acts.[79] Regardless of their employment law status, the remuneration of all public service office-holders is taxable under the Schedule E.[80]

As for private sector officers, the only modern legislation affecting them as such is Schedule E of the Income Tax Act, 1967, which renders the emoluments deriving from any 'office or employment' subject to tax under that schedule.[81] Among the principal private sector offices are directorships of companies and certain senior positions in trade unions and in various voluntary, social, sporting or philantropic bodies.

Whether a particular office-holder is an employee for the purposes of employment legislation will depend on all the incidents of the office; the tests for determining employee status, described above, will be applied in the same way. In *In re Dairy Lee Ltd*,[82] it was held that, for the purposes of

73. *Lee Ting Sang v. Chung Chi-Keung* [1990] 2 AC 374, *Lynch v. Limerick County Council* [1926] IR 176 and *Galvin v. Minister for Industry and Commerce* [1932] IR 216.
74. *Edwards v. Clinch* [1981] 1 Ch.1, at p.5.
75. See post p.318.   76. See post p.290.
77. *Garvey v. Ireland* [1981] IR 75.   78. *People v. Warren* [1945] IR 24.
79. *O'Brien v. Tipperary (South Riding) Board of Health* [1938] IR 761.
80. *Mitchell and Eldon v. Ross* [1960] Ch.498.
81. See post p.331.   82. [1976] IR 314.

preferential debts in a company's liquidation, a salaried full time executive director was an employee. According to Kenny J, when a company director other than a managing director is working whole time for the company 'the inference that he was a . . . salaried employee seems . . . to be justified unless there is evidence that he was a whole time director only and was paid as such.'[83] On occasion, even managing directors have been held in the circumstances to be employees of their company.[84] Among the matters which suggest that a director may be an employee are his being designated by the company as, for instance, managing director or technical director, his hiring being the subject of a special contract or it was specially minuted at a board meeting, his remuneration being by way of salary rather than directors' fees, that the main tasks contracted for were performed under the board's directions. Regardless of their employment law status, all company directors' remuneration is taxable under Schedule E.

Workers Occasionally employment legislation uses the term 'workers' instead of employees, most notably some of the E.C. rules regarding employment[85] and the definition of a 'trade dispute' in the Industrial Relations Act, 1990.[86] This term was also used in the Workmen's Compensation Acts; for the purposes of those Acts, workers were employees or apprentices. The now repealed Truck Act, 1831, which required payment of wages in cash and not in kind, applied to 'artificers', who were defined as 'workmen' engaged in manual labour.[87] Workers for the purposes of that Act have been held to include certain categories who would be regarded as self-employed under modern legislation, like as 'gangers' and their men working on railways, the 'butty' in coal mines and 'lumpers' in the building industry.

EMPLOYEES EXCLUDED FROM THE LEGISLATION

It has already been remarked that legislation which regulates various aspects of the employment relationship is very much a modern phenomenon. Most of these laws date from either the mid-1930s or from the 1970s and later. Some of these laws apply only to a particular type of workforce, such as those employed in factories or in offices or in shops; others purport to apply

---

83. Id. at p.316; compare *Parsons v. Albert J. Parsons & Sons* [1979] ICR 271.
84. E.g. *Folami v. Nigerline (U.K.) Ltd* [1978] ICR 272 and *Eaton v. Robert Eaton Ltd* [1988] ICR 302.
85. See post p.128.   86. S.8.
87. Employers and Workmen Act, 1875, sched. 2, para 2.

practically universally. A feature which runs through many of these laws is that certain categories of employees are excluded from their scope; some categories being excluded by only some of the laws, other categories being excluded by all or virtually all of the laws. Some of the laws empower the Minister by order, usually requiring the Oireachtas' approval, either to extend or to restrict the scope of these excluded categories.[88] None of these laws provide for an exempting technique that features in labour legislation in some countries, viz. if a collective agreement applicable to a category of workers provides for matters in a manner at least equivalent to what the legislation provides for them, then the legislation will not apply to them for so long as that agreement is in force.[89]

The public service Civil servants and numerous other categories of non-industrial public service workers are excluded from the scope of many of the employment Acts.[90] There is considerable divergence between the Acts as to which public sector employees are excluded and even as to the legislative technique used for making the exclusion. Because the public sector is highly unionised and elaborate procedures exist for dealing with employment grievances that arise there,[91] perhaps there is not quite the same need for protective legislation as there is in the private sector.

Thus, the Unfair Dismissals Act, 1977, does not apply to the following categories: *inter alia*,

> A person employed by or under the State;
> Members of the defence forces and of the Garda Síochána;
> Officers of a local authority or of a health board, vocational education committee or committee of agriculture;
> A person being trained by or apprenticed to FÁS.[92]

By contrast, for the purposes of the Employment Equality Act, 1977, an employee is defined as including

> a civil servant of the State or of the Government and an officer or servant of a local authority . . . , an officer or servant of a harbour authority, health board, vocational education committee or committee of agriculture.[93]

Although the Redundancy Payments Acts are concerned with the conse-

---

88. Cf. *Minister for Industry and Commerce v. Hales* [1967] IR 50.
89. Cf. Redundancy Payments Act, 1967, s.47.
90. See post p.290.   91. See *Industrial Relations Law*, ch.7.
92. S.2(1); the full text of these exclusions are reproduced at post p.290.
93. S.1(1).

quences of various changes in business, the term business there is defined
to include

> any activity carried on ... by a public or local authority or a Department
> of State, and the performance or its functions by a public or a local
> authority or a Department of State.[94]

However, since the redundancy legislation applies only to persons insured
for all benefits under the Social Welfare legislation,[95] most public service
officers are outside their scope. As has been explained, E.C. Directives
which have not been appropriately implemented by the State, if they contain
very specific requirements, can have 'horizontal effect' against the State
and State agencies, but probably not against State-owned public utilities.[96]
The entire position of public service workers is considered in Chapter Eight.

Temporary and part-time workers In order to obtain the protection of
many statutory provisions, especially with regard to dismissal from employment, the employee must have worked continuously for the employer in
question for a specified period—be it 13 weeks, 12 months or 2 years, as
the case may be.[97] Therefore, those who have worked for the employer for
less than the requisite period do not get the benefit of the relevant Acts.
Many of these Acts, moreover, only apply if the employee works for a
minimum period in each working day or week. Up to 1991 the commonest
requirement was being expected to work for not less than 18 hours in a week;
by the Workers Protection (Regular Part Time Employees) Act, 1991,
employees who worked for no less than 8 hours a day and for more than 13
continuous weeks with an employer, were afforded protection under most
of the modern Acts.[98]

These Acts also lay down or incorporate special rules for reckoning an
employee's duration of continuous employment, such as what interruptions
shall not be regarded as breaking continuity and whether time off work for
certain purposes shall be deemed to be time spent in employment for those
purposes.[99] Continuity of employment is discussed in Chapter Eight,
dealing with statutory rights regarding dismissal. There are no continuity
requirements for the laws against sex discrimination.

Beyond retiring age Several of the employment Acts exclude employees
who have reached the normal retiring age or pensionable age for similar

94. S.2(1).   95. S.4(1).
96. Cf. *Foster v. British Gas Corp.* (Case C-188/89) [1990] 2 CMLR 833, ante p.16.
97. See post p.189, 193 and 207-208.
98. See post p.187.   99. See post p.185.

employees, notably the Unfair Dismissals Act, 1977, and the Redundancy Payments Acts 1967–1979.[1] Sixty-six years of age is the maximum age for insurable employment under the Social Welfare Acts, and employees over that age are in any event excluded from the scope of several employment Acts, notably in respect of redundancy payments and maternity protection.

Under-aged workers Employers are legally free to employ persons over the age of 18; the Protection of Young Persons (Employment) Act, 1977, places various restrictions on employing children and young persons regarding the kinds of work they may do and the hours during which they may work.[2] The minimum age for being an insured worker under the Social Welfare legislation is 16 years, so that the requisite continuity of employment for the purposes of several employment Acts does not commence until that age, notably for redundancy compensation and maternity protection.

Employees not insurable for all benefits Employees who are not insured for all benefits under the Social Welfare Acts do not fall within the Redundancy Payments Acts, the Maternity Protection of Employees Act, 1981, or the Protection of Employees (Employers' Insolvency) Act, 1984.

Employer a close relative Several of the employment Acts exclude employees who are close family relations of their employers. The Shops (Conditions of Employment) Act, 1938, does not apply to a member of a shop's staff where the proprietor is a relative.[3] The Holidays (Employees) Act, 1973, and the three principal Acts dealing with dismissal from employment (the Minimum Notice and Terms of Employment Act, 1973, the Unfair Dismissals Act, 1977, and the Redundancy Payments Acts, 1967-1979) do not apply where the employer is a relative as defined in those Acts and, additionally, where both parties dwell in the employer's house or on his farm.[4] The legislative formula used for this purpose is that these Acts shall not apply to a person who is employed by his spouse, father, mother, grandfather, grandmother, stepfather, stepmother, son, daughter, grandson, granddaughter, stepson, stepdaughter, brother, sister, half-brother or half-sister, is a member of the employer's household and whose place of employment is a private dwelling-house or a farm in or in which both the employer and the employee reside.

---

1. See post pp.194 and 208. 2. See post p.78.
3. S.3(2)(a) and (c).
4. Hoidays etc. Act s.2(1)(g), Minimum Notice etc. Act s.3(1)(b), Unfair Dismissals Act s.2(1)(c) and Redundancy etc. Act, 1967, s.4(3).

Illegal employment A person's employment may be illegal in whole or in part. For instance, he may be a non-E.C. alien working in a job which has not been duly authorised by the Minister for Justice; he may be a child or young person employed in breach of the Protection of Young Persons (Employment) Act, 1977, or of apprenticeship regulations laid down under s.27 of the Industrial Training Act, 1967. Perhaps the commonest example of partial illegal employment is where the parties do not declare to the Revenue the full remuneration being paid; all or part of the agreed remuneration is 'paid under the table'. Apart from a 'trade dispute' case in the 1950s,[5] the Superior Courts do not appear to have given careful consideration to the employment law rights and obligations of persons in what may loosely be described as in illegal employment. In that case, it was held that a dispute about the dismissal of an under-age barman, who had just joined a trade union, could not be a trade dispute under the Trade Disputes Act, 1906.

It would seem to be the practice in the Employment Appeals Tribunal to dismiss claims being brought by illegally employed workers, even where the element of unlawfulness is tax evasion in collusion with their employer. A similar practice is followed in Britain.[6] In *Lewis v. Squash (Ireland) Ltd*,[7] the plaintiff's claim for unfair dismissal was rejected by the E.A.T. because much of his remuneration had been dressed up as expenses. There the Tribunal followed several English tribunal decisions that the maxim *ex turpi causa non oritur actio* debars enforcing statutory rights arising from an employment relationship which is significantly tainted by illegality. The justice of this reasoning does not appear to have been questioned on appeal.[8]

SPECIAL OCCUPATIONS

There are several occupations in respect of which the employment Acts make special provision, either designating them as employees or as self employed for particular purposes. Several of these occupations are difficult to classify as one or the other, so that the legislature intervened to avoid uncertainty regarding their position. The Social Welfare legislation classifies various groups as either employed or self-employed for the purpose of those Acts[9] and enables the Minister to further classify persons.[10]

5. *Corry v. National Union of Vintners* [1950] IR 315.
6. E.g. *Hyland v. J.H. Barker (North West) Ltd* [1985] ICR 861.
7. [1983] ILRM 363.
8. Cf. Mogridge, 'Illegal Employment Contracts: Loss of Statutory Protection', 10 *Ind.L.J.* 23 (1981).
9. Social Welfare (Consolidation) Act, 1981, 1st schedule.
10. S.5(4)-(6). Cf. *Hales v. Minister for Industry and Commerce* [1967] IR 50.

Trainees and apprentices The definition of employee in some of the employment Acts includes apprentices, notably the Minimum Notice etc. Act, 1973, the Holidays (Employees) Act, 1973, the Employment Equality Act, 1977, and the Redundancy Payments Acts; insured employments under the Social Welfare laws include apprenticeships. Special provision is made in ss.3 and 4 of the Unfair Dismissals Act, 1977, regarding the requisite continuity of employment of probationers, trainees and apprentices for protection under that Act. Where they are under 18 years of age, trainees and apprentices are covered by the Protection of Young Persons (Employment) Act, 1977. Persons undergoing training or receiving work experience are deemed to be employees for the purposes of the Safety, Health and Welfare at Work Act, 1989.

Where special legislative provision has not been made for them, the question then arises whether trainees and apprentices are employed under a contract of employment. The two major cases concern insurability of student nurses under the Social Welfare legislation.[11] In *Sister Dolores v. Minister for Social Welfare*,[12] the appellant was in charge of a children's hospital which trained young girls to nurse children by way of a two years course, for which modest fees were charged. During the first year the girls were given a small monthly allowance, which was doubled in the second year. It was held that these trainees were not employed under a contract of service. According to Budd J, while it was clearly implied that they should do certain valuable work in the hospital, 'the fact that a person does work of value to another does not of itself make that person an employee.'[13] The work they did was 'also part and parcel of their necessary training and part of the specialised training they receive.'[14] Although they were paid remuneration that had some bearing on the work they did, what they got was more 'properly described as "pocket money".'[15] Although they could be dismissed for neglecting their duties and for misconduct, it was held that the hospital's authority to dismiss them was not commensurate with an employer's ordinary dismissal powers. A very important consideration was that their training was 'a means to an end'—it was to 'fit them for a calling' and, when they are so fitted, they then 'will become properly speaking, employed in that calling.'[16] In *National Maternity Hospital v. Minister for Social Welfare*,[17] where the facts were very similar, Haugh J concluded that student nurses at Holles Street Hospital were not employees, because 'the preponderant feature of the relationship between the Hospital [and them]

11. A much earlier instance in *The Case of Pupil Teachers and Monitors* [1913] 1 IR 219.
12. [1960] 2 IR 77.   13. Id. at p.83.   14. Ibid.
15. Ibid.   16. Ibid.   17. [1960] IR 74.

was almost entirely that of student and master.'[18] In England, it has been held that police cadets are not employees for the purposes of the legislation on unfair dismissals[19] and that research fellows at Oxbridge Colleges are not employees for the purposes of laws against sex discrimination.[20] In New Zealand, paid student teachers were held not to be employees.[21] Whatever about their employment law status, trainee nurses, student nurses, pupil nurses and probationary nurses are now designated as being in insured employment for the purposes of the Social Welfare Acts.[22]

In the *Sister Dolores* case it was argued that, even if the student nurses there were not employees, they were apprentices, but that view was rejected by the Supreme Court. According to the Court, 'in order to establish the relation of apprentice and master there must be a binding agreement on the part of the apprentice to serve for a definite period and, on the part of the master, a reciprocal agreement to teach the apprentice his trade or calling.'[23] The evidence there did not disclose a reciprocal contractual undertaking to serve and to teach for the entire two years period; there was nothing to prevent student nurses from leaving at any time. No matter how practical the training is, there must be a 'binding' of the student to his teacher for there to be an apprenticeship.

Out-workers By out-workers is meant persons who perform their tasks on their own premises, like in their own homes. The numbers involved in this kind of work have increased considerably in recent years, mainly on account of developments in computer technology. Some employment Acts stipulate that they do not apply to out-workers, notably the Holidays (Employees) Acts, 1973, and parts of the Protection of Young Persons (Employment) Act, 1977. Out-work is an insurable employment under the Social Welfare Acts;[24] the expression is defined for the purpose of those Acts as 'a person to whom articles or materials are given to be made up, cleaned, washed, altered, ornamented, finished or repaired or adapted for sale in his own home or on other premises not under the control or management of the person who gave out the articles or the materials for the purposes of the trade or business of the last-mentioned person.'[25]

Whether an out-worker is employed under a contract of service or a

18. Id. at p.81.
19. *Wilts Police Authority v. Wynn* [1981] 1 QB 95.
20. *Hugh-Jones v. St. John's College Cambridge* [1979] ICR 848.
21. *New Zealand Educational Institute v. Director General of Education* [1981] 1 NZLR 538.
22. Supra n.9, para.9.   23. [1960] IR at p.92.
24. Supra n.9, except for s.38(3)(c).
25. Supra n.9, para.7; cf. Holidays Act, 1973, s.2(4).

contract for services depends on the entire nature of the arrangements with whoever he is working for. In *Minister for Industry and Commerce v. Healy*,[26] where the defendant worked in her own home making trousers in different styles for a tailoring firm, which supplied her with the materials, it was held that she was an independent contractor. It was said that 'a person does not cease to be an independent contractor because he is in a humble position.'[27] That case involved a prosecution under the Conditions of Employment Act, 1936, and the Court emphasised that the Act's penal provisions should be construed strictly in favour of the defendant. In a 1984 English case,[28] the Court of Appeal accepted the conclusions of an industrial tribunal that a group of out-workers there were employees. Their jobs involved sewing parts on to clothes, using machines provided by the company; they were paid in accordance with the amount of work they did, they had no fixed hours and they were not obliged to accept any particular quantity of work. It was held that '[t]he fact that the out-workers could fix their own hours of work, could take holidays and time off when they wished and could vary how many garments they were willing to take on any day or even to take none on a particular day . . . does not as a matter of law negative the existence of [an employment] contract.'[29]

Religious activities In what circumstances are priests, ministers, clergy-men, nuns and the like, going about their ordinary activities employed under a contract of employment? All depends on the entire circumstances sur-rounding the activity in question; the general practices of the different religious denominations vary considerably. The mere fact that an individual working is acting under the direction of religious superiors does not prevent him from being an employee. Thus, in *Dolan v. K.*,[30] which concerned a nun who was employed as a national teacher in a school managed by her order, it was held that her remuneration was taxable under Schedule E. That she handed her entire remuneration over to her religious superiors, as required by the rules of the Order, did not affect the taxable nature of those payments; she still was 'exercising an office in respect of which she [was] paid a salary.'[31]

In several English cases, which concerned religious officers being removed from their positions by their superior authorities, it was held that the relationship between them and their superiors could not be characterised

---

26. [1941] IR 545.   27. Id. at p.553.
28. *Nethermere (St. Neots) Ltd v. Gardiner* [1984] ICR 612.
29. Id. at p.634. Similarly, *Airfix Footwear Ltd v. Cope* [1978] ICR 1210.
30. [1944] IR 470.
31. Id. at p.477. Cf. *Barthope v. Exeter Diocesan Board* [1979] ICR 900.

as a contract either of service or for services. As Lord Templeman put it in a case involving the dismissal of a pastor in the Presbyterian Church of Wales, 'the duties owned by the pastor to the church are not contractual or enforceable. A pastor is called and accepts the call. He does not devote his working life but his whole life to the church and his religion. His duties are defined and his activities are dictated not by contract but by conscience. He is a servant of God. If his manner of serving God is not acceptable to the church, then his pastorate can be brought to an end by the church in accordance with [its] rules.'[32] On the other hand, it was accepted that 'it is possible for a man to be employed as a servant or as an independent contractor to carry out duties which are exclusively spiritual.'[33]

The Social Welfare legislation does not apply to employed persons 'in Holy Orders or other minister of religion or a person living in a religious community as a member thereof'.[34] Provision, however, is made for the Minister for Labour classifying ministers of a religion as being in insured employment where they are being remunerated by a stipend, salary or similar payment, where representatives of those ministers make appropriate representation to the Minister.[35]

32. *Davies v. Presbyterian Church of Wales* [1986] 1 WLR 323, at p.329.
33. Ibid. Cf. *Wright v. Day* [1895] 2 IR 337, *President of Methodist Conference v. Parfitt* [1984] 1 QB 368 and *Santokh Singh v. Guru Nanak Gurdwara* [1990] ICR 309.
34. Supra n.9, part II, reg.7.
35. Id., part I, reg.12.

3

Determining the terms

Before discussing the actual rights and obligations of employers and workers, the mode of ascertaining what the terms of employment are calls for consideration, in particular, ascertaining what duties are incorporated in the contract of employment.

THE EMPLOYMENT CONTRACT

Apart perhaps from certain public service offices, the employment relationship is founded on contract. Rights and obligations, and the remedies for their breach arising from the employment relationship, therefore, are governed mainly by the law of contract.

Formality The great majority of employment contracts are oral in the sense that there is no actual written contract; the employee agrees to work on certain terms that are explained verbally or which are set out in some written document drafted by the employer alone or with a trade union. Contracts for senior executive positions, which may impose certain elaborate duties and provide for complex remuneration arrangements, tend to take a written form; either the entire contract is a single document or it is a brief document which refers to terms and conditions that are set out in some other detailed document. The Appendix to this book contains model service contracts which may prove useful to the reader as precedents;[1] one is a standard terms and conditions of employment, the other an executive employment agreement for company directors.

There are two kinds of employment contract that the law requires to be written. Since 1797 the articles of agreement under which merchant seamen are hired must not only be in writing but must follow a prescribed form.[2] Although there is no equivalent absolute obligation in respect of apprentices, at common law, unless articles of apprenticeship are in writing and signed

1. Post pp.359 and 371.
2. Merchant Shipping Act, 1894, s.114 sets out the present requirements.

by both parties, the apprentice cannot enforce the employer's obligation to teach and the special restrictions against being dismissed. There are special statutory rules for apprentice solicitors[3] and for apprentice seamen.[4]

Express terms The express terms of the employment contract are the terms actually agreed on by the parties.[5] Where the contract is written, these terms will appear on the document; where it is oral, practical difficulties can arise in proving what was agreed. Certain terms are forbidden by law, especially terms that purport to exclude application of the protective legislation, like the Redundancy Payments Acts, 1967–1979, and the Unfair Dismissals Act, 1977.[6] Where a difference arises between the parties concerning a matter which is covered by an express term, then it is a question of the true construction of that term what the outcome should be.[7] The law does not lay down any special rules for the interpretation of employment contracts as such. However, the courts tend to require good faith observance of specific terms[8] and to insist that terms which confer a wide discretion on one party (usually the employer) should not be exercised unreasonably in the circumstances.[9] On the other hand, it is not for the courts to re-write extravagant terms to which the parties actually have agreed.[10]

Implied terms Frequently, differences will arise about a matter on which the parties never reached actual agreement. When the contract was being made, they may never even have considered the matter or they may have done so briefly without reaching any firm conclusion. A frequent example is sick pay—should the employee be paid his basic wages while absent on account of illness?[11] The courts may be able to answer such questions by implying a term into the contract and thereby filling the legal void.[12] Whether particular terms should be implied into employment, commercial and other contracts is a matter that often comes before the courts. Judges will not readily imply terms; generally the parties themselves and not judges should decide what terms they are contracting under.

3. Solicitors Act, 1954, ss.24-39.
4. Merchant Shipping Act, 1894, ss.105-109.
5. See generally, A.G. Guest ed., *Chitty on Contracts* (26th ed. 1989) ch.12.
6. 1967 Act ss.51 and 1977 Act s.13.
7. E.g. *Grehan v. North Eastern Health Board* [1989] IR 422
8. *Secretary of State for Employment v. A.S.L.E.F. (No.2)* [1972] 2 QB 455.
9. *Knox v. Down District Council* [1981] IRLR 452.
10. In Britain this proposition is now subject to the Unfair Contract Terms Act, 1977. Cf. *Johnstone v. Bloomsbury Health Authority* [1991] 2 WLR 1362.
11. See post p.86.
12. See generally, *Chitty on Contracts*, ch.13.

Implied by the facts: A common form of implied term is one which is implied by virtue of the particular facts of the case. In deciding whether to fill a gap in the contract by implying a term, the test usually adopted is, if the matter in question had been considered by the parties at the time they made their contract, would they almost certainly have agreed to the suggested term. The court attempts to guess what the parties would have decided had they faced up to the matter at that time. As an English judge put it in one instance,

> *prima facie* that which in any contract is left to be implied and need not be expressed is something that is so obvious that it goes without saying; so that, if while the parties were making their bargain, an officious bystander were to suggest some express provision for it in the agreement, they would testily suppress him with a common 'Oh, of course'.[13]

Perhaps a more exhaustive formulation of the test is that of Lord Simon of Glaisdale:

> for a term to be implied, the following conditions (which may overlap) must be satisfied: (1) it must be reasonable and equitable; (2) it must be necessary to give business efficacy to the contract, so no term will be implied if the contract is effective without it; (3) it must be so obvious that it 'goes without saying'; (4) it must be capable of clear expression; (5) it must not contradict any express term of the contract.[14]

Unless the existence of a term is practically compelled by these tests, it will not be implied by the courts. Merely because the term in question is a quite reasonable one is not sufficient. Thus, for instance, the courts have refused to imply into employment contracts a term that wages were not to be paid during absence on account of illness;[15] that the employer would take reasonable care to ensure that his employees' effects were not stolen;[16] that the employee would be appropriately insured in respect of injuries he suffered in the course of his work when he is working in some foreign country.[17] Because employment contracts establish a somewhat unique continuing relationship, the courts tend to imply some terms in circumstance where those terms might not be implied in ordinary commercial trans-actions.[18]

13. *Shirlaw v. Southern Foundries (1926) Ltd* [1939] 2 KB 206, at 227.
14. *B.P. Refinery (Westernport) Pty. Ltd v. Shire of Hastings* (1978) 52 A.J.L.R. 20, at p.26.
15. *Orman v. Saville Sportwear Ltd* [1960] 1 WLR 1055.
16. *Deyong v. Shenburn* [1946] KB 227.
17. *Reid v. Rush & Tomkins Ltd* [1990] 1 WLR 212.
18. Cf. *Mulcahy v. O'Sullivan* [1944] IR 336.

When determining whether a particular term should be implied, the courts take account of various indicia. One of these is the subsequent conduct of the parties; what they did after the employment commenced is a very useful indication of what term they would have agreed upon when the contract was being made. As is explained below, where they are not directly incorporated into the contract, provisions in collective agreements applying to the workplace are often implied into the contract.[19] Very relevant also are works rules and appropriate customs and practices obtaining in the workplace.[20] Because the implication of terms into a contract is regarded as a question of law rather than of fact,[21] a decision by a lower tribunal or court on such a question can be fully reviewed on appeal to a higher court on a point of law.

Implied by law: Exceptionally, a term will be implied as a matter of law. That is to say, because of the very nature of the legal relationship in question, the courts hold that the contract embodies certain common incidents. As Stephenson LJ explained,

> there are contracts which establish a relationship, e.g. of master and servant, landlord and tenant, which demand by their nature and subject matter certain obligations, and those obligations the general law will impose and imply, not as satisfying the business efficacy or officious bystander tests applicable to commercial contracts where there is no such relationship, but as legal incidents of those other kinds of contractual relationship. In considering what obligations to imply into contracts of these kinds which are not complete, the actions of the parties may properly be considered. But the obligation must be a necessary term; that is, required by their relationship. It is not enough that it would be a reasonable term.[22]

By implying a term as a matter of law, the court is in fact laying down a general rule of law, that in contracts of this type a particular term almost invariably will exist unless the express terms of the contract or special circumstances of the case indicate otherwise.[23] These terms in employment contracts include the employer's duty of care for the safety of his employees and the employee's reciprocal duty to take reasonable care in how he performs his duties,[24] and also the employee's obligation of confidentiality.[25] Another way of describing this type of implied term is the common

19. Infra p.62.   20. Infra pp.57 and 58.
21. *O'Brien v. Associated Fire Alarms Ltd* [1968] 1 WLR 1916.
22. *Mears v. Safecar Security Ltd* [1983] 1 QB 54, at p.78.
23. *Siney v. Dublin Corp.* [1980] IR 400.
24. *Lister v. Romford Ice & Cold Storage Co.* [1957] AC 555.
25. *Thomas Marshall (Exports) Ltd v. Guinle* [1979] 1 Ch.227.

law of employment rights and obligations. Although the obligations arising from such an implied term often correspond with obligations imposed on the basis of tort, it would seem that a duty of care in tort can exist in certain circumstances where a contractual obligation to take care would not be implied.[26]

Written statement of particulars Within one month of the employment commencing, employers are required by s.9 of the Minimum Notice and Terms of Employment Act, 1973, on request, to furnish employees with written particulars of various terms of their employment contracts. Employees who are expected to work at least eight hours a week are entitled to these particulars.[27] The particulars that must be given in this manner are the following:

(a) the date of commencement of his employment
(b) the rate or method of calculation of his remuneration
(c) the length of the intervals between the times at which remuneration is paid, whether weekly, monthly or any other period,
(d) any terms or conditions relating to hours of work or over-time,
(e) any terms or conditions relating to

(i) holidays and holiday pay
(ii) incapacity for work due to sickness or injury and sick pay and
(iii) pensions and pension schemes,

(f) the period of notice which the employee is obliged to give and entitled to receive to determine his contract of employment, or (if the contract of employment is for a fixed term) the date on which the contract expires.

The Minister may add to this list of particulars but so far has not done so.

Where the particulars in question are contained in some written document, like a collective agreement or works rules, it suffices to refer the employee to that document, provided however that he 'has reasonable opportunities of reading it' at work or that it is 'reasonably accessible to him in some other way'.[28] It will depend on the circumstances whether the document satisfies these requirements of readability and accessibility.

26. Supra n.17; such a case did not arise in the circumstances there.
27. S.3(1)(a), as amended by Worker Protection (Regular Part-Time Employees) Act, 1991, s.2. The 1973 Act does not apply to civil servants, to merchant seamen and to persons employed by a close relative on a farm or in a house where that person and also the employer reside.
28. S.9(4).

Contractual effects of particulars: Where particulars furnished have not elicited protest from the employee,[29] the courts tend to accept the employer's statement as the agreed terms of the employment contract. The precise relevance of these statements in determining the terms of the contract remain to be determined. There have been differences of opinion on the matter in England, where it has been held that, in general, the statement 'provides very strong *prima facie* evidence of what were the terms of the contract between the parties, but does not constitute a written contract between the parties. Nor are the statements of the terms finally conclusive; at most, they place a heavy burden on the employer to show that the actual terms of contract are different from those which he has set out in the statutory statement.'[30]

Among the questions that remain to be resolved include, does a signed acknowledgement that the document is a contract give it contractual status? Is the employee estopped from denying the particulars as stated merely because he did not raise a protest shortly after those particulars were furnished; does estoppel operate only where the employee's very actions indicated his acceptance of the particulars in question? Dealing with the extent to which these statements give rise to an estoppel against the employee, Browne-Wilkinson J has observed that the courts should be hesitant in this regard. In one instance, concerning the extent to which the employer was authorised to vary the work-place, under a term to that effect in the statement of particulars, it was said that to

> imply an agreement to vary or to raise an estoppel against the employee on the grounds that he has not objected to a false record by the employer of the terms actually agreed is a course which should be adopted with great caution. If the variation related to a matter which has immediate practical application (e.g., the rate of pay) and the employee continues to work without objection after effect has been given to the variation (e.g. his pay packet has been reduced) then obviously he may well be taken to have impliedly agreed. But where, as in the present case, the variation has no immediate practical affect the position is not the same. It is . . . asking too much of the ordinary employee to require him either to object to an erroneous statement of his terms of employment having no immediate practical impact on him or be taken to have assented to the variation. So to hold would involve

29. Cf. *Mears v. Safecar Security Ltd* [1983] 1 QB 54, where the employee disputed the terms contained in the statement.
30. *System Floors (U.K.) Ltd v. Daniel* [1982] ICR 54, at p.58.

an unrealistic view of the inclination and ability of the ordinary employee to read and fully understand such statements.

Even if he does read the statement and can understand it, it would be unrealistic of the law to require him to risk a confrontation with his employer on a matter which has no immediate practical impact on the employee.[31]

Another unresolved question is how relevant is the statement as furnished when some of the contract is written or the terms of a collective agreement are incorporated into the contract, either expressly or by implication?

Enforcement of obligation: In *Scally v. Southern Health and Social Services Board*,[32] it was held that there can be an implied term in the contract of employment to bring to the notice of employees certain changes in the terms of service. There a new system of contributions to a pension scheme was introduced by the employer but the plaintiffs were not notified of that change and, in consequence, they lost valuable pension entitlements. It was also argued that the employer should be held liable for breach of statutory duty—for not disclosing the altered terms as required by the U.K. equivalent of the 1973 Act. But it was held the Parliament did not intend that those who suffered loss by virtue of a breach of that Act's requirements should have a civil remedy for damages.

Scally might be distinguished here because there was a civil remedy prescribed in the legislation under consideration there, being the right to refer the matter to an industrial tribunal. Under the 1973 Act, the only mode of enforcement is the criminal sanction, which leads on to the question of when do penal provisions also give rise to a civil remedy. This Act does not lay down any special procedure for dealing with where an employer does not furnish particulars or sufficient particulars, or for where the employee disagrees with whatever particulars as have been provided. Section 11 of the Act gives the Employment Appeals Tribunal judisdiction over '[a]ny dispute arising out of any matter' under the Act except for disputes about the notice of particulars.

Works rules The employment contract may incorporate, either expressly or by implication, certain rules that are supposed to obtain at the workplace. At times these rules may have been drafted with the agreement of the employees' trade union. Many employers furnish employees with a book of rules regarding numerous aspects of the job. On other occasions rules

31. *Jones v. Associated Tunnelling Ltd* [1981] IRLR 477, at p.481.
32. [1991] 4 All ER 563.

may be displayed in notices at the workplace. These rules may relate only to disciplinary matters or they may cover a whole range of subjects, like times of work, meal breaks, calculation of remuneration, holidays, sick pay; grievance and disciplinary procedures may also be set out.

Works rules become express terms of the contract where the parties so agree. Agreement to this effect may be express, such as by a written acknowledgement that the employment terms shall include those laid down in the rules. Or the consent may be tacit, like working for some period when the rules purported to be in operation. But in this case, it must be shown that the employee was furnished with reasonable notice of the rules. What notice is reasonable for these purposes will depend on the circumstances, for instance, the nature of the document in question and what steps were taken to bring it to the employee's attention. Where rules obtaining at the time of the hiring are changed later, the employee may very well be bound by the new rules if his conduct indicates that he consented to the change, such as by working in accordance with these new rules.[33] Doing that may be regarded either as a consensual variation of the terms or as an estoppel from denying that the terms had been varied. Even where works rules do not become express terms of the contract, they may be considered by the court as containing certain implied terms.

Custom and practice   Some customs and practices prevailing at the workplace may be implied as terms of the employment contract. In order to attain contractual status in this manner, the alleged custom must satisfy four requirements; it must be notorious, certain, reasonable and is a custom that is regarded as obligatory. If the custom is not notorious, then it is impossible to say that the employee in question could have not been unaware of it on being hired. As in the case of works rules, it is essential to demonstrate that employees should have been fully aware of the custom or rule. In *Devonald v. Rosser & Sons*, it was said that 'a custom cannot be read into a written contract unless . . . it is so universal that no workman could be supposed to have entered into the service without looking to it as part of the contract.'[34] But it has been held that it is not essential that the employee in question was actually aware of the custom; that it 'is immaterial whether he knew of it or not'.[35] Secondly, the custom must be sufficiently certain. Thus, in the *Devonald* case, where it was contended that a custom existed whereby employers could temporarily close the workplace without paying their employees any remuneration, it was held that 'there was no element of

33. *Petrie v. MacFisheries Ltd* [1940] 1 KB 258.
34. [1906] 2 KB 728, at p.741.
35. *Sagar v. Ridehalgh Ltd* [1931] 1 Ch. 310, at p.336.

certainty about the alleged customs.'[36] Thirdly, before it will be implied into the contract, the custom must be a reasonable one. Thus in the *Devonald* case, the alleged custom just referred to was rejected for being 'eminently unreasonable'.[37] Indeed, if a mode of acting is most unreasonable it is difficult to understand how it can be an established custom.

The custom also must be one that was regarded as imposing an obligation. In *Meek v. Port of London Authority*,[38] the court refused to imply into the contract an alleged custom whereby the employer paid the employee's income tax. Even if this practice had satisfied the requirement of notoriety, the court characterised it as a windfall, observing that '[i]t would require a very strong case indeed to turn a practice apparently of bounty into a usage of obligation.'[39]

Collective agreements Collective agreements are agreements made between trade unions and employers or employers' associations. As is explained elsewhere, [40] these agreements have several functions and, although undoubtedly they are contracts, often the parties cannot enforce the agreements against each other because they were not intended to be legally enforceable.[41] Provision is made in the Industrial Relations Acts, 1946-1969, for registering collective agreements with the Labour Court and there is a mechanism for enforcing their terms through Labour Court procedures. But there are comparatively few agreements of this type.

Most collective agreements have a 'normative' function, in the sense that they purport to lay down certain terms and conditions under which specified employees shall be employed; for instance, hours of work, rates of pay, arrangements for overtime and holidays. The subject matter of these provisions varies considerably from industry to industry; some agreements are confined to the bare minimum rates of remuneration, while other agreements deal with a wide range of topics. Generally, it is the implicit threat of retaliatory action against breach that deters employers and unions from contravening obligations they undertook in collective agreements. But where the term of an agreement is incorporated into a contract of employment, breach of the term constitutes an actionable breach of the employment contract. In this way the employer has a legal right to hold the employee to the collective agreement's terms; the employee has a similar right.

Provisions of collective agreements become terms of employment contracts in three ways; by the union in question making the agreement as agent

36. [1906] 2 KB at p.741. 37. Id. at p.743.
38. [1918] 1 Ch. 415. 39. Id. at p.422.
40. *Industrial Relations Law*, ch.4.
41. *Ford Motor Co. Ltd v. Amalgamated Union of Engineering Workers* [1969] 2 QB 303.

of its employees, by express incorporation of the agreement and by way of an implied term. Even though a collective agreement purports to apply to a particular category of employee, those employees and their employer are legally free to agree between themselves on terms of employment that are inconsistent with those provided for in the collective agreement. Unlike the position in many countries, the normative terms in collective agreements normally, as a matter of law, do not override inconsistent terms in employment contracts.[41a]

Agency: Generally, trade unions do not conclude collective agreements as agents of their members. Thus in *Goulding Chemicals Ltd v. Bolger*,[42] where the defendants' trade union agreed with their employer regarding the terms on which the defendants should be make redundant, it was held that those terms were not legally binding on the defendants. O'Higgins CJ observed that he found it 'very difficult to accept that membership of an association like a union could bind all members individually in respect of union contracts merely because such had been made by the union'.[43] Unions in Ireland usually bargain for non-members as well as for their own members.

Occasionally a union will be deemed to have contracted as its members' agent, endowed with authority to legally bind them. It depends entirely on the circumstances whether the members gave their union that authority. An excellent example is *O'Rourke v. Talbot Motors Ltd.*[44] When the defendant company was contemplating extensive redundancies at its Santry plant, a group of its foremen-employees elected a small committee to negotiate with the company. At these negotiations, in return for assurances that the foremen would co-operate with management's re-organisation of production, the company guaranteed that they would not be made redundant and, at the committee's insistence, gave that guarantee in writing. When the defendants violated the guarantee, the foremen—and not their trade union or their negotiating committee—individually sued the company for breach of a term in their employment contracts, that term being that they would not be made redundant. It was held that the term of the agreement which had been reached with the committee had become a part of the plaintiffs' contracts because it was clear and unambiguous and had been negotiated by their agents, who throughout had been adamant that the agreement should be legally effective.[45]

Express incorporation: Often employment contracts expressly stipulate that they shall incorporate the terms of collective agreements. In unionised

41a. See generally, O. Khan-Freund, *Labour and the Law* (2nd ed. 1977) pp.140-149.
42. [1977] IR 211.   43. Id. at p.231.   44. [1984] ILRM 587.
45. Similarly, *Edwards v. Skyways Ltd* [1964] 1 WLR 349.

establishments it is not uncommon for new employees to be informed that their rates of remuneration and several other terms shall be those set down in designated collective agreements. Instead of providing a list of the various particulars that the Minimum Notice etc. Act, 1973, requires to be given to new employees, the employer may refer them to some 'document' containing the requisite particulars; frequently that document is a collective agreement. The fact that the agreement was referred to in this way does not mean that its contents form express terms of employment contracts but such reference may lead to those terms being incorporated by implication.

In *National Coal Board v. Galley*,[46] where the defendant's written contract stated that its terms shall be subject to national collective agreements in the coal mining industry, it was contended that those agreements' terms regarding overtime were not part of the employment contract because they were too vague. What the agreement provided was that employees 'shall work such days or part days in each week as may reasonably be required by the management.' It was held that the 'parties have expressly provided that reasonableness shall be the test' and that the 'fact that it is difficult to decide in a given case should not deter the court from deciding what is a reasonable requirement by the master in the light of the surrounding circumstances.'[47]

A somewhat similar case is *Knox v. Down District Council*,[48] which concerned the incorporation and application of what had been agreed at a national joint negotiating council. Those councils are among the commonest 'constitutive' features of collective agreements; they are permanent joint negotiating bodies, comprised of employers' and employees' representatives, which continually revise various terms and conditions. The clause in question here concerned loans to employees: it provided that '[t]he employing authority may on receipt of an application for financial assistance ... authorise the grant of a loan', subject to certain conditions being satisfied. The issue before the court was, where an employee indeed satisfied these conditions, had he a legal right to obtain a loan. It was held by the Northern Ireland Court of Appeal that this clause formed part of the plaintiff's employment contract and, while use of the term 'may' gave the employer some discretion regarding loan applications, that was far from being an unfettered discretion. Referring to the negotiations that preceded adoption of this clause, Lord Lowry LCJ commented that '[i]t would be unrealistic and contrary to legal principle to overlook the background to the conditions of service and merely treat them as if they were agreed between a single employer and a single employee. Every contract has to be construed in the

46. [1958] 1 WLR 16.   47. Id. at p.24.   48. [1981] IRLR 452.

light of the surrounding circumstances. Once this is done here the absurdity is recognised of confiding to the unfettered discretion of the employer the decision on what terms to make a loan or whether to make a loan at all.'[49] Consequently, the mere fact that the employer never put money by in order to provide for some loans was no lawful reason for refusing the plaintiff's application.

Implied incorporation: Where persons commence working in an establishment in which a collective agreement deals with conditions for employees in their category, the courts will readily imply the agreement's terms into their employment contracts, on the grounds that this almost certainly is what the parties intended. In the case of a collective agreement being introduced in an establishment where previously there were none, it will depend on all the circumstances whether its terms will be implied into the employment contracts.[50] In appropriate circumstances, a collective agreement's terms can even be implied where the employer in question was not even a party to nor was directly represented in the negotiation of the agreement.

Problem cases: There are a number of problems that often arise in connection with impliedly incorporating the provisions of collective agreements into individual employment contracts. These matters are not the subject of any reported Irish authorities. Although there are numerous English cases where similar questions were considered, the analysis in at least some of those cases is faulty and may possibly not be followed here.

Where, as usually is the case, the collective agreement is not legally enforceable *inter partes*, being described as binding in honour only, does this prevent some of its provisions from becoming legally binding terms of an employment contract? The answer is no, unless there are special circumstances which suggest that those terms were not intended to be so incorporated in a binding manner.[51]

Not all terms of collective agreements can be incorporated into employment contracts; only terms which are appropriate for incorporation can be rendered enforceable in this manner. A distinction is drawn between provisions regarding, for example, wages, hours of work, sick pay and holidays, which are readily incorporated and, on the other hand, provisions regarding trade union responsibilities and facilities, which have no direct bearing on

49. Id. at p.455.
50. Cf. *Young v. Canadian Northern Rly. Co.* [1931] AC 83 and *Re Andrew M. Paterson Ltd* [1981] 2 NZLR 289.
51. E.g. *Robertson v. British Gas Corp.* [1983] ICR 351 and *Marley v. Forward Trust Group Ltd* [1986] ICR 891.

individual employees. For instance in *National Coal Board v. National Union of Mineworkers*,[52] one question which arose was whether the conciliation procedures in a collective agreement between the parties were capable of incorporation into the Coal Board's employment contracts with the N.U.M. members. It was held that they were 'not . . . in the least apt for contractual enforcement by individual employees'.[53] Because the machinery was designed to be operated either by the union or by the Coal Board, and no employee had any direct part to play in it, it 'simply [did] not lend itself at all to enforceability at the suit of an individual mineworker'.[54] So far the cases have not set out a comprehensive test for determining which terms are and are not apt for incorporation. In one instance, it was held that employees, union members, were individually bound by a no-strike clause in a collective agreement, whereby their union undertook not to institute any strike action.[55]

The fact that the employee in question is not a member of a union-party to a collective agreement does not ordinarily prevent its terms from being incorporated into his employment contract.[56] Ordinarily, the employee either having left his union or being expelled from it does not prevent the provisions of a collective agreement with that union from being incorporated into his employment contract. However, the term in question may be one which is not appropriate to apply to non-union members, for instance a clause expressly providing for wage increases or certain benefits for union members only. The same applies where the employer ceases to be a member of an employers' federation which was a party to the relevant collective agreement.[57] That the agreement was subsequently terminated may not prevent its incorporation into the individual contract.[58]

Employees may be affected by several collective agreements, which contain inconsistent provisions. For instance, there may be a national industry-wide agreement, a plant agreement and also a craft agreement. There are no hard and fast rules for determining which agreement's provisions take precedence for the purpose of incorporation into the individual contracts.[59] Some assistance may be obtained from the statement of particulars given in accordance with the 1973 Act.

---

52. [1986] ICR 736.
53. Id. at p.773.
54. Ibid. Similarly *Tadd v. Eastwood* [1983] IRLR 320.
55. *Camden Exhibition & Display Ltd v. Lynott* [1966] 1 QB 555.
56. *Singh v. British Steel Corp.* [1974] IRLR 131.
57. *Burroughs Machinery Ltd v. Timmoney* [1976] IRLR 343.
58. *Morris v. C.H. Bailey Ltd* [1969] 2 LlLR 215
59. Cf. *Gascol Conversions Ltd v. Mercer* [1974] ICR 420, *Donelan v. Kirby Constructions Ltd [1983] IRLR 191 and Alexander v. Standard Telephones & Cables p.l.c.* [1990] ICR 291.

ALTERING THE CONTRACT

Since the employment relationship often is one which lasts for a prolonged period, some of its terms and conditions will be changed from time to time. Usually, those changes will be made by agreement between the employer and the employee or their representatives; for instance, salary increases will often be negotiated so that at least the employee's real earnings are not eroded by inflation. Neither party may change the contract unilaterally, except where the very terms of the contract authorise unilateral alteration. In such a case, the power to change the terms without the other party's agreement cannot be used unreasonably. It depends on the circumstances what kinds of changes amount to altering the very terms of the contract. Clearly, changes in agreed rates of pay, hours and place of work, intrinsic nature of the job fall into that category. But changes in the way the work is done may not usually be so classified. For instance, in *Cresswell v. Inland Revenue*,[60] the employer introduced computers to facilitate recording information at the workplace. The contention that this amounted to a unilateral change of the plaintiff's employment terms was rejected. Generally, an employee is expected to adapt to new methods and techniques in performing his duties provided the employer arranged for him to receive the necessary training in the new skills and the nature of the work did not alter so radically that it was outside the contractual obligations of the employee.

Where an alteration has been agreed to by a 'representative' of the employer, that representative must be someone who was duly authorised to agree to the change. In one instance where post office sorters claimed they had been given a fifteen minute break during their overtime shift, O'Hanlon J rejected the claim on the grounds that those who agreed to that break did not have authority to do so.[61] Nor does the willingness of an employee to give an alteration in the terms a trial constitute his acceptance of that change. In *McCarroll v. Hickling Pentecost & Co.*,[62] a foreman in a textile factory was ordered to revert to his original job as a machine operator, at which his employment conditions were less favourable. He obeyed the order, although he was clearly dissatisfied with it, but after ten days working as an operative he resigned. His claim that the employer had repudiated the employment contract, by unilaterally altering its terms, was upheld. The fact that he gave the changed terms a trial could not be taken as him having consented to the alteration.

60. [1984] 2 All ER 713.   61. *Kenny v. An Post* [1988] IR 285.
62. [1971] N.I. 250.

STATUTORY OBLIGATIONS

There are numerous statutory provisions that give rights to employers and employees and that impose obligations on them. Sometimes the statutory requirement is declared to be a very term of the employment contract; most notably the equal pay provision of the Anti-Discrimination (Pay) Act, 1974, s.2 of which stipulates that '[i]t shall be the term of the contract under which a woman is employed . . . that she shall be entitled to' equal pay for like work. The mechanism under Part IV of the Industrial Relations Act, 1946, for fixing compulsory minimum wages in exceptional circumstances operates similarly; the rate of remuneration as determined by the Labour Court is incorporated into the relevant employee's contract.

Most employment legislation, however, does not adopt this technique. Some of the laws, such as the statement of particulars requirement in the Minimum Notice and Terms of Employment Act, 1973, the Holidays (Employees) Act, 1973, the Protection of Employment Act, 1977, the Protection of Young Persons (Employment) Act, 1977, and the Safety, Health and Welfare at Work Act, 1989, declare action which contravenes the standards they impose to be criminal offences. Offences under the first four of these Acts may be prosecuted by the Minister for Labour; under the safety legislation they may be prosecuted by the Health and Safety Authority or by some body duly authorised by that Authority. Under the young persons legislation, prosecutions may also be brought by the person in question's trade union or his parent or guardian. Remuneration which is due to an employee under the holidays and under the young persons legislation is recoverable as a simple contract debt; those proceedings may be brought by the employee's trade union and, in the case of young persons, their parent or guardian. Breach of the health and safety legislation of 1989 is declared not to be an actionable wrong; yet the very circumstances of the breach may very well constitute the tort of negligence.[63]

The technique most commonly used in modern legislation, like the Unfair Dismissals Act, 1977, is to prescribe certain requirements and then to stipulate that they can be enforced by bringing appropriate proceedings in an administrative tribunal, most notably the Employment Appeals Tribunal or the rights commissioners or the equality officers who are attached to the Labour Commission.[64] The jurisdiction of these tribunals has been outlined earlier in this book. The form of redress which these tribunals most frequently provide is an award of compensation, for instance, for unfair dismissal or the lump sum award for employees who were made redundant.

63. See post p.124.   64. See ante p.22 et seq.

Several rules are laid down for calculating how much shall be awarded to a successful claimant and there is usually a ceiling imposed on what can be awarded even if the actual loss suffered exceeds that sum. Almost every one of these Acts expressly provide for their peremptory application, by declaring void any provision in an employment contract which purports to exclude application of the Act in question.

4

Incidents of the employment relationship

This chapter is concerned with the principal incidents of the employment relationship, i.e. the main rights and duties of the employer and employee *vis-à-vis* each other. As has been explained in the previous chapter, the primary source of these incidents is the employment contract's express and implied terms and the reader should consult Mark Freedland's *The Contract of Employment*[1] for a comprehensive account of those rights and obligations. Those are now supplemented by numerous statutory requirements, in particular, the Conditions of Employment Acts, 1936-1944, the Holidays (Employees) Act, 1973 and the Payment of Wages Act, 1991. The requirements regarding discrimination at work and health and safety at work are considered separately in the following chapters.

For employees who come within the scope of the Unfair Dismissals Act, 1977, there are in a sense two entirely separate sets of employment rights and obligations. One is the obligations described here arising either from the contract or from statute. The other is standards of conduct which either justify or do not justify dismissal under the 1977 Act. Sometimes breach of the contractual and statutory obligations will be held to justify a dismissal; on other occasions a breach will not be so treated. For instance, in *Flynn v. Power*,[2] where a young teacher in a convent school challenged her dismissal under the 1977 Act, she was dismissed because she was openly living with a married man, had a child by him and refused to change this aspect of her private life. In deciding the case, it was not necessary to determine what rights she had under her employment contract. The only question was whether, in all the circumstances, her dismissal was unfair.[3]

---

1. (1976), hereinafter referred to as *Freedland.*
2. [1985] IR 648.
3. See post p.203.

THE WORK OBLIGATION

A central feature of the employment relationship is the provision and the performance of work; during the agreed working hours and for the agreed remuneration, the employee should carry out the tasks assigned by the employer. If the employee refuses to perform those tasks then, provided the job definition encompasses them, the employer is not obliged to pay the agreed remuneration. The position is more complex where the employee renders defective performance, i.e. he does the job but performs it badly.

Employer providing work Generally, while the employee is contractually obliged to attend at the workplace during the agreed times for working, the employer is not obliged to furnish actual work to be done.[4] All that usually is required of the employer is to pay the agreed remuneration for the period during which the employee is at work. As a judge put it, '[i]t is true that a contract of employment does not necessarily, or perhaps normally, oblige the master to provide the servant with work. Provided I pay my cook her wages regularly she cannot complain if I choose to take any or all of my meals out.'[5] Although having no actual work to do may deprive the employee of job satisfaction, generally 'a loss of job satisfaction is always regrettable but by itself provides no cause of action.'[6] Thus in *Turner v. Sawdon & Co.*,[7] the plaintiff was hired for four years as a salesman at a fixed salary. Before the contract expired, his employer refused to provide him with any more work to do, although the employer was content to continue paying his salary. It was held that the employer was not thereby in breach of his obligations.

This general principle does not apply where the employee's remuneration depends entirely on being provided with tasks to perform, for instance, where remuneration is based on piece-rates or on commission. In those circumstances, absent express stipulation to the contrary, it is an implied term that the employee will be supplied with sufficient work to earn such remuneration as could reasonably be anticipated.[8] Where part of the agreed earnings are to be reckoned on a piece rate or a commission basis, the circumstances may warrant implying a similar term. Such a term was held to exist in *In re Rubel Bronze & Metal Co.*,[9] where the plaintiff was the company's general manager for three years at a fixed salary together with

---

4. See generally *Freedland*, pp.23-27.
5. *Collier v. Sunday Referee Publishing Co.* [1940] 2 KB 647, at p.650.
6. *Cresswell v. Inland Revenue* [1984] 2 All ER 713, at p.720.
7. [1901] 2 KB 653.
8. *R. v. Welch* (1853) 2 E & B 357.   9. [1918] 1 KB 315.

a commission based on the company's net profits. Because he could have earned a very large commission on the profits, if made, it was held that he 'had therefore the right to ask that he should have a full opportunity to earning such commission'.[10]

There are also certain types of jobs where it will be implied that the parties intended that the employee should be provided with actual work to do. On several occasions, actors who were hired on a fixed salary have been held entitled to be given parts in which they can show their talents.[11] This was because the employers were deemed, in one of these cases, to have contracted, 'not only to pay . . . a salary, but to give an opportunity of appearing before the public in a part which answered to the stipulated description'.[12] Where a person becomes employed, especially for a long period and at a low remuneration, in order to earn a skill or to gain business experience, the employer is obliged to furnish such work as is required to achieve those objectives.[13] There can be other exceptional situations where an obligation to furnish work will be implied. Thus, in *Collier v. Sunday Referee Publishing Co.*,[14] where the plaintiff was appointed as chief sub-editor of the defendants' newspaper, and where the defendants then sold the paper, it was held that they were in breach of contract by paying him a salary but not providing him with any work to do. Although, because of deferences in the law reports, it could be said that this was not exactly what was decided.

Employee performing work The employee's principal duty under the employment contract is to perform those tasks, within the job description, as are assigned to him during working hours and to obey all reasonable orders incidental to the performance of those tasks. Several features of these reciprocal duties are dealt with later in this chapter, like identifying the workplace, determining the agreed times of work and calculating how much remuneration must be paid; the question of job description, of defining what exactly the employee can be required to do, has been considered to an extent in the previous chapter. The express terms of the contract may set out in detail what the job in question entails. The terms of the contract may also indicate the extent to which the employer is free unilaterally to alter various incidents of the job. Over and above any express terms, employees are obliged to obey all reasonable instructions incidental to performing their

---

10. Id. at p.324. See too *Turner v. Goldsmith* [1891] 1 QB 544 and *Addis v. Gramophone Co.* [1909] AC 488.
11. *Marbe v. George Edwards (Day's Theatre) Ltd* [1928] 1 KB 269.
12. *Clayton & Waller Ltd v. Oliver* [1930] AC 209, at p.221.
13. *Turner v. Sawdon & Co.* [1901] 2 KB 653.
14. [1940] 2 KB 647.

job, they must co-operate with the employer in doing their work and they must exercise reasonable care in the performance of the work. They also have an obligation of fidelity to their employer.

Competence and care: An employee must be reasonably competent to perform the job for which he was hired. Extreme incompetence will warrant instant dismissal; it has been held to be 'very unreasonable that an employer should be compelled to go on employing a man who, having represented himself competent, turns out to be incompetent'.[15] Many employments have elaborate disciplinary procedures aimed at ensuring that the work is done with a reasonable degree of competence. It is an implied term of the employment contract that employees will exercise a reasonable degree of care and skill in the performance of their work. Consequently, it was held in *Lister v. Romford Ice & Cold Storage Co. Ltd*,[16] that where an employer suffered financial loss as a result of his employee's breach of this duty, the employee is under an obligation to indemnify the loss. In that case, an employee who negligently drove a van in the course of his work injured a fellow employee (who was his father). On the basis of vicarious liability, the employer had to compensate that fellow employee for his injuries. It was held that the van driver was under an implied contractual duty to indemnify the employer in respect of that sum.[17]

Employers are subject to an extensive duty of care which is based on an implied term of the employment contract,[18] which also is founded in tort and is the subject of elaborate statutory regulation, notably, the Safety in Industry Acts, 1955–1980, the Mines and Quarries Act, 1955, the Office Premises Act, 1958, the Safety, Health and Welfare (Offshore Installations) Act, 1987, and other comparable measures. Many provisions of these Acts have now been replaced by a comprehensive measure, the Safety, Health and Welfare at Work Act, 1989.[19] The employer's common law duty is owed to each individual employee and employers must take due account of the different physiques and other attributes of their various employees. For instance, an employer owes a greater duty to take care of a one-eyed man than a normal man in respect of risk of injuries to the eyes.[20]

15. *Harmer v. Cornelius* (1858) 5 CB (NS) 236.
16. [1957] AC 555.
17. Contrast *Harvey v. R.G. O'Dell Ltd* [1958] 2 QB 78.
18. *Matthews v. Kuwait Bechtel Corp.* [1959] 2 QB 57. On the interaction of contractual and tortious obligations, see *Johnstone v. Bloomesbury Health Authority* [1991] 2 WLR 1362.
19. Discussed in detail, post ch.5.
20. *Paris v. Stepney Borough Council* [1951] AC 367.

Obey reasonable orders: It depends on the circumstance of the case whether an employer's lawful orders are reasonable and, accordingly, must be obeyed by the employee. Generally, employers are not entitled to give orders regarding what employees do outside of their working hours but there are some jobs which warrant giving certain instructions about what an employee should or should not do while not actually at work.[21] The extent to which, under the Constitution, contractual stipulations may authorise employers to interfere with their employees' private lives has yet to be resolved by the courts. Indeed, there is no modern judicial exposition of when orders will be deemed to be unreasonable. Orders that concern what happens outside the employee's times of work would usually be regarded as unreasonable, unless the contract clearly envisaged giving those orders. But the courts would be most reluctant to strike down instructions given about how a particular task should be performed since, by the nature of the employment relationship, it is for the employer to determine how the work is to be done. An order would have to be wholly unconnected with the employee's job or be manifestly unreasonable before it would be rejected by the courts.

An example of orders which were held to be unreasonable is *Ottoman Bank v. Chakarin*,[22] involving a bank employee who had been based in London. Under his contract, he could be posted abroad to any branch in Turkey. He was ordered to go and work at a branch there where, to the employer's knowledge, his personal safety was at risk. He disobeyed. It was held that, on account of that risk, the order there was unlawful. Even where the contract expressly authorises the employer to give certain directions, ordinarily those must still take due account of the employee's health and safety.[23]

Co-operation: Over and above the question of obeying specific orders, employees are subject to an overriding duty to co-operate with their employers in the performance of their work. Because the employment contract envisages a continuing relationship between employer and employee, it would seem that the employee must perform the various contractual obligations with a degree of good faith. As with the duty of obedience, the full extent of this obligation has not been articulated by the courts in recent times. But it has been held that 'working to rule' in the course of industrial action, meaning observing the strict letter of the contract to such extent as frustrates the very enterprise which the employer is embarked upon, can contravene

21. Cf. *Flynn v. Power* [1985] IR 648.   22. [1930] AC 277.
23. *Johnstone v. Bloomesbury Health Authority* [1991] 2 WLR 1362.

the duty of co-operation.[24] In *Secretary of State for Employment v. A.S.L.E.F. (No. 2)*,[25] which concerned a work to rule by train drivers and which was held to be in breach of those drivers' employment contracts, the judges spoke of an implied term to perform the contract in such a way as not to undermine its commercial objective. Roskill LJ observed that it is an implied term that 'each employee will not, in obeying his lawful instructions, seek to obey them in a wholly unreasonable way which has the effect of disrupting the system, the efficient running of which he is employed to ensure.'[26]

Fidelity: Employees must serve their employer with fidelity and in good faith. As was observed in *Hivac Ltd v. Park Royal Scientific Instruments Ltd*,

> It has been said on many occasions that an employee owes a duty of fidelity to his employer. As a general proposition that is indisputable. The practical difficulty in any given case is to find how far that rather vague duty of fidelity extends. . . . [I]t must be a question on the facts of each particular case. . . . [T]he obligation . . . may extend very much further in the case of one class of employee than it does in others.[27]

That case concerned whether, during their spare time, employees can work for an employer in a rival business. In the special circumstances of the case—the primary employer was the only manufacturer of the product in question at the time, the spare time work was done in entire secrecy, the work involved was highly skilled labour—the court enjoined the employees from working for the rival, who was seeking to break into the plaintiff's market.

The whole question of employees competing with their former employer is dealt with separately below,[28] as is the closely related question of disclosing and using confidential information obtained about the employer's business.[29] Many of the leading authorities on the duty of fidelity concern using confidential information to compete with a former employer. Other illustrations of the duty of fidelity are the obligations of at least senior management to disclose the misconduct of their fellow employees[30] and the obligation to disclose to the employer information of value to him which the senior employee obtained in the course of employment.[31] But it has been

24. See *Industrial Relations Law*, pp.109-110.
25. [1972] 2 QB 455.   26. Id. at p.508-509.   27. [1946] 1 Ch. 169, at p.174.
28. Infra p.101.   29. Infra p.96.
30. *Sybron Corp. v. Rochem Ltd* [1984] 1 Ch. 112.
31. *Industrial Development Consultats Ltd v. Cooley* [1972] 1 WLR 443.

held that an employee is not under any implied obligation to disclose his own previous breaches of duty.[32]

Enforcing of the work obligation There are various categories of breach of contract, principally, breach of warranty, breach of a condition and, perhaps, fundamental breach. The legal sanctions that can be used in response to a breach of contract often depend on what category that breach falls into; this is also the case with breaches of employment contracts. Where the breach is so serious that it amounts to a repudiation of the entire agreement then the other party is entitled, in legal jargon, to accept that repudiation and to terminate the contract there and then. Thus, where the employer does something that amounts to repudiation, like going into liquidation, the employee is entitled to resign immediately and claim damages for wrongful termination.[33] Similarly in *In re Rubel Bronze & Metal Co.*,[34] which concerned a general manager whose remuneration was to include a commission on the company's profits, it was held that, by preventing him from managing the business, the company had repudiated the contract although it continued to pay him the agreed fixed salary. It depends on all the circumstances of the case whether a breach of the contract has such drastic ramifications. As was observed in that case, '[i]n every case the question of repudiation must depend on the character of the contract, the number and weight of the wrongful acts or assertions, the intention indicated by such acts or words, the deliberation or otherwise with which they are committed or uttered, and in the general circumstances of the case.'[35]

Resignation/dismissal: Where the breach of contract is sufficiently serious as to amount to a repudiation, the employee can forthwith resign or, in the case of repudiation by the employee, the employer is entitled to dismiss him there and then, without giving any notice or money in lieu of notice. Many of the reported cases on breach of employment contracts are concerned with whether the employee had repudiated the contract and, consequently, whether his summary dismissal was lawful.[36] This entire matter is considered in detail in Chapter Seven; unfair dismissals is dealt with in Chapter Eight.

Suspension from work: Another sanction which may be open to the employer is to suspend the employee, who was in breach of contract, from

32. *Bell v. Lever Bros. Ltd* [1932] AC 161.   33. See post p.154.
34. [1918] 1 KB 315.   35. Id. at p.322.
36. E.g. *Pepper v. Webb* [1969] 1 WLR 514 and *Carvill v. Irish Industrial Bank Ltd* [1968] IR 325.

work—for a day, a week, a month or whatever. The contract may expressly authorise suspension[37] and even set out a disciplinary procedure.[38] A contractual power to suspend normally implies suspension without payment of remuneration for the relevant period; it usually means that 'the contracting party, if he be an employer, never contracts to pay wages during the period referred to, any more than the other party, if he be a workman, contracts to work during that period.'[39] Statutory provisions governing a variety of employments in the public service often authorise suspension, without pay, in prescribed circumstances and in accordance with set procedures.[40]

Absent an express power along these lines, disciplinary suspension is governed by two main principles. Apart from the exceptional situation where the employer must provide the employee with actual tasks to perform, the employee may be suspended from work at any time provided the employer continues to pay the agreed salary. Unless clearly authorised by the contract to do so, the employer is not entitled to suspend an employee without paying his agreed remuneration; if the employee has contracted to work in exchange for remuneration from say Mondays to Fridays, he is entitled to be paid for those days even if the employer chooses to suspend him from work. Thus in *Hanley v. Pease and Partners Ltd*,[41] in breach of contract, the plaintiff did not turn up for work on one day and, on the following days when he arrived for work, he was suspended without pay because of the previous absence. It was held that, while the employers in the circumstances may have been entitled to dismiss the plaintiff, they had no implied right to suspend him without pay. This was because '[h]aving elected to treat the contract as continuing it was continuing. They might have had a right to claim damages against the servant, but they could not justify their act in suspending the workman for the one day and refusing to let him work and earn wages.'[42] Exceptional circumstances however may warrant implying into the contract a power of suspension without remuneration, although the courts have been markedly reluctant to imply such a term.[43]

An employee who is wrongfully suspended from work can claim against the employer for the remuneration he would have earned during the period of suspension and, generally, that suspension would constitute a repudiation of the contract, thereby entitling the employee to treat it as a dismissal.

---

37. See generally, *Freedland*, pp.80-86.   38. See post p.170.
39. *Bird v. British Celanese Ltd* [1945] 1 KB 336, at p.342.
40. See post pp.315 and 321. Cf. *Cox v. Electricity Supply Board (No.3)* [1944] IR 81.
41. [1915] 1 KB 698.   42. Id. at p.705.
43. E.g. *Bond v. CAV Ltd* [1983] IRLR 360.

Damages: The employer or employee, as the case may be, may choose to bring an action for damages for breach of the contract. Where the breach does not amount to a repudiation of their agreement, then both parties' primary legal remedy is a claim for damages. Because the amount of damages resulting from breach of the employment contract usually is relatively meagre (other than in cases of personal injury), damages actions between employers and employees are comparatively rare—especially claims brought against employees.[44] The employer's usual response to an employee's serious breach of contract is to suspend or to dismiss the employee; if the breach was not an extremely grievous one, the employer most likely would give the employee some weeks notice of the dismissal or, more often than not, dismiss the employee and pay him a salary in lieu of notice, i.e. the equivalent of what would have been earned if the employee had remained at work during the notice period.

Reduction of earnings: Where the employee was in breach of the work obligation, the employer may in the circumstances be entitled to respond to the breach by reducing the employee's earnings. In the first place, the employment contract may specifically authorise deductions from earnings; in that event, the grounds and procedures for making the deduction must be scrupulously followed. It has been held recently in England that where, in breach of contract, employees resort to forms of industrial action which would entitle their employer to claim damages against them, the employer may deduct the amount of damages from remuneration which is due, by way of a set-off.[45] This principle would very likely be followed in Ireland. As is explained in this chapter, however, the Payment of Wages Act, 1991, greatly circumscribes the power to make deductions from the earnings of employees.

Injunction: Generally, the courts will not compel an employer to continue employing an employee who was wrongfully suspended or dismissed, nor will the courts compel an employee who has wrongfully absented himself to perform his work. Because employment contracts involve the provision and acceptance of personal services, as a rule the courts will not use their equity jurisdiction to compel performance of such contracts.[46]

---

44. E.g. *National Coal Board v. Galley* [1958] 1 WLR 16.
45. *Sim v. Rotherham Metropolitan B.C.* [1987] 1 Ch.216; also *Miles v. Wakefield Council* [1987] AC 539 and *Wiluszynske v. Tower Hamlets B.C.* [1989] ICR 493. See *Industrial Relations Law*, pp.112-115.
46. See generally, I.C.F. Spry, *Equitable Remedies* (3rd ed. 1984) pp.111-117; post p.203.

THE WORKPLACE

Most work is performed at a particular workplace, such as at the employer's factory, shop, office or some other premises. But there are employments that are carried on in several locations and some jobs entail considerable travel from place to place. Indeed, much of a person's work may have to be done abroad.[47] It is for the employer and the employee to agree where the work is to be performed. Usually it will be quite obvious from the circumstances where that place is located.

Changing the workplace Often employers seek to move their employees from one location to another. An employer cannot require an employee to work somewhere that is not envisaged by their agreement; any unilateral attempt to impose on the employee another workplace would be in breach of the employment contract. One of the circumstances that constitutes redundancy for the purposes of the Redundancy Payments Acts, 1967–1979, is that the employer 'has ceased or intends to cease, to carry on that business in the place where the employee was employed'.[48] Thus, a unilaterally imposed change of the workplace can render an employee redundant, thereby entitling him to a lump sum compensation as provided for by those Acts.[49] A forced change in the workplace may also render a dismissal unfair under the Unfair Dismissals Act, 1977.[50]

Employers may stipulate in the employment contract for considerable discretion regarding the workplace, by providing that the employee shall work anywhere in a specified region to which he is posted. Whether such a power must always be exercised reasonably in the circumstances remains to be determined.[51] In appropriate circumstances the courts may imply a mobility clause into the employment contract.[52] Any implied clause of that nature can only be exercised reasonably;[53] what changes in a workplace are reasonable depends on all the circumstances of the case.

Establishment Some laws refer to the 'establishment' where persons are employed and many of the E.C. rules and requirements refer to the employer's one or more establishments. At times, what is an establishment in a particular context is defined with some precision. Thus, the Protection

47. See post ch.12 on 'transnational' employment.   48. 1967 Act s.7(2)(a).
49. See post p.216.   50. See post p.202-203.
51. Cf. *Rank Xerox Ltd v. Churchill* [1988] IRLR 280.
52. E.g. *O'Brien v. Associated Fire Alarms Ltd* [1968] 1 WLR 1916 and *Jones v. Associated Tunnelling Ltd* [1981] IRL.R. 477.
53. Ibid. and *Courtaulds Northern Spinning Ltd v. Sibson* [1988] ICR 451.

of Employment Act, 1977, *inter alia* gives employees in establishments, where more than 20 persons work, rights where there are 'collective redundancies'. An establishment for those purposes is identified as the 'location' where an employer carries on business or, if there are more than one location, 'each such location'.[54]

TIMES OF WORK

It is for the employer and employee to agree when the work shall be done. One of the particulars that the Minimum Notice etc., Act, 1973, requires to be provided to new employees is 'any terms or conditions relating to hours of work or overtime'.[55] In unionised establishments, working times, along with overtime and lay-off provisions, will usually be the subject of collective agreements. Occasionally employees may be given a degree of discretion as regards the precise working times.

Restrictions on working times Employers and employees are generally free to choose when work shall be done and the length of the working times. But the legislature has imposed restrictions on these matters with regard to certain categories of employee and certain types of work. Since early in the last century there have been special provisions regarding the times when young persons and women were permitted to work. The reduction of hours of work and in particular the eight hour day was one of the most constant demands of organised labour during the 19th century. Working times was also one of the major areas of concern of the International Labour Organisation in its early years, and the I.L.O. has promulgated Conventions on the standard eight hour day, the standard forty hour week, weekly rest, paid holidays and paid educational leave.[56] State parties to the European Social Charter undertake 'to provide for reasonable daily and weekly working hours, the working week to be progressively reduced to the extent that the increase of productivity and other relevant factors permit'.[57]

Women: The view that women should be protected against being required or agreeing to work for long hours is not as prevalent today as in the past. Some observers regard legislation professedly aimed at protecting women against unduly long working hours as an unfairly discriminatory form of paternalism. Although sex discrimination at work is now unlawful, s.14 of

54. S.6(3).   55. S.9(d).
56. See generally, N. Valticos, *International Labour Law* (1979) pp.134-140.
57. Art.2(1).

the Employment Equality Act, 1977, permits continuance of certain statutory restrictions on women working. The restrictions on the hours during which women may be employed in 'industrial work' were repealed by order in 1986.[58]

Young persons: Ever since the factories legislation in 1802,[59] the employment of children and young persons has been the subject of regulation and today is the subject of comprehensive international standards.[60] Persons may not be employed on any full time basis unless they have reached the minimum school leaving age. The employment of young persons between that age and 18 years of age is regulated by the Protection of Young Persons (Employment) Act, 1977. For those under 16 years of age, their normal working hours are 37½ hours in any week,[61] and they cannot be employed for more than eight hours in any day and more than 40 hours in any week.[62] For those between 16 and 18 years of age, their normal working hours is 40 hours a week and they cannot be employed for more than nine hours in any day, more than 45 hours in any week, more than 172 hours in any period of four consecutive weeks and more than 2,000 hours in any year.[63] Young persons must not be employed between 10.00 p.m. and 6.00 a.m. on the following day and at least 12 hours must elapse between them finishing work on one day and commencing the following day.[64] Children under 14 years of age can never be employed between 8.00 p.m. and 8 a.m. on the following day and more than 14 hours must elapse between their working days. The Act sets out the conditions under which children between 14 and 15 years of age may be engaged in light non-industrial work,[65] and provision is made for rest periods during the working day.[66] Double employment, i.e. working for two or more employers, is prohibited where the aggregate hours of work exceed the prescribed maxima.[67]

The Minister is empowered to make regulations restricting the employment of excessive numbers of juveniles in shops[68] and also regulations prohibiting and restricting the employment of juveniles in industrial work.[69]

Industrial work: The times during which all types of employees may work at industrial work is regulated in considerable detail by Part III of the

58. SI No. 112 of 1987; see post p.140.
59. Cotton Mills and Factories Act, 1802.
60. See generally, Valticos, supra n.56, at pp.180-190.
61. S.7(1)(b).   62. S.8.   63. S.7(1)(a) and 9.
64. S.14.   65. S.4.   66. S.13.
67. S.16.   68. Shops (Hours of Trading) Act, 1938, s.18.
69. Conditions of Employment Act, 1936, s.15.

Conditions of Employment Act, 1936-1944. Under this, an employer must have a licence to carry out shift work, which licence will only be given where the work involves some continuous process; the maximum length of the working day is fixed; controls are imposed on the amount of overtime which may be worked; at least a half an hour's interval must be given after five hours continuous work during any day and a break must be given before starting overtime; extensive restrictions are imposed on what work may be done on Sundays and on public holidays. It is a defence to proceedings under this Act that the breach was necessary in order to deal with an emergency.

Shop work: The times during which persons may work in shops is governed by the Shops (Hours of Trading) Act, 1938, which covers matters like Sunday trading, weekly half holidays and restrictions on what hours may be worked during weekdays.

Bakeries: The employment of bakery workers at night is regulated by the Night Work (Bakeries) Acts, 1936 and 1981.

Drivers: In 1969 the E.C. introduced regulations governing a wide category of drivers of vehicles, like bus drivers and lorry drivers. These contain rules regarding manning requirements, driving periods, daily rest periods and weekly rest periods; the tachograph, which is a special recording equipment, was made compulsory in order to ensure compliance with many of the requirements.[70]

Normal working hours and overtime The distinction between normal working hours and overtime is relevant for several purposes. Often the remuneration payable for overtime will be proportionately greater than that for normal working hours; overtime may be paid at time and a quarter or time and a half, or whatever. Overtime does not count for certain statutory requirements. Usually, it is his normal working hours that determines if an employee is protected by particular Acts; for instance, under the Minimum Notice etc. Act, 1973, the Unfair Dismissals Act, 1977, and the Redundancy Payments Acts, it is only weeks during which the employee is 'normally expected to work' at least 8 hours a day which count for the purposes of continuity of employment.[71] But where overtime is not entirely optional,

70. Regulation No. 543/69, as amended; E.C. (Road Transport) Regulations, 1986, SI No. 392 of 1986, and E.C. (Road Transport) (Recording Equipment) Regulations, 1986, SI No. 393 of 1986.
71. See post p.187.

then the employee is normally expected to work for those extra periods. Overtime pay is not included for the purpose of determining the 'normal weekly rate' of pay under the Holidays (Employees) Act, 1973.[72] In determining the amount to be paid to an employee being made redundant, the basis of measurement is his 'normal weekly remuneration' as defined in the legislation; where he is 'normally expect to work overtime', the relevant figure is his average weekly earnings.[73] When calculating the ceiling on compensation payable under the Unfair Dismissals Act, which is 104 weeks' remuneration, the relevant figure is the remuneration for 'normal hours'; where the employee is 'normally required to work overtime' then his average weekly overtime earnings are included.[74]

Overtime may be compulsory or voluntary. Ordinarily employees are not obliged to work overtime. But their contracts may stipulate that they must work a certain amount of overtime when called on to do so or, alternatively, they may be entitled to work a specified period of overtime should they choose to do so. Several of the reported cases concern provisions of this nature in collective agreements and the question to be considered was whether the overtime clause was incorporated into the employment contracts, either expressly or by implication. For instance in *Gascol Conversions Ltd v. Mercer*,[75] the issue was what were the employee's normal working hours for the purpose of calculating the amount of redundancy compensation which should be paid to him. When he commenced working in 1969, he agreed to work a 54½ hour week, with overtime when required, and was remunerated on a 40 hour week basis, all extra hours being paid at overtime rates. This arrangement was confirmed the following year in a national collective agreement applicable to him. But in the year after that, a local collective agreement was concluded for his area, which provided that 'working hours . . . will revert to 54 per week.' It was held that his normal working hours were not 54 but 40 hours per week because the statement of particulars furnished to him referred only to the national agreement and, additionally, the receipt he signed when he got those particulars described them as 'the contract'. Perhaps the main principle to be derived from this case is the very strong emphasis the courts tend to put on memoranda and writing when seeking to ascertain the true terms and conditions of employment. The Irish Acts do not contain anything comparable to the provisions of the United Kingdom Acts which define when overtime is to be regarded as part of the normal working hours.[76] The precise meaning of the ex-

---

72. S.1(1).   73. Redundancy Payments Act, 1967, sch.3, paras.13 and 14.
74. SI No. 287 of 1977, reg.4.   75. [1974] ICR 420.
76. Cf. *Gascol Conversions Ltd v. Mercer* [1974] ICR 420.

pression 'normally expected work' has not been settled by the Superior Courts.

Lay offs and short time Occasionally an employer may not have sufficient work to keep his employees busy and, accordingly, may want to lay them off for a comparatively short period. Whether, or to what extent, employers can do this depends on the terms of the employment contract. In the building industry, short time and lay offs on account of bad weather is so frequent that special 'wet time' provisions for that industry were adopted in 1942 until they were phased out in 1985.

Right to lay off: Absent a term in the contract to the contrary, the employer's fundamental obligation is to pay the agreed remuneration for the times of work during which the employee is prepared to work.[77] Ordinarily an employer is free to lay off workers for any reason provided he continues paying them. A lay off without paying the normal agreed remuneration can be treated by the employee as a dismissal.

Where remuneration is based on piece work and in similar employment, it is an implied term of the contract that reasonable amounts of work will be provided. An employer therefore is not free to lay off workers employed on those terms, leading to a significant reduction in their earnings. Thus in *Devonald v. Rosser*,[78] which concerned piece rate workers in the tin-plate trade, it was held that their employer could not lay off those workers merely because business had drastically fallen off and there was a serious shortage of orders. The contention that there was a custom which entitled employers to lay off in those circumstances was rejected on the grounds of un-reasonableness; such a custom would introduce undue uncertainty into the contract.

Where the workplace must be closed down for a period in order to do necessary repairs, an employer may have an implied contractual right to lay off workers. So it was held in *Browning v. Crumlin Valley Collieries Ltd.*,[79] concerning piece workers, where the employers felt compelled to close their coal mines for some weeks in order to repair mine shafts. Because, in the circumstances, the dangerous state of the mines there was not the employers' fault, it was held that both parties to the contract should share the burden of the temporary closure. Since the employers lost 'the advantages of con-tinuing to have their coal gotten and being compelled to undertake expensive repairs', it was found reasonable to imply a term that the employees should 'los[e] their wages for such time as was reasonably necessary to put the mine

77. *Hanley v. Pease & Partners* [1915] 1 KB 698.
78. [1906] 2 KB 728.   79. [1926] 1 KB 522.

into a safe condition'.[80] Whether this temporary *force majeure* principle applies to employees who are not paid on piece rates has not been determined. But this principle can never apply where the dangerous state of the workplace is due to the employer's fault.

Redundancy payments: As is explained later,[81] under sections 11-13 of the Redundancy Payments Act, 1967, an employee who is laid off without pay or who is put on 'short time' for four or more consecutive weeks, or for six or more weeks in a 13 week period, may be entitled to claim a lump sum redundancy payment as if he had been made redundant.

REMUNERATION

The employer's principal obligation under the contract of employment is to pay the agreed remuneration. If he does not do so, the employee can sue him for that sum and, generally, is entitled to treat the non-payment as a repudiation of the contract.

Defining 'remuneration' Remuneration in this context means what the employer has agreed to give an employee in exchange for the latter's work. There are various statutory provisions that deal with pay or remuneration and the question frequently arises of what exactly constitutes pay or remuneration for the statutory purposes. For instance, are pensions or employers' pension contributions 'pay' for those purposes? Article 119 of the E.E.C. Treaty, which establishes the principle of equal pay for equal work, uses the expression 'pay' and there is a substantial case law dealing with what precisely this term envisages.[82] Section 1(i) of the Anti-Discrimination (Pay) Act, 1974, which was enacted to render Article 119 fully effective in Ireland, defines 'remuneration' for the purposes of that Act as 'any consideration, whether in cash or in kind, which an employee receives, directly or indirectly, in respect of his employment from his employer.'[83] Section 7(3) of the Unfair Dismissals Act, 1977, contains a slightly different definition; under it 'remuneration', for the purpose of calculating the compensation to be paid to an employee who was unfairly dismissed, 'includes allowances in the nature of pay and benefits in lieu of or in addition to pay.'[84] For the purposes of the Payment of Wages Act, 1991, which provides for the modes of paying wages and imposes restrictions on deductions from them, the word 'wages' is defined as follows:

80. Id. at p.529.   81. Post p.213.   82. See post p.137.
83. See post p.137.   84. See post p.205.

any sums payable to the employee by the employer in connection with his employment including—

    (a) any fee, bonus or commission, or any holiday, sick or maternity pay, or any other emolument, referable to his employment, whether payable under his contract of employment or otherwise, and

    (b) any sum payable to the employee upon the termination by the employer of his contract of employment without his having given to the employee the appropriate prior notice of the termination, being a sum paid in lieu of the giving of such notice:

Provided however that the following payments shall not be regarded as wages for the purposes of this definition:

    (i) any payment in respect of expenses incurred by the employee in carrying out his employment,

    (ii) any payment by way of a pension, allowance or gratuity in connection with the death, or the retirement or resignation from his employment, of the employee or as compensation for loss of office,

    (iii) any payment referable to the employee's redundancy,

    (iv) any payment to the employee otherwise than in his capacity as an employee,

    (v) any payment in kind or benefit in kind.

Special concepts of remuneration exist under tax law, social welfare law and family law, and what amounts to remuneration for these purposes is not necessarily wages, pay or remuneration for the purposes of the employment legislation.[85] The term used in Part V of the Finance Act, 1967, which deals with Schedule E income taxation, is 'emoluments', which mean *inter alia*, 'all salaries, fees, wages, prerequisites or profits or gains whatsoever arising from an office or employment, or the amount of any annuity, pension or stipend as the case may be.'[86] The term used in s.2(i) of the Social Welfare (Consolidation) Act, 1981, for the purpose of determining remuneration on which social welfare contributions are to be calculated is 'reckonable earnings', which is defined as 'earnings derived from insurable employment'.[87] Section 3(i) of the Family Law (Maintenance of Spouses and Children) Act, 1976, which deals with the attachment of earnings, defines earnings as

---

85. Cf. *Pereira v. Hotel Jayapuri Bhd* [1986] 1 WLR 449.
86. S.111(4); see post p.331.
87. See post p.355. Cf. *Re Given* [1936] IR 20 and *Minister for Industry and Commerce v. Ussher* [1948] IR 133.

any sums payable to a person—

(a) by way of wages or salary (including any fees, bonus, commission, overtime pay or other emoluments payable in addition to wages or salary or payable under a contract of service);

(b) by way of pension or other like benefit in respect of employment (including an annuity in respect of past services, whether or not rendered to the person paying the annuity, and including periodical payments by way of compensation for the loss, abolition or relinquishment, or diminution in the emoluments, of any office or employment).

Fixing the remuneration In most cases the parties to the contract will determine, either expressly or by implication, what remuneration is to be paid and when it shall become payable.[88] Frequently, this matter would be settled through collective bargaining, the outcome of which may be incorporated into the employment contract.[89] Among the matters that must be notified to employees in the written statement of particulars, given under the Minimum Notice and Terms and Conditions of Employment Act, 1973, are the 'rate or method of calculation of [the] remuneration' and the 'length of the intervals between the times at which remuneration is paid, whether weekly, monthly or any other period'.[90] Accordingly, disputes about what exactly was agreed between the parties with regard to remuneration often can be resolved by reference to this statement. Subject to two principal qualifications, the parties are legally free to determine the remuneration to be paid. Unlike the position in some countries, generally the employer and employee are legally free to agree on terms of remuneration that differ from those set down in a collective agreement that purports to apply to that very employment.[91]

Minimum wages: Under Part IV of the Industrial Relations Act, 1946, compulsory minimum wages can be set by the Labour Court and all employers affected by those minimum wage orders are obliged to pay at least the statutory minimum. Part IV of the 1946 Act is the successor to the old trade boards, which were first established in 1909 in order to combat what were known as sweat shops. Not alone can payments due under a minimum wages order be recovered in a civil action but the employer can be prosecuted for not paying the prescribed rates of pay. An employer who

88. E.g. *Mulcahy v. O'Sullivan* [1944] IR 336.
89. See ante p.59.   90. S.9(1)(b) and (c).
91. See generally O. Kahn Freund, *Labour and the Law* (2nd ed., 1977),. pp. 140-149.

is convicted of that offence may be ordered to pay the difference between the statutory minimum and the actual wages paid for the preceding three years.[92] On 1 January 1992, minimum wages orders were in force for the industries and occupations set out below.[93]

Equal pay: Employers are prohibited by Article 119 of the E.E.C. Treaty and by the Anti-Discrimination (Pay) Act, 1974, from paying women less than men who do similar work, and vice versa. The whole question of 'equal pay' is considered in Chapter Six.

Normal remuneration Like the concept of normal working hours, an employee's normal pay can be central to measuring the exact extent of his entitlements under several legislative provisions. Statutory holiday pay is calculated on the basis of the employee's 'normal weekly rate' as defined in the Holidays (Employees) Act, 1973;[94] the lump sum statutory redundancy payment is based on the 'normal weekly remuneration' as defined in the Redundancy Payments Act, 1967;[95] compensation for employees who are unfairly dismissed is based on the 'week's remuneration' as defined in regulations issued under the Unfair Dismissals Act, 1977.[96]

Sick pay One of the particulars that the Minimum Notice etc. Act, 1973, requires to be provided to new employees are 'any term or conditions relating to incapacity for work due to sickness or injury and sick pay.' Where

92. Cf. *Minister for Labour v. Costello* [1988] IR 235.
93. Aerated Waters and Wholesale Bottling (former trade board) (1946) (Variation) Order 1956 under the terms of s.40 of the Industrial Relations Act, 1946). S.I. No. 92 of 1991; Agricultural Workers (formerly Agricultural Wages Board (JLC Est. 1976). S.I. No. 256 of 1991; Brush and Broom (former trade board) (1946). S.I. No. 225 of 1991; Catering Excluding Dublin Co. Borough and the Borough of Dun Laoghaire (Est. 1977). S.I. No. 155 of 1991; Contract Cleaning (City and County Dublin) (JLC Est. 1984). S.I. No. 131 of 1989; Hairdressing (Dublin County and County Borough and Dun Laoghaire Borough and Bray Urban District) (JLC Est. 1964). S.I. No. 132 of 1991; Hairdressing (Cork County Borough) (JLC Est. 1977). S.I. No. 153 of 1990; Handkerchief and Household Piece Goods (former Trade Board) (1946). S.I. No. 324 of 1991; Hotels (excluding County Borough of Dublin and Cork and the Borough Dun Laoghaire) (JLC Est. 1965). S.I. No. 154 of 1991; Law Clerks (JLC Est. 1947). S.I. No. 131 of 1991; Provender Milling (JLC Est. 1960). S.I. No. 91 of 1991; retail Grocery and Allied Trades (JLC Est. 1990) (Establishment Order only). S.I. No. 58 of 1991; Shirtmaking (former Trade Board) 1946. S.I. No. 321 of 1991; Tailoring (former Trade Board) 1946. S.I. No. 323 of 1991; Women's Clothing and Millinery (former Trade Board) 1946. S.I. No. 322 of 1991.
94. S. 1(1).   95. 3rd Schedule, paras. 13-23; see post p.217.
96. SI No. 287 of 1977; see post p.205.

these particulars are supplied then, generally, there is no great difficulty in determining whether or not the employee is to be paid when absent due to illness or incapacity. Where the parties have not agreed on this matter or where no particulars were supplied and accepted by the employee, the legal position is not entirely clear. For there is a division of opinion in the cases decided in Britain and the only reported Irish authority[97] does not take sides on the point of principle.

One view is that, unless there is a term to the contrary in the contract, employees are entitled to receive remuneration while absent by reason of illness. As was observed in *Marrison v. Bell*,[98] 'under a contract of service, irrespective of the question of the length of notice provided by that contract, wages continue through sickness and incapacity from sickness to do the work contracted for until the contract is terminated by [due] notice. . . .'[99] The reason for implying such a term was that 'the great majority of employed persons in this country are employed on terms of a week's or, at any rate, a month's notice . . . ; and consequently there is no social need for protecting the employer from the liability of having to go on paying wages which he is always able to terminate after a short time'.[1] It was held there that this implied term stood even where the employee was in receipt of sickness benefit under the National Insurance Acts.[2]

The other view does not quite go to the opposite extreme—that the presumption is 'no work, no pay' and it is for the employee to rebut that presumption. Instead, there is no presumption one way or another; account should be taken of all the circumstances of the case and those should indicate what the parties would have decided about sick pay had they addressed the question.[3] Among the relevant matters is how the parties acted with reference to sick pay after they make the contract. In *Mears v. Safecar Security Ltd*,[4] where this approach was endorsed, it was found that practically every relevant circumstance in that case indicated that there was to be no sick pay. The company's practice was not to pay sick pay and that was well known to the employees; the plaintiff had been sick for 7 out of 14 months and, at that time, never asked for sick pay; on leaving the job he only asked for holiday pay and it was some time later that he decided to claim sick pay. In *Flynn v. Great Northern Rly. (Irl.) Ltd*,[5] under the collective agreement which applied to the plaintiff, ex gratia payments were to be made to employees during temporary illnesses. Budd J held that this was inconsistent

97. *Flynn v. Great Northern Rly (Ir.) Ltd*, 89 ILTR 46 (1955) at pp.60-61.
98. [1939] 2 KB 187.   99. Id. at p.198.   1. Id. at p.204.
 2. Similarly, *Orman v. Saville Sportswear Ltd* [1960] 1 WLR 1055.
 3. *O'Grady v. Saper Ltd* [1940] 2 KB 469.
 4. [1983] 1 QB 54.   5. 89 ILTR 46 (1955).

with there being any legal right to sick pay; the ex gratia payment was a substitute for whatever right to wages as might exist.[6]

Paid holidays Another of the matters which the Minimum Notice etc. Act, 1973, requires to be notified to employees are the 'terms and conditions relating to holidays and holiday pay'. Usually, therefore, there would be no great difficulty in ascertaining what arrangements were made about taking holidays and the payment of remuneration during those times. Authority on the contractual right to paid holidays is almost non-existent, presumably because almost every employer makes the position about holidays abundantly clear. Additionally, under the Holidays (Employees) Act, 1973, employees are given a statutory right to a minimum period of paid annual leave and also rights regarding time off and pay on public holidays. This Act applies to practically all categories of employee other than those 'employed by or under the State' in an 'established capacity' or in non-industrial work.[7]

Annual leave: The normal required paid annual leave is three working weeks and at least two of those weeks must be for an unbroken period. This is the case where the employee worked for the employer (or predecessor who sold the undertaking) for 12 qualifying months or for at least 1,400 hours during the leave year. If the employee was with the employer for less than 12 months, his entitlement is proportionately reduced; if he has at least eight months qualifying service, he must get at least two weeks unbroken leave. An employee's union cannot negotiate down his length of minimum leave but may, if duly authorised, agree to break up the specified uninterrupted periods. A qualifying month for these purposes is one where the worker was employed for at least 120 hours. Holiday pay which is due under these provisions must be paid in advance and must be at the employee's 'normal weekly rate' as defined in s.1(1) of the 1973 Act. The actual times on which annual leave can be taken is determinable by the employer after having consulted either the employee in question or his trade union. Failure to give paid leave is a criminal offence and the employee is entitled to receive what he ought to have been paid. On the other hand, an employee is prohibited from recovering any reward due to him for working during his annual leave.

Public holidays: Those days which are public holidays are designated in the schedule to the 1973 Act as Christmas day, St. Stephen's day, St.

6. Similarly in *Petrie v. Mac Fisheries Ltd* [1940] 1 KB 258.   7. S.2(1).

Patrick's day, Easter Monday and any other day designated by regulation; at present those days are the first Monday in June, August Monday and the last Monday in October. Except for Christmas day and St. Patrick's day, an employer may substitute a church holiday for a public holiday; the church holidays are also set out in the schedule. An employee's entitlement regarding public holidays is, at the employer's choice, either a paid day off on that day, a paid day off within a month of that day, an extra day's annual leave or an extra day's pay. The rate payable is a full day's normal pay.

Cesser of employment: Where an employee ceases to be employed and at the time annual leave was due to him, he is entitled to compensation for losing the opportunity to avail of that leave. This compensation is payable on the basis of one quarter of his normal weekly rate of remuneration for each qualifying month of service; an extra day's pay or a day and a quarter's pay is due in specified circumstances.

Modes of payment Subject to the Payment of Wages Act, 1991, remuneration is to be paid in the manner agreed between the employer and the employee. In the past, payment in cash was the norm but today many 'white collar' workers are paid either by cheque or by a credit transfer to their bank accounts. There are some employees who are partly remunerated in kind, like agricultural workers who may receive produce from the farm, employees of financial institutions who get low interest loans and employees of various transport companies who benefit from cheap travel. Some employers provide their employees with luncheon vouchers and some have remuneration arrangements that involve issuing to employees shares in their employing company or in its holding company. The treatment of 'benefits in kind' is a major concern of income tax law.[8]

The Truck Acts, 1743-1896, were designed to ensure that workers were paid their entire wages in cash and not otherwise, to prohibit placing conditions on how wages are to be spent and to restrict what kinds of deductions may be made from wages. As described by Bowen LJ,

> The clear intention of the[se] Acts was to ensure to workmen the payment of the entire amount of their wages in actual current coin of the realm, unfettered by any promise or obligation that it should be spent in any particular manner, or at any particular shop. The legislature endeavoured to secure that the workman might have in his hand the very actual coin representing his wages, in order that he and his family might freely carry it home, or spend it without impediment

8. See post p.339.

in the open market. . . . The Truck Act of 1831 . . . attempted to enforce
this object by rendering illegal every payment, or contract of payment,
of wages, except in the mode provided by the Act.[9]

A feature of these Acts, which at times confused lawyers, is the extent to
which various requirements are stated repeatedly. As has been observed of
the 1831 Act, 'the statute was intended to be a charter of liberty to workmen
which they could easily understand; and in 1831 the education of the
working classes is not what it is today. It was for this reason important for
Parliament to make very plain—even to the point of repetition—the workman's right to receive his whole remuneration in current coin of the realm.'[10]

Over the years several unsatisfactory features of these Acts emerged.
They did not apply to all employees but only to manual workers and, to an
extent, to shop assistants. Several of their provisions were quite technical
and there was some confusion about their interpretation. Most importantly,
however, their insistence on employees being paid their wages in cash, as
compared with a cheque or similar instrument, was regarded as being out
of tune with the times. Today, a substantial body of the workforce have
access to banks and equivalent credit institutions, so that there is not quite
the same objection to paying wages by cheque as there was hitherto. In 1979
an Act was passed to facilitate payment by cheque.[11] It and also the Truck
Acts were repealed in 1991 by a comprehensive measure, the Payment of
Wages Act, 1991, which sets out the ways in which wages may be paid, the
information regarding wages which employees must be provided with and
the restrictions on deductions from wages. Complaints under the 1991 Act
must first be made to a rights commissioner, with a full right of appeal to
the Employment Appeals Tribunal.[12]

Workers covered by the Payment of Wages Act: The personal scope of the
1991 Act is very extensive. As well as covering employees, apprentices and
persons holding office in the public service, including members of the Garda
Síochána and the Defence Forces, this Act applies to persons who have
agreed to 'do or perform personally any work or service for a third party'.[13]
However, the Act does not apply were that agreement creates a professional
person-client relationship or a business undertaking-customer relationship.

---

9. *Hewlett v. Allen & Son* [1892] 2 QB 662, at p.664.
10. *Kenyon v. Darwen Cotton Mf. Co.* [1936] 2 KB 193 at p.211.
11. Payment of Wages Act, 1979.
12. The procedure is set out in the Payment of Wages (Appeals) Regulations, 1991; S.I. No. 351 of 1991.
13. S.1(1).

'Wages': What are wages for these purposes is also defined very extensively. Practically every sum payable to an employee in connection with his work is deemed to be a wage, whether payable under the employment contract or otherwise, including any sum payable on the termination of the employment, like an amount paid in lieu of notice.[14] But certain payments are not wages, for instance, payments in respect of expenses incurred by the employee, redundancy payments and compensation for loss of office, pensions and benefits in kind. Accordingly, the full wages need no longer be paid in money, be it cash or cheque; payments in kind fall outside the 1991 Act.

Modes of payment: The century and a half old requirement that wages must always be paid in full in cash in now replaced by s.2 of the 1991 Act. This authorises payment of the money due either in cash or by cheque, bill of exchange or several similar forms of payment. Other modes of payment may be laid down by the Minister. However, where before 23 July 1991 an employee was being paid in cash, he must continue to be paid in cash unless he or his union agree that he should be paid by one of the other permissible modes.[15] This also applies where, by agreement, the employee was being paid otherwise than in cash; if that agreement or arrangement is terminated, he again becomes entitled to be paid in cash unless he or his union agrees otherwise.

Deductions from remuneration Subject principally to the provisions of the Payment of Wages Act, 1991, the employer and the employee can agree to make deductions from the latter's remuneration, for instance, for trade union subscriptions, for contributions to a pension fund and also in respect of defective work or for other disciplinary purposes. The contractual duty to pay the full amount of wages earned is qualified by any agreement regarding deductions. Furthermore, it has been held that the employer is not obliged to pay any remuneration in respect of periods during which the employee was deliberately absent from work.[16] There are certain deductions that are specifically forbidden by statute; in particular, to cover the employer's redundancy contribution under the Redundancy Payment Acts[17] or his contribution under the Social Welfare Acts.[18] On the other hand, there are deductions that employers are legally obliged to make without getting their employee's consent, notably P.A.Y.E. and P.R.S.I. contributions.[19] At

14. S.1(1); reproduced supra p.83.   15. S.3.
16. E.g. *Sim v. Rotherham Metropolitan B.C.* [1987] 1 Ch.216; see infra p. 93.
17. Redundancy Payments Act, 1967 s.28(4), as amended.
18. Social Welfare (Consolidation) Act, 1981, s.10(5).   19. See post pp.349 et seq.

one time a judgment creditor of an employee could obtain from a court a garnishee order attaching his salary, in which event the employer had to pay over to the judgment creditor whatever sum had been attached. That form of redress was stopped by the Wages Attachment Abolition Act, 1870. However, Part III of the Family Law (Maintenance of Spouses and Children) Act, 1976, contains an elaborate mechanism for attaching the earnings of an employee against whom a maintenance order has been made.[20] Section 73 of the Finance Act, 1988, confers extensive authority on the Revenue to attach debts and other sums owing to taxpayers who owe tax to the Revenue; but this power does not apply to taxable remuneration payable to an employee or an office-holder.[21]

'Deduction': A major theme of the Truck Acts was regulating the circumstances in which employers could make deductions from wages; that matter is now dealt with by s.5 of the Payment of Wages Act, 1991. As is explained above,[22] the categories of workers covered by this Act and what constitutes wages for its purposes is defined very extensively. What is a deduction for these purposes is also defined very widely, as any difference between the total amount of wages properly payable to the employee and the amount he receives.[23] Accordingly, transfer payments as well as sums retained by the employer are in principle deductions. But what may appear at first sight to be a deduction may not be so because it is really the consequence of how the amount of wages payable is calculated. For example, in *Deane v. Wilson*,[24] the plaintiff was employed in a shirt factory and was to be paid 8 shillings a week; there was also 'an attendance bonus' of 2 shillings which would be paid if there was full attendance at work throughout the week. One week when she was absent for a quarter of a day, she was not paid this 2 shillings. It was held that there was no breach of the Truck Act because that sum had not been deducted from her wages; it was money that was never earned and never even became payable to her. Therefore, 'a mode of calculating the wages to be paid in which deductions are made may take the case outside the [1991] Act altogether'.[25] Where a worker is suspended from employment for a period without pay, the Truck Acts were not been contravened because 'he ceases to be under any present duty to work, and the employer ceases to be under any consequent duty to pay.'[26]

20. See generally, A.J. Shatter, *Family Law* (3rd ed. 1986) ch.14.
21. S.73(1)(b) proviso (ii).   22. Supra p.89.
23. 1991 Act s.5(6).   24. [1906] 2 IR 405.
25. *Sagar v. Redehalgh Ltd* [1931] 1 Ch. 310, at p.327.
26. Ibid. and *Bird v. British Celanese Ltd* [1945] 1 KB 336.

Transfer payments: Transfer payments made by an employer to a third party fell outside the Truck Acts provided the employee agreed that part of his remuneration should be paid over to some third party.[27] Payments of that nature are allowed by the 1991 Act provided the employee gave his prior consent to them in writing and the third party notified the employer that the sum or sums in question are owed by the employee.[28] Transfer payments can be made without the employee's consent where, by virtue of any statutory provision, the employer is obliged to deduct a sum from wages and pay it over to a 'public authority';[29] for instance P.R.S.I. deductions.

Court orders: Subject to some exceptions, described below, an employer cannot set-off against wages payable by him a sum he is owed by the employee; this was so even where the employee's debt to the employer had been upheld by a court or tribunal.[30] But if the employee agreed in writing in advance to a deduction of that nature, it is permitted by the 1991 Act.[31] Deductions may also be made on foot of a court order in respect of debts owed by an employee to a third party or an amount payable into court or the tribunal.[32] In this case, the 1991 Act does not require the employee's prior consent.

Rectifying over-payments: Another permitted deduction is in order to rectify an over-payment made to the employee in respect of his wages or of expenses incurred by him in carrying out his work.[33] That deduction must not exceed the amount of the over-payment.

Employee taking industrial action: Certain deductions can be made from the wages of employees who have gone on strike or who have taken part in other industrial action. This gives legislative recognition to recent case law developments in Britain but the 1991 Act does not specify exactly what sums may be deducted from employees resorting to industrial action; all it says is that the deductions may be made 'on account of having taken part in' that action.[34]

Where an employee refuses to perform duties required by the contract, it has been held that, even if the contract does not expressly authorise deductions from remuneration, his employer may in effect make such deductions. By 'in effect' here is meant, where the employer is entitled to damages in respect of the breach but the employee sues for wages for the period during

27. *Hewlett v. Allen* [1894] AC 383.   28. S.5(5)(d).   29. S.5(5)(c).
30. *Williams v. North's Navigation Collieries (1889) Ltd* [1906] AC 136.
31. S.5(5)(f). Contrast *Penman v. Fife Coal Co.* [1936] AC 45.
32. S.5(5)(g).   33. S.5(5)(a).   34. S.5(5)(e).

which that breach was committed, the employer is entitled to set-off those damages against whatever wages the employee would be entitled to. By virtue of the right of set-off,[35] the employer is in effect authorised to make the deductions. Thus in *Sim v. Rotherham Council*,[36] as a form of industrial action and in breach of their contracts, secondary school teachers refused to provide 'cover' during school hours for absent colleagues. Instead of dismissing them, their employer deducted a sum from their monthly earnings; it was accepted that the amount of those deductions was at least equivalent to any damages the teachers would have been required to pay if they had been sued for breach of contract. It was contended that, as a matter of legal principle, no deduction could be made in those circumstances. But it was held that the employer is entitled to set-off the damages that could be recovered against the employees' weekly or monthly wages, as the case may be. As Scott J put it, 'if an employee, in breach of contract, fails or refuses to perform his contractual services, his right or title to recover his salary for the period during which the failure or refusal occurred is impeached by the employer's cross-claim for damages. It would be manifestly unjust in such a case to allow the employee to recover his salary in full without taking into account the loss to the employer of those services.'[37]

Where the employee refuses to perform a particular task or tasks and, in response, the employer informs him that he is not needed at work during the period when those tasks call to be performed, it has been held that the employer's right to make deductions from remuneration is based on funda-mental principle and not merely on the law regarding set-off. That was in *Miles v. Wakefield Council*[38] where, in pursuance of industrial action and in breach of his obligations, the plaintiff refused to carry out his principal duties on Saturdays. Although he was willing to attend at the workplace on Saturdays, his employer told him that he should not do so for so long as he persisted in his refusal. His employer then deducted from his monthly salary a sum equivalent to what his earnings would have been had he actually worked on Saturdays. On the basis of the principle 'no work, no pay', it was held that the employer here was entitled to make those deductions. According to Lord Templeman,

> wages are remuneration which must be earned; in a claim for wages under a contract of employment, the worker must assert that he worked or was willing to work. . . . When a worker in breach of contract declines to work in accordance with the contract, but claims payment

35. See generally, S.R. Derham, *Set-Off* (1987) ch. 1.
36. [1987] 1 Ch. 216.
37. Id. at pp.261-262.   38. [1987] AC 540.

for his wages, it is unnecessary to consider the law relating to damages and unnecessary for the employer to rely on the defence of a abatement or equitable set-off. The employer may or may not sustain or be able to prove and recover damages by reason of the breach of contract for each worker. But so far as wages are concerned, the worker can only claim them if he is willing to work.[39]

The full implications of the 'no work no pay' principle have yet to be determined by the courts. But there is no inherent or implied right to withhold wages for bad work or as a disciplinary measure.

Disciplinary measures: Deductions may be made for any 'act or omission of' an employee provided that the stringent requirements of s.5(2) of the 1991 Act have been met. An exception is where the disciplinary deduction is made in consequence of disciplinary proceedings provided for by statute,[40] for instance the Garda Síochána Discipline Regulations. The general requirements for deductions are sixfold, being—

i. They must have been authorised by a term of the employment contract; that term may be implied as well as express.

ii. The amount deducted must be 'fair and reasonable', having regard to all the circumstances, including the employee's earnings.

iii. Before the act or omission being penalised ever occurred, the employee must have been given a written copy of the contractual term allowing deductions or he must have been given written notice of the existence and effect of that term.

iv. At least one week before the deduction was made, the employee must have been given written particulars of the act or omission which caused the deduction.

v. If the deduction was to compensate the employer for loss he suffered as a result of the employee's acts or inaction, the amount withheld must not exceed the amount of the loss or damage suffered.

iv. The deduction or, if more than one is being made, the first deduction must be made within six months of the employer discovering the employee's act or omission in question.

Goods or services necessary to do the work: Deductions are also permitted where the employer has provided the employee with goods or services

39. Id. at pp.564 and 565.   40. S.5(5)(b).

which are 'necessary to the employment', for instance, tools of the trade and the provision of training. Of course, equipment to do the work and training are often supplied by employers free of charge. Before any deduction can be made in respect of these matters, requirements similar to those just described for disciplinary measures must have been satisfied.[41]

Statement of wages and deductions Section 4 of the 1991 Act requires that all employees be given a written statement of what their gross wages are and of the nature and amounts of any deductions made from them. Employers are required to take reasonable steps to ensure that those statements are confidential. Ordinarily, this statement must be given at the time the wages are being paid. Where the wages are being paid by credit transfer, the statement here must be given very shortly afterwards.

Assignment and attachment of remuneration Most forms of property, including future property, can be assigned to someone else by the owner or the owner-to-be. On account of the uniquely personal nature of the contract of employment, contracts of that nature cannot be assigned. But wages or remuneration received by employees are assignable. In *Picton v. Cullen*,[42] where the court appointed a receiver over the salary of a teacher which was due and payable, all of the judges accepted that his future earnings could not be assigned or attached. Whether this principle applies equally to private sector employees has not been determined but there do not appear to be any compelling reasons why it should not be so extended.

As has been explained, subject to certain exceptions, wages cannot be attached in favour of an employee's creditor; in other words, future wages cannot be the subject of a garnishee order.[43] An exception to this is maintenance orders in family law proceedings.[44] That other creditors' remedy, the appointment of a receiver by way of equitable execution, cannot be applied to the future earnings of public officials and also of private sector employees. In *McCreery v. Bennett*,[45] a clerk to the petty sessions had assigned his official salary to the plaintiff to secure an annuity. When the annuity fell into arrears, the plaintiff sought to have a receiver appointed over the clerk's future salary. That application was rejected by Kenny J on the grounds that public policy protects the remuneration of judicial officers from such process. But Barton J would extend this principle much wider, observing that '[i]t makes no difference whether the judgment debtor is a

41. S.5(2). 42. [1900] 2 IR 612.
43. Wages Attachment (Abolition) Act, 1870.
44. Family Law (Maintenance of Spouses and Children) Act, 1976.
45. [1904] 2 IR 69.

public officer or a person earning a salary in private employment. Future earnings or salary could not have been attached by a writ of sequestration before the Judicature Act . . . and cannot be reached by the appointment of a receiver by way of equitable execution in any division of the High Court'.[46] He further observed that the court was not concerned at that stage about the legality of the deed of assignment which the clerk had executed; that matter could be raised in the action to enforce the deed.[47] But once remuneration has fallen due it can then be subject to the appointment of a receiver.

CONFIDENTIAL INFORMATION

The law protects persons, including employers and employees, against confidential information about their affairs being used or disclosed against their wishes.[48] The employment contract may expressly stipulate what information belonging to them is confidential and may not be disclosed. Even where there is no express provision, by virtue of an employee's general duty of fidelity, it is an implied term of almost all employment contracts that employees will not disclose or use their employer's confidential information without the latter's consent. That duty is broken, for instance, where the employee makes or copies a list of his employer's customers for use by him when the employment ends or indeed where he memorises that very list for that purpose.[49] The extent to which an employer's confidential information is protected varies depending on whether the employee's activities in question are taking place during his employment or afterwards.

Confidentiality What kinds of information are confidential for this purpose was summarised as follows:

> First . . . the information must be information the release of which the owner believes would be injurious to him or of advantage to his rivals or others. Second . . . the owner must believe that the information is confidential or secret, i.e. that it is not already in the public domain. Third . . . the owner's belief under the two previous headings must be reasonable. Fourth . . . the information must be judged in the light of the usage and practices of the particular industry or trade concerned. It may be that information that does not satisfy all these requirements

46. Id. at p.74.   47. Ibid.
48. See generally, W.R. Cornish, *Intellectual Property* (2nd ed. 1991) and M. Forde, *Commercial Law in Ireland* (1990) pp.329-333.
49. *Robb v. Green* [1895] 2 QB 315.

may be entitled to protection . . . ; but . . . any information which does satisfy them must be of a type which is entitled to protection.[50]

In *Faccenda Chicken Ltd v. Fowler*,[51] where an employee left his employment and went into the same business on his own account, taking other employees with him, the following considerations were stated to govern the question of improper use of confidential information:

> In order to determine whether any particular item of information falls within the implied term so as to prevent its use or disclosure by an employee after his employment has ceased, it is necessary to consider all the circumstances of the case. . . . [T]he following matters are among those to which attention must be paid:
>
> (a) The nature of the employment. Thus, employment in a capacity where 'confidential' material is habitually handled may impose a high obligation of confidentiality because the employee can be expected to realise its sensitive nature to a greater extent than if he were employed in a capacity where such material reaches him only occasionally or incidentally.
>
> (b) The nature of the information itself. . . . [T]he information will only be protected if it can properly be classed as a trade secret, or as material which while not properly to be described as a trade secret, is in all the circumstances of such a highly confidential nature as to require the same protection as a trade secret. . . . It is clearly impossible to provide a list of matters which will qualify as trade secrets or their equivalent. Secret processes of manufacture provide obvious examples, but in- numerable other pieces of information are capable of being trade secrets, though the secrecy of some information may only be short lived. In addition, the fact that the circulation of certain information is restricted to a limited number of individuals may throw light on the status of the information and its degree of confidentially. . . .
>
> (c) Whether the employer impressed on the employee the confi- dentiality of the information. Thus, thought an employer cannot pre- vent the use or disclosure merely by telling the employee that certain information is confidential, the attitude of the employer towards the information provides evidence which may assist in determining whether or not the information can properly be regarded as a trade secret. . . .

---

50. *House of Spring Gardens Ltd v. Point Blank Ltd* [1984] IR 611, at p.663, adopting *Thomas Marshall (Exports) Ltd v. Guinle* [1979] Ch.227, at p.248.
51. [1987] Ch. 117.

(d) Whether the relevant information can be easily isolated from other information which the employee is free to use or disclose. . . . [T]he seperability of the information [is not] conclusive, but the fact that the alleged 'confidential' information is part of a package and the remainder of the package is not confidential is likely to throw light on whether the information in question is really a trade secret.[52]

Permitted disclosure Although the Constitution guarantees freedom of expression, there is hardly a general constitutional right to disclose confidential information about an employer's or a former employer's affairs. Leaving aside any constitutional rights as may exist, disclosure may be permitted in the public interest, for instance where the information relates to fraud committed by the employer. But the public interest is not confined to fraud. In *Initial Services Ltd v. Putterill*,[53] it was held that disclosure applies to 'any misconduct of such a nature that it ought in the public interest to be disclosed to others'; this extends to 'crimes, frauds and misdeeds, both those actually committed and those in contemplation'.[54] It was held there that the public interest defence could very well, in the circumstances, apply to information about a price ring to which the employer was a party. A question which has confronted the English courts on several occasions in recent years is whether to award an interlocutory injunction restraining disclosure of confidential information where it is being claimed that disclosure is warranted in the public interest.[55]

INTELLECTUAL PROPERTY

The principal forms of intellectual property are copyright and patents; trade marks, merchandise marks and performers protection rights are not directly relevant to the discussion here. An author of any literary, dramatic or musical work is entitled to the copyright in it for the remainder of his life and copyright remains in his estate for fifty years after his death.[56] Copyright also vests in the original maker of a sound recording, the maker of a film, the broadcaster of any material and the direct publisher of any published

---

52. Id. at pp.129-130. For interlocutory proceedings, see *R. Bullivant Ltd v. Ellis* [1987] ICR 464.
53. [1968] 1 QB 396.   54. Id. at p.405.
55. E.g. *Hubbard v. Vosper* [1972] 2 QB 84, *Sheering Chemicals Ltd v. Falkman Ltd* [1982] 1 QB 1 and *Lion Labouratories Ltd v. Evans* [1985] 1 QB 526. See generally, Finn, 'Confidentiality and the Public Interest', 58 *Australian L.J.* 497 (1984)
56. Copyright Act, 1963, ss.8 and 9.

edition of a literary, dramatic or musical work.[57] A person who invents an invention is entitled to take out a patent in respect of that, which will entitle him to the exclusive exploitation of the invention for sixteen years, which period can be renewed.[58]

A question that often arises is, where an employee creates material which is protected by copyright or he invents something, is he entitled to the copyright or the patent, as the case may be, or does it belong to the employer. Frequently, this very matter will be determined by an express clause in the employment contract. A common practice among employers is to require their employees to give over rights in all inventions made during their employment. However, in one instance a clause of that nature was struck down for being an unreasonable restraint of trade.[59] That clause applied to all inventions made while the defendant was being employed, not just during the course of his employment. Accordingly, a vacuum cleaning company could not require a senior storekeeper to surrender rights in an invention which he made at home in his spare time, even though it was an adapter for vacuum cleaner bags.

Copyright Except where by agreement the parties have stipulated otherwise, the position regarding copyright is governed by s.10 of the Copyright Act, 1963. The general rule is that copyright material made 'in the course of [the author's] employment' belongs to his employer and not to the author. Sometimes it can be difficult to determine the precise scope of an employment for these purposes, especially regarding teachers who may spend considerable parts of their spare time on work-related activities. For instance, the teacher may write a play to be performed by his students, which turns out to be a great commercial success. The outcome in this kind of case will usually turn on a careful consideration of the facts. The *Stevenson, Jordan and Harrison* case,[60] where the 'integration test' for ascertaining whether the relationship was one of employer-employee was popularised, concerned lectures written by an accountant, dealing with the business in which he was employed, to be given at universities and learned societies. His employer encouraged this activity by paying the expenses he incurred in it. Nevertheless, it was held that those lectures were not prepared in the course of his employment.

Employee journalists[61] are not stripped entirely of the copyright in material they make in the course of their employment for the purpose of

---

57. Id. ss.17-20.   58. Patents Act, 1964, ss.25-27.
59. *Electrolux Ltd v. Hudson* [1977] FSR 312.   60. [1952] TLR 101.
61. Cf. *Beloff v. Pressdram Ltd* [1973], 1 All ER 241 and *Re Sunday Tribune Ltd* [1984] IR 505.

publication in the newspaper or whatever in question. What s.10(2) reserves to the proprietor-employer is the copyright in that material 'only in so far as it relates to publication of the work in a newspaper, magazine or similar periodical, or to its reproduction for the purposes of its being so published.'

Patents Where the employment contract does not directly deal with the matter the position regarding the ownership of patents is somewhat un-settled.[62] Formerly, there were two kinds of case where the employee-inventor was obliged to hold the invention for his employer. One was where he was employed to use his skill and inventive ingenuity to solve a technical problem—where in effect he was 'employed to invent'. Thus, an engineering draftsman who was instructed to design an unlubricated crane-brake was obliged to hold the resultant patent on trust for his employer.[63] The other was where the employee occupied a senior managerial position; his extensive duty of fidelity includes an obligation to give the employer the rights in whatever he may invent in connection with his employment. In one instance,[64] an American pump manufacturing company put a man in charge of its English business at a high salary and commission, making him vice-president of the company. He was held liable, under an obligation of good faith, to account for patents relating to developments in pumps.[65]

In a case in 1955, Lord Simonds purported to extend the rights of employers regarding their employees' inventions when he declared that 'it is an implied term in the contract of service of any workman that what he produces by the strength of his arm or the skill of his hand or the exercise of his inventive faculty shall become the property of his employer'.[66] It remains to be seen whether this statement of the law would be followed in Ireland.

Unlike the position with copyright, the Patents Act, 1964, does not attempt to determine when employees' inventions should belong to their employers. However, s.53 of that Act empowers the Controller of Patents, Designs and Trade Marks to decide disputes between them regarding rights in an invention. Unless the Controller is satisfied on the evidence that one or other of them owns the invention in its entirety, he may apportion between them the benefit of the invention. The criterion for that apportionment is whatever he considers just. His decision has the same effect as a judgment of a court. However, if during the proceedings he is of the view that any

62. See generally W.R. Cornish, *Intellectual Property* (1981) pp.216-218.
63. *British Reinforced Concrete Ltd v. Lind* (1917) 34 RPC 101.
64. *Worthington v. Moore* (1903) 20 RPC 41.
65. Contrast *Selz's Application* (1954) 71 RPC 158.
66. *Patchett v. Sterling* (1955) 72 RPC 50, at p.57.

particular matter would more properly be determined by the court, he can decline to deal with that matter. There is an appeal to the High Court from the Controller's decision under s.53.

POST-EMPLOYMENT RESTRAINTS

Employees are often subject to restrictions regarding what they may work at when they cease being employed with a particular employer. As has been explained, it is an implied term of their contract that they will not use or disclose confidential information in a way that damages their former employer's business.[67] Additionally, the contract may contain express restrictions on their freedom to work. Exactly how extensive any such restriction is depends on the true meaning of the contract. Where the ex-employee's activities are caught by the terms of a contractual restriction, that clause may be void and unenforceable by virtue of the doctrine of unreasonable restraint of trade.[68] Restraints on persons working or on being engaged in one or more lines of business by definition are restraints of trade. In the famous *Ballymacelligot Co-Op* case,[69] the test of whether such a restriction would be enforced by the courts was expounded as being two-fold;

> A contract which is in restraint of trade cannot be enforced unless (a) it is reasonable as between the parties; (b) it is consistent with the interests of the public.[70]

Public interest The public interest is that the community should not unnecessarily be deprived of talents and services which are valuable. As has been observed, 'the public interest . . . might be gravely endangered or contravened by a restriction or impairment of the liberty of the subject to enter the ranks of business or of labour and work for and earn his living.'[71] However, very few of the restraint of trade cases focus specifically on the public interest being adversely affected.

Reasonableness *inter partes* Regarding reasonableness between the parties, there is a presumption that all restrictions on work activities are

---

67. *Hivac Ltd v. Park Royal Scientific Instruments Ltd* [1946] 1 Ch.169. Cf. *A.F. Associates v. Ralston* [1973] NI 229.
68. See generally, A.G. Guest ed., *Chitty on Contract* (26th ed. 1989), pp.725 et seq. and M. Forde, *Commercial Law in Ireland* (1990) pp.309-320.
69. *McElligot v. Ballymacelligot Co-Op. Agricultural & Dairy Soc. Ltd* [1919] AC 548.
70. Id. at p.562.
71. *Mason v. Provident Clothing & Supply Co.* [1913] AC 724, at p.738.

unlawful unless the former employer can point to some very strong justification for the restraint in question and also show that the range and extent of that restraint does not go beyond the demands of that justification. An employer is not entitled to prevent his former employee from competing against him, either directly or as an employee of some third party. Thus in *Bull v. Pitney-Bowes Ltd*[72] the court refused to enforce a clause in a pension scheme whereby pensions would be forfeited if ex-employees should work for any firm which competed against their former employer. This is one of the few restraint of employment cases where the public interest was discussed by the court.

According to Lord Wilberforce in the leading recent authoritative case, *Stenhouse (Australia) Ltd v. Phillips,*

> the proposition that an employer is not entitled to protection from mere competition by a former employee means that the employee is entitled to use to the full any personal skill or experience, even if this has been acquired in the service of his employer: it is this freedom to use to the full a man's improving ability and talents which lies at the root of the policy of the law regarding this type of restraint. Leaving aside the case of misuse of trade secrets or confidential information . . . , the employer's claim for protection must be based upon the identification of some advantage or asset inherent in the business which can properly be regarded as, in a general sense, his property, and which it would be unjust to allow the employee to appropriate for his own purposes, even though he, the employee, may have contributed to its creation.[73]

An employer is entitled by contract to restrict a former employee from canvassing the employer's former clients, provided there is some element of goodwill attaching to that clientele and the extent of the canvassing restriction is not excessive. Thus in the *Stenhouse (Australia) Ltd* case, a clause was upheld which prohibited a formerly employed insurance broker, for a period of five years, from canvassing the employer's clients within a radius of 25 miles of the employer's headquarters in Sydney. And in *Home Counties Dairies Ltd v. Skilton*[74] a clause was upheld which prevented a milk roundsman from selling milk to his ex-employer's customers during the 12 months after his job came to an end. Occasionally, a restriction which does not expressively refer to former customers being part of the employer's goodwill will be construed as applying to them. Thus in *Marian White Ltd v. Francis,*[75] the court upheld a clause whereby an employee of a hairdresser had agreed not to work as a hairdresser within a half a mile of her former

72. [1967] 1 WLR 273.   73. [1974] AC 391, at p.400.
74. [1970] 1 WLR 526.   75. [1972] 1 WLR 1423.

employer's establishment in a provincial town. An express prohibition against working for a competitor may even be upheld where the employee is in a senior managerial position and there is a strong likelihood that he possesses trade secrets which will be put to use in that competitor's business.[76] It depends on the circumstances whether such a danger exists.

Both the duration and the geographical scope of any restriction on working must not be excessive. What is excessive depends very much on the nature of the work in question and the structure of the business. A canvassing restriction over a 25 mile radius of the centre of Sydney was upheld with regard to a senior executive insurance broker.[77] But a clause seeking to prevent a person who sold credit facilities for buying clothes from doing so within a 25 mile radius of the centre of London was declared to be unreasonable and void;[78] so too was a clause purporting to stop a senior executive insurance broker from acting in any town in Australia where a company within his former employer's group of companies had an establishment.[79]

Where the clause in question is capable of several interpretations, some of which render it unreasonable but one or more of which render it reasonable, the courts tend to give it the reasonable interpretation and thereby uphold the restraint. However, if in order to prevent the clause from being too wide it is necessary virtually to rewrite it and give it a different meaning from that of its proper construction, the courts will not so construe the clause.[80] Where an employment contract contains several restrictions on what an employee may do after his job ends, and one or more of them is an unreasonable restraint, it may be possible to 'sever' the offending parts and enforce the remainder.[81] However, where an attempted severance would give the remaining clause a meaning significantly different from what it was intended to possess, the clause cannot be saved in that manner.[82]

Restraints contained in an employer's pension scheme may be regarded as being part of the employment contract. Although the forfeiture of pension benefits for working for a competitor may not be as drastic as being enjoined by the court from engaging in that work, the loss of a pension in those circumstances falls within the restraint of trade principle.[83]

76. *Littlewoods Organisation Ltd v. Harris* [1977] 1 WLR 1472.
77. *Stenhouse Australia Ltd v. Phillips* [1974] AC 391.
78. *Mason v. Provident Clothing & Supply Co.* [1913] AC 724.
79. *Stenhouse Australia Ltd* case [1974] AC 391.
80. *Home Counties Dairies Ltd v. Skilton* [1970] 1 WLR 526.
81. E.g. *Stenhouse Australia Ltd* case [1974] AC 391.
82. E.g. *T. Lucas & Co. Ltd v. Mitchell* [1972] 1 WLR 938.
83. E.g. *Bull v. Pitney Bowes Ltd* [1967] 1 WLR 273 and *Wyatt v. Kreglinger & Fernau* [1933] 1 KB 793.

On several occasions, persons engaged in professional sport have challenged restrictions on their activities, imposed both by their employers and the governing sporting organisations. In determining the effectiveness of these restrictions, special consideration tends to be given to the public interest claims of the governing organisations. These considerations did not save the old 'retention and transfer' rules in English soccer[84] but were held to justify some restrictions placed by the New Zealand rugby league on the employment of players with overseas clubs.[85]

Injunction to enforce the restraint Breach of a valid restraint can give rise to liability in damages, although it can be difficult in cases of this nature to quantify the damages recoverable. Breach of the restraint can also be prevented by an injunction, which ordinarily will be granted subject to one major proviso. If enforcing the injunction has the practical effect of compelling the employee to continue working for his former employer, the injunction is almost an order for specific performance of an employment contract, which will not be granted.[86] But there is no comparable objection ordinarily to an injunction restraining an ex-employee from working for some third party.[87] It depends on all the circumstances of the case whether what is being sought is equivalent to specific performance. In an application for an interlocutory injunction, pending a full trial of the action, account will be taken of the general *American Cyanamid* considerations and other relevant circumstances, for instance, the likelihood of trade secrets being disclosed to others.[88] Where the duration of the restraint most likely would have expired before the trail took place, account will be taken of the likelihood of the plaintiff succeeding at the trial.[89]

APPRENTICES AND TRAINEES

The status and position of apprentices has been the subject of statutory regulation for centuries. By an Act passed in 1814,[90] the old system of compulsory apprenticeships to guilds which enjoyed some monopolies of

---

84. *Eastham v. Newcastle Utd. F.C.* [1964] 1 Ch. 413.
85. *Kemp v. New Zealand R.F. League Inc.* [1989] 3 NZLR 463. Cf. *Johnston v. Cliftonville F.C. Ltd* [1984] NI 9, striking down the Irish Football League (i.e. Northern Ireland) minimum signing on bonus and minimum weekly wage.
86. *Whitwood Chemical Co. v. Hardman* [1891] 2 Ch. 416.
87. Cf. *Warren v. Mendy* [1989] 1 WLR 853.
88. *Lawrence David Ltd v. Ashton* [1989] ICR 123.
89. *Lansing Linde Ltd v. Kerr* [1991] 1 WLR 251.
90. Apprentices Act, 1814.

trades was abolished. Thereafter, the rights and duties of apprentices became principally a matter of contract. Frequently, that contract would be a sealed indenture of apprenticeship, although neither a seal nor writing are essential to create the master-apprentice relationship. Sometimes the provisions of trade union rules contain guidelines on apprentices and, formerly, controlling the number of apprentices in a trade was one means by which trade unions regulated their members' earnings.

A contract of apprenticeship has been described as follows:

> [it] secures three things for an apprentice; it secures him first a money payment during the period of apprenticeship, secondly that he shall be instructed and trained and thus acquire skills which would be of value to him for the rest of his life and, thirdly, it gives him status because ... once a young man ... completes his apprenticeship and can show by certificate that he has completed his time with a well known employer, that gets him off to a good start in the labour market.[91]

Where the apprentice is a minor, that is under 18 years of age, then the general principles regarding contracts with minors apply to him. At common law, there is no implied term to pay wages to the apprentice, so that it is usual for the contract to expressly provide for remuneration.

In determining whether an apprentice is an employee for the purposes of employment protection legislation or otherwise, it depends entirely on the terms of the contract. In the *Sister Dolores* case[92] and the *National Maternity Hospital* case,[93] it was held that trainee nurses there were not employees for the purposes of the social welfare legislation. Many of the employment protection Acts apply as much to apprentices as well as to employees. However, certain categories of trainees and probationers are excluded from the Unfair Dismissal Act, 1977.[94] For apprentices who come within that Act, it would seem that their dismissal at the expiry of their contract would not ordinarily be regarded as an unfair dismissal. Most likely, the dismissal would be justified as being for some other substantial reason which warrants dismissal. It has been held in England that a dismissal of an apprentice when his contract expires ordinarily would not be treated as a dismissal by reason of his redundancy.[95]

Sections 27-40 of the Industrial Training Act, 1967, gives An Foras (before 1987, An Chomhairle) extensive authority to regulate the position

91. *Dunk v. George Waller & Sons Ltd* [1970] 2 QB 163, at p.169.
92. [1960] 2 IR 77; see ante p.47.
93. [1960] IR 74; see ante p.47.
94. Ss.3 and 4; see post p.195.
95. *North Eash Coast Shiprepairers Ltd v. Secretary of State* (1978) ICR 755.

of apprentices. This power is contingent on the employer being involved in a 'designated industrial activity' as classified by an industrial training order; the orders in force in early 1992 are set out hereunder.[96] The main objective of the 1967 Act is to foster training; to that end, levies are imposed on employers in designated activities and An Foras makes grants to encourage training from the proceeds of that levy. Regulations adopted by An Foras in respect of apprenticeship in a designated activity may deal with matters like minimum age for commencing employment, educational or other qualifications or suitability for employment, the circumstances in which trainees may be dismissed or suspended, the period of training to be undergone, the form of contract to be used and prohibiting the taking of any premium or other consideration for employing an apprentice. Employers in designated activities must first obtain the consent of An Foras before they may hire an apprentice. An Foras is authorised to declare that every person employed in a particular manner shall be deemed to be an apprentice for the purposes of the 1967 Act. An Foras may also require apprentices to attend training courses provided by a vocational education committee but the employer of an apprentice who attends a course of that nature is not obliged to pay remuneration in respect of the period attending the course.

96. Chemicals and Allied Products Industry Order, S.I. No. 294 of 1991; Clothing and Footwear Industry Order, S.I. No. 295 of 1991; Food, Drink and Tobacco Industry Order, S.I. No. 296 of 1991; Printing and Paper Industry Order, S.I. No. 297 of 1991; Textiles Industry Order, S.O. No. 298 of 1991; Construction Industry Order, S.I. No. 299 of 1991; Engineering Industry Order, S.I. No. 300 of 1991.

5

Health and safety at work

Every year a substantial number of persons suffer injuries in the course of their work or contract some disease at work. Over the last two years, an average of seventy persons have been killed at work every year; about half of these fatalities were on farms. In the past the workplace was often a very dangerous location but the enactment of health and safety legislation and greater awareness of the risks existing at work has led to a significant decline in injuries and fatalities. The entire question of safety and health at work was the subject of an enquiry chaired by Mr Justice Barrington, which reported in 1983.[1] This report led to the enactment of the Safety, Health and Welfare at Work Act, 1989, which is replacing much of the existing safety legislation. It is in connection with health and safety that the E.C. so far has adopted the most initiatives in the area of employment law.[2] Regulations and Directives issued for 'improv[ing] the working environment, as regards the health and safety of workers', require only a qualified majority in the E.C. Council of Ministers.[3]

1. *Report of Committee of Enquiry on Safety, Health and Welfare at Work* (1983).
2. The E.C. measures implemented in Ireland are regulations on exposure of workers to lead (SI No. 291 of 1988), to asbestos (SI No. 34 of 1989), to noise (SI No. 157 of 1990).
3. E.E.C. Treaty Art. 118 A. By the end of 1990, the following measures regarding occupational health and safety had been promulgated by the E.C.:
   Directive 76/579 laying down the revised basic safety standards for the health protection of the general public and workers against the dangers of ionising radiation (OJ LI87/12.7.76 p. 1).
   Directive 77/576 on the approximation of the laws, regulations and administrative provisions of the member states relating to the provision of safety signs at places of work (OJ L229/7.9.77 p. 12).
   Directive 78/610 on the approximation of the laws, regulations and administrative provisons of the member states on the protection of the health of workers exposed to vinyl chloride monomers (OJ L1997/22.7.78 p. 12).
   Directive 80/1107 on the protection of workers from the risks related to exposure to chemical, physical and biological agents at work (OJ L327/3.12.80 p. 8).
   Directive on the major-accident hazards of certain industrial activities (OJ L230/5.8.82 p 1); implemented by S.I. No. 292 of 1986.
   Directive on the protection of workers from the virus related to exposure to metallic

A full account of the law regarding health and safety at work would require an entire book—and a lengthy one at that.[4] This chapter can only provide a very brief exposition of the topic, focusing principally on the mechanics of the regulatory regime designed to prevent work-related accidents and diseases. The social welfare aspects of industrial injuries and diseases and the question of civil liability in respect of such events are concerned with providing redress for the victims of unsafe and unhealthy workplaces. Whether that redress is adequate and whether the means for securing redress and the amount of compensation being awarded are entirely satisfactory is a matter of some controversy.

lead and its ionic compounds at work (OJ L247/23.8.82 p. 12); implemented by S.I. No. 291 of 1988.

Directive 83/477 on the protection of workers from the risks related to exposure to asbestos at work; implemented by S.I. No. 39 of 1989 (OJ L263/24.9.83 p. 25).

Directive 86/188 on the protection of workers from the risks related to exposure to noise at work (OJ L137/24.5.86 p. 28); implemented by S.I. No. 157 of 1990.

Directive 88/364 on the protection of workers by the banning of certain specified agents and/or certain work activites (fourth individual Directive within the meaning of 80/1107 (OJ L179/9.7.88 p. 44).

Directive 89/391on the introduction of measures to encourage improvements in the safety and health of workers at work (OJ L183/29.6.89 p. 1).

Directive 89/392 on the approximation of the laws of the member states relating to machinery (OJ L183/29.6.89 p. 9).

Directive 89/654 concerning the minimum safety and health requirements for the use of work equipment by workers at work (second individual Directive within the meaning of 89/391, art 16(1)) (OJ L393/30.12.89 p. 1).

Directive 89/655 concerning the minimum safety and health requirements for the use of work equipment by workers at work (second individual Directive within the meaning of 89/391, art 16(1) ((OJ L393/30.12.89 p. 13).

Directive 89/656 concerning the minimum safety and health requirements for the use by workers of personal protective equipment at the workplace (third individual Directive with the meaning of 89/391, art 16(1) (OJ L393/30.12.89 p. 18).

Directive 90/269 concerning the minimum safety and health requirements for the manual handling of loads where there is a risk particularly of back injury to workers (fourth individual Directive within the meaning of 89/391, art 16(1) (OJ L156/21/90 p. 9).

Directive 90/270 concerning the minimum safety and health requirements for work with diaplay screen equipment (fifth individual Directive within the meaning of 89/391, art 16(1) (OJ L156/21.6.90 p. 14).

Directive 90/394 on the protection of workers from the risks related to exposure to carcinogens at work (sixth individual Directive within the meaning of 89/391, art 16(1)) (OJ L196/26.7.90 p. 38).

4. See generally, Redgrave, et al., *Health and Safety* (1990)

THE REGULATORY SYSTEM

Legislation designed to protect employees' health and safety at work can be traced back to the passing of the first factories statute in 1802, which was a response to the appalling conditions in which children worked in the Lancashire cotton mills.[5] Even before the establishment of the International Labour Organisation, questions of industrial hygiene and safety were being dealt with at the international level. For technological reasons and also because of simple economic and commercial reasons, adoption of measures to protect workers' health and safety is a particularly apt subject for international investigation and co-ordination; hence the recent E.C. initiatives in this area. A large part of the I.L.O.'s standards relate directly or indirectly to health and safety and deal with matters such as specific risks (e.g. white phosphorous, white lead, anthrax, benzene poisoning, occupational cancer, radiation protection, guarding machinery, maximum weight, pollution and noise in the work environment), special branches of activity (e.g. industrial establishments, building and construction sites, bakeries, dock work, merchant seamen) and preventative measures (e.g. preventing industrial accidents, protecting workers' health, occupational health services).[6] Many of these provisions have been incorporated into various regulations, and presumably particular account will be taken of the I.L.O. guidelines by the National Authority for Occupational Health and Safety when it is issuing its codes of conduct.

The pre-1989 Acts A whole mass of regulatory legislation going back for more than 60 years was replaced and consolidated by the Factories Act, 1955. By 1989 there were numerous Acts in force for different types of work environments, notably the Factories Act, 1955, as supplemented by the Safety in Industry Act, 1980, the Mines and Quarries Act, 1965, the Office Premises Act, 1958, and the Safety, Health and Welfare (Offshore Installations) Act, 1987, as well as provisions of the Shops (Conditions) of Employment Act, 1938, and of the Merchant Shipping Act, 1894. Mention should also be made of the E.C. (Major Accident Hazards of Certain Industrial Activities) Regulations, 1986, which are not aimed exclusively or even predominantly at protecting employees. Some sectors, notably agriculture, were virtually unregulated in this regard. The Factories Act and the Mines and Quarries Act are very bulky affairs, laying down an elaborate set of detailed prescriptions, which were supplemented by a body of statutory

---

5. An Act for the Preservation of the Health and Morals of Apprentices and others employed in Cotton and Other Mills, 42 Geo. III c.73.
6. See generally, N. Valticos, *International Labour Law* (1979) pp.147-157.

instruments that expanded on those prescriptions. However, many of the main provisions of these Acts were replaced by the Safety, Health and Welfare at Work Act, 1989, which adopts a radically different approach to the entire question.

There is a vast body of case law dealing with the interpretation of the Factories Acts and the other legislation now being revoked. The extreme technicality and even the artificiality of some of the distinctions made in these cases were referred to by Hailsham LC, in an action for damages for an accident where it was alleged that the moving parts of a machine had not been properly fenced as required by the regulations:

> While the policy of the [Factories] Act is well established, some of the protection to the workmen which at first sight may be thought to be available turns out on closer scrutiny to be illusory. Thus (1) since it is only parts of the machinery which have to be fenced, there is no obligation to fence a machine . . . if it is dangerous as a whole but without having dangerous parts; (2) it is now established that . . . what is referred to as part of the machine does not include a work-piece moving under power and held in the machinery by a chuck; nor does it include other material in the machine as distinct from parts of the machinery; (3) the dangers against which the fencing is required do not include dangers to be apprehended from the ejection of flying material from the machine whether this is part of the material used in the machine or whether it is part of the machine itself; (4) the workman is not ordinarily protected if what comes into contact with the dangerous part of a machine is a hand tool operated by the workman as distinct from the workman's body or his clothes, nor if the danger created arises because of the proximity of moving machinery to some stationary object extraneous to the machine.[7]

As with the body of case law on the Workmens' Compensation Acts, built up between 1897 and 1977, much of the vast *ratio decidendi* and *obiter dicta* on the Factories Acts and comparable legislation will become a dead letter when what remains of those Acts is repealed in accordance with s. 4(3) of the 1989 Act.

The 1989 Act Instead of laying down numerous detailed rules for various categories of employment, the 1989 Act's requirements bind every employer and apply to every employee. It therefore is no longer absolutely decisive whether the employee in question works in a factory or in a mine

---

7. *F.E. Callow (Engineering) Ltd v. Johnson* [1971] AC 335, at pp.342-343.

or in an office, which often involved consideration of whether the workplace fell within the complex definitions of a 'factory', a 'building operation', a 'work of engineering construction' and the like.[8] Regardless of the nature of the workplace, the 1989 Act's requirements apply. They apply throughout the public service as well as the private sector, even to prisons and places of detention except where their application is not compatible with 'safe custody, good order and security.' The other major difference between the 1989 legislation and its predecessors is the intrinsic nature of the 1989 requirements. Instead of being very detailed rules of conduct, these lay down broad standards of behaviour. For instance, the Factories Act, 1955, contains elaborate requirements concerning matters such as prime movers, transmission machinery, unfenced machinery, self-acting machines, hoists and lifts, cranes and other lifting machines, steam boilers and receivers, air receivers, gasholders, humid factories, underground rooms, laundries, lifting excessive weights etc. There is nothing comparable in the 1989 Act, which in ss.6-11 lays down several broadly formulated duties; the remainder of the Act deals with the different modes of enforcing and securing compliance with those duties.

The main employers' duties: An overriding duty of care is imposed on employers by s.6(1):

> It shall be the duty of every employer to ensure, so far as is reasonably practicable, the safety, health and welfare at work of all his employees.

The remainder of that section sets out several ways in which this duty may arise, being

> (a) as regards any place or work under the employer's control, the design, the provision and the maintenance of it in a condition that is, so far as is reasonably practicable, safe and without risk to health;
> (b) so far as is reasonably practicable, as regards any place of work under the employer's control, the design, the provision and the maintenance of safe means of access to and egress from it;
> (c) the design, the provision and the maintenance of plant and machinery that are, so far as is reasonably practicable, safe and without risk to health;
> (d) the provision of systems of work that are planned, organised, performed and maintained so as to be, so far as is reasonably practicable, safe and without risk to health;
> (e) the provision of such information, instruction, training and super-

8. Factories Act, 1955, s.3.

vision as is necessary to ensure, so far as is reasonably practicable, the safety and health at work of his employees;

(f) in circumstances in which it is not reasonably practicable for an employer to control or eliminate hazards in a place of work under his control, or in such circumstances as may be prescribed, the provision and maintenance of such suitable protective clothing or equipment, as appropriate, that are necessary to ensure the safety and health at work of his employees;

(g) the preparation and revision as necessary of adequate plans to be followed in emergencies;

(h) to ensure, so far as is reasonably practicable, safety and the prevention of risk to health at work in connection with the use of any article or substance;

(i) the provision and the maintenance of facilities and arrangements for the welfare of his employees at work; and

(j) the obtaining, where necessary, of the services of a competent person (whether under a contract of employment or otherwise) for the purpose of ensuring, so far as is reasonably practicable, the safety and health at work of his employees.

Duties to persons who are not employees: The statutory duty of care is not confined to safeguarding employees. For s.7 of the 1989 Act places an obligation of reasonable care on employers in respect of persons who are not their employees but who are exposed to risks to their safety or health as a result of how the employer's undertaking is being conducted. A similar obligation is placed on self-employed persons for unsafe or unhealthy activities they may be engaged in. Section 8 of the Act imposes a form of occupier's liability on every person in control of a workplace, in respect of self-employed persons and employees of third parties who approach or come on to their premises, where that control is exercised for carrying on some trade or business or other undertaking.

Defective equipment or premises: Section 10 imposes duties regarding defective equipment for use at work.[9] These duties apply to any person who designs, manufactures, imports or supplies any article for use at work; to any person who erects or installs any article for use at a workplace; and to any manufacturer, importer or supplier of any substance which may be used at or in connection with work. Designers, manufacturers and others involved

---

9. Modeled on the British Employers Liability (Defective Equipment) Act, 1969, enacted following *Davie v. New Merton Board Mills Ltd* [1959] AC 604.

in supplying defective equipment or substances have a defence where the fault lay beyond their control or did not occur in the course of their trade or business. Section 11 imposes a duty of care on the designer and on the builder of any workplace.

Duties on employees: Finally, section 9 of the Act subjects employees to a duty of care. They must *inter alia* take reasonable care of their own safety, health and welfare and that of others who may be affected by what they do at work.

Elaborating the duties: It will be necessary to give more precise content to these well-meaning but vague standards of conduct. To that end, the Minister is empowered to introduce regulations. A considerable number of regulations already exist under the Factories Act, 1955, for instance the Building (Safety, Health and Welfare) Regulations, 1959,[10] and the Manual Labour (Maximum Weights and Transport) Regulations, 1972.[11] As well as continuing these regulations for the time being, provision is made by the 1989 Act for issuing 'codes of practice', which are intended to 'provid[e] practical guidance with respect to the requirements or prohibitions' in that Act.[12]

Implementation As is the case with other walks of life which are the subject of extensive regulation, the modes of securing compliance with and of enforcing the prescribed standards are at least as important as the very content of those standards. For without adequate techniques for implementation, the standards would tend to be honoured more in the breach than in their observance. A distinctive feature of the 1989 Act is the extent to which it concentrates on ensuring that the standards laid down are being met in the great majority of workplaces. Additionally, breach of the 1989 Act's requirements often will also constitute the tort of negligence, for which the person injured can recover damages to cover his loss;[13] in the case of serious injury those damages will be substantial.

The Authority: An autonomous executive agency is set up by the 1989 Act to oversee implementation of its requirements—the National Authority for Occupational Health and Safety.[14] Among its principal functions, as defined, are 'to make adequate arrangements for the enforcement of the relevant statutory provisions' and to 'promote, encourage and foster the

10. SI No. 227 of 1959.
12. S.30.
14. See 1989 Act ss.14-26.

11. SI No. 283 of 1972.
13. See infra p.118.

prevention of accidents and injury to health at work. . . .'[15] The Authority is tripartite in the sense of some of its members must be nominees of a representative employers' organisation and of a representative workers' organisation; for practical purpose, this means nominees of the Federation of Irish Employers and of the Irish Congress of Trade Unions. Among the tasks entrusted to the Authority are issuing codes of practice, advising the Minister on draft regulations, applying to the High Court for prohibition orders, obtaining information about aspects of the workplace, appointing inspectors who visit workplaces and investigate accidents and working conditions, and conducting special investigations into workplace incidents and related matters. It remains to be seen how successful the Authority will be in accomplishing its mission.

Inspectors: A factory inspectorate has been in existence since around 1830. The National Authority and any other 'enforcing agency' is empowered to appoint inspectors, who are given wide-ranging powers by s.34 of the 1989 Act. For instance, at any time they may enter and inspect any premises which they believe is a workplace, carry out an inquiry there as to compliance with the legal safety and health requirements, demand the production of relevant books, registers, records and the like. Inspectors can issue 'improvement notices' directing that measures be taken to remedy alleged breaches of the 1989 Act,[16] and also issue prohibition notices that specified dangerous activities shall cease.[17]

Codes of practice: The adoption of codes of practice on various aspects of health and safety is a central feature of the 1989 Act.[18] Codes will be issued by the Authority, after consulting any appropriate Government Minister and other person or body, like employers' associations and trade unions. Presumably, codes will be issued for various categories of activity and for numerous operations and processes. These codes are intended not to lay down hard and fast rules but to 'provid[e] practical guidance' on the Act's requirements.[19] Breach of the standards laid down in a code does not automatically mean that the statutory requirements have been contravened, for the purpose of criminal proceedings.[20] However, in determining whether the Act was broken, the codes are admissible in evidence and the courts can take account of what they require.[21] Employers and others who do not comply with the codes of practice, therefore, run the distinct risk of being convicted. The Act does not state what weight, if any, the codes should have in civil proceedings.

---

15. S.16(1)(a) and (b).   16. S.36.   17. S.37.
18. S.30.   19. S.30(3).   20. S.31(1).   21. S.31(2).

Prosecution: The principal enforcement technique under the 1989 Act, and under the Safety in Industry Acts and the other legislation, is prosecuting employers and others for breach of the statutory requirements. How effective prosecutions are depends to an extent on the success rate of detecting breaches, the ratio of prosecutions which end in convictions and the sanctions imposed by the courts. No empirical research seems to have been done on the success of criminalisation in this regard. Efficient detection will require that the National Authority and its inspectors be given sufficient resources to carry out their task. Summary offences under the 1989 Act will be prosecuted by the Authority or by the relevant enforcing agency appointed for that purpose. For many of these offences, the maximum fine is £1,000[22] for summary convictions.

In order to secure a conviction, it must be proved beyond reasonable doubt that the employer or other defendant committed the offence in question.[23] Section 50 of the 1989 Act will assist prosecutors, however. This reverses the burden of proof where the issue is whether the defendant did whatever was practicable in the circumstances, or whether he acted so far as was reasonably practicable or he used the best practicable means to do something. It is for the defendant to show that he took all such steps as were practicable in the circumstances.

Prohibition orders: Where the use of any workplace or part of it constitutes a very serious risk to health and safety, the National Authority or other enforcing agency may make an *ex parte* application to the High Court for an injunction. Section 39 of the 1989 Act empowers the Court to make an interim or an interlocutory order restricting or prohibiting the use in question. Resort to this procedure will be exceptional and probably will be confined to urgent situations. The more usual procedure will be that under s.37 of the Act, whereby any of the Authority's inspectors can issue a 'prohibition notice' against an activity which he believes involves or may involve a risk of serious personal injury to persons at any workplace. An appeal can be made to the District Court against such a notice. Where activities are carried on in breach of a prohibition notice, an order of the High Court can be obtained enjoining continuance of those activities.

Licensing: Certain kinds of activity can be prescribed by the Minister which cannot be carried on without possessing an appropriate licence.[24] Presumably, it is particularly dangerous kinds of work which will be regulated

---

22. S.49(10).
23. Except for prosecution for breach of a licence condition: s.49(3).
24. S.59.

in this manner. The National Authority is the licensing agency, which may attach such conditions as it thinks proper to any license. Carrying on an activity without possessing the appropriate license or breach of the terms of a license is a very serious offence; where the offender is prosecuted on indictment, he may be imprisoned for up to two years.[25]

Investigations and reports: In addition to the extensive powers inspectors enjoy to enter any premises they believe to be a workplace and to carry out enquiries there into compliance with the 1989 Act's requirements, ss.46 and 47 of the Act provide for what may be termed special reports and inquiries. Under the former, the National Authority may appoint someone to investigate 'the circumstances surrounding any accident, disease, occurrence, situation or any other matter related to the general purposes of' the Act and to report thereon. Under s.47, the Minister may appoint a judicial tribunal to hold an inquiry into 'any accident, disease, occurrence, situation or any other matter related to the general purposes' of the Act and to report thereon. The reports made following either of these inquiries may be published by the Authority. Provision is made in s.56 for the conduct of a coroner's inquest where what killed the deceased may have been an accident at the workplace or a disease contracted there. Witnesses at the inquest may be questioned by *inter alia* a representative of the majority of the persons employed at that workplace or by someone appointed by a trade union to which the deceased belonged or which has one or more members in that workplace.

Safety representatives: The elaborate system of safety representatives, safety committees and safety delegates, introduced in 1980 for factories, is simplified by s.13 of the 1989 Act and extended to all workplaces. Employees are given a right to 'make representations to and consult their employer on matters of safety, health and welfare in their place of work.'[26] Employers are required to consult their employees in this regard and to take account of any representations made by them. For these purposes, employees may appoint a safety representative from among their number. Their representative is entitled to such information from the employer as is necessary to safeguard health and safety at the workplace; he must get time off from his normal duties, without loss of remuneration, in connection with his task; and he is given a range of powers to investigate accidents and dangerous occurrences, to carry out inspections and to investigate potential hazards and complaints, and to have various dealings with the safety

25. S.49(3).   26. S.13(2).

inspector. His independence and freedom of action are protected by the stipulation that '[a]rising from the discharge of his functions [he] shall not be placed at any disadvantage in relation to his employment.'[27] The Minister may adopt regulations in order to give effect to the general thrust of these provisions.

Safety statements: Section 12 of the 1989 Act requires all employers to have prepared a safety statement. The terms of this statement must be notified to employees and to any other persons at the workplace who may be affected by it. This statement must set out the manner in which employees' health and welfare will be secured, being based on an identification of the hazards and an assessment of the risks at work, and specifying the arrangements made and resources available for safeguarding employees, the co-operation required for that purpose and identifying who are responsible for the tasks being assigned. If the inspector decides that a safety statement is inadequate in any material particular, he can direct that it be revised. In the case of registered companies, their annual report of the directors must contain an evaluation of the extent to which the policy set out in the safety statement was realised during the relevant period. It is anticipated that, by getting employers to focus on possible dangers and modes of avoiding them in this manner, accidents will be greatly reduced.

EMPLOYERS' LIABILITY

An employee who is injured in the course of his work as a result of his employer's negligence can recover compensation for the losses he suffered in consequence of that injury.[28] Where the employer's negligence brought about the employee's death, his dependents and also his estate may be entitled to recover damages.[29] This exposure to potential claims for damages is a powerful incentive for employers to ensure that their workplaces are safe and healthy. Although these risks can be covered by insurance, where several successful claims are made against an employer his insurance premium is bound to rise steeply. It is sometimes claimed that the high cost of employers' liability insurance cover renders segments of Irish industry uncompetitive. Unlike the position in Britain[30] and in several other

27. S.13(9).
28. See generally, B. McMahon & W. Binchy, *Irish Law of Torts* (2nd ed. 1990) ch.18 and J. Munkman, *Employers' Liability at Common Law* (11th ed. 1990).
29. Civil Liability Act, 1961, Parts II and IV and McMahon & Binchy chs. 41 and 42.
30. Employers Liability (Compulsory Insurance) Act, 1969.

countries, there is no statutory obligation on employers to take out insurance, in the same way as the owners of motor vehicles must have their vehicles insured. Whether at common law there is some duty to be insured, either generally or at least in exceptionally dangerous workplaces, is a question that awaits final resolution.[31]

Negligence For employers' liability in damages to arise, the following must be shown.

Duty of care: The employer should have owed a duty of care to the plaintiff in the circumstances which arose. Almost always the duty question will be answered in the affirmative where the accident or damage occurred in the workplace. The classic formulation of the employer's duty of care is that he is required to provide competent staff, a safe place of work, proper plant and appliances and a safe system of work.[32] But these are far from being rigid sub-divisions; they are particular manifestations of the general duty not to subject employees to unreasonable and unnecessary risk.

Standard of care: Secondly, it must be shown that the employer did not live up to the standard of care to be expected of a reasonable employer. This is mainly a pragmatic question and one of fact; whether in all the circumstances the danger to the plaintiff was reasonably foreseeable and whether the employer took adequate precautions to prevent the risk of damages or to control that risk.[33] A classic instance is failure to provide clothing or other equipment which would have protected the employee.[34] The standard of care imposed is high and has become increasingly stringent over the years, to the extent that there is almost a presumption of employer liability where one of his employees was injured in the course of his work. In principle, however, the burden of proof resides with the plaintiff to show that, in all the circumstances, his employer did not exercise reasonable care. As Henchy J put it, '[t]he law does not require the employer to ensure in all circumstances the safety of his workmen. He will have discharged his duty of care if he

---

31. In *Sweeney v. Duggan* (31 July 1991) Barron J held that no such duty existed at common law. This decision is being appealed to the Supreme Court. In *Sweeney*, Barron J followed *inter alia*, *Reid v. Rush & Tompkins Group p.l.c.* [1990] 1 WLR 212.
32. *Wilsons & Clyde Coal Co. v. English* [1938] AC 57.
33. E.g., *Paris v Stephney B.C.* [1951] AC 367; *Latimer v. A.E.I Ltd* [1953] AC 643; *Kenneally v. Waterford C.C.* (1959) 97 ILTR 97; *Crowe v. Brennan* [1967] IR 5; *Thompson v. Smiths Ship Repairers (North Shields) Ltd* [1984] QB 405 and *Bradford v. Robinson Rentals* [1967] 1 All ER 267.
34. E.g., *Thompson* case, supra n. 33; *Bradley v. C.I.E.* [1976] IR 217 and *Kennedy v. Hughes Dairies Ltd* [1989] ILRM 122.

does what a reasonable and prudent employer would have done in the circumstances.'[35] As is explained below, workplace regulations are often treated by the courts as laying down what is the appropriate standard of care.[36] Where the accident occurs at some place other than the employer's premises, which is not under his constant supervision, the standard of care is not as exacting as for what occurs on his premieses.[37]

A great number of reported and unreported cases exist on the standard of care required in different circumstances. While these cases lay down a variety of general propositions about what kinds of action should be expected of employers in various situations, there is always the danger of exalting, into the status of propositions of law, statements made with reference to the facts of particular cases. As an English judge once remarked, a judge 'naturally gives reasons for the conclusions formerly arrived at by a jury without reasons. It may sometimes be difficult to draw the line, but if the reasons given by a judge for arriving at the conclusions previously reached by a jury are to be treated as "law" and citable, the precedent system will die from a surfeit of authorities'.[38]

Causation: Thirdly, it must be shown that what caused the employee's injury was the negligent act of the employer or his agents.[39] Occasionally, the real cause of the loss may have been some extraneous matter. For instance, in the case of defective equipment which the employee was using at work, which injures him, often the employer will not be held liable for that loss.[40] But he would be liable where the defect was one which could easily have been discoved on any reasonable inspection of that equipment.[41] Causation can give rise to difficult questions of proof, especially where the injury is some form of disease which progressed slowly over time.[42]

Defences: Very exceptionally, the employer can raise the defence of *volenti non fit injuria*, that is that the damage was caused entirely by the employee's own actions.[43] The scope of this defence has been radically diminished by

35. *Bradley v. C.I.E.* [1976] IR at p. 223.
36. See infra p. 120.
37. E.g., *Mulcare v. Southern Health Board* [1988] ILRM 689.
38. *Qualcast (Wolverhampton) Ltd v Haynes* [1959] AC 743.
39. E.g., *McGhee v. National Coal Board* [1973] 1 WLR 1, *Joblins v Associated Dairies Ltd* [1982] AC 794 and *Bailey v Rolls Royce Ltd* [1984] ICR 688.
40. E.g., *Davie v New Merton Board Mills Ltd* [1959] AC 604.
41. E.g., *Keenan v. Bergin* [1971] IR 192.
42. E.g., *Carey v Cork Consumers Gas Co.* (Supreme Court, 5 March 1958); *O'Mahony v. Henry Ford & Son Ltd* [1962] IR 146; *Tremain v. Pike* [1969] 1 WLR 1556 and *Brady v. Beckman Instruments (Galway) Ltd* [1986] IILRM 361.
43. *Imperial Chemical Industries Ltd v. Shatwell* [1965] AC 656.

s. 34(1)(c) of the Civil Liability Act, 1961, to situations where the plaintiff actually waived his legal rights before the event in question occurred.[44] However, the actual extent of the employer's liability can be reduced, perhaps significantly, where it is shown that the damage was partly caused by the plaintiff's contributory negligence.[45]

It is no defence for an employer that he delegated to a subordinate, no matter how expert, the responsibility of ensuring that adequate precautions were taken in the circumstances.[46] Even if the person who was the immediate cause of the injuries was some third party and not a fellow-employee, the employer may still be held liable for not maintaining a safe workplace.[47]

Tort or contract: Although the employer's duty of care is an implied term of the employment contract,[48] as well as arising in tort, generally actions for damages arising out of injuries suffered at work are framed in tort. The extent to which employees' liability can be excluded by contract provisions has not been considered by the courts.

Breach of statutory duty On top of the common law duties, the parts still in force of the Factories Acts and equivalent legislation for mines and quarries, for offices and shops and for several other workplaces are regarded as imposing absolute duties. If injury results from an employer's breach of any of the statutory or regulatory requirements, he could be made liable for the tort of breach of statutory duty;[49] non-observance of most of the statutory requirements constitutes *per se* negligence.[50] As described by Professor Fleming,

> Dominating the industrial field nowadays is a vast volume of statutory regulation imposing detailed duties upon employers for the protection of their workers, such as Factory Acts requiring the fencing of

44. Cf. *O'Hanlon v. E.S.B.* [1969] IR 75 and *Rafferty v. Parsons (C.A.) of Ireland Ltd* [1987] ILRM 98.
45. Cf. *Stewart v. Killeen Paper Mills Ltd* [1959] IR 436 and *O'Hanlon v. E.S.B.* [1969] IR 75.
46. *Connolly v Dundalk U.D.C.* [1990] 2 IR 1.
47. *McDermid v. Nash Dredging & Reclamation Co.* [1987] AC 906. Compare *Stevens v. Brodribb Sawmilling Co. Pty. Ltd*, 160 CLR 16 (1986).
48. *Matthews v. Kuwait Bechtel Corp.* [1959] 2 QB 57.
49. *Groves v. Lord Wimbourne* [1898] 2 QB 402. See generally, B.M. Mahon & W. Binchy, *Irish Law of Torts* (2nd ed. 1990) ch. 21 and B. Shillman, *The Factory Legislation of Ireland* (1956).
50. E.g., *Doherty v. Bowaters Irish Wallboard Mills Ltd* [1968] IR 217; *Gallagher v. Mogul of Ireland Ltd* [1975] IR 204 and *Boyle v. Kodak Ltd* [1969] 1 WLR 661.

dangerous machinery. These statutes have been construed to confer a claim for damages on any employee injured as the result of his employer's failure to comply even if, as is usual, the statute provides only a penal sanction for its enforcement. Not infrequently these statutory duties are couched in absolute terms demanding compliance even if it would render the work in question commercially in-practicable or mechanically impossible. Failure to conform to the legislative safety standard is negligence *per se*, and if the statutory command is peremptory rather than demanding merely all reasonable care, liability is in effect strict and independent of fault in the con-ventional sense.

Most commonly such regulations prescribe specific precautions to be taken for particular industrial operations, like the use of specified scaffolding for work above minimum heights, of guards around moving machinery or duck boards for work on glass roofs. Regulations of this type in effect merely spell out precisely and beyond argument what the general duty of reasonable care would in any event require. More drastic by far in promoting strict liability are regulations, increasingly common, which prescribe that certain equipment be of sound construction, suitable material and adequate strength. These in effect import a warranty of fitness, covering even latent defects, and thereby far transcend the common law duty of employers. Although this has in other areas . . . militated conclusively against attaching civil sanctions, no similar scruples have prevailed in the industrial context. This striking difference in judicial attitude, which has indeed for all practical purposes—at least in Britain—made the whole doctrine of statutory negligence an almost exclusive preserve of industrial accident law, is of course in no small measure due to a desire to make up for the lower level of workers' compensation.[51]

Until s. 4(3) of the Safety, Health and Welfare at Work Act, 1989, is implemented entirely, most of the statutory requirements in the pre-1989 legislation and statutory instruments remain in force. It is anticipated that in due course these will be replaced by regulations adopted under the 1989 Act but it probably will take many years before all the pre-1989 measures become defunct. The main measures still in force are as follows, although several provisions of these Acts were replaced by s. 4(1) of the 1989 Act or by orders made under that Act:

Factories Act, 1955,
Office Premises Act, 1958,

51. *The Law of Torts* (7th ed. 1987) at p. 487.

Mines and Quarries Act, 1965,
Dangerous Substances Act, 1972,
Safety in Industry Act, 1980,
Safety, Health and Welfare (Offshore Installations) Act, 1987,
Part VI of the Shops (Conditions of Employment) Act, 1938,
Factories (Notification of Accidents) Regulations, 1956,
Factories (Operations at Unfenced Machinery Regulations), 1956,
Docks (Safety, Health and Welfare) Regulations, 1960,
Factories (Woodworking Machinery) Regulations, 1972,
Factories Act, 1955 (Manual Labour) (Maximum Weight and Transport)
    Regulations, 1972,
Construction (Safety, Health and Welfare) Regulations, 1975,
E.C. (Major Accident Hazards of Certain Industrial Activities)
    Regulations, 1986.

A full list of all the Acts, orders and regulations in force regarding health
and safety is published by the Department of Labour in its annual Labour
Inspection Report.

Breach of many of the requirements laid down in the above measures is
a criminal offence as well as an actionable wrong. However, before liability
under either head will be proclaimed, it must be established that the injured
person falls within the category of persons to whom the rules in question
apply (e.g. he may be self-employed, although some of these rules also apply
to self-employed persons), the place where the damage was inflicted falls
within the category of places covered by the rule (e.g. a factory, as defined,
a mine, an office etc.) and that the precise requirements of the rules were
not complied with. In the past, many of the cases under this heading adopted
a perhaps over-technical interpretation of the rule in question; because civil
liability for the breach is strict, a narrow interpretation was often favoured.
Among the issues which arise frequently in the reported cases include
whether the workplace was a 'factory', whether there was 'safe access' to
the workplace, whether a safe workplace was maintained, whether
machinery was properly fenced, whether the activity which caused the
damage was a 'process' and whether or not it was 'reasonably practical' to
adopt prescribed steps or measures. A detailed account of the interpretation
of similar legislation and regulations in England is contained in Munkman's
Employer's Liability (5th ed. 1990)

Occupational diseases Diseases contracted in the course of work can be
radically different from accidental injuries. Accidents are dramatic and
discrete events where a very clear relationship exists between what

happened and the injury suffered. By contrast, diseases develop and manifest themselves over time and their origins often are far less obvious. On account of the very nature of disease, it is more difficult for an employee, who is suffering from a debilitating malady he probably acquired by working in a certain environment for a long period, to succeed in an employers' liability claim.[52] Where, however, it is demonstrated that the employer's negligence or breach of statutory duty caused the employee's disease, that employee or, if dead, his dependents should succeed in an action for damages.[53]

Employees have succeeded in obtaining damages for deafness they contracted due to excessive noise in the workplace. The leading case perhaps is the thoughtful judgment of Mustill J in *Thompson v Smiths Ship Repairers (North Shields) Ltd,*[54] where the plaintiffs were several labourers and skilled workers who had worked in the defendant's shipyard for many years. They claimed damages for the loss of hearing they suffered due to working in that yard. Extensive scientific evidence was given regarding the causes of deafness, especially at work, which is set out in detail in the judgment. The plaintiffs succeeded but were not compensated completely for the loss they had suffered. It was held that, although there had been actual knowledge for many years that employees in ship-building and ship-repair yards suffered from deafness as a result of excessive noise, the risk had been considered as an inescapable feature of the industry. Accordingly, any liability of the defendants in negligence for failing to protect their employees against the risk of deafness had to be considered against the general practice in the industry of inaction and acceptance of the situation. The defendants could only rely on the general practice while there was a lack of social awareness of the need to protect employees generally against industrial noise and there was not readily available information and the means of protecting employees against noise. But once information could be obtained and ear protection devices were available on the market, the defendants came under a duty of care because either they should have sought the knowledge or they should have known that effective precautions could be taken in their yards to protect their employees against the risk of deafness.

A particularly vexed question is disability caused by exposure to asbestos many years ago, which poses the additional problem of limitation of

---

52. E.g., *O'Mahony v. Henry Ford & Son Ltd* [1962] IR 146 (cancer).
53. E.g., *McGhee v. National Coal Board* [1973] 1 WLR 1 (dermatitis) and *Pape v. Cumbria County Council* [1992] ICR 132 (dermatitis).
54. [1984] QB 405.

actions.[55] Among the matters covered by E.C. Directives, which have been implemented in Ireland, are exposure to noise[56] and exposure to asbestos,[57] to lead[58] and to other unsafe agents.[59] For the purposes of the Safety, Health and Welfare at Work Act, 1989, the term personal injury is defined to include 'any disease and any impairment of a person's physical or mental condition'.[60] Moreover, s.6(3)(h) of that Act obliges employers to take appropriate measures to prevent risk to health at work.

Civil liability and the 1989 Act The obligations laid down in the 1989 Act to ensure that the workplace is a safe and a healthy place are enforced by criminal sanctions. Many of these obligations also arise at common law; however, there are obligations under this Act which in particular circumstances would not arise at common law, for instance, in relation to defective equipment. Thus, the question arises of when does breach of the 1989 Act also provide a civil remedy to persons who suffer damage in consequence of that breach. The Act takes an almost entirely neutral stance on this issue. Section 60(1) provides that nothing in the Act confers any right of action in civil proceedings in respect of breach of any duty imposed by ss.6-11 of the Act (summarised above). Against that, the Act does not in any way cut back on the existing scope of tort liability nor indeed does the Act cut back on any civil liability for breach of statutory duty under the pre-1989 safety legislation. Accordingly, the entire civil liability position as of mid-1989 is preserved by the Act.

Section 28 of the 1989 Act empowers the Minister to adopt regulations to deal with a very wide range of matters or otherwise to give effect to the Act. Breach of these regulations is deemed to be an actionable wrong unless the regulation provides otherwise. What constitutes damage which can be recovered under any such breach is defined to include death or personal injury; it remains to be seen whether a work-related disease will be regarded as damage for these purposes. Liability for damages for breach of any of these regulations cannot be contracted out of. As has been observed, codes of conduct may be issued under the 1989 Act but the express provision for the court taking account of them applies only to criminal proceedings. It is possible, nevertheless, that some account may be taken of the codes in claims for damages, as indicating what would constitute taking reasonable care.

55. Cf. *Keenan v. Miller Insulation & Engineering Ltd* (Piers Ashworth QC, 8 Dec. 1987), discussed in 105 *L.Q.R.* 19 (1989); also *Nurse v. Morgan Crucible Ltd* [1989] AC 692.
56. SI No. 157 of 1990.   57. SI No. 34 of 1989.
58. SI No. 219 of 1988.   59. SI No. 251 of 1989.
60. S.2(1).

SOCIAL WELFARE BENEFITS

Duly insured employees may be entitled to be paid social welfare injury benefit or disablement benefit when they are put out of work or are incapacitated due to an injury they incurred at work.[61] If the accident occurred in the course of the person's employment, it is deemed to have arisen out of that employment unless the contrary is established.[62] There is a substantial body of case law, which is supplemented by legislation, regarding when does an accident arise out of work for these purposes. The fact that the employee's contract of employment is unlawful or that he was acting unlawfully when the accident occurred does not prevent it from being the basis for a claim for either of these social welfare benefits.[63]

The benefits are payable in respect of personal injury caused at work to the claimant; it is payable where the claimant 'suffers as a result of the accident from loss of physical or mental faculty' from disablement to the prescribed extent.[64] There is also compensation for a disease which was contracted at work but cannot be attributed to a direct accident, for instance occupational deafness and pneumoconiosis.[65] Perhaps the most notorious of those diseases, although it rarely occurs in Ireland because of the absence of any substantial mining industry, is the 'black lung' disease which many coal miners suffer from. Several Conventions and Recommendations have been issued by the International Labour Organisation dealing with what ailments and maladies should be deemed to be occupational diseases for the purpose of receiving social security benefits.

61. Social Welfare (Consolidation) Act, 1981, s.37.
62. Id. s.39(1).
63. Id. ss.39(3) and 40.
64. Id. s.43(1).
65. S.I. No. 392 of 1983 and S.I. No. 391 of 1983. See generally, Note, 'Compensating Victims of Occupational Disease', 93 *Harv. L Rev.* 916 (1980) and Wilson, 'Occupational Disease—The Problems of a Comprehensive System of Coverage', 11 *Ind. L. J.* 141 (1982).

6

Discrimination in employment

Discrimination of many kinds occurs at the workplace. Choices must frequently be made between employees and the very process of choosing involves discrimination. Employers prefer to hire certain types of people rather than others. Some attributes are vital when it comes to allocating particular jobs or promotion. Other attributes or conduct influence the decision to dismiss a worker. At common law, employers are entirely free to discriminate between members of their workforce on whatever basis they choose. As Lord Davey once observed,

> An employer may refuse to employ a [worker] from the most capricious, malicious or morally reprehensive motives that can be conceived but the workman has no right of action against him—a man has no right to be employed by any particular employer and has no right to any particular employment if it depends on the will of another.[1]

However, this freedom is now circumscribed by legislation and by E.C. rules; discrimination against nationals of E.C. Member States and also discrimination on the basis of sex or of marital status are the subject of extensive prohibitions. Additionally, there is the Unfair Dismissals Act, 1977, which outlaws dismissals for unfair reasons; among the grounds which are presumptively unfair under that Act are the employee's religious or political opinions, race or colour, the employee's pregnancy or the fact that she exercised her rights to maternity leave.[2]

The question of discrimination must also be considered in the light of the Constitution, which forbids discrimination on religious or political grounds and unfair discrimination on the basis of a person's membership of a family. Article 40.1 of the Constitution goes further to some extent, in that it contains a broad affirmation of equality: that

> All citizens shall, as human persons, be held equal before the law. This shall not be held to mean that the State shall not in its enactments have

---

1. *Allen v. Flood* [1989] AC 1, at pp.172-173.   2. See post pp. 198-199

due regard to differences of capacity, physical and moral, and of social function.

Most of the cases arising under this guarantee have concerned claims that legislative provisions were unfairly discriminatory.[3] The extent to which the guarantee applies to employment practices in the public sector has not been considered by the courts, but it can hardly be doubted that discrimination by public service employers on the grounds of a worker's sex or status at birth would be unconstitutional. Nevertheless, until comparatively recently most women who were employed in the public service were obliged to resign when they got married.[4] Whether private sector employers and trade unions are bound by this guarantee remains to be resolved; for instance, whether refusing to employ persons because of their nationality or their race or political views would be unconstitutional.

FOREIGN WORKERS—E.C. NATIONALS

The employment of foreign workers, meaning persons who do not possess Irish nationality, is regulated by the Aliens Act, 1935, and the many statutory instruments made under that Act. An alien may be employed only where his employment is duly authorised by the Minister for Justice.[5] However, these restrictions never applied to British subjects and, since Ireland joined the European Communities, do not apply to nationals of the E.C. Member States. Being a country with a long and enduring tradition of emigration, the treatment of foreign and migrant workers in Ireland has never been a topic of great practical legal significance. What little immigration there is into the State tends to be from Northern Ireland and many of those persons either possess or are eligible to have Irish citizenship.

Discrimination against nationals of E.C. Member States is proscribed by Article 7 of the E.E.C. Treaty, within the general framework of that Treaty. One of the main policies in that Treaty is to promote the free movement of workers between E.C. Member States which, according to Article 48(2) of the Treaty,

> shall entail the abolition of any discrimination based on nationality between workers of the Member States as regards employment, remuneration and other conditions of work and employment.

3. See generally *Constitutional Law*, ch.16.
4. Prior to the Civil Service (Employment of Married Women) Act, 1973.
5. SI No. 395 of 1946, as amended by SI No. 128 of 1975.
6. O.J. No. L 254/2 (1968, sp.ed.), as amended and supplemented by Regulation 1251/70, O.J. No. L 142/24 (1970) and several Directives.

Article 48 of the Treaty is supplemented by Regulation No.1612/68,[6] which, along with Regulations on social security,[7] are the principal legislative measures giving effect to the principle of the free movement of workers. It has been held that Article 48(2) and the prohibition against discrimination contained in the 1968 Regulation are directly applicable in the courts of the Member States.[8] Accordingly, any worker who suffers treatment which is banned by these provisions is entitled to legal redress, even against employers in the private sector—the Regulation being equivalent to national legislation.

'Worker' In order to obtain the benefit of these provisions, the person must be a national of an E.C. Member State and also be a 'worker', whether he actually has a job or is seeking work. The concept of a worker for these purposes is similar to that of an employee for the purpose of employment legislation. But the concept of worker here is still a Community one; if the person falls within the category of worker under E.C. law, he obtains the protection regardless of whether he may be regarded as self-employed or otherwise under national law.[9] According to the European Court of Justice in one of the 'Spanish Fishermen' cases,

> the Community concept of 'worker' must be defined in accordance with objective criteria which distinguish the employment relationship by reference to the rights and duties of the persons concerned. The essential feature of an employment relationship, however, is that for a certain period of time a person performs services for and under the direction of another person in return for which he receives remuneration.[10]

It was held there that 'share fishermen' working on trawlers, who might be regarded as self-employed for the purposes of national law,[11] are 'workers' within E.C. law. Similarly, trainee teachers were regarded as workers for these purposes,[12] as were foreign language assistants employed in universities[13] and persons who were prepared to work only part time.[14] But persons

---

7. Principally, Regulation 1408/71, O.J. No. L 149/2 (1971).
8. *Van Duyn v. Home Office* (Case 41/74) [1974] ECR 1337.
9. *Levin v. Secretary of State* (Case 53/81) [1982] ECR 1035.
10. *R. v. Ministry of Agriculture, ex p. Agegate Ltd* (Case C-3/87) [1990] 1 CMLR 366, at p.397.
11. *D.P.P. v. McLoughlin* [1986] IR 355; see ante p.36.
12. *Lawrie–Blum v. Land Baden–Wurttemberg* (Case 66/85) [1986] ECR 2121.
13. *Allue and Coonan v. Universita Degli Studi di Venezia* (Case 33/88) [1991] 1 CMLR 283.
14. *Kempf v. Staatssecretaris van Justitie* (Case 139/85) [1974] ECR 359.

employed in a special rehabilitation scheme for the physically and mentally handicapped, in order to facilitate their social integration, were held not to be workers.[15]

The prohibitions Regulation No. 1612/68 seeks to guarantee equal treatment for E.C. nationals in obtaining employment and in the exercise of their employment. Article 1 of the Regulation provides that

> 1. Any national of a Member State, shall, irrespective of his place of residence, have the right to take up an activity as an employed person, and to pursue such activity, within the territory of another Member State in accordance with the provisions laid down by law, regulation or administrative action governing the employment of nationals of that State.
> 2. He shall in particular have the right to take up available employment in the territory of another Member State with the same priority as nationals of that State.

And according to Article 7 of the Regulation,

> 1. A worker who is a national of a Member State may not, in the territory of another Member State, be treated differently from national workers by reason of his nationality in respect of any conditions of employment and work, in particular as regards remuneration, dismissal, and should he become unemployed, re-instatement or re-employment. . . .
> 4. Any clause of a collective or individual agreement or of any other collective regulation concerning eligibility for employment, employment remuneration and other conditions of work or dismissal shall be null and void insofar as it lays down or authorises discriminatory conditions in respect of workers who are nationals of the other Member States.

Several successful cases have been brought by the E.C. Commission against Member States in connection with provisions in their legislation stipulating a national requirement in order to obtain certain jobs, most notably that only French nationals could become seamen in the merchant navy there.[16] In the *Trinity House London Pilotage Committee* case,[17] the body with statutory responsibility for allocating river pilots' licences formerly granted those licences only to U.K. nationals. On joining the

15. *Bettray v. Staatssecretaris van Justitie* (Case 344/87) [1991] 1 CMLR 459.
16. *E.C. Commission v. France* (Case 167/73) [1974] ECR 359.
17. [1985] 2 CMLR 413.

E.E.C., that practice had to change but, as an interim measure, to prevent unemployment among British pilots, this body adjusted the practice of refusing licences to foreign applicants. It was held that rejecting applications from fully qualified Danish and German nationals contravened the E.C. rules.

Indirect as well as direct discrimination comes within the prohibitions. In the *Allue and Coonan* case,[18] it was held that all covert forms of discrimination which, by applying other distinguishing criteria, obtain the same result as if a nationality criterion was used, are proscribed. There, the regulations allowed assistants in universities, who taught foreign languages, to be employed for no longer than five years; there was no comparable restriction on other university staff. Because the great majority of those assistants would be other E.C. nationals, it was held that those rules contravened Article 48(2). A common form of indirect discrimination against aliens is the imposition of a residency requirement; that the person must either reside in the State or have resided there for a prescribed period. In the *Spanish Fishermen* case,[19] such a practice was condemned by the European Court. As a condition of obtaining a licence to fish inside U.K. waters, the U.K. regulations required that 75 per cent of the crew of the applicant's vessel be U.K. residents. The justification given was that they would be fishing against the quotas allocated to the U.K. under the E.C.'s common fisheries policy. But it was held that this requirement contravened Community law.

Another common method of practising indirect discrimination is by refusing to give due weight to qualifications for the job which have been obtained abroad. For instance, qualified engineers are required for a job but the employer refuses to accept applicants with foreign engineering qualifications. Or the law may prevent employers from accepting persons with foreign qualifications. In the latter situation the law may contravene the E.E.C. Treaty. In *Union Nationale des Entraineurs etc. v. Heylers*,[20] the defendant was a Belgian football trainer who was hired by the Lille football club, which was in the French first division. He was prosecuted for breach of the Criminal Code on the grounds that he did not possess the requisite qualifications for the job. If the French regulations simply provided that only persons duly qualified in France could do that job, that clearly would contravene Article 48 of the Treaty because its substantial effect would be to discriminate against nationals of other E.C. States.[21] According to Advocate General Mancini, 'the existence of a straight-forward power to

18. Supra n.13.   19. Supra n.10.
20. [1989] 1 CMLR 901.
21. In any event, it would contravene Art. 8 of Regulation 1612/68.

negate the validity of certificates obtained outside the national territory but within the Community must be ruled out. . . . [M]ember States must recognise that such certificates are valid, at least in as much as they certify that the holders are in possession of qualifications equivalent to the competence certified by the corresponding national documents.'[22]

In this instance, France had a procedure for recognising foreign qualifications which were based on standards equivalent to those obtaining in France. The defendant sought to have his Belgian trainers' diploma accepted under this process but he was refused, without any reason being given. The European Court held that this refusal to assign reasons contravened the Treaty because it facilitated covert discrimination against other E.C. nationals. If reasons were given, which were untenable, the defendant could challenge them in the courts. Regarding how foreign qualifications should be treated, the Court held that the 'procedure for the recognition of equivalence must enable the national authorities to assure themselves, on an objective basis, that the foreign diploma certifies that its holder has knowledge and qualifications which are, if not identical, at least equivalent to those certified by the national diploma.'[23]

Measures have been taken by the E.C. authorities to ensure that certain qualifications are duly recognised in all Member States but this process is far from complete.[24] In cases concerning applicants for a job with quali-

22. [1989] 1 CMLR at p.907.
23. Id. at p.913 (para. 13).
24. By the end of 1990 the following measure had been promulgated:—Directive 75/362 concerning the mutual recognition of diplomas, certificates and other evidence of formal qualifications in medicine, including measures to facilitate the effective exercise of the right of esbablishment and freedom to provide services, O.J. L No. 167/1 (1975).
    Directive 77/452 concerning the mutual recognition of diplomas, certificates and other evidence of the formal qualifications of nurses responsible for general care, including measures to facilitate the effective exercise of the right of establishment and freedom to provide services, O.J. L No. 176/1 (1975).
    Directive 78/686 concerning the mutual recognition of diplomas, certificates and other evidence of the formal qualificatiosn of practitioners of dentistry, including measures to facilitate the effective exercise of the right of establishment and freedom to provide services, O.J. L No. 233/1 (1978).
    Directive 78/1026 concerning the mutual recognition of diplomas, certificates and other evidence of formal qualifications in veterinary medicine, including measures to facilitate the effective exercise of the right of establishment and freedom to provide services, O.J. L No. 362/1 (1978).
    Directive 80/154 concerning the mutual recognition of diplomas, certificates and other evidence of formal qualifications in midwifery, including measures to facilitate the effective exercise of the right of establishment and freedom to provide services, O.J. L No. 33/1 (1980).
    Directive 81/1057 supplementing 75/362, 77/452, 78/686 and 78/1026, O.J. L No. 385/25 (1981).

fications which have been the subject of an E.C. Directive, a public authority employer might be estopped from refusing to recognise the qualification obtained in another Member State;[25] but Directives which have not been implemented in national law do not 'horizontally' bind private sector employers.

Requiring a candidate for a job to have a knowledge of the Irish language, even if the job does not actually involve using Irish,[26] may be permissible. In *Groener v. Minister for Education*[27] it was held that requiring teachers in a V.E.C.-managed art school to demonstrate a knowledge of Irish was permissible. Although a degree of indirect discrimination may result, the status of the Irish language in the Constitution and the need to preserve cultural and linguistic diversity in the Community warranted upholding the language requirement. However, requiring persons to have an extremely advanced knowledge of Irish would not ordinarily be acceptable under the Treaty. Measures to encourage the language 'must not in any circumstances be disproportionate in relation to the aim pursued and the manner in which they are applied must not bring about discrimination against nationals of other Member States.'[28]

Exceptions Workers' rights to freedom of movement within the European Community are subject to two principal exceptions or qualifications. The first is that Article 48 of the E.E.C. Treaty, by its very terms, does 'not apply to employment in the public service'. Accordingly, it is permissible to exclude other E.C. nationals from public service employment. On several occasions, the European Court has explained that this exception will be construed narrowly. The mere fact that the State in question regards a job as a public service occupation is not sufficient to place it outside the freedom

Directive 85/384 on the mutual recognition of diplomas, certificates and other evidence of formal qualifications in architecture, including measures to facilitate the effective exercise of the right of establishment and freedom to provide services, O.J. L No. 223/15 (1985).
Directive 85/433 concerning the mutual recognition of diplomas, certificates and other evidence of formal qualifications in pharmacy, including measures to facilitate the effective exercise of the right of establishment relating to certain activities in the field of pharmacy, O.J. L No. 253/37 (1985).
Directive 87/540 on access to the occupation of carrier of goods by waterway in national and international transport and on the mutual recognition of diplomas, certificates and othere evidence of formal qualifications for this occupation, O.J. L No. 322/20 (1987).
Directive 89/48 on a general system for the recognition of higher-education and training of at least three years' duration, O.J. L No. 19/16 (1989).
25. *Foster v. British Gas p.l.c.* [1990] 2 CMLR 833; see ante p.16.
26. Cf. Agricultural Credit Corporation Act, 1978, s.18, Local Authorities (Officers and Employees) Act, 1983, s.2, and University College Galway Act, 1929, s.3.
27. [1990] 1 CMLR 401.   28. Id. at p.414 (para. 19).

of movement principle. Successful actions have been brought by the E.C. Commission against Member States which sought to confine to their own nationals jobs such as railway workers,[29] manual workers employed by local authorities,[30] nurses in public hospitals[31] and researchers in national research institutions.[32] In the *Lawrie Blum* case,[33] it was held that Germany could not exclude other E.C. nationals from becoming trainee teachers merely because those positions were classified as civil service jobs in Germany. According to the Court,

> access to certain posts may not be limited by reason of the fact that in a given Member State persons appointed to such posts have the status of civil servants. . . . '[E]mployment in the public service' [in this context] must be understood as meaning those posts which involve direct or indirect participation in the exercise of powers conferred by public law and in the discharge of functions whose purpose is to safeguard the general interests of the State or other public authorities and which therefore require a special relationship of allegiance to the State on the part of persons occupying them and reciprocity of rights and duties which form the foundation of the bond of nationality. The posts excluded are confined to those which, having regard to the tasks and responsibilities involved, are apt to display the characteristics of the public service in the spheres described above.[34]

The other exception to the principle of the free movement of workers within the Community is that this freedom is subject to 'limitations justified on grounds of public policy, public security or public health'. So far, all of the major cases on this exception have concerned aspects of immigration and deportation regulations and practices.[35]

SEX AND MARITAL STATUS

Prohibitions against discrimination on the grounds of sex and of marital status feature in the employment laws of most industrial states today. These measures were often adopted in order to encourage female participation in

29. *Re Public Employees: E.C. Commission v. Belgium et al.* (Case 149/79) [1980] ECR 3881.
30. Ibid.
31. *Re French Nurses: E.C. Commission v. France* (Case 307/89) [1987] 3 CMLR 555.
32. *Re Employees of Consiglio Nazionale delle Ricerche: E.C. Commission v. Italy* (Case 225/85) [1987] ECR 2625.
33. [1986] ECR 2121.   34. Id. at p.2147 (para. 27).
35. E.g. the *Van Duyn* case, supra n.8.

the workforce at a time of labour shortages. Some anti-discrimination laws were enacted for philosophical or ideological reasons: that it is wrong to handicap women who may wish to earn their living by obtaining employment. One such measure is the Sex Disqualification (Removal) Act, 1919, which put an end to many disqualifications based on sex and on marital status in the public sector and in the professions. According to s.1 of this very short Act, which is still in force,

> A person shall not be disqualified by sex or marriage from the exercise of any public function, or from being appointed to or holding any civil or judicial office or post, or from entering or assuming or carrying on any civil profession or vocation.

But this Act permitted exceptions to its requirements for civil service employments and married women could not work in the civil service until the 'marriage bar' was removed in 1973.[36] In 1958 the law permitted women to join the Garda Síochána[37] and in 1979 women were permitted to become members of the armed forces.[38]

For many years a major area of concern of international employment law has been to protect women from excessively arduous conditions at work, especially in case of maternity, and to ensure equality of rights and treatment for men and women workers. Numerous conventions and recommendations have been adopted by the International Labour Organisation on topics like maternity protection, night work, employment of women in unhealthy and dangerous occupations, equal remuneration, equality of treatment generally and the employment of women with family responsibilities. Article 8 of the European Social Charter gives employed women protection in several respects. However, none of these instruments have any direct legal effect in domestic law and one scans in vain the law reports to see any reference to them as guidelines for interpreting the Constitution or related statutory provisions.

The main anti-discrimination legislation currently in force, however, is very much the consequence of membership of the European Communities. For Article 119 of the E.E.C. Treaty lays down the principle of equal pay for equal work as between men and women. This principle is directly applicable in the courts of all E.C. Member States against employers and others, be they private sector or public sector bodies.[39] Article 119 has been

36. Civil Service (Employment of Married Women) Act, 1973.
37. Garda Síochána Act, 1958.
38. Defence (Amendment) Act, 1979.
39. *Defrenne v. Sabena* (Case 43/75) [1976] ECR 455. See generally, B. McMahon & F. Murphy, *European Community Law in Ireland* (1989) ch.'s 13 and 25.

supplemented by several Directives, which deal with aspects of equal pay,[40] with equality in other employment terms and conditions[41] and with equality in occupational pension schemes.[42] A very substantial body of case law has been handed down by the European Court of Justice on the question of equal treatment of the sexes at the workplace. The principal legislative measures, which given effect to the E.C. requirements, are the Anti-Discrimination (Pay) Act, 1974, the Employment Equality Act, 1977, and Part VII of the Pensions Act, 1990.[43] When interpreting national laws, even laws which were not intended to implement specific E.C. measures, the courts tend to interpret the provisions in a manner that is consistent with E.C. measures *in pari materia*.

The law regarding sex equality at work has become a vast and complex topic in its own right and a general book on employment law could never do full justice to the subject. Happily, an excellent monograph on the topic was published in 1989, Ms Deirdre Curtin's *Irish Employment Equality Law*,[44] which the reader should consult for a more detailed treatment of the matters covered in this chapter and related questions. Another reason for not covering this subject in great detail is that there have been very few High Court and Supreme Court decisions so far on the substantive aspects of the legislation. Accordingly, there are many important questions about which differences of view exist and which have yet to be resolved authoritatively. Under the 1974 and the 1977 legislation, sex discrimination claims commence before equality officers, attached to the Labour Relations Commission, who have both a conciliatory and an adjudicative function. From them, there is an appeal to the Labour Court and there is an appeal on a point of law from this tribunal to the High Court. To the extent that what actually is the law is reflected in the practice of first instance tribunals, the present Irish law on sex discrimination is primarily the principles and guidelines being adopted by the equality officers. In making their determinations, the Supreme Court has exhorted them to set out in their reports their conclusion of fact and a summary of the evidence on which those conclusions were found.[45]

---

40. See infra p.136.
41. See infra p.140.
42. See post p.260.
43. See post ch. 11.
44. Published by the Round Hall Press (hereinafter referred to as *Curtin*).
45. *North Western Health Board v. Martyn* [1987] IR 565. Most of the reported Irish cases concern the practice and procedure of the equality officers and of the Labour Court, e.g. *Aer Lingus Teo. v. Labour Court* [1990] ILRM 485, *Aer Rianta c.p.t. v. Labour Court* [1989] ILRM 193, *Chomhairle Oiliuna Talmhiochta v. Doyle* [1989] IR 33, *Caldwell v. Labour Court* [1988] IR 280, *Cork Corporation v. Cahill* [1987] IR 478.

Equal pay The legislation and rules are somewhat different depending on whether the focus is on disparities in remuneration or on disparate treatment other than regarding pay. By 'equal pay' in this context means that persons doing the same or very similar work for the same employer shall not be paid different remuneration because they are of different sexes. If men and women are doing similar work but are being paid differently, the burden is on the employer to demonstrate some reason other than their sexes why they are not receiving the same pay. This principle is proclaimed in Article 119 of the E.E.C. Treaty, according to which

> Each Member State shall during the first stage ensure and subsequently maintain the application of the principle that men and women should receive equal pay for equal work. For the purpose of this Article, 'pay' means the ordinary basic or minimum wage or salary and any other consideration, whether in cash or in kind, which the worker receives, directly or indirectly, in respect of his employment from his employer. Equal pay without discrimination based on sex means: (a) that pay for the same work at piece rates shall be calculated on the basis of the same unit of measurement; (b) that pay for work at time rates shall be the same for the same job.

In order to confer rights and to impose duties on individuals, Article 119 does not need to be embodied in an E.C. Regulation or in national legislation or regulations. In the second *Defrenne* case,[46] where an air hostess with the Belgian carrier Sabena sued it for damages, it was held that 'since Article 119 is mandatory in nature, the prohibition on discrimination between men and women applies not only to the action of public authorities but also extends to all agreements which are intended to regulate paid labour collectively, as well as contracts between individuals'.[47] Article 119's requirements are amplified in several respects by Directive No. 75/117 on equal pay.[48] Both Article 119's requirements and this Directive are given legislative form in the Anti-Discrimination (Pay) Act, 1974. The central provision of this Act is s.2(1), according to which,

> Subject to this Act, it shall be a term of the contract under which a woman is employed in any place that she shall be entitled to the same rate of remuneration as a man who is employed in that place by the same employer (or by an associated employer . . .), if both are employed on like work.

---

46. Supra n.39.   47. [1976] ECR at p.476 (par.39).
48. O.J. No. L 45/19 (1975).

Most of the 1974 Act is devoted to the procedures and other techniques for implementing this principle of equal pay.

Personal scope: The right to equal pay under the 1974 Act is not confined to employees and apprentices; it extends to persons who are technically self-employed provided they act under a contract 'personally to execute any work or labour' for another.[49] Unlike much of the modern employment legislation, the 1974 Act does not expressly exclude from its scope categories of public service employment and certain other categories of jobs. No form of employment is exempted from its or from Article 119's requirements.

'Pay': In order to succeed in an equal pay claim, the complainant must show that he or she is earning less than a comparable man or woman.[50] Remuneration, for this purpose, is defined by s.1(1) of the 1974 Act as including

> any consideration, whether in cash or in kind, which an employee receives, directly or indirectly, in respect of his employment from his employer.

Article 119 of the E.E.C. Treaty contains a similar definition. So far, the courts and tribunals do not seem to have drawn the analogy with the 'emoluments' from an employment or office for the purpose of income tax law.[51] An extensive concept of what constitutes pay has been adopted in equal pay cases as including, for instance, sick pay, bonus payments, overtime payments, skills allowances, marriage gratuities, free accommodation, redundancy payments, commissions to sales assistants and house purchase loans.[52] Pensions under occupational pension schemes have been held to be remuneration for this purpose.[53] Special provisions for equality in occupational pensions were adopted in the Pensions Act, 1990.[54]

Same employer and workplace: For the equal pay principle to apply, the relevant man and woman being compared must be working for the one employer in the same workplace.[55] There must be an actual identifiable man doing a job who is to be compared with a woman worker, or vice versa; a comparison with some hypothetical worker does not suffice under the 1974

49. S.1(1). Cf. *Mirror Group Newspapers Ltd v. Gunning* [1985] 1 WLR 394.
50. See generally *Curtin*, ch.4.
51. See post p.331.   52. See *Curtin* at p.124.
53. *Barber v. Guardian Royal Exchange Insurance Group* (Case C 262/88) [1990] 1 CMLR 513.
54. See post pp. 260-261.   55. See generally, *Curtin*, ch. 4.

Act, even a worker who was employed in a comparable job before the other employee was hired. The man and woman in question must be working for the same employer. However, it suffices if one of them was working with an 'associated employer' provided that either all the employees or the particular category or employees of both employers had the same terms and conditions of employment.[56] An associated employer is a company which controls the other, directly or indirectly, or where both are under common control.[57]

For a comparison to be made between them, the man and woman must be working in the same place, but the 1978 Act does not define the workplace for these purposes. Circumstances can arise where two different localities may be regarded as the one workplace.

Like work: The work of the persons being compared does not have to be entirely identical for the 1974 Act to apply; it suffices if they are engaged in 'like work'.[58] That term is defined by s.3 of the Act as follows:

Two persons shall be regarded as employed on like work—
(a) where both perform the same work under the same or similar conditions, or where each is in every respect interchangeable with the other in relation to the work, or
(b) where the work performed by one is of a similar nature to that performed by the other and any differences between the work performed or the conditions under which it is performed by each occur only infrequently or are of small importance in relation to the work as a whole, or
(c) where the work performed by one is equal in value to that performed by the other in terms of the demands it makes in relation to such matters as skill, physical or mental effort, responsibility and working conditions.

In other words, the jobs being compared may be either the same, similar or of 'equal value'. For the purposes of Article 119, it was held that two jobs can be alike where they are of equal value.[59] Most equal pay claims now are brought on the basis that the jobs in question are of equal value,[60] which

56. S.2(1).
57. S.2(2); that control can be directed or indirect. See generally, M. Forde, *Company Law* (2nd ed. 1991) para. 14.30.
58. See generally, *Curtin*, ch.6.
59. *Jenkins v. Kingsgate (Clothing Productions) Ltd* (Case 96/80) [1981] ECR 911.
60. E.g., as well as instances cited by *Curtin*, see *Hayward v. Cammell Laird Shipbuilders Ltd* [1988] AC 894, *Pickstone v. Freemans p.l.c.* [1989] AC 66, *Leverton v. Clwyd County Council* [1990] AC 706. See generally, Willburn, 'Equal Pay for Work of Equal

often involves using professional job evaluation techniques as evidence.[61] There is a burgeoning case law on the concept of equal value.

In *Murphy v. Telecom Éireann,*[62] Keane J held that a woman's job, which demonstrably was more exacting and rewarding than a job held by a comparable man, was not work of equal value to the man's job. However, that interpretation was rejected by the European Court of Justice,[63] as being inconsistent with the very objective of Article 119, which is to outlaw unfair discrimination on the grounds of sex with regard to remuneration. In the light of that ruling, Keane J then held that the 1974 Act should be given a 'teleological interpretation', meaning that whenever possible it should be construed in accordance with the requirements of Article 119.[64] The British courts demonstrated a similar reluctance to take account of Community requirements when interpreting their legislation on equality until eventually that approach was abandoned in the *Pickstone* case.[65] Whether two or more jobs are of equal value is entirely a matter for objective verification by evidence.

Grounds other than sex: An employer who is paying different remuneration to men and women, for like work being performed by them, has a defence if he can establish that the reason for the differential treatment is 'grounds other than sex'.[66] For the purposes of Article 119 of the E.E.C. Treaty, it has been held that, in order to defend an equal pay claim on these grounds, the employer must demonstrate objectively justifiable grounds for the pay differential and not merely that he had no intention to discriminate on the basis of sex. For this defence to succeed, the differential treatment must 'correspond to a real need on the part of the undertaking' and be 'appropriate with a view to achieving the objective being pursued and necessary to that end.'[67] As with the concepts of pay and like work, there are a great number of decisions on what considerations warrant paying different remuneration to men and women who do essentially the same job.[68]

Value: Comparable Worth in the United Kingdom', 34 *American J. Comparative L.* 415 (1986).
61. Cf. *Rummler v. Dato-Druck Gmbh* (Case 237/85) [1987] 3 CMLR 127, regarding these techniques.
62. [1986] ILRM 483. 63. [1988] ILRM 53. 64. Id. at p.60.
65. *Pickstone v. Freemans p.l.c.* [1989] AC 66.
66. Anti-Discrimination (Pay) Act, 1974, s.2(3).
67. *Rinner-Kuhn v. FWW Spezial–Gebaudereinigung GmbH* (Case 171/89) [1989] IRL.R. 493
68. Ibid. *Kowalska v. City of Hamburg* (Case C – 33/89) [1992] ICR 29 (part-time workers), *Handels–Og Kontorfunktionaerernes Forbundi Danmark v. Dansk Arbejdsgiverfor-*

Transparency: In the *Danish Clerical Union* case,[69] the question arose of how to regard a remuneration system in which all employees were paid the same basic rates, regardless of sex, but when account was taken of various mobility, training and seniority allowances, men on average were paid significantly more than women. It was held that in these circumstances the E.C. Directive transferred the burden of proof on to the employer. Where an employer operates an opaque pay system, such that workers are unable to compare their wages because no reasons are given for pay differentials, and where there is a substantial difference between the average men's and women's wages, it is presumed that the Directive is being contravened. Accordingly, it is up to the employer in those circumstances to demonstrate that his remuneration arrangements are non-discriminatory.

Employment equality By employment equality in this context means that, in matters other than pay or remuneration, persons should not be discriminated against at work on account of their sex or their marital status. Although the E.E.C. Treaty does not refer to employment equality in this sense, in 1976 the E.C. Council adopted Directive No. 76/207 on equal treatment of the sexes in employment.[70] In the following year the Employment Equality Act, 1977, was enacted, which gives effect to this Directive. Unlike Article 119 of the Treaty, this Directive is not directly applicable in the Irish courts. However, to the extent, if any, that the 1977 Act does not implement the Directive's clear and specific requirements, they can be invoked in court against the State and other public agencies *qua* employer.[71]

The key provisions of the 1977 Act are ss.2 and 3. Section 2 defines discrimination as directly or indirectly treating a person less favourably than another on account of their sex or, if of the same sex, on account of their marital status. What discrimination is forbidden is defined in s.3; principally,

> an . . . employer . . . shall not discriminate against an employee or a prospective employee . . . in relation to access to employment, conditions of employment, . . . training or experience for or in relation to employment, promotion or re-grading in employment or classification of posts in employment.

forening (Case 109/88) [1991] 1 CMLR 8, *Enderby v. Frenchay Health Authority* [1991] ICR 382 (perpetuation of discriminatory arrangements in collective agreements), *Bank of Ireland v. Kavanagh* [1990] 1 CMLR 87, *A.C.O.T. v. Doyle* [1989] IR 33, *Rainey v. Greater Glasgow Health Board* [1987] AC 224.

69. *Handels-Og Kontorfunktionaerernes Forbund i Danmark v. Dansk Arbejdsgiverforforening* (Case 109/88) [1991] 1 CMLR 8.
70. O.J. No. L 39/40 (1976) [1990] 2 CMLR 833.
71. *Foster v. British Gas p.l.c.* (Case C-188/89) [1990] 2 CMLR 833.

The remainder of s.3 elaborates on this prohibition and the following section forbids sex discrimination by trade unions, by employers' organisations, by professional associations, by bodies offering vocational training, by employment agencies, in advertisements relating to employment and in collective agreements and employment contracts.

Personal scope: The 1974 Act applies to all private sector employment other than employments in a private residence or by a close relative.[72] Unlike the case with equal pay, this Act does not apply to self-employed persons who, under their contracts, must personally perform the work.[73] But the 1974 Act applies to the public service; an employee for its purpose is defined as including 'a civil servant of the State or of the Government and an officer or servant of a local authority . . . [or] of a harbour authority, health board, vocational education committee or committee of agriculture . . . .'[74] An exception, however, is made for the Defence Forces;[75] the Act does not apply to them but it can be extended to them by ministerial order. Before 1985 the Garda Síochána and the prison service were also excepted.

Focus of discrimination: The kinds of discriminatory action by an employer which are rendered unlawful are spelt out in detail in s.3 of the 1977 Act. Discrimination in relation to access to work, i.e. in hiring employees, is defined to include

> (a) any arrangements [made] for the purpose of deciding to whom [the employer] should offer employment, or
> (b) specifying, in respect of one person or class or persons, entry requirements for employment which are not specified in respect of other persons or classes of persons where the circumstances in which both such persons or classes would be employed are not materially different.[76]

Discrimination in relation to employment conditions does not include pay or pensions but is defined to include if the employer

> does not offer or afford to a person or class of persons the same terms

---

72. Ss.1(1) and 12(1)(d).
73. There is an E.C. Directive on sex discrimination against the self-employed: Directive 86/631, O.J. No. L 359/56 (1986). Contrast the position in Britain: *Mirror Group Newspapers p.l.c. v. Gunning* [1985] 1 WLR 394.
74. S.1(1). Cf. *E.C. Commission v. United Kingdom* (Case 165/82) [1983] ECR 3431.
75. S.12(1)(a). Cf. *Johnston v. Chief Constable of the R.U.C.* (Case 222/84) [1986] ECR 165 and *Re Sex Discrimination in the Civil Service* (Case 318/86) [1989] 3 CMLR 663.
76. S.3(3).

of employment . . ., the same working conditions and the same treatment in relation to overtime, shift work, short time, transfers, lay-offs, redundancies, dismissals . . . and disciplinary measures as he offers or affords to another person or class of persons where the circumstances in which both such persons or classes are or would be employed are not materially different.[77]

Discrimination in relation to work training and experience is defined to include if the employer

refuses to offer or afford to that employee the same opportunities or facilities for employment counselling, training (whether on or off the job) and work experience as he offers or affords to other employees where the circumstances in which that employee and those other employees are employed are not materially different.[78]

Discrimination in relation to promotion opportunities is defined to include where an employer

offers or affords [an] employee access to opportunities for promotion in circumstances in which another eligible and qualified person is offered or afforded such access or if in those circumstances he refuses or deliberately omits to offer or afford that employee access to opportunities for promotion.[79]

Classifying a job by reference to sex[80] and also advertising a job in such way as indicates an intention or even a probability of discrimination[81] is proscribed. Discrimination in connection with 'vocational training', as defined in s.6 of the Act, is also forbidden; this applies to any person or any educational or training body offering a course of vocational training.

As well as excluding from its scope questions of remuneration, the 1977 Act does not apply to 'any term relating to an occupational pension scheme.'[82] It was held by the European Court that the rules of a pension scheme whereby women reach pensionable age and must then resign earlier than men contravened the Equal Treatment Directive.[83]

In order to make out a case of unlawful discrimination against an employer, the complainant must first show that, in respect of any of the above matters, she was treated less favourably than a man in the same or similar circumstances; or if the complainant is a man, that he was treated differently from a woman in like circumstances; or if the basis of the

77. S.3(4).   78. S.3(5).   79. S.3(6).
80. S.3(7).   81. S.8.   82. S.3(4).
83. *Beets Proper v. F. van Lanschot Bankiers N.V.* (Case 262/84) [1986] ECR 773.

complaint is marital status, that a person of the same sex as the complainant but of a different marital status was treated differently in like circumstances. Once differential treatment has been established it must then be shown that the reason for it was the complainant's sex or marital status. Throughout the burden of proof lays on the complainant, but the standard of proof is on the balance of probabilities.[84] Once a prima facie or plausible case of discrimination has been made out, it then falls on the employer to explain why he acted in that manner. Statistical evidence which shows a strong probability of discrimination may be enough to call for a satisfactory explanation from an employer. Sexual harassment at work can contravene the 1977 Act.[85]

Direct discrimination: Direct discrimination here connotes action whereby an employee is overtly 'treated less favourably' on account of his or her sex or marital status.[86] Examples include refusing to hire a person because she is a woman or requiring women employees to leave the job whenever they get married. The contrast is with indirect discrimination, where the action in question is not patently discriminatory but it gives rise to significant discriminatory consequences; the end result of the action is to produce discrimination. Both forms of discrimination are forbidden by s.2 of the 1977 Act.

Since neither the terms 'by reason of sex' and 'because of his marital status' are defined, it is far from clear whether the Act prohibits action by employers and others which is prompted by the employee's pregnancy, or being bisexual or homosexual, or because the employee is divorced. The hostility to homosexuality articulated by some judges[87] and the constitutional ban on divorce[88] probably precludes those two grounds falling within the 1977 Act in the foreseeable future. Courts in several countries have differed on the question whether distinctions made because of a person's pregnancy constitutes sex discrimination as such.[89] Since only women become pregnant, that distinction would usually amount to indirect discrimination. As is explained below, there are special statutory provisions which protect women who are or have been pregnant. In the *Dekker* case,[90] where the defendant refused to hire the plaintiff on account of her preg-

---

84. Cf. *Wallace v. South Eastern Education & Library Board* [1980] NI 38.
85. Cf. *Parcelli v. Strathclyde Regional Council* [1986] ICR 564.
86. S.2(a). See generally *Curtin*, ch.7.
87. *Norris v. Attorney General* [1984] IR 36.
88. Art. 41,3,iii.
89. E.g. *General Electric Co. v Gilbert*, 429 US 125 (1976).
90. *Dekker v. Stichting Vormingscentrum Voor Jonge Volwassen* (Case 177/88 [1991] IRLR 27.

nancy, the European Court held that there was direct discrimination in breach of the Directive. Where the most important reason for refusing to employ or to dismiss a person is something which applies exclusively to one sex, the Directive is broken. No justification, not even the financial detriment the employer may suffer, is permissible.

Genuine occupational qualification: Where the reason for the discrimination is shown to be 'an occupational qualification for the post' in question, the employer has a good defence.[91] There are certain types of work which, because of their very nature, should be segregated along sex lines; those kinds of work can only properly be done by persons of one particular sex. Indeed, there are many jobs which, under conventional sexual stereotyping, are regarded as either men's or women's work. But tradition is not the test under the 1977 Act; s.17(2) sets out a very limited category of cases where sex discrimination will be permitted. A person's married status is not one of these.

One is where the job involves entertainment and its performance would be very different if it were performed by a man or a woman, as the case may be. Thus, it is generally permissible to hire male actors for male parts; this perhaps may not be so for the leading 'boy' in the Christmas pantomime. Another is where the job demands a man's or a woman's physiology; for instance, a wet nurse or a sperm donor. But physical strength or stamina is not a sufficient ground; if strong and durable workers are being sought, both men and women must be considered. The occupational qualification defence exists where shared sleeping and sanitary accommodation is an essential feature of the job and it would be either unreasonable to expect an employer or impractical for him to provide separate accommodation for workers of each sex. Finally, if the job is 'likely to' involve working at some sex-segregated location abroad, the employer may discriminate on that basis; for instance, being sent to Saudi Arabia.

Indirect discrimination: Indirect discrimination is concerned with the discriminatory consequences or effects of an action rather than the act's inherent nature.[92] Indirect discrimination is concerned with actions which in form are perfectly fair and unobjectionable but which in fact operate to substantially disadvantage either men or women (married or unmarried), as the case may be. For example, a requirement that all applicants for a job be more than 6 feet high or weigh more than 11 stones is not on its face discriminatory; but its effect discriminates significantly because a far

---

91. S.17. See generally *Curtin*, ch.8.   92. See generally *Curtin*, ch.7.

smaller proportion of women than men can meet those requirements. The question is whether the requirement in question, in the light of present social and economic circumstances, is one which only a small number of persons of one sex or of one marital status can comply with. Thus, while there are women who can indeed meet the 6 feet or the 11 stones requirement, the vast majority of women cannot whereas a comparatively substantial proportion of men can meet those qualifications.

In the case of alleged discrimination on the grounds of marital status, the comparison is with persons of the same sex but who are unmarried or married, as the case may be. For instance, in *North Western Health Board v. Martyn*,[93] the complainant, a clerical officer with a Health Board, was compelled in 1967 by the 'marriage bar' to resign her full time job. She then got a part time job with the Board and, when the marriage bar was later abolished, she applied for a full time vacancy. Her application was rejected because she was older than the maximum age for applicants, being 28 years of age. In dealing with her claim for discrimination, the equality officer acted on the basis that far more women than men are disadvantaged by this age limit. It was held that that was the wrong approach; the focus should have been on whether the age requirement disadvantages far more married women in comparison to single women. It was also held that the equality officer should have acted on the basis of evidence and not just on widely-held assumptions about persons' behaviour.

Sections 3(2) and 2(c) of the 1977 Act prohibit indirect discrimination:

> An employer shall not, in relation to his employees or to employment by him, . . . apply or operate a practice which results or would be likely to [contravene this Act because it discriminates on the following grounds, viz.] where, because of his sex or marital status, a person is obliged to comply with a requirement, relating to employment . . . which is not an essential requirement for such employment . . . and in respect of which the proportion of persons of the other sex or (as the case may be) of a different marital status but of the same sex able to comply is substantially higher.

The practice being challenged must relate to employment, such as regarding access to the job, work conditions, training or experience, promotion, re-grading or classification of posts. Section 3(4) of the Act elaborates what aspects of employment are signified by the terms 'access', 'conditions' etc.[94] But questions of remuneration and any term relating to an occupational pension scheme fall outside the prohibition;[95] those matters are dealt with separately in rules regarding equal pay and pensions.

93. [1987] IR 565.   94. See supra pp.141-142   95. S.3(4).

In order to make out a case of indirect discrimination by an employer, it must first be shown that, in respect of any of the above matters, he is imposing some requirement; for instance, conditions regarding height or weight, age limits, forms of training. It must then be shown that a substantial proportion of women or men, married or unmarried, as the case may be, are not able to comply with that requirement. By being 'able to comply' here means that in practice most men or women, as the case may be, could not meet that requirement in the light of present day behaviour patterns. Exactly what proportion of men or women cannot satisfy whatever requirement is being challenged is not specified in the Act—whether 90%, 80%, 75% or what. It has been held that this particular matter must be established by evidence, which usually would involve use of statistics.

It must additionally be shown that such non-compliance is due to the person's sex or marital status. Merely because fewer men or women (married or unmarried), as the case may be, do not possess a particular required attribute does not suffice. The differential impact must be 'as a result of an attribute of a person's sex or the circumstance of a person's marital status that such persons are substantially more affected than persons of the other sex or of a different marital status . . . .'[96] For this reason, it was held that requiring possession of a full driving licence to be able to go on mobile patrol duties for the Revenue Commissioners was not unlawfully discriminatory, even though far more men than women hold licences.[97]

Essential requirement: Where the challenged requirement is shown to be 'essential' for the employment in question, it cannot then be discriminatory within the terms of the 1977 Act. If a *prima facie* case of discrimination is made out, the employer has good defence if he can demonstrate that, even though the requirement being challenged disproportionally burdens women or men (married or unmarried), as the case may be, that requirement nevertheless is absolutely essential in order to do the particular job.

Non-retrospective effects: It was held by the Supreme Court in *Aer Lingus v. The Labour Court*[98] that the 1977 Act does not have retrospective effect. The claimants there had been full time employees with Aer Lingus until they got married some time in the early 1970s. Because at that time the company operated a marriage bar for female employees, their jobs were terminated and they were paid a marriage gratuity. Subsequently, they were

96. *North Western Health Board v. Martyn* [1987] IR at p.577.
97. *Revenue Cmrs. v. Kelly* (EE 9/1987). On application of the 'last in, first out' principle, see *Australian Iron & Steel Pty. Ltd v. Banovic*, 64 ALJLR 53 (1990).
98. [1990] ILRM 485.

re-hired on a temporary basis. Eventually in 1980 they were re-hired permanently, but it was stipulated that their seniority should rank as from 1980. They claimed that they should have seniority from the time they were first employed by the company and that denying them that seniority, because they were forced to resign under the old marriage bar, discriminated against them on the basis of their marital status. That contention was rejected, on the grounds that the Act 'does not have retrospective effect' and that 'the original discrimination was exhausted and spent when it took effect.'[99] There was no suggestion that since the complainants were re-hired in 1980, they had been adversely treated because they were married, by comparison with the treatment of single women since that time.

MATERNITY

There are differences of view about whether distinctions made on the basis of pregnancy and its immediate aftermath are distinctions based on sex. The United States Supreme Court divided on this question,[1] with the majority holding that pregnancy was not a classification founded on sex, even though it is an attribute that only women can possess. But in the *Dekker* case,[2] the European Court came to the opposite conclusion; it held that when the most important reason for taking certain action is a reason which applies exclusively to persons of one sex, they are the subject of discrimination based on sex. If the plaintiff there had got the job she applied for her employer would suffer some adverse financial consequences in that its sickness insurance cover did not provide for confinement or any illness attributable to pregnancy. Because the refusal to hire her was found to be direct discrimination, in breach of the Equal Treatment Directive, that additional potential cost could not be a legal justification for the decision. In his conclusions to the Court, Advocate General Darmon remarked that 'the principles involved . . . ask the Court to decide on the place which we must give to maternity in a European society. For a long time economic life has been reserved to men and physiological differences between sexes did not have to be taken into account. This is no longer the case today. Now we must reconcile—with difficulty—the requirements of professional life with those of motherhood.'[3] Two related questions are posed by maternity in the workplace.

99. Id. at p.503.
1. *General Electric Co. v. Gilbert*, 429 US 125 (1976). See *Curtin*, pp.213-219.
2. *Dekker v. Stichting Vormingscentrum Voor Jonge Volwassen* (Case 177/88) [1991] IRLR 27.
3. Ibid.

Equality legislation Neither the Anti-Discrimination (Pay) Act, 1974, nor the Employment Equality Act, 1977, define the word 'sex', for the purpose of these Acts, as including pregnancy. Paying different remuneration to women who are and are not pregnant, doing like work, does not contravene the 1974 Act. It would seem, however, that paying a pregnant woman less than the sum paid to a man doing like work contravenes the equal pay rule, except where the differential treatment comes within the 'grounds other than sex' defence. Having different employment terms and conditions, other than pay, for men and for pregnant women does not constitute direct discrimination under the 1977 Act if distinctions based on pregnancy are not regarded as differences on the grounds of sex. However, the terms of s.16 of this Act suggest that the legislature regarded pregnancy-based discrimination as falling within the prohibition. This view is now fortified by the *Dekker* case, which most likely would be followed when construing s.16. In any event, subject to s.16, such treatment would constitute indirect discrimination, except where it is 'essential' for the job that the employee is not pregnant.

Section 16 of this Act makes an exception to the equality requirement by permitting arrangements which advance the interests of pregnant women; that

> Nothing in this Act shall make it unlawful for an employer to arrange for or provide special treatment to women in connection with pregnancy or childbirth.

Although it is not stated, the 'special treatment' referred to here must be in order to accommodate the woman's needs and not simply be to make life different for her. What constitutes 'special treatment' for these purposes does not seem to have been authoritatively determined. Under the E.C. Equal Treatment Directive, the derogation from the equality principle exists for pregnancy and 'maternity'.[4] But an equality officer in one instance declined to interpret s.16 as extending to the immediate aftermath of pregnancy.[5]

Maternity leave The Maternity Protection of Employees Act, 1981, entitles qualified women to take leave from their jobs during their pregnancy and to return to work on the expiry of their maternity leave. Whereas s.16 of the 1977 Act (above) permits employers to have voluntary maternity leave arrangements, the 1981 Act goes further by giving women the right to obtain unpaid maternity leave. This Act applies to all insured employees

4. Cf. *Hofman v. Barmer Ersatzkasse* (Case 184/83) [1984] ECR 3047.
5. *Aer Rianta* (EE 11/1987).

and to a wide range of office-holders in the public service, as well as to employed ministers of religion and to those employed on fishing vessels who take a share of the profit.[6] But some employees and office-holders are not covered by the Act, most notably those who are permanently employed for less than 8 hours in each week and those who are employed under fixed term contracts with a duration of less than 26 weeks.[7]

Fourteen weeks' leave: The minimum period of maternity leave is fourteen consecutive weeks.[8] Employers are not required by the 1981 Act to pay remuneration during that period. But the employee may qualify for the social welfare maternity benefit, which is relatively generous. When that period is to commence and end is a matter for the employee to determine, provided the period commences at least four weeks before the anticipated date of confinement and the period ends at least four weeks following that date.[9] However, if a medical practitioner so certifies, this minimum period shall commence at a date outside the limits just stated.[10] Additionally, these limits do not apply where the confinement occurred more that four weeks before the anticipated date of confinement; in such a case, the minimum period is extended.

These rights are contingent on the employer being duly notified in advance of the employee's decision.[11] To begin with, as soon as possible, but at least four weeks before the chosen commencement date, the employee must notify the employer of her decision to take maternity leave and must give the employer a certificate confirming the pregnancy and specifying the expected date of confinement and how long the leave she intends taking. Where the confinement occurred more than four weeks before the anticipated date, fourteen days' advanced notice suffices.[12] Where the confinement occurs a week or more later than the anticipated date and the employee wants to extend the period, she must as soon as possible notify the employer of her intentions and, following the confinement, must confirm in writing her decision to take extra leave and specify the duration of that extention.[13]

Additional four weeks' leave: An employee may choose to take four additional consecutive weeks' unpaid leave immediately after the normal maternity leave comes to an end.[14] This right is contingent on her employer being notified in writing of her intention to take leave, at least four weeks before her ordinary maternity leave was due to expire.

6. Definition of 'employee' in s.2(1).
7. Definition of 'employer' in s.2(1), as amended in 1991.
8. S.8.   9. S.10.   10. S.11.
11. S.9.   12. S.13(1).   13. S.12(2).   14. S.14.

Time off for ante-natal and post-natal care: The employee is also entitled to time off work for the purpose of receiving ante-natal and post-natal care.[15] Regulations on those questions were published in 1981.[16]

Return to work: On completion of the maternity leave or additional leave, the employee is entitled to return to work in the same job and under the same terms as she had before taking the leave.[17] If in the intervening period the ownership of the undertaking where she was employed changed hands, she is entitled to return to the same job and on the same terms with the successor employer.[18] Where it is 'not reasonably practical' for her to be reinstated in her old job, she is entitled to 'a suitable alternative employment' with her employer or a successor employer.[19] In that event, the job must be one that is suitable for her and appropriate to her circumstances, and the terms and conditions must not be substantially less favourable than those she previously had. If she was not doing her normal job at the time she took the leave, she is entitled to get back her normal job as soon as is practicable after her leave expired. If, for some reason or another, there was an interruption or cesser of work at her place of employment at the time she was due to return to work and it would be unreasonable in the circumstances to expect her to come back to work, she may return when work has resumed at the place or as soon as is reasonably practical after that.[20]

In order to become entitled to return to work as provided for here, the employee must have given notice in writing of her intention and the date she expects to return; notice must be given at least four weeks before that date.[21] This requirement is mandatory.[23]

Status during absence and leave: An employee who is absent on normal maternity leave is deemed to be still in employment,[24] except that the 1981 Act does not require that she be paid remuneration. Apart from that, her absence does not affect any rights she may possess under her contract, by statute or otherwise. If she takes the additional leave, she is not deemed to be employed for that extra period, but this absence does not break her continuity of employment.[25] Being absent on maternity or on additional leave is not to be treated as part of any other form of leave to which she is entitled, for instance, annual holidays or sick leave.[26]

15. S.16.   16. SI No. 358 of 1981.   17. S.20(1).
18. S.20(1)(a) and (c).   19. S.21.   20. S.23.   21. S.22.
23. *Ivory v. Ski-Line Ltd* [1988] IR 399 and *Lavery v. Plessey Telecommunications Ltd* [1983] ICR 534.
24. S.15(1).   25. S.15(2).   26. S.15(4).

Resignation: Not alone can an employee taking maternity or additional leave or time off not be dismissed or suspended from work during that period, but she is not allowed to resign during those times. Any notice of termination or purported termination of her contract during those periods is declared void.[27]

Dismissal A dismissal notice or a purported dismissal occurring while the employee is on maternity leave or taking time off is void and ineffective.[28] If she was served with a dismissal notice before she took the leave or time off, which was due to expire while she was absent, the length of that notice is extended by the period she was absent.[29] A dismissal on the grounds of pregnancy, or because the employee exercised her rights under the 1981 Act, is generally an unfair dismissal under the Unfair Dismissals Act, 1977. The main features of the 1977 Act are considered in Chapter Eight but it is convenient to treat pregnancy and maternity-related dismissals here.

In the case of an employee who qualified for protection under the 1977 Act,[30] there is a very strong presumption that her dismissal is unfair if it 'result[ed] wholly or mainly from [her] pregnancy . . . or matters connected therewith. . . .'[31] Whether what caused the employer to dismiss her was her pregnancy or some other reason depends on the facts.[32] In a well known case where a pregnant and unmarried primary school teacher employed in a convent school was dismissed, it was held that her pregnancy as such was not the reason for her dismissal.[33] Even if the dismissal was on account of pregnancy, the employer has a defence to a claim under the 1977 Act if he can show the following. Because of her pregnancy or related matters, she must have been unable adequately to do the job for which she was employed or the employer would have been in breach of some statutory obligation if he continued employing her. In addition, the employer had no vacancy suitable for her or she was offered another job on corresponding terms and conditions, so that she could be retained by the employer, but she refused the offer.

An employee whose dismissal 'result[ed] wholly or mainly' from exercising any of her rights under the Maternity Protection of Employees Act, 1981, is deemed to have been unfairly dismissed, except where the employer can point to some exceptional and overwhelming justification.[34] In order to

27. S.17.   28. Ibid.   29. S.18.
30. See post pp.193-196.   31. 1977 Act s.6(2)(f).
32. Cf. *Dekker*, supra n.1, *Handles – OG Kontorfunktionaererernes Forbund Danmark v. Dansk Arbeidgiverforening* (Case 109/88) [1991] 1 CMLR 8 and *Brown v. Stockton on Tees B.C.* [1989] AC 20.
33. *Flynn v. Power* [1985] IR 648.
34. 1977 Act, s.6(2)(g), inserted by Maternity etc. Act, 1981, s.25.

succeed in a claim on those grounds, the claimant need not have been continually employed for more than a year by that employer. Probationers, trainees and apprentices also can claim under the 1977 Act on these grounds, but an employee who had not given the requisite four weeks' written notice of her intention to return to work does not benefit from the protection from dismissal.[35] In the case of such an employee, whether her dismissal was unfair depends on all the circumstances of the case and the general considerations applicable under the 1977 Act.

35. *Ivory v. Ski-Line Ltd* [1988] IR 399.

7

Termination of employment

The termination of employment, especially termination at the employer's insistence (dismissal from employment), causes far more litigation than any other aspect of the employment relationship. Although disputes will arise when the relationship is subsisting, often those differences are resolved by negotiation, either between the parties directly or with the assistance of one or more trade unions. But when an employee resigns or an employer purports to dismiss an employee, the parties may have reached confrontation point. Where a dismissed employee may suffer a significant loss of earnings and indeed be faced with a prolonged period of unemployment, he will be inclined to challenge his dismissal, either in court or through industrial action. This chapter considers the various common law rules regarding termination of a job, especially by dismissal. The next chapter then looks at the elaborate set of statutory restrictions and rights, established mainly in the last 25 years, affecting dismissal.

MODES OF TERMINATION

The employment relationship can be brought to an end by either the agreement of the parties, the unilateral act of one of them, in the form of a dismissal or a resignation, or by operation of law, which can take several forms.[1]

Agreement The employment contract can come to an end through the agreement of the parties. If the contract is for a particular task, once that task has been done the contract will have been performed. Similarly, if the contract is for a specified period, the contract comes to an end when that time has elapsed. Although termination following performance of a specific task or on the expiry of a fixed term is not a dismissal, those terminations are often characterised by legislation as dismissals, thereby attracting certain statutory protection.

1. See generally, M.R. Freedland, *The Contact of Employment* (1976) chs. 5-9 (hereinafter referred to as *Freedland*).

With regard to contracts which are terminable on giving notice, either by the employer or the employee, the parties may agree that the contract shall be terminated. Sometimes that agreement is made subject to a period elapsing before termination occurs. Alternatively, the employee may be paid a sum in lieu of notice on the understanding that the relationship shall come to an end forthwith or the parties may agree to immediate termination without any payment being made. At times, disputes arise regarding whether the employee indeed resigned or was forced to resign, because forcible resignation is in law and in fact a dismissal. The answer will depend on the entire circumstances of the case—whether the employee's action was truly voluntary or whether he was virtually compelled to resign.[2]

Dismissal A dismissal is a unilateral termination of the contract by the employer; by word or by deed, the employer tells the employee that their relationship has or shall come to an end. Where the employer did not give the agreed notice of dismissal, he repudiates his most fundamental obligation under the contract, which is to pay wages in return for work done. Usually, the employee will accept that repudiation, in the sense of accepting that the relationship has come to an end, although he may well bring an action for damages for wrongful dismissal. Generally, an unequivocal dismissal puts an end to the legal relationship there and then. Exceptionally, a dismissed employee may take the view that the legal relationship has not ended; in that event, the contract will still subsist until the proper period of notice expires,[3] although this state of affairs affords few practical benefits to the employee.

Repudiation As well as in cases of outright dismissals and forced resignations, an employer repudiates the contract, for example, by not paying any remuneration for a period when the employee was at work, by unilaterally reducing the remuneration it was agreed would be payable,[4] by unilaterally changing the entire nature of the job[5] or the place where[6] or times during when[7] it was agreed the work was to be performed. The

2. Cf. *Birch v. University of Liverpool* [1985] ICR 470.
3. *Gunton v. Richmond-Upon-Thames L.B.C.* [1981] Ch. 448.
4. *Rigby v. Ferodo Ltd* [1988] ICR 29. Cf. *Hogg v. Dover College* [1990] ICR 39 and *Murco Petroleum Ltd v. Forge* [1987] ICR 282.
5. *Woods v. W.M. Car Services (Peterborough) Ltd* [1982] ICR 693, *Norwest Holst Group Administration Ltd v. Harrison* [1985] ICR 668 and *Lewis v. Motorworld Garages Ltd* [1986] ICR 158.
6. *Courtaulds Northern Spinning Ltd v. Sibson* [1988] ICR 451, *Jones v. Associated Tunnelling Ltd* [1981] IRLR 477 and *O'Brien v. Associated Fire Alarms Ltd* [1986] 1 WLR 1916.
7. Cf. *Hogg v. Dover College* [1990] ICR 39.

question is whether the employer has broken or has threatened to break one of the main terms of the contract. It has been held, for instance, that there was repudiation where, when there was a severe break down of personal relationships between employees, their employer insisted that one of them, a consultant surgeon, underwent a psychiatric examination and then suspended him for refusing to do so.[8] In the circumstances, the employer had no reasonable cause to insist on that examination and, by doing so, the employer had acted 'in a manner calculated or likely to destroy or seriously damage the relationship of confidence or trust between [them].'[9] The question of employer repudiation has become particularly significant in legislation regarding dismissal, through the concept of 'constructive dismissal', that is if an employee leaves a job in response to a repudiation by the employer, the employee is deemed for the purposes of the Act in question to have been dismissed.

However, except where there has been an unequivocal dismissal or a forced resignation, the employer's repudiation as such does not put an end to the contract. Thus, in *Rigby v. Ferodo Ltd*,[10] when the plaintiff's employer was in serious financial difficulties, it unilaterally imposed wage reductions on the workforce. The plaintiff sued for damages, while remaining in the job. According to Lord Oliver, the basic principle is that

> the unilateral imposition by an employer of a reduction in the agreed remuneration of an employee constitutes a fundamental and repudiatory breach of the contract of employment which, if accepted by the employee, would terminate the contract forthwith. . . . [But], as a general rule, an unaccepted repudiation leaves the contractual obligations of the parties unaffected. . . .
>
> Whatever may be the position under a contract of service where the repudiation takes the form either of a walk out by the employee or of a refusal by the employer any longer to regard the employee as his servant, [there is] no principle of law that any breach which the innocent party is entitled to treat as repudiatory of the other party's obligations brings the contract to an end automatically.[11]

The repudiatory conduct may be on the part of the employee and not the employer. In that case the same principles as just explained apply. If the employee unambiguously leaves the job then, generally, that operates to terminate the contract there and then. But other breaches of the contract, no matter how fundamental they are, do not bring it to an end. The employer

---

8. *Bliss v. South East Thames Regional Health Authority* [1987] ICR 700.
9. Id. at p.715.   10. [1988] ICR 29.   11. Id. at pp.33 and 34.

always has the option of either accepting the repudiation, thereby treating the contract as ended or, alternatively, chosing to continue that relationship. According to Templeman LJ in *London Transport Executive v. Clarke*,[12] a case where the employee deliberately absented himself from work for seven weeks,

> If a worker walks out of his job or commits any other breach of contract, repudiatory or otherwise, but at any time claims that he is entitled to resume or to continue his work, then his contract of employment is only determined if the employer expressly or impliedly asserts and accepts repudiation on the part of the worker. Acceptance can take the form of formal writing or can take the form of refusing to allow the worker to resume or continue his work. . . . [T]he acceptance by an employer of repudiation by a worker who wishes to continue his employment notwithstanding his repudiatory conduct constitutes the determination of the contract of employment by the employer.[13]

An employee who does not perform his work because he is serving a prison sentence has not repudiated his contract—except were the very terms of the contract require that he not put himself in jeopardy of being imprisoned or otherwise similarly detained.[14] However, prolonged imprisonment may in the circumstances bring the contract to an end by way of frustration.[15]

Frustration One of the fundamental rules of the law of contract is that a contract will be discharged by frustration; if circumstances arise that amount to frustration, the contract automatically comes to an end. Frustration arises where performance of the contract becomes impossible, such as by the death of either of the parties,[16] or where performance becomes illegal. The underlying principle was formulated as follows:

> frustration occurs whenever the law recognises that without default of either party a contractual obligation has become incapable of being performed because the circumstances in which performance is called for would render it a thing radically different from that which was undertaken by the contract. *Non haec in foedera veni*. It was not this that I promised to do. . . . [I]t is not hardship or inconvenience or material loss itself which calls the principle of frustration into play. There must be as well such a change in the significance of the

12. [1981] ICR 355.   13. Id. at p.368.
14. *F.C. Shepherd & Co. Ltd v. Jerrom* [1987] 1 QB 301.   15. Infra.
16. Cf. Redundancy Payments Act, 1967, schedule 2.

obligation that the thing undertaken would, if performed, be a different thing from that contracted for.[17]

Thus, if either of the parties become physically or legally incapable of performing their obligations under the contract, it is frustrated and they no longer have any legal obligations under it.

In determining whether an employment contract has been frustrated,[18] it is often necessary to construe its terms—to ascertain precisely what obligations were assumed and in what circumstances the parties had undertaken them. That exercise in construction may demonstrate that the parties either did or did not intend that their obligations should continue in the light of the event in question. According to Hanna J in *Herman v. Owners of the S.S. Vica*, 'frustration depends on the terms of the contract and the surrounding circumstances of each case, as some kinds of impossibility may not discharge the contract at all.'[19] That case concerned seamen who had been hired to serve on a Finnish registered ship during World War II. For about six months the ship had the protection of a British ship's warrant and when that was not renewed the owners were assured by British shipping agents that its ship would not be seized by the British authorities. The ship arrived in Dublin three months after diplomatic relations between Britain and Finland were broken off. Some weeks later the master paid off the crew, claiming that the imminence of war between Britain and Finland rendered further performance of their contracts practically impossible. Two weeks later, war was declared between the two countries. The plaintiffs sued for breach of the express term in their contracts that they would be repatriated at their employers' expense at the end of their service. It was held that their contracts had not been frustrated in the circumstances obtaining when the crew were discharged; at that time it was not obvious that the ship would probably be seized by the British on leaving port. In any event, even if there were frustration then, that could not affect the 'accrued right [to be repatriated], vested in the seamen under their contracts before the alleged frustration'.[20]

In another war-time seamen's case, *Byrne v. Limerick S.S. Co. Ltd*,[21] the plaintiff was discharged by the master in Dublin because the British shipping authorities did not give him clearance when the crew list was submitted to them. Overend J accepted that it was 'impossible, from a practical point of view, to undertake this voyage save under the aegis and with the facilities afforded by the British.'[22] Nevertheless, the contract was not frustrated

17. *Davis Contractors Ltd v. Fareham U.D.C.* [1956] AC 696, at p.729.
18. See generally, *Freedland*, ch.8.   19. [1942] IR 305, at p.321.
20. Id. at p.325.   21. [1946] IR 138.
22. Id. at p.149.

because, 'where an essential licence or permission is refused, the defendants must prove that they have taken all reasonable steps to have such refusal withdrawn.'[23] In the circumstances here, it was probable that the refusal to give clearance for the plaintiff would have been revoked had the owners seriously questioned the British authorities' decision.[24]

Destruction of the workplace: One of the earliest cases to recognise the doctrine of frustration in the law of contract concerned the destruction of the very subject matter of the contract; in that instance a music hall which the defendant had agreed to make available for four days for concerts.[25] Whether destruction, through fire or whatever, of the workplace automatically puts an end to the contracts of those employed there depends on the nature of the employer's business, the resources available to him and to the terms of the contracts. There are no leading modern authorities that deal with the application of the principle in this situation.

Employee's illness: An employee's illness can result in his employment contract being terminated by frustration but whether illness has that effect depends on the nature of the job and the terms of the contract. If an employee is hired for a task to be performed at a particular time but then falls ill at that very time, the contract will be automatically terminated.[26] By contrast, if the job is permanent and the employee falls ill for a few days or indeed for several weeks, the contract will subsist. Terms of employment for permanent posts usually contain express provisions regarding illness. In the case of the vast majority of employment contracts, which are terminable at comparatively short notice, there is a view that the doctrine of frustration, at least in the context of the employee's disability, has no application. It has been observed that '[i]n the employment field the concept of discharge by operation of law, that is frustration, is normally only in play where the contract of employment is for a long term which cannot be determined by notice.'[27] But this view has also been rejected in England, where it has been held that, 'the mere fact that the contract can be terminated by the employer by relatively short notice cannot of itself render the doctrine of frustration inevitably inapplicable.'[28]

In many of the instances where an employer is contending that a contract

23. Ibid.
24. Compare *Horlock v. Beale* [1916] 1 AC 486.
25. *Taylor v. Caldwell* (1863) 3 B & S 826.
26. E.g. *Poussard v. Spiers* (1876) 1 QBD. 410.
27. *Harman v. Flexible Lamps Ltd* [1980] IRLR 418, at p.419.
28. *Notcutt v. Universal Equipment Co. (London) Ltd* [1986] 1 WLR 641, at p.646.

was terminated by frustration, the employer would be seeking to dismiss an employee who became ill and wants to avoid statutory obligations that arise in dismissal situations (e.g. compensation for unfair dismissal or a redundancy award) by claiming that the contract was terminated by way of frustration and not by way of dismissal. Because of this, generally the illness would need to be serious and lengthy before it would be characterised as bringing about frustration. In Britain the Employment Appeals Tribunal has formulated criteria for determining when an employment contract is frustrated on account of illness.[29] The central consideration is whether, looked at before the purported dismissal, the employee's incapacity was of such a nature, or did the illness appear likely to continue for such a period, that further performance of his obligations in the future would either be impossible or would be a thing radically different from that undertaken by him and accepted by the employer under the agreed terms of his employment.[30]

Employee's imprisonment: An employee's imprisonment or other form of compulsory detention can also cause his employment contract to be frustrated.[31] It would be very rare for one week's imprisonment to have this effect but commencement of a long sentence almost always would bring the contract to an end.[32] Occasionally, employers treat the event of imprisonment as putting an end to the relationship without having to follow contractual dismissal procedures or complying with statutory rules applicable to dismissals.[33] In determining whether there was indeed frustration, all depends on the anticipated duration of the detention, the nature of the job and the terms of the contract.[34]

Dissolution of partnership: Generally, the dissolution of a partnership will put an end to employment contracts with the partnership. As stated in *Lindley*, the principle is that

> if the contract is of a personal character, to be performed by the individuals who have entered into it, or is dependent on the personal skill or honesty of the individual partners, a change in the firm will determine the contract by rendering its performance impossible. If on

29. *Marshall v. Harland & Wolff Ltd* [1972] 1 WLR 899, *Egg Stores (Stamford Hill) Ltd v. Leibovici* [1977] ICR 260 and *Hart v. A.R. Marshall & Sons (Bulwell) Ltd* [1977] 1 WLR 1067.
30. See *Flynn v. Great Northern Rly. Co. (Ir.) Ltd*, 89 ILTR 46 (1955) at pp.59-60.
31. E.g. *Morgan v. Manser* [1948] 1 KB 184.
32. E.g. *F.C. Shepherd & Co. v. Jerrom* [1987] 1 QB 301.
33. Ibid. and *Hare v. Murphy Bros. Ltd* [1974] 3 All ER 940.
34. Ibid. Cf. *Chakki v. United Yeast Co. Ltd* [1982] ICR 140.

the other hand, upon a true construction of the particular contract, it is determined that the party contracting with the partnership was intending that the contract should be performed by the partnership as from time to time constituted, then a change in the firm would not *per se* automatically determine the contract or constitute a breach of it. This is a pure question of the construction of each particular contract and no general principles can be laid down in relation thereto.[35]

Receivership and liquidation: Undoubtedly the actual dissolution of a company when the winding up procedure has been completed will cause the employment contracts of any of its remaining employees come to an end. But the actual commencement of a receivership or a liquidation does not automatically terminate the enterprises' employment contracts. The position, briefly,[36] is that the appointment by the court of a receiver operates as a dismissal of the employees but the appointment of a receiver by the debenture-holders does not usually have this effect. Similarly, a compulsory liquidation operates as a dismissal of the employees but commencement of a voluntary liquidation usually does not have that effect. This matter is considered in some detail in Chapter Ten, which deals with an employer's insolvency.

NOTICE OF TERMINATION

At common law, provided the requisite notice of termination was given or the salary in lieu of that notice was paid, the employer can dismiss and the employee can resign for any reason.[37] It was primarily to reduce abuses of the employer's common law prerogative to dismiss for any reason whatsoever that the Unfair Dismissals Act, 1977, was enacted.[38] Statutory protection aside, dismissal from employment in certain circumstances can constitute breach of the employee's constitutional rights, although the application of the Constitution to dismissals by private sector employers is largely unexplored terrain.

Notifying resignation The employment contract may stipulate, expressly or by implication, how much notice an employee must give of his intention to resign from his job. Absent such stipulation, reasonable notice must be

---

35. *Lindley on Partnership* (15th ed. 1984) p.50. See *Briggs v. Oates* [1990] ICR 473.
36. For details, see post pp.233-234.
37. See generally, *Freedland*, ch. 5.   38. Discussed post p.192 et seq.

provided; it depends on all the circumstances how long is reasonable notice in any particular case. An employee who is in a job for longer than thirteen weeks has a statutory obligation to give at least one week's notice of his resignation.[39]

Dismissal notice One of the terms of every employment contract will concern how much notice the employer must give in order lawfully to terminate the contract, be it an hour's notice, a day, a week, a month or whatever. Where the contract is written, almost invariably one of its express terms will deal with notice of termination. Where there is no express term then the court, if called upon, will have to imply a term. One of the particulars that s.9 of the Minimum Notice etc. Act, 1973, requires to be furnished to new employees are 'the period of notice which the employee is obliged to give and entitled to receive to determine his contract of employment. . . .'[40] Notice periods may be dealt with in a collective agreement applicable to the job.

Where the contract does not state or indicate how much notice an employer must give to terminate it, the courts hold that the employee must be given reasonable notice. If the employee is being dismissed for a very serious breach of contract on his part, he is not entitled to any notice. Otherwise, the duration of the requisite notice will depend on the nature of the job and other terms of the contract. Persons in well paid and prestigious jobs are entitled to relatively lengthy notices. In an instance in 1966, the managing director of a small bank was held entitled to one year's notice;[41] in a case in 1940 a teacher was held to be entitled to six months' notice.[42] Under the Minimum Notice etc. Act, 1973, there is a statutory minimum, notice period, ranging from one week to eight weeks, depending on the employee's length of service.[43]

Permanent employment The fact that a job is described as permanent or as permanent and pensionable does not mean that it cannot be terminated by reasonable notice. According to Budd J in *Walsh v. Dublin Health Authority*,

> The word 'permanent' has various shades of meaning. Generally, it means something lasting, as distinct from temporary. In the case of a contract of service, a person may be said in one sense of the word to be 'permanently' employed when he is employed for an indefinite

---

39. Minimum Notice and Terms and Conditions of Employment Act, 1973, s.6.
40. S.9(1)(f).
41. *Carvill v. Irish Industrial Bank Ltd* [1968] IR 325.
42. *McDonnell v. Minister for Education* [1940] IR 316.　　43. S.4; see post p.190.

period on the regular staff of the employer, as distinct from persons taken on casually or for a temporary or defined period. That does not necessarily mean that such a person has a contract of employment for life. On the other hand a person may be given 'permanent' and pensionable employment in the sense that under his contract he holds his employment for life or for life subject to the right of his employer to dismiss him for misconduct, neglect of duty or unfitness or again it may mean that his employment is to last until he reaches full pensionable age, subject to the rights of the employer just mentioned. As to what is meant, and should be implied as being in the contemplation of the parties, depends upon the true construction of the whole contract viewed in the light of the surrounding circumstances and all relevant matters.[44]

In that case it was held that a carpenter, employed by a hospital on a permanent and pensionable basis, could be dismissed from his job on being given reasonable notice. In the circumstances, the description of the job did not mean that he could not be dismissed, before retirement age, other than for misconduct.

But there are cases where it was held that the employer's freedom to dismiss was so restricted by the terms of the contract. In *McLoughlin v. Great Southern Railways Co.*,[45] the employer gave the Minister for Transport an undertaking not to dismiss specified staff, except for misconduct, and then only after following a grievance procedure. That undertaking was assented to by the plaintiff's trade union. Since he fell within the category of staff specified, the company was held to be precluded from dismissing him before retirement age other than for misconduct.[46] Similarly in *Grehan v. North Eastern Health Board*,[47] the plaintiff was a medical practitioner employed on terms which had been negotiated by the Dept. of Health and the Irish Medical Organisation. The contract's terms contained detailed provisions on dismissal, but did not say that the plaintiff could be dismissed on reasonable notice. Costello J refused to imply into the contract a term to that effect, principally because its terms relating to termination were very detailed and their comprehensive nature would strongly suggest that an implication of a further term, relating to the parties' right of termination, would not be justified. A narrowly divided House of Lords came to the same conclusion in *McClelland v. Northern Ireland General Health Service Board*,[48] where the plaintiff, a clerk employed by a Health Board, was given

44. 98 ILTR 82 (1964), at pp.86-87.   45. [1944] IR 479.
46. Constrast *Flynn v. Great Northern Rly. Co. (Ir.) Ltd*, 89 ILTR 46 (1955).
47. [1989] IR 422.   48. [1957] 1 WLR 594.

six months notice of dismissal because she got married. As in the *Grehan* case, the contract contained detailed terms regarding termination. It was held that these provisions 'all contain express powers of termination and... there is no ground for suggesting that it is necessary to imply a further power to terminate the contract in order to give [it] the efficacy which the parties must have intended it to have.'[49] Accordingly, 'so long as she did not render herself liable to dismissal on one or other of the grounds expressly stated in her contract and was willing and able to serve the Board, [she] was entitled to continue in her employment for her life.'[50]

Generally, therefore, where the contract sets out in some detail the circumstances in which it may be terminated by either party but does not state that the employer may dismiss on giving a specified period of notice or reasonable notice, the tendency is against implying a term to that effect. One of the decisive considerations in the *McClelland* case was that both parties regarded the job as in fact as secure as the civil service. And in the *Grehan* case, Costello J referred to the fact that the terms of the relevant collective agreement must have been the subject of protracted negotiations and, therefore, the reasonable inference was that the parties did not intend to confer a right to dismiss on giving reasonable notice.

SUMMARY DISMISSAL

Employers possess a common law right of summary dismissal, in the sense of dismissing an employee without giving him the requisite notice.[51] This power is exercisable in circumstances where the contract expressly authorises summary dismissal. It can also be exercised where the employee is guilty of serious misconduct, unless the contract precludes its exercise in the circumstances in question.

Serious misconduct Where the employment contract does not specify the grounds for summary dismissal, what constitutes serious misconduct for these purposes depends on the nature of the job in question and the terms of the contract. Certain actions almost invariably would be regarded as serious misconduct, like deliberately destroying the employer's valuable property, stealing from the employer and gross insubordination.[52] Often the line is difficult to draw between what misconduct justifies summary dis-

---

49. Id. at p.599.   50. Id. at p.613.
51. See generally, *Freedland*, ch.6.
52. E.g. *Pepper v Webb* [1969] 1 WLR 514 and *Blyth v Scottish Liberal Club* (1982) SC 140.

missal and what calls at most for temporary suspension or a severe warning or reprimand. According to Kenny J in *Glover v. B.L.N. Ltd*,

> It is impossible to define the misconduct which justifies immediate dismissal. . . . There is no fixed rule of law defining the degree of misconduct which will justify dismissal. . . . What is or is not misconduct must be decided in each case without the assistance of a definition or a general rule. Similarly, all that one can say about serious misconduct is that it is misconduct which the court regards as being grave and deliberate. And the standards to be applied in deciding the matter are those of men and not of angels.[53]

Some general propositions can be stated concerning misconduct in this context. It was held in *Carvill v. Irish Industrial Bank*,[54] that the misconduct in question usually must have been known to the employer at the time he decided on the dismissal. That is to say, the employer 'cannot, as a defence to an action for wrongful dismissal, rely on an act of misconduct on the part of his servant which was unknown to him at the time of the dismissal, unless the act is of so fundamental a character as to show a repudiation of the contract of employment by the servant.'[55] In that case, the managing director of a bank arranged for a carpet in his house to be fitted in his office and he bought a new carpet for his house. He then charged the company about 60% of the price of that new carpet. The Supreme Court overruled Kenny J's decision that this act constituted misconduct as would justify his summary dismissal.

A single isolated act can constitute sufficient cause to justify instant dismissal, like fraudulent conduct or wilful disobedience of an order which was lawful and reasonable. The *Glover* case, which also concerned a company director, provides several examples of the kinds of small scale profiting at the employer's expense which do and which do not amount to serious misconduct. Disobeying an order does not invariably warrant instant dismissal; rather, 'one act of disobedience or misconduct can justify dismissal only if it is of a nature which goes to show (in effect) that the servant is repudiating the contract, or one of its essential conditions.'[56] Moreover, the order must be within the scope of the employment. A worker hired to perform one kind of task cannot be compelled to do something entirely different; for instance a person hired in an executive capacity cannot ordinarily be expected to spend his working hours performing manual

53. [1973] IR 388, at p.405. See *North Island Wholesale Groceries Ltd v. Hewin* [1982] 1 NZLR 176.
54. [1968] IR 325.   55. Id. at p.346.
56. *Laws v. London Chronicle Ltd* [1959] 1 WLR 698, at p.701.

labour.[57] It depends very much on the circumstances of each case whether instructions given are reasonable.

There are no reported modern authorities on dismissal on the grounds of incompetence. If the employee represented to the employer that he possessed a certain skill or qualification, which was not in fact the case, his misrepresentation would be regarded as a form of serious misconduct, warranting his immediate dismissal.[58] However, mere inability of a worker to adapt to technical change ordinarily would not warrant summary dismissal. Inability to do a job may even be due to the employer's inadequate training methods or to inefficient techniques for selecting employees.

Grounds stipulated in contract At times the contract of employment will set out in detail the circumstances in which it can be terminated forthwith by one or by both parties. Where the contract sets out the grounds for immediate dismissal, a court may conclude that those grounds supercede and displace the common law right of summary dismissal. In *Glover v. B.L.N. Ltd*,[59] the plaintiff's contract enumerated the grounds and circumstances in which he could be instantly dismissed. Accordingly, it was held,

> because of the express provisions of this clause, no implied term is to be read into the contract that the plaintiff might be summarily dismissed for misconduct. On the contrary, the clause expressly provides that the plaintiff could not be validly dismissed for misconduct unless it was serious misconduct and was of a kind which, in the unanimous opinion of the board of directors . . ., injuriously affected the reputation, business or property of the [companies].[60]

The plaintiff in *Glover* had been employed as the technical director of a group of car assembly companies, which later merged with another car assembly group. One of the terms of the contract was that his 'appointment may be terminated without giving rise to any claim for compensation or damages upon the happening of any events following, namely:—. . . (c) if Mr. Glover shall be guilty of any serious misconduct or serious neglect in the performance of his duties or wilfully disobeys the reasonable orders directions or restrictions or regulations of the board of directors of any of the said companies which in the unanimous opinion of the board of directors for the time being of the holding company present and voting at the meeting injuriously affects the reputation business or property or management of either the holding company or the operating company or the sales company

---

57. *Price v. Movat* (1862) CB (NS) 508.
58. *Harmer v. Cornelius* (1858) 5 CB (NS) 236.
59. [1973] IR 388.   60. Id. at p.424.

or the factors company.' At a board meeting of the holding company, a report was presented by the chairman accusing the plaintiff of a long catalogue of improprieties, such as being a shareholder in a company that supplied automotive goods to the group, getting company employees to do work on cars he owned without charging himself for their services and getting company employees to work for several weeks on his own house without ever charging himself for their work. The board resolved that he should be instantly dismissed. It was held that the test of whether his dismissal was lawful was not whether he had been guilty of serious misconduct but whether he committed acts of misconduct as characterised by the above clause in his contract. If, in the circumstances, the directors could reasonably conclude that he had so misconducted himself, he could have been dismissed forthwith.

It was found that the conflict of interests arising by virtue of his involvement in a supplier to the group was not even misconduct, since its existence had been disclosed to the employer. It was held that, although getting work done on his cars without charge was misconduct, it was not serious misconduct as defined in the contract. While getting the work done on his house without charge amounted to such serious misconduct, his dismissal was held to be unlawful because he had been given no opportunity whatsoever to defend himself against the allegations made against him.

DISMISSAL PROCEDURES

Frequently the employment contract will specify or will incorporate dismissal procedures, that is procedures to be adopted before an employee can be dismissed. These procedures may be set out in relevant collective agreements or in works rules. Indeed, employers are obliged by statute to give all new employees, within a month of their commencing work, a notice setting out what the dismissal procedures are; where those procedures are changed, 28 days' notice must be given of the alterations made.[61] But this obligation to notify does not apply where no procedure was ever agreed with the employee or with his trade union or excepted body, or where no such procedure is based on custom and practice.

Where there are no agreed procedural arrangements for dealing with dismissals, at least for certain categories of employees the courts imply minimum standards of fair procedures; what are often referred to as the principles of natural justice or of constitutional justice.[62] By far the most

61. Unfair Dismissals Act, 1977, s.14.
62. See generally, G. Hogan & D. Morgan, *Administrative Law in Ireland* (2nd ed. 1991) pp.472-476.

important of these is summed up in the maxim *audi alteram partem*, that the decision-maker (that is the employer) must hear the employee's side to the argument before deciding to dismiss. The extent to which the maxim *nemo iudex in sua causa*, that nobody should be judge in his own cause, applies in this context is very unclear. Nor is it clear whether, for employments where these principles apply, they can be waived in the employment contract. To the extent that the principles are based on the common law, undoubtedly they can be waived. But in *Glover v. B.L.N. Ltd*,[63] the Supreme Court said that these principles also have constitutional underpinnings. Walsh J there observed that 'public policy and the dictates of constitutional justice require that . . . agreements setting up machinery for taking decisions which may affect rights or impose liabilities should be construed as providing for fair procedures'.[64] Walsh J then remarked that, in the circumstances there, it was 'not necessary to decide to what extent the contrary can be provided for by agreement between the parties.'[65]

Public and private sector employment Most of the leading reported cases on the application of the maxim *audi alteram partem* to dismissals from employment concern jobs in the public service.[66] In *Garvey v. Ireland*,[67] it was held that the decision to remove the plaintiff, the Commissioner of the Garda Síochána, abruptly and without giving him any reason whatsoever, contravened natural justice and constitutional justice. Earlier in *State (Gleeson) v. Minister for Defence*,[68] it was held that the decision to discharge the plaintiff from the army was invalid because he 'should have been given an opportunity of being heard before being discharged.'[69] Constitutional law consideration aside, the requirement to give a fair hearing to persons facing some significant deprivation has been a principle of administrative law for centuries. As summarised by McCarthy J in a case that did not concern dismissal procedures,

> in all judicial or quasi-judicial proceedings, it is a fundamental requirement of justice that persons or property should not be at risk without the party charged being given an adequate opportunity of meeting the claim as identified or pursued. If the proceedings derived from statute then in the absence of any set fixed procedures, the relevant authority must create and carry out the necessary procedures; if the set or fixed procedure is not comprehensive, the authority must

63. [1973] IR 388.
64. Id. at p.425. Also, *Gunn v. Bord Cholaiste Naisiunta Eolaine is Dearta* [1990] 2 IR 168.
65. Id. at p.425.   66. See post pp.296-299.   67. [1981] IR 75.
68. [1976] IR 280.   69. Id. at p.295.

supplement it in such a fashion as to ensure compliance with constitutional justice.[70]

Practically all of the reported cases on applying fair procedures when dismissing public service workers have concerned office-holders and persons with high ranking or middle ranking jobs. It remains to be determined if these maxims apply to public sector workers who could not be regarded as officers, such as dustmen employed by the Corporation, road sweepers employed by the County Council, hospital attendants in Health Authority hospitals and bus drivers and conductors who work for Bus Éireann. Perhaps the reason why the courts have not yet been called upon to decide this question is that practically all employees in the categories just described are unionised and work under collective agreements which provide for dismissal procedures. Nor has it been determined if the *audi alteram* and *nemo iudex* maxims apply to dismissals in most private sector employments or, if they do, whether or to what extent they can be set aside by provisions in the employment contract. Of course, many of these employees work under collective agreements or some customary arrangements that have dismissal procedures. But this is far from being the case with all private sector employees. In a public sector case, Walsh J observed, *obiter*, that the application of the rules of natural justice 'does not depend upon whether the person concerned is an office-holder as distinct from being an employee of some other kind. . . . The quality of justice does not depend on such distinctions.'[71]

Most private sector employees, however, are protected by the Unfair Dismissals Act, 1977. In determining whether a particular decision was unfair the Employment Appeals Tribunal or the Circuit Court will usually insist on the employer having given the employee in question a fair hearing prior to deciding to dismiss.

Fair hearing The common law imposed no requirement on an employer, outside of the public service, that he should issue a warning before treating certain conduct as warranting dismissal or that the employee be given an opportunity to defend himself against any allegations made against him. As explained by Budd J in 1953, 'while a fair minded employer could undoubtedly give an employee an opportunity to answer a charge and state his case, an employer may if he sees fit to make up his mind from what he has learnt from other sources and observed himself.'[72] However, in the *Carvill*

70. *State (Irish Pharmaceutical Union) v. Employment Appeals Tribnal* [1987] ILRM 36, at p.40.
71. The *Gunn* case, supra n.64, at p.181.
72. *Flynn v. Great Northern Railways Co. (Ir.) Ltd*, 89 ILTR 46 (1955) at p.54.

case[73] and the *Glover* case[74] some of the traditional views about wrongful dismissal law were rejected by the Supreme Court and it is probable that the legal position as just stated would also be rejected.

With regard to senior executive level employees who are being dismissed on specific allegations of misconduct, *Glover v. B.L.N. Ltd* establishes that they are entitled to a fair hearing into the accusations. Because of the very formulation of the dismissal power in the plaintiff's contract there, it was held that there was 'necessarily an implied term of the contract that this inquiry and determination' by the directors into the allegations 'should be fairly conducted.'[75] And as the plaintiff was not told of the charges against him nor given any opportunity to defend himself, there was a breach of that implied term, since 'failure to allow a person to meet the charges against him and to afford him an adequate opportunity of answering them is a violation of an obligation to proceed fairly.'[76] Moreover, even if it could be shown that the employer would have come to the same conclusions if fair procedures had been followed, that does not validate a dismissal made in breach of those procedures. As Walsh J put it, '[t]he obligation to give a fair hearing to the guilty is just as great as the obligation to give a fair hearing to the innocent.'[77] The reasoning here should apply as much to dismissal for serious misconduct where the contract does not expressly deal with the dismissal powers.

This reasoning was applied in *Connolly v. McConnell*,[78] which was an action by the dismissed financial secretary of a trade union against the union's trustees. The governing principles in dismissals cases were stated by Griffin J as follows:

> The law is quite clear. When a person holds a full-time pensionable office from which he may be removed, and thus be deprived of his means of livelihood and of his pension rights, the domestic tribunal or body having the power to remove him are exercising quasi-judicial functions. Therefore, they may not remove him without first according to him natural justice. He must be given the reasons for his proposed dismissal, and an adequate opportunity of making his defence to the allegations made against him—*audi alteram partem*. The members of the tribunal must be impartial and not be judges in their own cause—*nemo iudex in causa sua*. They must ensure that the proceedings are conducted fairly. In determining whether the tribunal is impartial, a member is not to be regarded as impartial if his own interest might be

---

73. [1968] IR 325. 74. [1973] IR 388. 75. Id. at p.425.
76. Id. at pp.425-426. 77. Id. at p.429. 78. [1983] IR 172.

affected by the decision; and this interest is not necessarily to be confined to pecuniary interest.[79]

In that case, the plaintiff had been given an adequate opportunity to defend himself. But his accusers and others with an interest in upholding those charges participated in the decision to dismiss him, one of them even presiding at the meeting and voting on the proposal to dismiss. That action was a fragrant breach of the *nemo iudex* principle, which invalidated the decision taken. Whether the same principle applies to jobs which are not pensionable offices remains to be determined.

Procedures stipulated in contract Where the express terms of the employment contract, be they in the document itself or incorporated from some other document, lay down procedures to be followed when persons are being dismissed on specified grounds, then those procedures must be carried out in such cases. In *McLoughlin v. Great Southern Railways Co.*,[80] where the plaintiff had been summarily dismissed on suspicion of having stolen goods, it was held that the combined effect of relevant collective agreements was that 'while he could be dismissed for misconduct, neglect of duty or breach of discipline, he was entitled to demand that the procedure laid down' in the agreements for dismissal should be followed.[81] Accordingly, the employer was in breach of contract for dismissing him for alleged theft without affording him the stipulated hearing. In *Flynn v. Great Northern Railways Co.*,[82] which concerned substantially the same dismissals procedures, it was found that all of the prescribed steps had been followed by the employer. It has been held that where a public service employee's contract provides for a disciplinary procedure, the fact that he was given full notice before being dismissed for misconduct does not cure the failure to afford the agreed procedures.[83] Due notice is not a proper substitute for the procedures laid down.

Where the contract does not state what shall happen in certain circumstances, the decision-making body is the master of its own procedure, provided it acts fairly and reasonably. For instance, except where provided for expressly, the disciplinary tribunal need not follow the ordinary rules of evidence.[84]

---

79. Id. at pp.178-179.   80. [1944] IR 479.
81. Id. at p.484.   82. 89 ILTR 46 (1955).
83. *Marlboro Harbour Board v. Goulden* [1985] 2 NZLR p.378.
84. Id. at p.54. Also, *Ali v. Southwark L.B.C.* [1988] ICR 567.

Consequences of not affording a hearing Where the requisite procedures have not been followed, it depends on the employee's reaction whether his purported dismissal is legally ineffective or whether that dismissal took effect, leaving him with a right of action in damages. If he treats his dismissal as an effective albeit unlawful dismissal, he is left to a remedy in damages. In the jargon of the law of contract, the employee accepted the employer's repudiation of their agreement.[85] But the employee may choose to treat his contract as still subsisting, since it was not terminated in accordance with its terms. This is because, generally, a contractual breach or 'repudiation' by one party standing alone does not terminate the contract. It takes two to end it—by repudiation, on one side, and acceptance of the repudiation on the other.[86] In was held in *Dietman v. Brent L.B.C.*[87] that, accordingly, in an appropriate case the court will enjoin the employer from dismissing an employee until the procedures laid down in the contract have been followed.

Whether the court should give an injunction in such cases depends on the entire circumstances. If the employee accepted the employer's repudiation, the the question of an injunction does not even arise. For that reason, Hodgson J counselled in the *Dietman* case, the employee 'should make the position plain at once and at once bring proceedings and seek interlocutory relief. The [employer] can then decide whether, in cases of alleged procedural impropriety, to correct the impropriety or fight its corner with the consequences which may follow.'[88] Since the plaintiff there commenced injunction proceedings far too late in the day, her only redress for breach of the procedure was damages. Moreover, if in the circumstances it is plain that the employer has lost all confidence and trust in the employee, an injunction will not issue to keep him in employment pending exhaustion of grievance procedures.[89] If, however, it can be shown that a claimed loss of confidence by the employer is based on some irrational ground, an injunction may issue. And it may be possible to obtain an interlocutory injunction despite the loss of confidence.[90]

In the case of office-holders whose positions were terminated without the requisite procedures having been followed, the decision to remove them is void and they continue in their offices. In *Garvey v. Ireland*,[91] the Government dismissed the Commissioner of the Garda Síochána without

---

85. E.g. *Gunton v. Richmond-upon-Thames L.B.C.* [1981] Ch.448.
86. *Heyman v. Darwins Ltd* [1942] AC 356, at p.361.
87. [1987] ICR 737.　　　　　　　　　　　　　88. Id. at p.756.
89. E.g., *Ali v. Southwark L.B.C.* [1988] ICR 567.
90. E.g., *Robb v. Hammersmith & Fulham L.B.C.* [1991] ICR 514 and *Irani v. Southampton & South West Hampshire Health Authority* [1985] ICR 590.
91. [1981] IR 75. Similarly *Marlborough Harbour Board v. Goulden* [1985] 2 NZLR 378.

giving him any notice or indication of why he was being discharged. Under the legislation governing the Gardaí, his status was that of a statutory office-holder and not merely an employee of the State. Accordingly, it was held that his purported removal from office, without following fair procedures, was *ultra vires* and, therefore, a nullity so that he had never been validly removed from the office. In the event, the plaintiff did not seek an injunction restraining attempts to prevent him from exercising the powers of that office; instead he settled for damages. Although company directors are office-holders, where they are executive directors holding employment contracts with the company, their rights then are primarily based on the contract. Accordingly, the principles stated in the *Dietman* case regarding injunctions apply to them. The plaintiff in *Glover v. B.L.N. Ltd* only sought a declaration and damages.

REMEDIES FOR WRONGFUL DISMISSAL

The principal legal remedy open to a person who is wrongfully dismissed is damages for breach of the employment contract. Alternatively, the employee may have a claim for unfair dismissal under the 1977 Act; if he pursues that claim, he is precluded from seeking damages for breach of the contract.[92] Exceptionally, the employee may obtain a declaration that the dismissal was unlawful or may even obtain an injunction restraining the dismissal. Employees in many parts of the public sector are entitled to seek judicial review of the decision to dismiss them and, if that was unlawful, obtain orders of *certiorari* quashing that decision or a declaration that the decision is invalid. Extra-legal modes of redress may also be open to the employee, notably resort to industrial action. A dispute about a dismissal, even if that dismissal in the event is perfectly lawful, is a trade dispute for the purpose of the Industrial Relations Act, 1990. However, the immunities under that Act from liability in tort for taking industrial action do not apply where the subject matter of the dispute is covered by individual grievance procedures which have not been exhausted.[93]

Declaration In the case of many public sector jobs, decisions regarding dismissal can be challenged in court through the procedure known as judicial review. Alternatively, the employee may seek the declaration in ordinary plenary proceedings.[94] An office-holder or public service employee who

92. 1977 Act s.15.
93. Industrial Relations Act, 1990, s.9(2); see *Industrial Relations Law*, pp.144-146.
94. E.g. *Maunsell v. Minister for Education* [1940] IR 213 and *Cox v. Electricity Supply Board (No.2)* [1943] IR 231.

sought to challenge the legality of his dismissal would seek a declaration that the dismissal or the decision to dismiss was unlawful. Strictly there is no particular benefit in having a mere declaration, in that the employer is not thereby obliged to reinstate the employee or to pay compensation. All that a declaration does is to state that the plaintiff was wrongfully dismissed. However, public sector employers are inclined to adjust their circumstances so as to bring them in line with the legal position as pronounced in a judicial declaration.

Even in the private sector, circumstances can arise where a declaration can be a useful remedy and the courts will grant a declaration in such cases.[95] *Kingston v. Irish Dunlop Co. Ltd*[96] was not a dismissal case but concerned the correct interpretation of the terms on which an earlier action between the plaintiff and the defendant had been settled. The plaintiff sought a declaration to the effect that, under the settlement, he was entitled to be employed on light work in one section of the defendant's factory; he also sought damages but no loss was proved. It was argued that the Court could not make a bare declaration of his rights but that contention was rejected on the grounds that Order 19 r.29 of the Rules of the Superior Courts, gives an extensive jurisdiction to make declarations in appropriate cases. Ó Dálaigh CJ, giving judgment for the Supreme Court, pointed out that the declaration being sought there was not entirely valueless because it would establish what the parties' rights and duties were under the settlement. A court probably would not make the declaration if it was sought only to prove some hypothetical point. One of the reasons given for not granting a declaration that an employee was unlawfully dismissed is the principle that specific performance of an employment contract will not be ordered. But in *Glover v. B.L.N. Ltd* Walsh J 'expressly reserved [his] opinion on the correctness of this statement if it is intended to convey that a court cannot make a declaration which would have the effect of reinstating a person wrongfully dismissed.'[97]

Injunction It has been a fundamental principle of employment law for many years that, ordinarily, the courts will not order specific performance of an employment contract[98] or, what is the same thing, grant a mandatory injunction compelling an employer to continue employing somebody he does not wish to employ. Because employment is a personal relationship

95. See *Freedland*, pp.278-291.
96. [1969] IR 233.
97. [1973] IR at p.427.
98. See generally, I.C.F. Spry, *Equitable Remedies* (3rd ed. 1984) pp.111-117 and *Freedland*, pp.272-277. Cf. *Warren v. Mendy* [1989] 1 WLR 853.

involving a degree of mutual confidence, the view was, and indeed still is, that there is little point in seeking to compel an employer to continue employing someone he does not really want. Also, the courts are reluctant to issue orders that might require continual supervision by them. But this principle is not a hard and fast rule. The complete position is that

> the court will not by injunction require an employer to let a servant continue in his employment, when the employer has sought to terminate that employment and to prevent the servant carrying out his work under the contract, unless it is clear on the evidence not only that it is otherwise just to make such a requirement but also that there exists sufficient confidence on the part of the employer in the servant's ability and other necessary attributes for it to be reasonable to make the order.
>
> Sufficiency of confidence must be judged by reference to the circumstances of the case, including the nature of the work, the people with whom the work must be done and the likely effect upon the employer and the employer's operations if the employer is required by injunction to suffer the plaintiff to continue in the work.[99]

On several occasions in recent years the English courts have enjoined dismissing public service employees before grievance procedures available to them had been exhausted.[100]

However, if an employee wants to have his dismissal enjoined, he must move swiftly to seek relief of that nature.[1] Injunctions are discretionary remedies and there are several circumstances where the courts will refuse to make those orders. For instance, if the award of damages would be an adequate remedy, the tendency would be against granting an injunction in this type of case. The more senior the job is in the employer's hierarchy, the greater the likelihood that damages are not an adequate form of redress. If the employer demonstrates that he has lost all trust and confidence in the employee, he will not be obliged to keep him in his employment.[2]

Damages In the private sector and probably for jobs in the public sector that could not be characterised as offices, the principal legal remedy for the wrongfully dismissed employee is damages. Since the essence of the claim

---

99. *Powell v. Brent L.B.C.* [1988] ICR 176, at p.194.
100. E.g. the *Powell* case, ibid, the *Irani* and the *Robb* cases, supra n.90; see too *Hill v. C.A. Parsons Ltd* [1972] 1 Ch. 305 (all interlocutory applications).
   1. *Dietman v. Brent L.B.C.* [1987] ICR 737.
   2. *Ali v. Southwark L.B.C.* [1988] ICR 567 and *Alexander v. Standard Telephones & Cables Ltd* [1990] ICR 291.

is for damages for breach of contract, the measurement of these damages is determined by the general principles of the law of contract.[3] The normal measure of the damages is what the employee would have earned had he been allowed to remain working during the period for which notice should have been given. Thus, if under the contract he should have got two months notice, his damages ordinarily would be two months' salary. In the leading case *Addis v. Gramophone Co. Ltd*,[4] the plaintiff was employed by the defendants as a manager, under a contract entitling him to six months' notice of dismissal, his remuneration being £60 per month together with commission. He brought an action for wrongful dismissal and the central issue was how much damages he was entitled to in the circumstances. This amount was held to be six months' normal salary together with the commission he would have earned during that period.

Remuneration in lieu of notice: It is for this reasons that employers frequently pay an employee who is being dismissed salary in lieu of notice. Generally, if the employee is given what he would have earned during the due notice period, he has no action for breach of contract even though he was dismissed without any proper notice.

Additional damages: Are there special circumstances where an employee is entitled to damages in excess of what he would have earned during the remaining part of his notice period? Where the dismissal takes place in a particularly unfair manner or in notably unjust circumstances, which causes the employee great distress and perhaps lowers him in the estimation of others, is he entitled to additional damages for the loss he suffered? A categorical answer cannot be given about the position in Ireland because the superior courts have not ruled in the matter in recent years; although the general belief is that additional damages may be awarded in appropriate circumstances.

In *Addis v. Gramophone Co. Ltd*, the House of Lords held that additional damages cannot be awarded in such cases. According to Lord Loreburn LC there,

> I cannot agree that the manner of dismissal affects those damages. Such considerations have never been allowed to influence damages in this kind of case.... If there be a dismissal without notice the employer must pay an indemnity; but that indemnity cannot include com-

---

3. See generally, A.G. Guest ed, *Chitty on Contracts* (26nd ed. 1989) ch. 26, H. McGregor, *The Law of Damages* (15th ed. 1988) ch.27 and *Freedland* pp.244-171.
4. [1909] AC 488.

pensation either for the injured feelings of the servant, or for the loss he may maintain from the fact that his having been dismissed of itself makes it more difficult for him to obtain fresh employment.[5]

It was held that the employee may have a separate action in tort for defamation or for deliberately causing nervous shock or whatever, but that the damages for breach of the employment contract are limited to what would have been earned during the notice period. In 1976 the English High Court departed from this principle[6] but in 1985 the Court of Appeal endorsed the position as stated in the Lords in 1909 in the *Addis* case.[7] In 1909 the *Addis* rule was described as 'too inveterate to be now altered, even if it were desirable to alter it';[8] this view was reiterated by the Appeal Court in 1985.[9]

However, additional damages may be recoverable under what is known as the 'second rule' in *Hadley v. Baxendale*.[10] In the *Addis* case it was emphasised that the plaintiff's claim for additional damages was not being advanced under this rule. According to the 'second rule', one measure of damages in an action for breach of contract is the sum 'as may reasonably be supposed to have been in the contemplation of both parties, at the time they made the contract, as the probable result of the breach of it.'[11] Accordingly, if at the time they made the contract the parties were aware of exceptional losses which would result from a wrongful dismissal, then if those losses did indeed take place the employee must be compensated for them.

Mitigation: As with other successful plaintiffs in breach of contract actions, the wrongfully dismissed employee must mitigate his loss; he must take all reasonable steps to reduce the loss he stands to suffer. In this context, the employee must do what is reasonably necessary in order to find another job. If the employee got another job during the notice period, what he earned in that job for the remainder of that period will be deducted from the damages he otherwise would have obtained. An employer may contend that the dismissed employee can get or should have got other work during the notice period; it depends on the entire circumstances of the case whether that

---

5. Id. at p.491.
6. *Cox v. Phillips Industries Ltd* [1976] 1 WLR 638.; compare *Shove v. Downs Surgical p.l.c.* [1984] ICR 532.
7. *Bliss v. South East Thames Regional Health Authority* [1987] ICR 700.
8. [1909] AC at p.491.
9. *Bliss* case [1987] ICR at p.718. Compare *Vorvis v. Insurance Corp. of British Columbia* [1989] SCR 1085.
10. (1854) 9 Exch. 341.   11. Id. at p.355.

contention will succeed, thereby reducing the amount of damages to be paid.[12]

Collateral benefits: Collateral benefit which the employee received during the notice period may be deducted from the damages otherwise payable for the breach of contract. Those benefits include unemployment benefit payable under the Social Welfare Acts.[13] But the Irish courts have not considered in detail which particular benefits are so deductible.

Taxation: Is the amount of damages recoverable by the employee in respect of lost remuneration the pre-tax or post-tax earnings? It was held in *Glover v. B.L.N. Ltd (No. 2)*[14] that damages recovered for wrongful dismissal, albeit measured by reference to lost earnings, are not intrinsically earnings or 'emoluments'; accordingly, those damages cannot be taxed as the employee's income under Schedule E. But that still leaves the question of, in measuring the damages payable, should account be taken of what tax would have been deducted if the employee had remained on earning remuneration in his job and only the net amount after tax be paid in damages. This is a matter which has divided courts in many common law jurisdictions. In the *Glover (No. 2)* case, Kenny J followed the English precedents[15] on this point and held that the amount of tax which would have been paid must be deducted from the gross earnings which the plaintiff lost. This was because

> An award of damages by a court is intended to compensate the plaintiff for the loss which he has suffered. . . . Therefore, it is irrelevant that the defendant will profit by an allowance being made for tax against the loss. If the damages . . . are not chargeable to tax while the lost remuneration would have been, the plaintiff would be getting an award which would exceed the loss which he had suffered by being deprived of the remuneration. Income tax enters into the lives of so many of our citizens that the law cannot ignore it when assessing damages.[16]

However, in Canada[17] and New Zealand[18] the courts have rejected this reasoning, so that it is conceivable that, if this issue went on to the Supreme Court, the rule as stated here would be overturned. Among the arguments

12. E.g. *Herman v. Owners of the S.S. Vica* [1942] IR 305.
13. *Parsons v. B.N.M. Laboratories Ltd* [1964] 1 QB 95.
14. [1973] IR 432.
15. *British Transport Comm. v. Gourley* [1956] AC 185.
16. [1973] IR at p.441. See *Shove v. Downs Surgical p.l.c.* [1984] ICR 532.
17. *R. (in right of the Province of Ontario) v. Jennings* (1966) 57 DLR 2d 644.
18. *North Island Wholesale Groceries Ltd v. Hewin* [1982] 2 NZLR 176.

against the present rule is that the income tax legislation provides a comprehensive code for the tax consequences of loss of office and it is unsatisfactory that serious tax questions be dealt with by the employer and employee in the complete absence of the Revenue authorities. Indeed, in a case involving compensation for dismissal without giving adequate notice, as required by the Minimum Notice and Terms of Employment Act, 1973, Barrington J[19] refused to follow a recent House of Lords decision on a similar question under English law. It was held that the employer was not entitled to deduct from the sum stipulated in that Act the unemployment benefit which the plaintiff had been receiving during the relevant period.

REMEDY AGAINST EMPLOYEE'S WRONGFUL TERMINATION

Actions by employers against their former employees who have left their jobs, in breach of their employment contracts, are comparatively rare. Presumably in an appropriate case an employer might obtain a declaration that the employee broke his contract. The usual measure of damages is the cost of obtaining another person to do the work, less what would have been paid to the ex-employee under the contract.[20] Where a substitute for him cannot easily be obtained, the measure of the damages is the value of work lost by reason of the defection, less what remuneration the ex-employee would have earned.[21] Exceptionally, the employer may be able to recover expenditure which was rendered futile by the employee's breach of contract.[22]

Ordinarily, an employee will not be enjoined from leaving or from working for others, because that would be tantamount to ordering specific performance of the contract. But where the employee possesses confidential information which he is likely to disclose to a rival, or where a valid restraint of employment clause exists, an injunction can be obtained against the employee working for a named or for designated third parties.[23] There may be an exception where, practically speaking, there is only one other person for whom that employee can work using his own special skills and expertise.[24]

---

19. *Irish Leathers Ltd v. Minister for Labour* [1986] IR 177; see post p.191.
20. *Richards v. Hayward* (1841) 2 M & G 574.
21. *Ebbw Vale Steel Co. v. Tew* (1935) 79 SJ 593.
22. *Anglia Television v. Reed* [1972] 1 QB 60.
23. See ante p. 104.
24. Cf. *Warren v. Mendy* [1988] 1 WLR 853.

In recent years an exception to the general principle about enjoining a breach of employment contract has been recognised. This is where the employee left without giving proper notice. If the employer undertakes to continue paying him during the remainder of the notice period, a court may enjoin him from working for rival employers during that period.[25] Interlocutory relief can also be given in those circumstances.

---

25. E.g. *Evening Standard Co. v. Henderson* [1987] ICR 588 and *Provident Financial Group p.l.c. v. Hayward* [1989] ICR 160.

8

Statutory rights on dismissal

If employers and employees always had equal bargaining power, perhaps the substantial corpus of legislation regulating dismissals would never have been enacted. The position might then be as it is in the United States; such protection as employees have against being dismissed lies in their employment contracts and in provisions contained in collective agreements applicable to them—an exception to this pattern being made for race and sex discrimination. By contrast, the labour laws of Continental European counties have for many years regulated the employer's general prerogative to dismiss. In 1963 the International Labour Organisation adopted a Recommendation concerning Termination of Employment at the Initiative of the Employer (No. 119), which has proved extremely influential in this regard. It partly contributed to the enactment in Britain of legislation on redundancy (1965) and on minimum notice and unfair dismissals (1971). Similar measures were enacted in Ireland not too long afterwards—the Redundancy Payments Acts, 1967–1979, the Minimum Notice and Terms of Employment Act, 1973, and the Unfair Dismissals Act, 1977.

DISMISSAL

Before the merits of a claim for any of the statutory remedies relating to dismissal will be considered, the claimant or plaintiff must have been dismissed. The ordinary meaning of dismissal connotes an employer unequivocally telling his employee that he is no longer being employed; this message may be conveyed either with or without giving due notice or tendering money in lieu of notice. Whether the expiry of a fixed term contract or a contract to perform a specified task amounts to a dismissal is debatable. In order to avoid any confusion and to ensure that the statutory protections apply to all forms of dismissals in a very wide sense of the term, the various Acts contain a wide definition of what is a dismissal for their own purposes.

The term is defined in s.1 of the Unfair Dismissals Act, 1977, as follows:

(a) the termination by his employer of the employee's contract of employment with the employer, whether prior notice of the termination was or was not given to the employee,

(b) the termination by the employee of his contract of employment with his employer, whether prior notice of the termination was or was not given to the employer, in circumstances in which, because of the conduct of the employer, the employee was or would have been entitled, or it was or would have been reasonable for the employee, to terminate the contract of employment without giving prior notice of the termination to the employer, or

(c) the expiration of a contract of employment for a fixed term without its being renewed under the same contract or, in the case of a contract for a specified purpose (being a purpose of such a kind that the duration of the contract was limited but was, at the time of its making, incapable of precise ascertainment), the cesser of the purpose.

There are similar, but not identical, definitions in s.9 of the Redundancy Payments Act, 1967, s.1(i) of the Employment Equality Act, 1977, and s.1(i) of the Anti-Discrimination (Pay) Act, 1974. Accordingly, the word dismissal in this context has become a term of art, covering three main types of situation.

Unilateral termination by employer The first is the commonest case, where the contract is terminated by the employer, that is where the employer unilaterally makes it quite clear that the relationship has or shall come to an end. It is not essential that the employee has been furnished with due notice of dismissal. The principal problem which arises in this kind of case is where the employee has been virtually compelled to resign; has he resigned or was he dismissed? What matters is the substance and not the form of the transaction.[1]

Contracts for a fixed term or for a specified purpose Some employment contracts are not for an indefinite duration but are entered into for a fixed term or for a specified purpose. A dismissal is deemed by the various Acts to have taken place where the agreed term of the contract has expired and the contract has not been renewed. For the purposes of unfair dismissal, that non-renewal must be 'under the same contract',[2] meaning presumably a new contract with terms identical to those of the expired contract (except for the

---

1. Cf. *Birch v. University of Liverpool* [1985] ICR 470 and *Auckland Shop Employees Union v. Woolworths (N.Z.) Ltd* [1985] 2 NZLR 372.
2. (c) above.

actual dates). For the purposes of redundancy, there is a dismissal unless the fixed term contract was replaced by an identical or a similar contract.[3] Accordingly, giving a person whose fixed term contract expired a new contract, of indefinite duration and terminable by notice, constitutes a dismissal, even if many other terms of the new contract are more advantageous to the employee than the old contract. The non-renewal of a fixed term contract is not defined as a dismissal for the purposes of the laws against sex discrimination.[4]

Under the Unfair Dismissals Act, there is also a dismissal where a contract made for a specific purpose comes to an end.[5] This is a contract where the employee was to achieve a defined objective with a limited time but, at the time the contract was being entered into, it was not possible to tell how long it would take to realise that purpose. Non-renewal of a contract of this nature is not deemed to be a dismissal under the other Acts.

Constructive dismissal By constructive dismissal is meant where an employee leaves his job in circumstances where the employer's improper conduct drove him to resigning. In the Acts on unfair dismissals, redundancy and sex discrimination, a constructive dismissal occurs where, by reason of the employer's conduct, the employee is 'entitled to terminate' the contract.[6] In other words, the employer's conduct must have been so serious a breach of the agreement as to constitute a repudiation of it, thereby entitling the employee, should he choose, to rescind the agreement there and then. The test of what constitutes repudiation is based on ordinary contract law concepts and the express and implied terms of the contract in question.[7] Examples include where, unilaterally, the employer reduced the employee's remuneration,[8] changed the very nature of the task for which he was employed[9] or required him to work somewhere distant from the place it was agreed he should work.[10] Of course, alterations of this nature do not constitute repudiation where the contract's very terms enable the employer to change the terms in this manner. Repudiation occurs where there has been any breach of the implied term that the employer will not, without reasonable and probable cause, act in a manner calculated or likely to destroy or

---

3. 1967 Act s.9(1)(b).
4. Employment Equality Act, 1977, s.1(1).   5. (c) above.
6. Redundancy Payments Act, 1967, s.9(1)(c), Unfair Dismissals Act, 1977, s.1(b) and Employment Equality Act, 1977, s.1(1).
7. See ante pp.154-156.
8. E.g. *Rigby v. Ferodo Ltd* [1988] ICR 29.
9. E.g. *Lewis v. Motorworld Garages Ltd* [1986] ICR 157.
10. Cf. *Courtaulds Northern Spinning Ltd v. Sibson* [1988] ICR 451.

seriously damage the relationship of confidence and trust with the employee.[11]

For the purpose of the law regarding unfair dismissal and sex discrimination, the scope of constructive dismissal is even more extensive. The concept extends to where the employer's actions were such as rendered it 'reasonable' for the employee to terminate the contract without giving any prior notice.[12] In other words, even if in the circumstances the employer's actions did not amount to so serious a breach as would entitle the employee to rescind the contract, nevertheless those actions were sufficiently grave as a reasonable employee in that same position would easily have been driven to leave the job there and then. Whether an employee was constructively dismissed in this sense depends entirely on the particular facts of the case.[13]

CONTINUITY OF EMPLOYMENT

In order to benefit from many of the statutory rights regarding dismissal, the employee must have been continuously employed on a full time basis by his employer for a specified period; for instance, for one year under the Unfair Dismissals Act, 1977,[14] and for two years under the Redundancy Payments Acts.[15] Continuity is not required for certain types of dismissal under the 1977 Act[16] or for dismissals under the legislation on sex discrimination. Special rules are laid down for determining if the requisite continuity exists. There are two main sets of rules which differ in detail. Continuity for the purpose of claims for redundancy payments are dealt with in Schedule 3 of the Redundancy Payments Act, 1967;[17] for the purpose of unfair dismissals and other rights, continuity is dealt with principally in the first schedule of the Minimum Notice and Terms of Employment Act, 1973. Special legislation regarding some categories of employees in the public sector have their own unique rules regarding measuring continuity of service.

In the account of continuity here, the emphasis is placed on the rules under

11. *Bliss v. South East Thames Regional Health Authority* [1987] ICR 700.
12. 1977 Acts ss.1(b) (above) and 1(1).
13. See numerous instances in D. Madden & T. Kerr, *Unfair Dismissal Cases and Commentary* (1990) ch.3.
14. S.2(1)(a).
15. 1967 Act, s.7(5), as amended by 1971 Act, schedule. He must also have been an employed contributer for all social welfare benefits for the four years immediately preceding the redundancy: 1967 Act s.7(1)(b), as amended by 1971 Act schedule.
16. See infra p.193.
17. Paras 4-12, as amended by schedule to the 1971 Act.

the 1973 Minimum Notice etc. Act. There are very few decisions of the Superior Courts on these questions and many important matters of principle have not been considered by the tribunals.[18] Because there are significant differences between the continuity rules here and those in the British legislation, care should be taken in seeking solutions to problems here in the substantial body of case law in Britain.

Date of commencement The first matter to be ascertained is exactly when did the employee commence employment with that employer. This is principally a question of fact. The relevant time is not when the employee actually began working but when did the employment relationship commence. A person may have been working for the employer for some time as a trainee and not as an employee; in such a case, his period spent in training does not count.[19]

Date of dismissal In determining when the employment ended, the focus is not on when the employee actually ceased working but when did the employment relationship come to an end. The answer does not turn entirely on contract law concepts because the legislation on unfair dismissals and on redundancy contain definitions of the 'date of dismissal', which focus on two questions, viz. the requisite notice for dismissal and the position of fixed term contracts.[20]

Dismissal notice: Even though, as a matter of contract law, a summary dismissal may take effect immediately when the requisite notice was not given,[21] the employment relationship is not deemed to have ended at that time for the purposes of these Acts. Under the 1967 Act and the 1977 Act, where due notice was given, the contract ends when that notice expires, even if the employee departed earlier.[22] Where the due notice was not given, the dismissal is deemed to have occurred at the time such notice if given would have expired.[23] By due notice here is meant the notice required by the contract. For unfair dismissals it also means the statutory minimum notice under the Minimum Notice etc. Act, 1973; which ever of these notice periods is the longer in the circumstances. A specified period of notice has been held to be a period clear of the time the notice was given; for instance,

18. For examples, see Madden & Kerr, supra n.13, ch.4.
19. E.g. *Dempsey v. Grant Shopfitting Ltd* (UD 554/88) id. p.97.
20. Redundancy Payments Act, 1967, s.2(1) and Unfair Dismissals Act, 1977, s.1.
21. *Octavius Atkinson & Sons Ltd v. Morris* [1989] ICR 431.
22. Ss.2(1)(a) and 1(a), respectively.
23. Ss.2(1)(b) and 1(b) respectively.

seven days' notice means seven days after the day the employee was notified.[24] In England the courts are of the view that, once the decision to dismiss has been communicated, the parties can agree that the termination date should be earlier than that specified in the statutory definition.[25]

Fixed term or purpose contract: In the case of a fixed term contract which was not renewed or a contract for a specified purpose and that purpose has ceased, the dismissal date is the day on which the contract term expired or its purpose ceased, as the case may be.[26]

Presumption of continuous employment Having ascertained when the employment commenced and when it ceased, there is a statutory presumption that the employee was continuously employed between those dates. The employee's service is 'deemed to be continuous unless that service is terminated by [his] dismissal....'[27] The full effect of this provision does not appear to have been authoritatively decided. Its apparent meaning is that, unless it is shown that the employee was either dismissed or voluntarily left the job at an earlier stage, he shall be regarded as having been continuously employed between the dates of commencement and of dismissal.

Continuity not broken Several circumstances are specified which are deemed not to break continuity of service, even if the actual contractual relationship had been disrupted by them.

'Umbrella' contract: These special provisions do not even arise where the employee was employed under what may be termed an 'umbrella' contract, meaning a contract which envisaged that he would occasionally cease working for short periods and would later re-commence work. For instance, a ship's captain who sailed on voyages, interspersed with periods ashore during which he drew unemployment benefit, was held to be subject to such a contract.[28] The contention was rejected that each voyage was a separate contract and no contractual relationship existed between voyages. But in another instance, concerning trawlermen in similar circumstances, it was

---

24. *West v. Kneels Ltd* [1987] ICR 146.
25. *Crank v. Her Majesty's Stationery Office* [1985] ICR 1.
26. 1967 Act s.2(i)(c) (this does not deal with achievement of the contract's purpose *per se*) and 1977 Act s.1(c).
27. 1967 Act, schedule 3, para. 4, as amended by 1971 Act s.10 and Minimum Notice and Terms of Employment Act, 1973, schedule, para. 1.
28. *Boyd Line Ltd v. Pitts* [1986] ICR 244.

held that each voyage they sailed was under a separate contract;[29] the parties there were not subject to any mutual obligations at the times when there was no subsisting crew agreement.

Immediate re-employment: There is no break in continuity where the employee's dismissal was 'followed by [his] immediate re-employment'.[30] How short a time must elapse between these two events has not been determined.

Lay-off: That question is not particularly important because an employee who has been laid off for a period is deemed not to have been dismissed.[31] It depends on the circumstances whether there was a 'lay-off' as contrasted with a dismissal or a voluntary leaving. The term connotes a temporary severing of relations in the anticipation that the worker will be re-employed in the not too distant future.[32] There is a definition of the term for redundancy payments purposes.[33] In the British legislation, instead of 'lay off' the phrase 'temporary cessation of work' is used, which has generated substantial litigation in the superior courts there.[34]

Transfer of business: An employer may decide to sell or otherwise dispose of all or part of his business and, at the same time, arrange that one or more employees working in that business be employed by the transferee or successor company. In that event, the actual dismissal and commencement of the new job are deemed not to have broken the employees' continuity;[35] whatever continuity they had accrued with their former employer is carried over to their new employer.[36] This question and related matters are the subject of an E.C. directive and a statutory instrument, which are considered in detail in Chapter Ten. But no special provision is made in the legislation for where an employee is transferred from one company to an associated company within a group enterprise.

29. *Hellyer Bros. Ltd v. McLeod* [1987] 1 WLR 726; it was not argued here that the employees had been laid off during the intervals.
30. 1973 Act 1st schedule, para. 6; for redundancy claims, see 1967 Act, 3rd schedule para. 5A (inserted by 1971 Act).
31. 1973 Act, 1st schedule, para. 3 and 1967 Act, 3rd schedule, para. 5(1)(b)(i).
32. E.g. *Devonald v. Rosser & Sons* [1906] 2 KB 728.
33. 1967 Act, s.11(1). Cf. *Irish Leathers Ltd v. Minister for Labour* [1986] IR 177.
34. E.g. *Fitzgerald v. Hall, Russell & Co. Ltd* [1970] AC 984, *Ford v. Warwickshire C.C.* [1983] 2 AC 71 and *Flack v. Kodak Ltd* [1987] 1 WLR 31. Cf. *Corran Works Ltd v. Bell* [1967] NI 185.
35. 1973 Act, 1st schedule, para. 7 and 1967 Act, 3rd schedule, reg. 6 (inserted by 1971 Act).
36. *Nova Colour Graphic Supplies Ltd v. Employment Appeals Tribunal* [1987] IR 426.

Part-time employment Formerly, many part-time workers were not protected by the dismissals legislation because they did not work for at least 18
hours a week for the one employer. That period has now been reduced to 8
hours by the Worker Protection (Regular Part-Time Employees) Act, 1991.
The Redundancy Payment Acts do not apply to a person who is 'normally
expected to work' for his employer for less than eight hours in a week.[37]
There is not quite the same exclusion of part-time workers from the Unfair
Dismissals Act and other legislation. Instead, working weeks will not be
counted as weeks of continuous employment where the worker 'is not
normally expected to work for at least' eight hours in the relevant week.[38]
What exactly is meant by 'normally expected to work' in this context has
not been authoritatively decided; the comparable phrase in the British legislation is being under a contract 'which normally involves employment' for
a specified period. Where the position is not clear from the very terms of
the contract, account can be taken of the average hours the employee
worked,[39] although the average will not always be taken as conclusive.

It has been held that the times during which part-time firemen were on
call constituted working hours for these purposes.[40] In *Limerick Health
Authority v. Ryan*,[41] where a midwife sought redundancy compensation,
Kenny J observed that the then eighteen hours minimum 'does not apply
when the employer does not or cannot specify the hours during which the
employee is to do the work and when its nature requires that the person
employed has to be available to do it at all times.'[42] It has been held that
teachers are entitled to add to the actual hours they teach a period for
preparation for classes and for dealing with homework.[43]

Absences which are deemed weeks of service Unless special provision
was made, an employee who was temporarily absent on account of illness
or on holidays, or for some other reason, might not be entitled to credit for
those periods, although he would not suffer a complete break in his continuity of service. Accordingly, it is provided that a period of absence due
to a lay off, to sickness or injury or otherwise 'by agreement with his

---

37. 1967 Act s.4(2), as amended by 1991 Act.
38. 1977 Act s.2(4) and 1973 Act, 1st schedule, para. 8, as amended by 1991 Act.
39. E.g. *Dunne v. Cooney* (UD 532/86).
40. *Bartlett v. Kerry C.C.* (UD 178/78); compare *Suffolk C.C. v. Secretary of State* [1984] ICR 882.
41. [1969] IR 194.
42. Id. at p.198.
43. *Sinclair v. Dublin City V.E.C.* (UD 349/86). Compare *Girls Public Day School Trust v. Khanna* [1987] ICR 339.

employers' shall count as a period of service for these purposes.[44] But not more than twenty six weeks absence on these grounds, between consecutive periods of employment, can be so counted.[45] Any period of absence to serve in the Reserve Defence Force is counted.

Whether the absence was due to a lay off or to sickness or injury is a question of fact.[46] No express provision is made for counting an absence under statutory maternity leave.[47] What exactly is meant by 'agreement with' or 'arrangement with' the employer is another key concept calling for authoritative exposition. It has been held in England that employees who worked on alternate weeks could have their 'off weeks' counted for the purpose of continuity, because there was an arrangement with their employer that they could be absent on those weeks.[48] It was also held in England that where an employee was dismissed but was later re-employed, on the basis that he should be regarded as continuously employed from when he was first hired, the period during which he was dismissed was an absence from work by arrangement with his employer.[49] Holidays should fall within this term; they are expressly mentioned in the redundancy payments legislation.[50]

Industrial Action There are special rules for continuity of employment when the employees are on strike or have been locked out or the parties are engaged in some other forms of industrial action. These provisions are dealt with elsewhere.[51]

MINIMUM NOTICE OF DISMISSAL

As is explained in the previous chapter, under their employment contracts most employees are entitled to a period of notice before they can be lawfully dismissed, except in cases of summary dismissal for good cause. This right is supplemented by s.4 of the Minimum Notice and Terms of Employment Act, 1973, which gives employees covered by that Act a right to a minimum period of paid notice of dismissal, which cannot be contracted out of.

44. 1973 Act, 1st schedule, para. 10 and 1967 Act, 3rd schedule, para. 8.
45. Cf. 1967 Act, 3rd schedule, para. 8, where the maximum periods for the different kinds of absences vary.
46. E.g. *Harte v. Telecord Holdings Co. Ltd* (McWilliam J, 18 May 1979).
47. There is a reference to child-birth in the 1967 Act, 3rd schedule, para. 5(1)(d) (inserted by 1971 Act, schedule).
48. *Lloyds Bank v. Secretary of State* [1979] 1 WLR 498.
49. *Ingram v. Foxan* [1984] ICR 685.
50. 1967 Act, 3rd schedule, paras 5(1)(b)(ii) and 7.
51. See *Industrial Relations Law*, pp.118-119.

Workers covered On account of how s.1 of the 1973 Act defines the term 'employee' for the purposes of that Act, it would seem that some persons providing personal services who might strictly be self-employed fall within that Act. For the Act applies to a person working under a 'contract with an employer . . . whether it be a contract of service, of apprenticeship or otherwise . . . .' This Act does not apply to established civil servants, members of the permanent Defence Forces and of the Garda Síochána, merchant seamen and what may be described as close family/domestic employments. Also excluded from the Act are employees who are 'normally expected to work' for that employer for less than eight hours a week.[52]

Notice periods The 1973 Act does not deal with the actual form of a dismissal notice. As Henchy J observed, the Act 'is concerned only with the period referred to in the notice, and it matters not what form the notice takes so long as it conveys to the employee that it is proposed that he will lose his employment at the end of a period which is expressed or necessarily implied in the notice. There is nothing in the Act to suggest that the notice given should be stringently or technically construed as if it were analogous to a notice to quit.'[53] All that the Act does is require that notice be given which is of at least a specified duration.

Depending on the circumstances, a notice that an employee is being laid off can be a dismissal notice. In *Industrial Yarns Ltd v. Greene*,[54] as part of a settlement of an industrial dispute, a group of employees were laid off and could later apply to be made redundant. It was held that, in the circumstances there, their lay off constituted a dismissal because it was not really a lay off; the employer knew that there was no real prospect of them being re-employed in the foreseeable future. Since their employment contracts did not empower the employer to suspend employees without pay, by ceasing to employ these men and pay them wages the employer repudiated their contracts, thereby entitling them to treat his action as a dismissal. On the other hand, if an employee was indeed laid off by agreement, he was not dismissed. If subsequently a dismissal notice is served on him, the effect is that 'the contract of employment, the operation of which had been suspended, had been reinstated for the purpose of terminating it.'[55]

The length of notice which an employee is entitled to under the 1973 Act

---

52. S.3(1)(a), as amended by Workers Protection (Regular Part-Time Employees) Act, 1991.
53. *Bolands Ltd v. Ward* [1988] ILRM 382, at p.389.
54. [1984] ILRM 15.
55. *Irish Leathers Ltd v. Minister for Labour* [1986] IR 177, at p.181.

depends on how long he has worked for that employer. The initial qualifying period for the very minimum notice, of one week, is thirteen weeks continuous employment.[56] A week for these purposes is defined as seven consecutive days.[57] The maximum notice period under the Act, of eight weeks, is for employees with fifteen years or more continuous service. The entire lengths of notice for relevant service are as follows:

Period of Service	Length of Notice
13 weeks—2 years:	1 week
2 years—5 years:	2 weeks
5 years—10 years:	4 weeks
10 years—15 years:	6 weeks
15 years upwards:	8 weeks

These periods can be varied by ministerial order.

An employee who is guilty of such misconduct as would warrant his summary dismissal is not entitled to notice of dismissal under the 1973 Act.[58]

Where an employer gave notice but then finds that there is work for an additional period, he may extend the notice week by week or perhaps longer. Ordinarily, the fact that he did not terminate the employment on foot of the original notice does not mean that an entirely new notice must be given when the relationship is eventually terminated. Thus, in *Bolands Ltd v. Ward*,[59] a receiver appointed over the business gave bakery employees notices that complied with the Act. He then extended those notices for several weeks until the plant closed. It was held that the 1973 Act had been complied with. This would not be the case, however, where 'an employer was improperly or fraudulently manipulating contracts of employment and, consequently, the Act itself, so as to evade the requirements of the Act, by a series of such postponements.'[60]

Payment During the notice period required by the 1973 Act, the employee is entitled to be paid the remuneration provided for in his contract.[61] This is so even if he does not do any work. If the job has normal working hours, the employee is entitled to be paid in respect of all times, during those hours, when he is ready and willing to work;[62] if there aren't normal working hours, the remuneration payable is at least the average of what the employee earned during the thirteen weeks before the notice was given.[63]

---

56. S.4(1).   57. S.1.   58. S.8.   59. [1988] ILRM 382.
60. Id. at p.391.   61. 2nd schedule, para. 1.   62. Id. para. 2.
63. Id. para. 3.

In *Irish Leathers Ltd v. Minister for Labour*,[64] it was held that the full remuneration as prescribed in the Act must be paid and that an employer is not entitled in effect to set-off against that remuneration any unemployment benefit the employee may have been receiving during the notice period. According to Barrington J, the employee's entitlement is to 'receive from his employer a fixed sum of money determined in a manner set out by statute'; to hold otherwise 'would be to hold that the State in effect would be obliged to subsidise employers who fail to fulfil their statutory duties.'[65] If, on the other hand, the employee is re-employed on a temporary basis during the notice period, the employer can in effect set-off the remuneration he earned in that period against the sum prescribed by the Act. In *Irish Shipping Ltd v. Byrne*,[66] where workers were dismissed on their employer being wound up, but they continued to work for the liquidator on a temporary basis, it was held that the remuneration they got from the liquidator could be deducted from the sums payable to them under the 1973 Act.

Peremptory nature How the minimum notice requirements are translated into a legal obligation is by rendering them a term of the employment contract, should the contract provide for a shorter period for notice of dismissal.[67] The obligation to pay remuneration during the requisite period is rendered peremptory by stipulating that any provision in a contract which purports to exclude or limit this right shall be void.[68] However, an employee may accept payment of the remuneration he would have earned during the notice period in lieu of the prescribed notice.[69]

Additionally, 'on any occasion' the employee may waive his right to notice. In the *Industrial Yarns Ltd* case, it was held that any such waiver 'must be clear and unambiguous'.[70] There, applications sent in by workers, who believed they were laid off, for redundancy compensation were found not to be waivers of their right to be paid during the minimum notice period. It remains to be determined how the prohibition against contracting out of the right to the stipulated payments is to be reconciled with permitting a waiver of the right to notice.

UNFAIR DISMISSAL

A most unsatisfactory feature in the existing common law and contractual rules concerning dismissal was that, provided an employer paid the salary

---

64. [1986] IR 177. 65. Compare *Westwood v. Secretary of State* [1985] AC 20.
66. [1987] IR 468. 67. S.4(5). 68. S.5(3). 69. S.7.
70. [1984] ILRM at p.23.

in lieu of notice due, he could dismiss an employee for any reason whatsoever, no matter how arbitrary it might be, without paying any compensation. So far as the general law was concerned, a person's security of
employment depended entirely on the employer's whim. If for any reason
at all the employer took objection to an employee, the latter had no legal
protection against being sacked. Perhaps dismissal on the grounds of the
worker's sex, race or religion might be unconstitutional; that issue does not
appear to have been canvassed in the Superior Courts in the context of
private sector employment. A frequent cause of disputes was dismissals;
lacking any legal protection against what they saw as arbitrary dismissals,
employees would often resort to strike action in order to protect their jobs.
Disputes about dismissals are 'trade disputes' for the purpose of the law
regarding strikes, lock-outs and picketing but the usual immunity from
liability in tort is conditioned on all individual grievance procedures being
exhausted.[71] At times trade unions and employers negotiate dismissals
procedure agreements, which contain a mechanism for dealing with employees' grievances in this area. Depending on the nature of the agreed
procedure, it might become an implied term of the employment contract.
When most categories of public sector employees are faced with dismissals,
they can have their grievances aired in the appropriate conciliation and
arbitration scheme.[72]

The Unfair Dismissals Act In response to the inadequacies in the general
law, the Unfair Dismissals Act, 1977, was passed. As well as providing
protection for employees against arbitrary dismissal decisions, this Act was
also aimed at cutting down the number of industrial disputes, leading to
strikes, lock-outs and picketing.

The 1977 Act is modelled on similar legislation introduced in Britain in
1971 and now contained in the Employment Protection (Consolidation) Act,
1978.[73] However, the two measures are far from being identical and,
accordingly, British cases on unfair dismissals should be treated with great
caution as guides to what the position under the 1977 Act might be. Another
source of inspiration for this Act was the International Labour Organisation's Recommendation No.119 on the Termination of Employment; that
document was since reviewed by the I.L.O., eventually resulting in the
Termination of Employment Convention of 1982 and also a Recommendation of that name of 1982.[74] Ireland is not a party to this Convention. An

71. See *Industrial Relations Law*, pp.143-146.
72. See id. pp.200-206.
73. See generally, S. Anderman, *Unfair Dismissals* (2nd ed. 1985).
74. See generally, Napier, 'Dismissals—the New I.L.O. Standards', 12 *Ind. L.J.* 17 (1983).

excellent account of the place of the 1977 Act in Irish law shortly after its enactment can be found in Mary Redmond's *Dismissal Law*,[75] which remains the only authoritative survey of the law and practice. Perhaps that author might be tempted to bring out a second edition of this work, which is badly needed. Space permits giving only a bare outline of this important topic in a general book on Employment Law.

Although the 1977 Act has been in force for some fifteen years, its requirements have been the subject of only one reported Supreme Court case[76] and a few reported High Court cases.[77] But there has been a vast quantity of Employment Appeal Tribunal and Circuit Court decisions. An excellent selection of cases on the Act have been published by the Federation of Irish Employers,[78] which readers seeking enlightenment on the present practice should consult. Unlike the position in Britain, the Superior Courts here have not yet laid down general guidelines for applying the 1977 Act's central requirements. Accordingly, there is the inevitable degree of inconsistency between the approaches taken by different divisions of the Employment Appeals Tribunal (hereinafter referred to as the E.A.T.) and the several Circuit Court judges.

Employees not covered The Unfair Dismissals Act applies to employees and apprentices.[79] But not all employees are entitled to redress under this Act.

Continuity of employment: To begin with, they must possess the requisite continuity of employment,[80] which is one year's service, meaning fifty two weeks' continuous service in full-time or regular part-time employment.[81] It would seem that a week for these purposes means seven days. As explained above, special rules are contained in the 1st schedule to the Minimum Notice etc. Act, 1973, for calculating continuity of employment.

The requisite one year's continuity is not required where the employee was dismissed for any of the following reasons: trade union membership or activities, as defined in s.6(2)(a) of the Act;[82] pregnancy, in circumstances

---

75. 1982 (Incorp. Law Soc.).
76. *Halal Meat Packers (Ballyhaunis) Ltd v. Employment Appeals Tribunal* [1990] ILRM 293 (dealing with the jurisdiction of the E.A.T.: see ante p.23).
77. Most notably *Flynn v. Power* [1985] IR 648 and *McCabe v. Lisney & Co.* [1981] ILRM 289.
78. D. Madden & T. Kerr, *Unfair Dismissals: Cases and Commentary* (1990) (hereinafter referred to as *Cases*).
79. On employees, see ante pp.29 et seq.
80. See supra pp.183-188.   81. S.2(1)(a).
82. S.6(7); see *Industrial Relations Law*, pp.63-66.

set out is s.6(2)(f) of the Act;[83] because the employee exercised any of the statutory rights to maternity leave, to additional maternity leave or to time off for ante or post-natal care.[84]

Public service: Those public sector workers who are excluded are members of the Defence Forces and of the Garda Síochána,[85] persons employed 'by or under the State'[86] and 'officers' of any local authority, health board, vocational education committee or committee of agriculture.[87]

Part-time workers: Part-time workers, meaning those who 'are not normally expected to work for at least' eight hours a week, are excluded from the Act.[88]

Pensioners: Except for dismissals for protected trade union membership or activities, this Act does not apply to employees who have reached the pensionable age for social welfare purposes, which is 66 years of age.[89] Additionally, the Act excludes employees who, on or before the date they were dismissed, had reached 'the normal retiring age for employees of the same employer in similar employment. . . .'[90] For instance, a 'lad porter' with Iarnrod Éireann, who lost his job on reaching twenty years of age, was held to fall outside the 1977 Act because that age was the normal retiring age for that category of employee.[91] Where the employment contract does not stipulate any retirement age, it depends on the circumstances if there was a general practice that employees in the claimant's position would retire before the State pension age.[92] Even if there is a contractual provision, its requirements may be negated by the actual practice at the workplace of those employees' usually retiring at a later age.[93] The usual age here does not mean the statistical average age but the age at which those employees usually would expect to retire.[94] It remains to be seen when an assurance given to an employee, that he would be retired at a date after the normal age,

83. S.2(1)(a); see infra p.199.
84. S.6(2)(g), added by s.25 of the Maternity Protection of Employees Act, 1981; see infra p.199.
85. S.2(1)(d) and (e).
86. S.2(1)(h), except for 'industrial' civil servants; see post p.290.
87. S.2(1)(i) and (j); see post pp.291 and 318.
88. S.2(4), as amended by the Worker Protection (Regular Part Time Employees) Act, 1991.
89. Ss.2(1)(b) and 6(7).   90. Ibid.
91. *Humphries v. Iarnrod Éireann* (UD 1099/88) *Cases* p.109.
92. *Waite v. Government Communications Headquarters* [1983] 2 AC 714.
93. Ibid.
94. Cf. *Mauldon v. British Telecommunications p.l.c.* [1987] ICR 450.

will operate as an estoppel against the employer, regarding when his normal retirement age is for the purpose of the 1977 Act.[95]

Close family/domestics: Employees who are employed by a close member of the family in a domestic situation fall outside the Act.[96]

Trainees and probationers: Although the 1977 Act applies to apprentices, excluded from its scope are several categories of trainees and probationers, except for dismissals for protected trade union membership and activities.[97] One of these are employees who are undergoing training for any of the following purposes:[98] to become qualified or registered, as the case may be, as a nurse, pharmacist, health inspector, medical laboratory technician, occupational therapist, physiotherapist, speech therapist, radiographer or social worker. A statutory apprentice, within the terms of the Industrial Training Act, 1977, is not protected by the 1977 Act if he was dismissed either within six months after his apprenticeship commenced or within one month after the apprenticeship was completed.[99] Finally, in the case of any employee who is undergoing training or who is on probation, the Act does not apply where the contract is in writing and it stipulates that its duration shall not be longer than one year.[100] Apprentices employed by FÁS and also persons receiving a training allowance from or undergoing training or instruction by FÁS are excluded, provided they are not employees, even where their dismissal is for protected union membership activities.[1]

Fixed term contracts: The 1977 Act does not define what exactly it envisages as an employment contract for a fixed term. Obviously, it is the opposite of a contract for an indeterminate duration. It has been held in England that not alone does a contract for a specified or ascertainable duration fall into this category but there is a fixed term contract even where it contains a provision enabling its lawful termination prior to the specified expiry date. In *Dixon v. B.B.C.*,[2] a contract due to expire on 1 May 1976, unless previously determined by one week's notice in writing by either side, was held to be a fixed term contract. The reason principally is because otherwise the protective legislation could easily be evaded by the manipulation of contracts for specified terms, which could be extended but which also could be terminated at short notice. If contracts like that in *Dixon* were not fixed term contracts, their expiry on their specified due date and non-renewal would never constitute a dismissal as defined in the unfair

95. Cf. *Hughes v. Dept. of Social Security* [1985] 1 AC 776.
96. S.2(1)(c).   97. S.6(7).   98. S.3(2).   99. S.4.
100. S.3(1).   1. S.2(1)(f).   2. [1979] 1 QB 546.

dismissals legislation. The mere expiry of a term is only a dismissal in the case of fixed term contracts.

Where a fixed term contract expires and is not renewed or where a specified purpose contract ceases, the 1977 Act does not apply in the following case. This is where the contract itself is in writing, it is agreed by or for the employer and by the employee and it expressly states that the 1977 Act is not to apply to the contract expiring or ceasing.[3] But the termination of such contracts, other than by their normal expiry or cesser, can be a dismissal within the terms of the 1977 Act.

Replacement for employees away on maternity leave: The Act does not apply to a person who is replacing an employee who has taken maternity or additional matenity leave or time off for ante or post-natal care in the following circumstances.[4] Those are where, at the commencement of the job, he is informed in writing by the employer that the job will be terminated when the absent employee returns and, secondly, the actual dismissal was to enable that employee to return to work.

Transnationals: Special provision is made by s.2(3) of the 1977 Act for employees who ordinarily work outside the State.[5]

Dismissal In order to claim under the Unfair Dismissals Act, the employee must have been 'dismissed' from his work. What constitutes a dismissal, actual and constructive, for these purposes is defined in s.1 of the Act and has been considered above.[6]

Unfair or justifiable? Section 6 of the 1977 Act sets out when a dismissal shall be regarded as contravening that Act. Its general scheme is as follows. The burden of proof is not on the employee but falls on the employer; unless the employer can show that there were 'substantial grounds for justifying' the dismissal, it will be deemed to be unfair. What grounds justify a dismissal depends on all the circumstances of the case. Section 6 provides some help in this regard because it enumerates certain grounds which ordinarily would justify a dismissal—misconduct, inability to do the job and redundancy. It also lists grounds of dismissal which will be deemed unfair—union membership or activities, religious or political opinions, race or colour, pregnancy or taking maternity leave and what is termed unfair

---

3. S.2(2)(a) and (b).
4. S.2(2)(c), inserted by s.24 of the Maternity Protection of Employees Act, 1981.
5. See post p.269.   6. Supra pp.180-183.

redundancy. Special rules exist for dismissals of employees who are on strike or who have been locked out of their jobs.[7]

When considering claims, the Tribunal's and Circuit Court's approach is not so much determining if in all the circumstances the employee deserved to be dismissed; instead, the focus is on whether a reasonable employer would have dismissed him in those circumstances. As stated in *Bunyan v. United Dominions Trust (Ireland) Ltd*,[8] one of the few reported cases on the key 'fairness' question,

> the fairness or unfairness of dismissal is to be judged by the objective standard of the way in which a reasonable employer in those circumstances in that line of business would have behaved. The Tribunal therefore does not decide the question whether or not, on evidence before it, the employee should be dismissed. The decision to dismiss has been taken and our function is to test such decision against what we consider the reasonable employer would have done and/or concluded.[9]

In another instance, concerning dismissal for alleged dishonesty, it was said that

> It is not for the Tribunal to seek to establish the guilt or innocence of the claimant, nor is it for the Tribunal to indicate or consider whether we, in the employer's position, would have acted as [he] did in his investigation, or concluded as [he] did or decided as he did, as to do so would substitute our own mind and decision for that of the employer. Our responsibility is to consider against the facts what a reasonable employer in [the same] position and circumstances at that time would have done and decided and to set this up as a standard against which [the employer's] action and decision be judged.[10]

Considerable emphasis is placed on the employer following fair procedures, be they the actual grievance procedures obtaining at the workplace or the more general principles of fair play. Following fair procedures will ensure that the employer is more fully informed before he takes a serious decision; the employee also has the opportunity to defend himself against any allegations made against him. Thus in the *Bunyan* case, where the claimant was dismissed for allegedly having attempted to undermine his managing director's authority, the dismissal was held to have been unfair

---

7. See *Industrial Relations Law*, pp.115-118.
8. [1982] ILRM 404.   9. Id. at p.413.
10. *Looney & Co. Ltd v. Looney* (UD 843/1984) *Cases*, p.235.

because the employee had been denied natural justice.[11] The Tribunal's view there was that 'compliance with the requirements of natural justice could have resulted in the decision to dismiss the claimant not being taken.'[12] Exceptionally, however, a dismissal will be sustained even though the agreed or the customary procedures were not followed. According to Barron J in *Loftus and Healy v. An Bord Telecom*,[13] the question to be determined is 'not whether the plaintiffs were deprived of procedures to which they were entitled, but whether the denial to them of such procedures is such that the (employer) must be deemed to have failed to establish [the stated basis of that dismissal] as the whole or the main reason for and justifying their dismissal.'[14] It was held in England that, in cases where agreed or fair procedures were not followed, the issue should not then be whether the employer would have decided differently if he had adopted the proper procedures. According to the Law Lords, in such cases '[i]t is what the employer did that wants to be judged, not what he might have done'.[15]

Determining the reason: It must first be determined why the employee was dismissed. Employees have an express statutory right to be given a written statement of the reasons for their dismissal.[16] A request for this document must be made within 14 days of the dismissal. Where a claim is made under the 1977 Act, the employer is not confined to advancing the grounds contained in this statement; the Tribunal or court may take account of any other grounds which would justify the dismissal.[17]

Deemed unfair reasons: If it is demonstrated that the dismissal was wholly or mainly for any of the following reasons, it is deemed by s.6(2) of the Act to have been unfair. However, the catalogue of deemed unfair grounds in s.6(2) is stated to be '[w]ithout prejudice to the generality of' s.6(1) of the 1977 Act. It therefore would seem that this deeming is not an iron inflexible rule for most of these reasons; in other words, very exceptional circumstances may exist which may justify a dismissal on most of these grounds. The burden of proving that the dismissal was for one of these reasons is on the employee.[18]

11. Similarly, *Gearon v. Dunnes Stores Ltd* (UD 367/1988) *Cases*, p.138 and *McCarthy v. Córas Iompair Éireann* (Circuit Court, 10 May 1985) *Cases* p.140.
12. [1982] ILRM at p.413.
13. Barron J, 6 JISLL 135.   14. At p.138.
15. *Polkey v. A.E. Dayton Services Ltd* [1988] 1 AC 344, at p.355.
16. S.14(4); also Employment Equality Act, 1977, s.28.
17. Ibid.
18. See *Cases*, ch.7 for a selection of instances under s.6(2).

- *Trade union membership or activities:* This matter is dealt with elsewhere.[19]

- *Race or colour:* Although Ireland does not have legislation which comprehensively outlaws race discrimination generally, a dismissal motivated by racial considerations or on grounds of colour is deemed to be unfair.[20]

- *Religion or politics:* In addition to the constitutional guarantee of religious and political freedom, a dismissal of an employee for his religious or political opinions is deemed to be unfair.[21]

- *Pregnancy or maternity leave:* It is presumptively unfair to dismiss because of the employee's pregnancy or matters connected therewith.[22] However, there are special circumstances which may justify a dismissal for those reasons. On account of the particular reason, the employee must be unable to do her job adequately or without contravening some law or regulation; additionally, there must be no vacancy which would be suitable for her or she must have refused an offer of a different job on terms corresponding to those of the job from which she was dismissed. Where a woman is dismissed because she choose to exercise her rights, under the Maternity Protection of Employees Act, 1981, either to maternity leave, to additional maternity leave or to time off under that Act, her dismissal is deemed to be unfair for the purposes of the 1977 Act.[23] The woman must have been entitled under the 1981 Act to the right in question. She also must not fall within the category of employees who are excluded from the 1977 Act, except that she need not possess one year's continuous service in the job and she may even be an employed probationer or a trainee or a statutory apprentice.

- *Sex or marital status:* Even though the Employment Equality Act and the Unfair Dismissals Act were passed in the same year, dismissal on the grounds of a person's sex or marital status is not listed as one of the deemed unfair grounds under the latter Act. But dismissal on one of those grounds is proscribed by s.3(4) of the former Act and, accordingly, it is only in the most exceptional case that a dismissal for reason of sex or marital status would not be regarded as an unfair dismissal. If, however, the claimant falls within one of those categories of employees who are excluded from the Unfair Dismissals Act, her mode of redress is a claim

19. S.6(2)(a); see *Industrial Relations Law*, pp.63-64 and 65- 66.
20. S.6(2)(e).   21. S.6(2)(b).
22. S.6(2)(f). Cf. *Flynn v. Power* [1985] IR 648, infra p.203.
23. S.6(2)(g), added by Maternity Protection of Employees Act, 1981, s.25.

before the Labour Court for compensation under s.27 of the Employment Equality Act. The compensation recoverable in a claim of this nature is such amount as the Labour Court 'thinks reasonable', subject to a maximum of two years usual remuneration.[24]

• *Proceedings against employer:* A dismissal is deemed to be unfair where the reason was that the employee is either a party to or is a likely witness to civil or criminal proceedings which have been brought against the employer or which are proposed or threatened to be brought against the employer.[25] Additionally, where a person is dismissed solely or mainly for making an equal pay claim under the Anti-Discrimination (Pay) Act, 1974, or is dismissed for claiming discrimination on the grounds of sex or marital status under the Employment Equality Act, 1977, or under the Pensions Act, 1990, or notifying an intention either to bring a claim, to give evidence or to oppose unlawful action under either of these Acts, these Acts lay down special machinery whereby redress can be obtained.[26] Either a claim can be brought before the Labour Court or criminal proceedings can be instituted.

Justifying dismissal Section 6(4) of the Unfair Dismissals Act then sets out several grounds on which the dismissal can be justified by the employer. In other words, if the dismissal was 'wholly or mainly' for any of these reasons, there is a strong likelihood that it will not be unfair, viz. misconduct, inability for several reasons to do the job and redundancy. But these are not the exclusive reasons for upholding a dismissal; it will also be upheld where the employer can demonstrate 'other substantial grounds' which would justify the dismissal.

Misconduct. If an employee commits one or more acts of misconduct, which would cause an average employer in the circumstances to dismiss him, his dismissal would usually be upheld by the Tribunal or the Court, especially where fair or agreed disciplinary procedures were followed.[27] The actual term used in s.6(4)(b) is 'conduct' and not misconduct; the full significance of this remains to be determined. Among the questions which arise under this heading is whether the act or acts in the circumstances are sufficiently serious in general terms to warrant dismissal; would they warrant summary dismissal or only dismissal with full notice; should the employee have been warned in advance of the likely consequences of his acts; were the requisite

---

24. S.23.   25. S.6(2)(c) and (d).
26. 1974 Act ss.9 and 10, 1977 Act ss.25 and 26 and 1990 Act ss.80 and 81.
27. See *Cases* ch.9 for a selection of instances of misconduct.

procedures followed. The Tribunal has described its general approach to misconduct in these terms:

> In deciding whether or not the dismissal . . . was unfair we apply a test of reasonableness to
> (1) the nature and extent of the enquiry carried out by the [employer] prior to the decision to dismiss . . . and
> (2) the conclusion arrived at by the [employer] that on the basis of the information resulting from such enquiry, the [employee] should be dismissed.[28]

The overriding test is reasonableness: did the employer have reasonable grounds for believing that the employee had misconducted himself and was the sanction of dismissal proportionate to that conduct?

Incapacity for the job: Another justification for upholding a dismissal is that the employee is not capable, qualified or competent to do his work or it would be unlawful for the employer to continue employing him.[29] The catch-all heading 'incapacity' used here perhaps puts the position too strongly; in the words of the Act, the dismissal may be justifiable if it was due to

> (a) the capability, competence or qualifications of the employee for performing work of the kind which he was employed by the employer to do. . . . (or)
> (d) the employee being unable to work or continue to work in the position which he held without contravention (by him or by his employer) of a duty or restriction imposed by or under any statute or instrument made under statute.[30]

Allegations of incapability to do the work usually concern absences from work, such as on account of illness, or irregular or persistent late attendance at work. When considering allegations of incompetence, account must always be taken of the employer's apparent failure to detect that defect when hiring the employee and not remedying it by appropriate training. The Tribunal does not yet appear to have dealt with a dismissal caused by the employee not having the requisite 'qualification' for his job. Examples of where it would be illegal to continue employing a worker include where the requisite consents have not been obtained under the Aliens Act, 1935. As is the case with dismissals for misconduct, the overriding test is that of

---

28. *Hennessy v. Read & Write Shop Ltd* (UD 192/78) *Cases* p.211.
29. See *Cases* ch.8 for a selection of instances of incapacity.
30. S.6(4)(a) and (d).

reasonableness; had the employer reasonable grounds for believing that the worker was incapable as described here and, in all the circumstances, was dismissal a reasonable and fair response to the situation.

Redundancy: Another justification for upholding a dismissal is that the employee was made redundant.[31] Redundancy for these purposes has the same meaning as in the Redundancy Payments Acts, 1967-1979.[32] However, even if there was a redundancy, the employee may succeed in a claim under the Unfair Dismissals Act on the grounds that he was unfairly selected to be made redundant.[33] Many claims are made for compensation for so-called 'unfair redundancy' because employees often stand to recover a larger sum under the 1977 Act than the lump sum redundancy payment they would be entitled to under the 1967-1979 Acts. In order to succeed in a claim under this head, the employee must first demonstrate that 'the circumstances constituting the redundancy applied equally to one or more other employees in similar employment' with the employer and who were not dismissed. In other words, there were other employees doing that type of work and who could have been made redundant but were not dismissed. It is not always essential that the employees being compared here all work in the very same location or unit, provided they are in 'similar employment'.

Where this is established, the claimant will succeed if he shows that the actual reason why he, and not one of his comparable employees, was selected is a ground which would not justify his dismissal. These grounds may be any of the deemed unfair reasons referred to above or some other reason which, in all the circumstances, was unfair to the employee. If the employee's selection was in breach of an agreed or customary arrangement for dealing with redundancies it will be deemed to have been unfair unless there were 'special reasons' for departing from that procedure.

Other substantial grounds: In an appropriate case, a dismissal will be upheld where it was caused by grounds other than redundancy, incapacity or misconduct, as described above. What these grounds are and whether in any particular instance they would justify a dismissal depends on the entire circumstances of the case.[34] Thus, there are Tribunal cases where third party pressure to have the employee dismissed were held to justify[35] and not to justify[36] dismissal. Another ground which may justify dismissal is inability

---

31. S.6(4)(c).   32. See infra p.210.
33. S.6(3); see *Cases* ch.10 for a selection of instances.
34. See *Cases* ch.11 for a selection of instances.
35. E.g. *Jackson v. John McCarthy & Co.* (UD 297/78) *Cases* p.295.
36. E.g. *Merrigan v. Home Counties Cleaning Ireland Ltd* (UD 904/84) *Cases* p.293 and *McSweeney v. OK Garages Ltd* (UD 107/78) *Cases* p.295.

to obtain employer's liability insurance for the employee.[37] In *Flynn v. Power*,[38] the plaintiff was a school teacher employed by nuns at a convent school in a country town. She was openly living with a married man and had a child by him. Her employers asked her to terminate her relationship with that man on account of the example she was giving the school children. Costello J held that, in those circumstances, her employers were entitled to 'regard her conduct as a rejection of the norms of behaviour and the ideals which the school was endeavouring to instil in and to set for' the children.[39] They, accordingly, were entitled 'to foster in their pupils norms of behaviour and religious tenets which the school had been established to promote'.[40] Therefore, it was found, there were substantial grounds for dismissing her. As with the other grounds discussed above, the overriding test of the employer's actions is that of reasonableness and proportionality.

Redress Where a qualified employee has been unfairly dismissed, his redress may take the form of getting his job back or obtaining a different job or else the payment of compensation.[41] A claim for redress under the 1977 Act may be made to a rights commissioner or to the Employment Appeals Tribunal.[42] There is an appeal from the E.A.T. to the Circuit Court,[43] by way of a full re-hearing of the case; there is a further appeal to the High Court, also by way of a full re-hearing of the dispute.[44] Regulations have been adopted which regulate in detail the mode for bringing claims to the E.A.T.[45] A claim cannot be brought in the courts for damages for wrongful dismissal and at the same time a claim under the 1977 Act. Once an employee commences any common law proceedings for damages, he is precluded by s.15(3) from claiming unfair dismissal under the Act. But seeking exclusively injunctive relief does not forfeit the right to claim under the 1977 Act.

Notice of the claim must be given within six months of the date of dismissal.[46] Subject to some exceptions, the claimant must have been continuously employed by that employer at least fifty two weeks prior to

37. *Browne v. Aga Khan* (UD 332/87) *Cases* p.297.
38. [1985] IR 648.
39. Id. at p.657.
40. Ibid. Similarly, *Berrisford v. Woodword Schools (Midland Division) Ltd* [1991] ICR 564.
41. S.7. 42. S.8(1). 43. S.10(4).
44. *McCabe v. Lisney & Son* [1981] ILRM 289.
45. SI No. 286 of 1977 — Unfair Dismissals (Claims and Appeals) Regulations, 1977. Cf. *Halal Meat Packers (Ballyhaunis) Ltd v. Employment Appeals Tribunal* [1990] ILRM 293, on the overriding requirement that the Tribunal follows fair procedures; see ante p.23.
46. S.8(2); cf. *State (I.B.M. Ireland Ltd) v. Employment Appeals Tribunal* [1984] ILRM 31.

the dismissal date.[47] There is no indication in the 1977 Act of when any one of the modes of redress discussed below should be preferred over others, apart from what the tribunal 'considers appropriate having regard to all the circumstances.'[48] Before opting for any one or more remedies, the Tribunal or court should seek to ascertain the views of the parties on the matter,[49] although the Tribunal is not obliged always to follow their preference or the employee's preference.

Reinstatement: By reinstatement is meant the claimant getting his old job back as if he had never been dismissed. It is defined in the 1977 Act as re-instatement 'in the position which he held immediately before his dismissal. . . .'[50] Reinstatement is the preferred remedy always and, where it is ordered, will operate as from the date the employee was dismissed, thereby entitling him to remuneration for the entire intervening period. However, circumstances regarding the job itself, the employer or the claimant may dictate that some other redress should be awarded. Where the employee's actions substantially contributed to his dismissal, full re-instatement tends not to be ordered; instead the Tribunal directs re-engagement[51] or, at times, re-instatement but as from some time after the dismissal,[52] or compensation.[53] If the job no longer exists then reinstatement will not be ordered.

Re-engagement: By re-engagement is meant being re-employed by the employer either in the same job or in a suitable different job. It is defined in the 1977 Act as re-engagement 'either in the position which he held immediately before his dismissal or in a different position which would be reasonably suitable for him on such terms and conditions as are reasonable having regard to all the circumstances'.[54] Among the reasons for not directing re-engagement are that relationships between the parties had deteriorated badly or that, due to changes which have been made, no suitable job is available. There is a tendency not to require that senior executives be re-engaged, because their dismissal almost always would have ruptured the essential degree of confidence the parties should have in each other.[55]

47. S.2(1)(a); for details, see ante p.184.
48. S.7(1); see *Cases* ch.12 for a selection of instances.
49. *State (Irish Pharmaceutical Union) v. Employment Appeals Tribunal* [1987] ILRM 386.
50. S.7(1)(a).
51. E.g. *McDonald v. Des Gibney Ltd* (UD 329/85) *Cases* p.306.
52. E.g. *Lynch v. Sunbeam Ltd* (UD 20/77) *Cases* p.307.
53. E.g. *Gibney v. Riverside Mfg. Co. (Ir.) Ltd* (UD 732/87) *Cases* p.304.
54. S.7(1)(b).
55. E.g. *Bunyan v. United Dominions Trust (Ir.) Ltd* [1982] ILRM 404 and *Gibney*, supra n.53.

Compensation: Where neither of these two modes are appropriate, compensation will be awarded, up to a maximum of two years normal remuneration. But an award of compensation will not be made simply because that is what the claimant prefers; his views are not decisive where it appears that the employer would be prepared to take him back.

Measuring the loss: The criteria laid down in the 1977 Act for ascertaining the amount to be paid in compensation is 'in respect of any financial loss incurred by him and attributable to the dismissal as is just and equitable having regard to all the circumstances.'[56] Financial loss for these purposes is defined as 'includ[ing] any actual loss and any estimated prospective loss of income and the value of any loss or diminution, attributable to the dismissal, of the rights of the employee under the Redundancy Payments Acts . . . or in relation to superannuation'.[57] And remuneration is defined there as 'includ[ing] allowances in the nature of pay and benefits in lieu of or in addition to pay'.[58] Thus, not only loss of wages but all forms of financial loss reasonably resulting from the dismissal will be compensated.

Adding to or subtracting from that sum: Once the amount of the financial loss has been determined, an additional amount may be awarded because of how badly the employer acted in the circumstances or because agreed dismissal procedures or a code of practice for handling dismissals had not been complied with.[59] Conversely, a deduction may be made from that sum reflecting the fact that the employee had been substantially or partly at fault in causing his own dismissal. A deduction will also be made where the employee failed to mitigate his losses.

Ceiling on compensation: There is an overall ceiling on the amount of compensation which can be awarded, being 104 weeks of 'normal remuneration', as defined in the Unfair Dismissals (Calculation of Weekly Remuneration) Regulations, 1977.[60]

REDUNDANCY

In order for their business to survive, employers must compete in the market place, domestic and international. Successful competition will often require changes in the employer's establishment in response to new commercial pressures and technological innovation. At times, changes of that nature will involve a reduction of the workforce—be it an all-over reduction or the replacement of some existing employees by others who are more suitable

---

56. S.7(1)(c).   57. S.7(3).   58. Ibid.   59. S.7(2)(a) and (d).
60. SI No. 287 of 1977; for text, see Appendix.

for the changed nature of the job. In order to overcome the inevitable resistence by employees to their being put out of work through no fault of their own, it was found necessary at least to guarantee them compensation for loosing their jobs. Often trade unions negotiate the amount of compensation to be paid to employees being made redundant and, if the union is in a strong bargaining position, substantial sums can be secured on their members' behalf, the amounts usually being based on a multiplier of each employee's present salary and his seniority. Disputes about redundancy are 'trade disputes' for the purpose of the law regarding strikes, lock-outs and picketing but immunity from tort liability is conditional on individual grievance procedures being exhausted.[61]

For many years there have been provisions for paying redundancy compensation to several categories of employees in the public sector. Perhaps the best known of these, which gave rise to a very substantial body of litigation, was Article 10 of the 1922 Treaty between Ireland and Great Britain, whereby civil servants who retired in consequence of the change of regime and government were to be compensated.[62] Legislation governing local authorities often provided for compensating persons who lost their offices when the structures of local government were charged.[63] The first schedule to the Electricity (Supply) Act, 1927, is a scheme for compensating employees who were made redundant as a result of nationalising the electricity supply industry and there are numerous provisions in the many Transport Acts providing for redundancy compensation when C.I.E. employees lost their jobs in the many re-organisations of that business.[64]

The Redundancy Payments Acts The Redundancy Payments Acts, 1967-1979, were enacted principally to make it easier for employers to reorganise their businesses, by guaranteeing substantial lump sum payments to workers who stood to loose their jobs in the course of reorganisation. These Acts apply to public as well as private sector employees, except for those who are not insured for all social welfare benefits. The 1967 Act is modelled on its British predecessor of the previous year and many of the British cases

61. *Goulding Chemicals Ltd v. Bolger* [1977] IR 211; see *Industrial Relations Law*, pp.133-134 and 144-146.
62. Cf. *Wigg v. Attorney General* [1927] IR 285, *Lonsdale v. Attorney General* [1928] IR 35, *Re Compensation to Civil Servants* [1929] IR 44, *Birmingham v. Attorney General* [1932] IR 510, *Fitzgibbon v. Attorney General* [1930] IR 49, and *De Lacey Smith v. Attorney General* [1934] IR 139.
63. Cf. *O'Neill v. Tipperary C.C. (South Riding)* [1926] IR 397, *O'Sullivan v. Limerick C.C.* [1928] IR 493 and *O'Driscoll v. Cork C.C.* [1931] IR 92.
64. Cf. *Stenson v. Córas Iompair Éireann* [1967] IR 409. S. 48 of the Redundancy Payments Act, 1967, deals with overlaps with the special arrangements for C.I.E. employees.

are helpful for interpretation; these are analysed extensively in Grundfeld's *Law of Redundancy*.[65] But there are significant differences between parts of the Irish and British legislation, most notably, regarding what exactly constitutes becoming 'redundant'. As in the case with minimum notice and unfair dismissals, therefore, great care should be taken when relying on the British cases for guidance.

The 1967 Act was amended extensively in 1971 and again in 1979. What the Redundancy Payments Acts, 1967-1979, principally do is require that an eligible employee who is made redundant be paid a lump sum, the amount being determined with reference to his salary and seniority. In order to finance these payments, a special Redundancy Fund was established, into which all employers made contributions. In 1991 that Fund, which in 1984 became the Redundancy and Employers' Insolvency Fund, amalgamated with the general Social Insurance Fund;[66] it is now financed by the normal social insurance contributions. When any employer has to make a redundancy payment, he is entitled to be reimbursed 60 per cent of the amount from the Fund.[67] In addition to any lump sum, eligible employees who are about to be made redundant are entitled to notice of that fact and to time off to find a new job.[68] As well as the 1967-1979 Acts, there is the Protection of Employment Act, 1977, dealing with 'collective redundancies', which requires employers to consult with trade unions when they are considering making groups of employees redundant.[69]

Employees not covered The Redundancy Payments Acts, 1967-1979, apply to employees and apprentices.[70] But not all employees are entitled to obtain compensation under these Acts. In addition to the groups set out hereunder, s.14(1) of the 1967 Act disentitle employees who were lawfully dismissed for misconduct.

Continuity of employment: To begin with, they must have the requisite continuity of employment, which is 104 weeks (or two years) full-time or regular part-time employment.[71] A week in this context means a working

65. 3rd ed. 1989.
66. 1967 Act s.27, as amended by Social Welfare Act, 1991, s.39.
67. 1967 Act s.29, as amended by s.13 of the 1971 Act. The procedure for claiming rebates is laid down in the Redundancy (Rebates) Regulations, SI No. 122 of 1990. Rebates will be paid only where the lump sum was indeed payable under the legislation. Cf. *Secretary of State v. Cheltenham Computer Bureau* [1985] ICR 381.
68. Redundancy Payments Act, 1979, s.7; see infra p.212.
69. See *Industrial Relations Law*, pp.83-84.
70. See definition of 'employee' in 1967 Act s.2(1).
71. 1967 Act, s.4(2) as amended by the Worker Protection (Regular Part-Time Employment) Act, 1991.

week as contrasted with seven days.[72] Continuous employment is presumed unless the contrary is proved.[73] Special rules are contained in the 1967 Act's Third schedule for calculating continuity of employment.[74] In addition to having been continuously employed for the requisite period, the employee must have been employed at a job which is insurable for all benefits under the Social Welfare Acts, for a period of four years before he was dismissed.[75]

The continuity requirement applies only to the lump sum payment; it does not affect otherwise eligible employees' entitlements to notice under s.17 of the 1967 Act and to time off under s.7 of the 1979 Act.

Public service: Public sector employment falls within the general scope of these Acts because a business, for their purposes, is defined as including 'any activity carried on . . . by a public or a local authority or a Department of State, and the performance of its functions by a public or local authority or a Department of State'.[76] However, the requirement of the employee being insurable for all benefits under the Social Welfare Acts excludes a substantial number of public service workers from entitlement to redundancy compensation.[77]

Part-time workers: These Acts do not apply to part-time workers, meaning those 'normally expected to work' for the same employer for less than eight hours in a week.[78]

Pensioners: These Acts do not apply to employees who have reached the pensionable age under the Social Welfare Acts, which is 66 years of age.[79]

Close family/domestics: Employees who are employed by a close member of their family in a domestic situation are not covered by these Acts.[80]

Transnationals: Special provision is made by s.25 of the 1967 Act for employees who ordinarily work outside the State.[81]

---

72. *Gormley v. McCartin Bros. (Engineering) Ltd* [1982] ILRM 215.
73. 1971 Act s.10(a).
74. As amended extensively by the 1971 Act; see ante pp.183-188.
75. 1967 Act ss.4(1) and 7(1)(b), as amended by the 1971 Act.
76. 1967 Act s.2(1).
77. The (non-industial) civil service and other public officers are class B and class D contributors respectively.
78. Supra n.11.
79. 1967 Act s.4(1), as amended by 1979 Act s.5.
80. 1967 Act s.4(3), as amended by 1971 Act schedule.
81. See post pp.271-272.

Dismissal and its date In order to claim compensation under the Redundancy Payments Acts, the qualified employee must have been 'dismissed ... by reason of redundancy' or else was 'laid off or kept on short time'.[82] As has been explained, under s.9 of the 1967 Act, a dismissal for these purposes means a unilateral termination of the employment contract by the employer, the non-renewal of a fixed term contract which has expired and so-called 'constructive dismissal', where the employee leaves as a result of action by the employer amounting to a repudiation of the contract.[83] Unlike for unfair dismissals, the expiry of a 'specific purpose' contract and also constructive dismissal where the employee merely has acted reasonably in leaving his job do not constitute dismissals for redundancy purposes. Where an employer dies or some other event occurs which by law operates to terminate the employment contract, the employee is deemed to have been dismissed if his contract was not renewed or he was not re-engaged on the same terms and conditions.[84]

An employee is deemed not to have been dismissed where his contract has been renewed or where he is re-engaged by the same or by another employer in certain circumstances. In the case of renewal or re-engagement by his former employer,[85] the terms of the new contract must not differ from the corresponding terms in the previous contract; the re-employment must have commenced not later then four weeks after his dismissal and his employer must have made a written offer of re-employment before the dismissal. In the case of re-engagement by another employer,[86] that must have happened with the agreement of the employee and of both the previous and the new employer; it must have commenced immediately after the previous job ended; and before that the employer must have been given a written statement of the terms and conditions of the new job and the period of continuous service with the former employer which will be carried forward in the new job.

For the purposes of these Acts, the date of the dismissal is defined by s.2(1) of the 1967 Act, as either the date on which dismissal notice given expires; where notice of dismissal was not given, the dismissal date is when the termination actually took place or the date when a fixed term contract expired. But where no or very little notice is given, the contract cannot terminate until the requisite minimum notice period under the 1973 Minimum Notice etc. Act has expired. Unlike for unfair dismissals, no special provision is made for when less than the contractual notice is given. Where an employee receives notice of dismissal but he then notifies his

---

82. 1967 Act s.7(1).   83. 1967 Act s.9(1) and ante pp.154-156.
84. 1967 Act s.21; cf. id. 2nd schedule on effects of death on either party.
85. Id. s.9(2).   86. Id. s.9(3).

employer that he will leave on a date before that notice is to expire, the date of the dismissal is deemed to be the time when the employee's notice expired.[87] But the employer may require him to withdraw that notice and ask that he continue in employment until the notice given by the employer expires.[88]

Making employees redundant The concept of redundant for the purposes of the Redundancy Payments Act is a term of art, defined by s.7(2) of the 1967 Act. The original definition was extended in 1971.[89] An employee who has been dismissed is presumed to have been dismissed by reason of redundancy.[90]

'Redundant': According to s.7(2) of the 1967 Act, as amended,

> an employee who is dismissed shall be taken to be dismissed by reason of redundancy if the dismissal is attributable wholly or mainly to—
>
> (a) the fact that his employer has ceased, or intends to cease, to carry on the business for the purposes of which the employee was employed by him, or has ceased or intends to cease, to carry on that business in the place where the employee was so employed, or
>
> (b) the fact that the requirements of that business for employees to carry out work of a particular kind in the place where he was so employed have ceased or diminished or are expected to cease or diminish, or
>
> (c) the fact that his employer has decided to carry on the business with fewer or no employees, whether by requiring the work for which the employee had been employed (or had been doing before his dismissal) to be done by other employees or otherwise, or
>
> (d) the fact that his employer has decided that the work for which the employee has been employed (or had been doing before his dismissal) should henceforward be done in a different manner for which the employee is not sufficiently qualified or trained, or
>
> (e) the fact that his employer has decided that the work for which the employee had been employed (or had been doing before his dismissal) should henceforward be done by a person who is also capable of doing

---

87. 1967 Act s.10.   88. Id. s.10(3).
89. 1971 Act s.4; this amendment was prompted by *Limerick Health Authority v. Ryan* [1969] IR 194.
90. 1971 Act s.10(b).

other work for which the employee is not sufficiently qualified or trained.

This definition is very extensive; it sweeps far wider than the comparable definition in Britain. Although redundancy often connotes cut-backs as a result of contracting orders for the employer's output or relocation of the business and the necessary reorganisation in order to deal with harsher times, the concept under s.7(2) is not confined to that. Sub-section (a) and (b), which are similar to those in the British Act, deal with contractions of that nature— the type of business for which the employee was hired ceasing or relocating, or economic or technical changes diminishing the need for employees with particular skills or other attributes. But sub-sections (c)–(e) could be satisfied without the employer being under any economic pressure to shed some of the workforce. These cover situations where, for one reason or another, the employer decides to reduce the workforce or, without any reduction, to replace an employee with another who has different training or by replacing an employee with someone who will do both that job and other work as well, for which the departing employee is not adequately trained. Virtually all forms of rational reorganisation of a workforce fall within s.7(2). For instance, employees have been held to have been made redundant where the employer wanted them to change from day work to doing the same job at nights for part of the working week;[91] where the employer replaced full-time staff with part-time employees doing the same job;[92] where a long-standing employee was replaced by a member of the employer's family who had just finished secondary school.[93] Section 7(2)'s provisions have not yet been the subject of any exhaustive analysis in the Superior Courts and, indeed, do not seem to have caused much difficulty in the E.A.T. or the Circuit Court, on account of its extensive sweep.[94]

Because the 1967-1979 Acts presume a redundancy situation until the contrary is shown, the burden of proof is on the employer-defendant/respondent to show that the employee was not dismissed on account of redundancy. It would seem that these Acts apply even where there were several reasons for the dismissal, including redundancy, provided that redundancy was a significant reason. For s.7(1) of the 1967 Act states that a right to a lump sum arises once the plaintiff was dismissed 'by reason of redundancy'. Where redundancy is being invoked as a defence to an action for unfair dismissal, the burden of proof also falls on the employer, who

91. *Dimworth v. Southern Health Board* (284/77).
92. *Kelleher v. St. James Hospital Board* (59/77).
93. *Hallinan v. Gilligan* (UD 564/81).
94. See D. Madden & T. Kerr, *Unfair Dismissal: Cases and Commentary* (1990) ch.10 for a selection of instances.

must show that the dismissal resulted 'wholly or mainly from redundancy'.[95] The burden is also on the employer to show that the dismissal was not unfair in any of the ways described in s.6(3) of the 1977 Act.[96]

Redundancy notices and certificates: At least two weeks written notice of the proposed redundancy must be given to all eligible employees affected by the employer's decision.[97] Eligibility here requires two years' continuous service. Two weeks' notice must also be given to the Minister for Labour.[98] In the case of employees being made redundant but who do not have the requisite two years' continuous employment to obtain a lump sum, they must be furnished with redundancy certificates before they are dismissed.[99] In the case of 'collective redundancies' as defined in the Protection of Employment Act, 1977, the Minister for Labour must be given at least 30 days' written notice of the employer's proposals[100] and there should be consultations with employees' representatives and with the Minister.[1]

Paid time off: Section 7 of the 1979 Act gives every eligible employee being made redundant a right to 'reasonable time off . . . in order to look for new employment or make arrangements for training for future employment.' Eligibility here requires two years' continuous service. Before granting time off for this purpose, the employer can require evidence to show that the time will be spent on searching for work or making arrangements about re-training. The time during which this right arises is in the last two weeks of the redundancy notice period. During the employee's absence, he is entitled to be paid the appropriate hourly rate obtaining on the day he received his redundancy notice.

Lay off and short time A 'lay off' involves an employee being suspended from work without pay for some specified or indefinite period. Unless the employment contract gives a right to lay off in this manner, normally such action is a repudiation of the agreement by the employer, entitling the employee to treat it as a dismissal.[2] 'Short time' involves working for

95. See ante p.202; e.g. *Daly v. Hanson Industries Ltd* (UD 719/86).
96. *Caladom Ltd v. Hoare & Kelly* (Cir. Ct. 1985 no's 48 and 49).
97. 1967 Act s.17 and Redundancy (Notice of Dismissal) Regulations, 1991, S.I. No. 348 of 1991.
98. Ibid. and Redundancy Certificate Regulations, 1991, S.I. No. 347 of 1991.
99. 1967 Act s.18, as amended by the 1971 Act.
100. S.12 and infra p.218.
  1. *Industrial Relations Law*, pp.83-84.
  2. *Devonald v. Rosser & Sons* [1906] 2 KB 728; compare *Browning v. Crumlin Valley Colleries Ltd* [1926] 1 KB 522.

significantly less than the normal hours and, depending on the contract's terms, may also amount to a repudiation by the employer of the agreement. Where an employee is put on temporary lay off or short time work, he is not there and then entitled to claim compensation for having been made redundant. But if that lay off or short time exceeds a specified period, he then is entitled to be compensated, provided of course the other qualifying conditions have been satisfied.

A lay off, for these purposes is defined by s.11(1) of the 1967 Act as where the employer is unable to provide work of the kind which the employee was hired to do but it is reasonable in the circumstances for the employer to believe that he will be re-hiring the employee. Notice to that effect must have been given to the employee before being laid off. Short time, for these purposes, is defined by s.11(2) of the 1967 Act[3] as where, because of a fall in the kind of work the employee was hired to do, his weekly pay is reduced to less than half his 'normal weekly remuneration', or his working hours are correspondingly reduced, but it is reasonable in the circumstances for the employer to believe that this state of affairs will not be permanent. Again, notice to this effect must have been given to the employee before his earnings or working hours were cut. It depends on all the circumstances whether an employer was reasonable in believing that a lay off or short time would not be permanent.[4]

Entitlement to be paid the lump sum will arise when the lay off or short time exceeds the following periods.[5] One is where they last for four or more consecutive weeks. Alternatively, where within a period of thirteen weeks, the employee was laid off or put on short time for six or more weeks and more than three of those weeks were consecutive. In either of these events, the employee may notify the employer of his intention to claim a redundancy payment.[6] Such an intention is deemed to have been notified where the employee gives his employer notice that he is terminating the employment contract.[7] However, if at the time the employee notifies his claim, it was reasonable to expect that, within the next four weeks, the employee would be resuming full time employment for at least another thirteen weeks, the employee is not entitled to the payment.[8] For practical purposes, therefore,

---

3. As amended by 1979 Act s.10.
4. Cf. *Industrial Yarns Ltd v. Greene* [1984] ILRM 15 and *Irish Leathers Ltd v. Minister for Labour* [1986] IR 177.
5. 1967 Act s.12(1)(a), as amended by 1971 Act s.11.
6. 1967 Act s.12(1)(b), as amended by 1971 Act s.11.
7. 1967 Act s.12(2), as amended by 1971 Act s.11; cf. *Industrial Yarns Ltd v. Greene* [1984] ILRM 15.
8. 1967 Act s.13(1).

a lay off or short time can last for up to eight weeks before a right to a lump sum can arise. The additional four weeks referred to here apply only if the employer had notified the employee of his intention to contest any claim being made for a redundancy payment.

Offer of new employment Generally, the fact that an employee obtained another job immediately on or shortly after being made redundant does not disentitle him to a lump sum payment otherwise due to him under the Redundancy Payments Acts. There is no rule whereby the amount payable to him is subject to mitigation in those circumstances or can be reduced because of his bad behaviour. This principle is subject to one major set of exceptions. An employee who was dismissed for redundancy is not entitled to compensation where he was offered suitable new employment, in accordance with ss.15, 16 or 20 of the 1967 Act and he 'unreasonably refused' that offer. Additionally, an employee who has been re-engaged by or with the agreement of his old employer in accordance with s.9(2) and (3) of the 1967 Act, is not even deemed to have been dismissed for the purposes of the Redundancy Payments Acts.[9]

In order for a dismissed redundant employee to become disentitled to a payment, the following must have taken place. The employer must have offered to renew the employment or have offered the employee a new contract.[10] The terms and conditions of employment offered may either be the same as those under the old contract or may differ from those terms. If the same terms are being offered, the employment must be one which commences on or before the date the old job was due to end. If different terms are being offered, the employer's offer must be made in writing that the employment must be one which commences within four weeks of the old job ending. Moreover, the job offered must be 'suitable employment in relation to the employee'. It is only when an employee 'unreasonably refuses' an offer in these terms that he becomes disentitled to a payment. Considerable discretion is left to the tribunals and courts to determine what types of employment are 'suitable' for these purposes and when a refusal of an offer is 'unreasonable'. Special provision is made for where the offer comes from an associate company of the present employer[11] and also for where the employee continued working for a purchaser of the old employer's business.[12]

'Suitable' alternative employment: Where the terms and conditions offered are different from those of the existing job, the offer must be of 'suitable

9. See ante p.209.   10. 1967 Act s.15(1) and (2).
11. Id. s.16.   12. Id. s.20.

employment' for that employee. In determining suitability, presumably the focus is on determining whether, in the light of the employee's skills and experience, the job is one which he is well capable of performing and which also does not involve any significant element of demotion. According to Grunfeld,[13] the British courts and tribunals consider the following matters: *inter alia*, pay, greater distance from existing home, need to change place of residence, the employee's health, his skill and status, retraining, domestic circumstances and any collective offer.

'Unreasonable' refusal: Even where the job being offered is suitable, the employee may refuse it on reasonable grounds and thereby does not prejudice his entitlement to the lump sum. In determining what is reasonable and unreasonable, in practice account tends to be taken of the extent to which the old and the new terms and conditions diverge and also the suitability of the job for the employee, although the conflating of these matters has been criticised by judges in Britain. According to Grunfeld,[14] the most important consideration is personal domestic circumstances; others include pay, retraining, travelling time and expenses.

Offer by associated employer: Where the employer is a company, the alternative employment may be offered, for these purposes, by one of its associated companies.[15] An associated company for these purposes is a subsidiary company or, where the employer itself is a subsidiary, another subsidiary of the same parent company.

Offer by transferee of business: As is explained in detail in chapter 11, a transfer of business for the purposes of employment law involves the transfer of all or part of a business as a going concern. It is to be contrasted with a sale or other disposal of the assets and no more. Whether what was transferred was ownership of all or some of the business or was merely assets depends on the circumstances of the case.[16] Where an employee was made redundant 'immediately before' such a transfer and 'in connection with' that transfer, the following applies. If immediately after the change of

13. *The Law of Redundancy* (3rd ed. 1989) pp.182-189.
14. Id. pp.189-199.
15. 1967 Act s.16.
16. Cf. *Nova Colour Graphic Supplies Ltd v. Employment Appeals Tribunal* [1987] IR 426, *Marks v. Wellman* [1970] NI 236 and *Melon v. Hector Powe Ltd* [1981] 1 All ER 313. For instances of transfers or 'hive downs' by receivers, see *Dedway Trading Ltd v. Calverly* [1973] 3 All ER 776 and *Pambankian v. Brentford Nylons Ltd* [1978] ICR 665.

ownership the employee accepts employment with the transferee, he is deemed not to have been dismissed. If instead he is offered re-employment with the transferee which would be 'suitable' for him and he 'unreasonably' refuses that offer, he is not entitled to the lump sum payment.

Lump sum payments A qualified employee who was dismissed by reason of redundancy, or was laid off or placed on short time for the specified period, becomes entitled to a lump sum redundancy payment from the employer. A claim for a payment must be made to the employer within thirty weeks of the date the employee was dismissed or the contract was otherwise terminated.[17] Disputed claims are first referred to 'deciding officers', who are appointed for that purpose by the Minister;[18] there is an appeal from them, in the form of a full re-hearing to the Employment Appeals Tribunal.[19] Instead of determining the matter, the deciding officer at the very outset may refer it to the Tribunal.[20] The E.A.T.'s decision is final and conclusive but there is an appeal from the Tribunal to the High Court on a point of law.[21]

The rules for ascertaining the amount of the sum due are contained in the 3rd schedule to the 1967 Act, as amended. That amount is determined by reference to the length of the employee's 'continuous employment' and his 'normal weekly remuneration'. For these purposes, there is a different multiplier for service before and after the employee reached 41 years of age. Earnings in excess of £13,000 per annum are disregarded.[22] Because of the inflation in the last ten years, for practical purposes the normal earnings for which redundancy payments for most employees will be determined is £250 per week (i.e. £13,000÷52).

Continuous employment: As has been explained above, the 1967 Act's 3rd schedule lays down rules for ascertaining the length of a worker's continuous employment and reckonable service for these purposes,[23] dealing with what does and does not break continuity of service and when absences from work should be counted as periods of service.

Normal weekly remuneration: What an employee's 'normal weekly remuneration' is for these purposes is also dealt with in the 3rd schedule.[24] In the case of the average worker, whose remuneration does not vary with the actual amount of work done, his normal remuneration is

his earnings (including any regular bonus or allowance which does not

17. 1967 Act s.24.   18. Id. ss.37 and 38.   19. Id. s.39.
20. Id. s.39(16).   21. Id. s.39(14).   22. SI No. 18 of 1990.
23. Paras 4-12; supra p.183.   24. Paras 13-23.

vary in relation to the amount of work done and any payment in kind) for his normal weekly working hours as at the date on which he was declared redundant, together with, in the case of an employee who is normally expected to work overtime, his average weekly overtime earnings. . . .[25]

Computation: How the amount of the payment due is then determined is as follows.[26] The number of weeks continuous service is divided by 52, to get the yearly figure. The normal weekly remuneration is calculated as just described. Then for years of service with the employer between the ages of 16 and 41 years, the number of those years is multiplied by ▪▪▪▪▪ a half times the normal weekly remuneration. For years of service after 41 years of age (up to the State pension age), the number of those years is multiplied by the normal weekly remuneration. The employee is entitled in addition to one week's normal remuneration.

Collective Redundancies What are referred to as collective redundancies are regulated by the Protection of Employment Act, 1977, which is based on E.C. Directive 75/129.[27] A 'collective redundancy' for these purposes is the making redundant, over a period of 30 consecutive days, of a minimum number of employees, that minimum varying with the size of the establishment's workforce. For these purposes, redundant has the same meaning as under the 1967-1979 Acts [28] and, as in those Acts, a business is deemed to include any profession or undertaking or activity, including all public sector activities.[29] The 1977 Act's requirements do not apply to redundancies where the establishment in which the workers were employed was closed down following bankruptcy or winding up proceedings;[30] also where that close down was the result of any other decision of a competent court, for instance, where an examiner into the company's affairs had recommended the closure and the court then shut down the establishment.

Certain categories of employee are excluded from the Act, notably those employed by or under the State, with the exception of 'industrial' civil servants, officers of a local authority and merchant seamen employed under the prescribed agreement.[31] The due expiry of a fixed term contract or the

25. Para. 13, as amended. See also paras 14-15 and 17-23. Where employees are paid wholly or partly by piece rates, bonuses or commissions which are related directly to output, see para. 16 and elaborations in paras 17-23.
26. Paras 1-3.
27. O.J. No. L 48/29 (1975). Cf. *Re Collective Redundancies: E.C. Commission v. Belgium* (Case 215/83) [1985] 3 CMLR 624.
28. S.6(2); see supra p.210.   29. S.6(4).   30. S.7(2)(e).
31. S.7(2).

completion of an employment contract made for a specified purpose is not treated as a dismissal in this context.[32]

In order to trigger the 1977 Act's requirements, the minimum number of redundancies in a 30-day period for the employing 'establishment' is as follows:[33] in establishments 'normally employing' between 20 and 49 employees, at least five redundancies; in establishments normally employing between 50 and 99 employees, at least ten redundancies; in establishments normally employing between 100 and 299 employees, at least 10% of the workforce being made redundant; in establishments normally employing more than 300 employees, at least 30 redundancies. For these purposes, an establishment is the particular location or locations where the employer carries on a business or comparable activity.[34] For determining the average size of the workforce, the measure is the average over the 12 months preceding the date of the dismissal.[35]

Consultations with workers' representatives: The extent of the employer's obligation to consult with workers' representatives about the proposed redundancies has been described elsewhere.[36]

Notifying and consulting with the Minister: A common feature of employment law in Continental Europe is that, before they may take various types of decisions, employers are often required to notify the Ministry for Labour and enter into negotiations with officials of the Minister. Provisions along these lines are contained in the 1977 Act. Where the employer proposes to create collective redundancies, he must notify the Minister at the earliest opportunity; at the very least, notice must be given 30 days before the first dismissals are to occur.[37] A copy of that notice must be supplied promptly to the employees' representatives, who may submit to the Minister written observations on the matter. There is no obligation on employers to foresee or anticipate collective redundancies, for instance when they are in financial difficulties, nor does the Act affect their freedom to decide whether and with whom they should draw up plans for collective dismissals.[38]

Employers are required to supply certain 'relevant information' about the proposals to the employees' representatives; as soon as possible, a copy of that information must also be sent to the Minister.[39] That principally consists of details of the reasons for the proposed redundancies; the number,

32. S.7(2)(a).   33. S.6(1).
34. S.6(3).   35. S.8.
36. Ss.9 and 10; see *Industrial Relations Law*, pp.83-84.   37. S.12.
38. *Dansk Metalarbejderforbund i Danmark v. Nielsen & Son* (Case 284/83) [1986] 1 CMLR 91.
39. S.10.

description and categories of employees to be affected; the number of employees normally employed and the period during which the proposed redundancies are to take place.

At the Minister's request, the employer must enter into consultations with him or his chosen representative, with the objective of seeking solutions to the problem caused by the proposed redundancies.[40] Any information about the proposals as he may reasonably require must be supplied to the Minister.

Timing: Regardless of what notice the employees may be entitled to under their employment contracts or under the Minimum Notice etc. Act 1973, there is a 30 days' moratorium placed on collective redundancies.[41] Before the dismissals can take effect, at least 30 days must have expired after the Minister was notified by the employer about the proposed redundancies.

40. S.15.   41. S.14.

9

Transfer of employer's business

An employee may not always have the same employer throughout his working life. He may resign from his job or be dismissed and either move to another job or become unemployed. Or his present employer may dispose of the business or part of the business to a new owner and the employee may then become employed by that new owner. Business transfers are a comparatively frequent occurrence and take place for a variety of reasons. For instance, the present owner may want to retire entirely from business or he may see little future for the business he is disposing of or, indeed, that business may be insolvent and he is being compelled to liquidate it . The rights and duties of employees in business transfers may be the subject of special contractual arrangements or special statutory provisions. The position in this regard of most employees is regulated by the E.C.—inspired Transfer of Undertakings Regulations of 1980.[1]

SPECIAL ARRANGEMENTS FOR EMPLOYMENT PROTECTION

Before dealing with the 1980 Regulations, the position at common law and some of the special arrangements made for protecting employees of a business or undertaking which is being transferred call for consideration. Where a business is transferred to another employer, at common law the transferor's employees are deemed to have thereby been dismissed. Where part of the employer's business has been transferred, it depends on the entire circumstances which if any employees were thereby dismissed; a source of difficulty has been where there was a 'hive down' by a receiver of the viable part of the business.[2]

As regards the employee's position *vis-à-vis* the transferee or successor enterprise, the fundamental principle is that of privity of contract; the employee's contract is with the transferor of the business and cannot give

1. SI No. 306 of 1980, considered in detail infra.
2. E.g. *Pambaikian v. Brentford Nylons Ltd* [1988] ICR 665.

rise to enforceable rights against a third party, such as the transferee of the business. Statutory provisions aside, in order to acquire rights against and assume obligations to the transferee, the employee must have entered into an enforceable contract with him. At times such a contract may exist, most notably where the employee's trade union made an agreement with the transferee, on behalf of the employee, governing the terms of the business transfer. Or the transferor of the business, as agent for his employees, may have extracted terms from the transferee affecting them. In both cases, the employee will not have enforceable rights against the transferee unless the union or transferor negotiated terms as his agent; whether they acted as agent depends on the circumstances of the case.[3]

Generally, employment contracts cannot be unilaterally assigned. While a party to various types of contracts, for instance a creditor who is owed money, can assign his rights under the contract to a third party, who then can enforce that contract against the debtor, the obligations under a contract of employment cannot be transferred in that manner. This principle is illustrated in *Nokes v. Doncaster Amalgamated Collieries Ltd*,[4] a company law case, which involved a scheme of arrangement to reorganise the affairs of a company under the equivalent of ss.201-203 of the Companies Act, 1963. In order to become effective, these schemes must be approved by the High Court, which is empowered to make various directions to facilitate implementation of the agreed scheme. The Court may direct that one company's property shall be transferred to another company involved in the scheme; property for this purpose is defined as including 'rights and powers of every description'. Mr Nokes had been employed by one company as a coal miner and it was contended that, when the Court directed that all his employer's property and liabilities shall be transferred to the respondent colliery company, he thereby became an employee of that colliery. This view was rejected, on the grounds that the section of the Companies Act did not expressly provide for the assignment of employment contracts. It was held to be a 'fundamental principle . . . that a free citizen, in the exercise of his freedom, is entitled to choose the employer whom he proposes to serve, so that the right to his services cannot be transferred from one employer to another without his assent.'[5]

Express provision may be made by statute for transferring employees' rights and obligations from one employer to another. Provisions of that nature are often encountered in legislation which reorganises some part of the public service and where one body is being replaced by another. Frequently in these measures, it is stipulated that the employees of the

---

3.   See ante p.60.   4.   [1940] AC 1014.   5.   Id. at p.1200.

existing body shall be transferred to the new body, generally on the same terms as those on which they are presently employed. For instance, under the Postal and Telecommunications Services Act, 1983, where An Post and Bord Telecom Éireann took over the activities of the former Department of Posts and Telegraphs, s.45 of that Act stipulated that each of these companies 'shall accept into its employment' existing members of the Department's staff on terms and conditions of employment that are no less favourable than those they presently enjoyed. It was also provided that a transferred employee's previous service with the civil service shall be reckonable service for the purpose of legislation governing employees' rights on being dismissed from their jobs. Other examples of similar provisions include s.9 of the Transport Act, 1964, (reorganising Córas Iompair Éireann), s.37 of the Health Act, 1970, (establishing the Health Boards), s.7(4)–(8) of the Labour Services Act, 1987, (establishing An FAS), s.6 of the Agriculture (Research, Traning and Advice) Act, 1988 (establishing An Teogasc), s.20 of the Safety, Health and Welfare at Work Act, 1989 (establishing the National Authority for Occupational Safety and Health) and s.6 of the Insurance Act, 1990 (pre-privatisation of Irish Life).

The case of *Cox v. Electricity Supply Board* [6] concerned a former officer of Dublin Corporation who became an employee of the defendant, under s.39(2) of the Electricity (Supply) Act, 1927, when the defendant acquired the Corporation's electricity undertaking. Section 39(2) provided that the plaintiff was transferred to the Board's service 'on the same terms' as those he enjoyed when serving the Corporation. It was held that, accordingly, for him to be lawfully dismissed, the Board had to follow precisely the same procedures as the Corporation would have been bound to follow—including, at that time, obtaining the consent of the Minister for Local Government.

Under s.1(2) of the Holidays (Employees) Act, 1973, all qualified employees who 'continue in the undertaking' after it was transferred carry over their accrued holiday entitlements to their new employer. Provision is also made for business transfers in the Redundancy Payments Act, 1967. One of these,[7] which has since been extended to all contexts,[8] was that the transfer of all or part of a business or undertaking does not break an employee's continuous service and that continuous service with the transferor enterprise is carried over to the transferee. But this rule does not apply where all that has been transferred was assets, like plant and stock in trade, as opposed to

6. [1943] IR 94.
7. 3rd schedule, para. 6, as amended.
8. Minimum Notice and Terms of Employment Act, 1973, schedule, reg.7.

the on-going business or part of it.[9] Section 20 of the 1967 Act deals with where an employee, who is being made redundant by the transferor, loses his right to lump sum compensation where the successor business offers to re-employ him.[10] That right is lost where, by prior agreement between the employee and the successor, the new owner renews his contract or re-engages him. Unreasonable refusal by the employee of an offer of similar and suitable employment by the successor can also deny the employee the lump sum payment.

TRANSFER OF UNDERTAKINGS REGULATIONS

In 1977 the E.C. Council adopted Directive 77/187 on the approximation of laws 'relating the the safeguarding of employees' rights in the event of transfers of undertakings, businesses or parts of businesses.'[11] This Directive provides for the transfer of employees from the transferor to the transferee business, subject to certain exceptions, and for consultations with employees' representatives about aspects of the transfer. Its purpose, as described by the European Court, is

> to ensure, so far as possible, that the rights of employees are safe-guarded in the event of a change of employer by allowing them to remain in employment with the new employer on the terms and conditions agreed with the transferor.[12]
>
> It also aims to ensure, so far as possible, that the employment relationship continues unchanged with the transferee, particularly by compelling him to retain the conditions of employment stipulated by a collective agreement and by protecting employees against dismissal solely on the ground of transfer.[13]

This Directive was made effective in Ireland by the European Communities (Safeguarding of Employees' Rights on Transfer of Undertakings) Regulations, 1980.[14] These Regulations can have a very significant impact on

9. Cf. *Nova Colour Graphic Supplies Ltd v. Employment Appeals Tribunal* [1987] IR 426 and *Gibson v. Motortune Ltd* [1990] ICR 740, and cases cited ante p.215,. n.16.
10. See ante p.214.
11. O.J. No. L 61/26 (1977).
12. *Foreningen Af Arbejdsledeve i Danmark v. Daddy's Dance Hall A/S* (Case 324/86) [1989] 2 CMLR 517, at p.523 (para.9).
13. *Mikkelsen v. Danmols Inventar A/S* (Case 105/84) [1986] 1 CMLR 316, at p.326 (para.15.
14. SI No. 306 of 1980. See generally, Kerr, 'Transfer of Undertakings: The European Directive and its Implementation into Domestic Law', 7 *J.I.S.L.L.* 26 (1988) and Hepple, 'Workers' Rights in Mergers and Takeovers: The E.E.C. Proposals', [1976] *Ind. L. J.* 197.

calculations made when considering the sale or other disposition of a business or part of a business. Before examining the substantive rights conferred by the regulations, their interpretation and scope call for comment.

Interpretation Several cases have been referred from other jurisdictions to the European Court of Justice concerning the meaning of the 1977 Directive and a substantial body of case law now exists regarding its meaning, although there remain matters which require clarification. The terminology of the 1980 Regulations reproduces practically verbatim that of the Directive which, apart from other considerations, would suggest that the analysis adopted by the European Court would always be followed by Irish tribunals and courts. This matter is put beyond doubt by reg.2(1) of the Regulations, which states that any word or expression used in the Regulations 'shall . . . have the same meaning' as those in the Directive. An exception to this principle is made for where 'the context otherwise requires . . .' British decisions on the comparable provisions adopted in the United Kingdom[15] should be treated with caution because the terminology used there is not so similar to that in the Directive and several British tribunals and courts have not sought guidance on every point from the European Court. However, the House of Lords' decision in the *Litster* case[16] marks a departure from that approach, so that post-1989 British decisions may be more helpful guides to the Directive's meaning.

Relevant 'business transfers' The kinds of transaction which affect employees' entitlements under these Regulations are defined in the Directive as

> the transfer of an undertaking, business or part of a business to another employer as a result of a legal transfer or merger.[17]

What is an undertaking or a business here is not defined, which raises the question whether a transfer of a part of some public service agency or department, which is not engaged in business in the ordinary meaning of the term, is a relevant transfer for these purposes. As has been pointed out, transfers within the public service are often the subject of special legislative provisions, in order to ensure that all employees of the old service are

---

15. See generally, J. McMullen, *Business Transfers and Employee Rights* (1987); Collins, 'Dismissals on Transfer of a Business', 15 *Ind. L.J.* 244 (1986) and Collins, 'Transfer of Undertakings and Insolvency', 18 *Ind. L.J.* 144 (1989).
16. *Litster v. Forth Dry Dock & Engineering Co.* [1990] 1 AC 547.
17. Art.1(1).

re-employed in the new service on terms and conditions no less favourable than they hitherto enjoyed. Most likely the term 'undertaking' here would be given an expansive interpretation as applying to most if not all parts of the public service.[18]

Transfers of undertakings often take the form of legal transfers, notably sales of the business or mergers. But other forms of transfer can be affected by these Regulations. For instance, in the *Daddy's Dance Hall* case,[19] the employer leased premises to carry on a restaurant business. Because he was in breach of covenant, his lease was forfeited and another company took over the premises to run a restaurant business. It was held that the Directive applied to that transfer. The triangular nature of the transaction did not matter, 'provided that the economic unit in question retains its identity.'[20] According to Advocate General Mancini in a later case, also involving the forfeiture of a lease, 'no significance is to be attached to the nature of the transaction, be it a contract or a deed taking effect on death, an administrative measure or a judicial decision, as a result of which one business man succeeds another. . . . The sole requirement [is] the capacity of the business transferred to retain its 'identity', that is to say, to remain in operation as a going concern . . . only a part of the business is transferred.'[21] In cases of partial transfers, the criterion is 'whether or not a transfer takes place of the department to which [those employees] were assigned and which formed the organisational framework within which their employment relationship took effect.'[22] That the business was temporarily suspended prior to the transfer does not prevent the Regulations from applying, such as a restaurant business which was closed down during the winter season.

But if all that has happened is a mere sale of the transferor's assets and no more, the Regulations do not apply. It depends on the entire circumstances of the case whether the transaction is only a sale of assets and, in this regard, the courts are vigilant lest the employees' protections are evaded by sales of businesses being dressed up to look like mere disposals of assets. According to the European Court in the *Spijkers* case,[23] involving the sale of a slaughterhouse which had ceased to trade,

it is necessary to determine whether what has been sold is an economic

18. Cf. *Expro Services Ltd v. Smith* [1991] ICR 577.   19. Supra n.12.
20. [1989] 2 CMLR at p.523 (para.10).
21. *Landsorganisationen I Danmark v. Ny Molle Kro* (Case 287/86) [1989] 2 CMLR 468, at pp.472-473. See too, *P. Bork International A/S v. Foreningen Af Arbejdsledere I Danmark* (Case 101/87) [1990] 3 CMLR 701.
22. *Botzen v. Rotterdamsche Droogdok Maatschappij B.V.* (Case 186/83) [1986] 2 CMLR 50, at p.57 (para.14).
23. *Spijkers v. Gebroeders Benedik Abattoir B.V.* (Case 24/85) [1986] 2 CMLR 296.

entity which is still in existence, and this will be apparent from the fact that its operation is actually being continued or has been taken over by the new employer, with the same economic or similar activities.

To decide whether these conditions are fulfilled, it is necessary to take account of all the factual circumstances of the transaction in question, including the type of undertaking or business in question, the transfer or otherwise of tangible assets such as buildings and stocks, the value of intangible assets at the date of transfer, whether the majority of the staff are taken over by the new employer, the transfer or otherwise of the circle of customers and the degree of similarity between activities before and after the transfer and the duration of any interruption in those activities. . . . [E]ach of these factors is only part of the overall assessment which is required and therefore they cannot be examined independently of each other.[24]

The fact that the transferor is insolvent does not as such take the transaction outside the Regulations, although the position of disposals by the liquidator of an insolvent company is still to be clarified. In the *Abels* case,[25] it was held that the Directive applied to a disposal by a Dutch company which was in the process of *surséance van betaling*, which is similar to a scheme of arrangement under ss.201-203 of the Companies Act, 1963 and to the Court-supervised examination under the Companies (Amendment) Act, 1990. In *Mythen v. Employment Appeals Tribunal*,[26] Barrington J held that the Regulations applied to a disposal of part of the undertaking by a receiver who had been appointed by a debenture-holder. Of course where all that the liquidator or receiver disposes of is the bare assets of the company, the Regulations cannot apply. The position of disposals by liquidators is considered in the next chapter, dealing with employers' insolvency.

Workers covered Unlike many of the modern employment protection measures, the Transfer of Undertakings Regulations do not set out the categories of workers who fall within or outside its terms. The Regulations deal with a contract of employment or an employment relationship, so that self-employed persons obtain no rights under it. Many categories of employee who fall outside the scope of measures like the Unfair Dismissals Act and the Redundancy Payments Acts are protected by these Regulations,

---

24. Id. at p.303 (paras. 12 and 13).
25. *Abels v. Administrative Board of the Bedrijsvereniging Voor de Metaal-Industrie* (Case 135/83) [1987] 2 CMLR 406.
26. [1989] ILRM 844.

since they do not purport to exclude any categories of employee from their scope. As has been observed, it would seem that they apply to public service employees and office-holders.

Even if various categories of employees were excluded in the Regulations, as a matter of E.C. law the State would be in breach of its obligations under the Directive if it sought to exclude any group who, under Irish law, enjoyed protection in connection with dismissal from employment. Thus, where Belgium sought to exclude from its implementing measure temporary employees and employees over the pensionable age, it was held that the obligation to implement the Directive had not been fully met, because those categories of employee enjoyed some protection against dismissal under Belgian law. According to the European Court, the Directive 'applies to any situation in which employees affected by a transfer enjoy some, albeit limited, protection against dismissal under national law, with the result that, under the Directive, that protection may not be taken away from them or curtailed solely because of the transfer.'[27] Regarding who is an employee for the purpose of the Directive, it was held in another instance that there is no special European concept of employee for this purpose. Rather, these provisions can 'be invoked by persons who in one way or another are protected as employees under rules or law of the member-State concerned', that is 'any person who, in the Member State concerned, is protected as an employee under the national legislation relating to labour law.'[28]

A strategy which has been adopted in an attempt to avoid application of the Regulations is to dismiss the employees in question before the actual transfer of the undertaking occurs. It would seem, however, that devices of this nature would not be accepted by the courts. Although the Directive applies only to those employed by the transferor at the time of the transfer,[29] persons can be so employed even though not performing work for the transferor or not being paid by it. Additionally, it was held by the European Court in the *Bork* case[30] that workers who are dismissed by the transferor prior to and in order to facilitate the transfer are protected by the Directive. According to the Court, 'workers employed by the undertaking whose contract of employment or employment relationship has been terminated with effect on a date before that of the transfer, in breach of Article 4(1) ...,

27. *E.C. Commission v. Belgium* (Case 237/84) [1988] 2 CMLR 865, at p.872 (para.12).
28. *Mikkelsen v. Danmols Investar A/S* (Case 105/84) [1986] 1 CMLR 316, at p.329 (paras. 27 and 28).
29. *Wendelboe v. L.J. Music ApS* (Case 19/83) [1986] 1 CMLR 476 and *Mikkelsen* case, supra n.28.
30. *P. Bork International A/S v. Foreningen Af Arbejdsledere I Danmark* (Case 101/87) [1990] 3 CMLR 701.

must be considered as still employed by the undertaking on the date of transfer. . . .'[31]

Thus in the *Litster* case[32] in Britain a blatant attempt to avoid application of the Regulations there did not succeed because that would subvert the Regulations' very object. In order to facilitate the transfer of part of a company, which was in receivership, the receiver agreed to dismiss several employees one hour before the transfer was to occur. The transfer also took the form of the purchase of the company's tangible assets and the purchase of the lease on the property, on which it had traded; there was no disposal of goodwill. All of this was with the express object that the Regulations would not apply. But they were held to govern the case on account of that very objective.

Continuing rights and duties Where an employer's business is transferred, its then employees become in effect employees of the person or the company which acquired the business. What was not achieved in the *Doncaster Colleries*[33] case by the Companies Act—the assignment of the entire employment relationship to the successor or transferee company— is now the outcome of the Directive. According to Art. 3(i) of the Directive (reg.3 of the Regulations),

> The transferor's rights and obligations arising from a contract of employment or from an employment relationship existing on the date of a transfer . . . shall . . . be transferred to the transferee.

Accordingly, as from the date of the transfer, the transferor's employees are entitled to be employed on the very same terms and conditions by the transferee— save where they were dismissed for 'economic' etc. reasons, as described below. Continuity of employment which was built up while working for the transferor is carried over to the transferee. Any money owing by the transferor to the employee arising from his job can be recovered from the transferee. All of the transferor's duties as employer became vested in the transferee, including, presumably, liability in damages for injuries caused negligently in the course of employment. It remains to be seen whether rights to shares under an employees' share option scheme can be transferred in this manner. Not alone are obligations and rights automatically vested in the transferee but, at the same time, the transferor is completely divested of those rights and duties; he no longer has any legal redress against the ex-employee nor does that employee any longer have

31. Id. at p.713 (para.18).
32. *Litster v. Forth Dry Dock & Engineering Co.* [1990] 1 AC 546.
33. [1940] AC 1014; see ante p.221.

redress against him in respect of matters which arose prior to the date of the transfer.

The automatic vesting of rights and obligations in the successor has been held to be peremptory in two respects. The release of the transferor's obligations, on the occurrence of the transfer, is not conditional on the employee consenting to that release; it occurs automatically, regardless of the employee's wishes.[34] To an extent, therefore, the employee has become a chattel of his employing enterprise, capable of being assigned to a successor employer in the face of the most ardent objections. Of course, he cannot be compelled actually to work for his new employer. Secondly, rights acquired by the employee under these Regulations cannot be waived by him. The protection afforded to employees by the Directive has been described as 'a matter of public policy (*ordre public*) and, therefore, independent of the will of the parties to the contract of employment'.[35] Even if they are offered commensurate or even greater benefits for doing so, employees cannot contract out of their rights in this regard. However, this does not preclude them, following the transfer, from agreeing to a change in terms and conditions with their new employer.[36]

Express provision is made for carrying over any collective agreements affecting the employees, to which the transferor was a party. The transferee is required to continue observing those agreements' terms until they expire or are replaced.[37] Of course, if the collective agreement is not legally enforceable *inter partes*, it is not rendered so enforceable by these Regulations.

An exception to this 'carry over' principle is made in respect of supplementary company and inter-company pension schemes.[38] However, the transferee is placed under a more general obligation to ensure that acquired rights under such schemes to old age, invalidity or survivors benefits are protected. The nature and scope of this duty to protect the pension rights has yet to receive authoritative analysis.[39]

Redress for dismissal Subject to an exception, explained below, the Directive seeks to prevent dismissing employees on account of the undertaking or part of it being transferred. According to Article 4(1) of the Directive (reg.5(1) of the Regulations),

34. *Berg v. Ivo Marten Besselsen* (Cases 144-145/87), [1989] 3 CMLR 817, at p.826 (para.11).
35. *Daddy's Dance Hall* case, supra n.12, at p.524 (paras 14 and 15).
36. Id. at p.525 (paras 17 and 18).
37. Reg.4(1).   38. Reg.4(2).   39. See post p.258.

> The transfer . . . shall not in itself constitute grounds for dismissal by the transferor or the transferee and a dismissal, the grounds for which are such a transfer, . . . is hereby prohibited.

For employees covered by the Unfair Dismissals Act, 1977, what this appears to mean is that a dismissal, either by the transferor or the transferee, on account of the transfer, is deemed to be automatically unfair. An employee dismissed on those grounds is entitled either to reinstatement, reengagement or compensation, under the 1977 Act, as the case may be. An unsatisfactory feature of the 1980 Regulations is that they do not expressly give the Employment Appeals Tribunal jurisdiction to deal with complaints of dismissal in contravention of their requirements. In the *Mythen* case,[40] however, it was held that the absence of an express jurisdiction does not disentitle that Tribunal to hear claims of this nature. The claim in essence is one of unfair dismissal, which is entirely within the Tribunal's competence.

For employees who are excluded from the scope of the 1977 Act, however, it would seem that they may have a right of action for damages, for breach of statutory duty, that is breach of the Regulations, where they are dismissed because of the transfer. This result would seem to follow from the Regulations not confining the prohibition to employees who are covered by the 1977 Act.

What exactly is meant by the phrase, the transfer being the 'grounds for dismissal', will require elaboration by the courts. For instance, must the transfer be the only grounds for the dismissal, or must it be the principal grounds or does it suffice if one of the reasons for the dismissal is the transfer? A dismissal for these purposes includes constructive dismissal, that is where a substantial change for the worse in the employee's terms or conditions virtually forces him to resign.[41]

The prohibition against dismissals due to the business transfer does not apply where the employee was discharged 'for economic, technical or organisational reasons entailing changes in the workforce.'[42] Surprisingly, the exact meaning of this phrase has not yet been elaborated on extensively by the European Court.[43] Although these reasons have affinity with the concept of 'redundancy' under the Redundancy Payments Acts,[44] it may be that certain situations which would amount to redundancy would not fall

---

40. [1989] ILRM 844; see supra p.226.   41. Reg.5(2).   42. Reg.5(1).
43. Cf. *Wheeler v. Patel* [1987] ICR 631; *Berriman v. Delabole Slate Ltd* [1985] ICR 546 and *Anderson v. Dalkeith Engineering Ltd* [1985] ICR 66.
44. See ante p.210.

within the 'economic, technical or organisational' rubric in 1980 Regulations. Of course, under the Unfair Dismissals Act, 1977, while redundancy is a permitted grounds for dismissal, dismissal for that reason may nevertheless be unfair because of some improper way the employer went about the matter.[45]

Informing and consulting employees' representatives As had been explained elsewhere,[46] both the transferor and the transferee are obliged to inform representatives of employees affected about aspects of the proposed transfer and to consult with them on those matters.

45. See ante p.202.   46. *Industrial Relations Law*, pp.82-83.

10

Employer's insolvency

Occasionally, an employer may become insolvent—he may be an individual who is adjudicated a bankrupt or who enters into an arrangement with all his creditors, or the employer is a company which is wound up because it cannot pay its debts or it is placed in receivership or in court-supervised examination. For many years, the only special protection for employees in these circumstances was the preferential debts which they are entitled to be paid before the general creditors can get a penny. As a result of an E.C. initiative,[1] an insolvency fund was established to meet various debts to employees who an insolvent employer is unable to pay. The extent to which the Transfer of Undertakings Regulations apply to disposals made in the context of insolvency proceedings has not been fully clarified.

IMPACT ON THE EMPLOYMENT CONTRACT

An important preliminary question is the effect, under the general principles of contract law, of the insolvency in question on the workers' contracts of employment. Does the insolvency operate to frustrate these contracts or otherwise terminate them, or do the contractual rights and obligations survive the onset of insolvency? There may be express or implied terms in a contract which provide answers to these questions. In the absence of such terms, the matter turns on the nature of the insolvency proceedings involved.

Bankruptcy On a person being adjudicated a bankrupt, his property, subject to certain exceptions, immediately vests in the Official Assignee.[2] Since rights under an employment contract are not proprietary for these purposes, they will not vest in the Assignee once an employer is made bankrupt.[3] Whether the contract is thereupon lawfully terminated or is

---

1. Directive 80/987, O.J. No. L 283/23 (1980); see infra p.235.
2. See generally, M. Forde, *Bankruptcy Law in Ireland* (1990) pp.71-83.
3. *Re Collins* [1925] Ch. 556.

frustrated, or whether the bankruptcy operates to break the contract, depends on the bankrupt's own circumstances and the terms of the contract.

Liquidation Where an insolvent company is put into liquidation, that may be an out-of-court creditors' voluntary liquidation or an official liquidation (or compulsory winding up) by order of the High Court.[4] Where the winding up is by order of the Court, publication of the winding up order is deemed to be notice to the entire world, including the company's employees, that they are dismissed.[5] Under the Companies Acts, that order operates retrospectively to when the petition was presented,[6] so that the deemed notice of dismissal would also operate retrospectively in this manner. If, under their contracts, the employees were entitled to advance notice of termination, they would be entitled to damages for breach of that provision. This rule applies regardless of the employee's status within the company and regardless of whether the job is subject to a specified notice period or is for a fixed term or indeed for life.[7] Strictly, publication of the winding up order does not terminate the contract because, in principle, the employee can refuse to accept the unlawful repudiation of the contract; but for all practical purposes the contract is brought to an end at that time.

However, the liquidator may want to carry on the business for the time being and to continue all or some of the employees in their jobs. He therefore is entitled to waive the deemed notices of dismissal and to continue employing the relevant employees under their existing contracts.[8] Unless there has been an unequivocal waiver, the company's employees will be treated as having been dismissed, although they may be re-employed by the liquidator on new terms for the purpose of the winding up.

Occasionally, a provisional liquidator is appointed by the court prior to ordering a winding up, whose task is to safeguard the company's assets. If that provisional liquidator is authorised to carry on the company's business for the time being, his appointment does not operate to discharge the employment contracts of the workforce.[9]

A creditor's voluntary liquidation commences when the members of the company pass a resolution that it be wound up because it cannot pay its

4. See generally, M. Forde, *Company Law* (2nd ed. 1992) ch.18, and Graham, 'The Effect of Liquidation on Contracts of Service', 15 *Mod. L. Rev.* 48 (1952).
5. *Re General Rolling Stock Co.* (1866) 1 LR Eq 346.
6. Companies Act, 1963, s.220(2).
7. *Fowler v. Commercial Timber Co.* [1930] 2 KB 1. Cf. *Re R.S. Newman Ltd* [1916] 2 Ch. 309 and *Re T.N. Farrer Ltd* [1937] Ch. 352.
8. *Re English Joint Stock Bank* (1867) 3 Eq 341.
9. *Donnelly v. Gleeson* (Hamilton J, 11 July 1978). Cf. *Re McEvanhenry Ltd* (Murphy J, 15 May 1986).

debts. It has been held that the passing or indeed the publication of such resolution does not invariably operate as a notice of dismissal.[10] In particular circumstances, depending on the terms of the contract, the resolution to wind up may constitute notice of termination. The test is whether in all the circumstances the employee is justified in regarding the winding up as indicating an intention by the company to repudiate its obligations under the contract.[11] If employees are retained by the liquidator or are re-hired shortly after the resolution was passed, they are deemed to be still employed by the company.[12]

Receivership The appointment of a receiver over some or all of the employer's assets does not necessarily mean that it is insolvent, although that usually is the case. A receiver's task is to take control of and to sell off the relevant assets and, from the proceeds of the sale, to pay the appointing creditor what he is owed. Occasionally, a receiver is appointed by order of the court but the usual form of receivership is where the appointment is made by a secured creditor under the terms of a debenture.[13] Frequently the receiver is authorised to continue managing the business until a buyer can be found who will purchase it as a going concern and usually the receiver will be designated an agent of the company.

The effect on the employment relationship of the appointment of a receiver was analysed in *Griffiths v. Secretary of State*,[14] where the plaintiff was a managing director of a company when a debenture-holder appointed a receiver and manager over its entire assets. The position was explained by Lawson J as follows:

> the appointment by debenture-holders of a receiver and manager as agent of the company (the commonest case) . . . does not of itself automatically terminate contracts of employment previously made and subsisting between the relevant company and all its employees. There are three situations in which this may be qualified.
>
> The first situation is where . . . the appointment is accompanied by a sale of business; that will operate to terminate contracts of employment . . . because . . . there is no longer any business for which the employees can work.[15]

10. *Midland Counties Bank v. Attwood* [1905] 1 Ch. 357.
11. *Reigate v. Union Mfg. Co.* [1918] 1 KB 592.
12. *Collman v. Construction Industry Training Board* (1966) 1 ITR 52.
13. See generally, M. Forde, *Reorganising Failing Businesses* (1991) ch.5 and Davies & Freedland, 'The Effects of Receiverships Upon Employees of Companies', 9 *Ind. L.J.* 95 (1980).
14. [1974] 1 QB 468.
15. E.g. *Re Foster & Clarke Ltd's Indenture Trusts* [1966] 1 WLR 125.

The second situation is where . . . a receiver and manager enters into a new agreement with a particular employee that may be inconsistent with the continuation of his old service contract. . . .[16]

The third situation . . . is where . . . the continuation of the employment of a particular employee is inconsistent with the role and functions of a receiver and manager. The mere fact that he is labelled 'managing director' does not . . . indicate that because he is so labelled his employment in that capacity or office is inconsistent with the position, role and functions of a receiver and manager. . . .[17]

Where it is the Court which appoints the receiver and manager, 'the result of such an appointment is to discharge the servants from their service to their original employer and that [may be] a wrongful dismissal for which an action would lie.'[18] The reason for this rule perhaps is that this receiver is the agent of the Court.

Court-supervised examination There is no reason in principle why the appointment of an examiner into a company's affairs, under the Companies (Amendment) Act, 1990,[19] should bring an end to the employment contracts of the company's workforce. Even where the Court directs the examiner to take over the function of the company's directors,[20] that should not affect the employee's contracts.

TRANSFER OF UNDERTAKINGS REGULATIONS

The strict contract law position of employees of insolvent businesses may be significantly modified by the European Communities (Safeguarding of Employees' Rights on Transfer of Undertakings) Regulations, 1980,[21] as described in the previous chapter, although the precise application of these Regulations in insolvency situations requires further elaboration by the courts. The Regulations only apply to persons employed by the business in question at the date of the transfer. Therefore, if the insolvency operated as a dismissal before any transfer took place, the Regulations would not apply. This, of course, is not the case where the employee was dismissed in order

16. E.g. *Re Mack Trucks (Britain) Ltd* [1967] 1 WLR 780.
17. [1974] 1 QB at pp.485-486.
18. *Reid v. Explosives Co.* (1887) 19 QBD. 264, at p.267.
19. See generally Forde, supra n.13, ch.7.
20. Under s.9 of that Act; see id. at p.90.
21. SI No. 306 of 1980. See generally, Collins, 'Transfer of Undertakings and Insolvency', 18 *Ind. L.J.* 144 (1989).

to facilitate the transfer, other than for the specified 'economic' etc. reasons.[22] It furthermore would seem that if the transfer took place before the expiry of the employee's notice period, the employment relationship continued in existence after the dismissal took place provided the employee did not accept the repudiation of his contract.[23] In such a case, the Regulations would apply to any transfer of all or part of the business.

It was contended before the European Court of Justice that the E.C. Directive, which gave rise to these Regulations, does not apply where the transfer is being made in the context of insolvency administration. That view received some support from the European Commission and from Advocate General Slynn in the *Abels* case,[24] which concerned a transfer made by a Dutch company that was in *surséance van betaling*—a status resembling a stay on proceedings imposed by s.201 of the Companies Act, 1963. It was argued that, insolvency being a very technical field, which will be the subject of E.C. approximating measures at some stage, the Directive should not be regarded as applying in those circumstances unless it explicitly provided otherwise, which it does not. Should they so choose, Member States remain free, under the Directive, to apply its provisions to insolvent businesses. There were also practical considerations, that the Directive's actual objects would be frustrated rather than advanced if it applied to insolvency disposals. It was said that

> a potential purchaser may be deterred from buying up businesses which are insolvent, but which might be capable of rescue, if they are obliged to take on all the employees. The only way to save the business may be to reduce the number of staff. It is in the interests of the labour force as a whole that such rescue attempts should be made, even if some staff have to go. In fact, rather than in theory, more jobs may be lost if purchasers are deterred by a rule that they must take on the employees and satisfy all obligations to them.[25]

But the Court declined to be guided by this analysis in its entirety. Some insolvency disposals fall within the Directive, for instance the disposal in the instant case. The fact that a court has authorised an employer to suspend payments to his creditors does not take him outside the Directive.

In *Mythen v. Employment Appeals Tribunal*,[26] Barrington J held that a sale of part of the business by a receiver, appointed under a debenture, came

22. Reg.5(1).
23. *Quare* where employee accepts money in lieu of notice? Cf. *Gothard v. Mirror Group Newspapers Ltd* [1988] ICR 729.
24. *Abels v. Administrative Board of the Bedrijfsvereniging Voor de Metal-Industrie* (Case 135/83) [1987] 2 CMLR 406.
25. Id. at pp.412-413.   26. [1989] ILRM 844.

within the Directive. If receivers' disposals fell outside the Directive, its requirements could easily be avoided, because the most common form of receivership is an 'entirely extra-judicial process . . . which might be employed much more easily than a liquidation . . . to defeat the purposes of the Directive'.[27] The *Litster* case[28] in Britain, where the Directive was held to apply, also involved a sale by a receiver. Because a creditor's voluntary liquidation could relatively easily be used to avoid the Regulations' requirements, it would seem that a disposal in that situation also falls within the Regulations. Of course, the Regulations will not apply where all that is transferred is the bare assets and not the going concern or the goodwill of all or part of the business.

Where, however, the High Court adjudicated the employer a bankrupt or ordered that the employer be wound up as being insolvent, it was held that the Directive does not apply. According to the European Court in the *Abels* case,

> Article 1(1) of (the) Directive . . . does not apply to the transfer of an undertaking, business or part of a business where the transferor has been adjudged insolvent and the undertaking or business in question forms part of the assets of the insolvent transferor. . . .[29]

It remains to be determined whether the Directive applies in situations where the High Court is involved in the case but has not made a formal adjudication of insolvency, notably a scheme of arrangement under Part IV of the Bankruptcy Act, 1988, a scheme of arrangement under ss.201-203 of the Companies Act, 1963, and the supervised examination under the Companies (Amendment) Act, 1990.[30]

PREFERENTIAL DEBTS

Where an individual is bankrupt or a company is insolvent, there are certain creditors who are entitled to be paid out of the insolvent estate before any payments can be made to the general creditors. The traditional justification for preferring employees of the insolvent in this manner is that they are very much in an unequal position when dealing with an employer who is in financial difficulties. Preferential treatment was first accorded to them in an era when there was no welfare state and trade unions hardly existed. Under

27. Id. at p.853.
28. *Litster v. Forth Dry Dock & Engineering Co.* [1990] 1 AC 546.
29. [1987] 2 CMLR at p.422 (para.30).
30. For details of these legislative provisions, see supra n.13.

the Preferential Payments in Bankruptcy (Ireland) Act, 1889, arrears of salary owed to the bankrupt's employees, up to a specified amount, were made a preferential debt. The position is now covered by s.81 of the Bankruptcy Act, 1988, and by s.285(2) of the Companies Act, 1963, as amended in 1982. Under the companies and the bankruptcy legislation, the State is also a preferred creditor in respect of certain unpaid taxes. Employers are affected by these provisions in that unpaid tax deducted from the employee's remuneration and unpaid P.R.S.I. are preferred debts.[31]

Debts to employees Only employees who work under a contract of employment benefit from these preferential debts provisions. Thus in *In re Sunday Tribune Ltd*,[32] where several journalists with a Sunday newspaper claimed to be preferential creditors, some of those claims were rejected on the grounds that those journalists were independent contractors. In *Stakelum v. Canning*,[33] it was held that executive directors of companies, other than managing directors, can be employees for the purposes of this preference. Company liquidators and also company receivers are obliged to pay employees in accordance with the following preferences.[34]

Wages and salary: First and foremost are unpaid wages and salary owing for services rendered to the employer. This preference is subject to a financial ceiling; sums which are owing in excess of £2,500 are not preferred. In 1982 the ceiling for companies as employers was increased from £300;[34] this £2,500 sum may be varied by the Minister.[36] There is no general definition of what is a 'wage' or a 'salary' for these purposes but it must mean remuneration for work done; it includes remuneration for periods of absence from work for 'good cause' and on holidays.[37] In *In re M*[38] it was held that amounts deducted from earnings and credited to a holiday stamp scheme in the construction industry were wages, even though the employees were only entitled to have the sums deducted paid into what was described as a suspense account. The services in question must have been rendered during the four months immediately preceding the adjudication. Where the arrangement with a 'farm labourer' is to pay him a lump sum at the end of the hiring or at the end of the year, the Court is empowered to apportion how much of what is owing should be preferred.[39]

31. See generally, M. Forde, *Company Law* (2nd ed. 1992) paras 18.96-99.
32. [1984] IR 505.   33. [1976] IR 314.
34. Companies Act, 1963, ss.285 and 98.
35. Companies (Amendment) Act, 1982, s.10(b).
36. Companies Act, 1963, s.285(13) (inserted by 1982 Act s.10(e)). For individuals, see Bankruptcy Act, 1988, s.81(1)(b)-(f).
37. Id. s.285(11).   38. [1955] NI 182.   39. Companies Act, 1963, s.285(4).

Holiday pay: Accrued holiday remuneration at the date of the adjudication is preferred.[40]

Sick pay: Outstanding amounts due under an arrangement for sick pay are preferred.[41]

Pension contributions: Outstanding pension contributions, under any scheme or arrangement made for superannuation, are preferred, whether they are employer's contributions or those deducted from the employee's remuneration.[42]

Compensation for dismissal: Three major statutory schemes exist for compensating employees who have been dismissed from their jobs in specified circumstances, viz. where they were not given the requisite statutory minimum notice, where they were made redundant and where their dismissal was held to be unfair. Compensation which is awarded to a dismissed employee under any of these schemes is a priority debt.[43] Where the employer is unable to pay that compensation, the Protection of Employees (Insolvency) Act, 1984, requires those amounts to be paid by the Minister for Labour. In that event, the Minister is subrogated for the employees in respect of the amounts paid.

Compensation for accidents: In the case of insolvent companies, if the employee was injured in the course of his employment and has been awarded or stands to be awarded damages and costs in respect of that injury, the amount of those damages and the costs are a preferred debt.[44] However, this preference does not exist where the company is effectively indemnified by insurers against that liability. In such a case, the injured employee is in effect subrogated for the company and is entitled to be paid the full amount forthcoming on the insurance policy.[45]

Sums advanced to pay employees In the case of insolvent companies, where persons advanced money to the company for the purpose of paying employees' wages or salary, holiday remuneration or pension benefits, the lender is preferred to the extent that those employees would have been

40. Id. s.285(2)(d).
41. Id. s.285(2)(h) (inserted by 1982 Act s.10(a)).
42. Id. s.285(2)(i) (inserted by 1982 Act s.10(a)).
43. Minimum Notice and Terms of Employment Act, 1973, s.13, Redundancy Payments Act, 1979, s.42, as amended, Unfair Dismissals Act, 1977, s.12.
44. Companies Act, 1963, s.285(2)(g).   45. Civil Liability Act, 1961, s.62.

preferred if they had not been paid what was owing to them.[46] Thus, if a bank lends £20,000 to meet the payroll at the end of the week or the end of the month, it is a preferred creditor for that amount. Any form of 'advance' to the employer comes within this preference; it need not strictly be a loan if those wages would have been a preferred debt if unpaid.[47] But the fact that a bank debits wages cheques to a separate wages account does not always entitle it to the preference.

THE INSOLVENCY FUND

At times an employer may be so heavily insolvent that there is not enough in his entire estate to satisfy even the preferential debts. Whatever assets he possessed may have been captured by a prior charge or be subject to leasing, hire purchase or retention of title arrangements. Even if there are enough assets to cover the preferential debts, the employees may have to wait years for the liquidator or Official Assignee to make a distribution. It was to deal with these eventualities that the Protection of Employees (Employers' Insolvency) Act, 1984, was passed. This Act sets up a fund, administered by the Minister, from which the equivalent of certain debts to employees can be paid to them from the Fund; the Minister is then subrogated for those employees. This Act is based on the E.C. Directive 80/987 on the protection of employees in the event of the insolvency of their employer.[48] The Fund was known as the Redundancy and Employers Insolvency Fund but in 1991 was amalgamated with the general Social Insurance Fund.

Employees covered Like the redundancy payments legislation, the 1984 Act applies only to employees who are insurable for all benefits under the Social Welfare Acts.[49] But the Minister, by order, can extend or restrict the personal scope of the Act. In 1988 employees over 66 years of age who otherwise would be insured for all benefits were brought within the Act.[50]

Debts payable Those debts which eligible employees may recover from the fund are listed in s.6(2) of the 1984 Act. These are:

> Arrears of 'normal weekly remuneration'[51] not exceeding £250 per week[52] and for a duration of no more than eight weeks.

46. Companies Act, 1963, s.285(6) (as supplemented by 1982 Act s.10(c)).
47. *Waikato Savings Bank v. Andrews Furniture Ltd* [1982] 2 NZLR 520.
48. O.J. No. L 283/23 (1980).   49. S.3.   50. SI No. 48 of 1988.
51. As defined in s.6(9)—same meaning as for the Redundancy Payments Acts; see ante p.216.
52. S.6(4)(a), as amended by SI No. 17 of 1990.

Arrears under a sick pay scheme, subject to the same £250 per week and eight weeks ceiling; but also subject to a ceiling measured by reference to the injury or disability benefit and pay related benefit payable under the Social Welfare Acts.[53]

Arrears of holiday pay, subject to the same £250 per week and eight weeks ceiling.

Money in lieu of the minimum notice periods for dismissal prescribed by the Minimum Notice etc. Act, 1973, again subject to the same ceilings.

Damages, compensation, awards and fines payable under the Unfair Dismissals Act, 1977, the Redundancy Payments Acts 1967-79, the Anti-Discrimination (Pay) Act, 1974, the Employment Equality Act, 1979, and also remuneration payable under Part VI of the Industrial Relations Act, 1946. Where the amount payable under any of these heads is calculated on the basis of normal remuneration, the Fund will not pay out any on more than what represents £250 a week. The amount payable under some of these heads is subject to several other qualifications.

It was held by the House of Lords in the *Westwood* case[54] that payments made from a similar fund in Britain are subject to the collateral benefits principle. There the amount of unemployment benefit an employee drew immediately following his dismissal was deducted from the amount due to him in principle under the insolvency fund legislation and only the net sum was payable to him. This was because the mode of redress for not giving the minimum notice of dismissal required by statute is deemed to be an action for breach of contract. That being so, the successful plaintiff has a duty to mitigate his damages and it was previously held that, under the duty to mitigate, unemployment benefit received during the relevant period must be deducted from the overall sum due.[55] The legislative mechanism for recovery under the Minimum Notice etc. Act, 1973, is different from that in Britain but, s.12(1) of that Act speaks of 'recovering compensation for any loss sustained'. In *Irish Leathers Ltd v. Minister for Labour*[56] Barrington J declined to follow *Westwood* because it was unsafe to follow the English precedents where there are differences of detail in the legislation. It was held that the fund should pay the full amount of the outstanding salary without deducting any unemployment benefit the employee had

53. S.6(4)(b).
54. *Westwood v. Secretary of State for Employment* [1985] AC 20.
55. *Parsons v. B.N.M. Laboratories Ltd* [1964] 1 QB 95.
56. [1986] IR 177.

received. Under the 1973 Act, he has a right to be paid a specified sum of money and whether at the same time he received unemployment benefit is outside that Act's concerns; it is entirely a matter between the employee and the social welfare authorities. More recently it was held in Britain that the amount payable from the insolvency fund is the net amount after deducting income tax.[57]

Obtaining payments Payment from the Fund is obtained principally by making an application by or on behalf of the employee to the Minister.[58] If the Minister is satisfied that the employee falls within the Act, that his employer is insolvent and that all or part of any debt, described above, is owed to the employee, the Minister shall make the payment. What constitutes insolvency for these purposes is defined as an individual executing a deed of arrangement or being adjudicated bankrupt, and a company being put into receivership or being wound up, or possession being taken of company assets under a floating charge.[59] The Minister is empowered to require information regarding the debt in order to ascertain if the claim is well founded.[60] If there was some agreement between the employer and the applicant that an application should be made to the Fund in respect of a debt but the employer then had the means to pay that sum, the Minister can refuse to make a payment.[61]

In the case of an application for arrears of remuneration, sick pay or holiday pay, if the sum has been awarded by a court to the employee, then the obligation to make a payment from the Fund is immediate.[62] Where there has not been a court award under either of these heads, if an application for payment from the Fund is refused by the Minister the matter can be appealed to the Employment Appeals Tribunal.[63] Moreover, if the Minister is in doubt whether any particular claim should be paid, he may refer the matter to the Tribunal for its determination.[64]

---

57. *Secretary of State for Employment v. Cooper* [1987] ICR 766.
58. S.6(1). The procedure is set out in the Protection of Employees (Employer's Insolvency) (Forms and Procedure) Regulations, 1984, as amended in 1991 (S.I. 349 of 1991).
59. S.1(3); cf. s.4.   60. S.8.   61. S.6(8).   62. S.6(3).
63. S.9(1) and (4). Cf. *Re Solus Teo.* [1990] ILRM 180.   64. S.9(3).

11

Occupational pensions

Most full time jobs today are pensionable in the sense that provision is made by many employers to pay their employees a pension on their retirement from work.[1] In the past it was primarily public sector employments which were pensionable and one of the main attractions of working in the public service was the security of statutory pension arrangements.[2] More recently, however, occupational pensions have spread into the private sector and in 1991 it was estimated that approximately 55 per cent of the private sector workforce were in pensionable employment. As well as private pensions arrangements, retired workers may also be entitled to pensions under the Social Welfare Acts.[3]

Before the Pensions Act, 1990, came into force, occupational pensions and their administration were virtually unregulated. Although the 1990 Act established the Pensions Board to monitor pension schemes and to publish codes of practice regarding their administration, and lays down rules regarding funding, preservation of benefits, disclosure of information and equal treatment, the exact nature and terms of any particular scheme is left largely to be determined by the employers and employees affected. Different industries and different types of company and workforces may require somewhat distinctive pension arrangements. Matters to be decided when a company is adopting a pension scheme include, for example, eligibility—which employees can be members of the scheme, what conditions must be met to become a member of a scheme and is membership to be entirely voluntary; contributions—shall the employer pay all the

---

1. See generally N. Inglis-Jones, *The Law of Occupational Pension Schemes* (1989) and B. Escolme et al. eds., *Hosking's Pensions Schemes and Retirement Benefits* (6th ed. 1991).
2. E.g., Superannuation Acts, 1834-1963, Local Government Superannuation Acts, 1956-1980, Health Act, 1970, s.20, Mental Treatment Act, 1945, Part V, as amended in 1961, Garda Pension Acts, 1933 and 1947, Army Pensions Acts, 1923-1947. These and other public sector pension arrangements have engendered a considerable amount of litigation.
3. Social Welfare (Consolidation) Act, 1981, ss.78-82 (contributory old age pension, ss.83-86 (retirement pension) and 157-194 (non-contributory pensions)

contributions or must the employees also pay contributions, and should provision be made for additional voluntary contributions; benefits—what benefits are to be paid under the scheme and how are the amounts of pensions to be determined; what is to happen where members leave the scheme before they reach the prescribed retirement age. An excellent collection of precedents for these schemes can be found in *Longman's Commercial Law Precedents* (Vol.II).

Occupational pension schemes are usually based on a trust deed, whereby the employer undertakes to pay specified contributions towards a pension fund. This deed will provide for the appointment of trustees of the fund and set out their obligations with regard to it, like the investment policy or criteria. The trustees then either manage the fund or appoint a committee of management for that purpose. Almost invariably one or more representatives of the employer will be appointed as fund trustees; there may also be trustees chosen by or on behalf of the employees and indeed by members who are in receipt of pensions.

APPROVED SCHEMES

Sections 13-23 of the Finance Act, 1972, give pension schemes which are approved by the Revenue Commissioners special tax advantages. For practical purposes, all pension schemes of any significance which are in existence have been so approved or else are the subject of an application for Revenue approval. In order to obtain approval, the scheme must satisfy the following general conditions and also conditions regarding benefits, laid down by s.15 of the Finance Act, 1972.

The general conditions are:

(1) the scheme is bona fide established for the sole purpose of providing relevant benefits in respect of service as an employee, being benefits payable to the employee or to his widow, children, dependents or personal representatives;

(2) the scheme is recognised by the employer and employees to whom it relates;

(3) every employee who is, or has a right to be, a member of the scheme has been given written particulars of all essential features of the scheme which concern him;

(4) there is a person resident in the State responsible for discharging all the duties imposed by Finance Act, 1972, Part II on the administrator of the scheme;

(5) the employer is a contributor to the scheme (there is no requirement for the employee to be a contributor, but he may be);

(6) the scheme is established in connection with some trade or undertaking carried on in the State by a person resident in the State (which may include a profession, an investment company or the management of property rents);

(7) no repayment can be made of any employee's contributions under the scheme.

The conditions as to benefits are:

(1) the maximum benefit for an employee is a pension on retirement not exceeding two thirds of his final remuneration (as defined), but for service of less than 40 years the maximum pension is:

n/60 x final remuneration

where n = the number of years of service;

(2) the pension must be one payable on retirement at a specified age not earlier than 60 (or, in the case of a woman, 55) and not later than 70 (except on earlier retirement due to incapacity);

(3) any pension payable to a widow of an employee who dies before retirement must not exceed two thirds of the maximum pension to which that employee would have been entitled if he had continued to serve in the employment until the normal retirement date at a remuneration equal to his final remuneration before his death;

(4) any lump sums payable to the widow, children, dependents or personal representatives of an employee who dies before retirement must not exceed, in the aggregate, four times the employee's final remuneration;

(5) any benefit for a widow of an employee payable on his death after the retirement must be a pension and must not exceed two thirds of any pension payable to the employee;

(6) any pensions for the children or dependents (other than the widow) of an employee who dies either before or after his retirement must not exceed in the aggregate, one half of the pension specified in (3) or (5) above (whichever is appropriate);

(7) the maximum lump sum which an employee may take, if permitted to do so under the terms of the scheme, is an amount equal to 1.5 times his final remuneration, but for service of less than 40 years the maximum lump sum is:

3n/80 x final remuneration

(where n = the number of years of service); and

(8) no other benefits, other than those specified above, can be payable under the scheme. In order to obtain Revenue approval, it is not

essential that the scheme provides for paying benefits up to the maximum levels mentioned here, nor that each and every type of benefit referred to here is paid.

In an appropriate case the Revenue will give approval to a scheme which does not meet all the prescribed requirements; they have a discretion to sanction schemes which they consider acceptable albeit not satisfying all of these conditions. For this purpose they have published guidelines. For an extensive treatment of this topic and of the various tax benefits given in connection with approved pension schemes, the reader should consult one of the specialised works on income taxation.[4]

FUNDING

The funding of pension schemes is concerned with how ultimate payment of the benefits in question is to be financed. A method which became common in France after the Second World War is the *répartition* scheme; subject to the accumulation of very modest sums to cover demographic factors, the whole of any year's contributions is paid out in benefit. Existing employed members finance the pensions presently being paid, in the anticipation that, when they in turn become pensioners, their successors will continue contributing to the scheme. Schemes like this are risky when they do not cover a substantial number of employees. The more common form of funding in this country and in Britain is to make advance provision, spread over the working life of a member, for benefits which it is intended to pay him on retirement. An infinite variety of ways exist for arranging the incidence of contributions during a working life. But the minimum requirement should be that, at any given time, sufficient assets exist in the fund to ensure that, if the fund were terminated, pensions can be provided for the remainder of the lives of those who are already retired, together with deferred pensions for existing members based on the duration of their service and their earnings up to that date.

The financial operation of pension schemes is based on the assumption that the contributions collected will accumulate to an extent that it will be possible to pay all of the promised benefits. Accumulation of funds will depend on the success of the fund's investment policy; badly-advised investment will result in deficits, sound investments may very well give rise to a surplus in the fund. One of the objectives of the Pensions Act, 1990, is

4.   See generally, N. Judge, *Irish Income Tax* (1986, loose leaf), ch.16.1.

to ensure that occupational pension schemes, which are not based on defined contributions, are properly funded. These are schemes where the amount of the ultimate pension is not related directly to the number of contributions made to the fund. Section 43 of the 1990 Act sets out a 'funding standard' for such schemes: the scheme's resources must be sufficient that, if the scheme were wound up, its liabilities and the expenses of the dissolution would be covered. Determining whether a scheme meets the standard is a matter for investigation and assessment by an actuary.

Every three and a half years, the scheme's trustees are required to submit to the Pensions Board an actuarial funding certificate.[5] This is to be based on the findings of the scheme's actuary and will state whether or not the funding standard is being met. In the event of that standard not being satisfied, the trustees are required to draw up a funding proposal, to be submitted to the Board, which is designed to ensure that the scheme is fully funded before the next certification period comes about. Unless an adequate proposal has been submitted to them, the Board are empowered to direct the trustees to reduce the benefits which would be payable under the scheme, in such manner that the funding standard would be satisfied. By this means, it is expected that any deficiencies which may occur in the scheme will be overcome. But the 1990 Act does not contain provisions regarding how any surplus which may arise in the fund should or should not be disposed of.

TRUSTEES

Overall responsibility for the pension fund and its administration will be conferred on trustees. Their rights and duties are based on the terms of the trust deed, the general principles of the law regarding trustees[6] and Part VI of the Pensions Act, 1990. The contention that the general law of trusts does not apply to pension fund trustees was rejected in *Cowan v. Scargill*,[7] a case which concerned what investment policy the National Union of Mineworkers' pension fund should follow. Megarry VC, could

> see no reason for holding that different principles apply to pension fund trusts from those which apply to other trusts. Of course, there are many provisions in pension schemes which are not to be found in private trusts, and to these the general law of trusts will be sub-ordinated. But subject to that, I think that the trusts of pension funds are subject to the same rules as other trusts. The large size of pension funds emphasises the need for diversification, rather than lessening it,

5. Pensions Act, 1990, s.42.
6. See generally, R. Keane, *Equity and the Law of Trusts in the Republic of Ireland* (1988) chs. 6-14.

and the fact that much of the fund has been contributed by members of the scheme seems to me to make it even more important that the trustees should exercise their powers in the best interests of the beneficiaries. In a private trust, most, if not all, of the beneficiaries are the recipients of the bounty of the settlor, whereas under the trusts of a pension fund many (though not all) of the beneficiaries are those who, as members, contributed to the funds so that in due time they would receive pensions. It is thus all the more important that the interests of the beneficiaries should be paramount, so that they may receive the benefits which in part they have paid for.[8]

This, however, may be overstating somewhat the true legal position. For a strong argument could be made that, as a general principle, pension schemes are different in vital respects from family trusts and wills. The latter are funded by the original settlor by way of gift, whereas pension schemes are a form of deferred remuneration which have been established in trust form, often in order to secure tax advantages for approved schemes. Moreover, in many of these schemes, the beneficiaries (employees who ultimately will become pensioners) contribute directly to fund their benefits. Unlike the usual private trust, the rules of pension schemes are often incorporated, wholly or in part, into their beneficiaries' employment contracts; the members have enforceable contractual rights to participate in the fund in various ways.[9] Given the very large sums that may be tied up in pension funds and the large number of potential beneficiaries, the limited scope of private trust law and that pension trust arrangements may have a substantial contractual element, it may perhaps be a mistake to apply rigidly traditional trust law rules. In the *Scargill* case,[10] the fund's trustees there sacked their lawyers and the case was argued by the N.U.M.'s president, who is not a lawyer, on mainly ideological grounds. If the arguments had focused more on legal principles and rules, it is possible that Megarry J might have modified the analysis stated above.

Appointment and removal Usually, the trustees are individuals who are appointed and removable in accordance with the terms of the trust deed. Occasionally instead, the trustees may be either an outside trust corporation, which specialises in acting as a trustee in various contexts, or an 'in-house'

7.   [1985] Ch. 270.
8.   Id. at p.290.
9.   This analysis of the hybrid nature of pension schemes was accepted in *Imperial Group Pension Trust Ltd v. Imperial Tobacco Co. Ltd* [1991] 1 WLR 589.
10. [1985] Ch. 270, supra.

trust company which is specially incorporated for this purpose.[11] The in-house company enables greater flexibility in managing the fund, its directors being in effect the trustees. Except where the trust deed provides to the contrary, the surviving trustees or trustee, or their personal representatives, possess a power under s.10 of the Trustee Act, 1893, to appoint new trustees. Section 23 and 25 of that Act empower the High Court to replace a trustee and to appoint additional trustees. The Court also has an inherent jurisdiction to remove a trustee where that is necessary for the proper execution of the trust.[12]

These powers are now supplemented by powers under the Pensions Act, 1990, which apply regardless of any contrary stipulation in the trust deed. Where there are no trustees or where the trustees cannot be found, the Pensions Board can intervene and appoint a new trustee or new trustees.[13] And where one or more trustees failed to carry out their legal duties, whether under the terms of the trust deed or under the general principles of law or the 1990 Act, or where they are acting in such a way as jeopardises the rights or interests of the members in the scheme, the High Court is empowered to remove those trustees and to appoint replacements.[14]

Powers and duties Section 59 of the 1990 Act sets out the obligations of pension scheme trustees in general terms:

> Without prejudice to the duties of trustees generally and in addition to complying with the other requirements of this Act, the duties of trustees of [pension] schemes shall include the following:
>
> (a) to ensure, in so far as is reasonable, that the contributions payable by the employer and the members of the scheme, where appropriate, are received;
>
> (b) to provide for the proper investment of the resources of the scheme in accordance with the rules of the scheme;
>
> (c) where appropriate, to make arrangements for the payment of the benefits as provided for under the rules of the scheme as they become due;
>
> (d) to ensure that the proper membership and financial records are kept.

Among the other main duties imposed on trustees by the 1990 Act are to ensure that the pension scheme is registered with the Pensions Board.[15] The

---

11. Cf. *Mettoy Pension Trustees Ltd v. Evans* [1990] 1 WLR 1587, at p.1605 on the difference between a trust company and a trust corporation.
12. *Arnott v. Arnott*, 58 ILTR 185 (1924).
13. S.64.   14. S.63.   15. S.60.

trustees must supply information on the following matters to the members of the fund and to some others: the scheme's constitution and its administration and finances, the rights and obligations that arise or may arise under the scheme, and such other relevant matters as may be prescribed by the Minister.[16] As well as disclosure to members and prospective members, that information must be provided to those persons' spouses, to persons who are within the scope of the scheme and who qualify or prospectively qualify for its benefits, and to any licensed trade union which represents members of the scheme.[17] The trustees must arrange to have the fund's accounts audited periodically[18] and also to have the scheme's assets and liabilities valued by an actuary.[19] They must prepare an annual report on the scheme in the form prescribed by the Minister.[20] They have certain duties with regard to the funding standard and the preservation of benefits,[21] as indicated below. Several powers and duties will be laid down in the trust deed, which most likely will follow a standard format.

Being fiduciary agents, pension fund trustees are subject to the exacting fiduciary duties imposed by the principles of equity.[22] Except where provision to do so is made, they are not entitled to any remuneration for their services; they are not allowed to deal in or to purchase property belonging to the trust; they must not permit themselves to get into a situation where a substantial conflict exists or could very well exist between their own personal interests and the interests of the beneficiaries. Trust powers should not be used for any personal advantage. And, as it was put in the *Scargill* case, they must

> exercise their powers in the best interests of the present and future beneficiaries of the trust, holding the scales impartially between different classes of beneficiaries. . . . They must of course obey the law; but subject to that they must put the interests of their beneficiaries first. When the purpose of the trust is to provide financial benefits for the beneficiaries, as is usually the case, the best interests of the beneficiaries are normally their best financial interests.[23]

Among of the commonest powers conferred on trustees are to invest the scheme's contributions, to pay benefits to the dependents of a member who dies during his service, to amend the scheme in various ways and to close it to new members.

---

16. S.54(1). S.I. No. 215 of 1991.   17. S.54(2).   18. S.56.
19. Ibid.   20. S.55.   21. Parts III and IV.
22. See generally, Keane, supra n.6, ch.10 and P. Finn, *Fiduciary Obligations* (1977).
23. [1985] Ch. at pp.286-287.

Investment: The power of investment is also governed by the Trustee (Authorised Investments) Act, 1958, which lays down the types of securities in which trust funds may be invested. But the trust deed may confer an even more extensive investment power. In *Cowan v. Scargill*,[24] regarding the investment policy of the National Union of Miners' pension fund, it was held that some of the trustees had acted improperly by insisting that there should be no investment in industries which competed with coal and that investment outside of the United Kingdom should be substantially curtailed. That may have been the Union's own policy but it was held not to be in the best interests of the members of the fund, because it could have resulted in lower returns on investments. The power to invest, it was said, 'must be executed so as to yield the best return for the beneficiaries, judged in relation to the risks of the investments in question; and the prospects of the yield of income and capital appreciation both have to be considered in judging the return from the investment. . . . In considering what investments to make trustees must put on one side their own personal interests and views.'[25] However, the rules of any particular scheme may expressly or perhaps by implication permit what is termed 'social investment' by the trustees. Indeed, what at first sight may seem to be social investment may on closer scrutiny be in the members' best financial interests as well.[26]

A matter, which is often the source of considerable controversy, is the extent to which the fund may invest in the employer's own shares or business. This is not dealt with in the 1990 Act but may very well be the subject of codes of conduct issued by the Pensions Board. Conventional wisdom has it that too many eggs should not be placed in the one basket and there is always a danger that employers, facing financial difficulties, may raid the fund, thereby putting at risk the very solvency of the fund. The rules of many funds permit what is termed 'self-investment'. In an unreported English case,[27] concerning the London Co-Operative Society pension fund, the rules permitted the fund to make loans to the Society. When loans were made to the Society at below the going market interest rate, their propriety was challenged by one of the beneficiaries. The issue to be determined was whether, in all the circumstances, that arrangement was in the interests of the beneficiaries as a whole than was lending money to third parties at the market rate of interest. The Society there was short of working capital and could not have paid the market rates. With some reluctance, Brightman J held that the loans there were permissible, provided they were not for indefinite periods; to rule otherwise would require the trustees to allow the

---

24. [1985] Ch.270.   25. Id. at p.287.
26. E.g. *Withers v. Teachers Retirement System of New York*, 447 F Supp 1248 (1978).
27. *Evans v. London Co-Operative Soc. Ltd* (*The Times*, 6 July 1976).

Society to become insolvent, to the detriment of the scheme's members. If a substantial proportion of the scheme's members there were pensioners rather than present employees of the Society, the outcome might have been different. In the United States in 1978 the New York Teachers' Pension Fund were allowed to make loans to New York City at a time the City was facing bankruptcy[28]—nearly all of the teachers being City employees.

Closely related to self-investment is the question of the role of the fund when a take-over bid is made for the company. Where part of the fund's assets are shares in the company, in what circumstances should the general interests of the company, perhaps as seen by its directors and majority trustees, be placed before the immediate financial gain for the beneficiaries?

Amendment: A power which will be very carefully scrutinised by the courts is that of amending the scheme. It is common practice to provide in the deed for changes to be made to the scheme to meet new legislation or new circumstances of the employer's business, or to enlarge or restrict benefits, or for other unforeseen circumstances. The procedures laid down for making an amendment must be scrupulously followed. Where the reason for amendment is the merger of two or more schemes or to facilitate the wholesale transfer of membership, particular attention will be given to ensuring that the changes stay within the scheme's general objects and purposes. In *In re Courage Group's Pension Schemes*,[29] Millett J indicated that a power of amendment will not be unduly constricted, observing that

> there are no special rules of construction applicable to a pension scheme; nevertheless, its provisions should wherever possible be construed to give reasonable and practical effect to the scheme, bearing in mind that it has to be operated against a constantly changing commercial background. It is important to avoid unduly fettering the power to amend the provisions of the scheme, thereby preventing the parties from making those changes which may be required by the exigencies of commercial life. This is particularly the case where the scheme is intended to be for the benefit not of the employees of a single company but of a group of companies. The composition of the group may constantly change as companies are disposed of and new companies are acquired; and such changes may need to be reflected by modifications to the scheme.[30]

To what extent the exercise of the power of amendment will be reviewed by the courts depends on how it is formulated and who is entitled to exercise

28. Supra n.26.   29. [1987] 1 WLR 495.   30. Id. at p.505.

it. Where that power is given to the trustees, it is of a fiduciary nature. Accordingly, they must take due account of all the relevant considerations and must not exercise it for a self-serving purpose or other improper purpose. Frequently, the power to amend is exerciseable jointly by the trustees and the employer. That kind of a power formed the background to the *Mettoy Pension Trustees* case.[31] Under the original version of the scheme there, the trustees could decide to allocate all or part of the surplus towards increasing benefits. Subsequently, that was changed to give the employer an 'absolute discretion' in this regard. If the company were ever wound up, that discretion would be exercised by the liquidator, who would be much inclined to exercise it in the company's (and its creditors) favour. That amendment was set aside by the court on the grounds that, when they agreed to it, the trustees had failed to consider the full implications of what they were doing. That the trustees had acted on professional advice was no answer; their duty is 'to take into account all material considerations' and '[t]he extent of that duty is not affected by the amount or quality of the professional advice they may seek or obtain.'[32]

EMPLOYERS

Obviously, the employer plays a vital role in the scheme; it is his contributions which fund it and, in contributory schemes, he pays the wages from which employees' contributions are deducted. A vital role is also played by the employer in establishing the scheme; especially in non-unionised jobs, the employer is virtually free to dictate all the terms and conditions of the scheme.[33] Often, the employer is empowered to appoint and to remove all or any of the trustees. Often the employer is empowered to determine how the surplus or part of it shall be allocated. Frequently some major decisions regarding the scheme must be taken jointly by the employer and the trustees.

In was held in *Imperial Group Pension Trust Ltd v. Imperial Tobacco Ltd*[34] that powers of decision exerciseable by employers under pension schemes cannot be used for an improper purpose and must be referable to the financial and administrative interests of the scheme. In other words, employers cannot decide on one particular course of action just because it suits them. The reason for this is the hybrid nature of pension schemes; as Browne-Wilkinson VC put it,

31. *Mettoy Pensions Trustees Ltd v. Evans* [1990] 1 WLR 1587, infra p.257.
32. Id. at p.1626.
33. Regulations to be issued under s.62 of the 1990 Act may very well restrict this freedom.
34. [1991] 1 WLR 589.

> Pension scheme trusts are of quite a different nature to traditional trusts. . . . Pension benefits are part of the consideration which an employee receives in return for the rendering of his services. In many cases . . . membership of the pension scheme is a requirement of employment. In contributory schemes . . . the employee is himself bound to pay his or her contributions. Beneficiaries of the scheme, the members, far from being volunteers have given valuable consideration. The company employer is not conferring a bounty.[35]

Accordingly, the 'good faith' obligation, which underlies the employment relationship,[36] is carried over to pension schemes and employers must act in good faith when they exercise any powers they possess under these schemes. Those powers are 'subject to the implied limitation that the[y] shall not be exercised so as to destroy or seriously damage the relationship of confidence and trust between the company and its employees and former employees.'[37]

That case concerned the role of an employer in the amendment of a scheme; often the power to amend is exerciseable jointly by the employer and the trustees. When a company is taken over, often the new owners will attempt to acquire the surplus in the company's pension fund in order to help finance the acquisition. For that reason, pension fund rules regarding the surplus are often changed when a take-over bid is made, in order to close any further access to the surplus and thereby deter the bidder; this is one of the so-called 'poison pills'. In the *Imperial Tobacco* case, an amendment of that nature had been made but it failed to defeat the take-over. A new pension scheme was then established by the new owners for the company's new employees and proposals were made by the company to merge that scheme with the old one. One of the incentives being offered was that the new scheme provided for higher benefits. Although the old scheme was in a financial position to fund equally higher benefits, the employer indicated that it would never consent to make the amendments to the scheme which were necessary to permit payment of those higher benefits from the large surplus. But it was held that the employer was exercising this veto unlawfully. The employer's power under the scheme, to give or withhold consent to amendments, was not untrammelled and could not be used for a clearly improper purpose, such as to put pressure on members to abandon their existing rights and to transfer to a scheme which provided for higher benefits but which, if wound up, vested the entire surplus in the employer. Under the old scheme, the members got the entire surplus on a dissolution.

35. Id. at p.597.   36. See ante pp.71-72.   37. [1991] 1 WLR at p.598.

THE SURPLUS

A matter of considerable controversy is, where there is a surplus of the fund's assets over its liabilities, who is entitled to that surplus. In particular, does the surplus belong to the members? This question can arise in a variety of contexts, for instance, whether the employer can take a 'contributions holiday' in such circumstances, whether the rules can be amended so that the surplus can be extracted, how much must be paid out when a group of members transfer from one scheme to another? Ideally all of these problems should have been expressly provided for in the rules but that is not always done. And while many rules provide that, on the scheme being wound up, the surplus assets shall be returned to the employer, this is not always enough to answer the question being posed. To an extent, the answer depends on how the employer's contributions to the fund are characterised. If pensions represent deferred remuneration for services rendered to the employer, then it should follow that the employer cannot simply recapture the unanticipated fruits of that remuneration. But the employer's contributions may be regarded as conditional; as entitling the members to the agreed benefits but any excess over what would fund those benefits is in essence a gift from the employer, thereby entitling him, as resulting trustee, to claim any surplus over the sum which must be paid under the fund's rules. The matter has been touched on in several English decisions, without any conclusive answer being reached, although the trend there has been towards regarding the surplus as belonging to the employer.[38]

In *Davis v. Richards & Wallington Industries Ltd*[39] the question of surplus arose when a contributory scheme was being dissolved after the company had been put into liquidation. Like many of these schemes, the one there had a long and complicated history, being amended on numerous occasions, including absorbing other pension schemes. The issue to be determined was who was entitled to the surplus as represented by the employers' contributions and by the contributions made to the since-merged scheme. There was no express or clearly implied provision in the scheme about how those were to be allocated. Under the scheme, the employees' contributions were a fixed amount—five per cent of salary—and the employees were entitled to a specified pension and other benefits. The employer's obligation was to fund the scheme and, as the surplus proved, the employer had over-contributed. For that reason, it was held that the surplus represented by those over-contributions were held by the fund on a

38. See generally, Nobles, 'Who is Entitled to the Pension Fund Surplus?', 16 *Ind. L.J.* 164 (1987).
39. [1990] 1 WLR 1511.

'resulting trust' on the employer's behalf. This principle of a resulting trust applies where an owner of property conveys it to another to be held on certain trusts, which fail, either in whole or in part; in that event the beneficial interest reverts to the person who conveyed the property.[40] In an earlier pension case, it was held that

> Where a trust deed is silent as to the destination of a surplus the law will supply a resulting trust in favour of the provider of the funds in question. This is something which arises out of the trust deed as an implication of law. The trust deed may include a clause which prevents a resulting trust from operating and in that case it will operate according to its terms.[41]

An intention to exclude this resulting trust in favour of the provider of the funds can also be implied into the deed, but there must be very persuasive grounds to raise an implied term of that nature. It was held that the circumstances of the case did not justify an inference that the surplus should go to the employees.

It was possible that some of the surplus there represented employees' contributions, either to the fund or to the funds which had been merged. But it was held that there was no resulting trust of those sums for the employees' benefit, for practical reasons. Each employee paid his contributions in return for specified financial benefits from the fund. The value of those benefits would be different for each employee depending on how long he had served, how old he was when he joined and how old he was when he left. Two employees might have paid identical sums in contributions but have become entitled to benefits of a very different value. The point is particularly striking of the employees who exercised their option to a refund of contributions. How could a resulting trust work as between the various employees *inter se*? Furthermore, the scheme was established to take advantage of the legislation relevant to an exempt approved scheme and a contracted-out of scheme. Those very requirements, it was held, prevent imputing to the employees an intention that any surplus deriving from their contributions should be returned to them under a resulting trust. On the other hand, because the employer did not provide those funds, there could be no resulting trust in his favour. Accordingly, it vested in the Crown as *bona vacantia*.[42]

In *Mettoy Pension Trustees Ltd v. Evans*,[43] the employer had been forced

40. See generally, Keane, supra n.6, ch. 12.
41. *Re A.B.C. Television Pension Scheme* (Knox J, 22 May 1973).
42. See State Property Act, 1954, ss.27 and 29.
43. [1990] 1 WLR 1587.

into liquidation but, in contrast with the above case, the deed contained a clause concerning the surplus. It stated that any surplus remaining 'may at the absolute discretion of the employer' be applied to secure further benefits, within prescribed limits; any further balance is payable to the employers. Because company directors become *functus officio* on a winding up, the company's discretion vested in the liquidator. What he would have liked to do was decide not to apportion any of the surplus towards increasing pension benefits; his primary responsibility was to safeguard the creditors' interests and, obviously, if he decided not to allocate the surplus in that way, it could be used to pay the creditors. However, it was argued on behalf of the employees that the discretion given here was not absolute but was a fiduciary power, which required the liquidator to give due consideration to the interests of the employees in increased benefits. Discretions conferred in deeds fall into several categories and it was contended that several features of the scheme here rendered this discretion a fiduciary one, including the fact that the beneficiaries were not volunteers obtaining a gift:

> Their rights have contractual and commercial origins. They are derived from the contracts of employment of the members. The benefits provided under the scheme have been earned by the service of the members under those contracts and, where the scheme is contributory, *pro tanto* by their contributions.[44]

In construing the rules of a 'balance of cost' pension scheme, it was said that '[o]ne cannot . . . start from an assumption that any surplus belongs morally to the employer.'[45] Accordingly, it was 'not correct to say that the rights of the beneficiaries [here] are satisfied when they have received their mandatory benefits and that anything more lies in the bounty of the employer.'[46]

EARLY LEAVERS

A criticism levelled against many occupational pension schemes is that they penalise the early leaver, that is the person who left the pensionable employment before his due retirement age, often to work in some other job. Whether he could recover all or any of the contributions he had made to the scheme and the contributions made by the employer on his behalf depended on the rules of the particular scheme. Perhaps the most commonly adopted solution in those cases was to refund him his own contributions, together with a

44. Id. at p.1610.   45. Id. at p.1619.   46. Ibid.

portion of the value accumulated on them. Especially for employees working for one employer for a long time before leaving, the loss of their
employer's contributions was a heavy financial penalty they suffered. Those
outcomes were a distinct obstacle to personal freedom and to the mobility
of labour.

Perhaps the most significant innovation in the 1990 Act Part III (ss.27-39)
is to protect the early leaver by providing for portable pensions. Once an
employee has served more than five years of reckonable service, the trustees
are obliged to preserve his benefit. This can be done by him choosing to
transfer to another pension scheme, which he is joining, an amount of money
from the fund which is equal to the amount of his preserved benefit.
Alternatively, that money can be used to purchase insurance annuities,
which will yield him a pension; in defined circumstances the trustees may
choose to preserve his benefit in this manner. A member who is entitled to
have his pension preserved in accordance with the Act is not permitted to
opt for a repayment of contributions made to the fund by him or on his
behalf.

ASSIGNMENT AND ATTACHMENT

In the absence of a statutory prohibition, a person may assign a pension
given to him entirely for past services. A receiver by way of equitable
execution may be appointed of a pension. For instance, in *Manning v.
Mullins*,[47] it was held that a receiver could be appointed of the pension of a
former sargeant in the Royal Irish Constabulary. The terms of the appropriate order are set out at the end of the judgment there. Many public service
pensions are rendered non-assignable by statute.[48]

EMPLOYER'S INSOLVENCY

Where an employer becomes insolvent, if the pension scheme was properly
funded it ought to be able to meet the obligations owed to the members. If
the fund itself is insolvent, then questions arise about whether the trustees
exercised their investment powers with all due care. Where an employer's
contributions are owing to the fund, those sums are preferential debts in a
winding up; this is also the case with employees' contributions to be
deducted from their remuneration and payable by the employer.[49] It is only

47. [1898] 2 IR 34.   48. E.g. Mental Treatment Act, 1945, s.87.
49. Companies Act, 1963, s.285(2)(i).

funds for the provision of 'superannuation benefits' to which this preference applies. Provision is made by s.7 of the Protection of Employees (Employers' Insolvency) Act, 1984 for the payment by the Minister of those outstanding contributions from the assets of the insolvency fund. On making such a payment, the Minister becomes subrogated for whatever rights and remedies the fund's trustees may have against the employer.[50] But ceilings are placed on the amounts of an employer's and employees' contributions which may be recovered in this manner from the Minister.

DISCRIMINATION ON GROUNDS OF SEX AND MARITAL STATUS

Most Irish pension schemes treat men and women equally and the State social welfare pensions do not discriminate between men and women. However, there are private schemes which contain one form or another of sex discrimination; for instance, in 1989 approximately 19 per cent of schemes which were surveyed had a lower normal retirement age for women than for men. For many years there was a belief that qualification rules for occupational pension schemes were not caught by Article 119 of the E.E.C. Treaty, a view which obtained some support from decisions of the European Court of Justice.[51] However, in the *Bilka-Kaufhaus* case,[52] which concerned rules that excluded part-time workers from a German supplementary pensions scheme, it was held that the ordinary private pension is a form of 'pay'. Accordingly, rules which discriminated, directly or indirectly, on the basis of sex regarding eligibility for such pensions contravened Community law. Since far more women than men are engaged in part-time work in Germany, the eligibility rule in question was unlawful. However, if it could be demonstrated convincingly that there was a sound reason other than sex for excluding part-time workers from the scheme, there then would not be a breach of Article 119. Later in the *Barber* case,[53] which concerned differential retirement rules in a British 'contracted out' pension scheme, it was held that Article 119 required that the actual amounts of the pension paid to men and women with equal seniority must always be the same. There, the Court condemned a rule whereby women qualified for a pension at the age of 57 and men at 62, and women qualified for an early pension at 50 years of age whereas men had to wait until they reached 55.

50. S.10(3); see ante p.242.
51. *Burton v. British Railways Board* (Case 19/81) [1982] QB 1080.
52. *Bilka-Kaufhaus GmbH v. von Hartz* (Case 170/84) [1987] ICR 110.
53. *Barber v. Guardian Royal Exchange Assurance Group* (Case C-262/88) [1990] 2 CMLR 513.

The full implications of the cases remain to be worked out;[54] they deal with a very complex set of matters, where the Community legislators up to now have refrained from imposing across-the-board rules of equality. In between the times they were decided, the Directive 86/378 on equal treatment in occupational social security schemes was enacted.[55] When the Pensions Bill was first published in 1989, it contained provisions on equal treatment in this field. However, the *Barber* case, decided in May 1990, forced the draftsman back to the drawing board, to eventually produce Part VII of the Pensions Act, 1990, which was enacted two months later. Equality between men and women is provided in ss.66 and 67 of this Act;

> every occupational benefit scheme shall comply with the principle of equal treatment [meaning] there shall be no discrimination on the basis of sex in respect of any matter relating to an occupational benefit scheme.

The principle of equal treatment proclaimed here also applies to discrimination on the basis of marital status and to indirect as well as to direct discrimination. In the case of indirect discrimination on each of these grounds, the burden is placed on those seeking to justify it to show that there are objectively compelling reasons for the rule in question which is not based on sex or marital status.[56]

Where a scheme discriminates contrary to these provisions, the relevant rules are declared void.[57] Additionally, there is a 'levelling up' in favour of those who were discriminated against; the void rule is replaced by the one which granted the more favourable treatment. However, the Minister is empowered to prescribe a period, not longer than ten years from the time of enactment, during which existing obligations and rights are not made subject to this levelling up.[58]

Several exceptions to the equality principle are permitted by the 1990 Act. Whether all of these are fully consistent with Article 119, as expounded in *Bilka-Kaufhaus* and in *Barber* is debatable, even though they are provided for in the Directive of 1986. Most notably there is the exception for defined contribution schemes which have differential treatment that is wholly explained on actuarial grounds.[59] Since women on average live longer than men, this permits either paying lower pensions to women than to men who have made the same amount of contributions to the fund. If the actual rate of the pension is to be the same, then the women must either have made

---

54. See generally, Curtin, 'Scalping the Community Legislator: Occupational Pensions and "Barber"', 27 *Cmn. Mkt. L. Rev.* 475 (1990).
55. O.J. No. L 225/40 (1986).
56. S.68.   57. S.71.   58. S.71(3).   59. S.69(1)(b).

higher contributions or retire later from the job; or there may be an 'equal benefit' package which extends to survivors, where the initial discrepancy is evened out because widows live longer than widowers. However, in the *Barber* case, it was said that the 'application of the principle of equal pay must be ensured in respect of each element of remuneration and not only on the basis of a comprehensive assessment of the consideration paid to workers.'[60] In other words, what matters is not the over-all package; on account of the comparative ease with which equality can be avoided when seeking to take account of complex demographic factors, the only way of guaranteeing equal treatment is that 'each element of remuneration' must be equal. It, therefore, would appear that s.69(1)(b) of the 1990 Act con-travenes Article 119. This too may be the case with the exception for benefits paid to a member's surviving spouse or other dependents (s.69(1)(d)). An argument to that effect could also be made with regard to the exception for any optional provisions, for instance, one which permits women to buy additional years of cover should they choose to do so (s.69(1)(c)).

As is the case with all the other rules regarding sex discrimination, 'special treatment' is permitted for women in connection with pregnancy or child birth.[61] Additionally, women are not to be disadvantaged in any scheme on account of their absence from work, either paid or unpaid, in connection with maternity.[62]

---

60. [1990] 2 CMLR at p.557 (para 35).   61. S.72(1).   62. S.72(2).

12

Transnational employment

By transnational employment is meant situations where an employee does not work exclusively in one country but his job involves spending some or all of his time abroad. Merchant seamen and aircraft personnel are engaged in uniquely transnational work; so too are non-local diplomatic personnel. Modern developments in transport and the opening up of foreign markets, especially within the European Community, have resulted in an increasing number of personnel working for significant periods of time away from their employer's headquarters. Employments of this nature give rise to their own special legal problems, such as what law governs the employment relationship, what courts are competent to hear disputes arising from these relationships and to what extent do the labour laws of one State affect the legal position of employees who are working in another State. Many of the questions which arise in this particular context require consideration of the principles of the conflict of laws—otherwise known as private international law.[1] As has already been explained, aliens (other than nationals of E.C. Member States) need administrative authority to become employed in Ireland[2] and, within the European Community, discrimination against nationals of E.C. States is prohibited.[3]

ADJUDICATIVE JURISDICTION

A vital preliminary point in transnational employment situations is what court or courts have jurisdiction to hear the case if a dispute arises. Even where the applicable law, say, is French law, an Irish court or tribunal may still be able to hear the matter and decide it in accordance with the law of France, expert testimony being given of that law. Or the applicable law may be that of Ireland but a French court may be able to decide the dispute applying Irish law. Where several countries' courts are competent to hear

1. See generally, W. Binchy, *Irish Conflicts of Law* (1988) (hereinafter referred to as *Binchy*).
2. See ante p.127.   3. See ante p.129.

the case then practical considerations govern the decision regarding which of them a plaintiff should proceed in, like convenience in presenting the evidence, suitable procedural rules, availability of legal aid and ease of enforcing any judgment obtained against the defendant. The criteria governing adjudicative jurisdiction vary from state to state; in some countries the nationality of one of the parties is a vital matter, in other states it is important that the defendant, either personally or through an agent, is present in the country. Within the European Community there are now uniform rules concerning adjudicative jurisdiction in civil and commercial matters, including employment.

E.C.-based defendants Where the defendant is an E.C.-based individual, company or other kind of body, this question is regulated by the Brussels Convention on Jurisdiction and the Enforcement of Judgments of 1968, as amended, which is in force in all the E.C. Member States. This Convention was implemented in Ireland by the Jurisdiction of Courts and Enforcement of Judgments (European Communities) Act, 1988.[4] Regarding employment-related disputes,[5] the position is as follows; unlike in the Rome Convention on the Conflict of Laws,[6] there is no article specially devoted to employment cases.

The key concept is a person's 'domicile'; persons can be sued in the courts of the State where they are domiciled.[7] Thus an Irish-registered company doing business in Ireland can be sued in this country and a French-registered company which is trading in France can be sued there. A person or body can be sued other than at their domicile in the following circumstances:

> In an action arising out a contract, the courts 'for the place of performance of the obligation in question' also have jurisdiction.[8] For instance, if an Irish company hires a person to work for it in France, he may sue the company for breach of contract in the French courts as well as in Ireland.
>
> Where the claim is being brought in tort or delict, the courts 'for the place where the harmful event occurred' also have jurisdiction.[9] For instance, if the employee of an Irish company, who is based in France, is injured during a brief working visit to Italy, he may sue the company in tort in the Italian courts as well as in Ireland.

4. See generally, *Binchy*, pp.181 et seq.
5. *Soc. Sanicentral v. Collins* (Case 25/79) [1979] ECR 3423.
6. See infra p.266.
7. Art.2. On what constitutes 'domicile', see *Binchy*, ch.6.
8. Art.5(1).   9. Art.5(3).

Where several defendants are being sued, proceedings can be brought against all of them in any court where any one of them is domiciled.[10] Thus, if a Belgian domiciliary had some involvement in the accident in Italy just referred to, he could be joined as a defendant in the Irish courts.

Occasionally the parties may have agreed in advance that all disputes arising between them shall be heard in one designated court or country; these provisions are commonly referred to as 'choice of forum' or '*prorogation*' clauses. A stipulation to that effect in an employment contract prevents the parties from proceeding against each other in any court other than the one or ones on which they had agreed to confer exclusive jurisdiction.[11] Instead of a choice of forum clause, the parties may have previously agreed that disputes arising between them should be decided by way of arbitration. In that case, generally they must then resort to arbitration and any court proceedings commenced in connection with the employment contract will be stayed.[12]

Non E.C.-based defendants Where the defendant is not present in Ireland and is not domiciled in any E.C. State, the question of the jurisdiction of the Irish courts is governed by Order 11 of the Rules of the Superior Courts. These rules set out the circumstances in which a notice of proceedings can be served on defendants who are outside the State.[13] In employment-related cases, they can be sued in the Irish courts in the following situations:

Where the defendant is either domiciled or ordinarily resident in the State, he may be sued here.

In an action arising out of a contract, he can be sued here if either (a) the contract was made here, (b) the contract was made by an agent who was trading or residing here or (c) the contract is governed by Irish law.

In a tort action, he may be sued here if the tort was committed here. Certain tort claims in the employment sphere can also be formulated as actions for breach of contract, like claims against the employer for negligence. Civil actions for breach of statutory duty are usually regarded as tort claims but not every right of action given by a statute will be characterised as a contract or a tort claim. The 'division of all

---

10. Art.6(1).   11. Art.17.
12. Arbitration Act, 1980, s.5. Cf. *McCormac Products Ltd v. Monaghan Co-Op. Ltd* [1988] IR 304.
13. See generally, *Binchy*, pp.123 et seq.

causes of action [at common law] into two classes, contract and tort' has been rejected by the Supreme Court.[14]

A 'necessary and proper party' to an action being brought here may be joined as a defendant in the action.

What was said above about choice of forum clauses and arbitration agreements applies equally to claims being brought against non-E.C. based defendants.

APPLICABLE LAW

Where an employee works exclusively within Ireland then his rights and obligations are determined exclusively by Irish law. If he works in some other State his legal position is subject to the laws of that State. But where his work takes him to two or more States, the question then arises of which State's laws determine his entitlements and duties.[15]

Contract Often this matter is resolved beforehand by the parties stipulating in the employment contract that it shall be governed by Irish law or by English law or by some other law, as the case may be. Generally, the parties' express choice of law will be accepted and given effect by the courts. Where the parties did not actually select a governing law, when a dispute arises the courts will attempt to ascertain, from all the circumstances, which law they chose by implication.[16] Certain features of how the contract was concluded, its terms and the performance of the work may indicate that the parties had in mind one particular national law. For instance, if the contract was concluded in Connemara, was in the Irish language and contained references to Irish legislation and Irish industrial relations procedures, this would suggest very strongly that they had intended that their relationship would be governed by the law of Ireland, even though much of the work under the contract was to be done abroad.

In the absence of an express or an implied choice of law, then the applicable law is that of the State with which the contract is most closely connected.[17] Sometimes there may be no difficulty in ascertaining what State this is; the overwhelming preponderance of features may relate to one

14. *Shipsey v. British & South American Steam Navigation Co.* [1936] IR 65, at p.103.
15. See generally, Forde, 'The Conflict of Individual Labour Laws and the E.E.C.'s Rules' [1979] *Legal Issues Eur. Integration* 85, Forde, 'Transnational Employment and Employment Protection', 7 *Ind. L.J.* 228 (1978) and F. Morgenstern, *International Conflicts of Labour Law* (1984).
16. See generally, *Binchy*, pp.518 et seq.   17. Ibid.

particular State. For instance, if the contract were made in Ireland, both parties are Irish nationals and residents, the employer's headquarters is in Ireland and a substantial amount of the employee's work must be performed here, then the relationship almost certainly is subject to Irish law. At times, however, the relationship's connections with two or more States may be approximately even. There is a tendency, where the connections with the State where a dispute is being heard are not less than those with another State, for the court to apply its State's laws. This is not entirely legal chauvinism; those laws have as strong a claim to apply as any other laws and those are the laws which the court understands best.

That judges can easily reach contrary conclusions on the question of which law should apply is illustrated by one of the principal modern cases dealing with this matter. In *Sayers v. International Drilling Co. N.V.*,[18] the plaintiff was injured when working on an oil rig off the coast of Nigeria. His employers were a Dutch company, which operated drilling rigs in many parts of the world. He was English; his contract was made in England and was in the English language; he was to be paid in pounds sterling and the contract was administered from London. A majority of the English Court of Appeal overcame the temptation to apply their own law in cases like this and held that the contract was governed by Dutch law. This was because the contract was in a standard form drawn up by a Dutch company to cater for workers of diverse nationalities who might be hired in different countries. Also, it contained an exclusion clause which would not be valid under English law.[19] The several English aspects of the contract were attributed by the Court more to administrative convenience than to any inferred intention as to which law shall apply.

The Rome Convention on the Law Applicable to Contractual Relations of 1980 was brought into force in Ireland by the Contractual Obligations (Applicable Law) Act, 1991.[20] This is a treaty which purports to lay down a comprehensive set of rules for determining which particular law shall govern nearly all types of contracts containing a transnational element. Article 6 of the Convention deals with employment contracts and provides as follows:

> 1. Notwithstanding [the principle of the parties' freedom to choose the applicable law], in a contract of employment a choice of law made by the parties shall not have the result of depriving the employee of the protection afforded to him by the mandatory rules of the law which would be applicable . . . in the absence of choice.

18. [1971] 1 WLR 1176.
19. Law Reform (Personal Injuries) Act, 1948, s.1(3).
20. See generally, *Binchy*, pp.552 et seq.

2. [A] contract of employment shall, in the absence of choice . . . , be governed

(a) by the law of the country in which the employee habitually carries out his work in performance of the contract, even if he is temporarily employed in another country; or

(b) if the employee does not habitually carry out his work in any one country, by the law of the country in which the place of business through which he was engaged is situated

unless it appears from the circumstances as a whole that the contract is more closely connected with another country, in which case the contract shall be governed by the law of that country.

Tort If the dispute is framed in tort rather than in contract, the outcome is determined by the 'proper law' of the tort, which means the law with which the several features of the alleged wrong is most closely connected.[21] In deciding what law that is, account is taken of similar considerations as affect the proper law of the contract. Often the law governing the contract and the proper law of the tort will be the same. For instance in the *Sayers* case, the tort action as well as the employment contract were held to be subject to Dutch law. Where the law of the contract and of the tort are different, complications can arise, such as when the contract contains a clause which purports to exclude liability in tort.[22]

Statutory rights and duties When the question arises whether a particular piece of legislation grants rights to or imposes duties on the parties to an employment contract, the answer does not always turn on what State's law governs their contract in general terms. A feature of several of the modern employment protection Acts is that they expressly provide for the transnational situations in which they apply or do not apply. Thus, s.2(3) of the Unfair Dismissals Act, 1977, excludes from the Act's scope employees who, under their contracts, 'ordinarily worked' outside of Ireland, subject to some exceptions. But there are some Acts which do not address themselves directly to this question.

Territoriality: One of the general principles of international law is the territoriality of regulatory legislation. This principle has two aspects. Generally, regulatory legislation will be applied to all relevant circumstances

21. See generally, *Binchy*, Ch.32.
22. E.g. in the *Sayers* case [1971] 1 WLR 1176. Compare *Coupland v. Arabian Gulf Petroleum Co.* [1983] 3 All ER 226.

occurring within the legislating State. Thus, the Irish Road Traffic Acts apply to all situations involving road traffic in Ireland; the fact that the car in question was manufactured abroad or is owned or is being driven by a foreigner, or some other extra-territorial feature exists, does not prevent the Irish legislation from applying. Similarly, all consumer credit transactions occurring in Scotland are subject to the Scottish Consumer Credit Rules, regardless of whether some aspects of the transaction are not Scottish.[23]

In the employment law context, the territoriality principle is illustrated by two cases on the since-repealed Workmens' Compensation Acts. In *Scanlon v. Hartlepool S.S. Co.*,[24] the plaintiff was employed by an English shipping company which did not have any registered office in Ireland. He was injured while unloading cargo from one of the company's ships, which presumably was registered in England. However, that accident occurred in Ireland and the plaintiff claimed compensation under the Workmens' Compensation Act, 1906. The contention that the extraterritorial features of the employment relationship prevented this Act from applying to the case was rejected. According to Sullivan P, 'a person entering into a contract in the State is subject to all the conditions attached by our law to his contract, including, in the present case, liability to pay [workmen's] compensation ... and to have the question of such liability determined in the courts of this State.'[25] The circumstances in *Santry v. Coast Line Ltd*,[26] were similar. The plaintiff was employed by a British company on a British registered ship under articles entered into in London. He was injured while the ship was proceeding down the river Lee in Cork. It was held that he was entitled to proceed in this country with his workmen's compensation claim.

The second part of the territoriality principle is that, generally, a State's regulatory legislation does not apply to events occurring outside the jurisdiction even though the events in question may have some connection with that State. Of course, this is not the case where the Act by its very terms asserts an extra-territorial reach. Criminal laws are presumed not to be extra-territorial unless the legislation in question stipulates otherwise. Relying on the territoriality principle, the English courts declined to apply the Workmen's Compensation Act to events occurring abroad, despite their close connection with England, such as a fatal accident occurring in Malta to an English worker employed there by an English company for a temporary duration.[27] But in *Keegan v. Dawson*[28] the Supreme Court refused to follow these decisions, on the grounds that they carried territoriality to

23. *English v. Donnelly* (1958) S.C. 494.   24. [1929] IR 96.
25. Id. at p.97.   26. [1964] IR 439.
27. *Tomalin v. Pearson & Son Ltd* [1909] 2 KB 61.
28. [1934] IR 232.

an unjustifiable extreme. There the plaintiff, who was employed in Ireland by a Kildare horse trainer, was injured during the course of his work at Aintree racecourse in England. Fitzgibbon J remarked that '[i]t has been said that hard cases make bad law, but it is often the laying down of bad law that makes the hard case, and . . . it would be a misinterpretation of the Workmen's Compensation Act to hold that a groom or a drover in charge of a wagon load of horses or cattle from, say, Sligo or Bundoran to Greenore for shipment to England, lost and recovered his right to compensation under the Act half a dozen times in the course of his journey according to the particular side of the [Northern Ireland] border upon which the railway track chanced for the moment to be.'[29] Accordingly, it would be wrong to say that regulatory laws will never be given any extra-territorial effect. The nature of the rights and duties imposed by the law in question may dictate that it should apply to certain special circumstances occurring outside of the State but which are almost overwhelmingly connected with this State.

Some modern employment protection laws do not state the circumstances when they may have some extra-territorial application, notably the Minimum Notice and Terms of Employment Act, 1973, the Anti-Discrimination (Pay) Act, 1974, the Employment Equality Act, 1977,[30] the Maternity Protection of Employees Act, 1981 and the Transfer of Undertakings Regulations, 1980. Accordingly, account should be taken of the kind of considerations referred to in the *Keegan* case in determining when sanctions provided for in these Acts would not apply to such events.

Unfair dismissals: The question of the transnational impact of the Unfair Dismissals Act, 1977, is dealt with in s.2(3) of that Act: subject to some exceptions, the Act

> shall not apply in relation to the dismissal of an employee who, under the relevant contract of employment, ordinarily worked outside the State. . . .

Accordingly, if the employee worked predominantly abroad, he cannot claim protection of this Act. What exactly is meant by 'ordinarily worked' abroad; does it mean more than fifty per cent of the time, more than sixty per cent or whatever? Probably the nature of the particular job will affect how this question is answered. In *Wilson v. Maynard Shipbuilding Consultants A.B.*,[31] several propositions were laid down with reference to a

29. Id. at p.250. Compare *Equal Employment Opportunities Comm. v Arabian American Oil Co.*, 111 Supreme Court 1227 (1991)
30. Compare the position in Britain, e.g. *Deria v. General Council of British Shipping* [1986] 1 WLR 1207 and *Haughton v. Olau Line (U.K.) Ltd* [1986] 1 WLR 502.
31. [1978] 1 QB 665.

similar provision in the English legislation. Firstly, a person can ordinarily work in one place only; he cannot simultaneously ordinarily work abroad and in the State. Secondly, what matters is not the actual time worked abroad prior to the dismissal; the court should ascertain where, for the entire period envisaged by the contract, the employee was intended to be employed. Of course, the places where he worked prior to being dismissed may throw light on this question. Where the nature of the job involves considerable foreign travel, then the ordinary workplace may be the employer's base, even though he spends less than half of his working time there; for instance, in the case of airline pilots and stewards.[32] In difficult cases account can be taken of matters like where, under the contract, his travels are to begin and end, where his home is expected to be, what currency he is to be paid in and in what country is he covered by social security. Where an employee actually worked all his time in one place, the fact that under his contract he could have been posted to some other country does not mean that he did not ordinarily work where he had actually been employed.[33]

A person who ordinarily worked abroad, as contemplated by this sub-section, is not excluded from the 1977 Act's protection if either of the following conditions obtained. One is where, during the entire term of the contract, he was ordinarily resident in Ireland. The other is where, for that period, the employee was domiciled in Ireland and his employer was ordinarily resident here or, if a company, its principal place of business was in Ireland during the contract period.

Redundancy payments: Leaving aside entirely the question of working abroad, in order to fall within the Redundancy Payments Acts, 1967-1979, the employee must be significantly connected with the State because he must be insured for all benefits under the Social Welfare Acts. The social welfare legislation and regulations under it contain provisions regarding when persons are deemed to be insured even though their work has some extra-territorial features;[34] within the E.C., this matter is dealt with in Regulation No. 1408 of 1971.[35] Extra-territorial application of the redundancy law is dealt with in s.25 of the 1967 Act, which uses the same general criterion as the Unfair Dismissals Act—whether 'under his contract of employment he ordinarily worked' in the State or abroad.

An employee who ordinarily worked outside the State is denied the lump

32. E.g. *Maulik v. Air India* [1974] ICR 528 and *Todd v. British Midland Airways Ltd* [1978] ICR 959.
33. *Janata Bank v. Ahmed* [1981] ICR 791 and *Somali Bank v. Rahman* [1989] ICR 314.
34. Social Welfare (Consolidation) Act, 1981, ss.8 and 307.
35. O.J. No. L 149/2 (1971). See generally, Forde, 'The Applicable Law Under the E.E.C. Social Security Rules' 14 *Ir. Jur.* 83 (1979).

sum compensation if, at the time he was dismissed, 'he is outside the State'. Thus, being abroad on the very day the dismissal occurred is fatal for these purposes. Even if the employee ordinarily working abroad is in the State at that time, he is denied compensation unless he establishes the following: that immediately before he commenced working abroad he was (1) domiciled in Ireland, (2) employed by his present employer and (3) in the State at the time of his dismissal in accordance with his employer's instructions or, alternatively, was not given a 'reasonable opportunity' by his employer to be in the State at that time. What is meant by being denied a reasonable opportunity to be in Ireland at the date of dismissal will require clarification; does it mean that the employer should have offered him a reasonable opportunity to return, that is a positive obligation, or merely that the employer must not have unreasonably prevented him from returning?

Section 25 of the 1967 Act adds two riders, for which there is no equivalent in the Unfair Dismissals Act. Periods of service abroad are deemed to be service within the State for the purpose of calculating continuity of employment. Whether a similar provision is necessary to achieve this purpose for unfair dismissal is debatable. The other is that the employer may deduct from redundancy compensation payable any redundancy payment to which the employee may be entitled under some foreign statutory scheme where he is working.

SEAFARING

Employment in seafaring is perhaps the most highly regulated occupation of all. Legislation laying down the rights and duties of seafarers and the incidents of their employment can be traced back for centuries. Many of these measures were consolidated in the mammoth Merchant Shipping Act, 1894, which remains in force. Space does not permit any thorough account of the 1894 Act's requirements, but the extent of their range can be gathered from the headings in ss.92-226 of that Act, under the general heading 'Masters and Seamen':

> Certificates of competency,[36]
> Apprenticeship to the sea service,
> Licences to supply seamen,
> Engagement of seamen,
> Agreements with lascars,
> Rating of seamen,

36. Cf. by Merchant Shipping (Certification of Seamen) Act, 1979.

Discharge of seamen,[37]
Payment of wages,
Advance and allotment of wages,
Seamen's money orders and savings banks,
Rights of seamen in respect of wages,[38]
Mode of recovering wages,
Power of courts to rescind contracts,
Property of deceased seamen,
Reimbursement of relief to seamen's families,
Destitute seamen,
Leaving seamen abroad,[39]
Distressed seamen,
Volunteering into the navy,
Provisions, health and accommodation,
Facilities for making complaint,
Protection of seamen from imposition,
Provisions as to discipline,
Official logs, local marine boards and mercantile marine officers,
Registration of and returns respecting seamen,
Sites for sailors' homes.

These provisions apply to Irish-registered ships, their owners, masters and crew.[40] But they also apply in prescribed circumstances to foreign-registered ships.[41] Special provision is made in the 1894 Act for employment on fishing boats.[42] All of the major employment laws of general application also apply in principle to seafaring, provided the situation in question falls within their general transnational scope, for instance the Unfair Dismissals Act, 1977, and the Employment Equality Act, 1977. These measures and the other laws of general application do not expressly lay down the special circumstances when they are applicable to seafaring.[43]

Because of its very nature, seafaring is one of the most international of activities. Prescribing standards for employment at sea has been a major concern of the International Labour Organisation, which has adopted over fifty conventions and recommendations on maritime work.[44] These are

---

37. Cf. *Herman v. Owners of S.S. Vicia* [1942] IR 305.
38. Cf. *Byrne v Limerick S.S. Co.* [1946] IR 138 and *Motokov Foreign Trade Corp. v. Fermoyle Investments Ltd* (McMahon J, 25 Jan. 1985).
39. Cf. Merchant Shipping Act, 1906, s.32.
40. 1894 Act s.260.   41. Id. s.261.   42. Id. ss.376-416.
43. Compare position in Britain, e.g. in *Wood v. Cunard Line Ltd* [1991] ICR 13 and *Haughton v. Olau Line (U.K.) Ltd* [1986] 1 WLR 503.
44. See generally, N. Valticos, *International Labour Law* (1979) pp.191-199.

sometimes described as the International Seafarers' Code and deal with matters such as minimum age and protection of young seafarers, vocational training, certificates of competency, articles of agreement, hours of work and paid holidays, safety and hygiene, inspection.

Section 12 of the Merchant Shipping Act, 1947, gives the Minister for Industry and Commerce very extensive authority by regulation to prescribe employment standards and rules for seafarers. Under this, he may

> make such provisions as he thinks proper for promoting the welfare of seamen in Irish ships or at ports within the State or for maintaining in Irish ships suitable conditions of employment for seamen. . . .

The usual means by which international labour conventions for seamen are implemented is by statutory instrument under these powers. But the Minister's prescribing authority under s.12 is not confined to giving effect to the international standards.

FOREIGN EMBASSY AND CONSULAR EMPLOYEES

All of the senior staff in foreign embassies would be civil servants of their employing government and their rights and duties would be governed by their appropriate civil service regulations. Frequently, local so-called 'contract staff' are employed for comparatively menial tasks, like typists and secretaries, drivers and gardeners. There are no modern authorities regarding what law governs the employment contracts of these personnel— the *lex loci laboris* or the law of the employer-State. Although the Unfair Dismissals Act, 1977, and many other of the laws of general application do not apply to officers employed by or under the State or by local authorities, there is no express exclusion for those employed by foreign governments and foreign public agencies.

To the extent that these Acts may be applicable in principle to foreign governments, the statutory requirements may be unenforceable because of the 'sovereign immunity' principle, which is now incorporated into the Diplomatic Relations and Immunities Act, 1967. This Act gives effect to the Vienna Conventions on Diplomatic Relations of 1961 and on Consular Relations of 1963. For the purposes of the 1961 Convention, personnel are categorised as 'diplomatic agents', 'administrative and technical staff', 'service staff' and 'private servants';[45] the extent of the immunity enjoyed depends on the category the individual falls into. However, this Act does

45. Defined in Art.1.

not confer immunity on the foreign government as such, as contrasted with suing embassy officials. Most countries possess up to date legislation dealing with the immunities of foreign governments and agencies as such[46] but measures along those lines have not so far been enacted in Ireland. The position, therefore, is governed by the 'common law' for foreign sovereign immunity.

This matter came before the Supreme Court in *Government of Canada v. Employment Appeals Tribunal.*[47] A driver/messenger employed in the Canadian embassy was sacked and commenced proceedings for unfair dismissal. The Canadian Government contended that the sovereign immunity principle deprived the courts and the E.A.T. of jurisdiction to hear the claim. It was held that the old doctrine of 'absolute' immunity was no longer the law but immunity would still be afforded to actions which relate to the actual business or policy of a foreign government. Anything to do with the embassy prima facie concerns the foreign government. In particular, the 'element of trust and confidentiality that is reposed in the driver of an embassy car creates a bond with his employers that has the effect of involving him in the employing government's public business organisation and interests.' The Canadian government were entitled to claim the immunity. In a similar English case[48] it was held that there was no jurisdiction to hear an unfair dismissal complaint by a clerk employed by the Indian High Commission in London. This was because his contractual duties involved exercising the Indian Government's public function and any hearing of the case most likely would involve an investigation into that public function. Accordingly, the very nature of the employee's job has a very significant bearing on whether the employer is entitled to claim immunity. Where the employer is not the State as such but a foreign public agency, the nature of its particular function also determines whether it would be entitled to claim immunity. Of course the foreign government or agency may always choose to waive any immunity and contest the merits of the case.

---

46. E.g. the British State Immunity Act, 1978.
47. Unrep., 12 March 1992.
48. *Sengupta v. Republic of India* [1983] ICR 221. See too, *Nelson v. Saudi Arabia*, 923 F 2d 1528 (1991).

13

Employees and Company Law

At one time the principal technique used to accommodate employee interests in companies was to grant workers and their representatives greater negotiating power in their dealings with employers. To this end, the Industrial Relations Act, 1990, makes strikes and peaceful picketing in the context of a trade dispute lawful and confers extensive immunities from suit on trade unions. Over and above the employment legislation considered in the previous chapters, legislation dealing with companies as such rather than *qua* employers contain provisions specific to employees, although Irish law in this regard is far behind that of most other Western European countries.[1]

ENTITLEMENT TO ACCOMMODATE EMPLOYEE'S INTERESTS

Unless there was authority in the memorandum and articles of association to do so, formerly major decisions within companies could not be made with the primary object of furthering their employees' interests. The law identified companies almost exclusively with their shareholders. Directors must exercise their powers bona fide in what they consider is in the interests of the company;[2] special resolutions of shareholders, or any class of shareholders, are unlawful where they are not adopted bona fide for the benefit of the company as a whole.[3] And by the company as a whole was meant the shareholders in general or the hypothetical average shareholder. Ambiguous though these formulae may be, it was not permissible to place employees' interests squarely before those of the shareholders. The classic instance is *Parke v. Daily News Ltd*,[4] where a newspaper company, that had sold off its assets, proposed to distribute most of the proceeds among its employees as *ex gratia* redundancy pay. That proposal was enjoined because such massive benevolence was *ultra vires* the company.

---

1. On company law generally, see M. Forde, *Company Law* (2nd ed. 1992) — hereafter referred to as *Company Law*.
2. See *Company Law*, ch.V.   3. See id. ch.X.

The position has been changed somewhat by s.52 of the Companies Act, 1990, according to which

> The matters to which directors of a company are to have regard in the performance of their functions shall include the interests of the company's employees in general, as well as the interests of its members.

This does not entirely reverse the position under the *Daily News* case. It deals only with the position of the directors and not alone allows them to take account of employees' interests but actually requires them to do so. However, s.52(2) adds that this obligation is owed only to the company and that the employees do not have a right of action to enforce compliance with its requirements. Where the benevolence towards employees would be *ultra vires* or unfairly discriminates against minority shareholders, it is not validated by s.52, in the sense that an objecting shareholder is entitled to have the proposed action blocked and, possibly, to recover extravagant payments that were made. Section 52 nevertheless is likely to have an indirect influence as indicating a general legislative policy in favour of upholding measures adopted by companies for the benefit of their employees.

Even in the past devoting company resources to employees was permissible where that was incidental to and within the general scope of the company's business. As Bowen LJ put it in *Hutton v. West Cork Rly. Co.*,

> most businesses require liberal dealings. The test . . . is . . . whether [the transaction is] done bona fide [and] is done within the ordinary scope of the company's business and whether it is reasonably incidental to the carrying on of the company's business for the company's benefit.
>
> Take this sort of instance. A railway company, or the directors of the company, might send down all the porters at a railway station to have tea in the country at the expense of the company. Why should they not? It is for the directors to judge, provided it is a matter which is reasonably incidental to the carrying on of the business of the company, and a company which always treated its employees with Draconian severity, and never allowed them a single inch more than the strict letter of the bond, would soon find itself deserted—at all events unless labour was very much more easy to obtain in the market than it often is. The law does not say that there are to be no cakes and ale, but there are to be no cakes and ale except such as are required for the benefit of the company.[5]

4. [1962] 1 Ch. 927.   5. (1883) 23 Ch.D. 645, at pp.672-673.

FINANCIAL PARTICIPATION BY EMPLOYEES

Some companies encourage and even help their employees to acquire shares in them. The view is that by having a financial stake in the firm and being entitled to participate in its distributed profits, employees will more readily identify with the company and indeed become participants in a form of economic democracy. On the other hand, there is a danger that workers who invest most of their savings in their employer's business will lose everything if it fails. It is for companies themselves to decide whether and on what terms shares should be offered to employees. There is no legal obligation on companies to allot shares to their employees as exists, for example, in France.[6] But a p.l.c. may not allot shares in exchange for any service contract.[7] One of the matters that the Pensions Board no doubt will regulate in due course is 'self-investment' by occupational pension schemes, that is the fund investing heavily in the employing enterprise. The Finance Acts of 1982 and 1986 provide a variety of tax incentives for schemes facilitating employees to purchase shares in their company.[8]

Financial assistance to acquire shares Section 60 of the Companies Act, 1963, not alone prohibits companies from giving financial assistance for or in connection with the purchase of their own shares but goes so far as to make this practice a criminal offence.[9] This prohibition is formulated in very extensive terms and also applies to assisting the acquisition of shares in the company's holding company, if it has one. However, it does not apply in two related circumstances as regards acquisitions of shares by a company's own employees.

One is where a private company loans money to any of its bona fide employees to enable them to acquire for themselves shares in it or in its holding company.[10] The other is where a private company provides money under a scheme whereby its shares are to be held by or on behalf of its employees or former employees, or employees of its subsidiaries.[11] Loans under the former cannot be made to directors who are also employees; but the scheme under the latter can include salaried directors. Furthermore, p.l.c.s can also give financial assistance for these two purposes, provided the funds come out of profits available for distribution or the company's net assets are not thereby reduced.[12]

6. Law n.80-834 of 24 Oct. 1980.
7. Companies (Amendment) Act, 1983, s.26(2).
8. See generally, N. Judge, *Income Tax* (1986, loose leaf) par.10.112 and ch.11.4-6.
9. See *Company Law*, para. 7.59 et seq.
10. 1963 Act s.60(13)(c).   11. Id. s.60(13)(b).
12. Id. s.60(15A)-(15C) (amended in 1983).

Authority and pre-emption when allotting additional shares Sections 20 and 23 of the Companies (Amendment) Act, 1983, place certain restrictions on the freedom of companies to allot additional shares.[13] Under s.20, any share allotment must have received prior shareholder approval but there are several qualifications to this rule. Under s.23, the new shares must first be offered to the existing members on a pro-rata basis before they can be offered to existing members otherwise or to persons who are not at present members of the company. This rule too is subject to several qualifications.

An exception is made to these authority and pre-emption requirements in respect of employee share schemes. They are defined as 'any scheme for the time being in force, in accordance with which a company encourages or facilitates the holding of shares or debentures in the company or its holding company by or for the benefit of employees or former employees of the company or of any subsidiary',[14] including salaried directors. The requirement of shareholders' prior authority does not apply to shares being allotted in pursuance of such a scheme.[15] Shares being allotted in connection with these schemes need not be offered on a pre-emptive basis and employees offered shares under a scheme are not prevented by the 1983 Act from renouncing or assigning the offer, even to persons who are outside of the scheme.[16] P.l.c.s are not forbidden to allot shares under such schemes where less than one-quarter of their shares' nominal value has not been paid up.[17]

Share options as remuneration Share option schemes have become a popular method of remuneration for executive employees and for directors of companies, and there is a notable trend towards extending these schemes to employees further down the company's hierarchy. These schemes encourage loyalty to the company and provide a distinct incentive to employees to work harder and more enthusiastically for it. The basic principle is very simple. The employees in question are given options to purchase a number of the company's shares at set prices and at set times; say the option is to buy 200 shares at say £1.20, £1.50 and £1.80 per share, respectively, during the next three years. If the company prospers during those years, the actual value of the shares when purchased will exceed the price at which the option may be exercised. For instance, say in year three here, the market value of the shares had risen to £2.50; accordingly, the employee stands to make a profit of 70 pence a share if he exercises his option then—assuming he immediately disposed of the shares. Formerly, the value of the option was measured for tax purposes at the time the

13. See *Company Law*, para. 6.24 et seq.   14. 1983 Act s.2(1).
15. Id. s.20(10)(a).   16. Id. s.23(13)(b).   17. Id. s.28(4).

employee became free to exercise it, regardless of whether or not he had exercised it.[18]

The option price and conditions: Obviously the most lucrative share options are those where the option price, that is the amount which must be paid for the shares, is much less than the actual share price at the time the option is exercised. As a matter of Company Law, ordinarily it is entirely a matter for the company's directors to determine what the option price shall be and when and under what conditions it may be exercised. There is no overriding duty on the directors or the company to allot shares for as high a premium as can be obtained in the market; nor is it *per se* wrong to allot shares at par even though other investors are prepared to pay a substantial premium for them. In *Hilder v. Dexter*[19] a company, in order to raise working capital, issued shares at par and gave its executives options to take further shares at par at some later stage. When the price of its shares rose in the market the holders of those options sought to exercise them. It was held that there is no 'law' which obliges a company to issue its shares above par because they are saleable at a premium in the market.

The exercise of options will be made subject to certain terms and conditions, for instance, the times they may be exercised and in respect of how many shares, and when do the options lapse. Several conditions are very common in consequence of the tax legislation—notably those laid down in s.19 of the Finance Act, 1976, and in the second schedule of that Act for obtaining Revenue approval for the scheme.[20]

That conditions in an option scheme will be strictly construed is illustrated by *Thompson v. ASDA-MFI Group p.l.c.*,[21] where an employee was perhaps unfairly deprived of the benefits of a scheme which applied to him. The plaintiff was employed by a department store company which was the defendant's wholly-owned subsidiary. By virtue of his employment, he could participate in a savings-related option scheme established by the defendant for the benefit of all of its employees and those employed by its subsidiaries. One of the conditions of the scheme, to obtain maximum advantage under the tax rules, was that options could only be exercised by persons presently employed by a company in the group.[22] If the plaintiff

18. *Abbott v. Philbin* [1961] AC 352. See generally, Samuels, 'Tax on Shares from Employees', 26 *Conv.* 411 (1962). Today the relevant time is when the option is exercised or is otherwise realised: Finance Act, 1986, s.9 and see *Judge* par. 10.112.
19. [1902] AC 474.
20. See *Judge*, supra n.8, ch.11.5 and precedent E10 in *Longman's Practical Commercial Precedents*, Vol. II.
21. [1988] 1 Ch. 241.
22. Compare Finance Act, 1986, 2nd schedule, para. 5(2).

had been wrongfully or unfairly dismissed, presumably he would have been compensated for the loss of his options.

What happened here was that the defendant sold off to third parties its entire shareholding in the subsidiary which employed the plaintiff. The question to be decided was whether the plaintiff's options had thereby lapsed. He contended that they had not lapsed; either it was an implied term of his employment contract that the subsidiary would not be disposed of in such a way as might cause the options to lapse or, alternatively, the options survived the actual disposal. Those arguments were rejected. The court would not imply a term preventing the defendant from disposing of its subsidiary because any term of that nature lacked the requisite 'business efficacy' for implying terms into contracts; such a term lacked all commercial reality. Moreover, in view of the U.K. Finance Act's condition that options must only be exercised by existing employees of the holding or group companies, it was not possible to imply a term that the option survived the disposal of the subsidiary, because the scheme was drawn up to secure maximum tax advantages.

Selling the shares: Many share option schemes place restrictions on the time and occasionally the circumstances in which those who have acquired shares under them may sell their shares. Under the 1986 rules for approved share option schemes, the shares cannot be made subject to any restrictions other than those applying to all of the shares in their class.[23] In addition to any restrictions on disposal which may exist under the scheme, the company's own articles of association may place restrictions on disposing of shares. Those restraints most likely apply to all categories of members, regardless of how they acquired their shares. The commonest of these in private companies is to give the directors an unfettered veto over whom shares may be transferred to.[24] This is often coupled with a pre-emption requirement, whereby the existing members or directors, as the case may be, are given a first option over shares being put up for sale, usually at a price to be determined by the company's auditors.

Termination of employment: Most share option schemes provide that the options shall cease once the individual ceases to be an employee of the company or of a company in the group, as the case may be. Sometimes they go so far as providing that shares acquired under the scheme shall revert to the company or one of its nominees. For instance, in *Walsh v. Cassidy &*

23. Id. para.9(c).
24. Companies Act, 1963, Table A, Part II, art.3. Cf. *In re Hafner* [1943] IR 426.

Co.[25] the plaintiff acquired shares in the company under a provision in its articles whereby shares were to be allotted to all company employees. But another of these regulations authorised the directors to expropriate the shares of any member who is 'employed in the company in any capacity [and who] ceases to be so employed by [it].' It is implicit in Kingsmill Moore J's judgment that such a power should be construed as narrowly as is reasonably possible. He suggested that the clause there might not authorise expelling a member who acquired shares for full value and who subsequently took up some employment in the company. But he emphasised that any expulsion falling four square within the clause's terms would not be set aside merely because it would result in considerable hardship. On the other hand, 'fraudulent' exercises of the expulsion power would be restrained.

In *Micklefield v. S.A.C. Technology Ltd,*[26] the employee shareholder was most unfortunate but it was not argued that he had been treated fraudulently. He was a company director and, under his contract, was entitled to six months notice in writing of dismissal. He was entitled under a share option scheme to subscribe for shares at the end of a three year period. When that period had almost expired, there was a very substantial difference between the option price and the price of the shares in the market, so that he stood to make a large profit. But he was peremptorily dismissed and given six months salary in lieu of notice. He nonetheless sought to exercise his options a few days later, when they fell due, but the company refused to allot him the shares on the grounds that he was no longer its employee. It was held that, once he was dismissed with salary in lieu of notice, he had ceased to be an employee of the company; accordingly, he was ineligible under the very terms of the scheme to exercise the options. Although certain aspects of the employment contract may survive termination of that contract, the status or relationship of employer/employee comes to an end. The doctrine that a person would not be permitted to take advantage of his wrongs was held not applicable here because the dismissal was not unlawful. Nor would the court imply a term that no dismissal could take effect until notice of termination had expired in full.

Where an employee succeeds in a claim for unfair dismissal, he may be compensated for losing benefits under a share option scheme. Whether he will be so compensated when he claims for wrongful dismissal depends on the very terms of the option arrangements. Under the scheme which was considered in the *Micklefield* case, one of the terms was that, once any employee ceased to be employed for any reason, not alone did the options come to an end but he waived any entitlement to compensation for loss of any benefits under the option scheme.

25. [1951] Ir Jur Rep 47.   26. [1991] 1 All ER 275.

DIRECTORS' SERVICE AGREEMENTS

Not all directors have service contracts with their companies. But most full-time executive directors have those contracts and the rights and duties of some non-executive directors may be set out in contracts with their company.[27] The Employment Law aspects of these agreements must be viewed against the backdrop of Company Law, for the Companies Acts, 1963-1990, lay down special rules for directors' service contracts and their remuneration.

Remuneration The question of directors' remuneration[28] is a sensitive matter in many companies. In closely-held companies tax considerations bear heavily on whether the directors are to be rewarded by emoluments that are subject to Schedule E or by generous expenses, both of which are deductible from the company's own tax bill; or else by way of dividends or, indeed, loans. At times, there may be concern that majority shareholders will occupy all the seats on the board, pay themselves handsome directors' fees and leave little or nothing for distribution by way of dividends. In large companies with many shareholders, the dilemma may be whether the directors are being adequately rewarded to ensure that they will give of their best in advancing the company's interests. 'Golden handshakes' paid to retiring directors can give rise to concern among shareholders about whose benefit the company in fact is being run:—for the professional directors or for the shareholders.

The Companies Acts do not state who shall determine whether or how much the directors should be paid in fees and salaries, other than that no such payment may be made free of income tax.[29] The right given by s.50 of the 1990 Act to inspect directors' service contracts with a duration exceeding three years[30] now enables every shareholder to ascertain exactly how much those directors are being paid, in what manner and for what services. Every set of annual accounts must contain or be accompanied by a statement showing the aggregate of *inter alia* directors' 'emoluments'.[31]

A pension is a form of deferred salary that an employer may be obliged by contract to pay or that may be paid as a gratuity. It depends on the circumstances whether a sum paid to a retiring or retired director is a pension or more in the nature of a 'golden handshake'; although for the purpose of disclosure in the company's accounts, there are elaborate definitions of each

27. See model Executive Service Agreement in Appendix, post p.371.
28. See *Company Law*, para. 5.50 et seq.
29. Companies Act, 1963, s.185.   30. Infra p.284.
31. 1963 Act s.191(1) and (2).

of these terms. All that the Companies Acts require is that directors' pensions may not be paid free of income tax[32] and the aggregate amount of pensions must be shown in a company's annual accounts.[33] Companies in business have implied powers to agree to pay pensions to executive directors and, after those directors have died, may agree to pay pensions to their dependents.

'Golden handshakes' The term 'golden handshake' signifies sizeable payments made to company directors on their retirement other than by way of ordinary pensions. In ss.186-189 of the 1963 Act these are called 'compensation for loss of office or as consideration for or in connection with retirement from office'.[34] These payments usually used to be made in lump sums but tax considerations now compel companies to space them out over a number of years.[35] Golden handshakes may be either the estimated cost of removing a director from office prematurely or may be more in the nature of a gratuity. The Companies Acts require that these payments must not be made tax free[36] and the aggregate amount of them in any year must be disclosed in or along with the annual accounts.[37]

In order to be valid, the particulars, including the amount of any proposed payment connected with retirement, must be disclosed to the company's members, who must give their approval in general meeting.[38] Disclosure must be made while the payment is still only a proposal and it must be made to all the company's members, even to those who do not have full voting rights in general meeting,[39] like many preference shareholders. Parallel provisions exist for such payments intended to be made in the context of full or partial take-overs and purchases of sizeable assets from the company in question.[40] Any directors who are responsible for paying golden hand-shakes which have not been duly authorised by the members can be held liable for misapplication of the company's funds. And the recipients of unauthorised payments must repay the money.

'Golden umbrellas' A golden umbrella is a phrase often used to describe service contracts of a very long duration. The gilded element is that, if the employer wants to terminate the contract, he must pay the equivalent of the

---

32. Supra n.29.
33. 1963 Act, ss.191(1) and (3).
34. 1963 Act ss.186-189. See definition in s.189(3), which excludes *inter alia* 'any bona fide payment by way of damages for breach of contract.'
35. Finance Act, 1967, s.114 and schedule 3, as amended by Finance Act, 1980, s.10; see post p.348.
36. Supra n.29.   37. 1963 Act s.191(1) and (4).
38. 1963 Act s.186.   39. *Re Duomatic Ltd* [1969] 2 Ch. 365.

remuneration which would have been earned during the remainder of the contract. Thus the longer the duration the higher the price to be paid in order to rid the company of the director. Section 28 of the Companies Act, 1990, prohibits the conclusion of golden umbrellas with a duration of longer than five years, without the prior approval of an ordinary resolution of the company's members. That approval is required whether the contract is one of service or for services, that is whether under the contract the director is an employee or is to be treated as self-employed. Shareholder approval must be given to any service contract which the company is not completely free to terminate lawfully within five years of the service commencing. In the case of a director of one or more companies within a group of companies, the approval must come from the members of the holding company. Before any approval can be given to these contracts, a written memorandum of the proposed terms must be available for inspection for at least fifteen days prior to the general meeting taking place; that memorandum must also be available at the meeting. The terms of any service contract which contravenes these requirements are void and can be determined by the company at any time on giving reasonable notice of dismissal.

Inspecting service contracts Another of the innovations introduced in 1990 is to entitle every shareholder to inspect a copy or a memorandum of the terms of many director's service contracts, regardless of who is entitled to appoint directors or determine their remuneration. Section 50 of the 1990 Act requires that a copy or memorandum of the contract be kept at either the registered office, the principal place of business or where the register of members is kept. This information must be open for inspection during business hours by any member, without charge. Similar information regarding directors of subsidiaries must be kept by the holding company. In the case of directors who work 'wholly or mainly outside' the State, only the name of the director and the duration of the contract need be disclosed in this manner. Disclosure of a contract's terms is not required in this manner where it can be terminated by the company, without payment of compensation, by less than three years' notice.

Dismissing directors Apart from their disqualifying provisions,[41] the Companies Acts do not set down grounds for removing directors from office. It used to be the case that, in the absence of express provision to the contrary in the company's regulations or in a service contract, shareholders did not possess the 'inherent' power to remove directors of registered

40.   1963 Act ss.187, 188 and 189(4).
41.   Companies Act, 1990, ss.159-169; see *Company Law*, para 5.20 et seq.

companies appointed for a definite period until that period has expired.[42] Article 99 of Table A provides that any or all of the directors can be removed by an ordinary resolution of the members. The regulations of some companies empower the directors themselves to remove any of their number from the board.

Right to dismiss: One of the most important rules in company law is s.182 of the 1963 Act whereby shareholders, by passing an ordinary resolution, may remove any or all of the directors from the board before their periods of office expire.[43] That is to say, a simple majority of the members voting may immediately sack even the entire board. Consequently, the ultimate control over the running of companies lies with whoever owns or has influence over 50% of the voting shares. Persons seeking to take over a company may be satisfied with a 50% stake, in that this brings them control of the management; although more often they may prefer at least a 75% stake, so that they are in a position to alter the articles of association. In order to entrench the principle of simple majority rule on this matter, s.182 of the 1963 Act adds that the power to remove directors by ordinary resolution cannot be excluded by the articles of association or by a service contract; that power exists notwithstanding anything in the articles or in an agreement between the company and the director. But the section does not prohibit a contrary provision in the memorandum of association, nor separate voting agreements between shareholders, or between shareholders and directors, not to exercise their statutory power.[44]

A director of a private company who, under the articles of association, holds office for life is exempted from this rule.[45] Table A does not make any provision for life directors.

Damages: A director, especially an executive director, may hold office under a contract that runs for a set period or until terminated on expressly stated or impliedly provided for grounds. Section 182(7) of the 1963 Act and also article 99 of Table A stipulate that the statutory power to remove them by ordinary resolution shall not deprive the directors of any entitlement to damages or compensation they may possess. A director may lawfully be removed from office only in accordance with the service contract's provisions regarding notice and procedures, except where he has broken a major term of the contract, in which case he may be dismissed *instanter* once he

42. *Imperial Hydropathic Hotel Co. v. Hampson* (1882) 23 Ch.D 1.
43. See *Company Law*, para 5.36 *et seq.*
44. *Bushell v. Faith* [1970] AC 1099.
45. 1963 Act, s.182(1).

has been given a fair opportunity to defend himself. The contractual terms may be express or implied. On account of s.182(7), it can be very expensive for the company to remove directors who have service contracts, especially where the members gave them golden umbrellas.

Whether a director was in fact removed from office depends on the circumstances of each case, the question being whether the company's conduct amounted to a repudiation of the service agreement. For instance in *Harold Holdsworth & Co. (Wakefield) Ltd v. Caddies*,[46] the plaintiff was appointed director of a company for a five year period, his function being defined as running the company and its associated companies in such manner as may from time to time be assigned to or vested in him by the board. Following differences that arose between them, the board resolved that the plaintiff should confine his attentions to just one company in the group. It was held that this was not a breach of the service agreement because, under its terms, the board reserved the power to limit his responsibilities as it saw fit. The mere appointment out of court by creditors of a receiver and manager to act for the company does not *ipso facto* amount to a repudiation of the service contract with a managing director.[47]

In *Glover v. B.L.N. Ltd*[48] the plaintiff's contract as managing director provided that he could be removed without compensation for serious misconduct, serious neglect of duties, wilful disobedience of reasonable orders and the like. One issue before the court was whether, when dismissing him, the defendant's board possessed sufficient evidence of serious misconduct and neglect on his part. It was held that only one of the many allegations made against him provided grounds for summary dismissal. At times the required standard of performance must be implied from the surrounding circumstances. A director whose conduct repudiates the service agreement can be removed almost instantaneously. In *Carvill v. Irish Industrial Bank Ltd*[49] what, to use a neutral term, was unwise conduct on the part of a small bank's managing director was held by Kenny J to warrant his immediate dismissal. But the Supreme Court concluded that, in the circumstances, his indiscretion was not sufficiently repudiatory for that purpose. Unless the contract provides for a fixed term of service or for dismissal only on stated grounds, a director may lawfully be removed for any reason whatsoever if given proper notice. Proper notice means the period stipulated in the contract or, where the contract is silent, a reasonable period. In *Carvill*, for example, it was found that twelve months was a reasonable period.

46. [1955] 1 All ER 725.
47. *Griffiths v. Secretary of State for Social Services* [1974] QB 468.
48. [1973] IR 388, discussed ante p.165.   49. [1968] IR 325, discussed ante p.164.

Requirements similar to natural justice must be complied with before the members can pass a resolution under s.182 of the Companies Act, 1963, to remove a director. The proposed resolution must follow the s.142 extended notice procedure[50] and a copy of it must be forwarded by the company to the director in advance. Ordinarily, he is entitled to have written representations circulated to the shareholders and to speak at the general meeting on the resolution. It was held in the *Glover* case that it is an implied term of a director's service contract, especially one that lays down grounds for removal from the board, that the removal procedures be fair. If, for example, the grounds stated for dismissal are misconduct or neglect of duty, then the director must be 'told of the charges against him [and be] allow[ed] to meet the charges ... and afford[ed] and adequate opportunity of answering them. . . .'[51] It is of no relevance to this that the director is an employee and not an office-holder. Refusal to accord these procedural rights is a breach of contract regardless of how guilty the director may have been. The court in *Glover* did not consider whether or to what extent these rights could be excluded or waived by contract.

50. I.e. 1963 Act, s.182; see *Company Law*, para. 4.17.
51. [1973] IR at p.425.

14

The public service

The State is by far the largest employer in the country, if by the State is conceived central, regional and local government and all the other public sector agencies and bodies. Because of the *de facto* security of employment and the various public sector pension schemes, jobs in the public service are often regarded as particularly attractive. Special conciliation and arbitration schemes have been established in order to cater for claims regarding remuneration and other employment grievances. From a legal point of view, public service employment is very different from that in the private sector because the position of many public employees is affected by detailed regulations which have no equivalent in the private sector. Moreover, the legal grievances of many public service employees are amenable to resolution through the procedure of judicial review.

EXCLUSIONS FROM EMPLOYMENT LEGISLATION

Much of the employment legislation considered so far in this book does not apply to certain parts of the public sector; the categories of public employees excluded from the legislation varies considerably from Act to Act. The reasons for these exclusions also differ. For instance, there may already exist adequate negotiating machinery within a category of employment in question that renders it unnecessary to have the statutory rules made applicable there. The public sector is very highly unionised, which significantly diminishes the need for employment protection legislation in that sector.

Before considering any particular statutory provisions, one general principle of statutory interpretation calls for mention. This is the principle, which originally was founded on the royal prerogative of the Crown not being bound by statutes, that legislative provisions do not bind the State except where the Act in question expressly or by implication is so binding. As formulated by Walsh J in *Byrne v. Ireland*,[1] a case which concerned the

1. [1972] IR 241.

old crown immunity from suit at common law, the general words of a statute ought not to include the Government, or affect its rights, unless that construction be clear and indispensable upon the construction of the Act.

Application to the public sector Several of the employment laws make it clear that they apply to the State and other public bodies as employers. Thus, the Industrial Training Act, 1967, applies even where the employer is the State. The definition of employee in the Employment Equality Act, 1977, covers all categories of public service workers but this Act does not yet apply to the Defence Forces.[2] The Anti-Discrimination (Pay) Act, 1974, applies to all employed persons without indicating whether or not the public service comes within this category. However, this Act's requirements replicate Article 119 of the Treaty of Rome and that Article is directly applicable to and can be enforced in the courts against all public sector employers.[3] Employees under the Payments of Wages Act, 1991, include all central and local public service workers, as well as members of the Defence Forces and the Garda Síochána. For the purposes of the Safety, Health and Welfare at Work Act, 1989, an employee within that Act includes civil servants and officers of various local and regional authorities. This Act even applies to prisons and places of detention, 'unless its application is incompatible with safe custody, good order and security'.[4] Because the Protection of Young Persons (Employment) Act, 1977, stipulates that certain of its requirements do not apply to the Defence Forces,[5] the inference must be that this Act applies to the rest of public sector employment.

The Maternity Protection of Employees Act, 1981, the Redundancy Payments Acts, 1967-1979, and the Protection of Employees (Employer's Insolvency) Acts, 1984, apply to the public sector as well as to the private sector. Indeed, s.2(1) of the 1967 Act defines the term 'business' for purposes of the Redundancy Acts as including 'any activity carried on . . . by a public or local authority or a Department of State, and the performance of its functions by a public or local authority or a Department of State'. Nevertheless, because these Acts apply only to persons in fully insured employment, many public sector employees, such as established civil servants and officers of local authorities and state agencies do not benefit from their protection.

Categories excluded Many public sector workers are excluded from the Holidays (Employees) Act, 1973, the Minimum Notice and Terms of

---

2. S.12(1)(a). Before 1985, the Garda Síochána and the prison service were also excluded from this Act.
3. See ante p.136.   4. S.57.   5. S.3(2). Cf. s.1(2).

Employment Act, 1973, the Unfair Dismissals Act, 1977, and the Protection of Employment Act, 1977. The most extensive exclusions are those in the Unfair Dismissals Act, which does not apply *inter alia* to the following categories:[6]

A member of the Garda Síochána;

A person in employment as a Member of the Defence Forces, the Judge Advocate-General, the Chairman of the Army Pensions Board or the ordinary member thereof who is not an Officer of the Medical Corps of the Defence Forces.

A person employed by or under the State other than persons standing designated for the time being under s.17 of the Industrial Relations Act, 1969.

Officers of a local authority for the purposes of the Local Government Act, 1941.

Officers of a health board, a vocational education committee established by the Vocational Education Act, 1930, or a committee of Agriculture established by the Agriculture Act, 1931.

'Persons employed by or under the State': The Unfair Dismissals Act, 1977, and also the Protection of Employment Act, 1977, and the Holidays (Employees) Act, 1973, stipulate that their requirements do not apply to 'persons employed by or under the State', subject to certain qualifications. It can hardly be doubted that this category covers all civil servants and members of the Defence Forces and of the Garda Síochána. Since the Unfair Dismissals Act expressly excludes the Gardaí and the Defence Forces and there is no similar provision in the other two Acts, an argument could be made that these groups do not come within the 'employed by or under the State' category in those Acts. But that contention does not seem very convincing. What of those who work for public agencies that receive their entire funding from the State but who are not civil servants in the strict legal sense, such as personnel in the Central Bank, solicitors who work for the Law Centres, primary and other teachers, and those employed in bodies like the Industrial Development Authority and Coras Trachtála? There has been no authoritative exposition of what is meant by being 'employed under' the State.[7]

Certain groups who are employed by or under the State are covered by the above Acts. Unestablished civil servants who are engaged on 'subordinate duties' and also anybody engaged in 'industrial work' come within the terms of the Holidays Act.[8] Persons designated under s.17(2) of

6. S.2(1)(d)-(j).   7. Cf. *Loat v. Andrews* [1986] ICR 679.
8. S.2(1)(f).

the Industrial Relations Act, 1969, come within the Unfair Dismissals Act;[9] they are, principally, those who might be described as the non-'white collar' or 'industrial' civil service.

'Officers' of local and regional authorities: The Unfair Dismissals Act, 1977, does not apply to 'officers' of local authorities or of a health board, a vocational education committee or a committee of agriculture; local authority officers are excluded from the Protection of Employment Act, 1977. But it is not each and every employee of these authorities and committees who are excluded. The question of who are officers as distinct from employees is dealt with earlier in this book.[10]

PUBLIC LAW RIGHTS AND REMEDIES

The term public law is a convenient label for constitutional law and administrative law. In Continental European countries, where there are special court structures for constitutional and administrative law cases (somewhat like the common law and the chancery courts structures in the past), the distinction between public and private law is of particular significance. A treatise on employment law is not the appropriate place to speculate on whether there exists in Ireland a body of public law in the Continental European sense. But the relevance of the distinction in the present context is that the State and public bodies and agencies, as employers, are subject to the general principles of constitutional and administrative law that are not generally applicable to private sector employments. All employers in dealing with their employees are subject to legal constraints, notably, their obligations under the contract of employment and also the law of tort and general legislative provisions. The State and other public sector employers are subject to the same constraints; whatever element of sovereign immunity from tort liability as existed in 1922 has been declared unconstitutional[11] and there are no Continental European-style special principles and rules for contracts in the public sector, like the doctrine of *imprévision*.[12] Public sector employers must observe the rules of natural justice or constitutional justice, must respect substantive constitutional rights and must not abuse their discretionary powers.[13] There is

9. S.2(1)(h).
10. See ante p.41.
11. *Byrne v. Ireland* [1972] IR 241.
12. See generally, D. Harris & D. Tallon eds., *Contract Law Today, Anglo-French Comparisons* (1989) pp.228-232.
13. See generally, G. Hogan & D. Morgan, *Administrative Law in Ireland* (2nd ed. 1991).

also a vitally important procedural distinction, redress by way of judicial review.

Judicial review Disputes with public authorities can be brought to court through what is known as the judicial review procedure, which is provided for in Order 84V of the Rules of the Superior Courts.[14] Thus, where a public service office-holder or his trade union or professional association believe that his employer has acted or proposes to act unlawfully, the matter can be litigated through this procedure. As well as awarding damages or granting an injunction or making a declaration, the High Court when exercising judicial review can make orders of prohibition and mandamus, and quash decisions through orders of certiorari. Where redress by way of judicial review is not available, before he can succeed an aggrieved party must be able to point to a breach of contract, a tort, a breach of fiduciary duty or of statutory duty. If his claim is based on a breach of statutory duty, it must be a duty which in the circumstances is owed to him and not just an obligation owed to the public at large. A more extensive range of legal defects can be raised when proceeding by way of judicial review. Where the plaintiff does not have an employment contract, as would seem to be the position with civil servants and with many other public service office-holders, their normal mode of legal redress would then be by way of judicial review. Before judicial review proceedings will even be considered by the Court, the applicant must have *locus standi*.[15]

There are certain disadvantages in bringing a claim by way of judicial review. Proceedings can only be brought in the High Court. Proceedings should be brought within six months of the alleged illegality occurring, although the Court has a wide discretion to extend the time in an appropriate case. Even if the applicant's legal argument is upheld, he will not invariably be given the remedy he seeks. For the Court has a discretion to refuse to grant a declaration, an injunction, certiorari, prohibition or mandamus in an appropriate case. Relief will be refused where the applicant did not show absolute good faith and did not make full disclosure of his circumstances. Relief will be withheld because of the applicant's general conduct and the reason for the application. And relief will be denied where the applicant did not act promptly, even within the six months period. For instance, in *State (Cussen) v. Brennan*,[16] the unsuccessful applicant for an office in the

---

14. See generally, A. Collins & J. O'Reilly, *Civil Proceedings and the State in Ireland* (1990), ch.4.
15. E.g. *The State (Kerry County Council) v. Minister for Local Government* [1933] IR 517 (ratepayers lack *locus standi* to challenge irregular appointment of county solicitor).
16. [1981] IR 181.

Southern Health Board challenged the appointment which was made, on the grounds that a test of proficiency in Irish was unlawfully introduced into the selection criteria. As is explained below, the Supreme Court upheld his argument. But the Court declined to quash the irregular appointment because the applicant delayed for four months before bringing the proceedings and, in the meantime, the person appointed and the Health Board had entered into new commitments.

Public law or private law dispute? If the dispute is between private individuals or organisations, it is not amenable to judicial review. Even if the dispute is with the State or with some other public body or agency, if it concerns an essentially 'private law' matter it is not appropriate for judicial review. In the various Continental European countries, there is a vast and complex jurisprudence regarding what types of disputes are private law or public matters; if they address public law questions, they must be heard by administrative tribunals as contrasted with the civil courts. Over the last ten years or so, the English courts have sought to draw a similar line, for the purpose of determining what kinds of claim can be brought by way of judicial review.[17] To an extent, the Irish courts have not engaged in a similar exercise.

Two main questions arise. One is what employers are sufficiently a part of the public sector apparatus for at least some employment-related disputes with them to be amenable to judicial review. Undoubtedly, the State, local and regional authorities, health boards, vocational educational committees and the like fall within this zone. But what of State-owned public utilities and enterprises, like Radio Telefís Éireann, Coras Trachtála, the Electricity Supply Board? The conventional wisdom is that employment disputes with these latter bodies and equivalent organisations fall outside judicial review and instead must follow the same procedures as for private sector employments. It was held in Britain that the old National Coal Board was not a 'public body' for the purpose of the Prevention of Corruption Acts.[18]

Secondly, regarding employers within the public zone, are all of their staff entitled to proceed by way of judicial review to assert their employment rights or is this procedure reserved for office-holders? Or does the matter turn on the exact nature of the claim being made? For instance, if the office-holder also has an employment contract and the dispute relates to the

17. Cf. *R. v. Derbyshire County Council, ex p. Noble* [1990] ICR 808, *McClaren v. Home Office* [1990] IRLR 338 and *R. v. Chief Constable of Thames Valley Police, ex p. Cotton* [1990] ICR 824. See generaly, Carty, 'Aggrieved Public Workers and Judicial Review', 54 *Mod. L. Rev.* 129 (1991) and Fredman & Morris 'Public or Private? State Employees and Judicial Review', 107 *L.Q.R.* 298 (1991).
18. *R. v. Newbould* [1962] 2 QB 102.

contract, is it then a private law matter and unsuitable for judicial review? If the applicant commenced private law proceedings but then decided instead to go by way of judicial review, is he estopped from taking that action? The conventional wisdom is that if the plaintiff works under an employment contract, ordinarily he cannot air his employment-related grievances by way of judicial review. A practical reason for excluding ordinary employees from judicial review is that, unlike many public service office-holders, they are protected by all the main employment protection legislation. In *O'Neill v. Beaumont Hospital Board*,[19] where a consultant surgeon contested disciplinary decisions made against him by the management of the largest public hospital in the State, the Supreme Court expressed its doubt about 'the basis of an application for judicial review concerning the decision by an employer provided for specifically in a contract of employment....'[20] However, the respondents there conceded that the matter could be dealt with by way of judicial review.

This matter came before the Supreme Court again in *O'Neill v. Iarnród Éireann*,[21] where the applicant sought to contest disciplinary measures taken against him by the State-owned railway undertaking. Those proceedings were the initial application for leave to seek judicial review, which is an *ex parte* proceeding. For that reason, it was decided to allow the claim for relief to be instituted and the whole matter of the appropriateness of proceedings in the manner could then be fully argued in court in *inter partes* proceedings. Finlay CJ and McCarthy J reiterated the reservations about bringing what in essence are claims for breach of an employment contract in this manner. Hederman J went further, concluding that the Order 84 procedure 'lies only against public authorities in respect of duties conferred upon them by law' and that leave to proceed with the action should be refused there and then.

Political activities Many public officials are subject to restrictions regarding active involvement in politics. In 1932 the Minister for Finance set out in the form of a circular the kinds of political activities which civil servants are not allowed to undertake; in particular officials should not

(i) be a member of an association or serve on a committee having for its object the promotion of the interests of a political party or the promotion or the prevention of the return of a particular candidate to the Dáil,

(ii) support or oppose any particular candidate or party either by public statement or writing,

19. [1990] ILRM 419.   20. Id. at p.437.   21. [1991] ILRM 129.

(iii) make any verbal statements in public (or which are liable to be published) [or] contribute to newspapers or other publications any letters or articles, conveying information, comment or criticism on any matter of current political interest, or which concerns the political action or position of the Government or of any member or group of members of the Oireachtas.[22]

But industrial civil servants are allowed to take part in any of these activities and to stand for election to local authorities.[23] Within the civil service conciliation and arbitration scheme, any staff association which is 'affiliated to, or associated in any way with, any political organisation', will not be recognised by the Minister or, if recognised, will lose its recognition for that reason.

It is almost always provided in legislation regulating various national public agencies that officers and employees of the agency in question may not at the same time be members of the Dáil or of the Seanad or of the European Parliament. If any of them becomes a member of any of these bodies, it is often provided that he shall stand seconded from his employment, without pay, for the duration of such membership.[24] A member of a local authority is not permitted to hold any remunerated office or employment with that authority.[25] For these purposes, membership of the authority is deemed to continue for the 12 months following its having ceased.

Fair procedures Many of the leading cases on the right to fair procedures, under the rubric of natural justice or constitutional justice, have concerned the treatment of public service office-holders and employees.[26] Where the relevant regulations lay down a procedure, then those procedures must be followed or, at least, only in very exceptional cases will departure from the prescribed procedure be permitted. Departure from procedures so prescribed or from procedures required under general principles of fairness generally will be upheld where the aggrieved party actually consented to or acquiesced in that departure.[27] The extent of informed consent to constitute a waiver of procedural rights has not been explained by the courts and it would seem

22. Circular 21/32.   23. Circular 22 of 1974.
24. E.g. (this list is not exhaustive) Law Reform Commission Act, 1975, s.13; Agricultural Credit Act, 1978, s.18; Broadcasting Authority (Amendment) Act, 1979, s.4; Udaras na Gaeltachta Act, 1979, s.16; Postal and Telecommunications Services Act, 1983, s.38; Labour Services Act, 1987, s.10; Radio and Television Act, 1988, schedule para 10; Forestry Act, 1988, s.34; Agriculture (Research, Training and Advice) Act, 1978, s.10.
25. Local Government Act, 1955, s.21.
26. See generally, Hogan & Morgan, supra n.13, ch.9.
27. E.g. *Corrigan v. Irish Land Commission* [1977] IR 317.

that extremely serious breaches of procedural propriety may be incapable of being waived.[28] What procedural rights are enjoyed by workers who only have employment contracts are dealt with in Chapter Seven.

Matters other than discipline or dismissal: There is very little judicial guidance as to when individual employees should be consulted before a decision is taken which adversely affects them to a significant degree, other than regarding disciplinary charges or dismissal.[29] Where an employer's action adversely affects a group of persons, the circumstances may require some prior consultation with their trade union or other representative association. Thus, in Britain an obligation to consult was held to exist when the G.C.H.Q. 'spy' agency unilaterally amended employment conditions to prohibit employees from being trade union members.[30] It was also held there that a health authority should have consulted representatives of general practitioners before temporarily shutting down a hospital.[31]

Suspension without pay: Where a person is suspended from work without pay, while certain matters are being investigated or considered, the suspension should not be unduly prolonged. In *Flynn v. An Post*,[32] the plaintiff was suspended, in accordance with the suspension procedures for civil servants, in order to investigate allegations that he had stolen postal packages from his employer. At the same time, criminal charges were being brought against him in connection with the same circumstances and the employer decided to prolong his suspension pending the outcome of the trial. The Supreme Court held that ordinarily a suspension of this nature should not continue indefinitely pending the outcome of the criminal case. Considerations of fair play for the individual demand that the administrative investigation into the allegation against him should proceed promptly; the contractual power is not one of virtual indefinite suspension. However, the individual may acquiesce in the prolongation of his suspension or there may be other exceptional circumstance which warrant its extension.

Adequate hearing: One of the main tenets of administrative law is that a serious decision adverse to an individual should not be taken unless he is

28. Id. at p.334 (Kenny J).
29. The exceptions include *Maunsell v. Minister for Education* [1940] IR 213.
30. *Council of Civil Service Unions v. Minister for the Civil Service* [1985] AC 374.
31. *R. v. Hillingdon Health Authority, ex p. Goodwin* [1984] ICR 800; contrast *R. v. National Coal Board, ex p. National Union of Mineworkers* [1986] ICR 791 and *Connor v. Strathclyde Regional Council* [1986] SLT 530.
32. [1987] IR 68.

first given a fair hearing: the maxim *audi alteram partem*. In *State (Gleeson) v. Minister for Defence*,[33] the applicant, a three-star private in the army, was discharged on the grounds that his conduct was unsatisfactory. But he had never been informed of what allegations were being made against him and got no opportunity whatsoever to put his side of the story to the military authorities. It was held that his discharge was invalid because those authorities had not acted in accordance with natural or constitutional justice. According to Henchy J,

> We are not here concerned with discharges for creditable or neutral reasons. Where . . . as in this case, the discharge is for a reason that is discreditable, the fundamentals of justice require that the man shall have an opportunity of meeting the case for discharging him for that reason . . . . [W]here (as happened in this case) the reason for the discharge of a soldier is proposed to be established for the first time by the army authorities for the purpose of the discharge, with the result in that event that not only will his army career be abruptly terminated but that he will be cast out into civilian life with a permanent slur on him in the record of his military service—which may seriously damage his opportunities in life—and when he is to be marked down as a permanent reject for the purpose of enlistment again, it would be an affront to justice if the law were to hold that a decision with such drastic consequences for the man involved, and possibly for his dependants, could be made behind his back.
>
> [T]he law applicable to a case such a this is clear and well established. The requirements of natural justice imposed an inescapable duty on the army authorities, before discharging the prosecutor from the army for the misconduct relied on, to give him due notice of the intention to discharge him, of the statutory reason for the proposed discharge, and of the essential facts and findings alleged to constitute that reason; and to give him a reasonable opportunity of presenting his response to that notice.[34]

Thirteen years later, the principles laid down here were extended to the dismissal of one of the most important office-holders in the State, the Commissioner of the Garda Síochána, by the Government of the day. In *Garvey v. Ireland*,[35] the plaintiff, the Garda Commissioner, was dismissed without any warning by the Government and was not given any reason for his discharge nor any opportunity to make representations against it. The Supreme Court held that his dismissal was void and ineffective. According

33. [1976] IR 280.   34. Id. at p.296.   35. [1981] IR 76.

to O'Higgins CJ, 'even if the office of Commissioner . . . were stated to be an office from which the holder could be removed at [the Government's] pleasure, this would not relieve those who sought to exercise that power from the obligation and requirement to act in accordance with natural justice.'[36] Before they could lawfully remove him, the Government was 'bound to act fairly and must tell [him] of the reason or reasons for the proposed action and give him an opportunity of being heard.'[37]

Even where a dismissal does not involve or carry undertones of improper conduct or inefficiency by the official, he may be entitled to a hearing before being discharged. In *Maunsell v. Minister for Education*,[38] the plaintiff was an assistant national teacher employed in Ballyduff National School, Co. Kerry. Under a system then prevailing, described as 'contrived to make a junior assistant teacher in a very real sense insurer of the average attendance of pupils at the school', if average school attendance over a certain period fell by a specified average, the assistant's salary was no longer payable; in effect, he would be dismissed. On the basis of the returns made by the headmaster to to the Department of Education, the plaintiff's salary was withdrawn—having taught at that school for the previous twenty years. No advance warning of this decision was given to him and he got no opportunity to present his case. Relying on Seneca's formulation of the *audi alteram partem* principle,[39] Gavan Duffy J declared the decision invalid. The plaintiff had not received 'fair notice that an inquiry was to be held to determine his fate, fair notice of the case against him and a fair opportunity to meet it.'[40] But this case is something of an exception; ordinarily there must be some significant connotation of misconduct or impropriety before a right to a hearing can arise. In a later instance, *Maunsell* was explained as 'turn[ing] upon the individual provisions of the regulation concerning assistant teachers' and as not being authority for the proposition that office holders must be given some hearing before being made redundant in accordance with established redundancy procedures.[41]

Authority is sparse on the question of exactly what procedures should be followed at the hearing. But it has been held that the ordinary rules of evidence need not apply,[42] that on-going enquiries can be abandoned and a new enquiry commenced[43] and, when Health Boards are investigating allegations against general practitioners, that doctors should be furnished

36. Id. at p.97.   37. Ibid.
38. [1940] IR 213.   39. See infra p.324.
40. [1940] IR at p.234. Similarly, *Malloch v. Aberdeen Corp.* [1971] 1 WLR 1578.
41. *Hickey v. Eastern Health Board* [1991] IR 208 at p.212.
42. *Dietman v. Brent L.B.C.* [1987] ICR 737.
43. *McGowan v. Wren* [1988] ILRM 744.

with copies of documentation relevant to the complaints which are in the Board's possession.[44] Among the questions still to be answered are how precise must the charges against the person be; how detailed an outline should he be given in advance of the evidence it is proposed to use against him;[44a] is he entitled to have legal representation[44b] and be allowed to cross-examine witnesses? In *Collins v. Cork County Vocational Education Committee,*[45] a case concerning the disciplinary suspension of a vocational school head-master, Murphy J reiterated the observation that '[t]here are ... no words which are of universal application to every kind of enquiry and every kind of domestic tribunal. The requirements of natural justice must depend on the circumstances of the case, the nature or the enquiry, the rules under which the tribunal is acting, the subject matter that is being dealt with and so forth.'[46] Murphy J's elaborate judgment in that case provides an excellent example of how the requirements of due process must be reconciled with somewhat cumbersome administrative structures.

In a case involving disciplinary sanctions imposed on a naval officer, Lavan J adopted the following statement of general principle:

> Where a tribunal is required to act judicially, the procedures to be adopted by it must be reasonable having regard to this requirement and to the consequences for the person concerned in the event of an adverse decision. Accordingly, procedures which might afford a sufficient protection to the person concerned in one case and so acceptable might not be acceptable in a more serious case. In the present case, the principles of natural justice involved relate to the requirement that the person involved should be made aware of the complaint against them and should have an opportunity both to prepare and to present their defence. Matters to be considered are the form in which the complaint should be made, the time to be allowed to the person concerned to prepare a defence, and the nature of the hearing at which that defence may be presented. In addition depending upon the gravity of the matter, the person concerned may be entitled to be represented and may also be entitled to be informed of their rights. Clearly, matters of a criminal nature must be treated more seriously than matters of a civil nature, but ultimately the criterion must be the consequences for the person concerned of an adverse verdict.[47]

44. *O'Flynn v. Mid Western Health Board* [1989] IR 429.
44a. Cf. *Gallagher v. Revenue Commissioners* [1991] ILRM 632.
44b. Ibid.   45. Murphy J, 27 May 1982, aff'd 18 March 1983.
46. At pp.68-69; see too pp.65-71.
47. *McDonough v. Minister for Defence* [1991] ILRM 115, at p.121, adopting *Flanagan v. University College Dublin* [1989] ILRM 469, at p.475.

Absence of bias: Another of the central tenets of administrative law is that no one should act as a judge in his own cause; the maxim *nemo iudex in sua causa*. The test applied by the courts for this purpose, 'in determining whether a tribunal . . . is impartial is that a member is not impartial if his own interest might be affected by the verdict, or he is so connected with the complainant that a reasonable man would think that he would come to the case with prior knowledge of the facts or that he might not be impartial'.[48] Whether there is a real possibility of bias in any particular instance depends on the entire circumstances of the case. For instance, in *Heneghan v. Western Regional Fisheries Board*,[49] the plaintiff, an office-holder with the Board, had a dispute with his regional manager, which the Board arranged to investigate under its procedures. That investigation was carried out by the very same regional manager, who recommended the plaintiff's dismissal. His dismissal was held to be void because of the flagrant contravention of the *nemo iudex* principle. In *O'Neill v. Beaumont Hospital Board*,[50] the plaintiff was a consultant surgeon at the Hospital who was on a one-year probationary period. At the end of that period, the Hospital's chief executive certified that his service had been unsatisfactory and the plaintiff then launched court proceedings challenging that certificate. In the meantime, the Hospital established an inquiry to investigate the plaintiff's service. Among the members of that committee of inquiry was the chief executive of the Hospital and two others who had expressed views adverse to the plaintiff. The Supreme Court awarded an injunction against them participating in the inquiry because 'a person in the position of the plaintiff who is a reasonable man and not either over-sensitive or careless of his own position, would have good grounds for fearing that he would not get, in respect of the issues involved, . . . an independent hearing.'[51]

Legitimate expectations It has been recognised in recent years that public officers have certain 'legitimate expectations' which do not amount to fully enforceable rights but which nevertheless acquire a degree of legal protection. This doctrine closely resembles the so-called 'acquired rights' principle in the civil service laws of Continental European countries whereby, even though as a matter of strict law the State is empowered unilaterally to change employment terms and conditions in whatever way it sees fit, there are certain kinds of drastic changes it will not be allowed to make, or only make on certain conditions being satisfied.[52] That condition may be

48. *O'Donoghue v. Vetrinary Council* [1975] IR 398, at p.405.
49. [1986] ILRM 225.   50. [1990] ILRM 419.   51. Id. at p.439.
52. See generally, Baade, 'Acquired Rights of International Public Servants', 15 *American Journal of Comparative Law*, 251 (1967).

entirely procedural; in other words, some form of prior consultation or hearing is required before the change could be made, as in the British *G.C.H.Q.* case.[53] That condition may be substantive; for instance, the proposed change may be permitted provided the persons affected are adequately compensated in some way. Or the change may be one which can be implemented only when those affected have adequate opportunity to rearrange their affairs.

The principle of legitimate expectations in public law has been recognised by the Supreme Court. In the *Derrynaflan Chalice* case, Finlay CJ stated that:

> It would appear that the doctrine of 'legitimate expectation', sometimes described as 'reasonable expectation', has not in those terms been the subject matter of any decision of our courts. However, the doctrine conoted by such expressions is but an aspect of the well-recognised equitable concept of promissory estoppel (which has been frequently applied in our courts), whereby a promise or representation as to intention may in certain circumstances be held binding on the representor or promisor. The nature and extent of that doctrine in circumstances such as those of this case has been expressed as follows.
>
> When the parties to a transaction proceed on the basis of an underlying assumption—either of fact or of law—whether due to misrepresentation or mistake makes no difference—on which they have conducted the dealing between them—neither of them will be allowed to go back on that assumption when it would be unfair or unjust to allow him to do so. If one of them does seek to go back on it, the courts will give the other such remedy as the equity of the case demands.[54]

An excellent example of the application of this principle to public officials is *Duggan v. An Taoiseach*,[55] which concerned civil servants affected by the discontinuance of the farm tax in early 1988. The plaintiffs were assigned to the farm tax division and were placed in grades, in an acting capacity, which were higher than the actual grades they held in the service; they were never actually 'established' in those higher grades. The farm tax was instituted in 1985 and three years later, for policy reasons, the Government discontinued collecting that tax before bringing in repealing legislation. In consequence, the plaintiffs were to be moved elsewhere in the civil service, probably at their established grades. They sought various

53. Supra p.. n.30.
54. *Webb v. Ireland* [1988] IR 353, at p.384. See generally, G. Hogan & D. Morgan, *Administrative Law in Ireland* (2nd ed. 1991) ch.13.
55. [1989] ILRM 710.

reliefs against this occurring, such as orders that the tax shall continue to be collected until the Act was repealed and that they should thenceforth remain in the grades they were temporarily occupying. There was a general civil service practice that when a person was put into a higher grade on an acting basis, he was never actually taken out of that grade.

Hamilton P refused to order that the tax should continue to be collected. He then pointed out that, whatever the general practice in the civil service was, it was made perfectly clear to the plaintiffs that they would be occupying higher grades in an acting capacity only and they accepted their appointments in writing on that basis. Accordingly, he could 'find no basis for an expectation, reasonable or otherwise, on the[ir] part . . . that they would be continued in th[ose] posts or positions . . . in an established or permanent capacity'; the circumstances could not 'give rise to a reasonable expectation by them that on the termination of the work of the Farm Tax Office, they would continue in the grades to which they had been appointed.'[56] However, they all had a 'reasonable and legitimate expectation' that their positions would be continued until the work of that office had been completed or been terminated lawfully. But that work was not completed. Nor was collecting the tax terminated lawfully; that required repealing legislation. Accordingly, their legitimate expectations had been terminated unlawfully. It was held that the Minister was entitled, under the Civil Service Acts, at any time to reassign them to their established grades, and an order would not be made requiring that they be continued in their acting grades for a temporary period. However, Hamilton P found that '[t]he equity of their case . . . demands that they be compensated in damages for the frustration or breach of the[ir] legitimate expectations. . . .'[57] He therefore ordered that, for a specified period, they should continue to be paid the salary and they should benefit from the other terms and conditions attaching to their acting grades.

Double jeopardy Where a person has been tried by a court and fully acquitted of charges, he cannot then be made undergo disciplinary proceedings which in effect amount to a re-trial of those charges.[58] Nor can he be charged with a disciplinary offence of bringing the force or service or whatever into disrepute by virtue of his having being charged with offences. In *McGrath v. Commissioner Garda Síochána*,[59] the plaintiff was acquitted of embezzlement charges. Disciplinary proceedings were then brought against him for corruptly and dishonestly taking money, in circumstances

56. Id. at p.727.   57. Id. at p.731.
58. *State (O'Callaghan) v. O'hUadhaigh* [1977] IR 42.
59. [1991] 1 IR 69.

identical to those in the charges which failed. Lynch J held that, while the exact circumstances about taking the money might be the subject of disciplinary proceedings, it was 'not now open to the inquiry to investigate these matters on the basis that there was any element of corruption or dishonesty on the part of the applicant in relation to them.'[60] Nor could the plaintiff be disciplined simply for having being charged with a criminal offence. In this case, the garda was acquitted by the jury because of insufficiency of evidence establishing fraud. His trial and the disciplinary proceedings would have focused on that very same issue—whether he had acted dishonestly. If the disciplinary tribunal found against him, that would in effect set at nought the outcome of the jury trial. Moreover, the normal practice in garda discipline was not to seek to have matters re-tried in this manner and, indeed, under the present garda regulations, a re-trial of this nature is no longer possible. Upholding the judgment, the Supreme Court found that there was an element of issue estoppel between the two proceedings. But Finlay J emphasised that 'there cannot . . . be any general principle that an acquittal on a criminal charge in respect of an offence, irrespective of the reasons for such acquittal or the basis on which it was achieved, could be inevitably an estoppel preventing a disciplinary investigation arising out of the same set of facts'.[61]

Grounds for discipline and dismissal Usually the relevant statute, regulation or document will state the grounds on which office-holders can be disciplined and dismissed. The grounds on which workers with employment contracts only can be dismissed are dealt with in Chapter Seven. It is a matter of interpretation of the relevant instrument or document whether the grounds stipulated are the exclusive grounds on which office-holders may be disciplined or dismissed.[62] The same general approach as was applied in the *Grehan* case[63] and in the *McClelland* case[64] would apply. Generally, the stated grounds for dismissal are the exclusive grounds unless the relevant instrument indicates the contrary. This is especially the case where it is within the employer's powers unilaterally to change the rules of appointment. As was stated in an English case concerning the dismissal of a probationary police officer, '[i]t is plain from the wording of the regulation

---

60. [1989] IR at p.246. Compare *R. v. Secretary of State, ex p. Thornton* [1987] QB 36.
61. [1991] 1 IR at p.71. Cf. *Harrison v. Northland Poyltechnic Council* [1991] 2 NZLR 593 on whether the disciplinary hearing should precede the criminal trial.
62. E.g. *Maunsell v. Minister for Education* [1940] IR 213.
63. *Grehan v. North Eastern Health Board* [1989] IR 422; see ante p.162.
64. *McClelland v. Northern Ireland General Health Services Board* [1957] 1 WLR 594; see ante p.162.

that the power . . . to dispense with the services of a person accepted as a probationer constable is to be exercised, and exercised only, after due consideration of the specified [grounds]. It is not a discretion that may be exercised arbitrarily and without accountability.'[65]

A person cannot be disciplined or dismissed on grounds which would be unconstitutional, for instance, on account of his religious beliefs or affiliations.[66] In the past sex discrimination was endemic in the public service, with married women the target of uniquely discriminatory treatment; but that 'marriage bar' was lifted in 1973.[67] Although there is a constitutional right, of uncertain degree, to privacy, it would seem that persons can be dismissed for how they conducted their own private lives where that behaviour significantly affects their work or work environment.[68] The freedom of senior civil servants to engage in politics is greatly circumscribed.[69] Formerly, all civil servants, including post men and post office sorters, were banned from political activity, a rule which hardly would have withstood constitutional challenge.[70]

In *Garvey v. Ireland*,[71] which concerned the Garda Commissioner who was peremptorily dismissed without any reason being given, it was held that unless an office is defined as being 'at the Government's pleasure' it is not tenable at pleasure. The plaintiff was dismissed under s.6(2) of the Police Forces Amalgamation Act, 1925, which stipulates that the Garda Commissioner 'may at any time be removed by' the Government. This, it was held, did not empower removal at the Government's whim without any reason whatsoever being assigned and affording the incumbent no opportunity to challenge the reason. In such cases, provided that fair procedures were followed and the grounds of dismissal were not unconstitutional, the Government 'has the widest possible discretion as to the reasons or grounds upon which it may decide to act.'[72] The tenure of civil servants is defined as being 'at the will and pleasure of the Government'.[73]

Where the grounds for dismissal are stipulated, the employing authority

---

65. *Chief Constable v. Evans* [1982] 1 WLR 1155, at p.1171.
66. See generally, 'Developments in the Law—Public Employment', 97 *Harv. L. Rev.* 1611 (1984), at pp.1738 et seq.
67. Civil Service (Employment of Married Women) Act, 1973. See too, Garda Síochána Act, 1958, and Defence (Amendment) Act, 1979.
68. *Stroker v. Doherty* [1991] 1 IR 23 and *Flynn v. Power* [1985] IR 648.
69. Circular 21/32; see ante p.294.
70. *United States Civil Service Comm. v. National Ass'n of Letter Carriers*, 413 US 548 (1973). Cf. *Glasenapp v. Germany*, 9 EHRR 25.
71. [1981] IR 75.   72. Id. at p.97; see too id. at p.109.
73. Civil Service Regulation Act, 1956, s.5; see infra p.315. Cf. *R. (McMorrow) v. Fitzpatrick* [1918] 2 IR 103.

must satisfy itself, through the prescribed procedures, that those grounds exist in the circumstances. If the official seeks to challenge his dismissal in the courts, the question to be determined is not so much whether he should have been dismissed as whether sufficient grounds were established as would warrant a reasonable employer to dismiss him. For instance, in *State (McGarritty) v. Deputy Commissioner Garda Síochána*,[74] the applicant contested the decision to dismiss him from the Garda Síochána during his probationary period. His challenge to that decision on the merits was rejected by McWilliam J because

> The Regulations vest the opinion-forming function exclusively in the Commissioner. . . . I cannot reject his opinion because I may have reached a contrary opinion. I am confined to deciding whether the opinion he did form is supported by the documentary material he had before him when he made his order.[75]

This approach was endorsed by the Supreme Court in *Hynes v. Garvey*,[76] another Garda probationer case, and in *Stroker v. Doherty*,[77] a case concerning a permanent Garda officer, which emphasised the Court's reluctance to second-guess the disciplinary tribunal's assessment of the substantive merits of the case. Where, in the light of the evidence, the decision taken lacked factual basis or where it was not bona fide or it was unreasonable, the court may declare the decision void. In this way the court can become involved to a degree in the actual merits of the decision, while still deferring to the employing authority's opinion. If in all the circumstances there was an unreasonable decision, it will not be left stand. Unreasonableness here means, not that the Court might have taken a different view of the evidence, but that the decision 'plainly and unambiguously flies in the face of fundamental reason and common sense.'[78]

In *State (Daly) v. Minister for Agriculture*,[79] a probationer civil servant, who was employed 'at the will and pleasure of the Government', was dismissed. No reasons were given and when the decision was challenged in court the Minister still refrained from offering a reason. It was held by Barron J that the Minister's decision, even under such a discretionary power, was subject to judicial review. The Minister's view 'must be seen to be *bona fide* held, to be factually sustainable and not unreasonable.'[80] Because the Minister persisted in not giving a reason, the Court could not then properly

74. 112 ILTR 25 (1978).   75. Id. at p.30.
76. [1978] IR 174.   77. [1991] 1 IR 23.
78. Id. at p.29, quoting *The State (Keegan) v. Stardust Victims Compensation Tribunal* [1986] IR 642, at p.658.
79. [1987] IR 165.   80. Id. at p.172.

exercise its review functions. Accordingly, it was concluded, the Court must presume that there was no proper basis for the applicant's dismissal and that decision was held to be void.

THE CIVIL SERVICE

There is no statutory definition of who a civil servant is, although the term 'established civil servant' is defined as a civil servant 'whose service is in a capacity in respect of which a superannuation allowance may be granted.'[81] The derivation of the term civil servant was explained by Kingsmill-Moore J as follows:

> The words 'civil service' and 'civil servant', though in frequent use on the lips of politicians and members of the general public, are not terms of legal art. The British Royal Commission on the Civil Service which reported in 1931 stated that 'there is nowhere any authoritative or exhaustive definition of the civil service.' The phrase seems to have been first used to describe the non-combatant service of the East India Company, and was well established in English political language by the middle of the nineteenth century.
>
> Though it may be difficult to frame an exact definition, it does not seem in any way impossible to reach an approximation to the meaning of the words sufficient to meet the requirements of the present case. In Britain civil servants were servants of the Crown, that is to say servants of the King in his politic capacity, but not all servants of the Crown were civil servants. Those who used the strong arm—military, naval and police forces—were excluded from the conception, for the service was civil, not combatant; and so also, by tradition, were judges and holders of political offices. Civil servants were paid out of monies voted by Parliament and, if permanent, had the benefit of the Super-annuation Acts. In theory, as servants of the King, they held their positions at pleasure but in practice they were treated as holding during good behaviour. . . .
>
> The bulk of British civil servants working in Ireland were taken into the service of Saorstát Éireann and the phrase, with the ideas attached to it, was assimilated into Irish political life. Soon it made its appearance in the Irish statute book, and, after the passing of our present constitution, in statutes of the Republic. Borderline cases have been

81. Civil Service Regulation Act, 1956, s.1(1). See generally, S. Dooney, *The Irish Civil Service* (1976).

dealt with by special legislation. Persons have been deemed to be civil servants for one purpose and deemed not to be civil servants for another. But, if we substitute 'State' for 'King' the summary which I have already given corresponds to the present conception of civil servant in Ireland.[82]

The principal incidents of civil servants' positions are governed by the Civil Service Regulation Act, 1956; the machinery for appointing them is governed by the Civil Service Commissioners Act, 1956, and their pensions are governed by the Superannuation Acts, 1834-1963.

These Acts draw a distinction between civil servants of the Government and of the State. Again, as Kingsmill-Moore pointed out, this is something of a contradiction:

The expression, 'civil service of the Government', unless given a restricted interpretation is a contradiction in terms. The status of a civil servant is that of a servant of the State. He may indeed be assigned to serve in any civil department of the State, or in the service of any organ of the State, including the Government, and the power of so assigning him may be conferred by law on the Government; but he is still a servant of the State. If, however, his service happens to be in one of the Departments of the Government he may conveniently be described as being also a servant of the Government.[83]

Accordingly, since, under the Constitution, the Attorney General's office is separate from the Executive, persons working in that office are civil servants of the State as opposed to of the Government. An ordinary member of the Labour Court was found to be a civil servant of the State[84] although, since he is appointed by and is under the control of the Minister for Labour, he would also seem to be a civil servant of the Government.

Another distinction is that between the holders of designated offices and civil servants generally. A host of particular offices exist under legislation, for instance the Master of the High Court, the Taxing Master, the Director of Public Prosecutions, the Chief State Solicitor, the Chairman of An Bord Pleanála, the Director General of Consumer Affairs and Fair Trade, the Data Protection Commissioner. The incidents of many of these distinct office-holders are regulated, in whole or in part, by legislation particular to the function being carried on. Except for the case involving the Garda Commissioner, there is no modern case law dealing with the incidents of these high offices.

82. *McLoughlin v. Minister for Social Welfare* [1958] IR 1, at pp.14-15.
83. Id. at p.16.   84. *Murphy v. Minister for Social Welfare* [1987] IR 295.

Appointment Generally, civil servants are appointed only after their taking part in a competition organised by the Civil Service Commissioners and their being selected for appointment by the Commissioners. The objective of this procedure is to place civil service appointments outside of political control, thereby ensuring that applicants for posts who support the Government of the day are not given undue preference. The general qualifications for appointment laid down by s.17 of the Civil Service Commissioners Act, 1956, is that the candidate

> (a) possesses the requisite knowledge and ability to enter on the discharge of the duties of that position,
>
> (b) he is within the age limits (if any) prescribed . . .,
>
> (c) he is in good health and free from any physical defect or disease which would be likely to interfere with the proper discharge of his duties in that position and possesses the physical characteristics (if any) prescribed for the position . . .,
>
> (d) he is suitable on grounds of character, and,
>
> (e) he is suitable in all other relevant respects for appointment to that position.

Among the appointments to which this Act does not apply are some positions which can be filled by the Government,[85] certain 'excluded positions' as defined in that Act[86] and 'scheduled occupations',[87] being what may be termed industrial civil servants, those hired on a part-time basis and persons employed by the Department of Foreign Affairs abroad in a clerical or ancillary capacity.

The only across-the-board legislative disqualification from appointment was s.34(3) of the Offences Against the State Act, 1939. Any person who was convicted of a scheduled offence under that Act by the Special Criminal Court was disqualified, for the next seven years, from holding any office or employment which is remunerated out of the Central Fund or from money provided by the Oireachtas. A person holding such a job forfeited it on being convicted as described here. But the Government had an 'absolute discretion' to remit the disqualification or forfeiture in whole or in part. In 1990 this section was held to be unconstitutional[88] because of its entirely indiscriminate impact. It would seem that counsel for the State did not argue that, by virtue of the doctrine of the presumption of constitutionality,[89] the complete discretion given to the Government to waive application of the rule in any individual case saved the section from invalidity. The E.C. rules

---

85. S.6(2)(a)(i).   86. Ss.5 and 6.   87. S.4.
88. *Cox v. Ireland* (Sup. Ct. 11 July 1991).
89. See generally *Constitutional Law*, pp.88-92.

regarding the free movement of workers and banning discrimination against nationals of E.C. Member States to that end do not apply to 'employment in the public service.'[90]

Status Are civil servants employed under a contract of employment or are they office-holders without any contract? If they are appointed by the Government for a specified period or task, they may very well have employment contracts as well as being office-holders. The exact status of civil servants generally has not yet been clarified, principally because the various labour enactments and the social welfare laws usually make it clear whether or not their provisions apply to the civil service. In Britain it was confirmed in 1987 that civil servants there are not appointed under an employment contract on the grounds that, when they are appointed, there is no intention by the Crown to create a contractual relationship with them.[91] On account of the very wide discretion the Minister for Finance is given over civil servants' terms and conditions of service and remuneration, whereby he may make 'such arrangements as he thinks fit' and he may 'cancel or vary those arrangements',[92] an Irish court may very well come to the same conclusion.

In *Cogan v. Minister for Finance*,[93] where regulations affecting civil servants' salaries were challenged, Gavan Duffy J described their position in these terms:

> There is no contract as to salary between the Minister and any one of [them], but each of them, with a tenure at will, enjoys an appointment under the State, carrying such remuneration as the Minister may from time to time determine, and the Minister has wide [statutory] powers for controlling and varying remuneration. . . . The Minister could not, even if he would, divest himself of the powers thus entrusted to him for the public weal and any circulars issued and communicated to candidates for appointment would seem to me quite irrelevant. . . .[94]

In a case in 1987, concerning the liability of an ordinary member of the Labour Court to pay social welfare contributions, Blayney J found it 'not necessary to go into the question of whether the applicant had any contract with the Minister.'[95]

---

90. See ante pp.132-133.
91. *R. v. Civil Service Appeal Board, ex p. Bruce* [1988] ICR 649.
92. Civil Service Regulations Act, 1956, s.17(2).
93. [1941] IR 389.   94. Id. at p.401.
95. *Murphy v. Minister for Social Welfare* [1987] IR 295, at p.303.

Incidents of the office The rights and duties of civil servants and their positions generally are regulated by the Minister for Finance. Under s.17 of the Civil Service Regulation Act, 1956, he may 'make such arrangements as he thinks fit' in connection with the following matters:

(a) the regulation and control of the Civil Service,
(b) the classification, re-classification, numbers and remuneration of civil servants,
(c) the fixing of (i) the terms and conditions of service of civil servants, and (ii) the conditions governing the promotion of civil servants.

The remuneration to be paid and other terms and conditions of service are usually set out in circulars which the Minister issues from time to time. Section 16(1) of the 1956 Act endorses the aphorism 'no work, no pay', by stipulating that a civil servant 'shall not be paid remuneration in respect of any period of unauthorised absence from duty.'

Altering the incidents: Section 17(2) of the 1956 Act says that the Minister 'may cancel or vary these arrangements' referred to above. According to Gavan Duffy J in the *Cogan* case,[96] the circulars issued by the Minister do not give rise to contractual entitlements and their contents may be altered by the Minister whenever he deems appropriate. Whatever the strict legal situation may be, the civil service is highly unionised and there are conciliation and arbitration schemes which process differences that arise between the Minister and civil servants regarding employment terms and conditions.[97] Accordingly, a substantial degree of negotiation and consultation actually takes place before changes of any significance are implemented.

While accepting that the Minister in Britain has similar powers unilaterally to change the employment incidents of civil servants, it was held in the *G.C.H.Q.* case[98] that, before actually making changes which would substantially affect those incidents to the detriment of civil servants, the Minister must consult with their trade union or other representative organisation. Because the Minister previously had consulted regularly with those organisations on comparable matters, they had acquired a 'legitimate expectation' to continue to be so consulted. In *Duggan v. An Taoiseach*,[99] Hamilton P applied this principle when civil servants were assigned to work in the Farm Tax Office, holding grades on an acting basis higher than their

96. Supra n.13.
97. See *Industrial Relations Law*, pp.200-205.
98. *Council of Civil Service Unions v. Minister for the Civil Service* [1985] AC 374.
99. [1989] ILRM 710.

actual grades. Because the Government had not acted properly in ceasing to collect the farm tax, without repealing the relevant legislation, the plaintiffs' legitimate expectations to occupy higher grades were unlawfully interfered with. That loss, therefore, had to be compensated by their continuing to be paid at the higher grade levels for a period.

Common law and equitable rights and obligations: It would seem that what may be termed entitlements under the various Ministerial circulars may not be enforced against the Government as if they were binding contracts. There then is no way in which civil servants can compel compliance with those circulars, unless they resort to industrial action. Since 1982, industrial action by civil servants can be a 'trade dispute', thereby qualifying those taking part in disputes to the immunities from liability for the economic torts contained in ss.10-12 of the Industrial Relations Act, 1990, if they are members of licensed trade unions.[100] Whether the Minister can enforce his circulars by way of court action is a matter that seems never to have been considered but, since they are neither contracts nor statutory instruments, it would appear that they are not directly enforceable. Of course they can be enforced indirectly by the Minister imposing disciplinary sanctions, up to even dismissal, where their requirements are being flouted.

A matter which does not appear to have been considered by the Irish courts in modern times is whether civil servants have rights and obligations under the common law and under general equitable principles. The legal position, as expounded by the courts mainly in the last century, is that 'public officers', including civil servants, are regarded as the repositories of the public's trust and confidence and, on grounds of public policy, the common law and equity ensure that that trust is not abused.[1] Abuse of public office is a criminal offence at common law. The classic formulation is that of Lord Mansfield in *R. v. Bembridge*:

> if a man accepts an office of trust and confidence, concerning the public, . . . he is answerable to the King for his execution of that office; and he can only answer to the King in a criminal prosecution. . . . [W]here there is a breach of trust, a fraud, or an imposition on a subject concerning the public, which as between subject and subject, would only be actionable by a civil action, yet as that concerns the King and the public (I use them as synonymous terms), it is indictable.[2]

100. See *Industrial Relations Law*, pp.15-16 and 210-211.
  1. Cf. *City of Boston v. Dolan*, 10 NE 2d 275 (1937).
  2. (1783) 3 Doug. KB 327, at p.332. See generally, Finn, 'Public Officers: Some Personal Liabilities', 51 *Australian L.J.* 313 (1977) and J. Gabbett, *A Treatise on the Criminal Law* (1842) Vol.I ch.41.

Since there have been no prosecutions brought under this broad common law offence in recent times and as many forms of abuse of public office constitute statutory offences, it is possible that the common law offence has become obsolete. But prosecutions of this nature are occasionally brought in Britain.[3] The Prevention of Corruption Acts, 1889-1916, have been made applicable to all persons who are remunerated from the Central Fund, which includes civil servants.[4]

The State or whichever public authority employs the official in question has certain civil remedies against him. The procedure used in the past for those claims was the information for equitable relief on the Revenue side of the Exchequer.[5] An official who makes an improper gain from his office will be held liable for it.[6] An officer who derives any personal profit from his misuse of public funds must account for that profit to the authority from whom he holds the office. For instance, in *Attorney General v. Edmunds*,[7] a civil servant was held liable to the Crown for having used public funds to buy quantities of stamps at a discount, which he then sold at full value. A public official is subject to the equitable duty to maintain the secrecy of information acquired by virtue of his office, at least in cases where the public interest or the interests of his employing authority so require. In *Attorney General v. Jonathan Cape Ltd*, Widgery CJ could 'not see why the courts should be powerless to restrain the publication of public secrets, whilst enjoying the *Argyll* powers in regard to domestic secrets.'[8] There, publication by the former Cabinet Minister Richard Crossman of what happened at numerous British Cabinet meetings was enjoined.[9] But the confidences of civil servants of foreign governments are not so readily enforceable.[10]

There is a tort of malicious abuse of public authority—or misfeasance of public office—where a public official who abuses his powers can be held liable in damages to persons who are the victims of that abuse.[11] What must be established to found a right of action was summarised in *Newell v. Starkie* as follows:

    1. some legal right vested in the plaintiff;
    2. the infraction or violation of that right;

3.   E.g. *R. v. Llellwyn-Jones* [1968] 1 QB 429.
4.   S.R. & O. No. 37 of 1928. Cf. Central Bank Act, 1989, s.17.
5.   *Attorney General v. Cochrane* (1810) Wright 10.
6.   *Reading v. Attorney General* [1951] AC 507.
7.   (1868) LR 6 Eq 381.   8. [1976] QB 752 at p.769.
9.   See too, *Attorney General v. Guardian Newspapers Ltd (No.2)* [1990] AC 109 and *Lord Advocate v. Scotsman Publications Ltd* [1990] AC 812.
10. *Attorney General for England and Wales v. Brandon Book Publishers Ltd* [1987] ILRM 135.
11. See generally, B. McMahon & W. Binchy, *Irish Law of Torts* (2nd ed. 1990) pp.345-348.

3. the violation or the procuring of such violation knowingly and intentionally and without lawful justification.[12]

In that case a school inspector sued two of his superiors for unlawfully causing him to be reprimanded several times, then suspended and finally compelled to resign on a diminishing allowance. However, his claim failed because it was not brought within the prescribed limitation period.[13] Where this tort is established, the official's employer can also be held vicariously liable in damages and the circumstances may well warrant the award of exemplary damages or punitive damages.

Statutory rights and duties: Most of the legislation giving employees rights do not apply to civil servants, the principal exception being the Employment Equality Act, 1977, where the term employee includes *inter alia* 'a civil servant of the State or of the Government. . . .' Civil servants and other public officials fall within Article 119 of the Rome Treaty, which gives a right to equal pay for equal work.[14] A question which has yet to be answered is whether civil servants' employment situation can be affected by Directives of the E.C. under its approximation of laws powers. Although they are excluded from application of the free movement of labour principle,[15] there is no such exclusion in the Rome Treaty from the approximation of laws powers.

There are some Acts which apply with particular force to the duties of civil servants and other public officers. One is the Official Secrets Act, 1963, which renders it a criminal offence for any person to disclose official secrets as defined in that Act or retain in his possession any official document or other information. What constitutes official information is defined very extensively, as

> any secret official code word or password, and any sketch, plan, model, article, note, document or information which is secret or confidential or is expressed to be either and which is or has been in the possession, custody or control of a holder of a public office, or to which he has or had access, by virtue of his office, and includes information recorded by film or magnetic tape or by any other recording medium.[16]

Secret information may be retained or disclosed where the person is duly authorised to do so or doing so is in accordance with the duties of his office.[17] Secret information also may be disclosed where doing so is in the person's

---

12. [1917] 2 IR 73, at p.80.
13. Public Authorities Protection Act, 1893 (repealed in 1954).
14. *Johnston v. Chief Constable of the R.U.C.* (Case 222/84) [1987] QB 129.
15. See ante pp.132-133.   16. S.2(1).   17. S.4(1).

'duty in the interest of the State to communicate it.'[18] The mere certificate by the Minister that certain information is secret or confidential for these purposes is deemed to be 'conclusive evidence' of that fact.[19]

Probation Civil service appointments are usually subject to a period of probation. Where the individual fails to fulfil the conditions of probation, s.7 of the 1956 Act enables his appointment to be terminated. He can challenge that decision in court on the grounds that unfair procedures were followed. That decision can also be challenged on the grounds that it is not bona fide held, is not factually sustainable or is wholly unreasonable.[20]

Discipline and dismissal Section 15 of the Civil Service Regulation Act, 1956, lays down the framework for disciplinary measures, other than suspension from duty. These apply where, in the opinion of the appropriate supervisory authority, the civil servant has 'in relation to his official duties, been guilty of misconduct, irregularity, neglect or unsatisfactory behaviour. . . .' What procedures should be followed in these cases is not prescribed in the 1956 Act, other than that the civil service regulations may prescribe for the matter to be referred to the Minister. There are no reported cases on what procedures must be followed in order to comply with natural justice or constitutional justice in these cases. The disciplinary sanctions which can be imposed are a reduction in remuneration or a reduction in grade or rank; both of these can be imposed together where a loss of public money or public funds resulted from the individual's action.

Section 9 of the 1956 Act sets out the procedures for discharge on medical grounds, where an established civil servant becomes 'by reason of infirmity of mind or body, incapable of discharging the duties of his position and such infirmity is likely to be permanent.'[21] If, after examining him, the medical officer concludes that he is so disabled, he can be required to tender his resignation. If he does not do so he will be deemed to have resigned.

Section 13 of the 1956 Act sets out when a civil servant can be suspended from duty without pay: where

> (a) it appears to the suspending authority that the civil servant has been guilty of grave misconduct or grave irregularity warranting disciplinary action, or

18. Ibid.
19. S.2(3). This provision may be unconstitutional; cf. *Maher v. Attorney General* [1973] IR 140.
20. *State (Daly) v. Minister for Agriculture* [1987] IR 165 and *Wheelan v. Minister for Justice* [1991] 1 IR 462.
21. Cf. *Ahern v. Minister for Industry and Commerce* [1991] 1 IR 462.

(b) it appears to the suspending authority that the public interest may be prejudiced by allowing the civil servant to remain on duty, or

(c) a charge of grave misconduct or grave irregularity is made against the civil servant and it appears to the suspending authority that the charge warrants investigation.

If the individual is acquitted of the disciplinary charges, he must be paid his 'ordinary remuneration' for the period of his suspension; in other cases, a direction may be made to pay all or some of that remuneration where 'considerations of equity so require.' There are no reported judicial guidelines regarding the procedures to be adopted when a civil servant is being suspended, other than that the suspension should not be unduly prolonged, for instance, to await the outcome of criminal proceedings being brought against the individual.[22]

Section 5 of the 1956 Act gives the Government a very extensive power to dismiss civil servants:

Every established civil servant shall hold office at the will and pleasure of the Government.

In the light of what was held in the *Garvey* case,[23] the Government have an extremely wide discretion regarding why a civil servant should be dismissed, provided the grounds are not unconstitutional. It is not clear whether the individual must be furnished with reasons and given an opportunity to rebut them. In 1971, in a case concerning the dismissal of a Scottish school teacher[24] in circumstances which would not have adversely reflected on her, the House of Lords held that an office held at pleasure means that the person being dismissed need not be given the exact reasons but still must be afforded a hearing. According to Lord Wilberforce, 'the very possibility of dismissal without reasons being given—action which may vitally affect a man's career or his pension—makes it all the more important for him, in suitable circumstances, to be able to state his case. [B]ut the courts will necessarily respect the right, for good reasons of public policy, to dismiss without assigned reasons. . . .'[25] Nevertheless, it would seem that, in Ireland, if judicial review is sought of the merits of the decision to dismiss, the Government must provide the court with some basis for accepting that the decision was 'bona fide held, sustainable and not unreasonable.'[26] In *State (Daly) v. Minister for Agriculture*,[27] it was held by Barron J that, where the Minister will not even disclose to the court the grounds for his decision to

---

22. *Flynn v. An Post* [1987] IR 68.   23. *Garvey v. Ireland* [1981] IR 75.

24. *Malloch v. Aberdeen Corp.* [1971] 1 WLR 1578.

25. Id. at p.1597.   26. See ante p.305.   27. [1987] IR 165.

dismiss a probationer, it must then be presumed that no good reason existed. Therefore, the decision was declared invalid.

LOCAL AND REGIONAL AUTHORITIES

The principal local and regional authorities are the urban corporations, county councils, regional health authorities, county committees of agriculture, vocational educational committees,[28] fisheries boards and harbour boards. Legislation regarding these bodies contain detailed provisions on the appointment, remuneration, terms and conditions of employment, discipline and dismissal of officers; notably, Part II of the Local Government Act, 1941, as amended, Part II of the Health Act, 1970, Part II of the Agriculture Act, 1931, and ss.25-33 of the Fisheries Act, 1980. Appointments to most of the offices under these Acts must be made with the approval of the Local Appointments Commission, which was established in 1926 in order to reduce political influence in local government staffing.[29] Elaborate pension arrangements exist principally under the Local Government (Superannuation) Act, 1956.

A pronounced feature of all this legislation is the detailed control the Minister for Local Government or other relevant Ministers exercise over all personnel matters. Thus, under ss.19-23 of the Local Government Act, 1941, the Minister is empowered to make regulations regarding the following matters: procedure for appointments, the remuneration, travelling expenses, hours of duty, attendance records, sick and other leave, security for the due performance of functions, continuance in and cesser of office, age limits; regarding specified offices, the duties of the holders and the places or limits within which those duties should be performed; also, qualifications regarding character, age, health, physical characteristics, education, training, experience, residence. A qualification regarding sex may be prescribed only where 'the duties of such office so require'.[30] Local government is highly unionised and special conciliation and arbitration schemes exist for that sector.[31] Indeed, under s.14(5)(b) of the Health Act, 1970, it is provided that, when a health board chief executive officer is determining the remuneration and other terms of conditions of his staff, he must follow the Minister's directions. In doing so he 'shall have regard to any arrangements in operation for conciliation and arbitration for persons

28. The postion of V.E.C. employees is considered infra p.322.
29. Local Authorities (Officers and Employees) Act, 1926.
30. Local Government Act, 1941, s.21(2).
31. See *Industrial Relations Law*, pp.205-206.

affected by the determination.' The precise legal consequences of this requirement do not appear to have been considered by the courts.

Appointment Although the appointing authority usually is the relevant local government unit for which the person will work, generally the officer must first have been selected by the Local Appointments Commission.[32] No qualifications for the various local offices are prescribed by the legislation but the Minister has extensive powers to stipulate what qualifications shall be required.[33] Persons convicted by the Special Criminal Court of scheduled offences under the Offences Against the State Act, 1939, were disqualified for the following seven years from holding any local government office or employment, but in 1990 that prohibition was declared unconstitutional.[34]

In *State (Cussen) v. Brennan*,[35] the plaintiff was an unsuccessful applicant for a position as paediatrician to the Southern Health Board. Qualifications for that job had been set by the Minister but the Local Appointments Commission decided to give extra credit to applicants who had a good knowledge of the Irish language. The plaintiff attended the interview but did not submit himself for the Irish test. The Supreme Court held that the Commissioners had exceeded its powers by adopting the language test; their function was to select the best candidate with reference to the qualifications laid down by the Minister and they could not 'add a new dimension' to those qualifications. As Henchy J pointed out, the Commission could not award extra credit to a candidate because of his 'knowledge of Sanskrit, his skill at chess, his talent as a musician, his proficiency at hurling or, for that matter, because of any abilities, achievements or qualities which were unrelated to the performance of the duties of the office.'[36] At the very outset the Minister might have included proficiency in Irish as one of the qualifications, because 'a law may provide that proficiency in Irish be a qualification for an office when [that] is relevant to the discharge of the duties of the office.'[37] But the Commission went beyond its terms of reference in adopting that test. In the *Groener* case,[38] it was held that requiring applicants for vacancies, as art teachers in a V.E.C. school, to demonstrate a working knowledge of Irish did not contravene the free movement of workers under the Rome Treaty.

32. Cf. *State (Minister for Local Government) v. Cork Mental Hospital* [1932] IR 207 and *State (Minister for Local Government) v. Ennis Mental Hospital* [1939] IR 258.
33. Local Government Act, 1941, s.19.
34. *Cox v. Ireland* (Sup. Ct. 11 July 1991).
35. [1981] IR 181.   36. Id. at p.192.
37. Id. at p.194. Cf. Local Authorities (Officers and Employees) Act, 1983, s.2 and Agricultural Credit Act, 1978, s.18.
38. *Groener v. Minister for Education* (Case 379/87) [1990] 1 CMLR 401; see ante p.132.

Status The various Acts dealing with local government service distinguish between employees and office-holders. But they do not define which groups of workers fall into each of these categories. It often is left to the court to decide in particular instances whether a local government worker is an officer or an employee. The context in which this question is posed varies. Many of the old cases concerned whether the person was an employed contributor for the purpose of the Social Welfare Acts. For instance, officials of a poor law union and the crier of the Belfast Recorders' Court were held not to be employees[39] whereas a school attendance inspector fell into that category.[40] The standing solicitor to the Carrickmacross Rural District Council was held to be an officer in order to claim compensation for loss of office;[41] the Dublin City rate collector was held not to be a 'clerk or servant' of the Dublin Corporation for the purpose of s.17 of the Larceny Act, 1916;[42] a messenger and assistant keeper at the Cork Court House was held to be an officer for the purpose of qualifying for a pension,[43] whereas a messenger-labourer with the Dublin Corporation was merely an employee.[44] Section 11(1) of the Local Government Act, 1955, empowers the Minister to determine whether a person is an officer for the purpose of the Local Government Acts and adds that his decision on this question shall be final.[45]

Perhaps the context in which the question arises most often these days is to determine whether the Unfair Dismissals Act, 1977, applies; excluded from the scope of this Act are *inter alia* 'officers' of local authorities, of health boards, of vocational education committees and of committees of agriculture.[46] In *Western Health Board v. Quigley*[47] it was held that a registered psychiatric nurse, holding a temporary appointment in a Galway hospital, was an officer of the Western Health Board. She accordingly could not claim under the Unfair Dismissals Act. However, this does not mean that officers can be arbitrarily dismissed, because the various Acts have set up the grounds on which they can be dismissed and prescribe procedures which must be followed to that end.[48]

Incidents of the office Local and regional government officers' remuneration and terms and conditions of employment are usually fixed by the

---

39. *Re National Insurance Act, 1911 — Officers of South Dublin Union,* 1 IR 244 and *Irish Insurance Cmrs. v. Craig* [1916] 2 IR 59.
40. *O'Callaghan v. Irish Insurance Cmrs.* [1915] 2 IR 262.
41. *Phelan v. Minister for Local Government* [1930] IR 542.
42. *People v. Warren* [1945] IR 24.
43. *Flaherty v. Minister for Local Government* [1941] IR 587.
44. *R (Dillon) v. Minister for Local Goverment* [192?] IR 474.
45. Local Government Act, 1955, s.11. Cf. *State (Raftis) v. Leonard* [1960] IR 381.
46. S.2(1)(j).   47. [1982] ILRM 390.   48. See infra pp.320-321.

Minister or by reference to his directions.[49] It would seem that, as a matter of law, these incidents of the job may be unilaterally altered, to the office-holder's detriment, by the Minister or the authority empowered to determine these matters. *Thistle v. Monaghan County Council* [50] was one of a series of cases in the late 1920s when the remuneration of many local government workers was cut as an economic measure. The plaintiffs were attendants at the Monaghan and Cavan District Mental Hospital whose remuneration had been so reduced. The argument for upholding this wage cut was that, under the relevant Act, the Council could appoint such officers as it considered necessary and they 'shall perform such duties and be paid such remuneration as the council may [decide].'[51] Under the Interpretation Act, 1889, where an Act grants a power or imposes a duty, it 'may be exercised or performed from time to time as occasion requires' unless the contrary intention appears. Accordingly, it was held, the power to determine remuneration may be exercised from time to time, by either increasing it or by reducing it.[52] Emphasis was placed on the fact that the plaintiffs were officers and not employees with contracts. Whether this construction would be followed today is debatable. If a power of unilateral reduction still exists, not alone must the prescribed procedure for doing so be scrupulously followed but 'legitimate expectations' must be respected and constitutional justice and fair play must be observed.[53] In addition, the local government trade unions must be reckoned with.

What has been said above with regard to civil servants' common law and equitable rights and obligations also applies generally to local government officials. The Prevention of Corruption Acts, 1889-1916, apply to them.[54] It has been held that only local government employees and not officers can be convicted of embezzlement under the Larceny Act.[55] Whether the Official Secrets Act, 1963, applies to confidential information held by local government bodies could be debated.

Discipline and dismissal The grounds and procedures for disciplining and dismissing the various categories of local government officials is laid down in the relevant Acts in different degrees of detail. Officers of vocational educational committees and of committees of agriculture can be removed

49. Local Government Act, 1941, ss.19-21, as amended by Local Government Act, 1955, ss.14-16; Vocational Education Act, 1930, s.23(2), Agriculture Act, 1931.
50. [1931] IR 381.
51. Local Government (Ireland) Act, 1898, s.84(1)(b).
52. Approving *Chambers v. Mayo Mental Hospital* [1930] IR 154. Cf. *Woods v. Dublin Corp.* [1931] IR 396.
53. See ante pp.300-302.
54. S.R. & O. No. 37 of 1928.   55. *People v. Warren* [1945] IR 24.

from office where the Minister considers that they are 'unfit or incompetent to perform [their] duties.'[56] Before deciding to remove them, the Minister must hold a 'local inquiry' and consider the report made by the person who conducted that inquiry.[57] The power to suspend without pay officers of vocational education committees has been the subject of considerable litigation in recent years.[58]

Permanent officers of health boards may be removed 'because of misconduct or unfitness'.[59] If the grounds of dismissal is being absent from his duties without reasonable cause, he may be removed on the Minister's direction.[60] Where misconduct or unfitness are alleged, the matter must first be considered by a committee comprising a chairman, chosen by the Minister, persons chosen by him from a panel of names supplied by the chief executive officer of the health board concerned and an equal number of persons selected by the Minister from a panel of names supplied by a trade union or trade unions representatives of the officer's own class or grade.[61] Provision is also made for suspending health board officers without pay while allegations against them of misconduct or unfitness are being investigated.[62]

The suspension and removal of the officers of a local government body are regulated by ss.24-27 of the Local Government Act, 1941. An officer can be required to resign where he never possessed the requisite qualifications for the job; also where, due to changes in the conditions of service or the nature or extent of the duties attached to the job, it is in the public interest that he resigns.[63] Where an officer refuses to resign, as requested in these circumstances, he can be removed from office. An officer can be suspended without pay where either the Minister or the relevant authority has reason to believe that he has 'failed to perform satisfactorily the duties' of the office, that he 'misconducted himself' in relation to the office or that he was 'otherwise unfit' to hold that office.[64] What amounts to being otherwise unfit for the office has not so far been clarified by the courts. Where the suspension ends, the Minister has a discretion to pay all or part of the remuneration which the officer would have earned during that period.[65]

A local government officer may be removed from office for the following reasons:

56. Vocational Education Act, 1930, s.27 and Agriculture Act, 1931, s.23.
57. Ibid. Cf. *State (Curtin) v. Minister for Health* [1953] IR 93.
58. See infra p.322, n.80.   59. Health Act, 1970, s.23(2).
60. Id. s.23(3).   61. Id. s.24.
62. Id. s.22. Cf. *Cox v. Electricity Supply Board (No.3)* [1944] IR 81.
63. Local Government Act, 1941, s.24.
64. Id. s.27.   65. Id. s.27(4).

(a) Unfitness of such holder for such office;

(b) the fact that such holder has refused to obey or carry into effect any order lawfully given to him as the holder of such office or has otherwise misconducted himself in such office.[66]

The normal procedure for removal from office is to conduct a 'local inquiry' into allegations, in order to determine if any of these grounds can be established.[67] But where the Minister otherwise comes to the view that these grounds exist, he can notify the officer in question in writing of his intention to dismiss.[68] That officer then has seven days to make representations to the Minister, who can then order that the individual be removed from office. The Minister may empower local authorities to remove officers and may lay down the procedures to be followed in such cases.[69]

TEACHERS

There are four principal categories of teachers—national, secondary, vocational and university teachers. The legal rights and duties of secondary teachers and of university teachers have rarely been the subject of litigation, with the noted exception of the *McGrath v. Maynooth College* case.[70] The status and incidents of secondary and university teachers are principally regulated by the contract between the teacher and the employing institution. They are not employed by the State. Whether they could be regarded as being employed 'under the State' and thereby, for instance, are excluded from the scope of the Unfair Dismissals Act is a matter which remains to be resolved.

University teachers Professors and some senior personnel in the National University of Ireland are statutory officers under the Irish Universities Act, 1908. This Act and also the Charter for Trinity College Dublin provide for a visitor,[71] who has authority to decide disputes between members of the universities and the colleges and those institutions. In *Thomas v. University of Bradford*,[72] the jurisdiction of a visitor to deal with employment-related disputes was considered by the House of Lords but the issue of a visitor's

---

66. Local Government Act, 1941, s.25(1).
67. Id. s.25(2). Cf. *State (Curtin) v. Minister for Health* [1953] IR 93.
68. Id. s.25(3).
69. Id. s.26. Cf. *Cox v. Electricity Supply Board* [1943] where the previous dismissals procedure was outlined in considerable detail.
70. [1979] ILRM 166. See *Constitutional Law*, pp.532-534.
71. Charter of National University of Ireland, ch. IV and Statutes of Trinity College, ch.III.
72. [1987] AC 795.

exclusive or parallel jurisdiction has not yet received any extensive consideration by the courts in this country. It was held in the *Thomas* case, and also in other cases involving disputes with Queen's University Belfast[73] and with a college which is part of the University of London,[74] that a visitor has an extensive exclusive jurisdiction, which can extend to the dismissal of lecturers and professors. But a visitor's decision can be challenged in the courts by way of judicial review.[75]

Vocational teachers The position of vocational teachers is regulated by the Vocational Education Act, 1930, as amended in 1944; their status, rights and duties are very similar to those of officers of local authorities.[76] The appointment, qualifications and remuneration of vocational teachers is regulated by the Minister for Education.[77] Provision is made for the suspension without pay of any V.E.C. office-holder where there is reason to believe he failed to perform his duties satisfactorily or he otherwise misconducted himself or was otherwise unfit for the office.[78] The statutory grounds for removal are unfitness to hold the office, refusal to obey or carry out a lawful order or other misconduct.[79] On several occasions the proper procedures for suspending and for dismissing vocational teachers were considered by the courts.[80]

National teachers An extensive body of case law exists regarding the status, rights and duties of national teachers.[81] A minority of national teachers are employed directly by the State, most notably those who teach in the model schools. The great majority of national teachers are employed under the management system whereby, even though their salary is paid by

---

73. *Re Wislang's Application* [1984] NI 63.
74. *Hines v. Birkbeck College* [1986] Ch. 526.
75. E.g. the *Thomas*, the *Wilsang* and the *Hines* cases; also *Pearce v. University of Aston* [1991] 2 All ER 461, 469 and *R. v. Hull University Visitor, ex p. Page* [1991] 1 WLR 1277.
76. Supra pp.318-321.
77. Vocational Education Act, 1930, s.23(2).
78. Vocational Education (Amendment) Act, 1944, s.7.
79. Id. s.8(1).
80. Mainly concerning whether the prescribed procedures and fair procedures had been followed; e.g. *State (Donegal V.E.C.) v. Minister for Education* [1985] IR 56, *Collins v. Co. Cork V.E.C.* (Murphy J, 27 May 1982; Sup. Ct. 18 Mar. 1983); *Ni Bheolain v. Dublin V.E.C.* (Carroll J, 28 Jan. 1983) *O'Callaghan v. Meath V.E.C.* (Costello J, 20 Nov. 1990). See too, *Gunn v. Bord An Cholaiste Naisiunta Ealaine is Deartha* [1990] 2 IR 168.
81. See generally, Osborough, 'Irish Law and the Rights of the National Schoolteacher', 14 *Ir. Jur.* 36 and 304 (1979).

the State, the hiring and directions regarding their work is done by or under local management boards. As described by Murnaghan J, the managerial system

> was adopted to obviate difficulties connected chiefly with religious belief. In most cases schools were not the property of the [State] but they were recognised by it as national schools. A manager, e.g. the parish priest or rector of the Church of Ireland, was nominated by an outside authority and the nomination was sanctioned by the [State]— when sanctioned the duties and functions of the manager were minutely provided for in Rules and Regulations made by the [State].
>
> The selection of the teacher, who should, however, have the prescribed qualifications, was left to the manager, but the salary of the teacher was in general provided by the [State]. The teacher had, under the Rules . . . , to be appointed under an agreement in writing on one of the approved forms and the agreement so approved of contained a clause stating that the duties of teachers should be such as were prescribed in the Rules. . . .[82]

There was a view that the national teacher's employer was the school manager and not the Department of Education, but that was rejected by the Supreme Court in 1940. In *McEneaney v. Minister for Education*[83] a school manager who 'did not own the school and was not carrying it on for his personal benefit' was described as being 'in the position of a trustee of an educational trust.'[84] Two of the principal reported cases, *Leyden*[85] and *McEneaney*, concerned unilateral alterations to the plaintiffs' employment contracts; in both cases the plaintiffs were backed by their trade union, the Irish National Teachers Organisation. In both cases, the teachers were appointed under regulations which contained 'rule 108(c)', whereby the State 'reserve[d] the right to alter the rates of grade salary and of continued good service salary. . . .' In *Leyden*, as an economy measure in 1923, the State cut teachers' salaries by 10 per cent. Although those salaries had been determined some years earlier by an arbitration award, it was held that rule 108(c) would permit reductions of that nature. The legal effects of the arbitration award were described there as follows: 'if the award is put forward as an alteration of a legal contract between manager and teacher, no evidence of authority to make such alteration on the part of the teacher has been shown. In reality what took place was negotiation through collective bargaining, without any intention to alter legal contracts between

---

82. *McEneaney v. Minister for Education* [1941] IR 430, at p.439.
83. [1941] IR 430.   84. Id. at p.440.   85. [1926] IR 334.

managers and teachers, although such alteration would naturally follow subsequently.'[86] Later in *McEneaney* the Supreme Court 'recognise[d] a power in the Department to make general reduction of pay as the necessities of the time may require'.[87] However, the Court would not permit the unilateral imposition of new qualifications for existing teachers—in that case, a certificate of competency to give bilingual instruction. A change of terms of that nature was not contemplated by rule 108(c). In 1955, the Supreme Court held that the Department could introduce a higher salary scale for married teachers[88]—an arrangement which now of course would contravene the E.E.C. Treaty and, apart from that, probably would be unconstitutional.

National teachers may fall into the category of persons who are employed by or under the State and are thereby excluded from the Unfair Dismissals Act. If that is so, then their rights regarding dismissal are principally to have the terms of their contracts adhered to; they can be lawfully dismissed for the reasons and in accordance with the procedures laid down in their contracts. One of the earliest cases on the right of public officials to fair procedures if they are to be dismissed was *Maunsell v. Minister for Education*,[89] where the Minister ceased to pay a teacher's salary on the grounds that enrolments at his school fell below a specified level. The reason for the fall in numbers had been investigated by the Department, without any reference to that teacher. Gavan Duffy J found guidance in the lines of Seneca,

> Quicunque aliquid statuerit, parte inaudita altera,
> Aequum licet statuerit, haud aequus fuerit.

Accordingly, it was held, the

> plaintiff was entitled to express notice of such an inquisition as that [carried out by the Department]. The principle is long and firmly established; it is elementary justice; it applies even where the person affected has no merits; it applies though the enactment does not seem to have contemplated notice; and it applies to every body having authority to adjudicate upon matters involving civil consequences to individuals.[90]

---

86. Id. at pp.360-361.   87. [1941] IR at p.444.
88. *O'Callaghan v. Minister for Education* (Sup. Ct. 30 Nov. 1955).
89. [1940] IR 213.
90. Id. at p.234. Distinguished unconvincingly in *Hickey v. Eastern Health Board* [1991] 1 IR 208.

THE GARDA SÍOCHÁNA

In contrast with civil servants and military personnel, the employment rights and obligations of police men and women are the subject of a considerable amount of litigation. Although they may not join trade unions, members of the Garda Síochána have their own representative associations for putting their case regarding remuneration and employment conditions.[91] A conciliation and arbitration scheme, similar to that for civil servants, exists for the Gardaí.[92] The legal position of members of the Garda is governed by the Garda Síochána Act, 1924, as amended, and regulations made under them. Several of the leading cases on fair procedures for disciplining and dismissing public officials have involved members of the Garda, including the *Garvey* case,[93] where the head of the force was dismissed peremptorily and without being offered any reason for that action or any opportunity to rebut allegations that might be made against him.

In *Attorney General v. Dublin United Tramways Co. Ltd*,[94] it was held that members of the Garda are employed under contracts of employment. Maguire P's reasoning was that 'members of the Garda Síochána are . . . servants of the public in the employment of the Government. . . . [W]hile he remains a member of the Garda Síochána, [the Guard] is bound to render services to the public.'[95] Accordingly, this was sufficient to create the relationship of master and servant. It is questionable whether the reasoning there would be followed today. Indeed, the appropriateness of proceeding by way of judicial review to assert the employment rights of Gardaí appears never to have been challenged.

Appointments of Gardaí, their promotion and disciplining and retirement are now regulated by statutory instruments issued in 1987, 1988, 1989 and 1990.[96] What is said above regarding civil servants' common law, fiduciary and statutory rights and duties applies as well to members of the Garda Síochána.

A special statutory scheme to compensate them or their dependents for malicious injuries and death occasioned in the performance of their duties was established by the Garda Síochána (Compensation) Act, 1941, as amended. In order to obtain compensation under this scheme, the applicant must show that, when the Garda in question was injured, he either was on

---

91. Garda Síochána Act, 1924, s.13, as amended in 1977. See *Industrial Relations Law* at p.195.
92. See id. at p.206.   93. *Garvey v. Ireland* [1981] IR 75.
94. [1939] IR 590.   95. Id. at p.597.
96. SI No. 164 of 1988 (Admissions and Appointments), No. 39 of 1987 (Promotions), No. 94 of 1989 (Discipline) and No. 318 of 1990 (Retirement).

duty and performing his duties or, if not on duty, was acting in his general capacity as a policeman; or the applicant may show that the injury resulted from something the Garda had done as a member of the force or merely because of such membership.[97] The injuries in question must have been maliciously inflicted. In the *Harrington* case[98] in 1945 involving two Gardaí stationed at Nenagh, who were both found shot dead in the station store-room, it seemed that one Guard shot the other and then committed suicide; there was evidence of private and personal differences between them. A claim by one of their dependents for compensation under the scheme was rejected because there was no evidence that the injuries were inflicted in relation to the deceased's duties as a Guard or his membership of the force.

Members of the Garda can be disciplined and dismissed for the reasons and in accordance with the procedures laid down in the 1989 Disciplinary Regulations.[99] Provided the requisite procedures were followed, the courts are loath to second-guess the findings of a disciplinary tribunal regarding whether the garda in question deserved to be punished or dismissed, once it is shown that a reasonable tribunal could have come to that conclusion on one view of the evidence.[100] Its determination will not be upset unless it took account of wholly irrelevant matters or it did not have regard to to very relevant matters, or the determination 'plainly and unambiguously flies in the face of fundamental reason and common sense.'[1] In *Stroker v. Doherty*,[2] where a garda stationed in a small country town was dismissed for having used obscene language in connection with his wife in a public house and, on another occasion, for not assisting his wife to leave the public house when she was asked by the barman to go, McCarthy J was 'not prepared to hold that the conclusion . . . involved a rejection of, or disregard for fundamental reason or common sense.' The judge observed that 'in a small country community, members of the gardaí should be setting an example of decent conduct.'[3] The Supreme Court there emphasised the general undesirability of the courts interfering with the merits of decisions taken by a body which is particularly well equipped for dealing with such matters.

---

97. 1941 Act s.2. There is a considerable body of case law on this Act, e.g. *O'Brien v. Minister for Finance* [1944] IR 392, *O'Brien v. Minister for Finance (No.2)* [1946] IR 314, *McLoughlin v. Minister for Public Service* [1985] IR 631, *O'Looney v. Minister for Public Service* [1986] IR 543, *Conroy v. Commissioner An Garda Síochána* [1989] IR 141.
98. *Harrington v. Minister for Finance* [1946] IR 320.
99. SI No. 94 of 1989. Cf. Garda Síochána (Complaints) Act, 1986.
100. See ante p.305. Cf. *McHugh v. Commissioner An Garda Síochána* [1986] IR 228.
   1. *Stroker v. Doherty* [1991] 1 IR 23 at p.29
   2. [1991] 1 IR 23.   3. Id. at p.29.

THE DEFENCE FORCES

It is unusual for a book on employment law to deal with the position of members of Defence Forces, but a brief account of their situation is called for, especially since, by the Defence (Amendment) Act, 1990, members of those forces are permitted to have their own representative associations for considering remuneration and other employment-related matters. Members of the Defence Forces are governed by Defence Act, 1954, which is a very bulky measure that has been amended on several occasions. Unlike the position for instance in the United States, the rights and obligations of members of these forces (the Army, the Navy and the Air Force) have been the subject of very little litigation, except for the question of army pensions. However, one of the leading authorities on the maxim *audi alteram partem* is *The State (Gleeson) v. Minister for Defence*,[4] concerned the proper procedures for discharging members of the forces. More recently in *McDonagh v. Minister for Defence*,[5] Lavan J castigated disciplinary action taken against a member of the naval service for having consulted the service's legal officer as 'unfair and capricious'. The penalty imposed on the naval officer there was completely disproportionate to the alleged offence and, additionally, he was never given the opportunity to answer the charges made against him.

Members of the forces do not hold their appointments under contracts of employment but have a status as defined by the Defence Acts. Unlike civil servants, however, it has been established that members of the forces have a legal right to be paid such remuneration as is owing to them under regulations made on foot of the Defence Acts. In a case in 1946[6] the Supreme Court gave a declaration that a captain in the Army Medical Service was entitled to the same rate of pay as for Commandants, as laid down in regulations in force at the time. What is said above regarding civil servants' common law, fiduciary and statutory rights and obligations applies as well to members of these forces,[7] with the principal exception of the Employment Equality Act, 1977, which does not apply to these forces.[8]

---

4. [1976] ILRM 115.   5. [1991] ILRM 115.
6. *Fitzpatrick v. Minister for Finance* [1946] IR 481.
7. Supra pp.311-313. E.g. *Reading v. Attorney General* [1951] AC 507.
8. S.12(1)(a). Cf. Defence (Amendment) Act, 1979, authorising women to become members of the armed forces.

15

Income taxation

Income tax is a very significant feature of many employment relationships, especially in Ireland where tax rates are high. Under the Finance Act, 1991, the rates of tax payable by a single person on taxable income were as follows: the first £6,700 at 29%, the next £3,100 at 48% and the remainder at 52%. The marginal rate of tax for most workers therefore is 52%. On account of the comparatively high tax rates, employers and workers often seek ways to minimise their tax bills and, when evaluating various kinds of rewards for working, will be concerned more with the after-tax worth than the face value. In recent years profit-sharing and employee share schemes have become a feature of private sector employment in prosperous companies and legislation has been enacted to remove several fiscal deterrents against participating in these schemes. Only a general outline of the tax features of employment can be given here; for a more detailed treatment the reader should consult a specialist work on income tax.[1]

EMPLOYMENT OR OFFICE

The rules for taxing income differ somewhat depending on which schedule the income in question is being taxed under. Income earned by working for others can fall under schedule D or schedule E of the Income Tax Acts. Schedule D is concerned with the income of self-employed persons; it is relatively favourable to them in that, *inter alia*, losses incurred in some years can be set off against gains made in other years, a wider range of earnings-related expenses are deductible from income and, before 1990, the actual amount of tax payable was calculated on a previous year basis. Schedule E deals with the income of employees and office-holders. Accordingly, the employee/self-employed distinction considered earlier in Chapter Two is vital for income tax purposes and, indeed, one of the main incentives for employees seeking to become self-employed is to avail of the more favourable schedule D tax regime.

---

1. Notably N.E. Judge, *Irish Income Tax* (1986 – loose leaf) (hereinafter referred to as *Judge*). See too, Whiteman, *Income Tax* (3rd ed. 1988) chs. 14 and 15.

Those who are taxable under schedule E are the holders of

> every public office or employment of profit, and in respect of every
> annuity, pension or stipend payable out of the public revenue of the
> State. . . . [E]very person having or exercising an office or employment
> of profit . . . to whom any annuity, pension or stipend . . . is payable
> . . . in respect of all salaries, fees, wages, perquisites or profits what-
> soever therefrom.[2]

The same criteria and tests apply in determining if a person is an employee
for tax purposes as apply for employment legislation and social security.[3]
That the parties have described their relationship as one of self-employment
is not conclusive on the matter.[4] What a tribunal and court will look for
principally is the right to control in detail how the work is done and the
absence of a significant entrepreneurial element.[5]

Several of the leading cases on the distinction in this context concern
persons claiming to be exercising their profession or vocation entirely or
predominantly for one employer. For instance, in *Fall v. Hitchin*[6] the
question was whether a professional dancer, who had a written contract with
the Sadlers Wells Company, was an employee or self-employed. Under the
contract, he was to be paid a weekly 'fee' regardless of whether or not he
was called on to dance in that week. During the tax year he had sought but
was unsuccessful in securing other dancing engagements. But he did not
intend to remain at Sadlers Wells and he regarded his engagement there as
an interim one. It was held that he was an employee.[7] His position was
contrasted with that in *Davies v. Braitwaite*,[8] where an actress argued that
every one of her separate theatrical engagements were distinct contracts of
employment for tax purposes. That contention was rejected and it was
observed that

> Where one finds a method of earning a livelihood which does not
> consist of the obtaining of a post and staying in it, but consists in a
> series of engagements and moving from one to the other . . . then each
> of those engagements cannot be considered an employment but is a
> mere engagement in the course of exercising a profession, and every
> profession and every trade does involve the making of successive
> engagements and successive contracts and, in one sense of the word,
> employments.[9]

2. Income Tax Act, 1967, ss.109(1) and 110(1).
3. *Fall v. Hitchen* [1973] 1 WLR 286.
4. *Narich Pty. Ltd v. Commissioner of Pay Roll Tax* [1984] ICR 286.
5. E.g. *McDermott v. Loy* (Barron J, 29 July 1982).
6. [1973] 1 WLR 286.   7. Similarly the *Narich* case, supra n.4.
8. [1931] 2 KB 628.   9. Id. at pp.635-636.

Where the person in question can be classified as an 'office-holder' then, regardless of his status under employment law, his earnings from the office are taxable under schedule E. In *Edwards v. Clinch*,[10] which concerned whether an inspector who was specially appointed to hold a planning inquiry fell into this category, the term 'office' was described

> as a post which can be recognised as existing, whether it be occupied for the time being or vacant, and which, if occupied, does not owe its existence in any way to the identity of the incumbent or his appointment to the post. . . . [T]he office must owe its existence to some constituent instrument, whether it be a charter, statute, declaration of trust, contract (other than a contract of personal service) or instrument of some other kind. . . . [T]he office must have a sufficient degree of continuance to admit of its being held by successive incumbents; it need not be capable of permanent or prolonged or indefinite existence, but it cannot be limited to the tenure of one man. . . .[11]

The second schedule to the Income Tax Act, 1967, contains a list of offices in respect of which tax under schedule E must be paid on their incomes.[12] This list is not intended as a comprehensive statement of the office-holders who are taxable in this manner.

The taxpayer in *Edwards v. Clinch*[13] was one of a panel of 60 engineers who the Department of the Environment could call on to hold public enquiries. When so invited, there was no obligation to accept the nomination. A duly appointed inspector was responsible for the entire conduct of the enquiry and was remunerated exclusively by fees paid on a daily basis. Because each appointment was an ad hoc one and no question ordinarily arose of appointing an incumbent inspector's successor, it was held that the

10. [1981] 1 Ch. 1.
11. Id. at p.6.
12. The following offices are listed:—
    (a) offices belonging to either House of the Oireachtas;
    (b) offices belonging to any court in the State;
    (c) public offices under the State;
    (d) officers of the Defence Forces;
    (e) offices or employments of profit under any ecclesiastical body;
    (f) offices or employments of profit under any company or society, whether corporate or not corporate;
    (g) offices or employments of profit under any public institution, or on any foundation of whatever nature, or for whatever purpose established;
    (h) offices or employments of profit under any public corporation or local authority, or under any trustees or guardians of any public funds, tolls, or duties;
    (i) all other public offices, or employments of profit which are of a public nature.
13. [1981] 1 Ch. 1.

inspector there was not an office-holder. By contrast, a part-time consultant with a regional hospital board was held to be taxable under schedule E,[14] as were non-executive directors of companies[15] and indeed a Scottish law firm which acted as the registrars of several companies.[16]

TAXABLE BENEFITS

What is taxable under schedule E is described as 'emoluments', which may be either cash payments or benefits in kind. Occasionally, very substantial payments made to employees, which are not emoluments, may be taxable as gifts under the Capital Acquisitions Tax Act, 1976. Emoluments are defined as

> all salaries, fees, wages, perquisites or profits or gains whatsoever arising from an office or employment, or the amount of any annuity, pension or stipend, as the case may be.[17]

Thus, not alone money but anything representing money's worth can be emoluments and thereby taxable. In the case of benefits in kind, tax will only be charged to the extent that they can be converted into money.

Money payments Not every payment made by an employer to his employee will be subject to income tax. The fact that the payment has some connection with the job does not always render it taxable; the payment must 'arise from' the office or employment. This general principle was enunciated in the leading case of *Hochstrasser v. Meyes* as follows:

> it is a question to be answered in the light of the particular facts of every case whether or not a particular payment is or is not a profit arising from the employment. . . . [N]ot every payment made to an employee is necessarily made to him as a profit arising from his employment. Indeed, . . . to be a profit arising from the employment the payment must be made in reference to the services the employee renders by virtue of his office, and it must be something in the nature of a reward for services, (past) present or future.[18]

14. *Mitchell and Eldon v. Ross* [1960] Ch. 145.
15. *McMillan v. Guest* [1942] AC 561.
16. *Inland Revenue v. Brander & Cruickshank* [1971] 1 WLR 212; contrast *McMenamin v. Diggles* [1991] 1 WLR 1249 (complex arrangement with barristers' head clerk).
17. Income Tax Act, 1967, s.111(4).
18. [1960] AC 376, at p.388. The word 'past' in this passage may be open to question.

Not alone must the payment be made to an employee but it must have been paid to him 'in return for acting as or being an employee.'[19] There are several categories of payment which do not 'arise from' the employment and therefore are not taxable in principle, although special rules have been enacted to subject some of these payments to income tax, like 'golden handshakes'.

The *Hochstrasser* case concerned a scheme whereby certain employees of Imperial Chemical Industries Ltd were compensated by the company in respect of losses incurred by them on sales of their houses when they were moved from one location to another by the company. The company employed a very large workforce in a number of establishments in Britain. In their service contracts, these employees agreed to serve the company wherever they were posted. In order to facilitate transfers from one establishment to another, a scheme existed whereby married male employees could obtain interest free loans from the company to purchase houses. Additionally, if on being transferred they incurred a loss on the sale of their house, the company would make up that loss. When the taxpayer was transferred to a factory in Liverpool in 1950, he lost £350 on the sale of his house and he was then reimbursed that amount by the company. It was held that this money was not a taxable emolument because the circumstance which brought about the payment was not any service rendered by him but rather 'his personal embarrassment in having sold his house for a smaller sum than he had given for it.'[20] The payment was 'no more taxable as a profit from his employment than would a payment out of a provident or a distress fund set up by an employer for the benefit of employees whose personal circumstances might justify assistance'.[21]

Gifts and other voluntary payments: That the payment is gratuitous, in the sense that it is not being made under a binding obligation, does not mean that it never falls within the tax net. The governing principle is that taxable income includes 'all payments made to the holder of an office or employment as such, that is to say, by way of remuneration for services, even though such payments may be voluntary, but they do not include a mere gift or present (such as a testimonial) which is made to him on personal grounds and not by way of payment for his services'.[22] Of course, if the gift is not remuneration but it exceeds £2,000, it falls subject to capital acquisitions tax.

There is a strong tendency to treat gratuitous payments by employers as taxable remuneration, especially when similar gifts are made to other

19. Id. at p.392.   20. [1960] AC at p.392.   21. Ibid.
22. *Reed v. Seymour* [1927] AC 554 at p.559.

employees. For instance, in *Laidler v. Perry*,[23] a group of companies gave each of its employees, who had worked for it for longer than one year, a voucher for £10 as a Christmas present, which could be exchanged for goods in the shop of the employee's own choice. These were held to be taxable emoluments. It did not matter that the gifts were made to 'help to maintain a feeling of happiness among the staff and to foster a spirit of personal relationship between management and staff.'[24] This objective was described '[i]n less roundabout language' as simply 'in order to maintain the quality of service given by the staff', meaning for 'each recipient to go on working well.'[25] Consequently, the vouchers arose from the employment itself.

Even a payment to a single employee which is given and is received as a gift may in the circumstances be remuneration for services rendered. That was held to be the case in *Wing v. O'Connell*,[26] where the owner of the horse that won the Irish Derby in 1921 subsequently sent the jockey a cheque for £400. The letter described the payment as 'a present', congratulated the jockey for his 'very fine riding' of the horse and expressed the hope that he 'will soon ride him again to victory'. According to Kennedy CJ, this payment was given for 'professional work done and vocational services rendered in successfully steering the horse . . . to victory, in other words, for successfully accomplishing the object of his professional engagement, and that it was in the nature of a bonus or voluntary addition to the prescribed fee under the regulations'.[27] The payment therefore was taxable income.

A rare instance of a gratuitous payment by an employer not being taxed is *Ball v. Johnson*,[28] concerning a bank clerk whose terms of employment required him to sit the examinations of the Institute of Bankers 'in order to better qualify himself for his duties in the service of the bank'. He duly worked for those examinations in his spare time and, having passed them, was paid £130 by his employer, in accordance with the long established practice. The payment was held not to be a profit arising from his employment and, accordingly, escaped tax. Similarly, when in 1940 the Governing Body of University College Dublin voted its retiring President, Dr Coffey, a sum of £1,000 to mark his retirement and to show the Governors' high estimation of his contribution to the College, the payment was held to be in the nature of a gift and not taxable.[29]

Depending on the circumstances, gifts made by persons other than the recipient's employer may be taxable income. Examples of such payments include tips received by a taxi driver in the ordinary course of his work,[30]

23. [1966] AC 16. 24. Id. at p.31. 25. Id. at p.36.
26. [1927] IR 84. 27. Id. at p.108. 28. (1971) 47 TC 155.
29. *Mulvey v. Coffey* [1942] IR 277. 30. *Calvert v. Wainwright* [1947] KB 526.

the Easter offering made to a Church of England parson[31] and the customary presents of cash given to a huntsman at Christmas by other members of the hunt who were also his personal friends.[32]

Special contractual payments: Where the payment is made on foot of a contractual stipulation, in return for something other than services rendered, then that money may not be a taxable emolument. The best example is the *Hochstrasser* case,[33] where the payments to cover losses incurred when the I.C.I. employees changed their houses were made under the terms of an enforceable contract and were not pure gifts. According to Lord Radcliffe, 'while it is not sufficient to render a payment assessable that an employee would not have received it unless he had been an employee, it is assessable if it has been paid to him in return for acting or as being an employee.'[34] In reaching their decision that the payment there was not for acting as an employee, the Lords laid stress on the fact that the taxpayer's salary compared favourably with that of employees in comparable circumstances but whose employers did not operate this kind of scheme. Similarly, when an amateur rugby football player got a signing-on-fee for turning professional and playing for his new club, the payment was held to be a capital sum received to compensate for the loss of amateur status, not a taxable emolument.[35]

But an inducement or signing on fee, where some special extra ingredient does not exist, would not escape the income tax net.[36] In *Vaughan-Neill v. Inland Revenue*,[37] where a successful barrister agreed to give up his practice and work full-time for a large civil engineering company, an inducement fee of £40,000 paid to him by the company was held to be taxable. This was because the taxpayer was not giving up something exceptional in order to do the new job; the payment in fact was 'an inducement to [him] to accept the professional and social consequences which flowed from his taking the proffered employment.'[38] A similar conclusion was reached in *Glantre Engineering Ltd v. Goodhand*,[39] where a lump sum was paid to a chartered accountant, who worked with a major international accountancy firm, to leave the firm and take up the position as financial director of a rapidly expanding engineering company. The view that this payment was made to

31. *Blaikston v. Cooper* [1909] AC 104.
32. *Wright v. Boyce* (1958) 38 TC 138.
33. [1960] AC 376.   34. Id. at pp.391-392.
35. *Jarrold v. Boustead* [1964] 1 WLR 1357.
36. *Riley v. Coglan* (1967) 44 TC 481.   37. [1979] 1 WLR 1283.
38. Id. at p.1293. Curiously, the Revenue did not attempt to tax this as an ordinary emolument but under special statutory provisions.
39. [1983] 1 All ER 542.

compensate for the loss of professional status as a chartered accountant in a very large firm, the loss of the prospects of becoming a partner in that firm and the loss of security in the future, was rejected.

Payments made in connection with a change in the terms of employment are almost invariably taxable. Thus in *Holland v. Geoghegan*,[40] a dustman received a lump sum for giving up the right he had enjoyed to a share in the proceeds from a sale of salvage. In the previous year, when his employer sought to remove his and his co-employees' right to share in the salvage, they went on strike. The lump sum was offered by way of a settlement of the strike and to induce him back to work, although he did not agree to remain in the job for any longer than one week's notice. Nevertheless, the payment was held to be taxable because its main purpose was to get him back to work and it was 'a form of substituted remuneration for his former rights to share in the proceeds of sale of the salvage'.[41] The same conclusion was reached in a case where an employee, whose remuneration was based on a salary and a commission, agreed to give up his right to any commission in return for a lump sum.[42]

In *Hamblett v. Godfrey*,[43] the taxpayer was a civil servant employed at 'G.C.H.Q.' in Cheltenham, a famous information-gathering and secret service establishment. On account of the Government's concern about trade unionism and possible industrial action there, many employees were persuaded to sign agreements that they would resign from trade union membership, would not join any trade union and not even discuss with the officials of any union their terms of employment. For that undertaking, they were paid £1,000 each. It was held that this sum was taxable because its very source was the civil servants' employment. The rights which had been surrendered 'had been enjoyed within the employer/employee relationship, [t]he removal of the rights involved changes in the conditions of service [and t]he payment was in recognition of th[ose] changes. . . .'[44] The view that what was surrendered were special personal rights was rejected since, whatever they were, they were still directly connected with the taxpayers' employment. A case could be made that the position in Ireland is different because the rights to join a trade union and to take part in its activities enjoy constitutional protection.

In *Clayton v. Gothorp*,[45] the taxpayer's wife obtained a loan from her employer to follow a course leading to a certificate for health visitors. She was employed as an assistant health visitor and, when getting the loan, agreed to serve the employer for at least eighteen months after she obtained

40. [1972] 1 WLR 1473.   41. Id. at p.1481.
42. *McGregor v. Randall* [1984] 1 All ER 1092.
43. [1987] 1 WLR 357.   44. Id. at p.370.   45. [1971] 1 WLR 999.

that qualification, at the end of which time the money then would become irrecoverable. The loan was paid to her in monthly instalments throughout the duration of the course. Having succeeded in obtaining the qualification, she remained with the employer for eighteen months and three days. It was held that the loan was a reward for past services and thereby taxable. The consideration given for the loan was the promise to follow the course and then work for at least eighteen months, and it was working for that period which turned the loan into an absolute payment.

A lump sum payment made in return for a restrictive covenant was held not to fall within Schedule E, whether the covenant applies during the currency of the employment or on its termination. However, special rules now exist for taxing restrictive covenants.[46] Compensation paid for having resigned a position or as an inducement to resign—so-called golden handshakes—also are the subject of special rules.[47]

Payments by third parties: Where the payment is made not by the employer but by a third party, it may still be a taxable emolument. For it is not essential that the payment was for services rendered or to be rendered; the tax net falls once the payment is 'from employment'. The famous English goalkeeper, Peter Shilton, fell foul of this rule when he was transferred from Nottingham Forest to Southampton in 1982.[48] Southampton agreed to pay him a regular remuneration and also a £75,000 signing on fee, which manifestly was taxable. But Nottingham also agreed to pay him £80,000 for agreeing to transfer clubs. That too, it was held, was a taxable emolument. There was nothing in the statutory definition of that term to justify the inference that tax will only be imposed on 'an emolument provided by a person who has an interest in the performance by the employee of the services which he becomes bound to perform when he enters into the contract of employment'.[49]

Payments to third parties: A payment made directly to a third party may in the circumstances constitute a taxable emolument. This is where the employer discharges an obligation incurred by the employee. For instance, in *Glynn v. C.I.R.*[50] the taxpayer was employed as an executive director at a monthly remuneration but his contract provided that a stipulated sum would be paid by the employer towards the costs of his children's education. School fees were paid directly by the employer to the child's school. Those

46. Finance Act, 1967, s.525; see *Judge*, par. 8.208.   47. See infra p.348.
48. *Shilton v. Wilmhurst* [1991] 1 AC 684.   49. Id. at p.693.
50. [1990] 2 AC 298.

were held to be taxable because money paid at an employee's request is the equivalent of money paid directly to him.

In *Rendell v. Went*,[51] while driving a car on the company's business, the taxpayer struck and killed a pedestrian. He intended to obtain legal advice from the Automobile Association but, when his employers learned that he would be prosecuted for serious driving offences, they instructed their own solicitors to spare no expense in the employee's defence. Leading Counsel were hired for the purpose and secured the employee's acquittal. As in the Christmas presents case, it was not seriously contested that the payment made by the employers for the legal defence here was not a taxable benefit in kind. The main issue was how to value that benefit for tax purposes. It was argued that tax should be assessed only on the excess over the amount which the employee would have expended on his own defence; that the extra paid by the employers in the circumstances was primarily for their own benefit—to ensure that a valued employee would not be convicted and imprisoned. That contention was rejected because the entire amount was spent for the employee's advantage, to prevent his going to prison. Expenditure is 'not the less advantageous to an [employee] because it suits or advantages the company to make it'.[52] Payments by employers to a superannuation fund are ordinarily taxable income under this principle[53] but special tax rules have been adopted for pension schemes.[54]

Arrangements, however, can exist whereby members of an employee's family obtain some financial benefit from his employer but that benefit is not his taxable income. Thus in *Barclays Bank Ltd v. Naylor*,[55] a company had a scheme for providing scholarships to some of its employees' children. Under the scheme, payments would be made to cover the educational expenses of the children of I.C.I. employees who were based abroad. It was not a term of the employees' contracts that those payments would be made, although the employees confidently anticipated that their children would obtain the scholarships. On account of the manner in which the scholarships were paid, they were deemed not to be the employees' taxable income. For instead of I.C.I. directly paying all or part of the school bills, the scheme provided the children directly with income which would then be used by them for that purpose. Although the employees benefited to an extent from this arrangement, in order to be assessed for tax it must be shown that 'the very money which was paid into [the child's] account by the trustees become his father's income when the account was debited with the payment of the

51. [1964] 1 WLR 650.
53. *Bruce v Hatton* (1921) 8 TC 180.
54. Finance Act, 1972, s.16(5); see *Judge* part 16.1.

52. Id. at p.659.
55. [1961] 1 Ch.

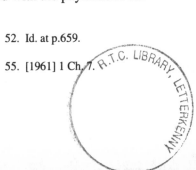

school bills for which his father had incurred a liability'.[56] In this case, the money was the child's and not the parent's income.[57]

Deductions from remuneration: It is not essential that the remuneration arising from the job be actually paid over to the employee; the earnings are taxable even though he has directed that part or all of them shall be retained by the employer. For instance, in *Mahon v. McLoughlin*,[58] under his contract an attendant at an asylum was obliged to pay 50p a week out of his salary towards his board and lodgings. It was held that the gross salary was taxable because that was the sum which accrued to him from his employment. It did not matter that he could not have been taxed on the value of board and lodgings, which would be provided free of charge. According to Rowlatt J,

> If a person is paid a wage with some advantage thrown in, you cannot add the advantage to the wage for the purpose of taxation unless that advantage can be turned into money. But when you have a person paid a wage with a necessity—the contractual necessity if you like—to expend that wage in a particular way, then he must pay tax upon the gross wage, and no question of alienability or inalienability arises.[59]

Similarly in *Dolan v. 'K'*,[60] a nun of the Order of St. Louis who was a qualified schoolteacher was employed in that capacity at a school run by her Order. Although she was paid a salary, in accordance with the Order's rules she handed it all over to the Order. It was held that her salary was still subject to income tax. But an employee is not liable for tax if he voluntarily renounced the emoluments before they were credited to him.

Payments for expenses: As is explained below,[61] only a very narrow category of expenses incurred in connection with a person's employment are deductible expenses for income tax purposes. Where the employee is reimbursed for a genuine expense incurred on his employer's behalf in the course of his work, generally that payment is not taxable. But payments in respect of expenses which are personal to the employee will be taxed. Perhaps the best example is the cost of travelling to or from work. Normally, that cost is not a deductible expense. Accordingly, in *Owen v. Pook*,[62] it was held that payments to an employee reimbursing him for the expense of travelling from one workplace to another was a taxable emolument. All payments to an employee arising out of his work are perquisites other than

---

56. Id. at p.21.   57. Similarly, *O Coindealbhain v. O'Carroll* [1989] IR 229.
58. (1926) 11 TC 83.
59. Id. at p.89. See too *Heaton v. Bell* [1969] 2 WLR 735.
60. [1944] IR 470.   61. Infra p.341 et seq.   62. [1970] AC 244.

refunding deductible expenses. Taxable remuneration cannot be placed outside the tax net by describing it as expenses.

Benefits in kind Income tax under Schedule E is charged on non-cash benefits provided to employees as well as on cash payments made, provided the benefit is something that is capable of being converted into money.

Value of benefits: Tax is chargeable on the 'full amount' of emoluments and the word amount 'denotes that in order to be taxable a perquisite must be either a cash or money payment or must be money's worth or of money value in the sense that it can be turned to pecuniary account.'[63] An example of the general principle is *Wilkins v. Rogerson*,[64] where the taxpayer's employer decided to make a Christmas present to all the male members of his staff of a new suit of clothes up to the value of £15. Arrangements were made with a well known firm of tailors to supply appropriate suits to all the employees who accepted this offer. The issue to be determined was not whether these suits were benefits in kind, for incontrovertibly they were. What was in dispute was the value of the benefits for tax purposes. It was held that their value was what they were worth to each employee, meaning the price an employee could fetch if he sold his new suit. The principle is that a benefit in kind 'should be assessed to income tax at its money value in the taxpayer's hands, that is to say, what he could get for it if he sold it as soon as he received it'.[65] Some of the leading cases on share options, before special rules were adopted for them, concern their proper valuation for these purposes.[66] There also are special rules for what are called preferential loans,[67] that is loans made directly or indirectly to an employee or his spouse at below-market interest rates in order to purchase a dwelling house to be occupied by the borrower.

Benefits not capable of being converted into money: Merely because a benefit is of some value to the recipient does not always render it taxable under schedule E, although there now are extensive statutory exceptions to this principle. This was decided in *Tennant v. Smith*,[68] where a bank manager resided free of charge in a house provided for him by the bank. He was required by the terms of his employment to live there. On the grounds that whatever benefit he may have derived from that arrangement could not be

63. *Heaton v. Bell* [1969] 2 WLR at p.754.
64. [1961] 1 Ch.133.   65. Id. at p.147.
66. E.g. *Abbott v. Philbin* [1961] AC 352. Special rules are now laid down in Finance Act, 1986, ss.9 and 10; see *Judge* par.10.108 and 10.112.
67. Finance 1982, s.8, as amended by Finance Act, 1989, s.6; see *Judge*, par.10.210.
68. [1892] AC 150.

converted by him into money, it was held that tax could not be assessed on it. The principle is that there is a 'limitation on the taxability of benefits in kind which are of a personal nature; it is not enough to say that they have a value to which there can be assigned a monetary equivalent'.[69] In any event, residing in the bank house was an obligation imposed on the employee there and might not even be regarded as a benefit to him, although the case was not decided on this point.[70] The free use of a car or of other property, which could not be assigned, would escape taxation on this basis, as would the provision of free meals and insurance cover. However, s.117 of the Finance Act, 1967, brings within the tax net many benefits that, under the above principle, would have escaped taxation.

Section 117 applies whenever

> a body corporate incurs expenses in or in connection with the pro-
> vision, . . . for any person employed by it . . . of living or other
> accommodation, of entertainment, of domestic or other services or of
> other benefits or facilities of whatsoever nature and, apart from this
> section, the expense would not be chargeable to income tax. . . .

In order to come within the tax net, the expense incurred by the employer does not have to derive from the employment as some form of remuneration for services. Once any expense as described here is incurred by the employer, liability to tax under s.117 is triggered. Once the employer incurs expense in providing living or other accommodation, entertainment etc. for an employee or a member of his family, that employee is treated as having received a benefit in kind, the value of which can be measured by criteria set out in s.118 of the 1967 Act.

An exception is made for meals provided in a canteen, once those meals are provided for the staff generally.[71] An exception is also made for living accommodation where, traditionally, an employee of that particular type was required to reside on premises provided by his employers.[72] The tax net was extended to benefits provided not by the employer but by a 'connected person', that is by some other person who is connected with the employer in the manner defined in s.117(8) of the 1967 Act.[73]

How benefits within s.117 are to be valued is as follows.[74] The gross amount of expense incurred by the employer (or connected person) or deemed to have been incurred in providing the benefit is ascertained. If the employee reimbursed any part of that expenditure, that sum is deducted from

69. *Heaton v. Bell* [1969] 2 WLR at p.754.
70. Compare *Heaton v. Bell* [1969] 2 WLR 735.
71. Income Tax Act, 1967, s.117(4).   72. Id. s.117(3).
73. Id. s.117(7)(8).   74. For a detailed account, see *Judge* para. 10.204 et seq.

the gross amount. The taxable benefit is the net expense after any deduction. There are special computation rules for where the benefit consists of a transfer of property or permitting an employee to make use of property, for instance living accommodation.[75] Regarding accommodation, the Revenue generally follow a rule of thumb, which has no statutory basis; they assume that the premises' annual value is 8% of its actual market value at the beginning of the tax year. All expenses incurred in connection with accommodation, like insurance, repairs and improvements are treated by s.118(4) as covered by the assumed market value rental of the premises. There also are special rules for where a motor car is made available for the employee's private use.[76] Of course, if the benefit in question is one which is capable of being converted into money, sections 117 and 118 do not apply to the situation; the ordinary approach to valuation applies instead.

ALLOWABLE EXPENSES

It is notorious that the kinds of expenses which are allowable against schedule E income are very limited; a considerably more extensive range of expenses can be deducted from schedule D income. Those expenses incurred by employees in connection with their work which can be deducted from their remuneration in order to determine their income tax liability are defined as follows:

> If the holder of an office or employment of profit is necessarily obliged to incur and defray out of the emoluments thereof the expenses of travelling in the performance of the duties of the office or employment, or of keeping or maintaining a horse to enable him to perform the same, or otherwise to expend money wholly, exclusively, and necessarily in the performance of the said duties, there may be deducted from the emoluments to be assessed the expenses so necessarily incurred and defrayed.[77]

Accordingly, for an employee to be able to deduct a work-related expense from his tax bill, the expense must have been incurred 'wholly, exclusively and necessarily in the performance of [his] duties.' But all business entertainment expenses, even when they come within this demanding requirement, are not deductible.[78]

75. Income Tax Act, 1967, s.118(2) and (3) and *Judge* para. 10.205.
76. Finance Act, 1982, s.4 and *Judge* para. 10.207-209.
77. Income Tax Act, 1967, schedule II, reg.3.
78. Finance Act, 1982, s.20; see *Judge* para. 10.303.

Necessarily and exclusively incurred In order for an expense incurred to be deductible, it must have been impossible to hold the job in question without making that expenditure; in incurring those expenses there must have been nothing optional on the part of the employee. The leading case on employees' expenses is *Ricketts v. Colquhoun*,[79] which concerned a London-based barrister who also held the part-time office of Recorder of Portsmouth. He would travel regularly from London to Portsmouth in order to perform his duties there. He then sought to have deducted the travelling expenses from his remuneration. Had he travelled in the course of work as a barrister, those expenses would be allowable from his self-employed remuneration. But they were not allowable from his Schedule E earnings as a Recorder. They were incurred, not in performing the tasks of that office, but only in order to get to and from the workplace. Had the taxpayer chosen to live in Portsmouth, those expenses would never have arisen. It would be different if travelling to there from London was an intrinsic requirement of the job, as with commercial travellers.

The classic exposition of the rule is Lord Blanesburgh's:

> Undoubtedly its most striking characteristic is its jealously restricted phraseology, some of it repeated to heighten the effect. . . . [T]he language of the rule points to the expenses with which it is concerned being only those which each and every occupant of the particular office is necessarily obliged to incur in the performance of its duties—to expenses imposed on each holder *ex necessitate* of his office and to such expenses only.[80]

Very few of the reported cases have been decided in favour of employed tax payers on this point. The commonest kinds of allowable expenditure are for special clothing and tools which are needed to do the work in question. The Revenue have agreed to appropriate rates for many kinds of occupation which require such expenditure.

In *O'Broin v. McGiolla Merdhre*,[81] the taxpayer was the County Engineer for Clare County Council. He claimed deductions from his salary in respect of subscriptions to professional associations, renewals of books and journals and expenses of a telephone at his home. These expenses were disallowed because they were not absolutely necessary for him to do his job, nor were they incurred exclusively for that purpose.[82] In *Kelly v. Quinn*,[83]

79. [1926] AC 1.   80. Id. at p.7.   81. [1959] IR 98.
82. Similarly, *Owen v. Burden* [1971] 1 All ER 356 and *Simpson v. Tate* [1925] 2 KB 214. Contrast *Smith v. Abbott* [1992] 1 WLR 201 (newspapers and periodicals purchased by juornalists).
83. [1964] IR 488.

the taxpayer was an army officer who was transferred to Athlone, leaving his family home in Dublin. Under army custom, a 'batman' was assigned to him, whose main duties were to maintain the officer's uniform, keep his quarters clean and tidy and make sure that he would be fit for parade at all times. The batman was appointed and paid by the army but, by a long standing custom, the officer paid him a £1 per week. It was held that this sum was not an allowable expense. According to Kenny J,

> [T]he gratuities were not paid in the performance of his duties; they were . . . paid for the purpose of making it possible for him to perform his duties. . . . [I]n addition, . . . the gratuities were not monies expended necessarily in the performance of the taxpayer's duties because . . . he could have performed his duties without the assistance of a batman.[84]

Even if a particular kind of expenditure is required by the employment contract's very terms, that does not always render it an allowable expense. For it must have been incurred in the actual performance of the employee's duties. Thus, generally, living expenses are not deductible, even if the employee is required to live in a designated place, because he has to live somewhere. By concession the Revenue may allow the costs of living away from home provided the employee has a permanent residence. Other examples of what is not deductible include expenses incurred in obtaining a job or in becoming qualified for a job. In *Lupton v. Potts*,[85] a solicitor's clerk claimed an allowance for what he had to pay to sit and pass the Law Society's examination, as required by the terms of his articles. These were held not to be allowable expenses, for his duties as an articled clerk were quite capable of being performed without incurring that outlay. The test is 'not whether the employer imposes the expense but whether the duties do, in the sense that, irrespective of what the employer may prescribe, the duties cannot be performed without the particular outlay'.[86] Similarly, the expenses incurred by a bank manager in joining several social clubs, on his employer's instructions in order to foster business contacts, were held not to be allowable.[87] Membership of those clubs was not absolutely essential in order to perform his duties as a bank manager. Exceptional circumstances can arise, however, where passing a particular examination or membership of a particular club is indeed necessary to do a job properly.[88]

Travel expenses As the Portsmouth Recorder's case[89] illustrates, ordin-

84. Id. at p.495.   85. [1969] 1 WLR 1749.
86. Id. at p.1754.   87. *Brown v. Bullock* [1961] 1 WLR 1095.
88. E.g. *Elwood v. Utitz* [1960] NI 93.
89. *Ricketts v. Colquhoun* [1926] AC 1; see ante p.342.

arily expenses incurred in going to and from work are not deductible expenses. Similarly, in *Phillips v. Keane*,[90] where a schoolteacher acquired a pony and trap to travel five miles to school because he could not find suitable accommodation where the school was located, it was held that none of those expenses were deductible.

But where actually doing the job for which the person is employed requires travel, then expenses necessarily incurred in travelling are deductible, because they are exclusively and also necessarily incurred in the performance of the duties.[91] An example is *Marsden v. I.R.C.*,[92] which concerned an investigator in the audit department of the Revenue, whose job involved travelling throughout Lancashire. It was accepted that costs necessarily incurred by him in the course of his travel were deductible. He used a car for travelling and the issue to be determined was whether the full costs of travelling by car were deductible. On the grounds that it was not a condition of employment that he should have a car and also because no evidence was given to show that he could not have used public transport, it was held that only a part of the car costs incurred were deductible. That part was in fact met by a car allowance paid by his employers.

Where an employee has two entirely separate workplaces, the cost of travel between them may in special circumstances be deductible. This principle is illustrated by *Owen v. Pook*,[93] which concerned a medical practitioner, whose practice was in one town where he lived but who also held part-time appointments in a hospital 15 miles form there. From the evidence, it was quite clear that his duties usually began once he was called from his practice and set out for the hospital. On receiving a call, he frequently would telephone ahead instructions to the hospital staff and advise treatment. If car phones existed at the time, presumably he would have continued obtaining information and giving instructions in the course of the journey. For those reasons it was held that his travelling costs were necessarily incurred in the performance of his duties. Those expenses arose from the nature of his job and not merely from the fact that he choose to live 15 miles from the hospital. As Lord Wilberforce explained, 'the hospital management committee required the services of doctors on a part-time basis for emergencies; [they] would have to appoint a doctor with a practice of his own and also with suitable . . . experience: he might live and practice within 15 miles or one mile or 100 yards from the hospital: the choice in the matter, if any exists, does not lie with the doctor, who is there in his practice, but with the committee which decides, however near or far he works, to

---

90. [1925] IR 48.
92. [1965] 1 WLR 734.

91. E.g. *Jardine v. Gillespie* (1906) 6 TC 263.
93. [1970] AC 244.

appoint him and to require him to discharge a part of his duty at his practice premises.'[94]

Where employees are paid a travelling allowance by their employer, that is often a taxable emolument, especially when the sum is intended to defray expenses in travelling to and from work. However, where travelling costs are a deductible expense, as explained above, the employer's allowance is simply a reimbursement of those expenses. For instance, in *Owen v. Pook*,[95] where the doctor was paid a mileage allowance for travelling to the hospital when called out, those sums were held to be reimbursements of expenses. The travel allowance may be very generous, in which case the excess over the actual costs of travelling will be taxed as an emolument. Thus, where the allowance paid to a county council rent officer included the cost of putting the car on the road and maintaining it for the owner's use, that part of it was held not to be deductible.[96]

TERMINATION PAYMENTS

At times when persons' jobs come to an end special payments are made to them in addition to their ordinary remuneration. At the 'blue collar' level, these payments would often be described as compensation for redundancy; at the executive level, they may be described as golden handshakes. The reason for making special payments in these circumstances can vary considerably; it may be to induce the employee to leave his job or as a special reward for the work he had done for the employer, or it may simply be to compensate him for his reduced earnings when he leaves the job. How the special payments are made also varies; they may be a single big sum or may comprise several payments. Occasionally, instead of the job ending entirely, its terms and conditions may have been altered radically and the special payment is made in respect of the change of terms. Where the payment can be characterised as an emolument, it is taxable in the ordinary way. Where it is not an emolument, it may still fall within the special rules in ss.114-115 of the Income Tax Act, 1967, for golden handshakes.[97] Any compensation paid under the Redundancy Payments Acts is deemed not to be a taxable emolument.[98]

---

94. Id. at p.263. Similarly, *Taylor v. Provan* [1975] AC 194.
95. [1970] AC 244.   96. *Perrons v. Spackman* [1981] 1 WLR 1411.
97. See generally, *Judge* part 10.4 and Corrigan, 'Taxation on Termination of Employment' [1983] *J.I.S.L.L.* 37 and Kerridge 'Dismissing Employees—Golden Handshakes and the Gourley Confusion' [1982] *Brit. Tax Rev.* 87.
98. Finance Act, 1968, s.37(2).

Taxable emoluments Where the making of a special termination payment is provided for in the employment contract, then that sum is taxable remuneration regardless of how it may have been described by the parties. For clearly the sum is part of the payment being made for the services rendered. Even where payment of the special sum is not provided for in the original contract, the circumstances may indicate that it is an emolument of the job. There is always a strong presumption that payments made by an employer to an employee in connection with his job is indeed a taxable emolument.

Personal gifts: Exceptionally the payment may be a pure gift to the employee in recognition of his past services rather than in payment for them. Where the payment is made to a number of employees, the burden of demonstrating that it is in the nature of a gift is particularly difficult. In *Mulvey v. Coffey*,[99] where a lump sum was paid to the President of University College Dublin on his retirement from that office, it was held that the payment was not taxable. The taxpayer had held that office for more than thirty years and, when he was retiring, the Governing Body of the College resolved to pay him £1,000 'on account of a great number of services unrewarded, as expressed in a labour of lengthened overtime work' during many years. It was held that there was evidence on which the Special Commissioners could have concluded that this sum was not an emolument.[100]

Compensation for loss of rights: Exceptionally, the payment may be by way of compensation for the loss of some rights occurring when the job came to an end or its nature was drastically changed. It is often very difficult to determine the character of a payment to a holder of an office when his tenure of the office is determined or the terms on which he holds it were altered, and in each case the question is whether, on the facts of the case, the lump sum paid is in the nature of remuneration or profits in respect of the office or is in the nature of a sum paid in consideration of the surrender by the recipient of his rights in respect of the office. Thus, damages paid for wrongful dismissal were held in *Glover v. B.L.N. Ltd (No. 2)*[1] not to be emoluments. According to Kenny J, in such an action, 'the damages are not an award of the remuneration which would have been earned: they are intended to compensate the plaintiff because he has not been allowed to earn it.'[2] In *Henley v. Murray*,[3] the managing director of a company was asked

99. [1942] IR 277.
100. Followed in *McGarry v. R.* [1954] IR 64.
  1. [1973] IR 432.   2. Id. at p.438.   3. [1950] 1 All ER 908.

to resign and was then paid a sum described as 'compensation for loss of office.' This was held not to be a taxable emolument because it was not a payment to him under his contract but instead compensation for abrogating that contract. Here the 'contract itself goes altogether and some sum becomes payable for the consideration of the total abandonment of all the contractual rights which the other party had under the contract'.[4] A feature of this case is that the lump sum paid was the equivalent of what he would have earned had he worked out his normal notice period, but that was immaterial to the outcome. For the same reason, a payment made in settlement of a dispute about the lawfulness of a dismissal is not an emolument.[5] A payment made by an employer to his employee in the course of his employment in commutation of his pension rights is not an emolument.[6] Statutory redundancy payments are designated as tax free.[7]

A case which has caused some difficulty is *Hunter v. Dewhurst*,[8] involving the chairman of a company, the articles of association of which provided that its directors should be paid 'compensation for loss of office' on their retiring after serving for at least five years. If the taxpayer simply retired and was then paid the compensation, that would have been taxable.[9] Instead, he had intended retiring but was persuaded to stay on. Again, if he was only paid an inducement to remain on with the company, that sum would have been taxable.[10] But the arrangement made here was that his work load would be lightened and his fees correspondingly reduced; he would also forego all claims to 'compensation' under the terms of the articles of association, in return for which he was paid a substantial lump sum. By a bare majority, it was held that this sum was not an emolument. It was not received under the employment contract itself but was paid to obtain a release from a contingent liability under that contract.

Golden handshakes The expression golden handshake commonly refers to many types of payments made when a person's job has come to an end; such payments are often made to company directors. As was demonstrated in *Mulvey v. Coffey*,[11] occasionally these payments are not taxable as emoluments of the office. However, the tax net was extended by ss. 114-115 of the Income Tax Act, 1967, to catch most kinds of termination payments; at the same time, the actual tax liabilities can be reduced by spreading out those payments over a period of years. These rules do not apply to the following kinds of payments. One is where the office or employment came

4. Id. at p.909.
5. *Du Cross v. Ryall* (1935) 19 TC 444.
6. *Tilley v. Wales* [1943] AC 386.
7. Finance Act, 1968, s.37(2).
8. (1932) 16 T.C. 605.
9. *Henry v. Foster* (1931) 16 TC 605.
10. *Cameron v. Prendergast* [1940] AC 549.
11. [1942] IR 277.

to an end by virtue of the holder's death, injury or disability. Payments from specified pension schemes are exempted, as are payments where the job involved a proportion of foreign service. Special provisions exist for payments made for restrictive covenants.

Subject to these exceptions, the payments which are rendered taxable by ss. 114-115 are

> any payment (not otherwise chargeable to income tax) which is made, whether in pursuance of any legal obligation or not, either directly or indirectly in consideration or in consequence of, or otherwise in connection with, the termination of the holding of the office or employment or any change in its functions or emoluments, including any payment in commutation of annual or periodic payments (whether chargeable to tax or not) which would otherwise have been made as aforesaid.[12]

The kind of payments which are caught by this section include personal gifts or testimonials received when leaving a job; compensation paid when being dismissed from a job or where the job was otherwise terminated; salary in lieu of notice and damages for breach of the employment contract; redundancy payments (in excess of the statutory ceiling); a lump sum commuting pension rights. It does not matter if the payment is voluntary or is by legal obligation, or was made directly or indirectly; that it was paid to or to the order of the employee's spouse, relative or dependent;[13] that the consideration was in kind and not in cash. The reference to a payment connected with a 'change of functions or emoluments' covers situations like in *Hunter v. Dewhurst*,[14] where there was not a complete termination of the employment. But it is doubtful if payments like those made in *Hochstrasser v. Mayes*,[15] to cover losses on the disposal of a house when changing job location, is really in connection with a change of function. It would seem that inducement payments which are not emoluments, like the payment to the amateur rugby footballer for becoming a professional,[16] are not connected with a change of function. There are no reported authorities so far on the meaning of this expression.

The amount of tax which is payable in respect of payments that fall within ss. 114-115 is significantly less than what would be paid if they were emoluments. Although they are deemed to be emoluments, the first £6,000 (sometimes less or more) is tax free and what is called 'top slicing relief'

12. Income Tax Act, 1967, s.114(2).
13. Id. s.114(3).   14. (1932) 16 TC 605.
15. [1960] AC 376.
16. *Jarrold v. Boustead* [1964] 1 WLR 1357.

enables the payments to be spread over several years and in effect taxed at the average rate of tax paid over that period. There are two related kinds of relief to this end, contained in the 3rd schedule to the Income Tax Act, as amended in 1980 and again in 1990. Paragraph 6 of that schedule provides a relief by way of reduction of the sums chargeable and paragraph 8 a relief by way of reduction of tax.[17]

P.A.Y.E.

For over thirty years, employees and pensioners have had a system of withholding income tax at source. What is known as 'pay as you earn', or P.A.Y.E. for short, was first introduced in the Finance Act, 1959, and detailed rules regarding its operation were prescribed in the Income Tax (Employments) Regulations, 1960. At present the basis for P.A.Y.E. is ss. 124-133 of the Income Tax Act, 1967, where the basic rule is laid down in s.126 as follows:

> On the making of any payment of any emoluments . . . , income tax shall . . . be deducted or repaid by the person making the payment. ...

And the term emoluments, which are made subject to P.A.Y.E., is defined in s.124 as

> anything assessable to income tax under Schedule E and references to payments of emoluments include references to payments on account of emoluments.

The remaining sections in the Income Tax Act on this question deal principally with making regulations in order to implement s.126 and related administrative matters, such as interest due, payment by way of stamps, recovery of sums deducted and priority in bankruptcy. How the system is administered is still governed mainly by the Regulations of 1960, which have been amended on several occasions.

P.A.Y.E. was adopted in order to relieve employees of the difficulty of having to pay all of their income tax at once at the end of the tax year. Unless they saved up to make this payment or could borrow for that purpose, it often was extremely difficult to raise the necessary money. What P.A.Y.E. does is to spread the tax payment across the entire year, so that all or almost all tax due will have been paid over by the time the fiscal year comes to an end. Every time an employee is paid remuneration in cash, a sum is deducted

---

17. For a full account of these reliefs, see *Judge* ch.10.4.

on account in respect of his prospective income tax liability. A commentator has described the system as 'combin[ing] the expedient with the objectionable. It is a rough and ready system which garnishes taxpayers' incomes, sometimes for debts they do not owe but subject in this event to refund. . . . It is surprising that this withholding system, to which so strong objections may be raised on grounds of principle, has aroused so little comment. It has probably done more to increase the tax collecting power of central government than any other one tax measure in any time in history.'[18]

The rules for collection are designed to ensure, so far as is reasonably possible, that the aggregate of deductions made during the year will approximate to the tax payable on the employee's schedule E income. This is done through a method of tax free allowances, which spreads each employee's personal allowances and other deductions evenly through the year and by a set of P.A.Y.E. tax tables under which tax is deducted from the net taxable pay at a rate or rates estimated according to the employee's expected income for the year.

Income subject to P.A.Y.E. Anything which is assessable to income tax under schedule E is an emolument for these purposes, including payments on account. Accordingly, all 'salaries, fees, wages, perquisites or profits or gains . . . arising from . . . employment', including pensions,[19] in principle are subject to P.A.Y.E. Foreign-source income which does not come within schedule E falls outside P.A.Y.E., although Irish residents in receipt of foreign earnings may choose to have their income tax dealt with under the P.A.Y.E. system. Although benefits in kind often are taxable emoluments, P.A.Y.E. is not directly deducted in respect of those benefits because they are not payments.

Impracticable to apply P.A.Y.E. Where an employer or employee can convince the Revenue that the deduction of income tax in their case under P.A.Y.E. is 'impracticable', they can be exonerated from the system. But this exemption only applies where the Revenue have notified the employer of the exemption. Exemptions of this kind are rarely given by the Revenue; one situation where an employer could be exempted is where he is a foreign resident and is paying remuneration outside the State.

Operating the system How the P.A.Y.E. system operates can be summarised as follows.[20]

18. McGregor, 4 *Canadian Tax Journal* (1956), at p.173.
19. Income Tax Act, 1967, s.111(4).
20. For a fuller account, see *Judge* ch.11.1.

Registration by employers: Every employer who makes any payments of emoluments to any employee is required to register as an employer. He is thereafter required to implement the P.A.Y.E. procedure in respect of all emoluments paid by him and to account monthly to the Collector General for all tax deducted from employees. An employer who fails to deduct any tax which should have been deducted from any payments of emoluments may be held directly liable for that tax, but there are some relieving provisions in certain cases. The employer is also required to make returns of employees and tax deducted at the end of each tax year.

Certificates of tax free allowances: Every employee should obtain a certificate of the tax free allowances which are deducted throughout each tax year from the emoluments paid to him to arrive at his net taxable pay for each pay period on which the income tax deductible (or repayable) by his employer is calculated. The certificate of tax free allowances also specifies which P.A.Y.E. tax table is to be applied. The total tax free allowances for any year are estimated as the total personal allowances and other reliefs due to the employee, but may be reduced by any of these allowances applicable to other employments or required to offset benefits in kind (see below) and sometimes other income.

The P.A.Y.E. tables: These are tax tables designed to spread each employee's tax payable each year as equally as possible over the year and to collect the tax on his emoluments at the rate expected to be payable by him as estimated by reference to his probable taxable income from all sources. The tax table selected, as considered appropriate to the individual's circumstances, applies one main rate for the year on the emoluments paid up to the expected net taxable pay for the year, but with provision for the application of higher rates if the cumulative net taxable earnings should exceed the estimated amount used at the beginning of the year in determining the relevant tax table. The main tax rate is linked to the individual's expected highest rate for the year. A separate tax table allowance is included in the tax free allowances to adjust for the non-application of tax rate bands below the main tax rate used.

Taxable pay: The employer deducts income tax computed at the appropriate P.A.Y.E. tax table rate as applied to each employee's cumulative taxable pay at the time of each payment of emoluments. 'Taxable pay' is 'gross pay' less the employee's contributions (if any) to an exempt approved pension scheme or to a statutory scheme and his tax free allowances. 'Gross pay' is, in effect, all payments of emoluments subject to P.A.Y.E. before any deductions for P.R.S.I. contributions, pensions scheme contributions etc.

Benefits in kind, expenses payments etc.: Section 126 of the 1967 Act and the Regulations provide for the deduction of P.A.Y.E. on the 'payment' of emoluments. A benefit in kind (including the amount taxable in respect of an employer's provided car or an employer-preferential loan) is not regarded as a payment for this purpose. Consequently, the amount taxable in respect of any such benefit is not included in 'gross pay' or 'taxable pay' and tax is not, therefore, deducted directly on such benefits in kind. However, the inspector of taxes seeks where possible to bring such benefits indirectly within the P.A.Y.E. system by deducting them from the individual's tax free allowances. If he does not deal with them in this way, he is able to make direct assessments under schedule E on the benefits in kind.

By contrast, if payments in respect of expenses taxable under s.116 of the 1967 Act are made in the form of a round sum allowance, that is a payment of emoluments to the employee and should be included in gross and taxable pay. Payments by the employer to the employee as a direct reimbursement of actual expenses incurred wholly, exclusively and necessarily by the employee in performing the duties of his employment are not in practice, normally included in taxable pay subject to P.A.Y.E.

Deduction and repayment of tax: The employer normally uses a tax deduction card supplied by the inspector for each employee for calculating the P.A.Y.E. deduction (or repayment) for each pay period throughout the year. This card provides for the calculation of cumulative taxable pay (cumulative pay less cumulative tax free allowances) for each period. The application of the relevant tax table rate to the cumulative taxable pay produces the cumulative tax payable at the end of the period. The tax actually deductible by the employer for a given pay period (e.g. month ending 5 August) is the excess of the cumulative tax payable at the end of that period over the corresponding figure of cumulative tax payable at the end of the previous period (e.g. month ending 5 July). If the cumulative tax payable at the end of the previous period should exceed the cumulative tax payable at the end of the current period, the employer should repay the excess to the employee on paying his emoluments for the current period.

Year end adjustments: After the end of each tax year, the employee's position should be reviewed by reference to his total earnings (and any other income) as chargeable to tax for the year and, of course, he should be given full allowance for his final personal allowances and reliefs. If the total income tax deducted (less any repayments) under the P.A.Y.E. system during the year results in an excess of total income tax payable (and paid) by him over his final income tax liability for the year, the employee is entitled to be repaid the excess by the Collector General. If the total income tax paid under P.A.Y.E. (and in any other way) is less than the final income tax payable, the inspector may assess the tax underpaid directly on the employee. Alternatively, the inspector may recover any underpayment by reducing the employee's tax free allowances for one or more of the following tax years.

Emergency card procedure: There is provision for the employer to deduct income tax through the emergency card procedure in any case where he has not received from the employee the necessary certificate of tax free allowances or, alternatively, an employment cessation certificate on form P45 from a previous employer. In that this emergency card procedure only gives the employee minimum tax free allowances for the first four weeks of a new employment (and no allowances thereafter until the necessary certificate is received), it is very important for all employees to ensure that they comply with the necessary formalities so that they can obtain their proper allowances as soon as possible. When the proper certificate is obtained, the employee is entitled to be repaid any excess tax suffered through the emergency procedure.

P.R.S.I. CONTRIBUTIONS AND LEVIES

The State social security system provides a variety of benefits for persons who are suffering financial distress in several ways, for instance, occupational injury benefit for those who were injured at work, disablement benefit for those who otherwise suffer from a disability, unemployment benefit, maternity allowance, pensions. The main benefits are contributory, in the sense that claimants for those benefits must have paid a specified number of contributions into the Social Welfare Fund.[21] Other benefits are non-contributory. Most modern social security systems are based on a contribution principle, which renders them a form of social insurance. In return for making a certain number of contributions to a fund, employees are insured against several kinds of social risk, like injury at work, disability, unemployment etc. Additionally, being a contributory to the social welfare system is one of the conditions of obtaining the lump sum redundancy

---

21. Social Welfare (Consolidation) Act, 1981, ss.9-17.

payment[22] and the payments made by the Minister for Labour when a person's employer becomes insolvent.[23]

Many social welfare benefits are financed partly by contributions made by the employees affected, partly by their employers' contributions and any deficit in the fund is subvented by the State. Rebates paid to employers who have made redundancy payments are also financed in this way, as are the payments made to those whose employer became insolvent. Prior to 1990 there were four separate funds which financed payments to employees or their dependents—the Redundancy Fund, the Employers' Insolvency Fund, the Occupational Injuries Fund and the Social Insurance Fund. These have now been amalgamated into a single Social Insurance Fund.[24] On top of the social insurance contributions, employers must also pay a 1.25 per cent health contribution and a 1 per cent training levy to the Fund. Between 1983 and 1986, the Finance Acts imposed a 1 per cent income levy on all earnings but that exaction no longer applies.

Insured employees' earnings Employers and employees social insurance contributions are based on each employee's earnings. The employee in question must be in insured employment, be over 16 years of age and under 66 years of age.[25] Subject to conditions, persons outside this category may make voluntary contributions to the Fund.[26] Those persons who are in insured employment are set out in Part I of the first schedule to the Social Welfare (Consolidation) Act, 1981, being principally, all persons employed in the State under a contract of employment, out-workers, midwives, certain ministers of religion, managers of an employment office, share fishermen and practically everyone working in the public service. However, the Minister is empowered by regulation to exclude most of these groups from the insured employment category.[27] Workers who are not deemed to be in insured employment for these purposes are listed in Part II of that schedule. Special provision is made for where the employment in question possesses a substantial foreign element.[28] Health contributions and the employment levy are not confined to persons in insured employment or under 66 years of age.[29]

Social insurance contributions are calculated by reference to what are called 'reckonable earnings'. Those are taxable earnings derived from

22. Redundancy Payments Act, 1967, s.4, as amended.
23. Protection of Employees (Employer's Insolvency) Act, 1984, s.3.
24. Social Welfare Act, 1990, ss.23 and 24 and Social Welfare Act, 1991, ss.39 and 40.
25. Social Welfare (Consolidation) Act, 1981, s.5(1).
26. Id. s.11.   27. Id. s.7.
28. Id.s.8. Also, E.C. Regulation no.1408/71, O.J. No. L 149/2 (1971).
29. See *Judge* para. 3.604.

insurable employment; accordingly, the basis for the exactions are the earnings which are subject to P.A.Y.E. The full definition of the term is:

> emoluments derived from insurable employment or insurable (occupational injuries) employment to which [the Social Welfare (Consolidation) Act, 1981, applies] (other than non-pecuniary emoluments) reduced by so much of the allowable contribution referred to in regulations 59 and 60 of the Income Tax (Employment) Regulations, 1960 . . . as is deducted on payment of those emoluments.[30]

Reckonable earnings, as here defined, are the main basis for health contributions and for the employment levy but these imposts also apply to what are called 'reckonable emoluments'. Reckonable emoluments effectively are all non-pecuniary Schedule E emoluments which are not reckonable earnings.[31]

Operating the system How P.S.R.I. contributions and the employment levy operate can be summarised as follows.[32] The main legislative provisions are ss.9-16 of the Social Welfare (Consolidation) Act, 1981 (social welfare contributions), ss.4-11 of the Health Contributions Act, 1979 (health contributions), ss.15-22 of the Youth Employment Agency Act, 1981 (employment and training levy). The principal regulations are the Social Welfare (Collection of Employment Contributions by the Collector General) Regulations, 1979,[33] the Health Contributions Regulations, 1979,[34] and the Youth Employment Levy Regulations, 1982.[35]

Accounting by employers: Every employer who makes payments which are charged to tax under Schedule E is required to pay over P.R.S.I. contributions when he is remitting to the Collector General tax deducted under P.A.Y.E. Employers' contributions and employees' contributions must be paid over at that time. Failure to make these payments is an offence and the amount due may be recovered in civil proceedings brought by the Minister for Social Welfare. There are similar provisions for the health contributions and the levy.

Employees' P.R.S.I. contributions: Contributions are levied on all employees who have reckonable earnings.[36] Ordinarily those are deducted

---

30. Social Welfare (Collection of Employment Constributions by the Collector General) Regulations, 1979, reg.4.
31. See *Judge* para. 3.604.
32. For a fuller account, see *Judge* ch.11.3.
33. SI No. 77 of 1979.
34. SI No. 107 of 1979.
35. SI No. 84 of 1979.
36. Social Welfare (Consolidation) Act, 1981, s.10.

from the remuneration and paid over by the employer at the prescribed intervals. In January 1992 the amount of this contribution was 5.5 per cent of the reckonable earnings, up to a maximum of £18,000 per annum. In addition, the employee must pay a 1.25 per cent health contribution, up to the same ceiling on earnings, and also a 1 per cent employment and training levy.

Employers' P.R.S.I. contributions: Employers with employees in insurable employment must pay contributions in respect of each of those employees.[37] Those must be paid from the employer's own resources; it is an offence to deduct the sum from his employees' earnings.[38] In January 1992 the amount payable was 12.2 per cent of reckonable earnings, up to a maximum income of £19,300 per annum.

Health contributions: Originally fixed at 1 per cent, since 1987 the health con- tribution payable in respect of employees is 1.25 per cent of their reckonable income, regardless of how much they are earning. For the purpose of their collection and recovery, the sum due is deemed to be an employment contribution to be deducted from earnings.[39]

Employment and training levy: The employment and training levy has always been 1 per cent of employees' reckonable income, regardless of how much they are earning. It too is deemed to be an employment contribution for the purpose of collection and recovery.[40]

37. Ibid.   38. Id. s.115(2)(b).
39. Health Contributions Act, 1979, s.5.
40. Youth Employment Agency Act, 1981, s.16.

APPENDIX

Standard Terms and Conditions of Employment

1 Name

_____

2 Commencement of employment

2.1 Your employment began on _____.

[2.2 Your employment with any previous employer does not count as part of your period of continuous employment.]

[2.2 Your employment with _____ from _____ will be treated as continuous with your employment by the Company.]

[2.2 Your employment with:

(1) from _____ to _____ , and
(2) from _____ to _____ , and
(3) from _____ to _____ , and

will be treated as continuous with your employment by the Company.]

3 Job title

3.1 Your job title is _____ .

[3.2 Your normal duties are as detailed in the job description [attached] [to be provided to you by the Personnel Department].]

3.3 In addition to your normal duties, you may be required to undertake other duties from time to time.

3.4 Until otherwise notified by the Company you are required to report to _____

4 Probationary period

4.1 The first _____ weeks of your employment will be probationary.

4.2 Your employment may be terminated on one week's notice given in writing by the Company at any time during or at the end of this period.

4.3 Your continued employment will be reviewed at the end of your probationary period [and if your continued employment is confirmed your [salary] [wages] may be increased from that date].

5 Salary/wages

5.1 Your [basic] [salary] [wages] at the commencement of your employment will be _____ per [annum] [week] [hour].

5.2 Your [salary] [wages] will be paid [monthly] [weekly] [in arrears] [_____ week[s] in advance and _____ week[s] in arrears] [by credit transfer] [unless an alternative method of payment has been agreed] [by cheque] [by cash] on the _____ day of each [month] [week] [four week payment period].

5.3 Your [salary] [wages] will be reviewed [annually] [with effect from _____ in each year.]

5.4 You will be notified in writing of any change to your [salary] [wages].

6 Bonus payments

[6.1 You will participate in the [_____] bonus scheme, full details of which are available on request from the Personnel Department. The Company reserves the right in its absolute discretion to terminate or amend [any] [the] bonus scheme without notice at any time or to exclude you from participation in [any] [the] bonus scheme without giving any reason.

[6.1 [Profit-sharing] [Personal Performance Related] bonus payments may be made from time to time at the Company's absolute discretion.]

6.2 Bonus payments will normally be paid in _____ in each year.

7 Commission

7.1 You [may] [will] be entitled to commission [according to] [calculated by reference to] _____.

7.2 Commission payments will be paid by [credit transfer] [cheque] [cash] [on the _____ day of each [month] [day] [in each _____ year] in respect of the period _____.

7.3 The Company reserves the right in its absolute discretion to terminate or amend the commission arrangements applicable to you without notice at any time or to exclude you from participation in any commission arrangements without giving any reason.

[8 Deductions

8.1 The Company has the right to deduct from your pay, any sums which you may owe the Company, including, without limitation, any overpayments or loans made to you by the Company, or losses suffered by the Company as a result of your negligence or breach of Company rules.

[9 Normal hours of work

9.1 You are normally required to work _____ hours per week, but the Company has the right to require you to remain away from work on full pay for such period and on such conditions as the Company may specify.

9.2 Your normal hours of work are _____ am to _____ pm [Monday to Friday] with a break of _____ for lunch [which must be taken between _____ [am] [pm] and _____ pm] and breaks of _____ for tea which must be taken between _____ am and _____ am and _____ pm and _____ pm respectively.

[9.3 You are also required to work such additional hours as may be necessary for the proper performance of your duties. There will be no additional payment for hours worked in excess of your normal hours of work [but you may, with the prior written consent of [the Company] [your Manager] be permitted to take time off in lieu of such excess hours worked provided you comply with such conditions as [may be imposed by the Company] [he may impose]].]

[9 Flexitime scheme

9.1 The Company currently operates a flexitime scheme ('the Scheme') which will apply to you until further notice.

9.2 The rules of the Scheme are as follows:

9.2.1　Your normal days of work are [Monday to Friday] inclusive.

9.2.2　You are required to work a minimum of _____ hours in any one flexitime period (as defined in clause 9.2.3 below) unless you are a part-time employee, in which case you will be notified separately of the hours applicable to you. All hours worked in excess of your minimum hours of work in any one flexitime period will be credited to you as 'excess hours worked'.

9.2.3　A flexitime period is a period of _____ weeks. The date of commencement of each flexitime period will be notified to you by the Company, either individually or by way of a general notice.

9.2.4 On the commencement of your employment you are required to work a minimum of seven hours in respect of each day remaining in the then current flexitime period. You will be credited with seven hours for each day before the commencement of your employment in the then current flexitime period. Thereafter you will be required to work the hours specified in clause 9.2.2 above.

9.2.5 On the days on which you are required to attend for work, you must be present at work during the Company's flexitime core time. The Company's flexitime core time is from _____ am to _____ .

9.2.6 You may commence work at any time between _____ am to _____ am and may finish work at any time between _____ pm and _____ pm subject always to the needs of the business. You will not be credited for hours worked before _____ am and after _____ pm except with the prior written consent of [your Manager] [the Company].

9.2.7 Lunch must be taken between _____ and _____ pm and these hours may not be varied except with the prior written consent of [your Manager] [the Company].

9.2.8 Provided that you are credited with a total of not less than _____ hours in respect of any one flexitime period (or such other minimum number of hours as may have been notified to you if you are a part-time employee) you may [with the prior consent of [your Manager] [the Company] take up to a maximum of two half days or one whole day off work in any one flexitime period (subject always to the needs of the business) provided that you have sufficient excess hours already credited to you to cover such absence.

9.2.9 The maximum credited time which may be carried forward to the following flexitime period is _____ hours.

9.2.10 You will be credited with _____ hours for each day of your basic Company holiday entitlement, each public holiday and each day of certified sickness absence.

9.3 The procedure for recording flexitime is that when you start or finish work you are required to clock in or out in accordance with the procedure in clause 10 below.

9.4 The Company reserves the right in its absolute discretion to terminate or amend the Scheme or to terminate your participation in it at any time.]

10 Clocking procedure

10.1 You are required to clock in on [entering the Company's premises] [attending your place of work] and to clock out on leaving [the Company's premises] [your place of work] for any reason.

10.2 You must only use the clock [card] [key] assigned to you for this purpose and must not interfere in any way with it or the clocking equipment.

10.3 You must not clock in or clock out any other employee or permit someone to clock in or out for you or interfere with the clock card of any other employee for any reason.

11 Shift working

11.1 You may be required to undertake shift working from time to time [if so instructed by [the Company] [your Manager]].

11.2 Reasonable notice of such shift working will be given.

11.3 When you are required to work shifts the following hours of work will apply: _____ .

11.4 When payable shift working rates will be as follows: _____ .

12 Overtime

12.1 You [are] [may be] required to work overtime from time to time [if so instructed by [the Company] [your Manager]].

12.2 Reasonable notice of such overtime will be given.

12.3 All overtime must be authorised by [the Company] [your Manager].

12.4 No payment for overtime will be made unless it has been previously authorised by [the Company] [your Manager].

12.5 Overtime rates will only apply to hours worked in excess of _____ hours per week.

12.6 When payable overtime rates will be as follows _____ .

12.7 Payment for overtime will be made on your normal pay day for the pay period in which the overtime was worked.

13 Reductions in normal hours of work

13.1 The Company reserves the right to lay you off without pay or to make temporary reductions to your normal hours of work and to reduce your pay proportionately if in the view of the Company this should become necessary.

13.2 You will be given as much notice of lay-off or reduction in normal hours as the Company reasonably can give.

14 Basic company holiday entitlement

14.1 The Company's holiday year runs from _____ to _____ .

14.2 In each holiday year your basic Company holiday entitlement will be as follows:

Number of completed years of service before	*in each year*	*Number of working days paid holiday*
Nil to _____ years		_____ days
_____ to _____ years		_____ days
Over _____ years		_____ days]

14.3 You must give at least _____ weeks' notice, of proposed holiday dates and these must then be agreed with the Company. [You may not take more than _____ weeks holiday in any _____ month period.]

[14.4 You are required to retain a sufficient number of days from your basic Company holiday entitlement to cover the Company's [annual] [summer] [Christmas] shut down period. You will be notified by the Company either individually or by way of a general notice to staff no later than _____ in each year of the number of days holiday you are required to retain for this purpose.]

[14.5 If you are absent from work due to sickness tor a continuous period of [four weeks or more] or for a total period of [eight weeksl in any one Company holiday year the Company reserves the right in its absolute discretion to reduce your basic Company holiday entitlement in respect of the Company holiday **year** in question as follows:

Total length of absence/ absences in the company holiday year in question	*Number of days reduction in basic company holiday entitlement in the company holiday year in question*
4 weeks	_____ days
5 weeks	_____ days
6 weeks	_____ days
7 weeks	_____ days
8 weeks	_____ days

3 months	_____ days
4 months	_____ days
5 months	_____ days
6 months	_____ days
7 months	_____ days
8 months	_____ days
9 months	_____ days
10 months	_____ days
11 months	_____ days
12 months	_____ days]

14.6 You may not carry any unused basic Company holiday entitlement forward to a subsequent holiday year. You will not be entitled to receive pay in lieu of holiday which is not taken except in accordance with clause 13.7 below.

[14.7 If you start or leave your employment during a holiday year your basic Company holiday entitlement in respect of the Company holiday year in question will be calculated at the rate of _____ days for each complete month of service in that holiday year.]

[14.7 If you start or leave your employment during a holiday year your basic Company holiday entitlement will be calculated as follows:

Number of complete months of service before the end of the holiday year in question	Number of working days paid holiday
1	_____ days
2	_____ days
3	_____ days
4	_____ days
5	_____ days
6	_____ days
7	_____ days
8	_____ days
9	_____ days
10	_____ days
11	_____ days]

14.8 Upon termination of your employment you will be entitled to pay in lieu of any unused basic Company holiday entitlement [unless your employment is terminated by the Company for gross misconduct] or be required to repay to the Company pay received for holidays taken in excess of entitlement under clause 14.7. Any sums so due may be deducted from any money owing to you. The Company reserves the right to require you to take any unused holiday entitlement during your notice period, even if booked to be taken after the end of the notice period.

[14.9 For the purpose of calculating any pay due to you or owed by you to the Company in accordance with clause 14.7 above one day's pay shall be [$\frac{1}{365}$] [$\frac{1}{261}$] [$\frac{1}{253}$] [$\frac{1}{7}$] [$\frac{1}{5}$] of your [basic] [annual] [weekly] [salary] [wages].]

[14.9 Any pay due to you or owed by you to the Company in accordance with clause 14.7 above will be calculated by reference to your [basic] [annual] [weekly] [salary] [wages] and will be as follows:

Number of complete months of service before the end of the holiday year in question	Number of working days paid holiday accrued

1	_____ days
2	_____ days
3	_____ days
4	_____ days
5	_____ days
6	_____ days
7	_____ days
8	_____ days
9	_____ days
10	_____ days
11	_____ days

For this purpose one day's pay shall be [¹⁄₃₆₅] [¹⁄₂₆₁] [¹⁄₂₅₃] [¹⁄₇] [¹⁄₅] of your [basic] [annual] [weekly] [salary] [wages].]

15 Public holidays

15.1 You are entitled to all public holidays applicable to the country in which your normal place of work is situated in addition to your basic Company holiday entitlement and will be paid for each public holiday.

15.2 If a public holiday falls within the dates ot your basic Company holiday entitlement you will be entitled to an additional day's paid holiday for each public holiday.

15.3 The Company reserves the right to require you to work on a public holiday, in return for which you shall be entitled to extra holiday, equal to the period worked, to be taken as agreed with [your manager] [the Company].

16 Notification of sickness or other absence

16.1 If you are absent from work for any reason and your absence has not previously been authorised by [the Company] [your Manager] you must inform [the Company] [your Manager] by _____ am on your first day of absence.

16.2 Any unauthorised absence must be properly explained and you must keep the Company informed daily until you have provided the Company with a medical certificate.

16.3 If you are absent from work due to sickness or injury which continues for more than seven days (including weekends) you must provide the Company with a medical certificate by the eighth day of sickness or injury. Thereafter medical certificates must be provided to the Company to cover any continued absence.

16.4 Immediately following your return to work after a period of absence which has not previously been authorised by [the Company] [your Manager] you are required to complete a Self-Certification form in the terms annexed stating the dates of and the reason for your absence, including details of sickness on non-working days as this information is required by the Company for calculating Statutory Sick Pay entitlement. Self-Certification forms will be retained in the Company's records.

17 Sick pay

17.1 If you are absent from work due to sickness or injury and comply with the requirements in this clause and clause 15 above regarding notification of absence, you will be paid Company Sick Pay in accordance with the terms of the Company's Sick Pay Scheme.

17.2 Under the provisions of the Company's Sick Pay Scheme you [will] [may] be entitled to Company Sick Pay [if you have completed _____ months continuous service] [at the Company's absolute discretion].

17.3 Company Sick Pay [will] [may] be paid for up to a maximum of _____ [weeks] [months] in any _____ month period and when payable will be as follows:

For the first _____ [week] [month] period or periods in any such absences

(1) Full salary less any Social Welfare Benefits recoverable by you (whether or not recovered); or

(2) Full salary in which case you must refund to the Company on demand an amount equal to any Social Welfare Benefits recoverable by you (whether or not recovered).

For the second _____ [week] [month] period or periods of any such absences

(1) Half salary less any Social Welfare Benefits recoverable by you (whether or not recovered); or

(2) Half salary in which case you must refund to the Company on demand an amount equal to any Social Welfare Benefits recoverable by you (whether or not recovered).

17.4 The Company reserves the right to require you to be examined at any time by an independent doctor at its expense and to cease payment of Company Sick Pay if it is advised by the doctor that you are fit to return to work.

17.5 If you are absent from your duties due to sickness or injury for a period or periods in excess of your maximum Company Sick Pay entitlement the Company will not be obliged to make any further payments to you. However if the Company does decide, in its absolute discretion, to make any further payments to you (in whatever amount the Company may decide), any such further payments may be varied or discontinued at any time.

17.6 If you are absent from work for any reason (excluding annual and public holidays) for a period or periods in excess of _____ working days in any period of 12 months the Company will be entitled to terminate your employment at any time by written notice on the date specified in the notice.

18 Pension

[18.1 You are entitled to join the Company's [contributory] [non-contributory] pension scheme [when you first become eligible for membership]. [Full details of the Company's Pension Scheme may be obtained from _____ .] [A copy of the current explanatory booklet giving details of the Pension Scheme is attached].]

[18.2 There is no pension scheme applicable to your employment.]

[18.3 The Company shall be entitled at any time to terminate the scheme or your membership of it [subject to providing you with the benefit of an equivalent pension scheme ('the New Scheme') each and every benefit of which shall be not less favourable than the benefits provided to you under the existing scheme and to ensuring that you are fully credited in the New Scheme for your pensionable service in the existing scheme as if those years had been under the New Scheme].]

19 Notice

19.1 If your employment is confirmed at the end of your probationary period the period of notice to be given in writing by the Company or by you to terminate your employment is:

19.1.1 one week's notice if you have been continuously employed for less than two years; and then

19.1.2 one week's notice for each completed year of continuous service up to a maximum of 12 weeks' notice after 12 years continuous service.

19.2 The Company reserves the right to pay [salary] [wages] in lieu of notice.

19.3 Nothing in terms and conditions of employment shall prevent the Company from terminating your employment without notice or [salary] [wages] in lieu of notice in appropriate circumstances.

20 Grievance procedure

20.1 If you have any grievance relating to your employment you should raise the matter initially with _____ . You may be required to put any such grievance in writing.

20.2 Having enquired into your grievance the _____ will discuss it with you and will then notify you of his decision.

20.3 If the decision of the _____ is not acceptable you may then refer the matter in writing to _____ whose decision will be final and binding.

[20.4 When stating grievances you may be accompanied by fellow employee of your choice [or by a representative of [a] [any recognised] Trade Union of which you are a member.]]

21 Disciplinary procedures

21.1 The purpose of the disciplinary procedures is to ensure that the standards established by the Company's rules are maintained and that any alleged failure to observe the Company's rules is fairly dealt with. [The procedure will only apply to employees who have [successfully completed their probationary periods/completed 6 months/one two year[s] continuous employment.]]

21.2 All cases of disciplinary action under these procedures will be recorded and placed in the Company's records. A copy of the Company's relevant records will be supplied at your request.

21.3 Offences under the Company's disciplinary procedures fall into 3 categories namely:
misconduct
gross misconduct
incapability

21.4 The following steps will be taken, as appropriate, in all cases of disciplinary action:

21.4.1 *Investigations:* No action will be taken before a proper investigation has been undertaken by the Company relating to the circumstances of the matter complained of. If appropriate, the Company may by written notice suspend you for a specified period during which time such an investigation will be undertaken. If you are so suspended your contract of employment will be deemed to continue together with all your rights under your contract including the payment of [salary] [wages], but during the period of suspension you will not be entitled to access to any of the Company's premises except at the prior request or with the prior consent of the Company and subject to such conditions as the Company may impose. The decision to suspend you will be notified to you by the [Personnel Manager] and confirmed in writing.

21.4.2 *Disciplinary hearings:* If the Company decides to hold a disciplinary hearing relating to the matter complained of, you will be given details of the complaint against you [at least [three] working days] before any such disciplinary hearing. At any disciplinary hearing you will be given an opportunity to state your case. You may also be accompanied by a fellow employee of your choice [or by a representative of [a] [any recognised] Trade Union of which you are a member]. No disciplinary penalty will be imposed without a disciplinary hearing.

21.4.3 *Appeals:* You have a right of appeal at any stage of the disciplinary procedures to the [Personnel Manager] or if he was involved at an earlier stage to the [Managing Director]. You should inform the [Personnel Manager] in writing of your wish to appeal within [five working days] of the date of the decision which forms the subject of your appeal.

The [Personnel Manager] or [Managing Director], as appropriate, will conduct an appeal hearing as soon as possible thereafter at which you will be given an opportunity to state your case and will be entitled to be accompanied by a fellow employee of your choice [or by a representative of [a] [any recognised] Trade Union of which you are a member].

The decision of the [Personnel Manager] or [Managing Director], as appropriate, will be notified to you in writing and will be final and binding.

21.5 Misconduct

21.5.1 The following offences are examples of misconduct:
— Bad time-keeping
— Unauthorised absence
— Minor damage to Company property
— Minor breach of Company rules
— Failure to observe Company procedures
— Abusive behaviour
— Sexual or racial harassment

These offences are not exclusive or exhaustive and offences of a similar nature will be dealt with under this procedure.

21.5.2 The following procedure will apply in cases of alleged misconduct:

First warning: This will be given by [your Manager] and may be oral or written according to the circumstances. In either event you will be advised that the warning constitutes the first formal stage of this procedure. If the warning is verbal a note that such a warning has been given will be placed in the Company's records.

Final warning: This will be given by the [Personnel Manager] and confirmed to you in writing. This warning will state that if you commit a further offence of misconduct during the period specified in it your employment will be terminated.

Dismissal: The decision to dismiss you will not be taken without reference to the [Personnel Manager] [Managing Director]. Dismissal will be notified to you in writing.

21.6 Gross misconduct

21.6.1 The following offences are examples of gross misconduct:
— Theft or unauthorised possession of any property or facilities belonging to the Company or any employee
— Unauthorised acceptance of gifts in contravention of clause 24 below
— Serious damage to Company property
— Falsification of reports, accounts, expense claims or self-certification forms
— [Clocking in or out offences]
— Refusal to carry out duties or reasonable instructions
— Intoxication by reason of drink or drugs
— Having alcoholic drink or illegal drugs at your place of work, in your locker on your person or otherwise in your possession, custody or control on the Company's premises
— Serious breach of Company rules
— Dangerous or intimidatory conduct
— [Abuse of the Company's flexitime scheme]

These examples are not exhaustive or exclusive and offences of a similar nature will be dealt with under this procedure.

21.6.2 Gross misconduct will result in immediate dismissal without notice or pay in lieu of notice. The decision to dismiss will not be taken without reference to the

[Personnel Manager] [Managing Director]. Dismissal will be notified to you in writing.

21.7 Incapability

21.7.1 The following are examples of incapability:
— Poor performance
— Incompetence
— Unsuitability
— Lack of application

These examples are not exhaustive or exclusive and instances of a similar nature will be dealt with under this procedure.

21.7.2 The following procedure will apply in cases of incapability:

First warning: This will be given by your Manager and will be confirmed to you in writing. This warning will specify the improvement required and will state that your work will be reviewed at the end of a period of _____ month[s] after the date of the warning.

Final warning: This will be given by the [Personnel Manager] and confirmed to you in writing. This warning will state that unless your work improves within a period of 1/3 month[sl after the date of the warning your employment will be terminated.

Dismissal: The decision to dismiss you will not be taken without reference to the [Personnel Manager] [Managing Director]. Dismissal will be notified to you in writing.

21.8 Subject to satisfactory performance and conduct any warning under these procedures will be removed from the Company's records after [two] years.

21.9 The Company reserves the right in its absolute discretion to waive any of the penalties referred to in clauses 21.5.2, 21.6.2 and 21.7.2 above and substitute any one or more of the following penalties namely:

21.9.1 *Demotion:* The Company may demote you by notice in writing giving details of any consequential changes to your terms and conditions of employment. In particular the notice will give details of any reduction to your [salary] [wagesl and/or any loss of benefits and/or privileges consequent upon such demotion. Demotion will be limited to a reduction of [ ] grades.

21.9.2 *Suspension:* The Company may suspend you from work with or without pay by notice in writing to this effect. Such notice will specify the dates of your suspension and the conditions applicable to your suspension. Suspension will be limited to not more than [ ] working days.

21.9.3 *[Bonus Scheme]:* The Company may exclude you from participating in [any] [the] bonus scheme referred to in clause [6] above by notice in writing to this effect. Such notice will specify the period of your exclusion from participation in [any] [the] bonus scheme.

22 Cars

22.1 You may only use your own car on Company business with the prior approval of _____ and you are responsible for ensuring that the vehicle is adequately insured.

22.2 A Company car [will] [may] be provided for your use for the better performance of your duties in accordance with and subject to the Company's Car Policy as amended from time to time. The Company reserves the right in its absolute discretion to withdraw the use of the car from you at any time without giving any reason [without compensation].

22.3 It is a condition in your employment that you have and keep a current driving licence. If you are disqualified from driving for any period the Company reserves the right to dismiss you. You must promptly notify the Company of any accidents while driving on Company business, any charges of driving offences brought against you by the police and of any endorsements imposed.

23 [Expenses

23.1 The Company will reimburse to you all expenses properly incurred by you in the proper performance of your duties, provided that on request you provide the Company with such vouchers or other evidence of actual payment of such expenses as the Company may reasonably require.]

24 Acceptance of gifts

24.1 You may not without prior written consent of [the Company] [your Manager] accept any gift and/or favour of whatever kind from any customer, client or supplier of the Company or any prospective customer, client or supplier of the Company.

25 Normal retirement age

You shall retire on reaching _____ years of age.

26 Other employment

26.1 You must devote the whole of your time, attention and abilities during your hours of work for the Company to your duties for the Company. You may not, under any circumstances, whether directly or indirectly, undertake any other duties, of whatever kind, during your hours of work for the Company.

26.2 You may not without the prior written consent of [the Company] [your Manager] (which will not be unreasonably withheld) engage, whether directly or indirectly, in any business or employment [which is similar to or in any way connected or competitive with the business of the Company in which you work] outside your hours of work for the Company.

27 Place of work

27.1 Your normal place of work will be _____ but the Company reserves the right to change this to any. place within _____ . You will be given at least one month's notice of any such change. However, the Company will, where appropriate, under its Relocation Policy from time to time provide you with financial or other relocation assistance.

27.2 You may be required to work at any of the Company's premises or at the premises of its customers, clients, suppliers or associates within Ireland [or overseas] from time to time. You will be reimbursed for any expenses properly incurred in connection with such duties in accordance with the Company's Expenses Policy as amended from time to time.

28 Confidentiality

28.1 You may not disclose any trade secrets or other information of a confidential nature relating to the Company or any of its associated companies or their business or in respect of which the Company owes an obligation of confidence to any third party during or after your employment except in the proper course of your employment or as required by law.

28.2 You must not remove any documents or computer disks or tapes containing any confidential information from the Company's premises at any time without proper advance authorisation. All such documents, disks or tapes and any copies are the Company's property.

29 Inventions

29.1 If you make any invention whether patentable or not which relates to or is capable of being used in any business of the Company with which you are (at the time of making the invention or have heen (within the two years before that time) concerned to a material degree you must disclose it to the Company immediately.

29.2 As between you and the Company, the ownership of all inventions made by you will be determined in accordance with s. 53 of the Patents Act 1964.

30 Accommodation

30.1 For the better pertormance ot your duties for the Company you are required to live in [*details of property*] which you will occupy upon the terms ot the annexed licence agreement.

31 Health and Safety at work

31.1 The Company will take all reasonably practicable steps to ensure your health safety and social welfare while at work. You must familiarise yourself with the Company's Health and Safety Policy and its Safety and Fire rules. It is also your legal duty to take care for your own health and safety and that of your colleagues.

32 Changes to your terms of emplovment

32.1 The Company reserves the right to make reasonable changes to any of your terms and conditions ot employment.

32.2 You will be notified of minor changes of detail by way of a notice to all employees and any such changes take effect from the date of the notice.

32.3 You will be given not less than one month's written notice of any significant changes which may be given by way of an individual notice or a general notice to all employees. Such changes will be deemed to be accepted unless you notify the Company of any objection in writing before the expiry of the notice period.

[*Name of Company*]

SELF CERTIFICATION FORM

TO BE COMPLETED BY EMPLOYEE IN THE PRESENCE OF HIS/HER HEAD OF DEPARTMENT (in Block Capitals)

Name:

Department:

Period of incapacity: From:
  To:
  (Non-working days should be included)

Nature of incapacity: (State any illness, symptoms or describe injury)

Have you visited a doctor or hospital?
(If yes, state doctor or hospital, name and address and treatment or prescription received)

Signed:

TO BE COMPLETED BY YOUR HEAD OF DEPARTMENT
I am satisfied/I am not satisfied that the information above is correct.

Signed: Date:
Position:

LICENCE AGREEMENT

From: *[Name of Company]*

To: *[Name of Employee]*

Dated:

IN CONSIDERATION of and as a term of your employment by the Company and for the better performance of your duties as *[job title]* you are required to occupy the *[details of property]* upon the following terms and conditions:

(1) No rent will be payable in respect of such occupation.

(2) The Company will pay periodic outgoings payable in respect of the premises [other than telephone, water, gas and electricity charges].

(3) You will at all times keep the interior of the premises in a good state of decorative repair and not damage or injure the exterior of the premises.

(4) If at any time, for any reason, your employment by the Company in the above mentioned capacity shall cease, you will forthwith vacate the premises and your occupation shall cease immediately. If at any time, for any reason your place of work changes to a different location or you take up a new job with the Company and in either case the Company is not willing to continue providing you with accommodation you must vacate the premises within one calendar month.

(5) It is acknowledged by both parties that it is mutually intended that you will occupy the premises as service occupant and that nothing herein contained shall be construed to create the relationship of landlord and tenant.

SIGNED for and on behalf of _____
by _____
DIRECTOR

I agree that I occupy the said premises upon the terms above stated.

_____ *[Employee]*

Executive Employment Agreement

EMPLOYMENT AGREEMENT

Date: 19

Parties:

1 'The Company': _____ [Limited] [PLC] (registered no _____) whose registered office is at _____ .

2 'The Appointee': _____ of _____ .

Operative provisions:

1 Interpretation

1.1 The headings and marginal headings to the clauses are for convenience only and have no legal effect.

1.2 Any reference in this Agreement to any Act or delegated legislation includes any statutory modification or re-enactment of it or the provision referred to.

1.3 In this Agreement:

'ASSOCIATED COMPANY' means any company which for the time being is a company having an equity share capital (as defined in s. 155(5) of the Companies Act, 1963) of which not less than [25] per cent is controlled directly or indirectly by the Company [or its holding company] applying the provisions of s. 102 of the Corporation Tax Act, 1976, in the determination of control

'THE BOARD' means the Board of Directors of the Company and includes any committee of the Board duly appointed by it

'COMPANY INVENTION' means any improvement, invention or discovery made by the Appointee which is the property of the Company

'MANAGING DIRECTOR' means any person or persons jointly holding such office of the Company from time to time and includes any person(s) exercising substantially the functions of a managing director or chief executive officer of the Company

'PENSION SCHEME' means the _____

'RECOGNISED STOCK EXCHANGE' means any body of persons which is for the time being a Recognised Investment Exchange for the purposes of the Companies Act 1990.

2 Appointment and duration

2.1 The Company appoints the Appointee and the Appointee agrees to act as [Managing Director] [Production Manager] [Assistant Director—Public Relations] [an Executive Director] of the Company [or in such other appointment as may from time to time be agreed] [or in such other appointment as the [Board] [Managing Director] [Company] may from time to time direct (such other appointment not to be of lower status than the Appointee's original appointment under this Agreement)]. [The Appointee accepts that the Company may [in emergencies] [at its discretion] require him to perform other duties or tasks not within the scope of his normal duties and the Appointee agrees to perform those duties or undertake those tasks as if they were specifically required under this Agreement].

2.2 The appointment shall [be deemed to have] commence[d] on _____ 19 _____ and shall continue (subject to earlier termination as provided in this Agreement) *either* [for a fixed period of [months] [years] from then until _____ 19 _____ [(or if renewed such later date as may be agreed by the parties and endorsed under their signatures in Part A of Schedule 1)] *or* [for a fixed period of _____ [months] [years] from then until _____ 19 _____ provided that on each anniversary of the commencement the then unexpired period shall automatically be renewed for a further _____ [months] [years] (in place of the unexpired term) unless either party shall prior to any such renewal date give notice to the other party that the period will not be renewed whereupon the Agreement will instead terminate at the end of the then current fixed period.] *or* [for a period of _____ [months] [years] from then [or until such later date as may be agreed by the parties and endorsed under the signatures in Part A of Schedule 1] and afterwards until terminated by either party giving to the other not less than _____ [days] [calendar months] [years] prior notice expiring on or at any time after the end of the specified period.] *or* [until terminated by either party giving to the other not less than _____ [days] [calendar months] [years] prior notice [if given on or before _____ 19 _____ and after then not less than _____ [days] [calendar months] [years] prior notice.] *or* [until terminated by the Company giving to the Appointee not less than _____ [days] [calendar months] [years] prior notice or by the Appointee giving to the Company not less than _____ [days] [calendar months] [years] prior notice.]

2.3 [With the prior consent of the Appointee] The Company may from time to time appoint any other person or persons to act jointly with the Appointee in his appointment.

2.4 The Appointee warrants that by virtue of entering into this Agreement [or the other agreements or arrangements made or to be made between the Company or any Associated Company and him] he will not be in breach of any express or implied terms of any contract with or of any other obligation to any third party binding upon him.

3 Duties of appointee

3.1 The Appointee shall:
3.1.1 devote [substantially] [the whole of his time, attention and ability] [so much of his time, attention and ability as is reasonably required] [so much of his time, attention and ability as the Board consider necessary] to the duties of his appointment;
3.1.2 faithfully and diligently perform those duties and exercise such powers consistent with them which are from time to time assigned to or vested in him;
3.1.3 obey all lawful and reasonable directions of the Board;
3.1.4 use his best endeavours to promote the interests of the Company and its Associated Companies.

3.2 The Appointee shall (without further remuneration) if and for so long as the Company requires:
3.2.1 carry out [duties] [the duties of his appointment] on behalf of any Associated Company;
3.2.2 act as an officer of any Associated Company or hold any other appointment or office as nominee or representative of the Company or any Associated Company;
3.2.3 carry out such duties and the duties attendant on any such appointment as if they were duties to be performed by him on behalf of the Company.

4 Reporting

4.1 The Appointee shall at all times keep the [Board] [person designated as his immediate superior] promptly and fully informed (in writing if so requested) of his conduct of the business or affairs of the Company and its Associated Companies and provide such explanations as [the Board] [his immediate superior] may require.

5 Secondment

5.1 The Company may without the Appointee's consent second him to be employed by any Associated Company without prejudice to his rights under this Agreement.

6 Place of work

6.1 The Appointee shall perform his duties at [the head office] of the Company and/or such other place of business of the Company or of any Associated Company as the Company requires [whether inside or outside Ireland but the Company shall not without his prior consent require him to go to or reside anywhere outside Ireland except for occasional visits in the ordinary course of his duties. In this clause, the term 'Ireland' includes Northern Ireland.]

6.2 The Appointee shall at all times reside within a radius of _____ miles from [the head office of the Company] [his place of work] from time to time. [If the Company shall [relocate its head office] [change his place of work] such that the Appointee has to relocate his residence to remain within that radius, the Company shall reimburse him his removal and other incidental expenses in accordance with its then current policy for relocation of executives.]

[7 Service occupancy

7.1 During the continuance of his appointment and for the better performance of the duties of his appointment, the Appointee shall occupy as a licensee only [that part of] the premises [called] [comprising _____ at] _____ or such other premises as the Company may from time to time specify on the terms set out in Schedule 5.]

8 Inventions

8.1 If at any time during his appointment the Appointee (whether alone or with any other person or persons) makes any invention, whether relating directly or indirectly to the business of the Company, the Appointee shall promptly disclose to the Company full details, including drawings and models, of such invention to enable the Company to determine whether it is a Company Invention. If the invention is not a Company Invention the Company shall treat all information disclosed to it by the Appointee as confidential information the property of the Appointee.

8.2 If the invention is a Company Invention the Appointee shall hold it in trust for the Company, and at the request and expense of the Company do all things necessary or desirable to enable the Company, or its nominee, to obtain the benefit of the Company Invention and to secure patent or other appropriate forms of protection for it throughout the World.

8.3 Decisions as to the patenting and exploitation of any Company Invention shall be in the sole discretion of the Company.

[8.4 The Appointee irrevocably appoints the Company to be his Attorney in his name and on his behalf to execute, sign and do all such instruments or things and generally to use the Appointee's name for the purpose of giving to the Company or its nominee the full benefit of the provisions of clause 8.2 and a certificate in writing signed by any Director or the Secretary of the Company, that any instrument or act falls within the authority hereby conferred, shall be conclusive evidence that such is the case so far as any third party is concerned].

9 Copyright

9.1 The Appointee shall promptly disclose to the Company all copyright works or designs originated conceived written or made by him alone or with others (except only those works originated conceived written or made by him wholly outside his normal working hours and wholly unconnected with his appointment) and shall until such rights shall be fully and absolutely vested in the Company hold them in trust for the Company.

9.2 The Appointee hereby assigns to the Company by way of future assignment all copyright design right and other proprietary rights if any for the full terms thereof throughout the World in respect of all copyright works and designs originated, conceived, written or made by the Appointee (except only those works or designs originated conceived written or made by the Appointee wholly outside his normal working hours and wholly unconnected with his appointment) during the period of his employment hereunder.

9.3 The Appointee hereby irrevocably and unconditionally waives in favour of the Company any and all moral rights conferred on him by law for any work in which copyright or design right is vested in the Company whether by Clause 9 or otherwise.

9.4 The Appointee will at the request and expense of the Company do all things necessary or desirable to substantiate the rights of the Company under clause 9.2 and 9.3.

10 Conflict of interest

10.1 During this Agreement the Appointee shall not (except as a representative or nominee of the Company or any Associated Company or otherwise with the prior consent in writing of the [Board] [Managing Director]) be directly or indirectly engaged concerned or interested in any other business which:

10.1.1 is wholly or partly in competition with [the] [any] business carried on by the [Companyl[the Company or any Associated Companies] or any of the foregoing by itself or themselves or in partnership, common ownership or as a joint venture with any third party; or

10.1.2 as regards any goods or services is a supplier to or customer of [the Company] [any such company];

Provided that the Appointee may hold (directly or through nominees) any units of any authorised unit trust and up to [five] per cent of the issued shares debentures or other securities of any class of any company whose shares are listed on a Recognised Stock Exchange or in respect of which dealing takes place in The International Stock Exchange of the United Kingdom and Republic of Ireland or the Unlisted Securities Market or the Third Market. The prior written consent of [the Board] [Managing Director] shall be required before the Appointee shall hold in excess of [five] per cent of the issued shares debentures or other securities of any class of any one such company.

10.2 Subject to any regulations from time to time issued by the Company which may apply to him, the Appointee shall not receive or obtain directly or indirectly any discount rebate commission or other inducement in respect of any sale or purchase of any goods or services effected or other business transacted (whether or not by him) by or on behalf of the Company or any Associated Company and if he (or any firm or company in which he is directly or indirectly engaged, concerned or interested) shall obtain any such discount rebate commission or inducement he shall immediately account to the Company for the amount received by him or the amount received by such firm or company. For the purpose of this clause the Appointee shall be deemed not to be engaged. concerned or interested in such a company as is referred to in the proviso to clause 10.1 [and the requirement in that proviso for prior consent shall be ignored].

11 [Share dealings

11.1 The Appointee shall comply where relevant with every rule of law, every regulation of The International Stock Exchange of the United Kingdom and Republic of Ireland and every regulation of the Company from time to time in force in relation to dealings in shares, debentures or other securities of the Company or any Associated Company and unpublished price sensitive information affecting the shares, debentures or other securities of any other company. Provided always that in relation to overseas dealings the Appointee shall also comply with all laws of the State and all regulations of the stock exchange market or dealing system in which such dealings take place.

11.2 The Appointee shall not (and shall procure so far as he is able that his spouse and children shall not) deal or become or cease to be interested (within the meaning of Part IV of the Companies Act 1990) in any securities of the company except in accordance with the Company's 'Rules for Securities Transactions by Directors' from time to time.]

12 Confidentiality

12.1 The Appointee shall not either during his appointment or at any time for one year after its termination:

    12.1.1 disclose to any person or persons (except to those authorised by the Company to know or as otherwise required by law);

    12.1.2 use for his own purposes or for any purposes other than those of the Company; or

    12.1.3 through any failure to exrcise all due care and diligence cause any unauthorised disclosure of

any confidcntial information of the Company (including in particular lists or details of customers of the Company or information relating to the working of any process or invention carried on or used by the Company or any Company Invention) or in respect of which the Company is bound by an obligation of confidence to a third party. These restrictions shall cease to apply to information or knowledge which may (otherwise than through the default of the Appointee) become available to the public generally [without requiring a significant expenditure of labour, skill or money].

12.2 The provisions of clause 12.1 shall apply mutatis mutandis in relation to the confidential or secret information of each Associated Company which the Appointee may have received or obtained during his appointment and the Appointee shall upon request enter into an enforceable agreement with any such company to the like effect.

12.3 All notes, memoranda, rccords and writing made by the Appointee relating to the business of the Company or its Associated Companics shall be and remain the property of the Company or Associated Company to whose business they relate and shall be delivered by him to the company to which they belong forthwith upon request.

[12.4 It is agreed that the information disclosed by the Appointee in Schedule 6A is prior knowledge of the Appointee and is expressly excluded from the ambit of this clause.]

13 Statements

13.1 The Appointee shall not at any time make any untrue or misleading statement in relation to the Company or any Associated Company.

14 Medical examination

14.1 The Appointee shall at the expense of the Company submit annually to a medical examination by a registered medical practitioner nominated by the Company and shall authorise such medical practitioner to disclose to and discuss with the Company's medical adviser the results of the examination and the matters which arise from it so that the

Company's medical adviser can notify the Company of any matters he considers might impair the Appointee from properly discharging his duties.

15 Pay

15.1 During his appointment the Company shall pay to the Appointee:

[15.1.1] a [basic] salary at the rate of IR£ _____ per year which shall accrue day-to-day and be payable by equal [monthly] [four weekly] instalments. The salary shall be deemed to include any fees receivable by the Appointee as a Director of the Company or any Associated Company, or of any other company or unincorporated body in which he holds office as nominee or representative of the Company or any Associated Company; [and

15.1.2 a commission calculated in accordance with the provisions of Schedule 2 payable in respect of each financial period of the Company (subject to any payment on account) within 21 days after the adoption of the accounts for that financial period at the Annual General Meeting.]

[15.2 The Appointee's [basic] salary shall be reviewed by the [Board] [Managing Director] [from time to time] [as at _____ each year] and the rate of [basic] salary may be increased by the Company with effect from that date by such amount if any as it shall think fit;]

[15.2 The Appointee's [basic] salary shall be reviewed and increased with effect from from _____ each year in accordance with the provisions of Schedule [3].]

[15.3 Notwithstanding the provisions of sub-clause 15.2 the Company shall not be requred to increase the Appointee's salary if and to the extent only that the increased payment would be unlawful under the provisions of any legislation then in force during his appointment, or if the increased payment would not be an allowable cost for the purpose of increasing prices under the provisions of any legislation controlling prices or price increases.]

16 Pension

16.1 The Appointee shall be entitled to be and remain a member of the _____ Pension Scheme subject to the terms of its Deeds and Rules from time to time [details of which are available from _____]. [The Company shall be entitled at any time to terminate the Scheme or the Appointee's membership of it] [subject to providing him with the benefit of an equivalent pension scheme ('the New Scheme') each and every benefit of which shall be not less favourable than the benefits provided to the Appointee under the existing scheme and to ensuring that the Appointee is fully credited in the New Scheme for his pensionable service in the existing scheme as if such pensionable service had been under the New Scheme].

17 Insurances

17.1 The Appointee shall be entitled to participate at the Company's expense in the Company's permanent health insurance scheme and [for himself, his spouse [and dependant children]] in the Company's private medical expenses insurance scheme, subject always to the rules of such schemes [which are available from _____].

18 Car

18.1 [Subject to the Appointee holding a current full driving licence] the Company shall provide the Appointee with:

18.1.1 Option 1: a [*eg* Jaguar XJ6 Sovereign 3.6 litre] car or other car of equivalent price and status;

18.1.2 Option 2: a car of a make, model and specification [manufactured by a [EEC member state] company] of his choice provided that its manufacturer's list price (including Car Tax, Value Added Tax, extras, delivery and other similar charges) shall not be more than £_____ (such limit to be reviewed by the Company from time to time and increased commensurately with increases in new car prices) and subject to the [Managing Director][Board] approving such choice as commensurate with both the status of the Appointee and the image of the Company (which approval shall not be withheld unreasonably);

18.1.3 Option 3: a car of a make, model and specification selected by the Company (which in the reasonable opinion of the [Managing Director][Board] is commensurate with the status of the Appointee and the image of the Company);

18.1.4 Option 4: a car of a make, model and specification determined by reference to the Company's car [scheme][policy] in effect from time to time for his sole business use and private use by him [and his spouse].

18.2 The Company shall:

18.2.1 Option 1: bear all standing and running expenses of the car [except for fuel consumed during [private use of the car] [use of the car by the Appointee for holiday purposes]] and any additional insurance costs incurred to permit the Appointee to use the car outside Ireland for private purposes;

18.2.2 Option 2: reimburse the Appointee for his business use of the car at [eg a rate per mile to be determined annually by the Company by reference to the then current estimate of standing and running costs for cars of the same engine capacity as the Appointee's company car prepared by the Automobile Association];

and shall replace such car [with the same or equivalent model]

18.2.3 Option A: when it has travelled [*eg* 45,000] miles or (if sooner) on the [eg third] anniversary of its purchase by the Company;

18.2.4 Option B: as provided in the Company's car [scheme] [policy] in effect from time to time;

18.3 The Appointee shall always comply with all regulations laid down by the Company from time to time with respect to company cars, and on the termination of his appointment for whatever reason and whether lawfully or unlawfully the Appointee shall forthwith return his company car to the Company [at its head office].

19 Expenses

19.1 The Company shall reimburse to the Appointee on a monthly basis all travelling, hotel, entertainment and other expenses reasonably incurred by him in the proper performance of his duties subject to [the Appointee complying with such guidelines or regulations issued by the Company from time to time in this respect and to] the production to the Company of such vouchers or other evidence of actual payment of the expenses as the Company may reasonably require.

19.2 Where the Company issues a company sponsored credit or charge card to the Appointee he shall use such card only for expenses reimbursable under clause 19.1 above, and shall return it to the Company forthwith on the termination of his emplovment.

20 Holiday

20.1 In addition to public holidays the Appointee is entitled to [20] working days paid holiday in each [holiday] year [from _____ to _____] to be taken at such time or times as are agreed with the [Board] [Managing Director]. The Appointee shall not without the consent of the [Board] [Managing Director] carry forward any unused part of his holiday entitlement to a subsequent year.

20.2 For the [holiday] year during which his appointment commences or terminates, the

Appointee is entitled to [1½] working days holiday for each [calendar month] completed in the employment of the Company for that year. On the termination of his appointment for whatever reason the Appointee shall [not] [as appropriate either] be entitled to pay in lieu of outstanding holiday entitlement [and shall] [or] be required to repay to the Company any salary received for holiday taken in excess of his actual entitlement. The basis for payment shall be [½₅₃] x annual [basic] salary for each day.

21 Incapacity

21.1 If the Appointee shall be prevented by illness (including mental disorder) injury or other incapacity from properly performing his duties hereunder he shall report this fact forthwith to the Company Secretary's office and if the Appointee is so prevented for seven or more consecutive days he shall provide a medical practitioner's statement on the eighth day and weekly thereafter so that the whole period of absence is certified by such statements. Immediately following his return to work after a period of absence the Appointee shall complete a Self-Certification form available from the Company Secretary's office detailing the reason for his absence.

21.2 If the Appointee shall be absent from his duties hereunder due to illness (including mental disorder) accident or other incapacity duly certified in accordance with the provisions of sub-clause 21.1 hereof he shall be paid his full remuneration hereunder [(including bonus and commission)] for up to _____ working days absence in any period of 12 months and thereafter such remuneration if any as the Board shall in its discretion from time to time allow provided that such remuneration shall be inclusive of any social welfare sickness benefit to which the Appointee is entitled under the provisions of the Social Welfare Acts and any such sickness or other benefits recoverable by the Appointee (whether or not recovered) may be deducted therefrom.

22 Termination of agreement

22.1 Automatic termination

This Agreement shall automatically terminate:

22.1.1 on the Appointee reaching [retirement age as defined in the Rules of the Pension Scheme] [his 65th birthday]; or

22.1.2 if the Appointee becomes prohibited by law from being a director; or

22.1.3 if he resigns his office; [or

22.1.4 if the office of director of the Company held by the Appointee is vacated pursuant to the Company's Articles of Association save if the vacation shall be caused by illness (including mental disorder) or injury.]

22.2 Suspension

In order to investigate a complaint against the Appointee of misconduct the Company is entitled to suspend the Appointee on full pay for so long as may be necessary to carry out a proper investigation and hold a disciplinary hearing.

22.3 Immediate dismissal

The Company may by notice terminate this Agreement with immediate effect if the Appointee:

22.3.1 commits any act of gross misconduct or repeats or continues (after written warning) any other [material] [serious] breach of his obligations under this Agreement; or.

22.3.2 is guilty of any conduct which in the [reasonable] opinion of the Board brings him, the Company or any Associated Company into [serious] disrepute; or

22.3.3 is convicted of any criminal offence punishable with 6 months or more imprisonment (excluding an offence under road traffic legislation in Ireland or elsewhere for which he is not sentenced to any term of imprisonment whether immediate or suspended); or

22.3.4 commits any act of dishonesty [whether] relating to the Company, any Associated Company, any of its or their employees or otherwise; or

22.3.5 becomes bankrupt or makes any arrangement or composition with his creditors generally; or

22.3.6 is in the [reasonable] opinion of the Board incompetent in the performance of his duties.

22.4 Dismissal on short notice

The Company may terminate this Agreement as follows:

22.4.1 notwithstanding clause 21.2 by not less than [3] months' prior notice given at any time while the Appointee is incapacitated by ill-health or accident from performing his duties under this Agreement and he has been so incapacitated for a period or periods aggregating _____ [days] [calendar months] in the preceding 12 months. [Provided that the Company shall withdraw any such notice if during the currency of the notice the Appointee returns to full time duties and provides a medical practitioner's certificate satisfactory to the Board to the effect that he has fully recovered his health and that no recurrence of his illness or incapacity can reasonably be anticipated.]

22.4.2 By not less than [one] month's prior notice if the Appointee has been offered but has refused to agree to the transfer of this Agreement by way of novation to a person firm or company which has acquired or agreed to acquire the whole or substantially the whole of the undertaking (as defined in the E.C. Safeguarding of Employees' Rights on Transfer of Undertaking) Regulations 1980 in which he is employed.

22.5 Pay in lieu

On serving notice for any reason to terminate this Agreement or at any time thereafter during the currency of such notice the Company shall be entitled to pay to the Appointee his [basic] salary (at the rate then current) for the unexpired portion of the duration of his appointment or entitlement to notice as may be the case.

22.6 Miscellaneous

On the termination of this Agreement for whatever reason, the Appointee shall:

22.6.1 at the request of the Company:

(a) resign from office as a Director of the Company and from all offices held by him in any Associated Company and from all other appointments or offices which he holds as nominee or representative of the Company or any Associated Company; and

(b) transfer without payment to the Company or as the Company may direct any qualifying shares provided by it to him;

and if he should fail to do so within seven days the Company is hereby irrevocably authorised to appoint some person in his name and on his behalf to sign any documents or do any things necessary or requisite to give effect to these. Such resignation(s) shall be without prejudice to any claims which the Appointee may have against any company arising out of this Agreement or the termination thereof.

22.6.2 Immediately deliver to the Company or to its order all books, documents, papers, (including copies) materials, credit cards, keys and other property of or relating to the business of the Company or its Associated Companies then in his possession or which are or were last under his power or control.

23 Post termination obligations of the appointee

23.1 Non-competition

The Appointee shall not within the Prohibited Area for a period of _____ [months] [years] after the termination of his employment hereunder (however that comes about and whether lawful or not):

23.1.1 be directly or indirectly engaged concerned or interested [in any capacity] [whether as Director Principal Agent Partner Consultant Employee or otherwise] in any other business [of whatever kind] which is wholly or partly in competition with any business carried on by the [Company] [Company or any of its subsidiaries];

23.1.2 accept employment in any [executive] [technical] [sales] capacity with any business concern which is wholly or partly in competition with any business carried on by the [Company] [Company or any of its subsidiaries];

23.1.3 [provide [technical] [commercial] [or professional] advice to any business concern which is wholly or partly in competition with any business carried on by the [Company] [Company or any of its subsidiaries]];

23.1.4 be directly or indirectly engaged concerned or interested [in any capacity] [whether as Director Principal Agent Partner Consultant Employee or otherwise] in any business concern which has at any time during the last _____ [months] [years] of the Appointee's employment hereunder supplied any goods materials or services to or been a customer of the [Company] [Company or any of its subsidiaries].

The provisions of sub-clauses 23.1.1, 23.1.2, 23.1.3 and 23.1.4 shall not restrain the Appointee from engaging in or accepting employment with any business concern where the Appointee's duties or work shall relate [either solely or exclusively to part or parts of the world outside the Prohibited Area or] to services goods or materials of a kind or nature with which the Appointee was not concerned to a material extent during the period of _____ [months] [years] prior to the termination of his employment hereunder.

23.2 Non-solicitation

The Appointee shall not within the Prohibited Area for a period of _____ [months] [years] after the termination of his emplovment hereunder (howsoever that comes about and whether lawfully or not) directly or indirectly and whether on his own behalf or on behalf of any other business concern person partnership firm company or other body which is wholly or partly in competition with [the] [any] business carried on by the Company:

23.2.1 Canvass solicit or approach or cause to be canvassed or solicited or approached for orders in respect of any services provided or any goods dealt in by the [Company] [Company and/or its subsidiaries] in respect of the provision or sale of which the Appointee was engaged during the last _____ [months] [years] of his employment with the Company any person or persons who at the date of the termination of the Appointee's appointment was negotiating with the Company for the supply of services or goods or within _____ [months] [years] prior to such date is or was a client or customer of the Company [or of its subsidiaries] or was in the habit of dealing with the Company [or its subsidiaries] and with whom the Appointee shall have dealt. [Provided that this restriction shall not apply to those clients or customers named in Schedule 6B which are agreed to be those introduced to the Company by the Appointee on the commencement of his Appointment.]

23.2.2 Interfere or seek to interfere or take such steps as may interfere with the continuance of supplies to the Company [and/or its subsidiaries] (or the terms relating to such supplies) from any suppliers who have been supplying components materials or services to the Company and/or its subsidiaries at any time during the last _____ [months] [years] of his employment hereunder.

23.2.3 Solicit or entice or endeavour to solicit or entice away from the Company [or its subsidiaries] or offer or cause to be offered any employment to any person employed by the Company [or its subsidiaries] in an [executive] [technical] [sales] capacity at the date of such termination for whom the Appointee is responsible.

23.2.4 Deal with any person or persons who or which at any time during the period of _____ [months] [years] prior to termination of the Appointee's employment hereunder have been in the habit of dealing under contract with the Company [or its subsidiaries].

23.3 For the purposes of clause 23 'Prohibited Area' means _____ .

23.4 The parties agree that each of the covenants set out in clauses 23.1 and 23.2 above is separate and severable and enforceable accordingly [and that if any of the restrictions shall be adjudged to be void or ineffective for whatever reason but would be adjudged to be valid and effective if part of the wording thereof were deleted, they shall apply with such modifications as may be necessary to make them valid and effective].

24 [Change in control (unquoted or private company)

24.1 If there is a change in control of the Company or of its holding company (as defined in s. 155 of the Companies Act 1963), the Appointee shall be entitled to a severance payment in the event his appointment is terminated by dismissal or constructive dismissal (other than pursuant to clause 22.3) in connection with or within six months after the change in control. The amount of this payment shall [not be less than equivalent to _____ per cent of the Appointee's then salary for each full year of employment with the Company up to a maximum payment of _____ per cent of his then salary] [_____ months/years salary at the rate then payable] 'Control' means the holding of 50 per cent or more of the issued voting share capital of the Company or its holding company.

[24.2 The Appointee shall be entitled to terminate his employment by 30 days prior notice given at any time within six months of a change in control as defined in clause 24.1 [if that change in control was at any time opposed by the Company's or Holding Company's Board] and upon such voluntary termination the Appointee shall be entitled to a severance payment calculated in accordance with clause 24.1.]]

25 General
25.1 Other terms
The provisions of the Company's standard terms and conditions of employment (as amended from time to time) shall be terms of the Appointee's employment except so far as inconsistent with this Agreement.

25.2 Statutory particulars
The further particulars of terms of employment not contained in the body of this Agreement which must be given to the Appointee in compliance with s. 9 of the Minimum Notice and Terms of Employment Act, 1973, are given in Schedule 4.

25.3 Prior agreements
This Agreement [sets out the entire agreement and understanding of the parties and] is in substitution for any previous contracts of employment or for services between the Company or any of its Associated Companies and the Appointee (which shall be deemed to have been terminated by mutual consent).

25.4 Accrued rights
The expiration or termination of this Agreement however arising shall not operate to

affect such of the provisions of this Agreement as are expressed to operate or have effect after then and shall be without prejudice to any accrued rights or remedies of the parties.

25.5 Proper law

The validity construction and performance of this Agreement shall be governed by the law of the Republic of Ireland.

25.6 Acceptance of juristiction

All disputes claims or proceedings between the parties relating to the validity construction or performance of this Agreement shall be subject to the non-exclusive jurisdiction of the High Court of Ireland ('the High Court') to which the parties irrevocably submit. [Each party irrevocably consents to the award or grant of any relief in any such proceedings before the High Court and either party shall be entitled to take proceedings in any other jurisdiction to enforce a judgment or order of the High Court.]

25.7 Notices

Any notice to be given by a party under this Agreement must be in writing [in the English language] and must be given by delivery at or sending [first class] post or other faster postal service, or telex, facsimile transmission or other means of telecommunication in permanent written form (provided the addressee has [his or its own] facilities for receiving such transmissions) to the last known postal address or relevant telecommunications number of the other party. Where notice is given by sending in a prescribed manner it shall be deemed to have been received when in the ordinary course of the means of transmission it would be received by the addressee. To prove the giving of a notice it shall be sufficient to show it was despatched. A notice shall have effect from the sooner of its actual or deemed receipt by the addressee.

SCHEDULE 1
Variations

Part 1
Extension of duration

By their respective signatures in Columns 3 and 4 opposite the relevant entry in Column I on the date stated in Column 2, the parties agree that the Appointee's employment is extended to the latest date stated in Column 1.

1	2	3	4
New Expiry Date	Date of this Entry	Signed on behalf of Company	Signed by the Appointee

Part 2
Increase in salary

By their respective signatures in Columns 4 and 5 set opposite the relevant entry in Column 1 on the date stated in Column 3 the parties agree that the Appointee's [basic] salary payable under clause 15.1.1 is increased to the annual rate stated in Column 1 with effect from the date stated in Column 2.

1	2	3	4	5
Revised Annual Rate of Salary	Effective Date of increase	Date of this Entry	Signed on behalf of the Company	Signed by the Appointee

SCHEDULE 2
Commission entitlement

1. Subject to the following provisions the Appointee's entitlement to commission under clause 15.1.2 for each complete financial period of the Company during the currency of this Agreement is _____ per cent of the [amount by which the] net profits of the Company and its subsidiaries] [and its Associated Companies] [exceed IR£ _____] such net profits being ascertained as provided in paragraph 6 below.

[2. The Appointee's entitlement to commission is limited to a maximum of [IR£ _____] [[eg half] his basic salary] in respect of any financial period.]

[3. If during the currency of this Agreement any financial period of the Company shall have a duration other than 365 days (or 366 days in the case of a leap year) the figure of IR£ _____ in clause 15.1.2 shall be adjusted in the same proportion as the number of complete days of the financial period bears to 365.]

4. If the Agreement commences or terminates during the currency of any financial year paragraph[s] [1] [and 2] shall be read and construed as if the references to the net profits of the Company [and its subsidiaries] [and its Associated Companies] for the relevant financial period [and to the figure of IR£ _____] [and in paragraph 2 to the figure of IR£ _____] were references to such proportion of such figures of IR £ _____] and to such proportion of such figure of IR£ _____ as the number of days served by the Appointee under this Agreement during such financial period bears to the total number of days in that financial period.

5. The certificate of the auditors of the Company as to the amount of commission payable shall in the absence of manifest error be final and binding upon the parties and in so certifying the auditors shall be deemed to be acting as experts and not liable in negligence to any person in respect thereof.

6. The net profits of the Company [and its subsidiaries] [and its Associated Companies] means the [consolidated] net revenue profits for such financial period as shown by the audited [consolidated] Profit and Loss Account of the Company [and its subsidiaries] [and its Associated Companies] subject to the following adjustments (if not already taken into account in the Profit and Loss Accounts):

    6.1 Before deducting:

        6.1.1   (subject to 6.2 below) taxation shown by the audited [consolidated] Profit and Loss Account of the [Company];

        6.1.2   the commission payable to the Appointee and any other remuneration calculated on or variable with profits payable to any other director, officer or employee of the Company [and its subsidiaries] [and its Associated Companies];

        [6.1.3   inter-company charges debited for the financial period.]

    6.2 After deducting:

        6.2.1   overseas taxation (other than that for which credit or relief against Irish taxation has been or will be allowed);

        [6.2.2   income from fixed assets and trade investments].

    6.3 Before adding or deducting profits or losses on the revaluation of any assets or any adjustment arising on the translation into pounds IR of assets and liabilities denominated in foreign currencies.

    6.4 Before adjustment for extraordinary items not deriving from the ordinary activities of the Company and [its subsidiaries] [and its Associated Companies] as required by the Statement of Standard Accounting Practice No 6 (SSAP 6).

    6.5 Excluding profits or losses of a capital nature.

    6.6 [If the Company issues shares for consideration and the Board is of the opinion that the income arising from that consideration will result in the material enlargement of net profits then such adjustment shall be made in the calculation of net profits or the Appointee's rate of commission (or partly one and partly the other) as the Company and the Appointee may agree or failing agreement as the auditors in their absolute discretion determine to be fair and reasonable for the purpose of counteracting an enlargement of commission otherwise resulting from the acquisition of additional profits (directly or indirectly) through such increase of issued shared capital.] In so determining, the auditors shall be deemed to be acting as experts and not liable in negligence to any person in respect thereof.

7. The Company (acting by unanimous decision of the Board) may in its discretion pay to the Appointee from time to time during a financial period an interim payment or payments on account of commission. If the payments in any financial period exceed the commission ultimately payable for such year the Board will at its option either carry forward the balance on account of any remuneration due for the next financial period or require that it be repaid by the Appointee within 21 days after the adoption of the accounts for that financial period at the Annual General Meeting.

SCHEDULE 3
Cost of living increase

[1. For the purposes of this Schedule the Appointee's Notional Salary shall, at the date of this Agreement be IR£ _____].

2. If, at any review of the Appointee's salary under clause 15.1.3, the latest figure available of the index of retail prices maintained by the _____ ('the Index') is greater than the figure of the Index taken for the purpose of the last review (or in the case of the first review only, the latest figure of the Index published immediately before the date of this Agreement) then the Company shall with effect from the review date [increase the Appointee's salary by the same percentage as the percentage increase in the Index since the previous review] [increase the Appointee's Salary (as previously increased) by the money amount of the increase in Notional Salary caused by increasing it by the same percentage as the percentage increase in the Index since the last previous review].

3. If prior to the date of any such review the basis of computation of the said Index shall have changed from that subsisting at the date of this Agreement or at the date taken for the purpose of the last previous review as the case may be any official reconciliation between the two bases of computation published shall be binding upon the parties.

4. In the absence of such official reconciliation such adjustments shall be made to the figure of the said Index at the date of any such review to make it correspond as nearly as possible to the previous method of computation and such adjusted figure shall be considered for the purpose of this Schedule to the exclusion of the actual published figure and any dispute regarding such adjustment shall be referred to the auditors for the time being of the Company whose decision shall be final and binding on the parties. In so deciding, the auditors shall be deemed to be acting as experts and not liable in negligence to any person in respect thereof.

SCHEDULE 4
Minimum Notice and Terms of Employment Act, 1973, section 9

The following information is given to supplement the information given in the body of the Agreement in order to comply with the requirements of the Act above.

1. The Appointee's employment by the Company commenced on _____ .

[No employment of the Appointee with a previous employer] [The Appointee's employment with _____] counts as part of the Appointee's continuous employment with the Company [and his continuous employment began on _____].

2. The Appointee's hours of work are the normal hours of the Company from _____ am to _____ pm Monday to Friday each week together with such additional hours as may be necessary so as properly to fulfil his duties.

3. The Appointee is subject to the Company's Disciplinary Rules and Disciplinary Procedures copies of which have been given to the Appointee.

4. If the Appointee has any grievance relating to his employment (other than one relating to a disciplinary decision) he should refer such grievance to the [Managing Director] [Chairman of the Board] [and if the grievance is not resolved by discussion with him it will be referred to the Board for resolution.]

SCHEDULE 5

Service occupancy
See the form suggested ante p.

SCHEDULE 6

A   List of prior knowledge

B   List of clients/customers

Redundancy Payments Act, 1967

Number 21 of 1967

AN ACT TO PROVIDE FOR THE MAKING BY EMPLOYERS OF PAYMENTS TO EMPLOYEES IN RESPECT OF REDUNDANCY, TO ESTABLISH A REDUNDANCY FUND AND TO REQUIRE EMPLOYERS AND EMPLOYEES TO PAY CONTRIBUTIONS TOWARDS THAT FUND, TO PROVIDE FOR PAYMENTS TO BE MADE OUT OF THAT FUND TO EMPLOYERS AND EMPLOYEES, TO PROVIDE FINANCIAL ASSISTANCE TO CERTAIN UNEMPLOYED PERSONS CHANGING RESIDENCE, AND TO PROVIDE FOR OTHER MATTERS (INCLUDING OFFENCES) CONNECTED WITH THE MATTERS AFORESAID. [18th December, 1967.]

BE IT ENACTED BY THE OIREACHTAS AS FOLLOWS:—

PART I

PRELIMINARY AND GENERAL

1.—This Act may be cited as the Redundancy Payments Act, 1967.   Interpretation

2.—(1) In this Act—

"Act of 1952" means the Social Welfare Act, 1952;

"business" includes a trade, industry, profession or undertaking, or any activity carried on by a person or body of persons, whether corporate or unincorporate, or by a public or local authority or a Department of State, and the performance of its functions by a public or local authority or a Department of State;

"date of dismissal", in relation to an employee, means—

> (a) where his contract of employment is terminated by notice given by his employer, the date on which that notice expires,
>
> (b) where his contract of employment is terminated without notice, whether by the employer or by the employee, the date on which the termination takes effect, and
>
> (c) where he is employed under a contract for a fixed term, and that term expires without the contract being renewed, the date on which that term expires, and cognate phrases shall be construed accordingly;

"employee" means a person who has entered into or works under (or, in the case of a contract which has been terminated, worked under) a contract with an employer, whether the contract is for manual labour, clerical work or otherwise, is express or implied, oral or in writing, and whether it is a contract of service or apprenticeship or otherwise, and "employer" and reference to employment shall be construed accordingly;

"employee's redundancy contribution" has the meaning; assigned to it by section 27;

'the National Manpower Service' means the service known by that title and operated under the control of the Minister;"

"lay-off" has the meaning assifned to it by section 11(1);

"lump sum" has the meaning assigned to it by section 19;

"the Minister" mean the Minister for Labour;

"prescribed" means prescribed by regulations made by the Minister under this Act;

"rebate" has the meaning assigned to it by section 29;

"redundancy payment" has the meaning assigned to it by section 7;

"short-time" has the meaning assigned to it by section 11(2) or section 11(3) (as the case may be).

"sickness" or "illness" includes being incapable of work within the meaning of the Act of 1952;

"special redundancy scheme" has the meaning assigned to it by section 47;

"the Tribunal" has the meaning assigned to it by section 39(1);

"week", in relation to an employee whose remuneration is calculated weekly by a week ending on a day other than Saturday, means a week ending on that other day and, in relation to any other employee, means a week ending on Saturday, and "weekly" shall be construed accordingly;

"weekly payment" has the meaning assigned to it by section 30.

(2) In this Act a reference to a Part, section or schedule is to a Part or section of, or schedule to, this Act unless it is indicated that reference to some other enactment is intended.

(3) In this Act reference to a subsection, paragraph, sub-paragraph or other division is to the subsection, paragraph, sub-paragraph or other division of the provision (including a schedule) in which the reference occurs, unless it is indicated that reference to another provision is intended.

(4) For the purposes of the operation of this Act in relation to an employee whose remuneration is payable to him by a person other than his employer, reference in this Act to an employer shall be construed as reference to the person by whom the remuneration is payable.

Classes of persons to which the Act applies
4.—(1) Subject to this section and to section 47 this Act shall apply to employees employed in employment which is insurable for all benefits under the Social Welfare Acts, 1952 to 1966 and to employlees who were so employed in such employment in the period of [four] years ending on the date of termination of employment.

[Notwithstanding ..., this Act, that Act shall, with effect from the 6th day of April, 1980, not apply to a person who on the date of termination of his employment had attained the age which on that date is the pensionable age within the meaning of the Social Welfare Act, 1952.]

(2) This Act shall not apply to a person who is normally expected to work for the same employer for less than [8] hours in a week.

(3) (*a*) For the purpose of the application of this Act to an employee who is employed in a private household this Act (other than section 20) shall apply as if the household were a business and the maintenance of the household were the carrying on of that business by the employer.

(*b*) This Act shall not apply to any person in respect of employment where the employer is the father, mother, grandfather, grandmother, stepfather, stepmother, son, daughter, grandson, granddaughter, stepson, stepdaughter, brother, sister, halfbrother or halfsister of the employee, where the employee is a member of the employer's household and the employment is related to a private dwelling house or a farm in or on which both the employer and the employee reside

(c) In deducing any relationship for the purposes of paragraph (*b*)—

(i) a person adopted under the Adoption Acts 1952 and 1964, shall be considered the legitimate offspring of the adopter or adopters;

(ii) subject to clause (i) of this paragraph, an illegitimate person shall be

considered the legitimate offspring of his mother and reputed father;
(iii) a person *in loco parentis* to another shall be considered the parent of that other.

(4) The Minister may by order declare that this Act shall not apply to a class or classes of persons specified in the order and from the commencement of the order this Act shall not apply to that class or those classes.

(5) Notwithstanding subsection (2), the Minister may by order declare that this Act shall apply to a specified class of worker and from the commencement of the order this Act shall apply to that class.

(6) Thc Minister may by order amend or revoke an order under this section.

5.—(1) Whenever an order is proposed to be made under section 4(4), 4(5), 4(6), 19(3), 30(3) or 47 [or s. 17 of the Redundancy Payments Act, 1970], a draft of the proposed order shall be laid before each House of the Oireachtas and the order shall not be made until a rcsolution approving of the draft has been passed by each such House. Laying of regulations and certain draft orders

(2) Every regulation made under this Act shall be laid before each House of the Oireachtas as soon as may be after it is made and, if a resolution annulling the regulation is passed by either such House within the next twenty-one days on which that House has sat after the regulation is laid before it the regulation shall be annulled according but without prejudice to the validity of anything previously done thereunder.

PART II

REDUNDANCY PAYMENT

6.—In this Part— Definitions for Part II
"cease" means cease either temporarily or permanently and from whatever cause;
"lock-out" means the closing of a place of employment, or the suspension of work, or the refusal by an employer to continue to employ any number of persons employed by him in consequence of a dispute, done with a view to compelling those persons, or to aid another employer in compelling persons employed by him, to accept terms or conditions of or affecting employment;
"notice of intention" to claim has the meaning assigned to it by section 12;
"redundancy certificate" has the meaning assigned to it by section 18;
"strike" means the cessation of work by a body of persons employed acting in combination or a concerted refusal or a refusal under a common understanding of any number of persons employed to continue to work for an employer in consequence of a dispute, done as a means of compelling their employer or any person or body of persons employed, or to aid other employees in compelling their employer or any person or body of persons employed, to accept or not to accept terms or conditions of or affecting employment.

7.—(1) An employee, if he is dismissed by his employer by reason of redundancy or is laid off or kept on short-time for the minimum period, shall, subject to this Act, be entitled to the payment of moneys while shall be known (and are in this Act referred to) as redundancy payment provided— General right to redundancy payment
(*a*) he has been employed for the requisite period, and
(*b*) he was an employed contributor in employment which was insurable for all benefits under the Social Welfare Acts, 1952 to 1966, immediately before the date of the termination of his employment or had ceased to be ordinarily

employed in employment which was so insurable in the period of [four] years ending on that date.

(2) For the purposes of subsection (1), an employee who is dismissed shall be taken to be dismissed by reason of redundancy if the dismissal is attributable wholly or mainly to—

(a) the fact that his employer has ceased, or intends to cease, to carry on the business for the purposes of which the employee was employed by him, or has ceased or intends to cease, to carry on that business in the place where the employee was so employed, or

(b) the fact that the requirements of that business for employees to carry out work of a particular kind in the place where he was so employed have ceased or diminished or are expected to cease or diminish, or

(c) the fact that his employer has decided to carry on the business with fewer or no employees, whether by requiring the work for which the employee had been employed (or had been doing before his dismissal) to be done by other employees or otherwise, or

(d) the fact that his employer has decided that the work for which the employee had been employed (or had been doing before his dismissal) should henceforward be done in a different manner for which the employee is not sufficiently qualified or trained, or

(e) the fact that his employer has decided that the work for which the employee had been employed (or had been doing before his dismissal) should henceforward be done by a person who is also capable of doing other work for which the employee is not sufficiently qualified or trained.

(3) For the purposes of subsection (1), an employee shall be taken as having been laid off or kept on short-time for the minimum period if he has been laid off or kept on short-time for a period of four or more consecutive weeks, or for a period of six or more weeks which are not consecutive but which fall within a period of thirteen consecutive weeks.

(4) Notwithstanding any other provision of this Act, where an employee who has been serving a period of apprenticeship training with an employer under an apprenticeship agreement is dismissed within one month after the end of that period, that employee shall not, by reason of that dismissal, be entitled to reaundancy payment.

(4A) In ascertaining, for the purposes of subsection (2)(c), whether an employer has decided to carry on a business with fewer or no employees, account shall not be taken of the following members of the employer's family—

father, mother, stepfather, stepmother, son, daughter, adopted child. grandson, granddaughter, stepson, stepdaughter, brother, sister, halfbrother, halfsister.

(5) In this section "requisite period" means a period of [104] weeks continuous employment (within the mcaning of Schedule 3) of the employee by the employer who dismissed him, laid him off or kept him on short-time, but excluding any period of employment with that employer before the employee had attained the age of 16 years.

Qualification of general right under section 7

8.—(1) Notwithstanding anything in section 7, where an employee who had been dismissed by reason of redundancy or laid off has, during the period of the the the four years immediately preceding the date of dismissal or the lay-off, been laid off for an average annual period of more than twelve weeks, the following provisions shall have effect:

(a) that employee shall not become entitled to redundancy payment by reason of dismissal or lay-off until a period equal to the average annual period of lay-off over the said four-year period in relation to that employee has elapsed after the date of dismissal or lay-off;

(b) if, before the termination of the period required to elapse under paragraph (a), that employee resumes work with the same employer, that employee shall not be entitled to redundancy payment in relation to that diimissal or lay-off;

(*c*) if, before the termination of the period required to elapse under paragraph (*a*), the employer offers to re-employ that employee and that employee unreasonably refuses the offer, he shall not be entitled to redundancy payment in relation to that dismissal or lay-off.

(2) In a case where this section applies, the period of four weeks first referred to in section 12 or the period of thirteen weeks referred to in that section shall not commence until the expiration of the period (referred to in subsection (1)(*a*)) equal to the appropriate average annual period of lay-off.

9. (1) For the purposes of this Part an employee shall, subject to this Part, be taken to be dismissed by his employer if but only if— Dismissal by employer

(*a*) the contract under which he is employed by the employer is terminated by the employer, whether by or without notice, or

(*b*) where under the contract under which he is employed by the employer he is employed for a fixed term, that term expires without being renewed under the same or a similar contract, or

(*c*) the employee terminates the contract under which he is employed by the employer in circumstances (not falling within subsection (5)) such that he is entitled so to terminate it by reason of the employer's conduct.

(2) An employee shall not be taken for the purposes of this Part to be dismissed by his employer if his contract of employment is renewed, or he is re-engaged by the same employer under a new contract of employment, and—

(*a*) in a case where the provisions of the contract as renewed or of the new contract as to the capacity and place in which he is employed and as to the other terms and conditions of his employment, do not differ from the corresponding provisions of the previous contract, the renewal or re-engagement takes effect immediately on the ending of his employment under the previous contract.

(*b*) in any other case, the renewal or re-engagement is in pursuance of an offer in writing made by his employer before the ending of his employment under the previous contract, and takes effect either immediately on the ending of that employment or after an interval of not more than four weeks thereafter.

(3) (*a*) An employee shall not be taken for the purposes of this Part as having been dismissed by his employer if—

(i) he is re-engaged by another employer (hereinafter referred to as the new employer) immediately on the termination of his previous employment,

(ii) the re-engagement takes place with the agreement of the employee, the previous employer and the new employer,

(iii) before the commencement of the period of employment with the new employer the employee receives a statement in writing on behalf of the previous employer and the new employer which—

(A) sets out the terms and conditions of the employee's contract of employment with the new employer,

(B) specifies that the employee's period of service with the previous employer will, for the purposes of this Act, be regarded by the new employer as service with the new employer,

(C) contains particulars of the service mentioned in clause (B), and

(D) the employee notifies in writing the new employer that the employee accepts the statement required by this subparagraph.

(*b*) Where in accordance with this subsection an employee is re-engaged by the new employer, the service of that employee with the previous employer shall for the purposes of this Act be deemed to be service with the new employer.

(4) For the purposes of the application of subsection (2) to a contract under which the employment ends on a Friday, Saturday or Sunday—

(*a*) the renewal or rengageement shall be treated as taking effect immediately on the ending of the employment under the previous contract if it takes effect on or before the next Monday after that Friday, Saturday or Sunday, and

(*b*) the interval of four weeks mentioned in subsection (2)(*b*) shall be calculated as if the employment had ended on that Monday.

(5) When an employee terminates his contract of employment without notice, being entitled to do so by reason of a lock-out by his employer, subsection (1)(c) shall not apply to that termination.

(6) Where by virtue of subsection (2) an employee is treated as not having been dismissed by reason of a renewal or re-engagement taking effect after an interval, then, in determining for the purposes of section 7(1) whether he has been continuously employed for the requisite period, the period of that shall count as a period of employment.

(7) In determining for the purposes of this Act whether at a particular time before the commencement of this Act an employee was dismissed by his employer, the appropriate provisions of this section shall apply as if the matter to be decided occurred after such commencement.

Employee anticipating expiry of employer's notice

10.—(1) This section shall have effect where—

(*a*) an employer gives notice to an employee to terminate his contract of employment, and

(*b*) at a time within the obligatory period of that notice, the employee gives notice in writing to the employer to terminate the contract of employment on a date earlier than the date on which the employer's notice is due to expire.

(2) Subject to subsection (3), in the circumstances specified in subsection (1) the employee shall, for the purposes of this Part, be taken to be dismissed by his employer, and the date of dismissal in relation to that dismissal shall be the date on which the employee's notice expires.

(3) If, before the employee's notice is due to expire, the employer gives him notice in writing—

(*a*) requiring him to withdraw his notice terminating the contract of employment as mentioned in subsection (1)(*b*) and to continue in the employment until the date on which the employer's notice expires, and

(*b*) stating that, unless he does so, the employer will contest any liability to pay to him a redundancy payment in respect of the termination of his contract of employment,

but the employee unreasonably refuses to comply with the requirements of that notice, the employee shall not be entitled to a redundancy payment by virtue of subsection (2).

(3A) Where an employer agrees in writing with an employee to alter the date of dismissal mentioned in a notice under subsection (1)(*a*) given by him to that employee so as to ensure that the employee's notice under subsection (1)(*b*) will be within the obligatory period in relation to the notice under subsection (1)(*a*), the employee's entitlement to redundancy payment shall be unaffected and the employee shall, for the purposes of this Part, be taken to be dismissed by his employer, the date of dismissal in relation to that dismissal being the date on which the employee's notice expires.

(4) In this section—

   (*a*) if the actual period of the employer's notice (that is to say, the period beginning at the time when the notice is given and ending at the time when it expires) is equal to the minimum period which (whether by virtue of any enactment or otherwise) is required to be given by the employer to terminate the contract of employment, "the obligatory period", in relation to that notice, means the actual period of the notice;

   (b) in any other case.

"the obligatory period", in relation to an employer's notice, means that period which, being equal to the minimum period referred to in paragraph (*a*), expires at the time when the employer's notice expires.

11.—(1) Where an employee's employment ceases by reason of his employer's being unable to provide the work for which the employee was employed to do, and— Lay-off and short time

   (*a*) it is reasonable in the circumstances for that employer to believe that the cessation of employment will not be permanent, and

   (*b*) the employer gives notice to that effect to the employee prior to the cessation,

that cessation of employment shall be regarded for the purposes of this Act as lay-off.

(2) Where—

   (*a*) for any week an employee's remuneration is less than one-half of his normal weekly remuneration or his hours of work are reduced to less than one-half of his normal weekly hours,

   (*b*) the reduction in remuneration or hours of work is caused by a diminution either in the work provided for the employee by his employer or in other work of a kind which under his contract the employee is employed to do,

   (*c*) it is reasonable in the circumstances for the employer to believe that the diminution in work will not be permanent and he gives notice to that effect to the employee prior to the reduction in remuneration or hours of work,

the employee shall, for the purposes of this Part, be taken to be kept on short-time for that week.

12.—(1) An employee shall not be entitled to redundancy payment by reason of having been laid off or kept on short-time unless— Right to redundancy payment by reason of lay-off or short time

   (*a*) he has been laid off or kept on short-time for four or more consecutive weeks or, within a period of thirteen weeks, for a series of six or more weeks of which not more than three were consecutive, and

   (*b*) after the expiry of the relevant period of lay-off or short-time mentioned in paragraph (a) and not later than four weeks after the cessation of the lay-off or short-time, he gives to his employer notice (in this Part referred to as a notice of intention to claim) in writing of his intention to claim redundancy payment in respect of lay-off or short-time.

(2) Where, after the expiry of the relevant period of lay-off or short-time mentioned in subsection (1)(*a*) and not later than four weeks after the cessation of the lay-off or short time, an employee to whom that subsection applies, in lieu of giving to his employer a notice of intention to claim, terminates his contract of employment either by giving him the notice thereby required or, if none is so required, by giving him not less than one week's notice in writing of intention to terminate the contract, the notice so given shall, for the purposes of this Part and of Schedule 2, be deemed to be a notice of intention to claim given in writing

to the employer by the employee on the date on which the notice is actually given.

Right of
employer to
give
counter-notice **13.**—(1) Subject to subsection (2), an employee shall not be entitled to a redundancy payment in pursuance of a notice of intention to claim if, on the date of service of that notice, it was reasonably to be expected that the employee (if he continued to be employed by the same employer) would, not later than four weeks after that date, enter upon a period of employment of not less than thirteen weeks during which he would not be laid off or kept on short-time for any week.

(2) Subsection (1) shall not apply unless, within seven days after the service of the notice of intention to claim, the employer gives to the employee notice (in this Part referred to as a counter-notice) in writing that he will contest any liability to pay to him a redundancy payment in pursuance of the notice of intention to claim.

(3) If, in a case where an employee gives notice of intention to claim and the employer gives a counter-notice, the employee continues or has continued during the next four weeks after the date of service of the notice of intention to claim, to be employed by the same employer, and he is or has been laid off or kept on short-time for each of those weeks, it shall be conclusively presumed that the condition specified in subsection (1) was not fulfilled.

(4) For the purposes of section 12 and for the purposes of subsection (3)—

> (*a*) it is immaterial whether a series of weeks (whether it is four weeks or four or more weeks, or six or more weeks) consists wholly of weeks for which the employee is laid off or wholly of weeks for which he is kept on short-time or partly of the other;

> (*b*) no account shall be taken of any week for which an employee is laid off or kept on short-time where the lay-off or short-time is wholly or mainly attributable to a strike or a lock-out, whether the strike or lock-out is in the trade or industry in which the employee is employed or not and whether it is in the State or elsewhere.

Disentitlement
to redundancy
benefit
because of
dismissal for
misconduct **14.**—(1) Subject to subsection (2), an employee who has been dismissed shall not be entitled to redundancy payment if his employer, being entitled to terminate that employee's contract of employment without notice by reason of the employee's conduct, terminates the contract beacuse of the employee's conduct—

> (*a*) without notice,

> (*b*) by giving notice shorter than that which, in the absence of such conduct, the employer would be required to give to terminate the contract, or

> (*c*) by giving notice (other than such notice as is mentioned in subparagraph (*b*)) which includes, or is accompanied by, a statement in writing that the employer would, by reason of such conduct, be entitled to terminate the contract without notice.

(2) When an employee who has received the notice required by section 17 takes part, before the date of dismissal, in a strike and his employer by reason of such participation, terminates the contract of employment with the employee in a manner mentioned in subsection (1), that subsection shall not apply to such termination.

(3) Where an employee who has given notice to terminate his contract of employment by reason of lay-off or short-time takes part, before the expiry of the notice, in a strike and, by Disentitlement
to redundancy
payment for
refusal to
accept
alternative
employment reason of such participation, is dismissed, subsection (1) shall not apply.

15.—(1) An employee shall not be entitled to a redundancy payment if—

> (*a*) his employer has offered to renew that employee's contract of employment or to re-engage him under a new contract of employment,

(b) the provisions of the contract as renewed, or of the new contract, as to the capacity and place in which he would be employed and as to the other terms and conditions of his employment would not differ from the corresponding provisions of the contract in force immediately before the termination of his contract.

(c) the renewal or re-engagement would take effect on or before the date of the termination of his contract, and

(d) he has unreasonably refused the offer.

(2) An employee shall not be entitled to a redundancy payment if—

(a) his employer has made to him in writing an offer to renew the employee's contract of employment or to re-engage him under a new contract of employment,

(b) the provisions of the contract as renewed, or of the new contract, as to the capacity and place in which he would be employed and as to the other terms and conditions of his employment would differ wholly or in part from the corresponding provisions of his contract in force immediately before the termination of his contract.

(c) the offer constitutes an offer of suitable employment in relation to the employee,

(d) the renewal or re-engagement would take effect not later than four weeks after the date of the termination of contract, and

(e) he has unreasonably refused the offer.

(2A) Where an employee who has been offered suitable employment and has carried out, for a period of not more than four weeks, the duties of that employment, refuses the offer, the temporary acceptance of that employment shall not solely constitute an unreasonable refusal for the purposes of this section.

(2B) Where—

(a) an employee's remuneration is reduced substantially but not to less than one-half of his normal weekly remuneration, or his hours of work are reduced substantially but not to less than one-half of his normal weekly hours, and

(b) the employee temporarily accepts the reduction in remuneration or hours of work and indicates his acceptance to his employer,

such a temporary acceptance for a period not exceeding 52 weeks shall not be taken to be an acceptance by the employee of an offer of suitable employment in relation to him.

16.—(1) Where the employer is a company, any reference in this Part to re-engagement *Associated* by the employer shall be construed as a reference to re-engagement by that company or by *companies* an associated company, and any reference in this Part to an offer made by the employer shall be construed as including a reference to an offer made by an associated company.

(2) Subsection (1) shall not affect the operation of section 20 in a case where the previous owner and new onner (as defined by that section) are associated companies; and where that section applies, subsection (1) shall not apply.

(3) Where an employee is dismissed by his employer, and the employer is a company (in this subsection referred to as the employing company) which has one or more associated companies, then if—

(a) none of the conditions specified in section 7(2) is fulfilled, but

(b) one or other of those conditions would be fulfilled if the business of the employing company and the business of the associated company (or, if more than one, each of the associated companies) were treated as together constituting one business, that condition shall for the purposes of this Part be taken to be fulfilled in relation to the dismissal of the employee.

(4) For the purposes of this section two companies shall be taken to be associatcd companies if one is a subsidiary of the other, or both are subsidiaries of a third company, and "associated company" shall be construed accordingly.

(5) In this section—

"company" includes any body corporate;

"subsidiary" has the same meaning as, by virtue of section 155 of the Companies Act, 1963, it has for the purposes of that Act.

Notice of proposed dismissal for redundancy

17.—(1) An employer who proposes to dismiss by reason of redundancy an employee who has not less than [104] weeks service with that employer shall, not later than two weeks before the date of dismissal, give to the employee notice in writing of the proposed dismissal and send to the Minister a copy of that notice.

(2) The Minister may make regulations for giving effect to this section and, without prejudice to the generality of the foregoing, regulations under this section may relate to all or any of the following matters—

> (a) the particulars to be stated in the notice,
>
> (b) the method of service of the notice,
>
> (c) the furnishing to the Minister of a copy of the notice and the time for furnishing such a copy.

(3) An employer who fails to comply with this section or who furnishes false information in a notice under this section shall be guilty of an offence and shall be liable on summary conviction to a fine not exceeding fifty pounds.

Redundancy certificate

18.—(1) When an employer dismisses by reason of redundancy an employee who has not less than [104] weeks continuous employment, he shall give to the employee not later than the date of the dismissal a certificate (in this Part referred to as a redundancy certificate).

(2) Whenever an employee who has not less than [104] weeks continuous employment gives notice of intention to claim in accordance with section 12, his employer shall, subject to section 13, give him, not later than seven days after the service of the notice of intention to claim, a redundancy certificate.

(3) The Minister may make regulations for giving effect to this section and, without prejudice to the generality of the foregoing, may prescribe the particulars to be stated on a redundancy certificate.

(4) An employer who fails to comply with this section or who furnishes false information in a redundancy certificate shall be guilty of an offence and shall be liable on summary conviction to a fine not exceeding £200 pounds.

Payment of lump sum by employer

19.—(1) Upon the dismissal by reason of redundancy of an employee who is entitled under this Part to redundancy payment, or where by virtue of section 12 an employee becomes entitled to redundancy payment, his employer shall pay to him an amount which is referred to in this Act as the lump sum.

(2) Schedule 3 shall apply in relation to the lump sum.

(3) The Minister may by order amend Schedule 3.

Change of ownership of business

20.—(1) This section shall have effect where—

> (a) a change occurs (whether by virtue of a sale or other disposition or by operation of law) in the ownership of a business for the purposes of which a person is employed, or of a part of such a business, and

(*b*) in connection with that change the person by whom the employee is employed immediately before the change occurs (in this section referred to as the previous owner) terminates the employee's contract of employment, whether by or without notice.

(2) If, by agreement with the employee, the person (in this section referred to as the new owner) who immediately after the change occurs is the owner of the business or of the part of the business in question as the case may be renews the employee's contract of employment (with the substitution of the new owner for the previous owner or re-engages him under a new contract of employment, section 9(2) shall have effect as if the renewal or re-engagement had been a renewal or re-engagement by the previous owner (without any substitution of the new owner for the previous owner).

(3) If the new owner offers to renew the employee's contract of employment (with the substitution of the new owner for the previous owner) or to re-engage him under a new contract of employment, but the employee refuses the offer, section 15 (1) or section 15(2) (as may be appropriate) shall have effect, subject to subsection (4) of this section, in relation to that offer and refusal as it would have had in relation to the like offer made by the previous owner and a refusal of that offer by the employee.

(4) For the purposes of the operation, in accordance with subsection (3) of this section, of section 15(1) or 15(2) in relation to an offer made by the new owner,—

(*a*) the offer shall be treated as one whereby the provisions of the contract as renewed, or of the new contract, as the case may be, would differ from the corresponding provisions of the contract as in force immediately before the dismissal by reason only that the new owner would be substituted for the previous owner as the employer, and

(b) no account shall be taken of that substitution in determining whether the refusal of the offer was unreasonable.

(5) Subsections (1) to (4) shall have effect (subject to the necessary modifications) in relation to a case where—

(*a*) the person by whom a business, or part of a business, is owned immediately before a change is one of the persons by whom (whether as partners, trustees or otherwise) it is owned immediately after the change, or

(*b*) the persons by whom a business, or part of a business, is owned immediately before a change (whether as partners, trustees or otherwise) include the person by whom or include one or more of the persons by whom, it is owned immediately after the change,

as those provisions have effect where the previous owner and the new owner are wholly different persons.

(5A) In a case mentioned in subsection (1)(*a*), the new owner shall be estopped from denying that an employee was in continuous employment (within the meaning of Schedule 3) unless, within 26 weeks of the change of ownership, he notifies the employee of his intention so to deny.

(6) Nothing in this section shall be construed as requiring any variation of a contract of employment by agreement between the parties to be treated as constituting a termination of the contract.

[–(1) Where—

(i) a change relating to the control or management of a business (or part thereof) for the purposes of which a person is employed occurs, but a change in the ownership of the business (or part thereof) does not occur,

(ii) section 20 of th[is] Act would have applied to that change if it were a change in the ownership of that business (or part thereof), and

(iii) an employee of the previous owner accepts, before, on or within four weeks of the termination of his contract of employment with the previous owner, an offer by the new owner of employment in the same place of employment and on terms which are either the same as, or not materially less advantageous to the employee than, his existing terms of employment,

the said section 20 shall apply to that change as if a change of ownership of that business (or part thereof) had occurred.

(2) In this section "previous owner" and "new owner" mean, respectively, the persons who would have been the previous owner and the new owner within the meaning of the said section 20 if a change of ownership of a business (or part thereof) had occurred. [1971 Act, s. 6].

Implied or constructive termination of contract

21.—(1) Where, in accordance with any enactment or rule of law, any act on the part of an employer or any event affecting an employer (including in the case of an individual, his death) operates so as to terminate a contract under which an employee is employed by him, that act or event shall for the purposes of this Act be treated as a termination of the contract by the employer, if apart from this subsection, it would not constitute a termination of the contract by him.

(2) Where—

(a) subsection (1) applies,

(b) the employee's contract of employment is not renewed, and

(c) he is not re-engaged under a new contract, as provided by section 9(2),

he shall for the purposes of this Act be taken to be dismissed by reason of redundancy if the circumstances in which the contract is not renewed and he is not re-engaged (as provided by the said section 9(2)) are wholly mainly attributable to a fact specified in section 7 (2).

(3) For the purposes of subsection (2), section 7(2)(a), in so far as it relates to the employer ceasing or intending to cease to carry on the business, shall be construed as if the reference to the employer included a reference to any person to whom, in consequence of the act or event in question, power to dispose of the business has passed.

(4) In this section reference to section 9(2) includes reference to that section as applied by section 20(2).

Application of this part upon employer's or employee's death

22.–(1) Part I of Schedule 2 shall have effect in relation to the death of an employer.

(2) Part 2 of Schedule 2 shall have effect in relation to the death of an employee.

Modification of right to redundancy payment where previous payment has been paid

23.—(1) This section shall apply where—

(a) a lump sum is paid to an employee under section 19, whether in respect of dismissal, lay-off or short-time,

(b) the contract of employment under which he was employed (in this section referred to as the previous contract) is renewed, whether by the same or another employer, or he is re-engaged under a new contract of employment, whether by the same or another employer, and

(c) the circumstances of the renewal or re-engagement are such that, in determining for the purposes of section 7(1) or Schedule 3 whether at any subsequent time he has been continuously employed for the requisite period, or for what period he has been continuously employed, the continuity of his period of employment would, apart from this section, be treated as not having been broken by the termination of the previous contract and the renewal or re-engagement.

(2) In determining for the purposes of section 7(1) or section 19 in a case to which this section applies whether at any subsequent time an employee has been continuously employed for the requisite period, or for what period he has been continuously employed, the continuity of the period of employment shall be treated as having been broken at the date which was the date of dismissal in relation to the lump sum mentioned in subsection (1)(*a*), and any time before that date shall be disregarded.

(3) For the purposes of this section a lump sum shall be treated as having been paid if the whole of the payment has been paid to the employee by the employer or if the Minister has paid a sum to the employee in respect of the redundancy payment under section 32.

(4) This section shall not apply to any case to which section 19 of the Unfair Dismissals Act, 1977, applies.

24.—(1) Notwithstanding any other provision of this Act, an employee shall not be entitled to a lump sum unless before the end of the period of [52] weeks beginning on the date of dismissal or the date of termination of employment— *Time limits on claims for redundancy payments*

    (*a*) the payment has been agreed and paid, or

    (*b*) the employee has made a claim for the payment by notice in writing given to the employer, or

    (*c*) a question as to the right of the employee to the payment, or as to the amount of the payment, has been referred to the Tribunal under section 39.

(2A) Where an employee who fails to make a claim for a lump sum within the period of 52 weeks mentioned in subsection (1) makes such a claim before the end of the period of 104 weeks beginning on the date of dismissal or the date of termination of employment, the Tribunal, if it is satisfied that the employee would have been entitled to the lump sum and that the failure was due to a reasonable cause, may declare the employee to be entitled to the lump sum and the employee shall thereupon become so entitled.

(3) Notwithstanding subsection (2A), where an employee establishes to the satisfaction of the Tribunal—

    (*a*) that failure to make a claim for a lump sum before the end of the period of 104 weeks mentioned in that subsection was caused by his ignorance of the identity of his employer or employers or by his ignorance of a change of employer involving his dismissal and engagement under a contract with another employer, and

    (*b*) that such ignorance arose out of or was contributed to by a breach of a statutory duty to give the employee either notice of his proposed dismissal or a redundancy certificate.

the period of 104 weeks shall commence from such date as the Tribunal at its discretion considers reasonable having regard to all the circumstances.

25.—(1) An employee shall not be entitled to redundancy payment if on the date of dismissal he is outside the State, unless under his contract of employment he ordinarily worked in the State. *Employment wholly or partly abroad*

(2) Notwithstanding subsection (1), an employee who under his contract of employment ordinarily works outside the State shall not be entitled to redundancy payment unless, immediately before he commenced to work outside the State, he was domiciled in the State and was in the employment of the employer concerned and unless—

    (*a*) he was in the State in accordance with the instructions of his employer on the date of dismissal, or

    (*b*) he had not been afforded a reasonable opportunity by his employer of being in the State on that date.

(3) In computing, for the purposes of this Act, for what period of service a person was in continuous employment, any period of service in the employment of the employer concerned while the employee was outside the State shall be deemed to have been service in the employment of that employer within the State.

(4) Where an employee who has worked for his employer outside the State becomes entitled to redundancy payment under this Act, the employer in making any lump sum payment due to the employee under section 19 shall be entitled to deduct from that payment any redundancy payment to which that employee may have been entitled under a statutory scheme relating to redundancy in the State in which he was working.

PART III

REDUNDANCY FUND

Financing of Redundancy Fund **27.**—All moneys received by the Minister under this Act shall be paid into the Social Insurance Fund and all payments made pursuant to this Act shall be made out of that Fund.

Relates to employers **29.**—(1) Subject to this Part, the Minister shall make from the Redundancy Fund a payment to an employer of such sum (in this Part to as a rebate) as is equivalent in amount to 60 per cent of each lump sum paid by that employer under section 19.

(2) Notwithstanding subsection (1), whenever an employer fails to comply with any provision of section 17, the Minister may at his discretion reduce the amount of the rebate payable in respect of the lump sum paid under section 19 to that employer, but the amount of rebate when so reduced shall not be less than 40 per cent of the lump sum.

(3) The Minister may by regulation, made with the consent of the Minister for Finance, vary a rate of rebate specified in this section.

PART IV

MISCELLANEOUS PROVISIONS

Decisions by deciding officers **38.**—(1) Subject to this Act and in accordance with any relevant regulations, every question arising—

    (*a*) in relation to a claim for a payment,

    (*e*) as to who is the employer of an employee, or

    (*f*) on such other matter relating to this Act as may be prescribed,

shall be decided by a deciding officer.

Redundancy Appeals Tribunal **39.**—(1) There shall be a Tribunal (which shall be known as the [Employment] Appeals Tribunal . . .) to determine the appeals provided for in this section. . . .

(16) A deciding officer may if he so thinks proper, instead of deciding it himself, refer in the prescribed manner to the Tribunal for a section thereon any question which falls to be decided by him under section 38.

Voidance of purported exclusion of provisions of this Act **51.**—(1) Any provision is an agreement (whether a contract of employment or not) shall be void in so far as it purports to exclude or limit the operation of any provision of this Act.

SCHEDULE 2

DEATH OF EMPLOYER OR EMPLOYEE

SECTION 3

AMOUNT OF LUMP SUM

1.—The amount of the lump sum shall be equivalent to the aggregate of the following—

   (*a*) the produce of one-half of the employee's normal weekly remuneration and the number of years of continuous employment, with the employer in whose employment he was on the date of dismissal or by whom he was employed when he gave notice of intention to claim under section 12 between the date on which the employee attained the age of sixteen years and the date on which he attained the age of forty-one years, and

   (*b*) the product to the employee's normal weekly remuneration and the number of years of continuous employment, with the employer in whose employment he was on the date of dismissal or by whom he was employed when he gave notice of intention to claim under section 12 after the employee had attained the age of forty-one, and

   (*c*) a sum equivalent to the employee's weekly remuneration.

2.—In calculating the amount of the lump sum any part of the employee's earnings per annum in excess of [£13,000] shall be disregarded.

3.—(*a*) For the purpose of ascertaining for the purposes of paragraph 1, the number of *years of continuous* employment, the *number of weeks* in the period of continuous employment shall be ascertained in accordance with this Schedule and the result shall be *divided by 52.*

   (*b*) In ascertaining the number of weeks in the period of continuous employment, a week which under this Schedule is *not* allowable as *reckonable service* shall be disregarded.

   (*c*) When the division required under subparagraph (*a*) produces a *remainder of 26 or more weeks*, this remaining period of 26 (or more) weekly *shall be counted as a year* of continuous employment but if that division produces a remainder of less than 26 weeks that period shall be disregarded.

   (*d*) When the total number of years of continuous employment as ascertained in accordance with subparagraphs (*a*) to (*c*) falls to be divided for the purposes of paragraphs 1(*a*) and 1(*b*), any remaining parts of a year in those divisions shall be aggregated and the number of full years represented by this aggregation (when calculated in accordance with subparagraphs (*a*) to (*c*)) shall be added to the period of employment mentioned in paragraph 1(*a*).

Continuous employment (paras. 4-6).

Reckonable Service (paras. 7-12).

Normal Weekly Remuneration (paras. 13-22).

Redundancy Payments Act, 1971

Number 20 *of* 1971

AN ACT TO AMEND AND EXTEND THE REDUNDANCY PAYMENTS ACT, 1967, AND TO PROVIDE FOR OTHER MATTERS CONNECTED WITH THE MATTERS AFORESAID. [*27th July*, 1971.]

BE IT ENACTED BY THE OIREACHTAS AS FOLLOWS:

Presumptions by Tribunal

10.—For the purposes to the Tribunal—

(*a*) a person's employment during any period shall, unless the contrary is proved, be presumed to have been continuous;

(*b*) an employee who has been dismissed by his employer shall, unless the contrary is proved, be presumed to have been so dismissed by reason of redundancy;

(*c*) the Tribunal shall, after consultation with any person or body charged by statute with the fixing or determination of minimum wages or rates of pay, or the registration of employment agreements under the Industrial Relations Act, 1946, have regard to any such minimum as is appropriate or relevant.

Reciprocal arrangements

17.—(1) The Minister may make such orders as may be necessary to carry out any reciprocal or other arrangements, made with the proper authority under any other Government, in respect of matters relating to redundancy payments, and may by any such order make such adaptations of and modifications in the Principal Act as he considers necessary.

(2) The Minister may by order amend or revoke an order under is section.

Minimum Notice and Terms of Employment Act, 1973

Number 4 of 1973

AN ACT TO REQUIRE A MINIMUM PERIOD OF NOTICE TO TERMINATE THE EMPLOYMENT OF THOSE WHO HAVE BEEN EMPLOYED FOR A QUALIFYING PERIOD, TO PROVIDE FOR MATTERS CONNECTED WITH THE GIVING OF NOTICE, AND TO REQUIRE EMPLOYERS TO GIVE WRITTEN PARTICULARS OF THE TERMS OF EMPLOYMENT, AND TO PROVIDE FOR OTHER MATTERS CONNECTED WITH THE MATTERS AFORESAID. [9th May, 1973]

BE IT ENACTED BY THE OIREACHTAS AS FOLLOWS:

1.—In this Act—

"the Act of 1967" means the Redundancy Payments Act, 1967;

Interpretation

"employee" means an individual who has entered into or works, under a contract with an employer, whether the contract be for manual labour, clerical work or otherwise, whether it be expressed or implied, oral or in writing, and whether it be a contract of service or of apprenticeship or otherwise, and cognate expressions shall be construed accordingly;

"lay-off" has the meaning assigned to it by the Act of 1967;

"lock-out" has the meaning assigned to it by Part II of the Act of 1967;

"Minister" means the Minister for Labour;

"prescribed" means prescribed by regulations made by the Minister under this Act;

"short-time" has the meaning assigned to it by the Act of 1967;

"strike" has the meaning assigned to it by Part II of the Act of 1967;

"the Tribunal" means the Tribunal established under the Act of 1967;

"week" means any period of seven consecutive days;

"year" means any period of fifty-two weeks.

3.—(1) This Act shall not apply to—

Non-application of Act

(*a*) Employment of an employee who is normally expected to work for the same employer for less than [eight] hours in a week,

(*b*) employment by an employer of an employee who is the father, mother, grandfather, grandmother, stepfather, stepmother, son, daughter, grandson, granddaughter, stepson, stepdaughter. brother, sister, halfbrother or half-sister of the employer and who is a member of the employer's household and whose place of employment is a private dwellinghouse or a farm in or on which both the employee and the employer reside,

(*c*) employment in the Civil Service (other than in an unestablished position) within the meaning of the Civil Service Commissioners Act, 1956,

(*d*) employment as a member of the Pcrmanent Defence Forces (other than a temporary member of the Army Nursing Service),

(*e*) employment as a member of the Garda Síochána, and

(*f*) employment under an employment agreement pursuant to Part II or Part IV of the Merchant Shipping Act, 1894.

(2) The Minister may by order declare that any provision of this Act shall not apply to a class or classes of employment specified in the order and from the commencement of the order this Act shall not apply to that class or those classes.

(3) Notwithstanding subsection (1) or (2) of this section, the Minister may by order declare that any provision of this Act shall apply to a class or classes of employment specified in the order and from the commencement of the order this Act shall apply to that class or those classes.

(4) An order made by the Minister under this section may include such transitional and other supplemental and incidental provisions as appear to the Minister to be necessary or expedient.

(5) The Minister may by order amend or revoke an order made under this section, including this subsection.

Minimum period of notice

4.—(1) An employer shall, in order to terminate the contract of employment of an employee who has been in his continuous service for a period of thirteen weeks or more, give to that employee a minimum period of notice calculated in accordance with the provisions of subsection (2) of this section.

(2) The minimum notice to be given by an employer to terminate the contract of employment of his employee shall be—

> (a) if the employee has been in the continuous service of his employer for less than two years, one week,
> (b) if the employee has been in the continuous service of his employer for two years or more, but less than five years, two weeks,
> (c) if the employee has been in the continuous service of his employer for five years or more, but less than ten years, four weeks,
> (d) if the employee has been in the continuous service of his employer for ten years or more, but less than fifteen years, six weeks,
> (e) if the employee has been in the continuous service of his employer for fifteen years or more, eight weeks.

(3) The provisions of the First Schedule to this Act shall apply for the purposes of ascertaining the period of service of an employee and whether that service has been continuous.

(4) The Minister may by order vary the minimum period of notice specified in subsection (2) of this section.

(5) Any provision in a contract of employment, whether made before or after the commencement of this Act, which provides for a period of notice which is less than the period of notice specified in subsection (2) of this section, shall have effect as if that contract provided for a period of notice in accordance with this section.

(6) The Minister may by order amend or revoke an order under this section including this subsection.

Rights to employee during notice period

5.—(1) The provisions of the Second Schedule to this Act shall have effect in relation to the liability of an employer during the period of notice required by this Act to be given—

> (a) by an employer to terminate the contract of employment of an employee who has been in his continuous service for thirteen weeks or more, and
> (b) by an employee who has been in such continuous service to terminate his contract of employment with that employer.

(2) This section shall not apply in any case where an employee gives notice to terminate his contract of employment in response to a notice of lay-off or short-time given by his employer.

(3) Any provision in a contract which purports to exclude or limit the obligation imposed on an employer by this section shall be void.

6.—An employer shall, subject to the right of an employee to give counter-notice under section 10 of the Act of 1967 or to give notice of intention to claim redundancy payment in respect of lay-off or short-time under section 12 of that Act, be entitled to not less than one week's notice from an employee who has been in his continuous employment for thirteen weeks or more of that employee's intention to terminate his contract of employment. *Right of employer to notice*

7.—(1) Nothing in this Act shall operate to prevent an employee or an employer from waiving his right to notice on any occasion or from accepting payment in lieu of notice. *Right to waive notice*

(2) In any case where an employee accepts payment in lieu of notice, the date of termination of that person's employment shall, for the purposes of the Act of 1967, be deemed to be the date on which notice, if given, would have expired.

8.—Nothing in this Act shall affect the right of any employer or employee to terminate a contract of employment without notice because of misconduct by the other party. *Right to terminate contract of employment without notice*

9.—(1) An employee may, for the purposes of ascertaining or confirming any term of his employment (including the date of commencement of that employment), require his employer to furnish him with a written statement containing all or any of the following particulars in relation to the following matters, that is to say— *Written statement of terms of employment*

(*a*) the date of commencement of his employment,

(*b*) the rate or method of calculation of his remuneration,

(*c*) the length of the intervals between the times at which remuncration is paid, whether weekly, monthly or any other period,

(*d*) any terms or conditions relating to hours of work or overtime.

(*e*) any terms or conditions relating to—

(i) holidays and holiday pay,

(ii) incapacity for work due to sickness or injury and sick pay, and

(iii) pensions and pension schemes,

(*f*) the period of notice which the employee is obliged to give and entitled to receive to determine his contract of employment, or (if the contract of employment is for a fixed term) the date on which the contract expires.

(2) The Minister may by order provide that employees may require their employers to furnish such further or other particulars of their contracts of employment as may be specified in the order.

(3) Subject to subsection (4) of this section, an employer shall, within one month after he has been required so to do under subsection (1) of this section, furnish to his employee a written statement in accordance with that subsection.

(4) A statement furnished by an employer under subsection (3) of this section may, in lieu of specifying the particulars requested by the employee under this section, refer the employee to a document containing those particulars which the employee has reasonable opportunities of reading during the course of his employment, or which is reasonably accessible to him in some other way.

(5) An employer shall, within one month after an employee commences work with that employer, furnish to that employee the particulars specified in this section.

(6) The Minister may by order amend or revoke an order under this section, including this subsection.

[Where an employer issues to an employee a statement containing the particulars specified in [this Act], he shall retain a copy of such statement for a period of two years from the date on which that statement was issued and shall furnish such copy on demand to an inspector for inspection under section 114 of the Principal Act. (Social Welfare Act) 1991, s. 3).]

Failure of employer to furnish statement

10.—(1) An employer who fails to comply with the provisions of section 9 of this Act shall be guilty of an offence under this section and shall be liable on summary conviction to a fine not exceeding twenty-five pounds.

(2) An offence under this section may be prosecuted by the Minister.

Reference of disputes to Tribunal

11.—(1) Any dispute arising on any matter under this Act (other than a dispute arising on any matter under section 9 of this Act) shall be referred in the prescribed manner to the Tribunal.

(2) The decision of the Tribunat on any matter referred to it under this section shall be final and conclusive, save that any person dissatisfied with the decision may appeal therefrom to the High Court on a question of law.

(3) The Minister may, on the request of the Tribunal, refer any question of law for the decision of the High Court.

Rights of employee on default of employer

12.—(1) If an employer—

(a) fails to give to an employee the notice required by section 4(2) of this Act, or

(b) fails to comply with the provisions of section 5 of this Act in relation to the rights of the employee during the period of notice,

the employee may refer the matter to the Tribunal for arbitration and the Tribunal may award to the employee compensation for any loss sustained by him by reason of the default of the employer.

(2) The amount of any compensation awarded by the Tribunal under subsection (1) of this section shall be recoverable by the employee from his employer as a simple contract debt in a court of competent jurisdiction.

(3) Proceedings for the recovery of any sum due by way of compensation awarded by the Tribunal under subsection (1) of this section may be instituted and maintained on behalf of the employee by the Minister or by that employee's trade union. . . .

FIRST SCHEDULE

COMPUTATION OF CONTINUOUS SERVICE
Continuity of Service

1. The service of an employee in his employment shall be deemed to be continuous unless that service is terminated by—

(a) the dismissal of the employee by his employer, or

(b) the employee voluntarily leaving his employment.

2. A lock-out shall not amout to a dismissal of the employee by his employer.

3. A lay-off shall not amount to the termination by an employer of his employee's service.

4. A strike by an employee shall not amount to that employee's voluntarily leaving his employment.

5. An employee who claims and receives redundancy payment in respect of lay-off or short time shall be deemed to have voluntarily left his employment.

6. The continuous service of an employee in his employment shall not be broken by the dismissal of the employee by his employer followed by the immediate re-employment of the employee.

7. Where the whole or part of a trade, business or undertaking was or is transferred to another person either before or after the passing of this Act, tbe service of an employee in the trade, business or undertaking, or the part thereof, so transferred shall be reckoned as part of the service of the employee with the transferee and the transfer shall not operate to break the continuity of the scrvice of the employee.

Computable Service

8. Any week in which an employee is not normally expected to work for at least twenty-one hours or more will not count in computing a period of service.

9. If an employee is absent from his employment by reason of service in the Reserve Defence Force, such period of absence shall count as a period of service.

10. If an employee is absent from his employment for not more than twenty-six weeks between consecutive periods of employment because of—

(*a*) a lay-off,

(*b*) sickness or injury, or

(*c*) by agreement with his employer,

such period shall count as a period of service.

11. If, in any week or part of a week, an employee is absent from his employment because he was taking part in a strike in relation to the trade or business in which he is employed, that week shall not count as a period of service.

12. If, in any week or part of a week, an employee was, for the whole or any part of the week, absent from work because of a lock-out by his employer, that week shall count as a period of service.

13. If, in any week or part of a week, an employee is absent from his employment by reason of a strike or lock-out in a trade or business other than that in which he is employed, that week shall count as a period of service.

Second Schedule

Rights of Employee During Period of Notice

1. Subject to the provisions of this Schedule, an employee shall, during the period of notice, be paid by his employer in accordance with the terms of his contract of employment and shall have the same rights to sick pay or holidays with pay as he would have if notice of termination of his contract of employment had not been given.

Employments for which there are normal working hours

2. (*a*) (i) An employee shall be paid by his employer in respect of any time during his normal working hours when he is ready and willing to work but no work is provided for him by his employer.

(ii) In this subparagraph "normal working hours" in the case of any employee who is normally expected to work overtime, include the hours during which such overtime is usually worked.

(b) In any case where an employee's pay is not wholly calculated by reference to time, the pay which his employer is bound to pay him under subparagraph (*a*) shall be calculated by reference to the average rate of pay earned by the employee in respect of any time worked during the thirteen weeks next preceding the giving of notice.

Employments for which there are no normal working hours

3. Subject to paragraph 4 of this Schedule, an employer shall pay to an employee, if there are no normal working hours for that employee under the contract of employment in force in the period of notice, in respect of each week in the period of notice, a sum not less than the average weekly earnings of the employee in the thirteen weeks next preceding the giving of notice.

4. An employer shall not be liable to pay to his employee any sum under paragraph 3 of this Schedule unless the employee is ready and willing to do work of a reasonable nature and amount to earn remuneration at the rate mentioned in the said paragraph 3.

Holidays (Employees) Act, 1973

Number 25 *of* 1973

AN ACT TO MAKE IMPROVED PROVISION FOR HOLIDAYS FOR EMPLOYEES AND TO AMEND THE PUBLIC HOLIDAYS ACTS, 1871 TO 1924. [21*st November*, 1973]

BE IT ENACIED BY THE OIREACHTAS AS FOLLOWS:

1. (1) In this Act—   Interpretation
"annual leave" has the meaning specified in section 3(1);
"employ" means employ under a contract of service (whether the contract is expressed or implied or is oral or in writing) or a contract of apprenticeship, and cognate words shall be construed accordingly;
"leave year" means a year beginning on any 1st day of April;
"the Minister" means the Minister for Labour;
"normal weekly rate", in relation to remuneration, means—

> (a) in a case of payment wholly by a time rate or by a fixed rate or salary, and in any other case of payment not varying in relation to the work done—the sum (including any regular bonus or allowance which does not vary in relation to work done, but excluding pay for overtime) payable in respect of normal weekly working hours in the working week next before annual leave or cesser of employment,
>
> (b) in any other case—a sum equivalent to the average weekly earnings (excluding pay for overtime) for normal working hours calculated by reference to the earnings in respect of the time worked during the thirteen weeks ending on the day before annual leave or cesser of employment or, if no time was worked during those weeks, during the thirteen weeks ending on the day on which time was last worked before annual leave or cesser of employment;

"public holiday" is to be construed in accordance with the Schedule;
"regulations" is to be construed in accordance with section 14(1);
"wet time" means hours of intermittent unemployment in respect of which supplementary benefit is payable under section 28 of the Insurance (Intermittent Unemployment) Act, 1942.

(2) Where an employee continues in an undertaking after its transfer—

> (a) he shall, for the purposes of this Act, be regarded as having been employed by the new employer from either (whichever is the later) the beginning of his employment in the undertaking or the beginning of—
>> (i) the previous leave year in case the transfer occurs during the first half of the second or any subsequent leave year, or
>> (ii) the leave year in which the transfer occurs in any other case,
>
> (b) if he has been allowed annual leave before the transfer, it shall, for the purposes of this Act, be regarded as having been allowed by the new employer.

(3) A person in the service of a local authority shall be deemed for the purposes of this Act to be employed by the local authority.

Application   **2.**—(1) This Act shall, save as provided by regulations, not apply to—

(*a*) an outworker,

(*b*) an agricultural worker,

(*c*) a seafarer,

(*d*) a lighthouse or lightship employee, a

(*e*) a fisherman,

(*f*) persons employed by or under the State other than a person so employed on industrial work within the meaning of the Conditions of Employment Act, 1936 or on subordinate duties in an unestablished capacity in the civil service,

(*g*) an employee who is a relative of the employer maintained by the employer and dwelling in the employer's house or on his farm.

(2) Regulations for the purposes of subsection (1) may contain ancillary and supplemental provisions (including provisions modifying this Act).

(3) Regulations may exclude specified employees from the application of section 3 or section 4.

(4) In this section—

"outworker" means an employee to whom articles or materials are given out to be made up, cleaned, washed, altered, ornamented or repaired or adapted for sale in his own home or on other premises not under the control or management of the person who gave out the materials or articles:

"agricultural worker" means an agricultural worker to whom the Agricultural Workers (Holidays) Acts 1950 to 1969, apply;

"seafarer" means a master or a member of the crew of any sea-going vessel (not being a barge or a hopper), whether publicly or privately owned, engaged in the transport of cargo or passengers;

"relative" means a wife, husband, father, mother, grandfather, grandmother, step-father, step-mother, son, daughter, grand-son, grand-daughter, step-son, step-daughter, brother, sister, half-brother or half-sister.

Entitlement to   **3.**—(1) An employee shall be entitled to paid leave (in this Act referred to as annual leave)
annual leave   in respect of a leave year in which he has at least one qualifying month of service.

(2) Annual leave shall be equivalent to three working weeks where there are twelve qualifying months of service and, subject to the next subsection, to proportionately less where there are eleven or fewer such months.

(3) Annual leave shall also be equivalent to three working weeks where the employee works for the employer at least 1,400 hours (or 1,300 hours if under 18 years of age) during the leave year unless it is a leave year during which he changes his employment.

(4) A day which, apart from this subsection, would be a day of annual leave shall, if it is a day of illness in respect of which a certificate of a registered medical practitioner is furnished, be taken as not being a day of annual leave.

(5) (*a*) Where there are eight or more qualifying months of service, annual leave shall, subject to any registered employment agreement, employment regulation order or agreement with the employee's trade union, include an unbroken period equivalent to two working weeks.

(*b*) When ascertaining, for the purposes of this subsection, whether a period is equivalent to two working weeks, the fact that a day is a public holiday or a day of illness shall be disregarded.

(*c*) In this subsection "registered employment agreement" has the same meaning as in Part III of the Industrial Relations Act, 1946, and "employment regulation order" has the same meaning as in Part IV of that Act.

(6) Where board, lodging or board and lodging is part of remuneration, the employee may, subject to being given double pay, elect not to take annual leave.

(7) (*a*) In this section "qualifying month of service" means any month (January to December) during which the employee has worked for the employer at least 120 hours (or 110 hours if under 18 years of age).

(*b*) For the purposes of subsection (3) and of the previous paragraph—

(i) a day of annual leave shall be taken as if the employee worked thereon the hours he would have worked if not on leave, and

(ii) wet time shall be taken to be hours worked up to a maximum, in the case of subsection (3), of 480 hours in the leave year or, in the case of the previous paragraph, 40 hours in the month.

4.—(1) (*a*) An employee shall, in respect of a public holiday, be entitled to—

(i) a paid day off on that day, or

(ii) a paid day off within a month, or

(iii) an extra day's annual leave, or

(iv) an extra day's pay,

as the employer may decide.

Entitlement in respect of public holidays

(*b*) Nothwithstanding that a public holiday falls on a day on which an employee, if it were not a holiday, would normally work for less than a full day, "paid" and "pay" in this subsection refer, as respects that day, to a full day's pay.

(2) (*a*) In the case of day to day and part-time employments, the employee must, for entitlement under this section, have worked for the employer for at least 120 hours (or 110 hours if under 18 years of age) during the five weeks ending on the day before the public holiday.

(*b*) For the purposes of this subsection—

(i) time off allowed under this Act shall be taken to be time worked,

(ii) wet time shall be taken to be hours worked up to a maximum of 50 hours.

5.—(1) Where—

(*a*) an employee ceases to be employed, and

(*b*) annual leave is due to him in respect of the current leave year or, in case the cesser occurs during the first half of that year, in respect of that year, the previous leave year or both,

Compensation on cesser of employment

the employer shall pay compensation to him in respect of the annual leave consisting of one quarter of the normal weekly rate of remuneration for each qualifying month of service.

(2) Where employment on a day to day basis ceases and the employee, annual leave not being due to him, has, during the 30 days ending on the day before cesser of employment, worked for the employer for not less than 120 hours (or 110 hours if under 18 years of age), the employer shall pay compensation to him consisting of an extra day and a quarter's pay.

(3) Where employment ceases during the five weeks ending on the day before a public holiday and the employee has, during the part of that period before the cesser, worked for the employer for at least 120 hours (or 110 hours if under 18 years of age), the employer shall pay compensation to him in respect of the public holiday consisting of an extra day's pay.

(4) Compensation under this section shall, if the cesser is by the employee's death, be paid to his representatives.

(5) Where compensatlon is payable under subsection (3), the employee shall, for the

purposes of the provisions of the Social Welfare Act, 1952, relating to unemployment benefit, be regarded as not having been, on the public holiday, in the employment of the employer.

Times and pay for annual leave

6.—(1) Times at which annual leave is given shall be determined by the employer having regard to work requirements and subject—

(*a*) to his taking into account the opportunities for rest and relaxation available to the employee,

(*b*) to his having consulted (prior to one month ending at the time) the employee or his trade union, and

(*c*) to leave being given within the leave year in respect of which it is given or the six months thereafter.

(2) An employer failing to comply with subsection(1)(*b*) shall be guilty of an offence.

(3) The pay for annual leave shall—

(*a*) be given in advance

(*b*) be at the normal weekly rate of remuneration, and

(*c*) in a case in which board, lodging or board and lodging is part of the remuneration, include, subject to regulations, compensation for any board or lodging not received.

Failure to give annual leave

7.—If an employer, in the case of an employee whom he continues to to employ upon the expiration of the period during which annual leave should have been given, has not given the leave—

(*a*) the employer shall be guilty of an offence,

(*b*) the employer shall (whether proceedings have or have not been taken for the offence) give to the employee, in addition to any pay due, a sum equivalent to the pay that would have been paid to him for the leave if it had been given so as to end on the expiration of the period during which it should have been given.

Failure to pay sum due

8.—(1) If an employer, in a case in which a sum is due by him under this Act to an employee, fails to pay the sum—

(*a*) the employer shall be guilty of an offence,

(*b*) the employee may (whether or not proceedings have been taken for the offence) recover the sum as a simple contract debt in any court of competent jurisdiction.

(2) The court by which an employer is convicted of an offence under this Act may order him, if the offence relates to an employee to whom he is liable for a sum under this Act, to pay the sum to the employee.

(3) Proceedings pursuant to subsection (1)(*b*) may be instituted and maintained on behalf of the employee by his trade union.

Work during annual leave

12.—Reward for work done by an employee during annual leave shall be irrecoverable.

SCHEDULE

Days which are public holidays

1. Each of the following days shall, subject to the subsequent paragraphs, be a public holiday for the purposes of this Act:

(*a*) Christmas Day if falling on a weekday or, if not, the next Tuesday, (*b*) St. Stephen's Day if falling on a weekday or, if not, the next day,

(*c*) St. Patrick's Day if falling on a weekday or, if not, the next day,

(*d*) Easter Monday, the first Monday in June and the first Monday in August,

(*e*) a day appointed by regulations to be a public holiday for those purposes.

2. Regulations may, with respect to any day referred to in paragraph 1, substitute any other day.

3. An employer may substitute for any public holiday (other than Christmas Day or St. Patrick's Day) either—

(*a*) the Church holiday falling in the same year immediately before the public holiday, or

(*b*) the Church holiday falling in the same year immediately after the public holiday or, if the public holiday is a day which is a public holiday by virtue of paragraph 1 (b), the 6th day of January next following,

by giving to the employee notice of the substitution not less than fourteen days before the Church holiday (where that holiday is before the public holiday) or before the public holiday (where that holiday is before the Church holiday).

4. Each of the following days shall be a Church holiday for the purposes of paragraph 3:

(*a*) the 6th day of January, except when falling on a Sunday,

(*b*) Ascension Thursday,

(*c*) the Feast of Corpus Christi,

(*d*) the 15th day of August, except when falling on a Sunday,

(*e*) the 1st day of November, except when falling on a Sunday,

(*f*) the 8th day of December, except when falling on a Sunday,

(*g*) a day appointed by regulations to be a Church holiday for those purposes.

5. Regulations may, with respect to any day referred to in paragraph 4, substitute any other day.

6. A notice under this Schedule may be given by handing a copy to the employee or by posting a copy in a conspicuous position in the place of employment.

Anti-Discrimination (Pay) Act, 1974

Number 15 *of* 1974

AN ACT TO ENSURE EQUAL TREATMENT, IN RELATION TO CERTAIN TERMS AND CONDITIONS OF EMPLOYMENT, BETWEEN MEN AND WOMEN EMPLOYED ON LIKE WORK [1*st July*, 1974]

BE IT ENACTED BY THE OIREACHTAS AS FOLLOWS:

Interpretation

1.—(1) In this Act—

"collective agreement" means an agreement relating to terms and conditions of employment made between parties who are or represent employers and parties who are or represent employees;

"the Court" means the Labour Court;

"dismissal" shall be taken to include the termination by an employee of her contract of employment with her employer (whether prior notice of the termination was or was not given to the employer) in circumstances in which, because of the conduct of tho employer, the employee was or would have been entitled to terminate the contract without giving such notice, or it was or would have been reasonable for her to do so, and 'dismissed' shall be construed accordingly;

"employed" means employed under a contract of service or apprenticeship or a contract personally to execute any work or lahour;

"the Minister" means the Minister for Labour;

"place" includes a city, town or locality;

"remuneration" includes any consideration, whether in cash or in kind, which an employee receives, directly or indirectly, in respect of his employment from his employer.

(2) In this Act a reference to a section is to a section of this Act unless it is indicated that reference to some other enactment is intended.

(3) In this Act a reference to a subsection is to the subsection of the section in which the reference occurs unless it is indicated that reference to some other section is intended.

Entitlement to equal pay

2.—(1) Subject to this Act, it shall be a term of the contract under which a woman is employed in any place that she shall be entitled to the same rate of remuneration as a man who is employed in that place by the same employer (or by an associated employer if the employees, whether generally or of a particular class, of both employers have the same terms and conditions of employment), if both are employed on like work.

(2) For the purpose of this section two employers shall be taken to be associated if one is a body corporate of which the other (whether directly or indirectly) has control or if both are bodies corporate of which a third person (whether directly or indirectly) has control.

(3) Nothing in this Act shall prevent an employer from paying to his employees who are employed on like work in the same place different rates of remuneration on grounds other than sex.

Like work

3.—Two persons shall be regarded as employed on like work—

(*a*) where both perform the same work under the same or similar conditons, or where each is in every respect interchangeable with the other in relation to the work, or

(b) where the work performed by one is of a similar nature to that performed by the other and any differences between the work performed or the conditions under which it is performed by each occur only infrequently or are of small importance in relation to the word as a whole, or

(c) where the work performed by one is equal in value to that performed by the other in terms of the demands it makes in relation to such matters as skill, physical or mental effort, responsibility and conditions.

4. Where a woman is employed otherwise than under a contract, or is employed under a contract which does not include (whether expressly or by reference to a collective agreement or otherwise) a term satisfying section 2, the terms and conditions of her employment shall include an implied term giving effect to that section, and such an implied term shall, where it conflicts with an express term, override it. *Equal pay entitlement implied*

5—(1) Where after the commencement of this Act an agreement or order to which this section applies contains a provision in which differences in rates of remuneration are based on or related to the sex of employees, such a provision shall be null and void. *Collective agreements etc.*

(2) This section applies to—

(a) a collective agreement made after the commencement of this Act,

(b) an employment regulation order within the meaning of Part IV of the Industrial Relations Act, 1946, made after the commencement of this Act,

(c) a registered employment agreement within the meaning of Part III of the Industrial Relations Act, 1946, registered in the Register of Employment Agreements after the commencement of this Act, and

(d) an order made by the Agricultural Wages Board under section 17 of the Agricultural Wages Act, 1936, after the commencement of this Act. . . .

11.—Sections 2(1), 4, 9(1) and 10(1) shall be construed as applying equally, in a case converse to that referred to in those sections, to a man in relation to his remuneration relative to that of a woman. *Application of Act to men*

Protection of Employment Act, 1977

Number 7 *of* 1977

AN ACT TO PROVIDE FOR THE IMPLEMENTATION OF THE DIRECTIVE OF THE COUNCIL OF THE EUROPEAN COMMUNITIES DONE AT BRUSSELS ON THE 17th DAY OF FEBRUARY, 1975, REGARDING THE APPROXIMATION OF THE LAWS OF MEMBER STATES OF THOSE COMMUNUNITIES RELATING TO COLLECTIVE REDUNDANCIES, AND TO PROVIDE FOR OTHER MATTERS RELATING TO THAT MATTER. [*5th April,* 1977]

BE IT ENACTED BY THE OIREACHTAS AS FOLLOWS:

PART I

PRELIMINARY AND GENERAL

Interpretation

2.—(1) In this Act—

"authorised officer" means a person appointed by the Minister to be an authorised officer for the purposes of this Act;

"contract of employment" means a contract of service or of apprenticeship;

"employee" means a person who has entered into or works under (or, in the case of a contract which has been terminated, worked under) a contract of employment with an employer, whether the contract is for manual labour, clerical work or otherwise, is express or implied, oral or in writing, and "employer" and references to employment shall be construed accordingly;

"employees' representatives" means officials (including shop stewards) of a trade union or of a staff association with which it has been the practice of the employer to conduct collective bargaining negotiations;

"the Minister" means the Minister for Labour;

"prescribed" means prescribed by regulations under this Act;

"staff association" means a body of persons all the members of which are employed by the same employer and which carries on negotiations for the fixing of wages or other conditions of employment of its own members only;

"trade union" means a trade union which is the holder of a negotiation licence granted under the Trade Union Acts, 1941 and 1971.

Meaning of collective redundancies

6.—(1) For the purpose of this Act, "collective redundancies" means dismissals which are effected for a reason specified in subsection (2) (other than a reason related to the individual employees dismissed) where in any period of 30 consecutive days the number of such dismissals is—

    (*a*) at least five in an establishment normally employing more than 20 and less than 50 employees,

    (*b*) at least ten in an establishment normally employing at least 50 but less than 100 employees,

    (*c*) at least ten per cent of the number of employees in an establishment normally employing at least 100 but less than 300 employees, and (*d*) at least 30 in an establishment normally employing 300 or more employees.

(2) The reasons referred to in subsection (1) are—

(*a*) that the employer concerned has ceased, or intends to cease, to carry on the business for the purposes of which the employees concerned were employed by him, or has ceased or intends to cease, to carry on that business in the place where those employees were so employed,

(*b*) that the requirements of the business for employees to carry out work of a particular kind in the place where the employees concerned were so employed have ceascd or diminished or are expected to cease or diminish,

(*c*) that the employer concerned has decided to carry on the business with fewer or no employecs, whether by requiring the work for which the employees conccrned had been empoyed (or had been doing before their dismissal) to be done by other employees or otherwise,

(*d*) that the employer concerned has decided that the work for which the employees concerned had been employed (or had been doing before their dismissal) should henceforward be done in a different manner for which those employees are not sufficiently qualified or trained,

(*e*) that the employer concerned has decided that the work for which the employees concerned had been employed (or had been doing before their dismissal) should henceforward be done by persons who are also capable of doing other work for which those employees are not sufficiently qualified or trained.

(3) (*a*) In this section "establishment" means—

(i) where an employer carries on business at a particular location, that location, or

(ii) where an employer carries on business at more than one location, each such location.

(*b*) For the purposes of the definition in paragraph (*a*) of this subsection, each workplace, factory, mine, quarry, dockyard, wharf, quay, warehouse, building site. engineering construction site, electricity station, gas works, water works, sewage disposal works, office, wholesale or retail shop, hotel, restaurant, cafe, farm, garden or forest plantation shall be taken to be a separate location.

(*c*) In ascertaining for the purposes of this section the total number of employees employed in an establishment, account shall be taken of those employees who are based at the establishment but who also perform some of their duties elsewhere.

(*d*) The Minister may, for the purpose of extending the provisions of this section by order amend paragraph (*a*), (*b*) or (*c*) of this subsection and may by order amend or revoke such an order.

(4) For the purposes of this section, "business" includes a trade, industry, profession or undertaking, or any activity carried on by a person or body of persons whether corporate or unincorporate, or by a public or local authority or a Department of State, and the performance of its functions by a public or local authority or a Department of State.

7.—(1) Subject to subsection (2), this Act applies to all persons in employment on or after the commencement of this Act in an establishment normally employing more than 20 persons. Application and non-application of Act

This Act does not apply to—

(*a*) dismissals of employees engaged under a contract of employment for a fixed term or for a specified purpose (being a purpose of such a kind that the duration of the contract was limited but was, at the time of its making, incapable of precise ascertainment) where the dismissals occurred only because of the expiry of the term or the cesser of the purpose,

(*b*) a person employed by or under the State other than persons standing designated for the time being under section 17 of the Industrial Relations Act, 1969,

(*c*) officers of a body which is a local authority within the meaning of the Local Government Act, 1941,

(*d*) empoyment under an employment agreement pursuant to Part II or IV of the Merchant Shipping Act, 1894,

(*e*) employees in an establishment the business carried on in which is being terminated following bankruptcy or winding-up proceedings or for any other reason as a result of a decision of a court of competent jurisdiction.

(3) (*a*) The Minister may by order declare that this Act shall not apply to a class of employees specified in the order and from the commencement of the order this Act shall not apply to that class.

(*b*) The Minister may by order declare that this Act shall apply to a specified class of employee and from the commencement of the order this Act shall apply to that class.

(*c*) The Minister may by order amend or revoke an order under this subsection.

(4) Where a notice of dismissal by reason of redundancy which was given bofore the commencement of this Act expires after such commencement, sections 9, 10, 12 and 14 shall not apply to the dismissal concerned, but such a notice shall be in accordance with the Minimum Notice and Terms of Employment Act, 1973, and with the relevant contract of employment.

(5) In this section "establishment" has the same meaning as in section 6.

Calculation of normal number of employees

8.—For the purposes of this Act, the number of employees normally employed in an establishment (within the meaning of section 6) shall be taken to be the average of the number so employed in each of the 12 months preceding the date on which the first dismissal takes effect.

PART II

CONSULTATION AND NOTIFICATION

Obligation on employer to consult employees' representatives

9.—(1) Where an employer proposes to create collective redundancies he shall, with a view to reaching an agreement, initiate consultations with employees' representatives representing the employees affected by the proposed redundancies.

(2) Consultations under this section shall include the following matters

(*a*) the possibility of avoiding the proposed redundancies, reducing the number of employees affected by them or otherwise mitigating their consequences,

(*b*) the basis on which it will be decided which particular employees will be made redundant.

(3) Consultations under this section shall be initiated at the earliest opportunity and in any event at least 30 days before the first dismissal takes effect.

Obligation on employer to supply certain information

10.—(1) For the purpose of consultations under section 9, the employer ooncerned shall supply the employees' representatives with all relevant information relating to the proposed redundancies.

(2) Without prejudice to the generality of subsection (1), information supplied under this section shall include the following, of which details shall be given in writing—

    (*a*) the reasons for the proposed redundancies,

    (*b*) the number, and descriptions or categories, of employees whom it is proposed to make redundant,

    (*c*) the number of employees normally employed, and

    (*d*) the period during which it is proposed to effect the proposed redundancies.

(3) An employer shall as soon as possible supply the Minister with copies of all information supplied in writing under subsection (2).

12.—(1) Where an employer proposes to create collective redundancies, he shall notify the Minister in writing of his proposals at the earliest opportunity and in any event at least 30 days before the first dismissal takes effect. *Obligation on employer to notify Minister of proposed redundancies*

(2) The Minister may prescribe the particulars to be specified in a notification under this section.

(3) A copy of a notification under this section shall be supplied as soon as possible by the employer affected to the employees' representatives affected who may forward to the Minister in writing any observations they have relating to the notification.

PART III

COMMENCEMENT OF COLLECTIVE REDUNDANCIES

14.—(1) Collective redundancies shall not take effect before the expiry of the period of 30 days beginning on the date of the relevant notification under section 12. *Collective redundancies to take effect for 30 days*

(2) Where collective redundancies are effected by an employer before the expiry of the 30-day period mentioned in subsection (1) the employer shall be guilty of an offence and shall be liable on conviction on indictment to a fine not exceeeding £3,000.

15.—(1) For the purpose of seeking solutions to the problems caused by the proposed redundancies, the employer concerned shall, at the Minister's request, enter into consultations with him or an authorised officer. *Further consultations with Minister*

(2) For the purpose of consultations under this section, an employer shall supply the Minister or an authorised officer with such information relating to the proposed redundancies as the Minister or the officer may reasonably require.

16. Nothing in this Act shall affect the right of any employee to a period of notice of dismissal or to any other entitlement under any other Act or under his contract of employment. *Saver for employees' rights to notice etc.*

Unfair Dismissals Act, 1977

Number 10 of 1977

AN ACT TO PROVIDE FOR REDRESS FOR EMPLOYEES UNFAIRLY DISMISSED FROM THEIR EMPLOYMENT, TO PROVIDE FOR THE DETERMINATION OF CLAIMS FOR SUCH REDRESS BY RIGHTS COMMISSIONERS AND BY THE TRIBUNAL ESTABLISHED, FOR THE PURPOSE OF DETERMINING CERTAIN APPEALS, BY THE REDUNDANCY PAYMENTS ACT, 1967, TO PROVIDE THAT THAT TRIBUNAL SHALL BE KNOWN AS THE EMPLOYMENT APPEALS TRIBUNAL, TO MAKE PROVISION FOR OTHER MATTERS CONNECTED WITH THE MATTERS AFORESAID AND TO AMEND THE MINIMUM NOTICE AND TERMS OF EMPLOYMENT ACT, 1973. [6th April, 1977]

BE IT ENACTED BY THE OIREACHTAS AS FOLLOWS:

Definitions **1.**—In this Act—

"contract of employment" means a contract of service or of apprenticeship, whether it is express or implied and (if it is express) whether it is oral or in writing;

"date of dismissal" means—

(a) where prior notice of the termination of the contract of employment is given and it complies with the provisions of that contract and of the Minimum Notice and Terms of Employment Act, 1973, the date on which that notice expires.

(b) where either prior notice of such termination is not given or the notice given does not comply with the provisions of the contract of employment or the Minimum Notice and Terms of Employment Act, 1973, the date on which such a notice would have expired, if it had been given on the date of such termination and had been expressed to expire on the later of the following dates—

(i) the earliest date that would be in compliance with the provisions of the contract of employment,

(ii) the earliest date that would be in compliance with the provisions of the Minimum Notice and Terms of Employment Act, 1973,

(c) where a contract of employment for a fixed term expires without its being renewed under the same contract or, in the case of a contract for a specified purpose (being a purpose of such a kind that the duration of the contract was limited, but was, at the time of its making, incapable of precise ascertainment), there is a cesser of the purpose, the date of the expiry or cesser;

"dismissal", in relation to an employee, means—

(a) the termination by his employer of the employee's contract of employment with the employer, whether prior notice of the termination was or was not given to the employee,

(b) the termination by the employee of his contract of employment with his employer, whether prior notice of the termination was or was not given to the employer, in circumstances in which, because of the conduct of the employer, the employee was or would have been entitled, or it was or would have been reasonable for the employee, to terminate the contract of employment without giving prior notice of the termination to the employer, or

(c) the expiration of a contract of employment for a fixed term without its being renewed under the same contract or, in the case of a contract for a specified purpose (being a purpose of such a kind that the duration of the contract was limited but was, at the time of its making, incapable of precise ascertainment), the cesser of the purpose;

"employee" means an individual who has entered into or works under (or, where the employment has ceased, worked under) a contract of employment and, in relation to redress for a dismissal under this Act, includes, in the case of the death of the employee concerned at any time following the dismissal, his personal representative;

"employer", in relation to employee, means the person by whom the employee is (or, in a case where the employment has ceased, was) employed under a contract of employment and an individual in the service of a local authority for the purposes of the Local Government Act, 1941, shall be deemed to be employed by the local authority;

"industrial action" means lawful action taken by any number or body of employees acting in combination or under a common understanding in consequence of a dispute, as a means of compelling their employers or any employee or body of employees, or to aid other employees in compelling their employer or any employee or body of employees, to accept or not to accept terms or conditions of or affecting employment;

"the Minister" means the Minister for Labour;

"redundancy" means any of the matters referred to in paragraphs (a) to (e) of section 7(2) of the Redundancy Payments Act, 1967, as amended by the Redundancy Payments Act, 1971;

"statutory apprenticeship" means an apprenticeship in a designated industrial activity within tho meaning of the Industrial Training Act, 1967, and includes any apprenticeship in a trade to which an order, rule or notice referred to in paragraph (a) or (b) of section 49(1) of that Act applies;

"strike" means the cessation of work by any number or body of employees acting in combination or a concerted refusal or a refusal under a common understanding of any number of employees to continue to work for an employer, in consequence of a dispute, done as a means of compelling their employer or any employee or body of employees, or to aid other employees in compelling their employer or any employee or body of employees, to accept or not to accept terms or conditions of or affecting employment;

"trade union" means a trade union which is the holder of a negotiation licence granted under the Trade Union Acts, 1941 and 1971:

"the Tribunal" means the Employment Appeals Tribunal established by the Redundancy Payments Act, 1967.

2.—(1) This Act shall not apply in relation to any of the following persons: Exclusions

(a) an employee (other than a person referred to in section 4 of this Act) who is dismissed, who, at the date of his dismissal, had less than one year's continuous service with the employer who dismissed him and whose dismissal does not result wholly or mainly from the matters referred to in section 6(2)(f) of this Act,

(b) an employee who is dismissed and who, on or before the date of his dismissal, had reached the normal retiring age for employees of the same employer in similar employment or who on that date was a person to whom by reason of his age the Redundancy Payments Acts, 1967 to 1973, did not apply,

(c) a person who is employed by his spouse, father, mother, grandfather, grand-

grandmother, step-father, step-mother, son, daughter, grandson, grand-daughter, step-son, stepdaughter, brother, sister, half-brother or half-sister, is a member of his employer's household and whose place of employment is a private dwellinghouse or a farm in or on which both the employee and the employer reside,

(*d*) a person in employment as a member of the Defence Forces, the Judge Advocate-General, the chairman of the Army Pensions Board or the ordinary member thereof who is not an officer of the Medical Corps of the Defence Forces,

(*e*) a member of the Garda Síochána,

(*f*) a person (other than a person employed under a contract of employment) who is recciving a training allowance from or undergoing instruction by An Chomhairle Oiliúna or is receiving a training allowance from and under-going instruction by that body,

(*g*) a person who is employed by An Chomhairle Oiliúna under a contract of apprenticeship,

(*h*) a person employed by or under the State other than persons standing designated for the time being under section 17 of the Industrial Relations Act, 1969,

(*i*) officers of a local authority for the purposes of the Local Government Act, 1941,

(*j*) officers of a health board, a vocational education committee established by the Vocational Education Act, 1930, or a committee of agriculture established by the Agriculture Act, 1931.

(2) This Act shall not apply in relation to—

(*a*) dismissal where the employment was under a contract of employment for a fixed term made before the 16th day of September, 1976, and the dismissal consisted only of the expiry of the term without its being renewed under the same contract, or

(*b*) dismissal where the employment was under a contract of employment for a fixed term or for a specified purpose (being a purpose of such a kind that the duration of the contract was limited but was, at the time of its making, incapable of precise ascertainment) and the dismissal consisted only of the expiry of the term without its being renewed under the said contract or the cesser of the purpose and the contract is in writing, was signed by or on behalf of the employer and by the employee and provides that this Act shall not apply to a dismissal consisting only of the expiry or cesser aforesaid, or

(*c*) dismissal where the employee's employer at the commencement ot the employ-ment informs the employee in writing the the emplovment will terminate on the return to work with that employer of another employee who is absent from her work while on maternity leave or additional maternity leave or time off under the Maternity Protection of Employees Act, 1981, and the dismissal of the first-mentioned employee duly occurs for the purpose of facilitating the return to work of that other employee.

(3)(*a*) This Act shall not apply in relation to the dismissal of an employee who, under the relevant contract of employment, ordinarily worked outside the State unless

(i) he was ordinarily resident in the State during the term of the contract, or

(ii) he was domiciled in the State during the term of the contract, and the employer—

(I) in case the employer was an individual, was ordinarily resident in the State, during the term of the contract, or

(II) in case the employer was a body corporate or an unincorporated body of persons, had its principal place of business in the State during the term of the contract.

(*b*) In this subsection "term of the contract" means the whole of the period from the time of the commencement of work under the contract to the time of the relevant dismissal.

(4) The First Schedule to the Minimum Notice and Terms of Employment Act, 1973, as amended by section 20 of this Act, shall apply for the purpose of ascertaining for the purposes of this Act the period of service of an employee and whether that service has been continuous.

3.—(1) This Act shall not apply in relation to the dismissal of an employee during a period starting with the commencement of the employment when he is on probation or undergoing training— Dismissal during probation or training

(*a*) if his contract of employment is in writing, the duration of the probation or training is 1 year or less and is specified in the contract, or

(*b*) if his contract of employment was made before the commencement of this Act and was not in writing and the duration of the probation or training is 1 year or less.

(2) This Act shall not apply in relation to the dismissal of an employee during a period starting with the commencement of the employment when he is undergoing training for the purpose of becoming qualified or registered, as tho case may be, as a nurse, pharmacist, health inspector, medical laboratory technician, occupational therapist, physiotherapist, speech therapist, radiographer or social worker.

4.—This Act shall not apply in relation to the dismissal of a person who is or was employed under a statutory apprenticeship if the dismissal takcs place within 6 months after the commencement of the apprenticeship or within I month after the completion of the apprenticeship. Dismissal during apprenticeship

5.—(1) The disrnissal of an employee by way of a lock-out shall be deemed, for the purposes of this Act, not to be an unfair dismissal if the employee is offered re-instatement or re-engagement as from the date of resumption of work. Dismissal by way of lock-out or for taking part in a strike

(2) The dismissal of an employee for taking part in a strike or other industrial action shall be deemed, for the purposes of this Act, to be an unfair dismissal, if—

(*a*) one or more employees of the same employer who took part in the strike or other industrial action were not dismissed for so taking part, or

(*b*) one or more of such employees who were dismissed for so taking part are subsequently offered re-instatement or re-engagement and the employee is not.

(3) References in paragraphs (*a*), (*b*) and (*c*) of section 7(1) of this Act to dismissals include, in the case of employees dismissed by way of lock-out or for taking part in a strike or other industrial action, references to failure to offer them re-instatement or re-engagement in accordance with any agreement by the employer and by or on behalf of the employees, or, in the absence of such agreement, from the earliest date for which re-instatement or re-engagement was offered to the other employees of the same employer who were locked out or took part in the strike or other industrial action or to a majority of such employees.

(4) In this section a reference to an offer of re-instatement or re-engagement, in relation to an employee, is a reference to an offer (made either by the original employer or by a successor of that employer or by an associated employer) to re-instate that employee in the position which he held immediately before his dismissal on the terms and conditions on which he was employed immediately before his dismissal together with a term that the

re-instatement shall be deemed to have commenced on the day of the dismissal, or to re-engage him, either in the position which he held immediately before his dismissal or in a different position which would be reasonably suitable for him, on such terms and conditions as are reasonable having regard to all the circumstances.

(5) In this section—

"lock-out" means an action which, in contemplation or furtherance of a trade dispute (within the meaning of the Industrial Relations Act, 1946), is taken by one or more employers, whether parties to the dispute or not, and which consists of the exclusion of one or more employees from one or more factories, offices or other places of work or of the suspension of work in one or more such places or of the collective, simultaneous or otherwise conncected termination or suspension of employment of a group of employees;

"the original employer" means, in relation to the employee, the employer who dismissed the employee.

Unfair dismissal

6.—(1) Subject to the provisions of this section, the dismissal of an employee shall be deemed, for the purposes of this Act, to be an unfair dismissal unless, having regard to all the circumstances, there were substantial grounds justifying the dismissal.

(2) Without prejudice to the generality of subsection (1) of this section, the dismissal of an employee shall be deemed, for the purposes of this Act, to be an unfair dismissal if it results wholly or mainly from one or more of the following:

(a) the employee's membership, or proposal that he or another person become a member, of, or his engaging in activities on behalf of, a trade union or excepted body under the Trade Union Acts, 1941 and 1971, where the times at which he engages in such activities are outside his hours of work or are times during his hours of work in which he is permitted pursuant to the contract of employment between him and his employer so to engage,

(b) the religious or political opinions of the employee,

(c) civil proceedings whether actual, threatened or proposed against the employer to which the employee is or will be a party or in which the employee was or is likely to be a witness,

(d) criminal proceedings against the employer, whether actual, threatened or proposed, in relation to which the employee has made, proposed or threatened to make a complaint or statement to the prosecuting authority or to any other authority connected with or involved in the prosecution of the proceedings or in which the employee was or is likely to be a witness,

(e) the race or colour of the employee,

(f) the pregnancy of the employee or matters connected therewith, unless—

(i) the employee was unable, by reason of the pregnancy or matters connected therewith—

(I) to do adequately the work for which she was employed, or

(II) to continue to do such work without contravention by her or her employer of a provision of a statute or instrument made under statute, and

(ii) (I) there was not, at the time of the dismissal, any other employment with her employer that was suitable for her and in relation to which there was a vacancy, or

(II) the employee refused an offer by her employer of alternative employment on terms and conditions corresponding to those of the employment to which the dismissal related, being an offer made so as to enable her to be retained in the employment of her employer notwithstanding;

(g) the exercise by an employee to whom Part II of the Maternity Protection of Employees Act, 1981, applies (other than a person specified in section 2(1) of this Act) of her right under the Maternity Protection of Employees Act, 1981, to maternity leave, additional maternity leave or time off under that Act, provided that—

(i) the requirement of one year's continuous service with the employer who dismissed her does not apply to a case falling within this paragraph, and

(ii) sections 3 and 4 of this Act do not apply to such a case.

(3) Without prejudice to the generality of subsection (1) of this section, if an employee was dismissed due to redundancy but the circumstances constituting the redundancy applied equally to onc or more other employees in similar employment with the same employer who have not been dismissed, and either—

(a) the selection of that employee for dismissal resulted wholly or mainly from one or more of the matters specified in subsection (2) of this section or another matter that would not be a ground justifying dismissal, or

(b) he was selected for dismissal in contravention of a procedure (being a procedure that has been agreed upon by or on behalf of the employer and by the employee or a trade union, or an excepted body under the Trade Union Acts, 1941 and 1971, representing him or has been established by the custom and practice of the employment concerned) relating to redundancy and there were no special reasons justifying a departure from that procedure,

then the dismissal shall be deemed, for the purposes of this Act, to be an unfair dismissal.

(4) Without prejudice to the generality of subsection (1) of this section, the dismissal of an employee shall be deemed, for the purposes of this Act, not to be an unfair dismissal, if it results wholly or mainly from one or more of the following:

(a) the capability, competence or qualifications of the employee for performing work of the kind which he was employed by the employer to do,

(b) the conduct of the employee,

(c) the redundancy of the employee, and

(d) the employee being unable to work or continue to work in the position which he held without contravention (by him or by his employer) of a duty or restriction imposed by or under any statute or instrument made under statute.

(5) (a) Without prejudice to the generality of subsection (1) of this section, the dismissal by the Minister for Defence of a civilian employed with the Defence Forces under section 30(1)(c) of the Defence Act, 1954, shall be deemed for the purposes of this Act not to be an unfair dismissal if it is shown that the dismissal was for the purpose of safeguarding national security.

(b) A certificate purporting to be signed by the Minister for Defence and stating that a dismissal by the Minister for Defence of a civilian named in the certificate from employment with the Defence Forces under section 30(1)(g) of the Defence Act, 1954, was for the purpose of safeguarding national security shall be evidence, for the purposes of this Act, of the facts stated in the certificate without further proof.

(6) In determining for the purposes of this Act whether the dismissal of an employee was an unfair dismissal or not, it shall be for the employer to show that the dismissal resulted wholly or mainly from one or more of the matters specified in subsection (4) of this seclion or that there were other substantial grounds justifying the dismissal

(7) Where it is shown that a dismissal of a person referred to in paragraph (*a*) or (*b*) of section 2(1) or section 3 or 4 of this Act results wholly or mainly from one or more of the matters referred to in subsection (2)(*a*) of this section, then subsections (1) and (6) of this section and the said sections 2 (1), 3 and 4 shall not apply in relation to the dismissal.

Redress for
unfair
dismissal

7.—(1) Where an employee is dismissed and the dismissal is an unfair dismissal, the employee shall be entitled to redress consisting of whichever of the following the rights commissioner, the Tribunal or the Circuit Ciurt, as the case may be, considces appropriate having regard to all the circumstances:

(*a*) re-instatement by the employer of the employee in the position which he held immediately before his dismissal on the terms and conditions on which he was employed immediately before his dismissal together with a term that the re-instatement shall be deemed to have commenced on the day of the dismissal, or

(*b*) re-engagement by the employer of the employee either in the position which he held immediately before his dismissal or in a different position which would be reasonably suitable for him on such terms and conditions as are reasonable having regard to all the circumstances, or

(*c*) payment by the employer to the employee of such compensation (not exceeding in amount 104 weeks remuneration in respect of the employment from which he was dismissed calculated in accordance with regulations under section 17 of this Act) in respect of any financial loss incurred by him and attributable to the dismissal as is just and equitable having regard to all the circumstances.

(2) Without prejudice to the generality of subsection (1) of this section, in determining the amount of compensation payable under that subsection regard shall be had to—

(*a*) the extent (if any) to which the financial loss referred to in that subsection was attributable to an act, omission or conduct by or on behalf of the employer,

(*b*) the extent (if any) to which the said financial loss was attributable to an action, omission or conduct by or on behalf of the employee,

(*c*) the measures (if any) adopted by the employee or, as the case may be, his failure to adopt measures, to mitigate the loss aforesaid, and

(*d*) the extent (if any) of the compliance or failure to comply by the employer or employee with any procedure of the kind referred to in section 14(3) of this Act or with the provisions of any code of practice relating to procedures regarding dismissal approved of by the Minister.

(3) In this section—

"financial loss", in relation to the dismissal of an employee, includes any actual loss and any estimated prospective loss of income attributable to the dismissal and the value of any loss or diminution, attributable to the dismissal, of the rights of the employee under the Redundancy Payments Acts, 1967 to 1973, or in relation to superannuation;

"remuneration" includes allowances in the nature of pay and benefits in lieu of or in addition to pay.

Voidance of
certain
provisions in
agreements

13.—A provision in an agreement (whether a contract of employment or not and whether made before or after the commencement of this Act) shall be void in so far as it purports to exclude or limit the application of, or is inconsistent with, any provision of this Act.

Notice to
employees of
procedure for,

14.(1) An employer shall, not later than 28 days after he enters into a contract of employment with an employee, give to the employee a notice in writing setting out the procedure which the employer will observe before and for the purpose of dismissing the employee.

(2) Where there is an alteration in the procedure referred to in subsection (1) of this section, the employer concerned shall, within 28 days after the alteration takes effect, give to any employee concerned a notice in writing setting out the procedure as so altered.

(3) The reference in subsection (1) of this section to a procedure is a reference to a procedure that has been agreed upon by or on behalf of the employer concerned and by the employee concerned or a trade union, or an excepted body under the Trade Union Acts, 1941 and 1971, representing him or has been established by the custom and practice of the employment concerned, and the references in subsection (2) of this section to an alteration in the said procedure are references to an alteration that has been agreed upon by the employer concerned or a person representing him and by a trade union, or an excepted body under the Trade Union Acts, 1941 and 1971, representing the employee concerned.

(4) Where an employee is dismissed, the employer shall, if so requested, furnish to the employee within 14 days of the request, particulars in writing of the grounds for the dismissal, but in determining for the purposes of this Act whether the dismissal was unfair there may be taken into account any other grounds which are substantial grounds and which would have justified the dismissal.

15.—(1) Nothing in this Act, apart from this section, shall prejudice the right of a person to recover damages at common law for wrongful dismissal.

(2) Where an employee gives a notice in writing under section 8(2) of this Act in respect of a dismissal to a rights commissioner or the Tribunal, he shall not be entitled to recover damages at common law for wrongful dismissal in respect of that dismissal.

(3) Where proceedings for damages at common law for wrongful dismissal are initiated by or on behalf of an employee, the employee shall not be entitled to redress under this Act in respect of the dismissal to which the proceedings relate.

(4) A person who accepts redress awarded under section 9 or 10 of the Anti-Discrimination (Pay) Act, 1974, in respect of any dismissal shall not be entitled to accept redress awarded under section 7 of this Act in respect of that dismissal and a person who accepts redress awarded under the said section 7 in respect of any dismissal shall not be entitled to accept redress awarded under the said section 9 or 10 in respect of that dismissal.

Unfair Dismissals (Claims and Appeals) Regulations, 1977

SI No. 286 of 1977

2. In these Regulations—
"the Act" means the Unfair Dismissals Act, 1977 (No. 10 of 1977);
"appeal" means an appeal under section 9 of the Act;
"claim" means a claim under section 8(1) or section 8(4)(a) of the Act;
"the Minister" means the Minister for Labour;
"the Tribunal" means the Employment Appeals Tribunal established by the Redundancy Payments Act, 1967.

3.—A notice under subsection (2) of section 8 of the Act to the Tribunal or under subsection (4) of the said section 8 or section 9(2) of the Act shall specify—
    (*a*) the name and address of the person bringing the claim or appeal,
    (*b*) the name and address of the employer or the employee, as the case may be, concerned,
    (*c*) the date of the commencement of the employment to which the notice relates,
    (*d*) the date of the dismissal to which the notice relates, and
    (*e*) the amount claimed by the said person to be the weekly remuneration of the said person in respect of the said employment calculated in accordance with regulations under section 17 of the Act.

4.—A claim or appeal may be withdrawn by sending a notification in writing signifying such withdrawal to the tribunal.

5.—(1) A party to a claim or appeal who receives notice thereof under section 8 or 9, as the case may be, of the Act and who intends to oppose the claim or appeal shall enter an appearance to the claim or appeal by giving to the Tribunal, within 14 days of the receipt by him of the said notice, a notice in writing stating that he intends to oppose the claim or appeal, as the case may be, and containing the facts and contentions on which he will ground such opposition.

(2) A party to a claim or appeal who does not enter an appearance to the claim or appeal in pursuance of this Regulation shall not be entitled to take part in or be present or represented at any proceedings before the Tribunal in relation to the claim or appeal.

(3) A party to a claim or appeal may, before the expiration of the period referred to in paragraph (1) of this Regulation, apply, by giving to the Tribunal a notice in writing containing the facts and contentions on which he grounds the application, for an extension of the said period and the Tribunal may make such order in relation to the application as it thinks just.

6.—On receipt by the Tribunal of a notice referred to in Regulation 3 or 5 of these Regulations or a notification under Regulation 4 of these Regulations, the Tribunal shall cause a copy of the notice or notification, as the case may be, to be given to the other party concerned.

7.—The chairman of the Tribunal may, by certificate under his hand, correct any mistake (including an omission) of a verbal or formal nature in a determination of the Tribunal.

8.—(1) The Tribunal shall maintain a register, to be known as the Register of Unfair Dismissals Determinations (referred to subsequently in this Regulation as 'the Register'), and shall cause to be entered in the Register particulars of every determination by the Tribunal under section 8 or 9 of the Act.

(2) The Register may be inspected free of charge by any person during normal office hours.

(3) Where the chairman of the Tribunal makes a correction, pursuant to Regulation 7 of these Regulations, particulars thereof shall be entered in the Register.

(4) A copy of an entry in the Register shall be sent to the parties concerned.

9.—(1) A notice required by subsection (2) or (4) of section 8 or section 9 (2) of the Act or by these Regulations to be given to the Tribunal may be sent by registered post addressed to the Secretary, Employment Appeals Tribunal, Dublin 4, and a document required by these Regulations to be given to a party to proceedings before the Tribunal may be sent by registered post addressed to the party—

      (*a*) in case his address is specified in a notice referred to in Regulation 3 of these Regulations, at that address, and

      (*b*) in the case of a body corporate (being a case to which paragraph (*a*) of this Regulation does not apply) at its registered office, and

      (*c*) in any other case, at his known place of residence or at a place where he works or carries on business.

(2) Any such notice of notification as aforesaid that is sent or given to a person authorised to receive it by the person to whom it is required by these Regulations to be given shall be deemed to have been sent to the latter person.

10.—Regulations 10 to 17(2), 19, 20, 20A (inserted by the Redundancy (Redundancy Appeals Tribunal) (Amendment) Regulations, 1969 (SI No. 26 of 1969)), 23 and 24 of the Redundancy (Redundancy Appeals Tribunal Regulations, 1968 (SI No. 24 of 1968), shall, with any necessary modifications, and in the case of the said Regulations 20 and 20A, with tbe modification that a sum awarded by the Tribunal under either such Regulation shall, in lieu of being paid out of the fund referred to therein, be paid by the Minister for Labour with the consent of the Minister for Finance, apply in relation to a claim under Section 8 of the Act, an appeal under section 9 of the Act and proceedings in relation to such a claim or appeal as they apply in relation to appeals provided for by section 39 of the Redundancy Payments Act, 1967 (No. 21 of 1967).

Unfair Dismissals (Calculation of Weekly Remuneration) Regulations, 1977

SI No. 287 of 1977

2.—In these Regulations—

"the Act" means the Unfair Dismissals Act, 1977 (No. 10 of 1977);

"date of dismissal" has the meaning assigned to it by section 1 of the Act, and "date", in relation to a dismissal, shall be construed accordingly;

"relevant employment", in relation to an employee, means the employment in respect of which the weekly remuneration of the employee is calculated for the purposes of section 7 (1)(c) of the Act;

"week", in relation to an employee whose remuneration is calculated by reference to a week ending on a day other than a Saturday, means a week ending on that other day and, in relation to any other employee, means a week ending on a Saturday, and "weekly" shall be construed accordingly.

3.—(a) A week's remuneration of an employee in respect of an employment shall be calculated for the purposes of section 7(1)(c) of the Act in accordance with these Regulations.

(b) Where, at the date of his dismissal from an employment, an employee had less than 52 weeks' continuous service in the employment, a week's remuneration of the employee in respect of the employment shall be calculated, for the purposes of the said section 7(1)(c), in the manner that in the opinion of the Tribunal corresponds most closely with that specified in these Regulations.

4.—In the case of an employee who is wholly remunerated in respect of the relevant employment at an hourly time rate or by a fixed wage or salary, and in the case of any other employee whose remuneration in respect of the relevant employment does not vary by reference to the amount of work done by him, his weekly remuneration in respect of the relevant employment shall be his earnings in respect of that employment (including any regular bonus or allowance which does not vary having regard to the amount of work done and any payment in kind) in the latest week before the date of the relevant dismissal in which he worked for the number of hours that was normal for the employment together with, if he was normally required to work overtime in the relevant employment, his average weekly overtime earnings in the relevant employment as determined in accordance with Regulation 5 of these Regulations.

5.—For the purpose of Regulation 4 of these Regulations, the average weekly overtime earnings of an employee in the relevant employment shall be the amount obtained by dividing by 26 the total amount of his overtime earnings in that employment in the period of 26 weeks ending 13 weeks before the date of the dismissal of the employee.

6.—For the purpose of Regulations 5 and 7(b) of these Regulations, any week during which the employee concerned did not work shall be disregarded and the latest week before the period of 26 weeks mentioned in the said Regulation 5 or 7(b), as the case may be, of these Regulations or before a week taken into account under this Regulation, as may be appropriate, shall be taken into account instead of a week during which the employee did not work as aforesaid.

7.—(a) In the case of an employee who is paid remuneration in respect of the relevant employment wholly or partly at piece rates, or whose remuneration includes commissions (being piece rates or commissions related directly to his output at work) or bonuses, and in the case of any other employee whose remuneration in respect of the relevant employment varies in relation to the amount of work done by him, his weekly remuneration shall be the amount obtained by dividing the amount of the remuneration to be taken into account in accordance with paragraph (b) of this Regulation by the number of hours worked in the period of 26 weeks mentioned in the said paragraph (b) and multiplying the resulting amount by the normal number of hours for which, at the date of the dismissal of the employee, an employee in the relevant employment was required to work in each week.

(b) The remuneration to be taken into account for the purposes of paragraph (a) of this Regulation shall be the total remuneration paid to the employee concerned in respect of the employment concerned for all the hours worked by the employee in the employment in the period of 26 weeks that ended 13 weeks before the date on which the employee was dismissed, adjusted in respect of any variations in the rates of pay which became operative during the period of 13 weeks ending on the date of dismissal of the employee.

(c) For the purposes of paragraph (b) of this Regulation, any week worked in another employment shall be taken into account if it would not have operated, for the purposes of the First Schedule to the Minimum Notice and Terms of Employment Act, 1973 (No. 4 of 1973), to break the continuity of service of the employee concerned in the employment from which he was dismissed.

8.—(1) Where, under his contract of employment, an employee is required to work for more hours than the number of hours that is normal for the employment, the hours for which he is so required to work shall be taken, for the purposes of Regulations 4 and 7(b) of these Regulations, to be, in the case of that employee, the number of hours that is normal for the employment.

(2) Where, under his contract of employment, an employee is entitled to additional remuneration for working for more than a specified number of hours per week—

(a) in case the employee is required under the said contract to work for more than the said specified number of hours per week, the number of hours per week for which he is so to work shall, for the purposes of Regulations 4 and 7(b) of these Regulations, be taken to be, in his case, the number of hours of work per week that is normal for the employment, and

(b) in any other case, the specified number of hours shall be taken, for the purposes of the said Regulations 4 and 7(b), to be, in the case of that employee, the number of hours of work per week that is normal for the employment.

9.—Where, in a particular week, an employee qualifies for a payment of a bonus, pay allowance or commission which relates to work the whole or part of which was not done in that particular week, the whole or the appropriate proportionate part of the payment as the case may be, shall, for the purposes of Regulations 4 and 7(b) of these Regulations, be disregarded in relation to that particular week and shall for those purposes, be taken into account in relation to any week in which any of the work was done.

10.—An employee who is normally employed on a shift cycle and whose remuneration in respect of the employment varies having regard to the particular shift on which he is employed, and an employee whose remuneration for working for the number of hours that is normal for the employment varies having regard to the days of the week or the times of the day on or at which he works, shall each be taken, for the purposes of these Regulations, to be an employee who is paid wholly or partly by piece rates.

11.—Where, in respect of the relevant employment, there is no number of hours for which employees work in each week that is normal for the employment, the weekly remuneration of each such employee shall be taken, for the purposes of these Regulations, to be the average amount of the remuneration paid to each such employee in the 52 weeks in each of which he was working in the employment immediately before the date of the relevant dismissal.

12.—Where under these Regulations account is to be taken of remuneration paid in a period which does not coincide with the periods for which the remuneration is calculated, the remuneration shall be apportioned in such manner as may be just.

13.—For the purposes of Regulations 4 and 7 of these Regulations, account shall not be taken of any sums paid to an employee by way of recoupment of expenses incurred by him in the discharge of the duties of his employment.

Employment Equality Act, 1977

Number 16 of 1977

AN ACT TO MAKE UNLAWFUL IN RELATION TO EMPLOYMENT CERTAIN KINDS OF DISCRIMINATION ON GROUNDS OF SEX OR MARITAL STATUS, TO ESTABLISH A BODY TO BE KNOWN AS THE EMPLOYMENT EQUALITY AGENCY, TO AMEND THE ANTI-DISCRIMINATION (PAY) ACT, 1974 AND TO PROVIDE FOR OTHER MATTERS RELATED TO THE AFORESAID MATTERS. [1st June, 1977]

BE IT ENACTED BY THE OIREACHTAS AS FOLLOWS:

1.—(1) In this Act— Interpretation

"the Act of 1946" means the Industrial Relations Act, 1946,

"the Act of 1974" means the Anti-Discrimination (Pay) Act, 1974;

"act" includes a deliberate omission;

"advertisement" includes every form of advertisement, whether to the public or not and whether in a newspaper or other publication, on television or radio or by display of a notice or by any other means, and references to the publishing of advertisements shall be construed accordingly;

"the Agency" means the Employment Equality Agency established by section 34;

"close relative" means a wife, husband, parent, child, grandparent, grandchild, brother or sister;

"the Court" means the Labour Court;

"dismissal" shall be taken to include the termination by an employee of his contract of employment with his employer (whether prior notice of termination was or was not given to the employer) in circumstances in which, because of the conduct of the employer, the employee was or would have been entitled to terminate the contract without giving such notice, or it was or would have been reasonable for him to do so, and "dismissed" shall be construed accordingly;

"employee" means a person who has entered into or works under (or, in the case of a contract which has been terminated, worked under) a contract of employment with an employer, whether the contract is (or was) for manual labour, clerical work or otherwise, is (or was) expressed or implied, oral or in writing, and whether it is (or was) a contract of service or apprenticeship or otherwise, and includes a civil servant of the State or of the Government and an officer or servant of a local authority within the meaning of the Local Government Act, 1941, an officer or servant of a harbour authority, health board, vocational education committee or committee of agriculture, and cognate words or expressions shall be construed accordingly;

"employer", in relation to an employee, means the person by whom the employee is (or, in a case where the employment has ceased, was) employed under a contract of employment, and for the purposes of this definition a civil servant of the State or of the Government shall be deemed to be employed by the State or the Government (as the case may be) and an officer or servant of a local authority within the meaning of the Local Government Act, 1911, or of a harbour authority, health board, vocational educational committee or committee of agriculture shall be deemed to be employed by the local authority, harbour authority, health

board, vocational educational committee or committee of agriculture (as the case may be);
"employment agency" means a person who, whether for profit or otherwise, provides services related to the finding of employment for prospective employees or the supplying of employees to employers;

"functions" includes powers and duties;

"investigation" means an investigation under section 39;

"the Minister" means the Minister for Labour;

"non-discrimination notice" means a notice under section 44;

"profession" includes any vocation or occupation;

"trade union" has the same meaning as it has in the Trade Union Acts, 1871 to 1975.

(2) In this Act a reference to a section is to a section of this Act unless it is indicated that reference to some other enactment is intended.

(3) In this Act a reference to a subsection is to the subsection of the section in which the reference occurs unless it is indicated that reference to some other section is intended.

Discrimination for the purposes of this Act   **2.**—For the purposes of this Act, discrimination shall be taken to occur in any of the following cases—

>   (*a*) whereby reason of his sex a person is treated less favourably that a person of the other sex.

>   (*b*) where because of his marital status a person is treated less favoutably than another person of the same sex,

>   (*c*) where because of his sex or marital status a person is obliged to comply with a requirement, relating to employment or membership of a body referred to in section 5, which is not an essential requirement for such employment or membership and in respect of which the proportion of persons of the other sex or (as the case may be) of a different marital status but of the same sex able to comply is substantially higher,

>   (*d*) where a person is penalised for having in good faith—

>>   (i) made a reference under section 19 or under section 7 of the Act of 1974,

>>   (ii) opposed by lawful means an act which is unlawful under this Act or the Act of 1974,

>>   (iii) given evidence in any proceedings under this Act or the Act of 1974, or

>>   (iv) given notice of an intention to do anything referred to in subparagraphs (i) to (iii),

and cognate words shall be construed accordingly.

Discrimination by employers prohibited   **3.**—(1) A person who is an employer or who obtains under a contract with another person the services of employees of that other person shall not discriminate against an employee or a prospective employee or an employee of that other porson in relation to access to employment, conditions of employment (other than remuneration or any condition relating to an occupational pension scheme), training or experience for or in relation to employment, promotion or re-grading in employment or classification of posts in employment.

(2) An employer shall not, in relation to his employees or to employment by him, have rules or instructions which would discriminate against an employee or class of employee, and shall not otherwise apply or operate a practice which results or would be likely to result in an act which is a contravention of any provision of this Act when taken in conjunction with section 2(*c*).

(3) Without prejudice to the generality of subsection (1), a person shall be taken to discriminate against an employee or prospective employee in relation to access to

employment if—
>(*a*) in any arrangements he makes for the purpose of deciding to whom he should offer employment, or
>(*b*) by specifying, in respect of one person or class of persons, entry requirements for employment which are not specified in respect of other persons or classes of persons where the circumstances in which both such persons or classes would be employed are not materially different,

he contravenes subsection (1).

(4) Without prejudice to the generality of subsection (1), a person shall be taken to discriminate against an employee or prospective employee in relation to conditions of employment if he does not offer or afford to a person or class of persons the same terms of employment (other than remuneration or any term relating to an occupational pension scheme), the same working conditions and the same treatment in relation to overtime, shift work, short time, transfers, lay-offs, redundancies, dismissals (other than a dismissal referred to in section 25) and disciplinary measures as he offers or affords to another person or class of persons where the circumstances in which both such persons or classes are or would be employed are not materially different.

(5) Without prejudice to the generality of subsection (1), a person shall be taken to discriminate against an employee in relation to training or experience for or in relation to employment if he refuses to offer or afford to that employee the same opportunities or facilities for employment counselling, training (whether on or off the job) and work experience as he offers or affords to other employees where the circumstances in which that employee and those other employees are employed are not materially different.

(6) Without prejudice to the generality of subsection (1), a person shall be taken to contravene that subsection if he discriminates against an employee in the way he offers or affords that employee access to opportunities for promotion in circumstances in which another eligible and qualified person is offered or afforded such access or if in those circumstances he refuses or deliberately omits to offer or afford that employee access to opportunities for promotion.

(7) Without prejudice to the generality of subsection (1), a person shall be taken to discriminate against an employee or prospective employee where he classifies posts by reference to sex and the classification is not a case referred to in section 17 (2).

4.—(1) If the terms of a contract under which a person is employed do not include (whether directly or by reference to a collective agreement within the meaning of the Act of 1974 or otherwise) an equality clause, they shall be deemed to include one. *Equality clause*

(2) An equality clause is a provision which relates to terms of a contract (other than a term relating to remuneration or an occupational pension scheme) under which a person is employed and has the effect that where the person is employed in circumstances where the work done by that person is not materially different from that being done by a person of the other sex (in this section referred to as "the other person") in the same employment—
>(*a*) if (apart from the equality clause) any term of the contract is or becomes less favourable to the person than a term of a similar kind in the contract under which the other person is employed, that term of the person's contract shall be treated as so modified as not to be less favourable, and
>(*b*) if (apart from the equality clause) at any time the person's contract does not include a term corresponding to a term benefiting the other person included in the contract under which the other person is employed, the person's contract shall be treated as including such a term.

(3) An equality clause shall not operate in relation to a variation between a person's

contract of employment and the contract of employment of the other person if the employer proves that the variation is genuinely a consequence of a material difference (other than the difference of sex) between the two cases.

(4) Where a person offers a person employment on certain terms, and if on his acceptance of the offer any of those would fall to be modified or any additional term would fall to be included by virtue of this section, the offer shall be taken to contravene sections 3(1) and 3(4).

Discrimination in relation to membership of certain bodies prohibited

5.—A body which is an organisation of workers, an organisation of employers or a professional or trade organisation or which controls entry to a profession or the carrying on of a profession shall not discriminate against a person in relation to membership of such body (or any benefits provided by it) or in relation to entry or the carrying on of the profession.

Discrimination in relation to vocational training prohibited

6—(1) Any person or educational or training body offering a course of vocational training shall not, in respect of any such course offered to persons over the age at which those persons are statutorily obliged to attend school, discriminate against a person (whether at the request of an employer, a trade union or a group of employers or trade unions or otherwise)—

(*a*) in the terms on which any such course or related facility is offered,

(*b*) by refusing or omitting to afford access to any such course or facility, or

(*c*) in the manner in which any such course or facility is provided.

(2) In this section "vocational training" means any system of instruction which enables a person being instructed to acquire, maintain, bring up to date or perfect the knowledge or technical capacity required for the carrying on of an occupational activity and which may be considered as exclusively concerned with training for such activity.

Discrimination by employment agencies prohibited

7.—(1) An employment agency shall not discriminate—

(*a*) in the terms on which it offers to provide any of its services,

(*b*) by refusing or omitting to provide any of its services,

(*c*) in the manner in which it provides any of its services.

(2) References in subsection (1) to a service of an employment agency include guidance on careers and any service related to employment.

(3) Subsection (1) does not apply where the service concerns only employment which an employer could lawfully refuse to offer to the person concerned.

(4) An employment agency shall not be under any liability under this section if it proves—

(*a*) that it acted in reliance on a statement made to it by the employer concerned to the effect that, by reason of the operation of subsection (3), its action would not be unlawful, and

(*b*) that it was reasonable for it to rely on the statement.

(5) An employer who, with a view to obtaining the services of an employment agency, knowingly makes a statement such as is referred to in subsection (4)(*a*) and which in a material respect is false or misleading shall be guilty of an offence and shall be liable on summary conviction to a fine not exceeding £200.

Discriminatory advertising prohibited

8.—(1) A person shall not publish or display, or cause to be published or displayed, an advertisement which relates to employment and indicates an intention to discriminate, or might reasonably be understood as indicating such an intention.

(2) For the purpose of subsection (1), where in an advertisement a word of phrase is used defining or describing a post and the word or phrase is one which connotes a particular sex, is descriptive of or refers to a post or occupation of a kind previously held or carried on by

members of one sex only, the advertisement shall be taken to indicate an intention to discriminate unless the advertisement contains a contrary indication.

(3) A person who makes a statement which he knows to be false with a view to securing publication or display in contravention of subsection (1) shall upon such publication or display being made be guilty of an offence and shall be liable on summary conviction to a fine not exceeding £200.

9.—A person shall not procure or attempt to procure another person to do in relation to employment anything which constitutes discrimination.

Procuring or attempting to procure discrimination prohibited

10.—(1) (*a*) Where an agreement or order to which this subsection applies contains a provision constituting discrimination, the provision shall be null and void.

Discrimination in collective agreements etc.

(*b*) This subsection applies to—
(i) a collective agreement.
(ii) an employment regulation order within the meaning of Part IV of the Act of 1946, and
(iii) a registered employment agreement within the meaning of Part III of the Act of 1946 registered in the Register of Employment Agreements.

(2) Where a contract of employment contains a term (whether expressed or implied) constituting discrimination, that term shall be null and void.

11.—(1) The Midwives Act, 1944 (No. 10 of 1944), is hereby amended by the substitution for the definition of "midwife" in section 2 of the following:
"the word 'midwife' means a woman or man registered in the roll of midwives and, accordingly, every word importing the feminine gender shall be construed as if it also imported the masculine gender."

Provisions relating to midwives and public health nurses

(2) Notwithstanding any other provision of this Act, it shall not be a contravention of the Act for a person to give access to training or employment as a midwife or as a public health nurse to persons of a particular sex.

12.—(1) This Act does not apply to employment—
(*a*) in the Defence Forces,
(*b*) in a private residence or by a close relative.

Employments excludes from application of Act

(2) (*a*) Notwithstanding subsection (1), the Minister may by order declare that this Act shall apply to such class or classes of employment referred to in that subsection as may be specified in the order, and from the commencement of the order this Act shall apply to that class or those classes.
(*b*) Where the Minister proposes to make an order under this subsection, a draft of the proposed order shall be laid before each House of the Oireachtas and the order shall not be made until a resolution approving of the draft has been passed by each House.

(3) Sections 19, 20(*b*), 21 and 28 shall not apply to the selection, by the Local Appointments Commissioners or the Civil Service Commissioners, of a person for appointment to an office or position.

13.—Nothing in this Act shall require an employer—
(*a*) to employ in a position a person who will not undertake the duties attached to that position or who will not accept the conditions under which those duties are performed, or

Savers for certain cases relating to non-performance of duties etc.

(*b*) to retain in his employment a person not undertaking the duties attached to the position held by that person.

Saver for and reprove of amendment of certain statutory provisions

14.–(1) Notwithstanding any provision of this Act, nothing done by an employer in compliance with any requirement of or under an Act to which this section applies shall constitute discrimination in contravention of this Act.

(2) (*a*) The Minister may by order repeal or amend any Act to which this section applies or any provision of such an Act.

(*b*) Before making an order under this subsection the Minister shall consult such trade unions, employers' organisations and organisations of trade unions or of employers' organisations as he considers appropriate.

(*c*) Where the Minister proposes to make an order under this subsection, a draft of the proposed order shall be laid before each House of the Oireachtas and the order shall not be made until a resolution approving of the draft has been passed by each House.

(3) This section applies to—

(*a*) the Conditions of the Employment Act, 1936,

(*b*) the Shops (Conditions of Employment) Act, 1938,

(*c*) the Factories Act, 1955,

(*d*) the Mines and Quarries Act, 1965.

Saver for certain training courses etc.

15.—Nothing in this Act shall make it unlawful for any person to arrange for or provide training for persons of a particular sex in a type, form or category of work in which either no, or an insignificant number of, persons of that sex had been engaged in the period of twelve months ending at the commencement of the training, or to encourage persons of that sex to take advantage of opportunities for doing such work.

Saver for special treatment in connection with pregnancy etc.

16.—Nothing in this Act shall make it unlawful for an employer to arrange for or provide special treatment to women in connection with pregnancy or childbirth.

Exclusion of posts where sex is occupational qualification

17.—(1) This Act does not apply to any act connected with or related to the employment of a person where the sex of the person is an occupational qualification for a post in relation to which the act occurs.

(2) For the purposes of this section, the sex of a person shall be taken to be an occupational qualification for a post in the following cases—

(*a*) where, on grounds of physiology (excluding physical strength or stamina) or on grounds of authenticity for the purpose of a form of entertainment, the nature of the post requires a member of a particular sex because otherwise the nature of the post would be materially different if carried out by a member of the other sex,

(*b*) where the duties of a post involve personal services and it is necessary to have persons of both sexes engaged in such duties,

(*e*) where because of the nature of the employment it is necessary to provide sleeping and sanitary accommodation for employees on a communal basis and it would be unreasonable to expect the provision of separate such accommodation or impracticable for an employer so to provide.

(*f*) where it is necessary that the post should be held by a member of a particular sex because it is likely to involve the performance of duties outside the State in a place where the laws or customs are such that the duties can only be performed by a member of that sex.

Redundancy Payments Act, 1979

Number 7 *of* 1979

AN ACT TO AMEND AND EXTEND THE REDUNDANCY PAYMENTS ACTS, 1967 TO 1973, AND TO PROVIDE FOR OTHER CONNECTED MATTERS. [2o*th March*, 1979]

7.—(1) This section applies to an employee who has not less than 104 weeks' service with an employer and has been given notice of proposed dismissal by reason of redundancy.

(2) An employee to whom this section applies shall be entitled during the two weeks ending on the expiration of his notice of dismissal to be allowed by his employer reasonable time off during the employee's working hours in order to look for new employment or make arrangements for training for future employment.

(3) An employee who is allowed time off under this section shall be entitled to be paid remuneration by his employer for the period of absence at the appropriate hourly rate obtaining on the date of his notice of dismissal and to remuneration equal to this amount in a case where the employer unreasonably refuses time off under this section.

(4) The employer of an employee to whom this section applies may require the employee to furnish him with such evidence as he requests of arrangements made by the employee relating to effort to obtain new employment or training for future employment, and the employee shall furnish any evidence so requested if it is not prejudicial to the employee's interest.

(5) Any dispute arising under this section shall be deemed to be a decision referred to in section 39(15) of the Principal Act, and any amount ordered by the Employment Appeals Tribunal to be paid by an employer to an employee shall be recoverable as a simple contract debt in a court of competent jurisdiction.

European Communities (Safeguarding of Employees' Rights on Transfer of Undertakings) Regulations, 1980

SI No. 306 of 1980

2.—(1) In these Regulations—
"the Council Directive" means Council Directive No. 77/187/EEC of 14 February, 1977;
"the Minister" means the Minister for Labour.

(2) A word or expression that is used in these Regulations and is also used in the Council Directive shall, unless the context otherwise requires, have the meaning in these Regulations that it has in the Council Directive.

3.—The rights and obligations of the transferor arising from a contract of employment or from an employment relationship existing on the date of a transfer shall, by reason of such transfer, be transferred to the transferee.

4.—(1) Following a transfer, the transferee shall continue to observe the terms and conditions agreed in any collective agreement on the same terms applicable to the transferor under that agreement, until the date of termination or expiry of the collective agreement or the entry into force or application of another collective agreement.

(2) Regulation 3 of these Regulations and paragraph (1) of this Regulation shall not apply in relation to employees' rights to old-age, invalidity or survivors' benefits under supplementary company or inter-company pension schemes outside the Social Welfare Acts, 1952 to 1979, but the transferee shall ensure that the interests of employees and of persons no longer employed in the transferor's business at the time of the transfer in respect of rights conferring on them immediate or prospective entitlement to old-age benefits including survivors' benefits, under such supplementary company pension schemes are protected.

5.—(1) The transfer of an undertaking, business or part of a business shall not in itself constitute grounds for dismissal by the transferor or the transferee and a dismissal, the grounds for which are such a transfer, by a transferor or a transferee is hereby prohibited. However, nothing in this Regulation shall be construed as prohibiting dismissals for economic, technical or organisational reasons entailing changes in the work-force.

(2) If a contract of employment or an employment relationship is terminated because a transfer involves a substantial change in working conditions to the detriment of the employee concerned, the employer concerned shall be regarded as having been responsible for termination of the contract of employment or of the employment relationship.

6.—Where an undertaking or business, or part of a business, the subject of a transfer preserves its autonomy after the transfer, the status and function, as laid down by the laws, regulations or administrative provisions of the State, of the representatives or of the representation of the employees affected by the transfer shall be preserved by the transferee concerned.

7.—(1) The transferor and transferee concerned in a transfer shall inform the representatives of their respective employees affected by the transfer of—

(*a*) the reasons for the transfer,

(*b*) the legal, economic and social implications of the transfer for the employees, and

(*c*) the measures envisaged in relation to the employees,

and the information shall be given—

(i) by the transferor to the representatives of his employees in good time before the transfer is carried out, and

(ii) by the transferee, to the representatives of his employees in good time, and in any event before his employees are directly affected by the transfer as regards their conditions of work and employment.

(2) If the transferor or the transferee concerned in a transfer envisages measures in relation to his employees, he shall consult his representatives of the employees in good time on such measures with a view to seeking agreement.

(3) Where, in the case of a transfer, there are no representatives of the employees in the undertaking or business of the transferor or, as the case may be, in the undertaking or business of the transferee, the transferor or transferee, as may he appropriate, shall cause—

(*a*) a statement in writing containing the particulars specified in suhparagraphs (*a*),

(*b*) and (*c*) of paragraph (1) of this Regulation to be given in good time before the transfer is carried out to each employee in the business or undertaking, and

(*b*) notices containing the particulars aforesaid to be displayed prominently in good time before the transfer is carried out at positions in the workplaces of the employees where they can be read conveniently by the employees.

Maternity Protection of Employees Act, 1981

Number 2 of 1981

AN ACT TO ENTITLE FEMALE EMPLOYEES TO MATERNITY LEAVE. TO RETURN TO WORK AFTER SUCH LEAVE AND TO TIME OFF FROM WORK FOR ANTENATAL AND POST-NATAL CARE, TO EXTEND AS A CONSEQUENCE OF THE ABOVE-MENTIONED PROVISIONS THE PROTECTION AGAINST UNFAIR DISMISSAL CONFERRED BY THE UNFAIR DISMISSALS ACT, 1977, AND TO MAKE OTHER PROVISIONS CONNECTED WITH THE ABOVE-MENTIONED MATTERS. [*26th March*, 1981]

BE IT ENACTED BY THE OIREACHTAS AS FOLLOWS:

PART I

Preliminary and General

Interpretation   **2.**—(1) In this Act—

"the Act of 1977" means the Unfair Dismissals Act, 1977;

"additional maternity leave" has the meaning assigned to it by *section 14*;

"employee", except in *Part IV*, means a person who is in an employment for the time being specified in or under Part I (other than paragraph 7) of the First Schedule to the *Social Welfare (Consolidation) Act, 1981*, not being an employment specified in or under Part 11 of that Schedule;

"employer", in relation to an employee. does not include an employer who employs that employee—

    (*a*) on a permanent basis for less than [8] hours in each week, or

    (*b*) under a contract of employment, or otherwise, for a fixed term of either less than 26 weeks or of which there are less than 26 weeks still to run:

"maternity leave" has the meaning assigned to it by *section 8*;

"the Minister" means the Minister for Labour;

"the successor" has the meaning assigned to it by *section 20*.

(2) In this Act a reference to a Part or section is to a Part or section of this Act, unless it is indicated that reference to some other enactment is intended.

(3) In this Act a reference to a subsection or paragraph is to the subsection or paragraph of the provision in which the reference occurs, unless it is indicated that reference to some other provision is intended.

Persons to whom Parts II and III apply   **3.**—(1) *Parts II* and *III* apply to female employees.

(2) The Minister may by order, made with the consent of the Minister for Social Welfare, amend *subsection (1)* so as to vary the application of *Part II* or *Part III*.

Voidance or modification of certain provisions in agreements   **5.**—(1) A provision in any agreement (whether a contract of employment or not, and whether made before or after the commencement of this Act) shall be void in so far as it purports to exclude or limit the application of any provision of this Act or is inconsistent with any provision of this Act.

(2) A provision in any agreement (whether a contract of employment or not, and whether made before or after the commencement of this Act) which is or becomes less favourable in relation to an employee to whom *Part II* or *Part III* applies than a similar or corresponding entitlement conferred on her by either of those Parts shall be deemed to be so modified as to be not less favourable to her.

(3) Nothing in this Act shall be construed as prohibiting any agreement referred to in this section from containing any provision more favourable to an employee to whom *Part II* or *Part III* applies than any provision in either of those Parts.

(4) References in this section to this Act (other than the references to the commencement of this Act) or to a Part shall be construed as references to this Act or to the Part as amended or extended by or under this Act or any other Act.

PART II

Maternity Leave

7.—In this Part—
"the expected week of confinement" and "confinement" have the meanings respectively assigned to them by sections 24 and 28 of the *Social Welfare (Consolidation) Act, 1981*; "the minimum period of maternity leave" has the meaning assigned to it by *section 8*.

[margin: Definitions for Part II]

8.—(1) Subject to this Part, an employee to whom this Part applies shall be entitled to leave, to be known (and referred to in this Act) as maternity leave from her employment for a period (in this Part referred to as "the minimum period of maternity leave") of not less than 14 consecutive weeks.

[margin: Entitlement to maternity leave]

(2) The Minister may by order, made with the consent of the Minister for Social Welfare and the consent of the Minister for Finance, amend *subsection (1)* so as to extend the period mentioned in that subsection.

9.—(1) Entitlement to the minimum period of maternity leave shall be subject to an employee having—

[margin: Notification to employer]

    (*a*) as soon as reasonably practicable but not later than four weeks before the commencement of maternity leave notified in writing her employer (or caused him to be so notified) of her intention to take maternity leave, and

    (*b*) at the time of the notification, given to her employer or produced for her employer's inspection a medical or other appropriate certificate confirming the pregnancy and specifying the expected week of confinement.

(2) A notification under this section may be revoked by a further notification in writing by the employee concerned to her employer.

10.—Subject to *sections 11* to *13*, the minimum period of maternity leave shall commence on such day as the employee selects, being not later than four weeks before the end of the expected week of confinement, and shall end on such day as she selects, being not earlier than four weeks after the end of the expected week of confinement.

[margin: Allocation of minimum period of maternity leave]

11.—(1) Where it is certified by a registered medical practitioner or otherwise to the satisfaction of the Minister and the Minister for Social Welfare that for a person specified in the certificate, the minimum period of maternity leave should for a medical reason so specified commence on a date so specified, and the certificate is produced for inspection by the employer concerned within such period as may be prescribed by regulations under this

[margin: Variation in allocation of minimum period of maternity leave]

section, the minimum period of maternity leave for that person shall commence on the date so specified.

(2) Where a certificate under this section is issued and the requirement in *subsection (1)* relating to the production of the certificate for the employer's inspection is complied with, the employee specified in the certificate shall be deemed to have complied also with *section 9(1)(a)*.

Extension of maternity leave

12.—(1) Where the date of confinement of an employee to whom this Part applies occurs in a week after the expected week of confinement, the minimum period of maternity leave shall be extended by such number of consecutive weeks (subject to a maximum of four consecutive weeks) after the week in which the date of confinement occurs as ensures compliance with *section 10*.

(2) Where the minimum period of maternity leave is proposed to be extended under this section, the employee concerned shall—

    (*a*) as soon as practicable after the proposal for such extensionm notify in writing her employer (or cause him to be so notified) of the proposed extension, and

    (*b*) as soon as practicable after the date of confinement, confirm in writing to her employer the notification under *paragraph (a)* and specify the duration of the extension.

Commencement of maternity leave (early confinement)

13.—(1) Where, in relation to an employee to whom this Part applies, the date of confinement occurs in a week that is four weeks or more before the expected week of confinement, the employee shall, where the circumstances so require be deemed to have complied with *section 9(1)(a)* if the notification required by that section is given in the period of 14 days commencing on the date of confinement.

(2) Notwithstanding *section 10*, but subject to regulations under *section 11*, the minimum period of maternity leave for an employee referred to in *subsection (1)* shall be a period of not less than 14 consecutive weeks commencing on whichever of the following is the earlier—

    (*a*) the first day of maternity leave taken in accordance with *section 10*, or

    (*b*) the date of confinement.

Entitlement to additional maternity leave

14.—(1) Subject to this section, an employee who has taken maternity leave shall, if she so wishes, be entitled to further leave, to be known (and referred to in this Act) as "additional maternity leave", for a maximum period of four consecutive weeks commencing immediately after the end of her maternity leave.

(2) An employee shall be entitled to additional maternity leave, whether or not the minimum period of maternity leave has been extended under *section 12*.

(3) Entitlement to additional maternity leave shall be subject to an employee having notified in writing her employer (or caused him to be so notified) in accordance with *subsection (4)* of her intention to take such leave.

(4) Notification under *subsection (3)* shall be given either at the same time as the relevant notification under *section 9* or not later than four weeks before the date which would have been the expected date of return to work under *Part III* if the employee concerned had not taken the additional maternity leave.

(5) A notification under this section may be revoked by a further notification in writing by the employee concerned to her employer not later than four weeks before the date which would have been the expected date of return to work under *Part III* if the employee concerned had not taken the additional maternity leave.

(6) The Minister may by order amend *subsection (1)* so as to extend the period of four consecutive weeks referred to in that subsection.

15.—(1) During a period of absence from her work by an employee while she is on Maternity leave, such an employee shall be deemed to have been in the employment of her employer and, accordingly, while so absent she shall, subject to *section 19*, be treated as if she had not been so absent and such absence shall not affect any right (other than her right to remuneration during such absence), whether conferred on her by Statute, contract or otherwise, and related to her employment.

(2) In respect of a period of absence from her work by an employee while she is on additional maternity leave, the period of employment before such absence shall be regarded as continuous with her employment following such absence in respect of any right, whether conferred on her by statute, contract or otherwise, and related to her employment (other than her right to remuneration which. during such absence, shall stand suspended).

(3) Nothing in this section shall affect an employee's right to be offered suitable alternative employment under *section 21*.

(4) A period of absence from her work while on maternity leave or additional material leave shall not be treated as part of any other leave (including sick leave or annual leave) to which an employee concerned is entitled.

(5) An employee shall he deemed not to he an emploved contributor for the purposes of the *Social Welfare (Consolidation) Act, 1981*, for any contribution week (within the meaning of that Act) in a period of absence from her work on maternity leave or additional maternity leave if she does not receive any reckonable earnings (within the meaning of that Act) in respect of that week.

16.—(1) For the purpose of receiving ante-natal or post-natal care (or ante-natal and post-natal care), an employee to whom this Part applies shall be entitled to time off from her work in accordance with regulations made under this section by the Minister.

(2) Without prejudice to the generality of *subsection (1)*, regulations under this section may make provision in relation to all or any of the following matters—

    (*a*) the amount of time off to which an employee shall be entitled under this section;

    (*b*) the terms or conditions relating to such time off;

    (*c*) the notice to be given in advance by an employee so entitled to her employer (including circumstances in which such notice need not be given);

    (*d*) the evidence to be furnished by an employee so entitled to her employer of any appropriate medical or related appointment.

(3) *Section 15(1)* shall apply to an employee entitled to time off in accordance with regulations under this section as if the employee's period of absence from her work under this section were a period of absence from her work while on maternity leave.

17.—Each of the following shall be void:

    (*a*) any purported termination of the employment of an employee to whom this Part applies, while she is absent from her work on maternity leave or additional maternity leave;

    (*b*) any purported termination of the employment of an employee to whom this Part applies, while she is absent from her work on time off under *section 16*;

    (*c*) any notice of termination of the employment of an employee to whom this Part applies, given while she is absent from her work on maternity leave or additional maternity leave and expiring subsequent to such absence;

(*d*) any notice of termination of the employment of an employee to whom this Part applies, given while she is absent from her work on time off under *section 16* and expiring subsequent to such absence;

(*e*) any purported suspension from her employment of an employee to whom this Part applies, imposed while she is absent from her work on maternity leave, additional maternity leave or on time off under *section 16*.

Extension of certain notices of employment or of certain suspension

18.—Any notice of termination of her employment given in respect of an employee to whom this Part applies, or any suspension from her employment imposed on such an employee, before the receipt by her employer of a notification under *section 9, 12, 14* or *16* (or where appropriate, under *section 22*), or before the production for the employer's inspection of a certificate under *section 11*, and due to expire during her absence from work on maternity leave, additional maternity leave or time off under *section 16*, shall be extended by the period of her absence from work on maternity leave, additional maternity leave or such time off.

Provisions regarding periods of probation, training and apprenticeship

19.—(1) During her absence from her work while on maternity leave or additional leave by an employee to whom this Part applies and who, starting with the commencement of her employment with her employer, is on probation in her employment, is undergoing training in relation to her employment or is employed under a contract of apprenticeship, her probation, training or apprenticeship shall stand suspended during such absence and shall be completed by her on her return to work after such absence.

(2) The Minister may by regulations prescribe a period or periods of training in relation to which *subsection (1)* shall not apply.

Part III

Right to Return to Work

General right to return to work on expiry of maternity leave

20.—(1) Subject to this Part, on the expiry of a period during which an employee to whom this Part applies was absent from work while on maternity leave or additional maternity leave, she shall be entitled to return to work—

(*a*) with the employer with whom she was working immediately before the start of that period or, where during her absence from work there was a change of ownership of the undertaking in which she was employed immediately before her absence, with the owner (in this Act referred to as "the successor") of the undertaking at the expiry of her period of absence,

(*b*) in the job which she held immediately before the start of that period, and

(*c*) under the contract of employment under which she was employed immediately before the start of that period, or, where a change of ownership such as is referred to in *paragraph (a)* has occurred, under a contract of employment with the successor which is identical to the contract under which she was employed immediately before the start of that period, and (in either case) under terms or conditions not less favourable than those that would have been applicable to her if she had not been so absent from work.

(2) For the purpose of *subsection (1)(b)*, where the job held by an employee immediately before the start of the period of her absence on maternity leave or additional maternity leave was not her normal or usual job, she shall be entitled to return to work, either in her normal of usual job or in that job as soon as is practicable without contravention by her or her employer of a provision of a statute or instrument made under statute.

(3) In this section "job", in relation to an employee, means the nature of the work which she is employed to do in accordance with her contract of employment and the capacity and place in which she is so employed.

21.—Where an employee is entitled to return to work in accordance with *section 20* but it is not reasonably practicable for her employer or the successor to permit her to return to work in accordance with that section, she shall, subject to this Part, be entitled to be offered by her employer, the successor or an associated employer suitable alternative employment under a new contract of employment. *Right to suitable alternative employment in certain circumstances on return to work*

(2) The following provisions shall apply to a new contract of employment under this section:

> (*a*) the work required to be done under it shall be of a kind which is suitable in relation to the employee concerned and appropriate for her job to do in the circumstances;
>
> (*b*) its terms or conditions relating to the place where the work under it is required to be done, the capacity in which the employee concerned is to be employed and any other terms or conditions of employment are not substantially less favourable to her than those of her contract of employment immediately before the start of her period of absence from work while on maternity leave or additional material leave.

22.—(1) Entitlement to return to work in accordance with *section 20* or to be offered suitable alternative employment under *section 21* shall be subject to an employee who has been absent from work while on maternity leave or additional maternity leave in accordance with this Act having, not later than four weeks before the date on which she expects to return to work, notified in writing (or caused to be so notified) her employer or, where she is aware of a change of ownership of the undertaking concerned, the successor, of her intention to return to work and of the date on which she expects to return to work. *Notification of intention to return to work*

(2) A notification under *subsection (1)* shall subsequently be confirmed in writing not earlier than four weeks and not later than two weeks before the date on which the employee concerned expects to return to work.

23.—Where, because of an interruption or cessation of work at her place of employment, existing on the date specified in a nomination under *section 22* given by her, it is unreasonable to expect an employee to return to work on the date specified in the notification, she may return to work instead when work resumes at the place of employment after the interruption or cessation, or as soon as reasonbly practicable after such resumption. *Postponement of return to work*

PART IV

Amendment of Application of Other Enactments

26.—(1) This section applies to an employee who, having duly complied with *section 22*, is entitled under *Part III* to return to work but is not permitted to do so by her employer, the successor or an associated employer, and who is an employee to whom an Act referred to in the relevant subsection of this section applies. *Provisions applying where employee not permitted to return to work*

(2) For the purposes of the Redundancy Payments Acts, 1967 to 1979, an employee to whom this section applies shall be deemed to have been dismissed by reason of redundancy, the date of dismissal being deemed to be the date specified in the relevant notification under *section 22(1)*.

(3) For the purposes of the Minimum Notice and Terms of Employment Act, 1973, the contract of employment of an employee to whom this section applies shall be deemed to have been terminated on the date specified in the relevant notification under *section 22(1)*.

(4) For the purposes of the Act of 1977, an employee to whom this section applies shall be deemed to have been dismissed on the date specifed in the relevant notification under *section 22(1)*, and the dismissal shall be deemed to be an unfair dismissal unless, having regard to all the circumstances, there were substantial grounds justifying the dismissal.

Disputes regarding entitlement under this Act

27.—(1) Any dispute (other than a claim under section 8 of the Act of 1977, as extended by *section 26*) between and employee to whom the Act of 1977 applies and to whom *part II* or *Part III* applies and her employer, the successor or an associated employer, relating to the employee's entitlement under this Act (or to any matter arising out of or related to such an entitlement) may be referred by either party to the dispute to a rights commissioner or to the Tribunal.

(2) A rights commissioner or the Tribunal shall hear the parties to a dispute under this section and any evidence relevant to the dispute tendered by them and, in the case of a rights commissioner, shall make a recommendation in relation to the dispute and, in the case of the Tribunal, shall make a determination in relation to the dispute.

(3) Sections 8(3), 8(4)(*a*), 8(5) to 8(10), 9(1), 10 and 11 of the Act of 1977 shall apply in relation to a dispute under this section, subject to the following modifications:

> (*a*) references in those sections to a claim for redress under that Act shall be construed as references to a dipute under this section;
>
> (*b*) section 9(4)(*a*) shall be construed as if "refer the claim to" were substituted for "bring the claim before";
>
> (*c*) the reference in section 8(8)(*a*) to the bringing of claims under that section shall be construed as a reference to the referral of a dispute under this section, and sections 8(8)(*d*) and 8(8)(*g*) shall be construed accordingly;
>
> (*d*) section 8(10) shall be construed as if "under this section" were substituted for "in relation to a dismissal that is an unfair dismissal for the purposes of this Act";
>
> (*e*) section 10 shall be construed as if "for an order directing the employer to carry out in accordance with its terms the determination" were submitted for "for redress under this Act" in subsection (1), and as if the following subsection were substituted for subsection (2):
>
>> "(2) Where, in proceedings under this section, the Circuit Court finds that an employee is entitled to an order under subsection (1) of this section, it shall make such an order";
>
> (*f*) section 11 shall be construed as if "under this section" were substituted for "under this Act".

(4) The Minister may make regulations for the purpose of giving effect to this section and may by such regulations make any further modifications of the Act of 1977, or any modifications of regulations under that Act, as he thinks necessary.

(5) In this section "the Tribunal" means the Employment Appeals Tribunal.

Protection of Employees (Employers' Insolvency) Act, 1984

Number 21 of 1984

AN ACT TO CONFER, ON THE INSOLVENCY OF EMPLOYERS, CERTAIN RIGHTS ON EMPLOYEES, TO AMEND CERTAIN ENACTMENTS RELATING TO THE RIGHTS OF EMPLOYEES AND TO PROVIDE FOR OTHER MATTERS (INCLUDING OFFENCES) CONNECTED WITH THE MATTERS AFORESAID. [13th November, 1984]

BE IT ENACTED BY THE OIREACHTAS AS FOLLOWS:

1.—(1) In this Act—

Interpretation

"the Act of 1967" means the Redundancy Payments Act, 1967;

"the Act of 1973" means the Minimum Notice and Terms of Employment Act, 1973;

"the Act of 1974" means the Anti-Discrimination (Pay) Act, 1974;

"the Act of 1977" means the Unfair Dismissals Act, 1977;

"the Act of 1981" means the Social Welfare (Consolidation) Act, 1981;

"company" means, except when the context otherwise requires, a company within the meaning of section 2 of the Companies Act, 1963, or any other body corporate whether incorporated within or outside the State;

"employee" means a person who has entered into or works under (or, in the case of a contract which has been terminated, worked under) a contract with an employer, whether the contract is for manual labour, clerical work or otherwise, is express or implied, oral or in writing, and whether it is a contract of service or apprenticeship or otherwise, and "employer" and any reference to employment shall be construed accordingly;

"holiday pay" means—

    (a) pay in respect of a holiday actually taken; or

    (b) any holiday pay which had accrued at the date of the termination of the employee's employment and which, had his employment with the employer continued until he became entitled to a holiday, would under the employee's contract of employment in the ordinary course have become payable to him on becoming so entitled;

"the Minister" means the Minister for Labour;

"occupational pension scheme" means any scheme or arrangement which, forming part of a contract of employment, provides or is capable of providing, in relation to employees in any description of employment, benefits (in the form of pensions or otherwise) payable to or in respect of any such employees on the termination of their employment or on their death or retirement;

"prescribed" means prescribed by regulations under this Act;

"relevant officer" means an executor, an administrator, the official assignee or a trustee in bankruptcy, a liquidator, a receiver or manager, or a trustee under an arrangement between an employer and his creditors or under a trust deed for his creditors executed by an employer;

"the Tribunal" means the Employment Appeals Tribunal.

(2) Any reference in this Act to the assets of an occupational pensions scheme is a

reference to the funds or other property out of which the benefits provided by the scheme are payable from time to time, including the proceeds of any policy of insurance taken out, or contract entered into, for the purposes of the scheme.

(3) For the purposes of this Act, an employer shall be taken to be or, as may be appropriate, to have become insolvent if, but only if,

> (*a*) he has been adjudicated bankrupt or has filed a petition for or has executed a deed of, arrangement (within the meaning of section 4 of the Deeds of Arrangement Act, 1887); or
>
> (*b*) he has died and his estate, being insolvent, is being administered in accordance with the rules set out in Part I of the First Schedule to the Succession Act, 1965; or
>
> (*c*) where the employer is a company, a winding up order is made or a resolution for voluntary winding up is passed with respect to it, or a receiver or manager of its undertaking is duly appointed, or possession is taken, by or on behalf of the holders of any debentures secured by any floating charge, of any property of the company comprised in or subject to the charge, or
>
> (*d*) he is an employer of a class or description specified in regulations under *section 4(2)* of this Act which are for the time being in force and the circumstances specified in the regulations as regards employers of such class or description obtain in relation to him.

Application of Act

3.—Subject to *section 11* of this Act, this Act applies to employees employed in employment which is insurable for all benefits under the Social Welfare Acts, 1981 to 1984.

Insolvency for purposes of Act

4.—(1) An employer who is for the purposes of this Act insolvent shall for such purposes be regarded as having become insolvent on—

> (*a*) where the employer has been adjudicated bankrupt, the date of such adjudication,
>
> (*b*) where the employer petitioned for arrangement, the date on which the petition is filed,
>
> (*c*) where the employer executed a deed referred to in *section 1(3)(a)* of this Act, the date of such execution,
>
> (*d*) where the employer has died, the date of his death,
>
> (*e*) where the employer is a company within the meaning of section 2 of the Companies Act, 1963—
>
>> (i) in case either a receiver is appointed on behalf of the holder of any debenture secured by a floating charge, or possession is taken by or on behalf of such a debenture holder of any property of the company comprised in or subject to the charge, the date of the appointment of the receiver or possession being taken as aforesaid, as may be appropriate, or
>>
>> (ii) in any other case the date which, in relation to the company, is the relevant date within the meaning of section 285 of the Companies Act, 1963, and
>
> (*f*) where the employer is an employer of a class or description specified in regulations under *subsection (3)* of this section which are for the time being in force, the day on which under the regulations such an employer is for such purposes to be regarded as having become insolvent.

(2) The Minister may by regulations specify the circumstances in which employers who are of a class or description specified in the regulations are, for the purposes of the Act, to

be taken to be, or to have become, insolvent.

(3) The Minister may by regulations specify the day on which any employer who is of a class or description specified in the regulations and who is also an employer who for the purposes of this Act is insolvent, is to be regarded as having become so insolvent.

5.—(1) Where—

(*a*) by virtue of *section 1(3)(d)* of this Act, an employer becomes insolvent for the purposes of this Act, or

(*b*) an employer otherwise becomes insolvent for such purposes and there is not for the time being in relation to the insolvency a relevant officer,

the Minister may appoint as regards such insolvency a person under this subsection.

Appointment in certain circumstances of persons to perform functions assigned by Act

(2) Where the Minister makes an appointment under this section the following provisions shall apply:

(*a*) the functions assigned by this Act to a relevant officer shall, as regards the employer concerned, be performed by, and only by, the person to whom the appointment relates, or, if through illness or because his appointment is revoked or for any other reason the person so appointed is unable to perform such functions, another person so appointed, and

(*b*) for so long as the appointment remains in force, each of the references to a relevant officer in *sections 6, 7* and *8* of this Act shall be construed as including a reference to the person to whom the appointment relates.

6.—(1) If, on an application made to him in the prescribed form by or on behalf of an individual, the Minister is satisfied that—

Employees' rights on insolvency of employer

(*a*) the person by or on whose behalf the application is made (which person is in this section subsequently referred to as "the applicant") is a person to whom this Act applies, and that he was employed by an employer who has become insolvent, and

(*b*) the date on which the employer became insolvent is a day not earlier than the 22nd day of October, 1983, and

(*c*) on the relevant date the applicant was entitled to be paid the whole or part of any debt to which this section applies,

the Minister shall, subject to this section, pay to or in respect of the applicant out of the [Social Insurance] Fund the amount which, in the opinion of the Minister, is or was due to the applicant in respect of that debt.

(2) (*a*) Subject to *paragraph (b)* of this subsection, the following are debts to which this section applies—

(i) any arrears of normal weekly remuneration in respect of a period, or of periods in the aggregate, not exceeding eight weeks, and to which the applicant became entitled during the relevant period.

(ii) any arrears due, in repect of a period or periods not exceeding eight weeks in all under a scheme or arrangement which, forming part or an employee's contract of employment, provides or is capable of providing in relation to employees in any description of employment, payments payable to any such employees in respect of periods during which they are unable to fulfil their contract of employment due to ill health and to which the applicant became entitled during the relevant period.

(iii) any amount which an employer is required to pay, by virtue of an award under section 12 of the Act of 1973 made not earlier than the commencement of the relevant period, either for the period of notice required by section 4 of the Act of 1973 or by reason of a failure by him to give the period of notice required by the said section 4,

(iv) any holiday pay in respect of a period or periods of holiday not exceeding eight weeks in all, and to which the applicant became entitled during the relevant period.

(v) any amount which an employer is required to pay by virtue of a determination under section 8(1) or 9(1) or an order under section 10(2) of the Act of 1977 and made, in any case, not earlier than the commencement of the relevant period.

(vi) any amount to which a recommendation under section 8(1) of the Act of 1977 relates, being a recommendation which was made not later than the commencement of the relevant period,

(vii) any amount which an employer is required to pay by virtue of an employment regulation order within the meaning of Part IV of the Industrial Relations Act, 1946, being an amount by reference to which proceedings have been instituted against the employer for an offence under section 45(1) of that Act,

(viii) any amount—

    (I) specified in a recommendation issued under section 7(3) of the Act of 1974, or section 19(3) of the Employment Equality Act, 1977,

    (II) which an employer is required to pay by virtue of a decision or determination of an appeal by the Labour Court under subsection (1) of section 8 of the Act of 1974 or subsection (2) of section 21 of the Employment Equality Act, 1977, or, where appropriate, a decision of the High Court given by virtue of either subsection (3) of the said section 8 or subsection (4) of the said section 21,

(ix) damages awarded under section 24(3)(a) of the Employment Equality Act, 1977,

(x) a fine imposed undre section 8(4)(c)(i) or paragraph (a) (inserted by section 30 of the Employment Equality Act, 1977) of section 9(3) of the Act of 1974 or under section 25(3)(a)(iii) or 26(3)(a)(iii) of the Employment Equality Act, 1977, and

(xi) compensation directed to be paid under section 10(1)(d) (inserted by section 31 of the Employment Equality Act, 1977) or section 10(3)(a) (inserted by the said section 31) of the Act of 1974 or under section 26(1)(d)(iii) of the Employment Equality Act, 1977.

(b) Any amount, damages, fine or compensation referred to in *subparagraph (viii), (x)* or *(xi)* of *paragraph (a)* of this subsection shall be regarded as being a debt to which this section applies if, and only if, the relevant recommendation, decision, determination, award or order was made during, or after the expiration of the relevant period.

(3) Where—

    (a) legal proceedings are institute by or on behalf of an employee and on foot of all or any of the following—

        (i) a claim for arrears described in *subparagraph (i)* or *(ii)* of *subsection (2)* of this section,

        (ii) a claim for holiday pay described in *subparagraph (iv)* of the said *subsection (2),*

(iii) a claim for damages at common law for wrongful dismissal,

an award is made by the court in favour of the employee, and

(*b*) had the employee made an application under *subsection (1)* of this section in respect of any of the matters referred to in *subparagraph (i), (ii)* or *(iii)* of *paragraph (a)* of this subsection he would have satisfied the requirements of *paragraphs (a), (b)* and *(c)* of the said *subsection (1)*,

subject to *subsection (4)(a)* of this section, there shall be paid out of the [Social Insurance] Fund, to or in respect of the employee, an amount equal to—

(i) the amount of the award, or

(ii) the maximum which would have been payable out of the said Fund by virtue of this Act had the employee successfully sought redress under section 8(1) or 9(1) of the Act of 1977.

(4) (*a*) The amount payable to an employee in respect of any debt mentioned in *subsection (2)* or award mentioned in *subsection (3)* of this section shall, where the amount of that debt is or may be calculated by reference to the employee's remuneration, not exceed [£250.00] in respect of any one week or, in respect of any period of less than a week, an amount bearing the same proportion to [£250.00] as that period bears to the normal weekly working hours of the employee at the relevant date.

(*b*) An amount payable under this section in respect of a debt mentioned in *subsection (2)(a)(ii)* of this section as regards a particular period, shall not exceed the difference between the payment of any disability benefit or injury benefit payable under the Act of 1981 to the employee concerned as regards the period (together with, in either case, the amount of any pay-related benefit payable to such employee under the Act of 1981 as regards the period) and the amount of his normal weekly remuneration as regards the period.

(*c*) (i) A payment shall not be made under this section in respect of an amount which an employer is required to pay by virtue of a determination having been made under section 8(1) or 9(1) of the Act of 1977, unless—

(I) if proceedings are instituted under section 10 of the Act of 1977, the proceedings are withdrawn, or

(II) in case an appeal is brought under section 10(4) of the Act of 1977 from the determination, the appeal has been either withdrawn or determined, or

(III) in case there is no such appeal, the time for bringing such an appeal has expired.

(ii) A payment shall not be made under this section in respect of an amount to which a recommendation under section 8(1) of the Act of 1977 relates unless—

(I) in case an appeal from the recommendation is brought under section 9(1) of the Act of 1977, the appeal is withdrawn, or

(II) in case there is no such appeal, the time for bringing such an appeal has expired.

(iii) A payment shall not be made under this section as regards a recommendation referred to in *subsection (2)(a)(viii)(I)* of this section unless—

(I) the case an appeal is brought under section 8(1)(*a*) of the Anti-Discrimination (Pay) Act, 1974, or section 21(1) of hte Employment Equality Act, 1977, against the recommendation, the appeal is withdrawn, or

(II) in case there is no such appeal, the time for bringing such an appeal has expired.

(5) The provisions of *subsections (6)* and *(7)* of this section shall apply in a case where a relevant officer is neither appointed or required to be appointed.

(6) Subject to *subsection (7)* of this section, the Minister shall not in a case which is a case referred to in *subsection (5)* of this section make any payment under this section in respect of any debt until he has received a statement in the prescribed form from the relevant officer of the amount of that debt which appears to have been owed to the employee on the relevant date and to remain unpaid; and the relevant officer shall, on a request being made in that behalf, by the Minister, provide him, as soon as is reasonably practicable, with such a statement.

(7) Where—

(*a*) a period of six months has elapsed since the application for a payment under this section was received by the Minister, but no such payment has been made,

(*b*) the Minister is satisfied that a payment under this section should be made, and

(*c*) it appears to the Minister that there is likely to be further delays before he receives a statement referred to in *subsection (6)* of this section regarding the debt in question,

then, the Minister may, if the applicant so requests, or if the Minister thinks fit, without such a request, make a payment under this section notwithstanding the fact that no such statement has been received.

(8) Where an application is made to the Minister under this section and in relation to any or each of the debts to which the application relates, the Minister is satisfied that—

(*a*) there was an agreement between the applicant and the employer concerned that the whole or any part of the debt would be the subject of an application under this section, and

(*b*) when the agreement was made such employer had the means to pay such debt or the part thereof,

the Minister may either refuse the application or disallow it in so far as it relates to such debt or part.

(9) In this section—

"normal weekly remuneration" has the meaning assigned to it by Schedule 3 of the Act of 1967 for the purposes of that Schedule save that any reference in that Schedule to the date on which an employee was declared redundant may, where appropriate, be construed as including a reference to the relevant date;

"the relevant date" means—

(*a*) in relation to a debt which is an amount, damages, fine or compensation referred to in *subparagraph (iii), (v), (vi), (viii), (ix), (x)* or *(xi)* of *subsection (2)(a)* of this section, the date on which the relevant employer became insolvent or the date on which the relevant recommendation, decision, determination, award or oder is made, whichever is the later,

(*b*) in relation to any other debt to which this section applies—

(i) in case the relevant applicant's employment is terminated as a result of the relevant employer's insolvency, the date on which such employer became insolvent, or the date of such termination, whichever such applicant shall as regards the debt nominate, or

(ii) in any other case, the date on which such employer became insolvent;

"the relevant period" means in relation to a debt to which this section applies, the period of eighteen months immediately preceding the relevant date.

(10) No reference in *subsection (3)* of this section to an award shall be construed as including a reference to any amount allowed as regards costs.

7.—(1) If, on an application made to him in the prescribed form by an employee or by the persons competent to act in respect of an occupational pension scheme, the Minister is satisfied that—

> (*a*) an employer (being in case the application is made by a person otherwise than in his capacity as the person competent so to act the employer of the applicant) has become insolvent,
>
> (*b*) the date on which for the purposes of this Act the employer became insolvent is a day not earlier than the 22nd day of October, 1983, and
>
> (*c*) on that day there remained unpaid relevant contributions remaining to be paid by the employer to the scheme.

on the date on which the employer became insolvent, being a date not earlier than the said 22nd day of October the Minister shall, subject to this section, pay into the assets of the scheme out of the [Social Insurance] Fund the sum which in his opinion is payable in respect of the unpaid relevant contributions.

(2) In this section "relevant contributions" means contributions falling to be paid by an employer in accordance with an occupational pension scheme, either on his own account or on behalf of an employee; provided that for the purposes of this section a contribution of any amount shall not be treated as falling to be paid on behalf of an employee unless a sum equal to that amount has been deducted from the pay of the employee by way of a contribution from him.

(3) The sum payable under this section in respect of unpaid contributions of an employer on his own account to an occupational pension scheme shall be the lesser of the following amounts—

> (*a*) the balance of relevant contributions remaining unpaid on the date on which he became insolvent and payble by the employer on his own account to the scheme in respect of the period of twelve months ending on the day immediately preceding that date,
>
> (*b*) the amount certified by an actuary to be necessary for the purpose of meeting the liability of the scheme on dissolution to pay the benefits provided by the scheme to or in respect of the employees of the employer.

(4) Any sum payable under this section in respect of unpaid contributions on behalf of an employee shall not exceed the amount deducted from the pay of the employee in respect of the employee's contributions to the occupational pension scheme during the period of twelve months ending on the day immediately preceding the date on which the employer became insolvent.

(5) The provisions in *subsection (6), (7)* and *(8)* of this section shall apply in a case where a relevant officer is either appointed or required to be appointed.

(6) Subject to *subsection (8)* of this section, the Minister shall not in any case which is a case referred to in *subsection (5)* of this section make any payment under this section in respect of unpaid relevant contributions until he has received a statement in the prescribed form from the relevant officer of the amount of relevant contributions which appear to have been unpaid on the date on which the employer became insolvent and to remain unpaid; and the relevant officer shall, on request made by the Minister provide him, as soon as reasonably practicable, with such a statement.

(7) Subject to *subsection (8)* of this section, an amount shall be taken to be payable under *subsection (3)* or to have been deducted in the manner referred to in *subsection (4)* of this

Payment of unpaid contributions to occupational pension scheme

section, only if it is certified by the relevant officer as being so payable, or to have been so deducted.

(8) Where—

> (*a*) a period of six months has elapsed since the application for a payment under this section was received by the Minister, but no such payment has been made,
>
> (*b*) the Minister is satisfied that a payment under this section should be made, and
>
> (*c*) it appears to the Minister that there is likely to be further delay before he receives a statement or certificate about the contributions in question,

then, the Minister may, if the applicant so requests or, if the Minister thinks fit, without such a request, make a payment under this section, notwithstanding the fact that no statement or certificate referred to in *subsection (6) or (7)* of this section has been received.

Minister may require certain information and documents

8.—(1) Where an application is made to the Minister under *section 6 or 7* of this Act in respect of a debt owed or unpaid contributions to an occupational pensions scheme, the Minister may require—

> (*a*) the employer concerned or, in case a relevant officer is or is required to be appointed, that officer, to provide him with such information as the Minister may reasonably require for the purpose of determining whether the application is well-founded and
>
> (*b*) any person having the custody or control of any relevant record kept and retained pursuant to section 10 of the Holidays (Employees) Act, 1973, or any register, card, wages sheet, record of wages or other document which an officer of the Minister may reasonably consider to be relevant to the application to produce to such officer such document for examination by him.

(2) A requirement under this section shall be made by notice in writing given to the person on whom the requirement is imposed and may be varied or revoked by a subsequent notice so given.

Complaints to Tribunal

9.—(1) A person who has applied for a payment under *section 6* of this Act of a debt described in *subparagraph (i), (ii) or (iv) of subsection (2)(a)* of that section may within the period of six weeks beginning on the day on which the decision of the Minister on the application was communicated to him or, if that is not reasonably practicable, within such further period as the Tribunal considers reasonable, present a complaint to the Tribunal that—

> (*a*) the Minister has failed to make such a payment
>
> or
>
> (*b*) any such payment made by the Minister is less than the amount which should have been paid.

(2) Any person who has applied for a payment to be made under *section 7* of this Act into the resources of a pension scheme may, within the period of six weeks beginning on the day on which the decision of the Minister on that application was communicated to him, or, if that is not reasonably practicable, within such further period as the Tribunal considers pensionable, present a complaint to the Tribunal that—

> (*a*) the Minister has failed to make any such payment;
>
> or
>
> (*b*) any such payment made by him is less than the amount which should have been paid.

(3) Where a claim for payment is made under *section 6 or 7* of this Act and it appears to the Minister that a doubt exists as to whether or not such claim is allowable, either in whole

or in part, he may refer any matter arising in connection with the claim to the Tribunal for a decision by it as regards the matter.

(4) Where on the hearing of a complaint presented under this section the Tribunal finds that the Minister is liable to make a payment under *section 6* or *7* of this Act, it shall make a declaration to that effect and shall specify in the declaration the amount of such payment.

(5) Subsection (14) of section 39 of the Act of 1967 shall apply to a decision of the Tribunal on any matter referred to it under this section as it applies to a decision of the Tribunal on a question referred to it under that section.

10.—(1) Where, in pursuance of *section 6* of this Act, the Minister makes any payment to an employee in respect of any debt to which that section applies, any rights and remedies of the employee in respect of that debt (of, if the Minister has paid only part of it, in respect of that part) shall, on the making of the payment, become rights and remedies of the Minister. Transfer to Minister of certain rights and remedies

(2) Without prejudice to the generality of *subsection (1)* of this section, where rights and remedies become, by virtue of *subsection (1)* of this section, rights and remedies of the Minister, there shall be included amongst them any right to be paid in priority to all other debts under—

    (*a*) section 4 of the Preferential Payments in Bankruptcy (Ireland) Act, 1889; or

    (*b*) section 285, as amended by section 10 of the Companies (Amendment) Act, 1982, of the Companies Act, 1963.

and the Minister shall be entitled to be so paid in priority to any other unsatisfied claim of the employee concerned being a claim which, but for this subsection, would be payable to the employee in such priority; and in computing for the purposes of any of the provisions of the said section 4 or the said section 285, as so amended, any limit of the amount of sums to be paid, any sum paid to the Minister shall be treated as it they had been paid to the employee.

(3) Where in pursuance of *section 7* of this Act the Minister makes any payment in to the resources of an occupational pension scheme in respect of any contributions to the scheme, any rights and remedies in respect of those contributions belonging to the persons competent to act in respect of the scheme shall, on the making of the payment, become rights and remedies of the Minister.

(4) Any sum recovered by the Minister in exercising any right or pursuing any remedy which is his by virtue of this section shall be paid into the [Social Insurance] Fund.

Safety, Health and Welfare at Work Act, 1989

Number 7 *of* 1989

AN ACT TO MAKE FURTHER PROVISION FOR SECURING THE SAFETY, HEALTH
AND WELFARE OF PERSONS AT WORK, FOR PROTECTING OTHERS
AGAINST RISKS TO SAFETY OR HEALTH IN CONNECTION WITH THE
ACTIVITIES OF PERSONS AT WORK, FOR THE ESTABLISHMENT OF A
NATIONAL AUTHORITY FOR OCCUPATIONAL SAFETY AND HEALTH, TO
PROVIDE FOR THE REPEAL OF CERTAIN ENACTMENTS, TO PROVIDE FOR
THE FURTHER REGULATION OF DANGEROUS SUBSTANCES IN SO FAR
AS THEY MAY AFFECT PERSONS OR PROPERTY AND FOR MATTERS
CONNECTED WITH THE AFORESAID. [19*th April*, 1989]

BE IT ENACTED BY THE OIREACHTAS AS FOLLOWS:

PART I

PRELIMINARY AND GENERAL

Short title and commencement

1.—(1) This Act may be cited as the Safety, Health and Welfare at Work Act, 1989.

(2) This Act shall come into operation on such day or days as may be fixed therefore by order or orders of the Minister either generally or with reference to any particular purpose or provision, and different days may be so fixed for different purposes and different provisions of this Act and an order under this subsection may provide for the commencement of section 4 (3) upon different days as respects different existing enactments and different provisions of existing enactments.

Interpretation

2.—(1) In this Act—
"article" includes—

> (*a*) any plant, machinery, apparatus and equipment for use or operation (whether exclusively or not) by persons at work, and

> (*b*) any article designed for use as a component in any such plant, machinery, apparatus or equipment;

"associated statutory provisions" means the provisions of the enactments specified in the third column of the Third Schedule together with the instruments made under them for the time being in force;

"the Authority" means the National Authority for Occupational Safety and Health established by section 15;

"code of practice" includes a standard, a specification, and any other written or illustrated form of practical guidance, instruction or control, issued or approved of in accordance with section 30;

"contract of employment" means a contract of employment or service or of apprenticeship, whether it is expressed or implied and (if it is express) whether it is oral or in writing;

"employee" means a person who has entered into or works (or in the case of a contract which has been terminated, worked) under a contract of employment with an employer;

"employer" in relation to an employee, means the person by whom the employee is employed under a contract of employment; for the purpose of this definition a person holding office under or in the service of the State or of the Government shall be deemed to be employed by the State or the Government (as the case may be) and an officer or servant of a local authority or of a harbour authority, health board or vocational education committee shall be deemed to be employed by the local authority, harbour authority, health board or vocational education committee (as the case may be);

"enforcing agency" means a body prescribed to be an enforcing agency under section 32;

"establishment day" means the day appointed by the Minister under section 14 to be the establishment day;

"existing enactments" means the enactments specified in Part I of the Second Schedule, and any instruments under them, for the time being in force; and the regulations under the European Communities Act, 1972, for the time being in force specified in Part 11 of the said Second Schedule;

"functions" includes powers and duties;

"improvement notice" means a notice under section 36;

"improvement plan" means a plan under section 35;

"inspector" means an inspector authorised under section 33;

"local authority" includes—

     (*a*) the council of a county,

     (*b*) the corporation of a county borough, or

     (*c*) the Corporation of Dun Laoghaire,

and such local authority shall exercise its functions under this Act within its functional area;

"micro-organism" includes any microscopic biological entity which is capable of replication;

"the Minister" means the Minister for Labour;

"occupational medical adviser" means a person designated under *section 34(4)* to be an occupational medical adviser;

"personal injury" includes any disease and any impairment of a person's physical or mental condition;

"place of work" includes any place, land or other location at, in, upon or near which, work is carried on whether occasionally or otherwise and in particular includes—

     (*a*) a premises,

     (*b*) an installation on land and any offshore installation (including any offshore installation to which the Safety, Health and Welfare (Offshore Installations) Act, 1987, applies),

     (*c*) a tent, temporary structure or movable structure, and

     (*d*) a vehicle, vessel or aircraft;

"prescribed" means prescribed by regulations made under this Act by the Minister except in *sections 36(3), 37(6)(a)* and *42(4)(a)* where it means prescribed by regulations made under this Act by the Minister for Justice in consultation with the Minister;

"prohibition notice" means a notice under *section 37*;

"recognised trade unions and staff associations" means trade unions and staff associations recognised by the Authority for the purposes of negotiations which are concerned with the remuneration, conditions of employment or working conditions of employees;

"relevant statutory provisions" means existing enactments and the provisions of this Act and any instrument made under it for the time being in force;

"safety representative" means a safety representative appointed under *section 13*;

"safety statement" has the meaning assigned to it by *section 12*;

"self-employed person" means a person who works for profit or gain otherwise than under a contract of employment, whether or not he himself employs other persons;

"substance" includes any natural or artificial substance, preparation or agent in solid or liquid form or as a gas or vapour or as a microorganism;

"use" in so far as any article is concerned includes the manufacture, supply, operation. setting, repair, cleaning and maintenance of such articles; and in so far as any substance is concerned, includes any manufacture, process, operation, storage, treatment, mixing, packing, conveyance, supply, handling, filling or emptying, loading and unloading of such substance.

(2) (*a*) In this Act a reference to a section or a Schedule is to a section of, or a Schedule to, this Act unless it is indicated that reference to some other enactment is intended;

    (*b*) in this Act a reference to a subsection, paragraph or subparagraph is a reference to the subsection, paragraph or subparagraph of the provision in which the reference occurs unless it is indicated that reference to some other provision is intended; and

    (*c*) a reference in this Act to any enactment shall be construed as a reference to that enactment as amended or adapted by any subsequent enactment.

(3) References to an inspector in *sections 35, 36* and *37* shall, in any case in which the enforcing agency is a local authority, be construed as a reference to that local authority.

PART II

GENERAL DUTIES

General duties of employers to their employees

6.—(1) It shall be the duty of every employer to ensure, so far as is reasonably practicable, the safety, health and welfare at work of all his employees.

(2) Without prejudice to the generality of an employer's duty under *subsection (1)*, the matters to which that duty extends include in particular—

    (*a*) as regards any place of work under the employer's control, the design, the provision and the maintenance of it in a condition that is, so far as is reasonably practicable, safe and without risk to health;

    (*b*) so far as is reasonably practicable, as regards any place of work under the employer's control, the design, the provision and the maintenance of safe means of access to and egress from it;

    (*c*) the design, the provision and the maintenance of plant and machinery that are, so far as is reasonably practicable, safe and without risk to health;

    (*d*) the provision of systems of work that are planned, organised, performed and maintained so as to be, so far as is reasonably practicable, safe and without risk to health;

    (*e*) the provision of such information, instruction, training and supervision as is necessary to ensure, so far as is reasonably practicable, the safety and health at work of his employees;

    (*f*) in circumstances in which it is not reasonably practicable for an employer to control or eliminate hazards in a place of work under his control, or in such circumstances as may be prescribed, the provision and maintenance of such suitable protective clothing or equipment, as appropriate, that are necessary to ensure the safety and health at work of his employees;

    (*g*) the preparation and revision as necessary of adequate plans to be followed in emergencies;

    (*h*) to ensure, so far as is reasonably practicable, safety and the prevention of risk to health at work in connection with the use of any article or substance;

    (*i*) the provision and the maintenance of facilities and arrangements for the welfare of his employees at work; and

    (*j*) the obtaining, where necessary, of the services of a competent person (whether under a contract of employment or otherwise) for the purpose of ensuring, so far as is reasonably practicable, the safety and health at work of his employees.

(3) For the purposes of this section, a person who is undergoing training for employment or receiving work experience, other than when pursuing a course of study in a university, school or college, shall be deemed to be an employee of the person whose undertaking (whether carried on by him for profit or not) is for the time being the immediate provider to that person of training or work experience, and employee, employer and cognate words and expressions shall be construed accordingly.

7.—(1) It shall be the duty of every employer to conduct his undertaking in such a way as to ensure, so far as is reasonably practicable, that persons not in his employment who may be affected thereby are not exposed to risks to their safety or health. General duties of employers and self-employed to persons other than their own employees

(2) It shall be the duty of every self-employed person to conduct his undertaking in such a way as to ensure, so far as is reasonably practicable, that he and other persons (not being his employees) who may be affected thereby are not exposed to risks to their safety or health.

(3) In such cases as may be prescribed, it shall be the duty of every employer and self-employed person, in the prescribed circumstances, and in the prescribed manner to give to persons (not being his employees) who may be affected by the way in which he conducts his undertaking the prescribed information about such aspects of the way he conducts his undertaking as might affect their safety or health.

8.—(1) This section has effect for imposing on persons duties in relation to those who are not their employees but who are either the employees of another person or are self-employed and who for the purposes of carrying out work use a non-domestic place of work made available to them or in which they may for the purposes of carrying out work use any article or substance provided for their use there, and it applies to places of work so made available and other non-domestic places of work used in connection with them. General duties of parties concerned with places of work to persons other than their employees

(2) It shall be the duty of each person who has control, to any extent, of any place of work or any part of any place of work to which this section applies or of the means of access thereto or egress therefrom or of any article or substance in such place of work to take such measures as is reasonable for a person in his position to take to ensure, so far as is reasonably practicable, that the place of work, all means of access thereto, or egress therefrom available for use by persons using the place of work, and any article or substance in the place of work or, as the case may be, provided for use therein, is or are safe and without risks to health.

(3) Where a person has, by virtue of any contract or tenancy, an obligation of any extent as to—

    (*a*) the maintenance or repair of any place of work to which this section applies or any means of access thereto or egress therefrom; or

    (*b*) the safety of or the absence of risk to health arising from any article or substance in any such place of work;

that person shall be treated, for the purposes of *subsection (2)*, as being a person who has control of the matters to which his obligation extends.

(4) Any reference in this section to a person having control of any place of work or matter is a reference to a person having control of the place of work or matter in connection with the carrying on by him of a trade, business or other undertaking (whether for profit or not).

9.—(1) It shall be the duty of every employee while at work— General duties of employees

    (*a*) to take reasonable care for his own safety, health and welfare and that of any other person who may be affected by his acts or omissions while at work;

(b) to co-operate with his employer and any other person to such extent as will enable his employer or the other person to comply with any of the relevant statutory provisions;

(c) to use in such manner so as to provide the protection intended, any suitable appliance, protective clothing, convenience, equipment or other means or thing provided (whether for his use alone or for use by him in common with others) for securing his safety, health or welfare while at work; and

(d) to report to his employer or his immediate supervisor, without unreasonable delay, any defects in plant, equipment, place of work or system of work, which might endanger safety, health or welfare, of which he becomes aware.

(2) No person shall intentionally or recklessly interfere with or misuse any appliance, protective clothing, convenience, equipment or other means or thing provided in pursuance of any of the relevant statutory provisions or otherwise, for securing the safety, health or welfare of persons arising out of work activities.

General duties of designers, manufacturers etc.

10.—(1) It shall be the duty of any person who designs, manufactures, imports or supplies any article for use at work—

(a) to ensure. so far as is reasonably practicable, that the article is designed, constructed, tested and examined so as to be safe and without risk to health when used by a person at a place of work;

(b) to take such steps as are necessary to secure that persons supplied by that person with the article are provided with adequate information about the use for which it is designed or has been tested, and about any conditions relating to the article so as to ensure that, when in use, dismantled or disposed of, it will be safe and without risk to health; and

(c) to take such steps as are necessary to secure, so far as is reasonably practicable, that persons so supplied are provided with all such revisions of information provided to them by virtue of paragraph (b) as are necessary by reason of its becoming known that anything relating to the article gives rise to a serious risk to safety or health.

(2) It shall be the duty of any person who undertakes the design or manufacture of any article for use at work to carry out or arrange for the carrying out of any necessary research with a view to the discovery and, so far as is reasonably practicable, the elimination or minimisation of any risks to safety or health to which the design or article may give rise.

(3) It shall be the duty of any person who erects or installs any article for use at a place of work where that article is to be used by persons at work to ensure, so far as is reasonably practicable, that nothing about the way in which the article is erected or installed makes it unsafe, or a risk to health when in use at a place of work.

(4) It shall be the duty of any person who manufactures or imports or supplies any substance—

(a) to ensure, so far as is reasonably practicable, that the substance will be safe and without risks to health when it is being used by a person at a place of work;

(b) to carry out or arrange for the carrying out of such testing and examination as may be necessary for the performance of the duty imposed on him by *paragraph (a)* and whenever requested by an inspector provide or cause to be provided to him evidence, including documentary evidence of such testing and examination;

(c) to take such steps as are necessary to ensure that persons supplied by that person with the substance are provided with adequate information about any risk to safety or health to which the inherent properties of the substance may give rise, about the results of any relevant tests which had heen carried out on or in connection with the substance and about any conditions necessary to ensure that the substance will be safe and without risk to health when the substance is being used or being disposed of.

(5) It shall be the duly of any person who undertakes the manufacture of any substance, or in a case where the manufacture was undertaken outside the State it shall be the duty of the importer, to carry out or arrange for the carrying out of any necessary research with a view to the discovery and, so far as is reasonably practicable, the elimination or minimisation of any risks to safety or health to which the substance may give rise when in use.

(6) Nothing in the preceding provisions of this section shall be construed as requiring a person to repeat any testing, examination or research which has been carried out otherwise than by him or at his instance, in so far as it is reasonable for him to rely on the results thereof, for the purposes of those provisions.

(7) Any duty imposed on a person by any of the preceding provisions of this section shall extend only to things done in the course of a trade, business or other undertaking carried on by him (whether for profit or not) and to matters within his control.

(8) Where a person designs, manufactures, imports or supplies an article for use at work and does so for or to another person on the basis of a written undertaking by that other person to take specified steps that are sufficient to ensure, so far as is reasonably practicable, that the article shall be safe and without risks to health when it is being used at a place of work, the said undertaking shall have the effect of relieving the first mentioned person from the duty imposed by virtue of *paragraph (a)* of *subsection (1)* to such extent as is reasonable having regard to the terms of the said undertaking.

(9) Nothing in *subsections (7)* or *(8)* shall relieve any person who imports any article or substance from any duty in respect of anything which—

> (a) in the case of an article designed outside the State, was done by and in the course of any trade, profession or other undertaking carried on by, or was within the control of, the person who designed the article; or
>
> (b) in the case of an article or substance manufactured outside the State, was done by and in the course of any trade, profession or other undertaking carried on by, or was within the control of, the person who manufactured the article or substance.

(10) Where a person (hereinafter referred to in this subsection as "the supplier") supplies, including hires or leases, to another person (hereinafter referred to in this subsection as "the customer") any article or substance for use at work, under a hire-purchase agreement, a leasing agreement or credit-sale agreement, and the supplier—

> (a) carried on the business of financing the acquisition of goods by others by means of such agreements, and
>
> (b) in the course of that business acquired his interest in the article or substance supplied to the customer as a means of financing its acquisition by the customer from a third party (hereinafter referred to in this subsection as "the dealer"),

the dealer and not the supplier, shall be treated for the purposes of this section as supplying the article or substance to the customer, and any duty imposed by this section on suppliers shall, accordingly, fall on the dealer and not on the supplier.

(11) For the purposes of this section an absence of safety or risk to health shall be disregarded in so far as the case is or in relation to which it would arise is shown to be one the occurrence of which could not reasonably be foreseen; and in determining whether any duty imposed by virtue of *paragraph (a)* of *subsections (1)* or *(4)* has been performed regard shall be had to any relevant information or advice which has been provided to any person

by the person by whom the article has been designed, manufactured, imported or supplied or, as the case may be, by the person by whom the substance has been manufactured, imported or supplied.

(12) Without prejudice to the generality of this section, the Minister may prescribe specifications or other requirements with which the design, manufacture and construction of any article, which is of a prescribed class or description, shall comply.

(13) Where an article or substance is used at work, and a request is made in that behalf by an inspector, the employer shall give to the inspector the name and address of the person from whom the article or substance was purchased or otherwise obtained.

General duties of persons who design or construct places of work
11.—(1) It shall be the duty of any person who designs places of work to design them so that they are, so far as is reasonably practicable, safe and without risk to health.

(2) It shall be the duty of any person who constructs places of work to construct them so that they are, so far as is reasonably practicable, safe and without risk to health.

Safety statement
12.—(1) Every employer shall, as soon as may be, after the coming into operation of this section prepare or cause to be prepared, a statement in writing to be known and hereinafter referred to as a "safety statement".

(2) The safety statement shall specify the manner in which the safety, health and welfare of persons employed by an employer shall be secured at work.

(3) The safety statement shall be based on an identification of the hazards and an assessment of the risks to safety and health at the place of work to which the safety statement relates.

(4) Without preiudice to the generality of *subsection (2)*, the safety statement shall specify—

> (*a*) the arrangements made and resources provided, for safeguarding the safety, health and welfare of persons employed at a place of work to which the safety statement relates;
>
> (*b*) the co-operation required from employees as regards safety, health and welfare; and
>
> (*c*) the names, including the names of authorised deputies and job titles where applicable, of the persons responsible for the performance of tasks assigned to them by the said statement.

(5) Where a safety statement is prepared or revised pursuant to this section and an inspector is satisfied that the statement is inadequate in a material respect he may direct that the statement be revised and the employer shall comply with the direction within thirty days of the direction being given by the inspector.

(6) The report of the directors of a company under section 158 of the Companies Act, 1963, shall contain, in addition to the information specified in that section, an evaluation of the extent to which the policy set out in a safety statement was fulfilled during the period of time covered by the said report.

(7) It shall be the duty of a self-employed person to prepare a safety statement, in so far as is practicable in accordance with this section, so as to ensure his safety, health and welfare at work and that of other persons at the place of work.

(8) It shall be the duty of an employer or a self-employed person to bring the terms of a safety statement to the attention of persons employed by him and to other persons at the place of work who may be affected by the safety statement.

Consultation at place of work and safety representatives
13.—(1) It shall be the duty of every employer—

> (*a*) to consult his employees for the purpose of the making and maintenance of

arrangements which will enable him and his employees to co-operate effectively in promoting and developing measures to ensure their safety, health and welfare at work and in ascertaining the effectiveness of such measures;

(*b*) as far as is reasonably practicable, to take account of any representations made by his employees.

(2) Employees shall have the right to make representations to and consult their employer on matters of safety, health and welfare in their place of work.

(3) Without prejudice to the generality of *subsections (1)* and *(2)*, employees may, from time to time, select and appoint from amongst their number at their place of work a representative (in this Act referred to as "the safety representative") to represent them in consultations pursuant to this section with their employer.

(4) A safety representative shall have the right to such information from his employer as is necessary to ensure, so far as is reasonably practicable. the safety and health of employees at the place of work.

(5) It shall be the duty of every employer to take such steps as are practicable to inform a safety representative when an inspector enters a place of work for the purpose of making a tour of inspection.

(6) A safety representative may—

(*a*) make representations to an employer on any aspects of safety, health and welfare at the place of work;

(*b*) investigate accidents and dangerous occurrences provided that he shall not interfere with or obstruct the performance of any statutory obligation required to be performed by any person under any of the relevant statutory provisions;

(*c*) make oral or written representations to inspectors on matters of safety, health and welfare at work;

(*d*) receive advice and information from inspectors on matters of safety, health and welfare at work;

(*e*) suhject to prior notice to the employer and to agreement between the safety representative and the employer as to frequency, carry out inspections and in reaching such agreement, which shall not be unreasonably withheld by the employer, the parties shall consider the nature and extent of the hazards in the place of work in determining the frequency of inspections to be carried out by the safety representative at the place of work concerned;

(*f*) subject to prior notice to the employer, in circumstances in which it is reasonable to assume that risk of personal injury exists, to investigate potential hazards and complaints made by any employee whom he represents relating to that employee's safety, health and welfare at the place of work; and

(*g*) on a request being made in that behalf by him, accompany an inspector on any tour of inspection other than a tour of inspection made by the inspector for the purpose of investigating an accident.

(7) An employer shall consider and, if necessary, act upon any representations made to him by a safety representative on any matter affecting the safety, health and welfare at work of any employee whom he represents.

(8) (*a*) For the purpose of acquiring the knowledge necessary for the discharge of their functions under *subsection (1)(a)* of this section and to enable them to dischuge those functions, an employer shall afford employees who may be involved in arrangements under *subsection (1)(a)* or under *subsection (2)* such tirne off from their duties as may be reasonable having regard to all the circumstances without

　　　　loss of remuneration;

　　(*b*) an employer shall afford a safety representative such time off from his duties as may be reasonable having regard to all the circumstances without loss of remuneration, to enable him to—

　　　　(i) acquire the knowledge necessary to discharge his functions as a safety representative, and

　　　　(ii) discharge his functions as a safety representative.

(9) Arising from the discharge of his functions under this section, a safety representative shall not be placed at any disadvantage in relation to his employment.

(10) Notwithstanding the generality of *subsections (1)* to *(9)*, the Minister may prescribe such further requirements, arrangements, modifications or exemptions as he considers necessary, from time to time, in relation to the operation of this section.

PART III

NATIONAL AUTHORITY FOR OCCUPATIONAL SAFETY AND HEALTH

Establishment of authority

15.—(1) On the establishment day there shall stand established a body to be known in the Irish language as *An tÚdarás Náisiúnta um Shábháilteacht agus Sláinte Ceirde* and in the English language as the National Authority for Occupational Safety and Health (which body is referred to in this Act as "the Authority") to perform the functions assigned to it by this Act.

(2) The provisions of the *First Schedule* to this Act shall have effect with respect to the Authority.

PART IV

REGULATIONS AND CODES OF PRACTICE

Review of legislation

27.—(1) It shall be the duty of the Authority—

　　(*a*) to keep under review the relevant statutory provisions;

　　(*b*) to keep under review the associated statutory provisions;

　　(*c*) to submit, from time to time, to the Minister such proposals as it considers appropriate in relation to the relevant statutory provisions or for the making or revoking of any instruments under those provisions; and

　　(*d*) to submit, from time to time, to the Minister having responsibility for any of the associated statutory provisions such proposals as it considers appropriate in relation to those provisions or for the making or revoking of any instruments under those provisions.

(2) Before submitting proposals to the Minister in accordance with *subsection (1)(c)*, the Authority shall consult any Minister of the Government or other person or body that appears to the Authority to be appropriate in the circumstances or where the Minister so directs, and, in particular, without prejudice to the generality of the aforesaid, the Authority shall consult the Minister for the Environment in the case of any proposals in relation to controls on the design of or construction of buildings.

(3) The Authority shall consider any proposals for legislative change concerning occupational safety or health and related matters referred to it by the Minister or any other Minister of the Government responsible for any of the relevant statutory provisions or any of the associated statutory provisions as the case may be.

28.—(1) The Minister may make regulations for or in relation to any of the matters set Regulations out in the Fourth Schedule to this Act and any other matter necessary to give effect to this Act.

(2) Regulations made under this Act may apply to all work activities or to particular work activities and may relate to one or more chemical, physical or biological agents.

(3) Before the Minister makes any regulations in exercise of any power conferred on him by this Act (other than as a result of a proposal made by the Authority under *section 27*) he shall consult the Authority.

(4) Where the Minister proposes to make regulations so as to give effect with modifications to any proposal made by the Authority under *section 27*, he shall before making the regulations consult the Authority.

(5) Every regulation made by the Minister under this Act shall be laid before each House of the Oireachtas as soon as may be after it is made and if a resolution annulling the regulation is passed by either such House within the next twenty-one days on which that House has sat after the regulation is laid before it, the regulation shall be annulled accordingly, but without prejudice to the validity of anything previously done under it.

(6) The Minister may, by regulations made under this section, exempt from all or any of the provisions of the relevant statutory provisions any specified class of activity or any specified class of person or place of work on such conditions as may be prescribed, where he is satisfied that the application of such provisions is unnecessary or impracticable.

30.—(1) The Authority may draw up and issue codes of practice. Codes of practice

(2) The Authority may, as it thinks fit, approve of any code of practice or any part of any code of practice drawn up by any other body.

(3) Codes of practice issued or approved of under this section shall be for the purpose of providing practical guidance with respect to the requirements or prohibitions of any of the relevant statutory provisions.

(4) The Authority shall obtain the consent of the Minister before issuing or approving of a code of practice.

(5) The Authority shall, before seeking the consent of the Minister for the issue or approval of a code of practice, consult any Minister of the Government or other person or body that appears to the Authority to be appropriate or where the Minister so directs.

(6) Where the Authority issues or approves of a code of practice it shall publish a statement in the *Iris Oifigiúil* of its issue or approval of that code, identifying the code in question, specifying for which provisions of the relevant statutory provisions the code is issued or approved and the date from which the said code shall have effect.

(7) The Authority may, with the consent of the Minister and following consultation with any other Minister of the Government or any other person or body that appears to the Authority to be appropriate—

(a) revise the whole or part of any code of practice prepared by it,

(b) withdraw its approval for any code of practice or part of any code of practice.

(8) Where the Authority revises, withdraws or ceases to approve of a code of practice it shall publish notice to that effect in the *Iris Oifigiúil*.

31.—(1) A failure on the part of any person to observe any provision of a code of practice Use of codes of practice in criminal proceedings shall not of itself render him liable to any civil or criminal proceedings; but where in any criminal proceedings a party is alleged to have committed an offence by reason of a contravention of any requirement or prohibition imposed by or under any of the relevant statutory provisions being a provision for which there was a code of practice at the time of the alleged contravention, *subsection (2)* shall have effect with respect to that code in relation to those proceedings.

(2) Any provision of the code of practice which appears to the court to give practical guidance as to the observance of the requirement or prohibition alleged to have been contravened shall be admissible in evidence; and if it is proved that any act or omission of the defendant alleged to constitute the contravention is a failure to observe such provision of the code, or if it is proved that any act or omission of the defendant is a compliance with such provision of the code, then such failure or compliance shall be admissible in evidence.

PART V

ENFORCEMENT

Enforcing agencies

32.—(1) Subject to *section 16(1)(a)* and (3), the Minister, with the consent of the Minister for Finance, and after consultation with any Minister of the Government as the Minister considers appropriate, may prescribe persons (including local authorities) to be enforcing agencies (which said person shall be referred to in this Act as "an enforcing agency") in lieu of the Authority for the enforcement of such provisions of the relevant statutory provisions to such extent as may be prescribed.

(2) It shall be the duty of an enforcing agency to make adequate arrangements for the enforcement of the relevant statutory provisions to the extent that it is by regulations under *subsection (1)* made responsible for their enforcement and to perform that duty and any other functions conferred on it by any of the relevant statutory provisions in accordance with such guidance as the Authority may give it.

(3) It shall be the duty of every enforcing agency to furnish any reports and information relating to its functions and activities under this Act to the Authority as the Authority may, from time to time, require.

Civil liability

60.—(1) Nothing in this Act shall be construed—

    (*a*) as conferring a right of action in any civil proceedings in respect of any failure to comply with any duty imposed by or under *sections 6 to 11*, or

    (*b*) as affecting the extent (if any) to which breach of a duty imposed by any of the existing enactments is actionable.

(2) Breach of a duty imposed by regulations made under *section 28* shall, so far as it causes damage, be actionable except in so far as regulations provide otherwise.

(3) *Subsections (1)* and *(2)* shall apply without prejudice to any right of action which exists apart from the provisions of this Act.

(4) Any term of an agreement which purports to exclude or restrict the operation of *subsection (2)* of this section, or any liability arising by virtue of that subsection shall be void, except in so far as regulations made under *section 28* provide otherwise.

(5) In this section "damage" includes death of or personal injury to any person.

Pensions Act, 1990

Number 25 *of* 1990

AN ACT TO REGULATE OCCUPATIONAL PENSION SCHEMES AND TO PROVIDE FOR EQUAL TREATMENT OF MEN AND WOMEN UNDER OCCUPATIONAL BENEFIT SCHEMES, FOR THOSE PURPOSES TO PROVIDE FOR THE ESTABLISHMENT OF A BODY (TO BE KNOWN AS AN BORD PINSEAN— THE PENSIONS BOARD) TO SUPERVISE SUCH SCHEMES AND THEIR OPERATION, TO DEFINE THE FUNCTIONS OF THAT BODY AND TO PROVIDE FOR CONNECTED MATTERS. [24*th July*, 1990]

BE IT ENACTED BY THE OIREACHTAS AS FOLLOWS:

PRELIMINARY AND GENERAL

2.—(1) In this Act, unless the context otherwise requires— *Interpretation*

"actuarial value" means the equivalent cash value of a benefit (including, where appropriate, provision for any revaluation of such benefit) calculated by reference to appropriate financial assumptions and making due allowance for the probability of survival to normal pensionable age and thereafter in accordance with normal life expectancy on the assumption that the member of a scheme, at the effective date of calculation, is in a normal state of health having regard to his age;

"actuary", in relation to a scheme, means a person appointed in pursuance of this Act to act as actuary, for the purposes of this Act, of the scheme, and "actuarial" shall be construed accordingly;

"additional voluntary contributions" means such contributions (if any) as are paid on a voluntary basis by a member of a scheme and are designed to fully provide additional benefits;

"administrator" has the meaning assigned to it by section 13 (1) of the Finance Act, 1972;

"auditor", in relation to a scheme, means a person appointed in pursuance of this Act to act as auditor, for the purposes of this Act, of the scheme;

"benefits", in relation to a scheme, means, other than in *Part VII*, either or both of the following, that is to say—

(*a*) benefit for the member of a scheme at normal pensionable age or in respect of earlier retirement, or on leaving the relevant employment, and

(*b*) benefit for the member's widow, widower, or dependants or others, on the death of the member;

"the Board" means the body established by *section 9*;

"chairman of the Board" shall be construed in accordance with *paragraph 3* of the *First Schedule*;

"the chief executive" means the chief officer of the Board appointed under *section 15*;

"defined benefit scheme" means, subject to *section 27*, a scheme which is not a defined contribution scheme;

"defined contribution scheme" means, subject to *section 27*, a scheme which, under its rules, provides long service benefit, the rate or amount of which is in total directly determined by the amount of the contributions paid by or in respect of the member and includes a scheme the contributions under which are used, directly or indirectly, to provide—

(*a*) benefits, other than long service benefit, and

(*b*) long service benefit the rate or amount of which is in total directly determined by the part of the contributions aforesaid that is used for the provision of the long service benefit;

"the establishment day" means the day appointed by the Minister under section 8;

"functions" includes powers and duties;

"funded scheme" means a scheme under which some or all of its resources are set aside in advance to provide benefits in a manner which is independent of the employer's business activities;

"long service benefit" means the benefits which will be payable under a scheme in accordance with an obligation to or in respect of a member of a scheme on the assumption that he remains in relevant employment until such time as he attains normal pensionable age;

"member", in relation to a scheme, means any person who, having been admitted to membership under the rules of the scheme, remains entitled to any benefit under the scheme;

"the Minister" means the Minister for Social Welfare;

"normal pensionable age" means the earliest age at which a member of a scheme is entitled to receive benefits under the rules of the scheme on retirement from relevant employment, disregarding any provisions under such rules for early retirement on grounds of illhealth or otherwise;

"occupational pension scheme" means any scheme or arrangement—

(*a*) which is comprised in one or more instruments or agreements, and

(*b*) which provides or is capable of providing in relation to employees in any description of employment who reside within the State, benefits, and

(*c*) (i) which has been approved of by the Revenue Commissioner for the purpose of Chapter II of Part I of the Finance Act, 1972, or

(ii) the application for approval of which under Chapter II of Part I of the Finance Act, 1972, is being considered,

(iii) which is a statutory scheme to which section 17 of the Finance Act, 1972, applies;

"prescribed" means prescribed by regulations made by the Minister under this Act;

"preserved benefit" has the meaning assigned to it by *section 28(2)*;

"prospective member" means any person who is already in relevant employment and who, by virtue of his contract of service or the rules of the scheme is or will be eligible to join the scheme or will in any event join the scheme if his service in relevant employment continues and the relevant terms of his contract of employment or, as the case may be, the relevant terms of the rules of the scheme remain unaltered during that time;

"reckonable service" means service in the relevant employment during membership of the scheme but does not include service as a member of the scheme where either—

(*a*) the only benefit thereunder is in respect of death prior to normal pensionable age, or

(*b*) the member has been notified in writing by the trustees that such service does not entitle him to long service benefit;

"regulations" means regulations made by the Minister under this Act;

"relevant employment" means any employment (or any period treated as employment) to which a scheme applies;

"resources", in relation to a scheme, means the funds out of which the benefits provided by the scheme are payable from time to time, including the proceeds of any policy of insurance taken out, or annuity contract entered into, for the purposes of the scheme;

"revaluation percentage" has the meaning assigned to it by *section 33*;

"rules", in relation to a scheme, means the provisions of a scheme, by whatever name they are called;

"scheme" means an occupational pension scheme;

"trustees", in relation to a scheme, which is estalished under a trust, means the trustees of the scheme and, in relation to a scheme not so established, means the administrator of the scheme and, accordingly, references to trustees shall, except in *sections 59, 62, 63* and *64*, be construed as including references to administrators.

(2) In this Act

> (*a*) a reference to a Part is to a Part of this Act unless it is indicated that a reference to a Part of a Schedule to this Act or of some other enactment is intended,
>
> (*b*) a reference, to a section or a Schedule is a reference to a section of, or a Schedule to, this Act unless it is indicated that reference to some other enactment is intended,
>
> (*c*) a reference to a subsection, paragraph or subparagraph is a reference to the subsection, paragraph or subparagraph of the provision in which the reference occurs unless it is indicated that reference to some other provision is intended,

(3) In this Act a reference to an enactment shall be construed as a reference to that enactment as amended or excluded by any other enactment including this Act.

PART II

ESTABLISHMENT OF PENSIONS BOARD

PART III

PRESERVATION OF BENEFITS

PART IV

FUNDING STANDARD

PART V

DISCLOSURE OF INFORMATION IN RELATION TO SCHEMES

54.—(1) It shall be the duty of the trustees of a scheme to furnish information to the persons specified in *subsection (2)* on the following, that is to say— *Disclosure of information in relation to schemes*

> (*a*) the constitution of the scheme,
>
> (*b*) the administration and finances of the scheme,
>
> (*c*) the rights and obligations that arise or may arise under the scheme, and

(*d*) such other matters as appear to the Minister to be relevant to schemes in general or to schemes of a particular description to which the scheme belongs and are prescribed.

(2) The persons to whom *subsection (1)* relates are—

(*a*) the members and prospective members of the scheme,

(*b*) the spouses of members and prospective members of the scheme,

(*c*) persons within the application of the scheme and qualifying or prospectively qualifying for its benefits,

(*d*) an authorised trade union representing the members concerned.

(3) Notwithstanding *subsection (1)*, the Minister may by regulations provide that information in relation to such of the matters aforesaid as may be specified shall be furnished by the trustees of the scheme to such of the persons specified in *subsection (2)* as may be specified in the regulations only if so requested by those persons.

(4) (*a*) The trustees, the actuary or the auditor of a scheme may request an employer to whom the scheme relates to furnish them or him with such information as they or he may reasonably require for the purposes of their or his functions under this Act or regulations thereunder and the employer shall comply with any such request.

(*b*) The actuary or the auditor of a scheme may request the trustees of the scheme to furnish him with such information as he may reasonably require for the purposes of his functions under this Act or regulations thereunder and the trustees shall comply with any such request.

(5) A person who contravenes *subsection (1)* or *(4)* or regulations under *subsection (3)* shall be guilty of an offence and shall be liable on summary conviction to a fine not exceeding £1,000.

(6) In this section "authorised trade union" means a body to whom a negotiation licence (within the meaning of Part II of the Trade Union Act, 1941) was issued under the said Part II.

Annual reports **55.**—(1) The trustees of a scheme shall prepare an annual report containing information in relation to such matters as may be prescribed with the consent of the Minister for Finance concerning the operation of the scheme during whichever of the following periods the trustees may select, that is to say:

(*a*) each year beginning on the date specified for the purpose of the scheme—

(i) in any document comprising the scheme or which is included among the documents comprising it, or

(ii) in the rules of the scheme,

(*b*) each year being on the 1st day of January, or

(*c*) each year beginning on such other day as may be agreed upon by the trustees and the Board.

(7) *Subsection (1)* of this section shall not apply to a scheme—

(*a*) the only benefit which is in respect of death prior to normal pensionable age, and

(*b*) the members of which have been notified in writing by the trustees that service by a member in the relevant employment after the date of the notification does not entitle the member to long service benefit.

Audited accounts and actuarial valuations **56.**—(1) The trustees of a scheme shall cause the accounts of the scheme in respect of such periods as may be prescribed to be audited by the auditor of the scheme and shall cause the resources and liabilities of the scheme to be valued by the actuary of the scheme at such times as may be prescribed and, in respect of each such audit and valuation, shall cause to be prepared the documents to which this section applies.

(2) The documents to which this section applies are—

    (*a*) the audited accounts of the scheme concerned,

    (*b*) the auditor's report on the accounts specified in *paragraph (a)*, and

    (*c*) the actuary's report on his valuation of the assets and liabilities of the scheme.

(3) A person shall not be qualified for appointment as auditor for the purposes of this Act of a scheme—

    (*a*) unless he is a member of a body of accountants, membership of which is recognised by the Minister for Industry and Commerce under the Companies Acts, 1963 to 1986, as qualifying a person to be an auditor of a company, or is otherwise for the time being authorised by the said Minister under the said Acts to be appointed auditor of a company, or

    (*b*) if he is a member of a class of persons standing prescribed for the time being for the purposes of this section.

(4) A person shall not act as auditor of a particular scheme at a time when he is disqualified under this section, for appointment to that office and, if an auditor of the scheme becomes so disqualified during his term of office as such auditor, he shall thereupon vacate his office and give notice in writing to the trustees of the scheme that he has vacated his office by reason of such disqualification.

(5) The form and content of any document to which this section applies may be prescribed with the consent of the Minister for Finance and those documents shall comply with any regulation under this subsection.

(6) (*a*) *Paragraph (a)* and *(b)* of *subsection (2)* shall not apply to a scheme—

    (i) that is not a funded scheme,

    (ii) the only benefit under which is in respect of death prior to normal pensionable age, and

    (iii) the members of which have been notified in writing by the trustees that service by a member in relevant employment after the date of the notification does not entitle the member to long service benefit under the seheme.

(*b*) *Paragraph (c)* of *subsection (2)* shall not apply to a scheme—

    (i) that is a defined contribution scheme,

    (ii) that is not a funded scheme,

    (iii) the only benefit under which is in respect of death prior to normal pensionable age, and

    (iv) the members of which have been notified in writing by the trustees that service by a member in relevant employment after the date of the notification does not entitle the member to long service benefit under the scheme.

57.—Where the Minister considers that it would be unreasonable, having regard to their nature and character and the size of their membership, to require specified schemes or categories of schemes to comply fully with *sections 54, 55* and *56*, he may by regulations made with the consent of the Minister for Finance provide that those sections shall apply in relation to those schemes or categories of schemes with specified modifications, being modifications that, in the opinion of the Minister, are reasonable and are not such to relieve the trustees of the obligation to furnish such information under those sections as is appropriate in all the circumstances. _{Modification of Part V}

Conflict
between Part
V and
schemes

58.—(1) The provisions of this Part and of any regulations made thereunder shall override any rule of a scheme to the extent that that rule conflicts with those provisions.

(2) Any question as to—

    (*a*) whether any provision of this Part (including the application of any provision as modified by regulations) or any regulation made thereunder conflicts with any rule of a scheme, or

    (*b*) whether a scheme is a defined benefit scheme or a defined contribution scheme for the purposes of this Part,

shall be determined by the Board on application to it in writing in that behalf by a person who, in relation to the scheme, corresponds to a person mentioned in *section 38(3)* in relation to the scheme mentioned therein.

(3) An appeal to the High Court on a point of law from a determination of the Board under *subsection (2)* in relation to a scheme, may be brought by the person who made, or a person who was entitled to make, the application concerned under *subsection (2)*.

PART VI

TRUSTEE OF SCHEMES

General duties
of trustees of
a scheme

59.—Without prejudice to the duties of trustees generally and in addition to complying with the other requirements of this Act, the duties of trustees of schemes shall include the following:

    (*a*) to ensure, in so far as is reasonable, that the contributions payable by the employer and the members of the scheme, where appropriate, are received;

    (*b*) to provide for the proper investment of the resources of the scheme in accordance with the rules of the scheme;

    (*c*) where appropriate, to make arrangements for the payment of the benefits as provided for under the rules of the scheme as they become due;

    (*d*) to ensure that proper membership and financial records are kept.

Duty to
register
scheme

60.—(1) Subject to the following subsections, it shall be the duty of trustees of a scheme to ensure that the scheme is registered with the Board.

(2) A scheme shall be registered not later than—

    (*a*) in case the scheme commenced before the commencement of this section, one year after such commencement,

    (*b*) in any other case, one year after the commencement of the scheme.

(3) It shall be the duty of the trustees of a scheme to provide the Board, in such a manner as may be prescribed, with such information as may be prescribed for the purposes of this section.

Restriction of
Perpetual
Funds
(Registration)
Act, 1933

61.—Sections 7, 8, 10, 12 (2), and, in so far as it relates to those sections, section 14 of the Perpetual Funds (Registration) Act, 1933 shall not apply in the case of a scheme.

Selection by
members of
funded
schemes of
persons for
appointment
as trustees

62.—(1) The Minister shall provide by regulations, in respect of schemes having not less than a specified number of members, that the members of any such scheme may, if a majority of the members decide to do so, select or, at the option of such majority, approve of the selection by the employer concerned of, a person or a specified number of persons who shall be appointed to be trustees of the scheme and different numbers of persons (including one person) may be so specified for different schemes.

(2) Regulations under this section—

    (*a*) shall specify the manner in which decisions of members of schemes, and the selection of persons for appointmem as trustees of schemes by the members of schemes, for the purpose of *subsection (1)* shall be made,

    (*b*) may make such other provision as the Minister considers necessary or expedient for the purpose of this section and for enabling it to have full effect.

63.—(1) The High Court (in this Part referred to as "the court") may, on application to it by the Board by petition, make an order for the appointment of one or more new trustees of a scheme in substitution for the existing trustees of the scheme. _{Appointment and removal of trustees by High Court}

(2) The court may make an order under *subsection (1)* in relation to the trustees of a scheme, if it considers—

    (*a*) that the trustees have failed to carry out the duties imposed on them by law (including this Act), and

    (*b*) that the scheme is being or has been administered in such a manner as to jeopardise the rights and interests thereunder of the members of the scheme.

(3) (*a*) A petition under this section shall be served only on the existing trustees unless the court directs otherwise.

    (*b*) Upon the hearing of a petition under this section, the Board, the existing trustees of the scheme concerned, the employer concerned and the members of the scheme shall be entitled to be heard unless the court directs otherwise.

(4) A trustee of a scheme appointed under this section shall, as well before as after the resources of the scheme become by law vested in him have the same powers, authorities and discretions and may in all respects act as if he had been originally appointed a trustee by the rules of the scheme.

(5) An order under this section may make provision for such ancillary and consequential matters (including the vesting of the property of the scheme concerned in the trustees appointed by the order and (notwithstanding anything contained in the rules of the scheme) the making of payments from the resources of the scheme to the trustees appointed by the order in respect of fees, expenses or other matters relating to their duties as such trustees) as the court considers necessary or expedient.

(6) An order under this section shall not operate further or otherwise as a discharge to any former trustee of the scheme concerned than an appointment of new trustees under any power for that purpose contained in any instrument would have operated.

(7) Where any land of which the ownership is registered under the Registration of Title Act, 1964, becomes vested, by order under this section, in any person or persons, the registering authority under that Act shall, upon production of the relevant order under this section, and upon payment of the appropriate fee, register that person or those persons in the appropriate register maintained under that Act as owner (within the meaning of that Act) of the land.

(8) Where an order is made under this section, any assets vested by the order that immediately before the commencement of the order were standing registered in the books of any bank corporation or company or were entered in any register kept in pursuance of any enactment in the names of the former trustees of the scheme concerned shall, upon such commencement, be transferred unto the names of the new trustees of the scheme.

64.—(1) Where, in relation to a scheme, there are no trustees or the trustees cannot be found, the Board may, if it considers it necessary to do so, on application to it in that behalf by a person having an interest by order under its seal— _{Appointment and removal of trustees by Board}

(*a*) appoint a new trustee or new trustees of the scheme in substitution, where appropriate, for any existing trustee or trustees; and

(*b*) vest, subject where necessary to transfer in the books of any bank, corporation or company, the assets of the scheme in the persons appointed trustees of the scheme by the order.

(2) The Board shall—

(*a*) not less than 14 days before the date on which it proposes to make an order under this section, publish a notice in a daily newspaper circulating throughout the State stating the proposal and giving particulars of the proposed order,

(*b*) within 10 days after the date of the making of the order, publish a notice in a daily newspaper circulating throughout the State stating the proposal and giving particulars of the proposed order.

(3) Every trustee of a scheme appointed under this section shall, as well before as after the resources of the scheme become by law vested in him, have the same powers, authorities and discretions and may in all respects act as if he had been originally appointed a trustee by the rules of the scheme.

(4) (*a*) A person having an interest may, within 21 days after the publication of a notice under *subsection (2)(b)* (or such longer period as the court may fix, being a period that, having regard to the circumstances of any particular case, the court considers to be reasonable), appeal to the court against the making of the order to which the notice relates.

(*b*) On an appeal under this subsection the court may make such order confirming, annulling or varying the order concerned and such order as to costs as it thinks fit, but if the court annuls or varies an order under this section that has come into operation, the annulment or variation shall be without prejudice to the validity of anything previously done thereunder.

(*c*) The Board, the trustees, the employer and the members of the scheme concerned shall be entitled to be represented and heard on any appeal under this subsection.

(*d*) An order under this section shall not come into operation—

(i) during the period of 21 days from the date of the publication of the notice under *subsection (2)(b)* in relation to the order, or

(ii) if an appeal against the order is brought during the period aforesaid, before the final determination of the appeal or any appeal from such determination the withdrawal of either such appeal.

(5) An order under this section may make provision for such ancillary and consequential matters (including the vesting of property of the scheme concerned in the trustees appointed by the order andd (notwithstanding anything contained in the rules of the scheme) the making of payments from the resources of the scheme to the trustees appointed by the order in respect of fees, expenses or other matters relating to their duties as such trustees) as the Board considers necessary or expedient.

(6) An order under this section shall not operate as a discharge of any liabilities of a former trustee of the scheme concerned to any greater or different extent than the appointment of new trustees under any power for that purpose contained in any instrument would have operated.

(7) Where a body corporate is appointed under this section to be, or a body corporate appointed under this section becomes, sole trustee of a scheme the terms of which provide for or require the appointment of more than one trustee, then, during such time as the body corporate holds the office of trustee of the scheme and is the only such trustee—

> (*a*) the rules of the scheme shall be deemed to provide for or require the appointment of one trustee only, and
>
> (*b*) one trustee only shall be deemed to have been originally appointed under the terms of the scheme.

(8) Where any land of which the ownership is registered under the Registration of Title Act, 1964, becomes vested, by an order under this section, in any person or persons, the registering authority under that Act shall, upon production of a copy of the order sealed with the seal of the Board, and upon payment of the appropriate fee, register that person or those persons in the appropriate register maintained under that Act as owner (within the meaning of that Act) of the land.

(9) Where an order is made under this section, any assets vested by the order that immediately before the commencement of the order were standing registered in the books of any bank, corporation or company or were entered in any register kept in pursuance of any enactment in the names of the former trustees of the scheme concerned shall, upon production after such commencement of a copy of the order sealed with the seal of the Board, be transferred into the names of the new trustees of the scheme.

PART VII

EQUAL TREATMENT FOR MEN AND WOMEN IN OCCUPATIONAL BENEFIT SCHEMES

65.—In this Part, unless the context otherwise requires— Interpretation (Part VII)

"the Act of 1946" means the Industrial Relations Act, 1946;

"the Agency" means the Empoyment Equality Agency;

"the Court" means the Labour Court;

"employee" means a person who has entered into or works under (or, in the case of a contract which has been terminated, worked under) a contract of employment with an employer, whether the contract is (or was) for manual labour, clerical work or otherwise, is (or was) expressed or implied, oral or in writing, and whether it is (or was) a contract of service or apprenticeship or otherwise, and includes a civil servant of the State or of the Government and an officer or servant of a local authority within the meaning of the Local Government Act, 1941, an officer or servant of a harbour authority, health board or vocational education committee and any reference to employment shall be construed accordingly;

"employer", in relation to an employee, means the person by whom the employee is (or, in the case where the employment has ceased, was) employed under a contract of employment, and for the purposes of this definition a civil servant of the State or of the Government shall be deemed to be employed by the State or the Government (as the case may be) and an officer or servant of an authority within the meaning of the Local Government Act, 1941, or of a harbour authority, health board or vocational education committee shall be deemed to be employed by the local authority, harbour authority, health board or vocational educational committee (as the case may be);

"member" means any person who, having been admitted to membership under the rules of an occupational benefit scheme remains entitled to the benefits of such scheme;

"occupational benefit scheme" means any scheme or arrangement which is comprised in one or more instruments or agreements and which provides, or is capable of providing, occupational benefits to employed or self-employed persons but does not include—

> (*a*) any individual contract made by or on behalf of an employed or a self-employed person, or
>
> (*b*) any scheme which has only one member, or

(*c*) any scheme for the benefit of employees under which the benefits are provided in full by contributions paid by the employees;

"occupational benefits" means benefits, in the form of pensions or otherwise, payable in cash or in kind in respect of—

(*a*) termination of service,

(*b*) retirement, old age or death,

(*c*) interruptions of service by reason of sickness or invalidity,

(*d*) accidents, injuries or diseases arising out of or in the course of a person's employment,

(*e*) unemployment, or

(*f*) expenses incurred in connection with children or other dependants;

and, in the case of a member who is an employee, includes any other benefit corresponding to a benefit provided by virtue of the Social Welfare Acts, the Maternity (Protection of Employees) Act, 1981, or the Health Acts, 1970 to 1987, which is payable to or in respect of the member as a consequence of his employment;

"the Social Welfare Acts" means thc Social Welfare (Consolidation) Act, 1981, and every enactment, whether passed before or after this Act, which is to be construed with it as one Act.

Schemes to comply with principles of equal treatment

66.—Subject to *sections 69* and *72* every occupational benefit scheme shall comply with the principle of equal treatment.

Principle of equal treatment

67.—(1) The principle of equal treatment is that there shall be no discrimination on the basis of sex in respect of any matter relating to an occupational benefit scheme.

(2) The principle of equal treatment shall apply in relation to members' dependants as it applies in relation to members.

(3) For the purposes of this section, discrimination on the basis of sex shall be deemed to occur in respect of a matter relating to an occupational benefit scheme in but only in the following cases—

(*a*) where because of a person's sex the person is treated less favourably than a person of the other sex,

(*b*) where a person is treated, by reference to his marital or family status, less favourably than a person of the other sex with the same status,

(*c*) where because of a person's sex the person is unable to comply with a requirement or condition—

(i) in respect of which the proportion of persons of the other sex able to comply with such requirement or condition is substantially higher than the proportion of persons of the first mentioned sex so able, and

(ii) which is not justifiable irrespective of the sex of the persons to whom it applies,

(*d*) where because of a person's marital or family status the person is unable to comply with a requirement or condition—

(i) in respect of which the proportion of persons of the other sex with the same status able to comply with such requirement or condition is substantially higher than the proportion of persons of the first mentioned sex so able, and

(ii) which is not justifiable irrespective of the sex of the persons to whom it applies,

(*e*) where a person is penalised for having in good faith—

(i) made a reference under *section 75, 76* or *77*,

(ii) given evidence in any proceedings under this Part, or

(iii) given notice of an intention to do anything referred to in *subparagraphs (i)* and *(ii)*.

68.—If any question arises as to whether a requirement or condition, falling within paragraphs *(c)* and *(d)* of *subsection (3)* of *section 67* is justifiable irrespective of the sex of the persons to whom it applies, it shall be for those who assert such justificaction to prove it. Onus of proof in certain cases

69.—(1) In determining whether a scheme complies with the principle of equal treatment under *section 66*, account shall not be taken of— Supplementary provisions to section 66

(*a*) any difference, on the basis of the sex of members, in the levels of contributions which the employer makes, to the extent that the difference is for the purposes of removing or limiting differences, as between men and women in the amount or value of benefits provided under a defined contribution scheme,

(*b*) any difference, on the basis of sex, in the amount or value of benefits provided under a defined contribution scheme to the extent that the difference is justifiable on actuarial grounds,

(*c*) any special treatment for the benefit of women to whom *section 72(1)* relates,

(*d*) any difference of treatment in relation to benefits for a deceased member's surviving spouse or other dependants,

(*e*) any difference of treatment in relation to any optional provisions available.

(2) In this section—

"defined contribution scheme" has the meaning assigned to it under *section 2* but as if the reference therein to "benefits" were a reference to "occupational benefits";

"optional provisions available" means those provisions of a scheme—

(*a*) which apply only in the case of members who elect for them to do so, and

(*b*) whose purpose is to secure for those members—

(i) benefits in addition to those otherwise provided under the scheme, or

(ii) a choice with respect to the date on which benefits under the scheme are to commence, or

(iii) a choice between any two or more benefits.

(3) *Subsection (1)(d)* shall cease to have effect on such date as may be prescribed.

70.—An employer shall comply with the principle of equal treatment in relation to the manner in which he affords his employees access to an occupational benefit scheme. Equal treatment and access to schemes

71.—(1) Where a rule of an occupational benefit scheme does not comply with the principle of equal treatment it shall, to the extent that it does not so comply, be rendered null and void by the provisions of this Part and the more favourable treatment accorded by it to persons of the one sex shall be accorded by it to persons of the other sex. Non-compliance, compulsory levelling up

(2) Where more favourable treatment is accorded to any persons under a scheme by virtue of *subsection (1)*, the trustees of the scheme or (where appropriate) the employer shall take such measures as are necessary to give effect to that subsection.

(3) Where, on the commencement of this Part, any rule of the scheme is rendered null and void by *subsection (1)*, then, during such period as may be prescribed, beginning on such commencement and not being longer than ten years, nothing in this Part shall affect any rights accrued or obligations incurred under the scheme before such commencement, and different periods may be prescribed under this subsection in relation to different classes or rights and different classes of obligations.

72.—(1) Subject to the provisions of this section, nothing in this Part shall prevent a scheme from providing special treatment for women in connection with pregnancy or childbirth.

(2) Where an occupational benefit scheme contains a rule—

(*a*) which relates to continuing membership of, or the accrual of rights under, the scheme during any period of paid maternity absence in the case of a woman who—

(i) is, or

(ii) immediately before the commencement of such period, was,

an employee and which treats that woman in a manner other than that in which she would be treated under the scheme if she was not absent from work and was in receipt of remuneration from her employer during that period, or

(*b*) which requires the amount of any benefit payable under the scheme to or in respect of any such woman, to the extent that it falls to be determined by reference to her earnings during a period which includes a period of paid maternity absence, to be determined other than it would so be determined if she was not absent from work, and was in receipt of remuneration from her employer during that period,

it shall be regarded to that extent as not complying with the principle of equal treatment.

(3) Where a scheme is regarded as not complying with the principle of equal treatment by virtue of *subsection (2)*, the trustees of the scheme or (where appropriate) the employer concerned shall take such measures as are necessary to ensure that the treatment accorded to the woman concerned under the scheme is no less favourable than that which would be accorded to her thereunder throughout the period of maternity absence concerned if she were not absent from work and was in receipt of remuneration from her employer during that period.

(4) In this section "period of paid maternity absence" means any period—

(*a*) throughout which a woman is absent from work due to pregnancy or childbirth, and

(*b*) for which her employer, or (if she is no longer in his employment) her former employer, pays her any contractual remuneration.

73.—(1) Where an occupational benefit scheme contains a rule—

(*a*) which relates to continuing membership of, or the accrual of rights under, the scheme during any period of paid family leave in the case of a member who is an employee and which treats the member in a manner other than that in which he would be treated under the scheme if he were not absent from work, and was in receipt of remuneration from his employer, during that period, or

(*b*) which requires the amount of any benefit payable under the scheme to or in respect of any such member, to the extent that it falls to be determined by reference to his earnings during a period which includes a period of paid family leave, to be determined other than it would so be determined if he was not absent from work and was in receipt of remuneration from his employer during that period,

it shall be regarded to that extent as not complying with the principle of equal treatment.

(2) Where a scheme is regarded as not complying with the principle of equal treatment by virtue of *subsection (1)*, the trustees of a scheme or (where appropriate) the employer concerned shall take such measures as are necessary to ensure that the treatment accorded

to the member concerned under the scheme is no less favourable than that which would be accorded to him thereunder throughout the period of family leave concerned if he was not absent from work and was in receipt of remuneration from his employer during that period.

(3) In this section "period of paid family leave" means any period—

    (*a*) throughout which a member is absent from work for family reasons, and

    (*b*) during which the employer pays him any contractual remuneration.

74.—(1) (*a*) Where an agreement or order to which this section applies contains a rule which does not comply with the principle of equal treatment, the rule shall be null and void.

    (*b*) This section applies to—

        (i) a collective agreement,

        (ii) an employment regulation order within the meaning of Part IV of the Act of 1946, and

        (iii) a registered employment agreement within the meaning of Part III of the Act of 1946 registered in the Register of Employment Agreements.

(2) Where a contract of employment contains a term (whether expressed or implied) which does not comply with the principle of equal treatment, the term shall be null and void.

[margin note: Principle of equal treatment and collective agreements etc.]

Worker Protection (Regulation Part-Time Employees) Act, 1991

Number 5 of 1991

AN ACT TO EXTEND CERTAIN PROVISIONS OF ACTS RELATING EMPLOYMENT TO EMPLOYEES WHO ARE NORMALLY EXPECTED TO WORK NOT LESS THAN 8 HOURS PER WEEK FOR AN EMPLOYER AND, WHERE APPROPRIATE, HAVE SO WORKED FOR NOT LESS THAN 13 WEEKS CONTINUOUSLY FOR THE EMPLOYER, AND TO PROVIDE FOR OTHER MATTERS CONNECTED WITH THE MATTERS AFORESAID. [26th March, 1991

BE IT ENACTED BY THE OIREACHTAS AS FOLLOWS:

Interpretation **1.**—(1) In this Act—

"the Act of 1967" means the Redundancy Payments Act, 1967;

"the Act of 1984" means the Protection of Employees (Employers' Insolvency) Act, 1984;

"excluding provision" means"

> (*a*) (i) subsection (1) of section 4 of the Act of 1967 in so far as it has the effect of excluding employees from the application of that Act by virtue of the Social Welfare (Subsidiary Employments) Regulations, 1979 (S.I. No. 127 of 1979), the Social Welfare (Employment of Inconsiderable Extent) Regulations, 1991 (S.I. No. 28 of 1991), or any other regulations for the time being prescribed by the Minister under *subsection (3)(a)* of this section, or
>
> (ii) subsection (2) of the said section 4,
>
> (*b*) section 3 (1) (a) of the Minimum Notice and Terms of Employment Act, 1973,
>
> (*c*) (i) in relation to annual leave entitlement, section 3 of the Holidays (Employees) Act, 1973, in so far as it has the effect of excluding employees from the application of that Act by reference to the number of hours worked, or
>
> (ii) in relation to public holiday entitlement, section 4 (2) of that Act,
>
> (*d*) the definition of "employee" in section 1 (as amended by the Worker Participation (State Enterprises) Act, 1988) of the Worker Participation (State Enterprises) Act, 1977, in so far as it has the effect of excluding employees from the application of that Act by reference to the number of hours worked,
>
> (*e*) paragraph 8 (as amended by the Act of 1984) of the First Schedule to the the Minimum Notice and Terms of Employment Act, 1973, as applied for the purposes of the Unfair Dismissal Act, 1977, by virtue of section 2 (4) of the latter Act.
>
> (*f*) (i) the definition of "employee" in section 2(1) of Maternity Protection of Employees Act, 1981, in so far as it has the effect of excluding employees from the application of that Act by virtue of the Social Welfare (Subsidiary Employments) Regulations, 1979, the Social Welfare (Employment of Inconsiderable Extent) Regulations, 1991, or any other regulations for the

time being prescribed by the Minister under subsechon (3) (a) of this
section, or

(ii) paragraph (a) of the definition of "employer" in section 2 (1) of that Act,

(*g*) section 3 of the Act of 1984, in so far as it has the effect of excluding employees
from the application of that Act by virtue of the Social Welfare (Subsidiary
Employments) Regulations, 1979, the Social Welfare (Employment of
Inconsiderable Extent) Regulations, 1991, or any other regulations for the
time being prescribed by the Minister under subsection (3) (a) of this
section;

"the Minister" means the Minister for Labour;

"regular part-time", in relation to an employee under a relevant enactment, means an
employee who works for an employer and who—

(*a*) has been in the continuous service of the employer for not less than 13 weeks,
and

(*b*) is normally expected to work not less than 8 hours a week for that employer,
and to whom, but for this Act, a provision of the relevant enactment would not apply because
of an excluding provision;

"relevant enactment" means—

(*a*) the Redundancy Payments Acts, 1967 to 1990,

(*b*) the Minimum Notice and Terms of Employment Acts, 1973 and 1984,

(*c*) the Holidays (Employees) Act, 1973,

(*d*) the Worker Participation (State Enterprises) Acts, 1977 and 1988,

(*e*) the Unfair Dismissals Act, 1977,

(*f*) the Maternity Protection of Employees Act, 1981, or

(*g*) the Protection of Employees (Employers' Insolvency) Acts, 1984 and 1990;

"the Tribunal" means the Employment Appeals Tribunal.

(2) References in this Act to an employee or to an employer shall be construed as is
appropriate in the circumstances, by reference to an employee or an employer, respectively,
for the purposes of one or more than one relevant enactment as amended by this Act.

(3) (*a*) The Minister may, for the purposes of *paragraphs (a)(i), (f) (h)* and *(g)* or any of
them, of the definition of "excluding provision", by order, prescribe any
regulations made by the Minister for Social Welfare and to which either or both
subsection (1) of section 4 of the Act of 1967 and section 3 of the Act of 1984
relates and may by order amend or revoke any order so prescribing.

(b) The Minister may by order amend the definition of "regular part-time" so as to
alter either or both the minimum number of weeks of continuous service and
the minimum number of hours a week that a person is normally expected to
work, and may so amend where that definition has been previously amended
by virtue of this subsection.

(c) Where an order is proposed to be made under this subsection, a draft thereof shall
be laid before each House of the Oireachtas and the order shall not be made
until a resolution approving of the draft has been passed by each such House.

2.—(1) For the purpose of calculating the 13 weeks continuous service, with an employer   Continuous
referred to in the definition of "regular part-time", the provisions of the First Schedule to the   service
Minimum Notice and Terms of Employment Act, 1973, shall apply as if—

(*a*) references to employer and employee were to be construed in accordance with
section 1(2) of this Act, and references to employment and cognate words
were construed accordingly, and

(*b*) the reference to "eighteen hours" in paragraph 8 of that Schedule were a reference to "8 hours".

(2) Notwithstanding subsection (1) of this section, the Tribunal shall have a discretion, when hearing a dispute referred to it under section 5(I) of this Act, to consider whether—

> (a) dismissal, whenever occurring, of an employee by the employer followed by re-employment of the employee within 26 weeks of such dismissal, or
>
> (b) reduction, whenever occurring, of the weekly working hours of an employee by the employer,

was used by the employer for the purpose of avoiding obligations arising or likely to arise by virtue of this Act and, where the Tribunal considers that such dismissal or reduction was so used, it shall be deemed not to operate so as to break the continuity or affect the computability of service of the employee.

(3) (a) Where, for the purpose of the application of any relevant enactment or part thereof, a period of continuous service (being service in accordance with the provisions, however expressed, of that enactment) of not less than 13 weeks is required, then in ascertaining the period under that enactment the 13 weeks continuous service referred to in *subsection (1)* of this section shall be included as if it were 13 weeks continuous service in accordance with the provisions, however expressed, of that enactment.

> (b) For the purpose of calculating the part of a period of continuous service to which paragraph (a) of this subsection relates, but which is not calculable in accordance with *subsection (1)* of this section, that part shall—
>
> > (i) in respect of the Act of 1967, be calculated under that Act as if the reference therein in section 4(2) (as amended by the Act of 1984) to "18 hours" were a reference to "8 hours",
> >
> > (ii) in respect of the Minimum Notice and Terms of Employment Act, 1973, be calculated as if the reference in paragraph 8 of the First Schedule to that Act (as so amended) to "eighteen hours" were a reference to "8 hours",
> >
> > (iii) in respect of the Unfair Dismissals Act, 1977, be calculated as if the reference in the said paragraph of the said First Schedule (as so amended and as applied for the purposes of the said Act by virtue of section 2(4) thereof) to "eighteen hours" were a reference to "8 hours".

(4) Except where provided for by this Act, no benefit or right shall accrue under any relevant enactment, including the Holidays (Employees) Act, 1973, to a regular part-time employee in respect of the 13 weeks continuous service referred to in *subsection (1)* of this section and no period shall be ascertained so as to include all or any part of the said 13 weeks.

(5) The provisions of this section are, in so far as they concern matters to which the European Communities (Safeguarding of Employees' Rights on Transfer of Undertakings) Regulations, 1980 (S.I. No. 306 of 1980), relate, in addition to and not in substitution for those Regulations.

Application of relevant enactments

3.—Subject to section 2 of this Act and where appropriate, each relevant enactment, other than the Holidays (Employees) Act, 1973, shall apply to a regular part-time employee in the same manner as it applies, other than by virtue of this Act, to an employee to whom that enactment relates.

Application of Act of 1973

4.—(1) Subject to *section 2* of this Act and to the other provisions of this section and where appropriate, the Act of 1973 shall apply to a regular part-time employee in the same manner as it applies, other than by virtue of this Act, to an employee to whom the Act of

1973 relates.

(2) Notwithstanding *subsection (1)* of this section, subsections (2) and (3) of section 3, subsection (2) of section 4 and subsection (2) of section 5 of the Act of 1973 shall not apply to any regular part-time employee.

(3) For the purpose of the application of the Act of 1973 to regular part-time employees, that Act shall have effect—

(*a*) in the case of subsection (1) of section 3, as if the subsection read as follows:

"(1) An employee shall be entitled to paid leave in respect of a leave year (in this Act referred to as annual leave) at a rate of six hours for every 100 hours worked and to proportionately less where there are fewer hours worked.",

(*b*) in the case of subsection (7) of section 3, as if that subsection read as follows:

"(7) For the purposes of subsection (1) a day of annual leave shall be taken as if the employee worked thereon the hours he would have worked if not on leave.",

(*c*) in the case of paragraphs (a) and (b) of subsection (5) of section 3, as if those paragraphs read respectively as follows:

"(*a*) Where there are eight or more months of service, annual leave shall, subject to any registered employment agreement, employment regulation order or agreement with the employee's trade union, include an unbroken period equivalent to—

(i) the leave entitlement earned over the first eight months of service, or of the appropriate leave year, or

(ii) two-thirds of the total leave entitlement earned in the first year of service, or subsequently in the appropriate leave year,

and for the purpose of ascertaining an unbroken period of annual leave, regard shall be had to the average period over which a number of hours (being the same number of hours as those representing the unbroken period of annual leave) would be worked.

(*b*) When ascertaining for the purposes of this subsection, whether a period is a period of unbroken leave, the fact that a day is a public holiday or a day of illness shall be disregarded.",

(*d*) in the case of subsection (1) of section 5, as if that subsection read as follows:

"(1) Where—

(*a*) an employee ceases to be employed, and

(*b*) annual leave is due to him in respect of the current leave year or, in case the cesser occurs during the first half of that in respect of that year, the previous year or both,

the employer shall pay compensation to him in respect of the annual leave at a rate which is proportionate to the normal weekly rate.",

(*e*) in the case of subsection (3) of section 5, as if that subsection read as follows:

"(3) Where employment ceases during the five weeks ending on the day before a public holiday and the employee has, during the part of that period before the cesser, worked for the employer during at least four of those five weeks, the employer shall pay compensation to him in respect of the public holiday consisting of an extra day's pay.",

and

(*f*) in the case of paragraph (*b*) of subsection (3) of section 6, as if that paragraph read as follows:

"(*b*) be at a rate which is proportionate to the normal weekly rate of remuneration, and".

(4) For the purposes of the application of this Act to the Act of 1973, nothing in this Act shall be construed as permitting any ascertainment of annual leave entitlement or public holiday entitlement from a date before the commencement date provided for in an order under section 8(9) of this Act and which relates to the Act of 1973.

(5) In this section "the Act of 1973" means the Holidays (Employees) Act, 1973.

Disputes as to continuity of service etc.

5.—(a) Any dispute arising in respect of the calculation of the 13 weeks continuous service to which *section 2(1)* of this Act relates and any dispute relating to the number of hours a week actually worked or normally expected to be worked, shall be referred in the prescribed manner to the Tribunal.

(2) Subject to a right of appeal to the High Court on a question of law, the determination of the Tribunal by virtue of this section shall be final.

(3) In this section "prescribed" means prescribed by regulations made by the Minister under *section 6* of this Act.

Payment of Wages Act, 1991

Number 25 *of* 1991

AN ACT TO PROVIDE FURTHER PROTECTION FOR EMPLOYEES IN RELATION TO THE PAYMENT OF WAGES, TO FACILITATE THE PAYMENT OF WAGES OTHERWISE THAN IN CASH, FOR THAT PURPOSE TO REPEAL THE TRUCK ACTS, 1831 TO 1896, AND RELATED ENACTMENTS AND TO PROVIDE FOR CONNECTED MATTERS. [23*rd July*, 1991]

BE IT ENACTED BY THE OIREACHTAS AS FOLLOWS:

1.—(1) In this Act—

"cash" means cash that is legal tender;

"contract of employment" means—

> (*a*) a contract of service or of apprenticeship, and
>
> (*b*) any other contract whereby an individual agrees with another person to do or perform personally any work or service for a third person (whether or not the third person is a party to the contract) whose status by virtue of the contract is not that of a client or customer of any profession or business undertaking carried on by the individual, and the person who is liable to pay the wages of the individual in respect of the work or service shall be deemed for the purposes of this Act to be his employer,

whether the contract is express or implied and if express, whether it is oral or in writing;

"employee" means a person who has entered into or works under (or, where the employment has ceased, entered into or worked under) a contract of employment and references, in relation to an employer, to an employee shall be construed as references to an employee employed by that employer; and for the purpose of this definition, a person holding office under, or in the service of, the State (including a member of the Garda Siochana or the Defence Forces) or otherwise as a civil servant, within the meaning of the Civil Service Regulation Act, 1956, shall be deemed to be an employee employed by the State or the Government, as the case may be, and an officer or servant of a local authority for the purposes of the Local Government Act, 1941, a harbour authority, a health board or a vocational education committee shall be deemed to be an employee employed by the authority, board or committee, as the case may be;

"employer", in relation to an employee, means the person with whom the employee has entered into or for whom the employee works under (or, where the employment has ceased, entered into or worked under) a contract of employment;

"the Minister" means the Minister for Labour;

"strike" and "industrial action" have the meanings assigned to them by the Industrial Relations Act, 1990;

"the Tribunal" means the Employment Appeals Tribunal;

"wages", in relation to an employee, means any sums payable to the employee by the employer in connection with his employment, including—

> (*a*) any fee, bonus or commission, or any holiday, sick or maternity pay, or any other emolument, referable to his employment, whether payable under his contract of employment or otherwise, and

(*b*) any sum payable to the employee upon the termination by the employer of his contract of employment without his having given to the employee the appropriate prior notice of the termination, being a sum paid in lieu of the giving of such notice:

Provided however that the following payments shall not be regarded as wages for the purposes of this definition:

(i) any payment in respect of expenses incurred by the employee in carrying out his employment,

(ii) any payment by way of a pension, allowance or gratuity in connection with the death, or the retirement or resignation from his employment, of the employee or as compensation for loss of office,

(iii) any payment referable to the employee's redundancy,

(iv) any payment to the employee otherwise than in his capacity as an employee,

(v) any payment in kind or benefit in kind.

(2) Except in *section 5 (5) (f)*, a reference in this Act to an employer receiving a payment from an employee is a reference to his receiving such a payment in his capacity as the employee's employer.

(3) In this Act, a reference to a section is a reference to a section of this Act, unless it is indicated that reference to some other enactment is intended.

(4) In this Act, a reference to a subsection, paragraph or subparagraph is a reference to a subsection, paragraph or subparagraph of the provision in which the reference occurs, unless it is indicated that reference to some other provision is intended.

Modes of
payment of
wages

2.—(1) Wages may be paid by and only by one or more of the following modes:

(*a*) a cheque. draft or other bill of exchange within the meaning of the Bills of Exchange Act, 1882,

(*b*) a document issued by a person who maintains an account with the Central Bank of Ireland or a holder of a licence under section 9 of the Central Bank Act, 1971, which, though nor such a bill of exchange as aforesaid, is intended to enable a person to obtain payment from that bank or that holder of the amount specified in the document,

(*c*) a draft payable on demand drawn by a holder of such a licence as aforesaid upon himself, whether payable at the head office or some other office of the bank to which the licence relates,

(*d*) a postal, money or paying order, or a warrant, or any other like document, issued by or drawn on An Post or a document issued by an officer of a Minister of the Government that is intended to enable a person to obtain payment from that Minister of the Government of the sum specified in the document,

(*e*) a document issued by a person who maintains an account with a trustee savings bank within the meaning of the Trustee Savings Banks Act, 1989, that is intended to enable a person to obtain payment from the bank of the sum specified in the document,

(*f*) a credit transfer or another mode of payment whereby an amount is credited to an account specified by the employee concerned,

(*g*) cash,

(*h*) any other mode of payment standing specified for the time being by regulations made by the Minister after consultation with the Minister for Finance.

(2) Where wages fall to be paid to an employee by a mode other than cash at a time when,

owing to a strike or other industrial action affecting a financial institution, cash is not readily available to the employee, the employer concerned shall, if the employee consents, pay the wages by another mode (other than cash) specified in *sub-section (1)* and, if the employee does not so consent, pay them in cash.

(3) An employer who pays wages to an employee otherwise than by a mode specified in *subsection (1)* or contravenes *subsection (2)* shall be guilty of an offence and shall be liable on summary conviction to a fine not exceeding £1,000.

4.—(1) An employer shall give or cause to be given to an employee a statement in writing specifying clearly the gross amount of the wages payable to the employee and the nature and amount of any deduction therefrom and the employer shall take such reasonable steps as are necessary to ensure that both the matter to which the statement relates and the statement are treated confidentially by the employer and his agents and by any other employees. _{Statements of wages and deductions from wages}

(2) A statement under this section shall be given to the employee concerned—

(*a*) if the relevant payment is made by a mode specified in *section 2 (1) (f)*, as soon as may be thereafter,

(*b*) if the payment is made by a mode of payment specified in regulations under *section 2 (1) (h)*, at such time as may be specified in the regulations,

(*c*) if the payment is made by any other mode of payment, at the time of the payment.

(3) Where a statement under this section contains an error or omission, the statement shall be regarded as complying with the provisions of this section if it is shown that the error or omission was made by way of a clerical mistake or was otherwise made accidentally and in good faith.

(4) An employer who contravenes *subsecton (1)* or *(2)* shall be guilty of an offence and shall be liable on summary conviction to a fine not exceeding £1,000.

5.—(1) An employer shall not make a deduction from the wages of an employee (or receive any payment from an employee) unless— _{Regulation of certain deductions made and payments received by employers}

(*a*) the deduction (or payment) is required or authorised to be made by virtue of any statute or any instrument made under statute,

(*b*) the deduction (or payment) is required or authorised to be made by virtue of a term of the employee's contract of employment included in the contract before, and in force at the time of, the deduction or payment, or

(*c*) in the case of a deduction, the employee has given his prior consent in writing to it.

(2) An employer shall not make a deduction from the wages of an employee in respect of—

(*a*) any act or omission of the employee, or

(*b*) any goods or services supplied to or provided for the employee by the employer the supply or provision of which is necessary to the employment,

unless—

(i) the deduction is required or authorised to be made by virtue of a term (whether express or implied and, if express, whether oral or in writing) of the contract of employment made between the employer and the employee, and

(ii) the deduction is of an amount that is fair and reasonable having regard to all the circumstances (including the amount of the wages of the employee), and

(iii) before the time of the act or omission or the provision of the goods or services, the employee has been furnished with—

    (I) in case the term referred to in subparagraph (i) is in writing, a copy thereof,

    (II) in any other case, notice in writing of the existence and effect of the term,

and

(iv) in case the deduction is in respect of an act or omission of the employee, the employee has been furnished at least one week before the making of the deduction, with particulars in writing of the act or omission and the amount of the deduction, and

(v) in case the deduction is in respect of compensation for loss or damage sustained by the employer as a result of an act or omission of the employee, the deduction is of an amount not exceeding the amount of the loss or the cost of the damage, and

(vi) in case the deduction is in respect of goods or services supplied or provided as aforesaid, the deduction is of an amount not exceeding the cost to the employer of the goods or services. and

(vii) the deduction or, if the total amount payable to the employer by the employee in respect of the an or omission or the goods or services is to be so paid by means of more than one deduction from the wages of the employee, the first such deduction is made not later than 6 months after the act or omission becomes known to the employer or, as the case may be, after the provision of the goods or service.

(3) (*a*) An employer shall not receive a payment from an employee in respect of a matter referred to in *subsection (2)* unless, if the payment were a deduction, it would comply with that subsection.

    (*b*) Where an employer receives a payment in accordance with *paragraph (a)* he shall forthwith give a receipt for the payment to the employee.

(4) A term of a contract of employment or other agreement whereby goods or services are supplied to or provided for an employee by an employer in consideration of the making of a deduction by the employer from the wages of the employee or the making of a payment to the employer by the employee shall not be enforceable by the employer unless the supply or provision and the deduction or payment complies with *subsection (2)*.

(5) Nothing in this section applies to—

    (*a*) a deduction made by an employer from the wages of an employee, or any payment received from an employee by an employer, where—

        (i) the purpose of the deduction or payment is the reimbursement of the employer in respect of—

            (I) any overpayment of wages, or

            (II) any overpayment in respect of expenses incurred by the employee in carrying out his employment.

made (for any reason) by the employer to the employee, and

        (ii) the amount of the deduction or payment does not exceed the amount of the overpayment,

    (*b*) a deduction made by an employer from the wages of an employee, or any payment received from an employee by an employer, in consequence of any disciplinary proceedings if those proceedings were held by virtue of a statutory provision, or

    (*c*) a deduction made by an employer from the wages of an employee in pursuance of a requirement imposed on the employer by virtue of any statutory provision to deduct and pay to a public authority, being a Minister of the Government, the Revenue Commissioners or a local authority for the purposes of the Local Government Act, 1941, amounts determined by that authority as being due to it from the employee, if the deduction is made in accordance with the relevant determination of that authority, or

(*d*) a deduction made by an employer from the wages of an employee in pursuance of any arrangements—

(i) which are in accordance with a term of a contract made between the employer and the employee to whose inclusion in the contract the employee has given his prior consent in writing, or

(ii) to which the employee has otherwise given his prior consent in writing, and under which the employer deducts and pays to a third person amounts, being amounts in relation to which he has received a notice in writing from that person stating that they are amounts due to him from the employee, if the deduction is made in accordance with the notice and the amount thereof is paid to the third person not later than the date on which it is required by the notice to be so paid, or

(*e*) a deduction made by an employer from the wages of an employee, or any payment received from an employee by his employer, where the employee has taken part in a strike or other industrial action and the deduction is made or the payment has been required by the employer on account of the employee's having taken part in that strike or other industrial action, or

(*f*) a deduction made by an employer from the wages of an employee with his prior consent in writing, or any payment received from an employee by an employer, where the purpose of the deduction or payment is the satisfaction (whether wholly or in part) of an order of a court or tribunal requiring the payment of any amount by the employee to the employer, or

(*g*) a deduction made by an employer from the wages of an employee where the purpose of the deduction is the satisfaction (whether wholly or in part) of an order of a court or tribunal requiring the payment of any amount by the employer to the court or tribunal or a third party out of the wages of the employee.

(6) Where—

(*a*) the total amount of any wages that are paid on any occasion by an employer to an employee is less than the total amount of wages that is properly payable by him to the employee on that occasion (after making any deductions therefrom that fall to be made and are in accordance with this Act), or

(*b*) none of the wages that are properly payable to an employee by an employer on any occasion (after making any such deductions as aforesaid) are paid to the employee,

then, except in so far as the deficiency or non-payment is attributable to an error of computation, the amount of the deficiency or nonpayment shall be treated as a deduction made by the employer from the wages of the employee on the occasion.

6.—(1) An employee may present a complaint to a rights commissioner that his employer has contravened *section 5* in relation to him and, if he does so, the commissioner shall give the parties an opportunity to be heard by him and to present to him any evidence relevant to the complaint, shall give a decision in writing in relation to it and shall communicate the decision to the parties.

Complaints by employees in relation to contravention of section 5 by their employer

Index

accidents at work 70, 109-25
agricultural wages 85
aliens 127, 262
altering the terms of employment 64
apprentices 47-8, 104-6
arbitration 27-8, 264
armed forces 327
asbestos 124
attachment of earnings 91-2, 258

bakeries 79
Blackstone 1

children: *see* young persons
civil servants 43-4, 289-316
　appointment 308
　discipline and dismissal 314-15
　exclusion from employment
　　protection 290
　fair procedures 295-302
　obligations 310-13
　probation 314
　status 309
company law 275-87
　directors' service agreements
　　282-7
　dismissing directors 284-7
　financial assistance to purchase
　　shares 277
　golden handshakes 283
　golden umbrellas 283-4
　share options 278-81
compensation
　accidents at work 117-24

occupational diseases 122-4
redundancy 216-7
unfair dismissal 205
wrongful dismissal 174-8
conflict of laws 262-71
　applicable law 265-71
　choice of forum clauses 264
　contracts 265-7
　jurisdiction of courts 262-5
　redundancy payments 270-1
　territoriality 267-9
　tort 267-9
　unfair dismissals 269-70
collective agreements 59-63
collective redundancy 217-19
competing with ex-employer 101-4
confidential information 96-8, 313,
　319
constructive dismissal 182-3
co-operation, duty of 71-2
copyright 99-100
Constitution, the 6-12
　discrimination in employment
　　126-7
　dismissal from employment
　　167-70, 297-300
　double jeopardy 302-3
　fair hearing/procedures 167-70,
　　297-300
　non-governmental action 7-9
　work, right to 9-12
consultation with employees or their
　representatives 218, 301
continuity of employment 183-8,
　189, 193-4, 207-8

contract of employment: *see also*
  dismissal, remuneration,
  suspension from work, times of
  work and workplace
  alteration of 64
  apprentices 47-8, 104-6
  civil servants 309
  collective agreement and 59-63
  control test for 33-4
  dismissals procedures 166-72
  formalities for 51-2
  grounds for dismissal 163-6
  integration test for 34-5
  obligations under 68-104
  out-workers 48-9
  religious activities 48-50
  terms of 51-64
  work rules and 57-8
  written statement of particulars of
    55-7
  control test 33-4
  corruption, prevention of 312, 319
  custom and practice 58-9

damages
  breach of employment contract 75
  injury at work 118-22
  occupational disease 122-4
  wrongful dismissal 174-8
declaration 172-3, 292
dismissal from employment
  civil service 303-5, 315
  compensation for 174-8
  constructive 182-3
  date of 184-5
  definition of 180-3
  enjoining 173-4
  insolvency of employer and
    232-35
  local authority workers 303-5,
    320-1
  maternity and 151-2, 199
  minimum notice of 188-91
  notice of 160-3
  procedures for 166-72, 198,

    297-302
  reasons for 163-6, 198-203,
    210-11, 303-5
  redundancy and 206-19
  repudiation of employment
    contract 154-6
  sex discrimination and 199-200
  summary 163-66
  unfair 192-205
  wrongful 160-78
deciding officers 27
defence forces 327
discipline at work 71-5, 94, 163-6,
  201-3, 314-5, 320-1
discrimination in employment
  EC nationals 127-33
  equal pay 136-40
  marital status 140-7, 259-61
  maternity 147-52, 199
  political opinion 126-7, 199, 294-5
  religious beliefs 126-7, 199
  sex 126-7, 133-48, 199, 259-61
disease, occupational 123-4, 125
drivers 79

EC nationals 127-33, 309
emoluments 331-38
employers: *see* contract of
  employment
employers' liability: *see* negligence
employment and training levy (PRSI)
  253-6
Employment Appeals Tribunal 22-4,
  40, 65
employment equality: *see* sex
  discrimination
enterprise test 35-6
equal pay 85, 134-40
equality officers 25-6, 135
established civil servants 306-7, 308
establishment 76-7
European community
  charter of fundamental rights 14
  collective redundancies 217-9
  directives 15-6

discrimination and EC nationals 127-33
employer's insolvency 235-7, 240-2
employment equality 140-9, 260-1
equal pay 136-40, 259
health and safety at work 13, 107-8
law making competence of 13-14
maternity 147-8
occupational pensions 259-61
transfer of undertakings 23-231, 235-7
working abroad 263-4, 266-7
European Convention on Human Rights 17-18
European Social Charter 19-20

Factories Acts 2, 109-10, 121-2
fidelity, duty of 72, 96-8, 311-12
fixed term employment contracts 181-2, 195-6
foreign embassy and consular staff 273-4

Garda Síochána 325-6

health and safety: *see* safety and health
Health and Safety Authority 113-6
health contributions (PRSI) 355-6
holidays (paid) 87-8

illegal employments 46
illness 85-6, 123-4, 126, 158-9
implied terms of employment contract 52-5, 56, 58, 62
imprisonment of employee 159
income tax
benefits in kind 339-41
emoluments 331-9
employees 328-9
expenses, allowable 341-5
gifts 332-3, 346, 347-9
golden handshakes 347-9

office holders 330-1
P.A.Y.E. 349-56
P.R.S.I. 353-6
taxable remuneration 331
travel expenses 344-5
termination payments 345-9
industrial action 71-2, 74-5, 92-4, 188
industrial work 78-9
injunction 75, 104, 173-4, 178-9, 292
integration test 34-5
International Labour Organisations 19
insolvency of employer
bankruptcy 232
examination 235
insolvency fund 240-2
liquidation 233-4
preferential debts 237-40
receivership 234-5
transfer of undertaking 235-7
inventions of employees 10
Irish language 132, 317

Labour Court 26, 135
lay-offs 74, 81-2, 212-3
legitimate expectations 300-2
liquidation 233-4, 237-42
Local Government employees
appointment 317
discipline and dismissal 319-21
obligations 319
status 318

maintenance orders 91, 92
married workers 126-7, 140-7, 269-61
maternity 51, 271-3
merchant shipping 51, 271-3
minimum notice of dismissal
contract of employment and 161
notice periods prescribed 189-90
payment during notice periods 190-91
remuneration in lieu of notice 175
minimum wages 84-5

negligence
  breach of statutory duty 120-2
  causations 199
  deafness 123-4
  defences 119-20
  diseases 122-4
  duty of care 118
  insurance 118
  standard of care 118-19
noise 124
notice of dismissal
  contracted period 161-3
  'golden umbrellas' 283-4
  minimum notice 188-91
  summary dismissal 163-6
nurses 47-8, 316

occupational pension schemes
  amendment of 252-3
  approval for 244-6
  discrimination in 259-61
  early leavers from 257-8
  employers and 253-4
  financing of 246-7
  insolvency of employer 258-9
  investment of funds 251
  surplus 247-53
  trustees 247-53
office holders 41-2, 291, 309, 318
official secrets 313, 319
orders, reasonable 71, 163-6, 200-1
out-workers 48-9
overtime 79-80

P.A.Y.E. 349-53
P.R.S.I. 353-6
part-time workers 187
partnership (dissolution of) 159-60
patents 100
pensioners 194, 208
pensions: *see* occupational pensions
Pensions Board 27, 243
place of work: *see* workplace
pregnancy: *see* maternity
privacy 71

probation 195, 314
public service employment: *see also*
  civil servants, defence forces,
  gardaí, local government, teachers
  audi alteram partem 297-9
  bias, absence of 300
  double jeopardy 302-3
  discipline and dismissal 303-5,
    314-5, 319-21
  exclusions from employment
    protection legislation 43-4,
    288-91
  fair procedures 295-300
  judicial review 292-4
  legitimate expectations 300-2
  political activities 294-5
  public law 291-4
  suspension without pay 296,
    314-5, 320
private international law: *see* conflict
  of law
procedures of dismissal
  civil servants 314-5
  contract of employment 170
  enjoining breaches of agreed
    procedure 173-4
  fair hearing 168-70, 297-300
  local government workers 320-1
  redundancy 302, 217-19
  unfair dismissal 202, 217-19

racial discrimination 26-127, 199
receivers 234-5, 237
reckonable earnings 354-5
redundancy
  certificate of 212
  collective 217-19
  conflict of laws 270-1
  consultations 218
  continuity of employment 207-8
  definition of 210-11
  lay off 212-13
  lump sum payment 216-17
  notice of 212
  part time workers 187, 208

public sector employment 208
transfer of employer's business
    230
unfair dismissal and 202
religion 49-50
remuneration
    assignment and attachment of
        91-2, 258
    cash payments 88-9
    deduction from 90-6
    defining 82-4
    equal pay 85, 136-40
    holiday 87-8
    minimum 84-5
    modes of payment 88-90
    normal 85
    preferential debts 237-40
    sick 85-6
    statement of 95

safety and health at work
    codes of practice 114
    employee's duties 113
    employer's liability 111-2, 117-24
    Health and Safety Authority
        114-16
    inspectors 114
    investigations and reports 116
    prohibition orders 115
    safety representatives 116
    safety statements 117
seafaring 271-3
self-employed workers 30-2
sex discrimination
    conflict of laws 269
    Constitution, the 126-7

employment equality 140-7, 199,
    259, 261
equal pay 134-40
maternity 147-52, 199
sexual harassment 143
unfair dismissal 199
share option for employees 278-81
shift work 77-9
shop work 79
short time 81-2, 212-13
sickness 85-6, 123-4, 158-9
Social Charter of the EC 14
social welfare 19-20, 125
sovereign immunity 274
strikes: *see* industrial action
summary dismissal 163-6
suspension from work 74, 81-2,
    212-13, 296

tacograph 79
teachers
    national 322-4
    secondary 321
    university 321-22
    vocational 322
termination of employment (modes
    of) 154-60
times of work
    bakeries 79
    drivers 79
    industrial work 78-9
    normal working hours 79-80
    overtime 79-80
    women workers 77-8
    young workers 78
tort 3-6, 117-24